BYTE Guide to Optimizing Windows 95

About the Authors...

Lenny Bailes is a writer, teacher, and consultant who has been writing about computers since 1987. Known to product managers and tech support staffs from Redmond to Boca Raton, he is a contributing editor to *MicroTimes* and his columns and reviews have appeared in *PC Magazine, PC Computing, Computer Shopper, Boardwatch, Maximize,* and *OS/2 Magazine.* He also co-authored *BYTE's DOS Programmer's Cookbook.* He resides in the Bay Area in a house filled with cats and computers.

Charles Bermant has been a computer journalist for more than a decade, covering Windows in earnest since 1989. He is the Windows columnist for *Computer Currents,* and has written two previous Windows books. He has covered technology and multimedia for the *New York Times* and the *Washington Post,* among others, and helped to define the multimedia feature format for *Nautilus CD Magazine.* He lives in Silverton, Oregon with his wife, daughter, and two dogs.

Craig Menefee has extensive experience in the shareware world. He has coauthored other books with bound-in freeware, shareware, and custom programs, including *The PC User's Guide* and *BYTE's DOS Programmer's Cookbook.* His articles have appeared in *Boardwatch, Computer Shopper,* and *Internet World.*

John Heilborn, a 34-year veteran of the computer industry, is an internationally syndicated computer columnist, and the author of more than fifty computer books. His columns, "Ask Dr. John" and "ComputerTalk," appear in hundreds of newspapers and magazines worldwide, both in print and electronically.

BYTE Guide to Optimizing Windows 95

Lenny Bailes
with Charles Bermant,
Craig Menefee,
and John Heilborn

Osborne **McGraw-Hill**

Berkeley New York St. Louis San Francisco Auckland Bogotá Hamburg London Madrid Mexico City Milan Montreal New Delhi Panama City Paris São Paulo Singapore Sydney Tokyo Toronto

Acquisitions Editor
Scott Rogers

Project Editor
Nancy McLaughlin

Copy Editor
Kimberly Torgerson

Proofreader
Stefany Otis

Indexer
Richard Shrout

Computer Designer
Richard Whitaker

Illustrator
Lance Ravella

Quality Control Specialist
Joe Scuderi

Cover Design
emdesign

Series Design
Seventeenth Street Studios

Osborne **McGraw-Hill**
2600 Tenth Street
Berkeley, California 94710
U.S.A.

For information on translations or book distributors outside the U.S.A., or to arrange bulk purchase discounts for sales promotions, premiums, or fundraisers, please contact Osborne **McGraw-Hill** at the above address.

BYTE Guide to Optimizing Windows 95

1234567890 DOC 99876

ISBN 0-07-88120-7

CONTENTS

Acknowledgments

Thanks to all of the people and companies whose cooperation made this book possible. Special thanks to Osborne editor Scott Rogers, whose patience during a complicated project made it possible for us to assemble the kind of book we wanted to write. Special thanks also to co-authors Charles Bermant, Craig Menefee, and John Heilborn, who made it possible for us to cover the wide range of material that you'll find here.

I also want to acknowledge the various programmers, gurus, tech-support engineers and other people who lent me invaluable moral support: Robert Hess and Andy Thomas of Microsoft, Jeff Marchi, Sylvia Paull, and the entire Windows 95 Beta Support Team, who put up with my constant phone calls and attempted to answer an array of bewildering questions throughout the Win95 test period.

Thanks also to the hardware and software companies who assisted me during this project: American Megatrends, Inc., DTC, Inc., Toshiba, Winbook Computers, Hewlett-Packard, No. 9 Graphics, Hooked Net, and Slipnet.

And thanks to the producers, writers and cast of *Northern Exposure,* whose TV reruns kept me sane during late hour chapter rewrites.

Introduction: Why This Book Is for You

You may be surprised when you open the Windows 95 box to discover that this complex and powerful operating system ships with a slim, under-100 page welcome booklet instead of an operating manual. From word-of-mouth descriptions and magazines, you may know that Windows 95 includes built-in networking support, fax and telecommunication programs, a complete e-mail management system, Internet connectivity, and an entirely new desktop that differs considerably from the Program Manager/File Manager interface of Windows 3.1.

note *This book contains late-breaking information on the first Windows 95 Service Pack Update. See Appendix A for details.*

You may optimistically assume that although these features can't possibly be documented in a slim welcome booklet, you'll get all the instructions you need from the Windows 95 online help system.

Actually, it is conceivable that you might teach yourself basic competency in Windows 95 by successively pointing and clicking at various entries in Microsoft's online help system. This is what the authors of all the Windows 95 manuals in your local bookstore did. However, most of these people began their exploration of the operating system over two years ago as participants in Microsoft's beta program.

To be fair, there are some simple, intuitive aspects of Windows 95 that you should expect to pick up just by using the operating system. This was Microsoft's intent in its design philosophy. For instance, you should be able to find and run programs that were installed under Windows 3.1, save your work, and gain simple access to the file structure of your hard disk. These things will be easier than they were under Windows 3.1.

But how do you install Windows 95 and keep a backup copy of Windows 3.1, just in case? What installation choices should you make to avoid adding and changing things later on? How do you know that your computer is fast enough for Windows 95? Where's the hardware compatibility list? What about your network and your old system utilities? What do you need to know to install and run Windows 95 on a notebook computer?

How do you create an efficient, project-oriented desktop? Can you have more than one desktop? Can you send a Fax cover page to another computer? How do you make your e-mail manager automatically collect your messages every *X* hours or *Y* days? What if you want to collect CompuServe mail or Internet messages from more than one account? How do you set up an Internet connection, anyway? Suppose you want to view, copy, or rename only documents with a .DOC file extension? What if you want to do a differential file backup, but Microsoft's utility appears to allow only incremental ones (and there are no third-party utilities that will do the job)? How do you run QuickTime, MPEG, and AutoDesk movies with Microsoft's Media Player, or attach sound and video files to your documents? How do you set up your applications to use Adobe PostScript fonts, or print files to disk? Can you still use third-party Win 3.1 font management utilities? What about optimizing the Win95 swap file and CD-ROM cache, or changing the IRQ assigned to your modem?

How do you make it run faster? How can you do things in fewer steps? What are the pitfalls you should avoid? *Where are the hidden shortcuts?*

This book is designed for people who want to bend Windows 95 to their will with the least possible effort. You'll find answers here to all of the preceding questions, and a great deal more. We've attempted to cover all aspects of Windows 95 for people who want to cut to the chase and get their work done. You'll find in-depth treatments of partially documented and undocumented features plus sidebars, tips, and easy-to-follow numbered procedures for setting up and using the best of Win95's productivity utilities.

Guide to What's Inside

There are actually several books-within-a-book here:

Chapters 1, 2, and 3 are a tutorial guide to setting up your hardware and installing Windows 95. Despite Microsoft's design policy, which tells you that you must overwrite older versions of Windows and DOS and lose all your old program settings, you can actually have your cake and eat it too. Windows 95 can easily be set up to coexist on the same hard disk with older versions of Windows and with other operating systems, including OS/2 Warp and Windows NT. You can also transfer either the floppy disk or CD-ROM installation files for Windows 95 to a local hard disk. This makes it much easier to install and update the operating system on notebooks and other machines with no permanent access to a CD-ROM drive.

Chapter 4 shows you all of the desktop features and shortcuts that you won't discover in Microsoft's Windows 95 Tour. Here you'll find the kinds of tips and timesaving procedures that are typically the bread and butter of Windows magazines.

Chapter 5 is a short course on the bundled Microsoft applications and utilities included in the Windows 95 Accessories folder. You'll find a mini-manual for using Microsoft Fax, plus descriptions and productivity tips for Dial-Up Networking, Direct Cable Connection, HyperTerminal, Phone Dialer, Paint, WordPad and all of the other Win95 mini-apps.

Chapters 6 and 7 provide a guide to Windows 95 system architecture, addressing memory management issues and compatibility with older DOS and Windows 3.1 applications and utilities. You'll learn about the new 32-bit enhancements to the operating system and see how to take advantage of Win95's hidden boot menu and Startup options. We document the new commands that have been added to "DOS 7" through MSDOS.SYS and CONFIG.SYS, and show you how to replace real-mode device drivers with their protected-mode counterparts. You'll find productivity guides for optimizing the DOS aspect of Windows 95 with MemMaker, DriveSpace, and third-party products like QEMM, NETROOM, 386MAX, and Stacker. Chapter 7 provides a compatibility guide for DOS and Windows 3.*x* applications and shows you how to optimize their performance.

Chapter 8 is a complete guide to the Windows 95 Control Panel and all its hidden features.

Chapter 9 tells you what you need to know about managing printers and fonts. You'll find a description of the basic Win95 font features and see how to integrate TrueType and PostScript fonts into your productivity environment. You'll also find information about the new plug-and-play printer features, bi-directional printing, and enhanced spooler features, all of which improve the performance of the Windows 95 printing system.

Chapters 10 through 12 are your Win95 Connectivity and Internet guide. Here you'll find easy-to-follow, step-by-step tutorials on setting up the Microsoft Exchange Inbox (your full-featured e-mail manager), and Dial-Up Networking (your dial-up connection to remote LANs and the Internet). Chapter 10 provides diagnostic and troubleshooting information for configuring modems, serial ports, and Internet connections. Chapter 11 takes you surfing online. You can relax, look at the pictures of the Microsoft Network Online Service, and then take in the Internet Bestiary, which provides late-breaking details on World Wide Web browsers and Win95's built-in Internet utilities, and how to use them. Chapter 12 is the dedicated networking guide, showing you how to set up and use a Microsoft LAN and take advantage of Win95's easy-to-use, built-in file-sharing features.

Chapter 13 is devoted to multimedia. It provides tips on choosing and setting up a multimedia PC, and includes tutorials on all of Win95's multimedia applications. You'll learn about the new video standards and sound compression protocols built into Windows 95, see how to integrate third-party multimedia utilities, and get a brief survey of hot, must-have multimedia products.

Chapter 14 provides an overview of new applications written specifically for Windows 95. You'll find details on Microsoft Plus! (an enhancement that many users feel should have been directly included in the Win95 box) as well as Norton Utilities and Norton Navigator for Windows 95, Microsoft Office Professional, and a series of useful freeware and shareware utilities.

Chapters 15 and 16 are a bonus hardware primer thrown in specifically for MIS managers and others who are faced with the task of choosing a hardware platform for Windows 95. These chapters are designed specifically for users who want to gain some hardware literacy and make informed buying decisions. You'll find the answers to all of the questions you were afraid to ask about CPUs, motherboards, bus standards, hard disks, video controllers, etc. Plus, you'll find a special section on mobile computing.

Appendices A, B, and C contain a miscellany of tips and tricks worth knowing. We've devoted special sections to installing Windows 95 in network and multi-operating system environments, and to customizing the interface with RegEdit. Appendix A also contains late-breaking information on the first Windows 95 Service Pack Update #1.

How to Use This Book

You can use this book as a guided tour to various Windows 95 features, or browse the Table of Contents and Index for specific references to the information you need. You can also just cruise through for tips, tricks, and nuggets of information—be sure to watch for the Note, Tip, Remember, and Caution icons.

We hope that your experience with Windows 95 turns out to be pleasant and productive. And once you get your Internet connection set up, be sure to cruise the Web for our *Optimizing Windows 95* home page.

Lenny Bailes
January 1996

chapter 1

Welcome to Windows 95

- What's better about Windows 95?

    What's in it for me?

- How easy is it to upgrade?
- Hardware and software requirements

    What's new and what just grew?

- Is the documentation decrease irrelevant to most people?
- ...and a few questions you can ask yourself, to see if you really *need* to upgrade.

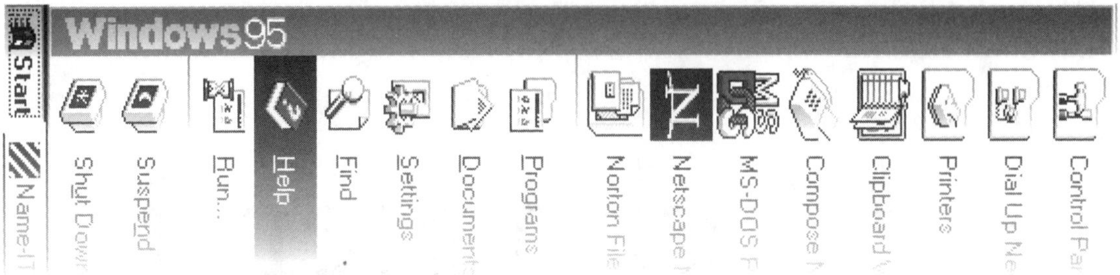

MICROSOFT executive Brad Silverberg: "Windows 95 is just software. It's not a cure for cancer. It doesn't grow hair. It's not a dessert topping, and it's not a floor wax. It's only software."

This declaration notwithstanding, Windows 95 talk is everywhere. If you live, work, or breathe anywhere near a PC, it would be impossible to remain aloof from the advertisements and press publicity urging you to upgrade your computer now or be preserved alongside the dinosaurs in the Museum of Natural History.

The Advantages of Windows 95

While it may take some time for PC novices to seek solace in Windows 95, veteran Windows 3.*x* users are getting the message right away. Here, after more than a decade of jerry-rigged operating system options and band-aid solutions, is the first wholesale revision of MS-DOS that integrates it with a graphical user interface. Windows 95 offers an improved interface, better multitasking, communications consistency, and a whole host of other features.

Easy Upgrade

Almost every popular DOS and Windows application works under Windows 95. (See Chapter 7 for information about the few incompatibilities in some application and utility software.) As you install Windows 95 for the first time, it upgrades the existing software environment, allowing you to use the same software you did before the upgrade.

Older Windows software takes on a new, enhanced 3-D appearance under Windows 95. The Microsoft Office suite of applications also adds some new menu options and dialog boxes.

Does Away with DOS?

You've probably heard this epithet used more than once by Microsoft. But, if it's true, then why are there Win95 files called COMMAND.COM, and MSDOS.SYS in the root directory of your boot drive? And why does the system execute a DOS CONFIG.SYS and AUTOEXEC.BAT before starting the graphic interface? The answer is that Microsoft has streamlined the link between the Windows 95 graphic interface and the text-based real-mode operating system that boots it onto the screen.

Windows 95 doesn't need the separate CONFIG.SYS or AUTOEXEC.BAT file required by DOS and Windows 3.*x*. Instead, Windows 95 commonly determines the required drivers and settings and loads the appropriate driver files or makes the appropriate configuration settings during its boot process. In the event that your system hardware configuration isn't directly supported, CONFIG.SYS can still be used to load the real-mode DOS drivers supplied by third-party manufacturers.

It's true that you can now start the Windows 95 desktop without a CONFIG.SYS or AUTOEXEC.BAT, although many users retain these files for the useful settings they enable prior to loading the graphic interface. (See Chapter 6 for details.) Windows 95 bootstraps itself from the real-mode DOS operating kernel. The WIN.COM file in the WINDOWS directory on your hard disk still loads the graphic interface, but you no longer have to type **WIN** at the C: prompt. The new real-mode DOS kernel runs WIN.COM automatically, just as it has always run COMMAND.COM.

You still have the option, for running eccentric or ill-behaved DOS programs, of pressing the F8 key at startup to boot to the C: prompt, instead of to the desktop.

Simplified Configuration

Perhaps the most striking feature about Windows 95—the one that new users will notice right away—is the new coordination of setup and productivity features. You no longer have to hunt for obscure configuration menus or scavenge up third-party driver diskettes to set up the operating system. (The menus are still there, but context-sensitive installation Wizards pop up, as needed, to find them and enter the correct information.) Video cards, disk controllers, PCMCIA peripherals, modems, and sound cards are usually detected and installed automatically. Where the operating system does require you to enter personalized information, help Wizards pop up to assist you. Fax support, multimedia support, and online connectivity options are all set up automatically.

Furthermore, the Windows 95 online Help system is directly linked to the system configuration utilities. If you open the Help index and enter **PRINTER**, the topic "To change printer settings" appears. The explanatory text includes a "click here" option to open the Printer Setup Wizard. Other Win95 setup Wizards can also be invoked through Help topics (see Figure 1-1). These Wizards walk you step-by-step through the process of adding new printers, modems, sound cards, and network components, sending a fax, or changing your video display.

Another obvious new feature of Windows 95 is the simpler, more flexible desktop interface. New users need no longer master the concepts of the Program Manager and the File Manager to start applications and access hard disk files. Running programs and managing the hard disk are integrated under a unified, more intuitive desktop. The Windows 95 desktop, before you start customizing it, contains a simple, obvious structure: a Start button for running programs, a My Computer icon for accessing files, a Recycle Bin for discarding unwanted files, and other icons for optional features you select during the installation process. The strict Windows 3.*x* restrictions on where icons can be placed on the desktop is gone. Programs, data files, and system

FIGURE 1-1

Setup Wizards embedded in Windows 95 online Help can automatically start and configure operating system features.

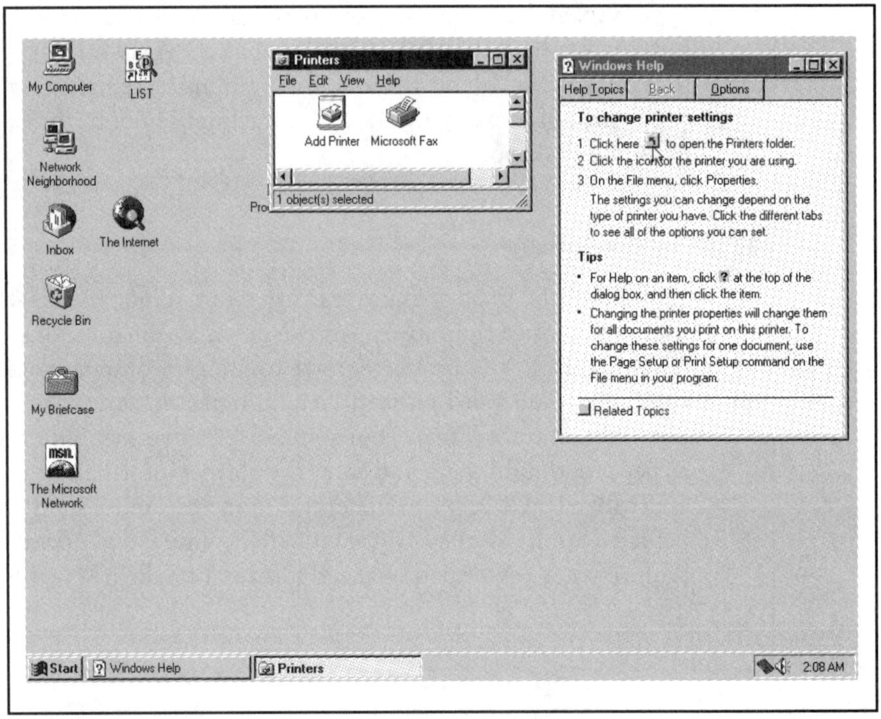

control icons can now be dragged out of their original locations and positioned anywhere you like for easy access.

More New User Features

The following capsule summaries describe other important new features you'll find in Windows 95. You'll find detailed discussions on how to use these features in subsequent chapters of this book.

A Modified GUI

The redesigned desktop is less cluttered and less explicit. Anyone who has seen OS/2 will notice a resemblance, although Windows 95 has added its own spin. The screen is wide open, with icons arranged to the user's convenience. Certain options are required—My Computer, Recycle Bin, Network Neighborhood—but most of it is your choice.

Windows 95 integrates the three major Windows 3.*x* interface components—the Program Manager, the File Manager, and the Task Manager—into a more cohesive whole. The desktop centers around the Start button, positioned at the lower left-hand corner of the desktop. This configurable program launcher brings the most needed features up front, and replaces the Program Manager's cumbersome groups with cascading menus. The new user interface includes hierarchical folders, new icon designs, and other enhancements to improve usability. The new shell makes a lot more sense than its predecessor. It's fairly easy to create nested menus, pull related applications and files into their own menu, and so on. The Recycle Bin, where you can drag files to purge them from the desktop, imitates a familiar Macintosh process and will save a lot of aggravation.

There are a number of new mouse tricks under Windows 95. In many cases, a single click will suffice where a double click was once required. Or you can just point and hover while the menus pop open. Like Warp OS/2, Windows 95 makes good use of the right mouse button. Before Windows 95, use of the right mouse button varied between programs; it was helpful but inconsistent. Now, there is uniformity. Highlight any desktop object or taskbar item, right click, and a context menu appears, as shown in Figure 1-2, full of utility features and configuration options. These menus can be basic, listing simple commands such as Move and Delete, or they can be specific to the application. For instance, a right click on a HyperTerminal icon starts the modem and makes the connection. Consistent mouse controls are a valuable improvement. If people know they can always pop up options

FIGURE 1-2

If you click on any desktop object with the right mouse button, a context menu of system options appears.

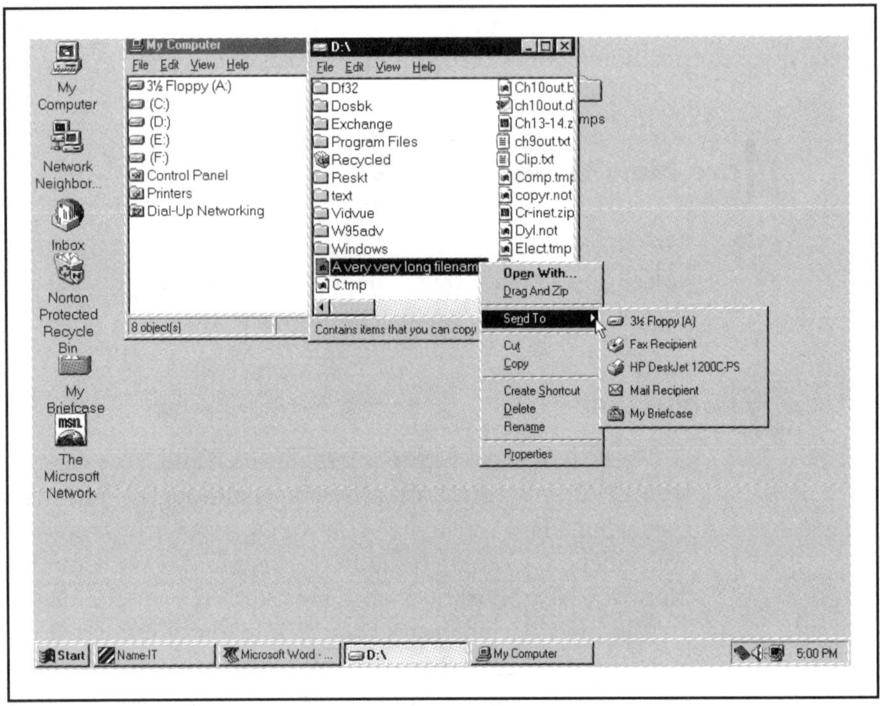

with a right click, they have more assurance in dealing with the operating system.

Windows 95 also emulates Warp OS/2's use of desktop shortcuts. In Windows 3.*x*, the icons in Program Manager groups were a kind of limited desktop shortcut. In Windows 95, any file or resource in the operating system can be represented by an icon link placed anywhere on the desktop or in another folder.

Microsoft supplies more than 30 QuickView file viewers that allow you to inspect files in a variety of formats without opening them in their source applications. You can open a Quattro Pro spreadsheet without owning a copy of Quattro Pro. The same applies for Ami Pro, Excel, Word for Windows, WordPerfect, and several vector and bitmap pictorial files.

A right-click Properties option for files, folders, and applications replaces many of the Windows 3.*x* Program Manager and File Manager options, DOS PIF editor, and some Control Panel options. Simply by right-clicking strategic desktop objects, you can directly access application settings, screen display properties, and other internal system functions. The Control Panel is still present in Windows 95, and it consolidates many functions that were formerly scattered throughout the operating system.

FIGURE 1-3

Clicking the Start button opens the Windows 95 Start Menu. From here you can access all the programs and utilities on your system.

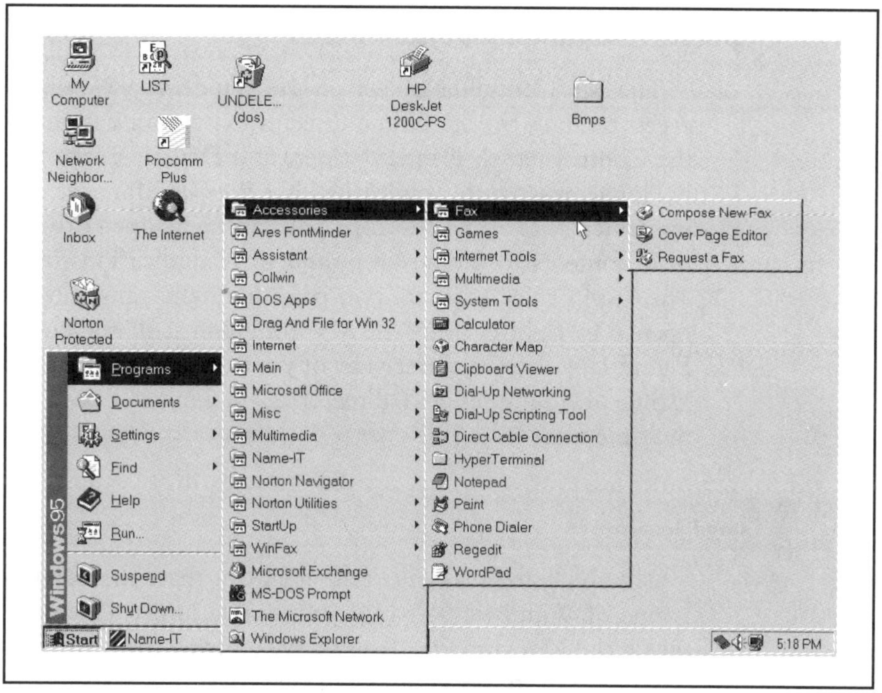

The Start button (located in the lower left-hand corner of the desktop) pops up the Start Menu (see Figure 1-3), which is first in a series of nested menus that take the place of the Windows 3.*x* Program Manager. By clicking the Start button, you gain quick access to all of your installed programs, the Printers folder, the Control Panel (under Settings), and the Windows 95 online Help system. A new Documents window tracks the most recently opened documents on the system, allowing you to gain quick repeat-access to a file.

The taskbar in Windows 95 takes the place of the Windows 3.*x* feature that minimized open windows to the bottom of the desktop. In addition to keeping track of your minimized open windows, the taskbar also contains the Start button, and has a section that provides quick access to several internal Win95 system utilities (the multimedia volume control, clock, printer/fax/modem status, and power management). Several third-party utility vendors now distribute Win95 software that enhances the taskbar's ability to serve as a system menu/program launcher; see Chapter 14 for details.

tip *You can still change the application shell in Windows 95, if you happen to prefer the Program Manager. It's extremely easy to do; we show you how in Chapter 4.*

Quick File Management and System Access

The My Computer object on the Windows 95 desktop provides quick access to all of the drives and directories on your computer. It also contains the Control Panel, Printers folder, and Dial-Up Networking components. No longer a separate application, like the File Manager, My Computer is an integrated part of the desktop. You can freely open drives and folders, drag their contents to the desktop, and start applications from My Computer. The Explorer is a special two-pane file management window that can be opened by right-clicking the My Computer icon and choosing Explore (see Figure 1-4). The Explorer view of your disk contents displays a hierarchical listing of your files and directories, making it easier to move and copy multiple files.

Long Filenames

The ability to break out of the eight-dot-three character file naming system is one of Windows 95's most noticeable improvements. (This is a luxury which the Mac and OS/2 folks have enjoyed for a while.) The ability to be more explicit in file naming will help users of all stripes: Imagine the ability

FIGURE 1-4

Using the Explorer

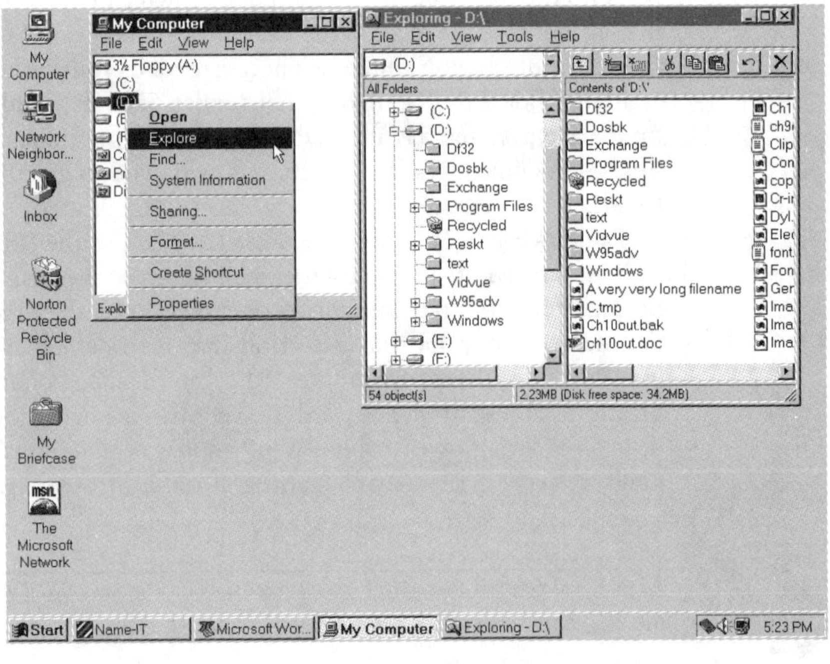

to write "What we did on our 1996 winter vacation" rather than VACATION.DOC. Such freedom makes your computer more hospitable and your hard disk more comprehensible. Having the freedom to be explicit in the naming of files is a tremendous convenience. It may not be an overriding reason to switch operating systems, but it is one of the first things you notice when you get there. Windows 95 supports filenames of up to 256 characters for all files, folders, and other desktop objects. Files with these long filenames also retain a conventional 8.3 DOS filename that can be accessed under DOS or on non-Windows 95 computers. Several third-party utility vendors now provide software that adds Win95 Long Filename recognition to ordinary Windows 3.*x* applications. See Chapter 14 for details.

Win95 Wizardry

Another demonstration of Win95's increased user friendliness is its implementation of Wizards: essential hybrids of macros and installation procedures. Microsoft has extended its use of this feature in its application software to the new operating system. Wizards are pop-up dialog sequences designed to perform complicated processes by breaking them into simple steps that are obvious to the user. The first Wizard that you're likely to see

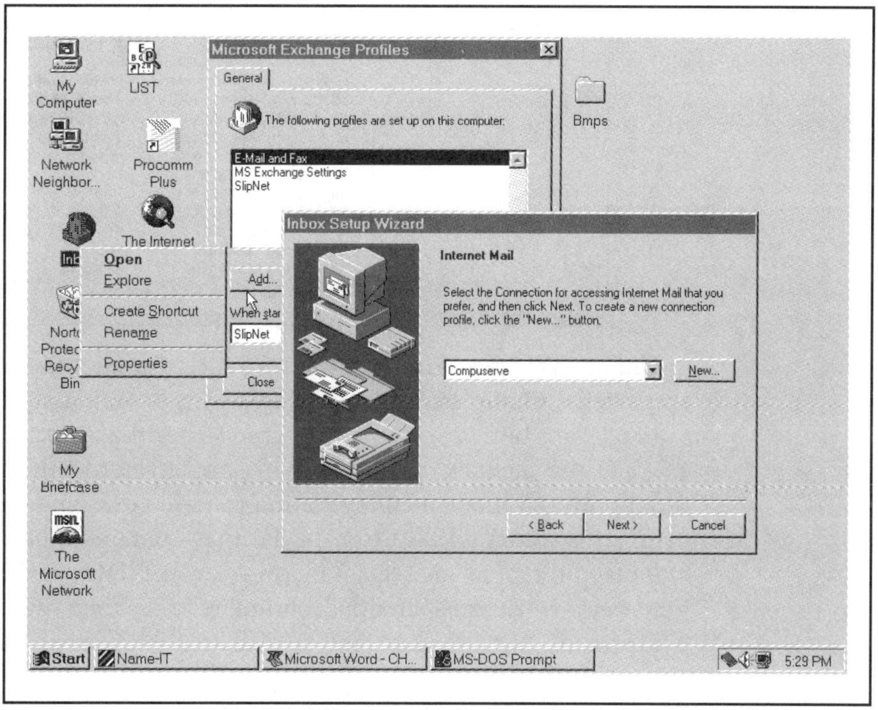

FIGURE 1-5 *The Inbox Setup Wizard configures your online mail services in an easy, step-by-step process.*

is the one that supervises the Windows 95 installation, taking you step by step through the decisions required for the setup of the new operating system. Previously, you needed to be equipped with knowledge and a printed manual to manage advanced configuration challenges. Now, Wizards attached to almost any menu can walk you through system setup options, the creation of document templates, or other computing processes that were too complex for the average person just 18 short months ago.

Communications

Windows 95 contains dramatic telecommunications enhancements. Microsoft Exchange is a near-universal mail management program that tracks received and transmitted faxes, e-mail from other users on a LAN, the Microsoft Network online service, CompuServe, and (with a downloadable attachment) the Internet. The Microsoft Exchange Inbox looks like this:

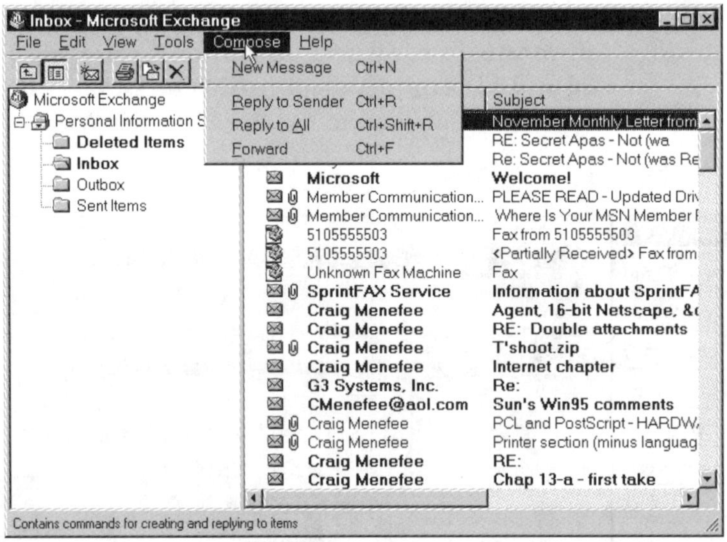

Unlike Windows 3.*x*, Windows 95 includes internal support for high-speed telecommunications, allowing you to manipulate the serial port's internal data buffer. Terminal programs specifically written for Windows 95 (like the included HyperTerminal applet) automatically know which serial port and modem configuration to use. Your modem is detected and configured automatically from a list that contains hundreds of different manufacturers and models. Windows 3.*x* and DOS communication programs also work transparently, continuing to use their own application-specific options, but taking advantage of shared, high-speed serial port drivers.

The Dial-Up Networking component of Windows 95 can seamlessly replace Windows 3.*x* TCP/IP Internet dialers like Trumpet, Chameleon, or CompuServe NetLauncher. It provides you with full 32-bit access to the Internet service provider of your choice, allowing you to use both 16-bit and 32-bit Internet software like Netscape, Air Mosaic, Emissary, WSFTP, and your other favorite packages. Microsoft also makes its own World Wide Web browser available for download, at no charge, in an Internet access kit. This Internet access kit can also be purchased as part of Microsoft Plus!, a collection of Microsoft add-ons for Windows 95 (see Figure 1-6). In addition to providing access to the Internet, Dial-Up Networking can be used to connect to a dedicated LAN through your modem.

Better Networking

Peer-to-peer networking in Windows 95 improves upon the support offered in Windows for Workgroups 3.11. In addition, Windows 95 features clients for Novell, Banyan, and SunSoft NFS networks. This support includes a protected mode installed directly through the graphic interface. Machines running Windows 95 can be integrated seamlessly into a Windows NT, Windows for Workgroups, or Novell/NetBIOS-compatible network. Sup-

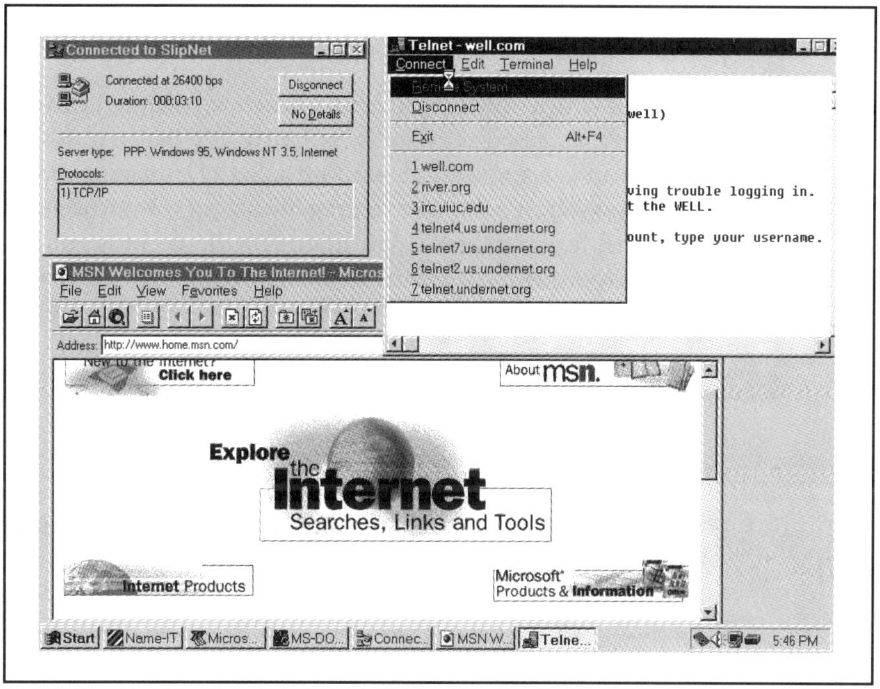

FIGURE 1-6 *Windows 95 includes built-in TCP/IP support for direct Internet connections, and a series of Internet access tools. The web browser shown in this picture can be downloaded or added to the system through the Microsoft Plus! package.*

port is also included for TCP/IP network connections, either through an adapter card, or through your modem.

The Windows 95 Dial-Up Adapter allows you to connect to a dedicated network via modem, establish an Internet connection, or (with the aid of a downloaded utility file) configure your local computer into a dial-up server. The Direct Cable Connection feature allows you to set up a peer-to-peer network connection between two computers through a serial or parallel cable. The Share option (built into the right-click context menu for all desktop objects) makes it easy to provide shared network access to selected folders, disk drives, or printers.

Better Multimedia

Windows 95 can automatically play audio CDs or start up programs on data CDs as they are inserted into the CD-ROM drive. The Media Player can handle larger video and audio files without generating out-of-memory errors, and a series of compression technologies are built into the operating system to reduce the overhead of storage space for multimedia presentations. A series of sound schemes includes a variety of 10-minute classical MIDI compositions and sound effects for all occasions. Improvements in the video handling system provide better performance for 3-D games and presentation graphics.

Object Linking and Embedding (OLE) 2.0

OLE 2.0 is the next generation of the Object Linking and Embedding feature contained in Windows 3.*x*. It lets the user control the embedded object and its application, without actually launching the application. Under Windows 95, it's possible to drag documents or portions of documents from properly programmed applications to the desktop, printer, or to another application with the mouse.

Support for DOS Programs

Windows 95 creates independent virtual machines for each of your DOS applications or DOS command sessions. These virtual machines have more memory protection than under Windows 3.*x*, and can be preemptively multitasked just like 32-bit Windows applications. Preemptive multitasking is the intelligent management by the operating system of the CPU time allocated to concurrently running programs. Each DOS session run in a desktop window can now have a toolbar of its own that includes functions for easy cut-and-paste, quick change of display font, and access to DOS session properties.

Because Windows 95 includes protected-mode drivers for disk compression, CD-ROM and other I/O peripherals, your DOS sessions will generally have more conventional memory available. DOS programs that use standard graphics modes can now be run in desktop windows as well as full screen sessions.

For the few DOS games and applications that can't run successfully under the Windows 95 GUI, a special feature can be invoked that shuts down the Windows 95 desktop and opens an exclusive MS-DOS mode session. Custom sets of CONFIG.SYS and AUTOEXEC.BAT startup files can be created for MS-DOS mode sessions that require specific real-mode drivers to be loaded at boot time.

More Fun

Some people actually dyed their hair blonde in order to have more fun in the 1960s. Upgrading to Windows 95 is a less daunting experience. Over time, you will see all kinds of powerful, innovative software: suites that do everything but your laundry, new multimedia, and fabulously realistic games. As a result, the time spent in front of the PC is a worthy pursuit.

New Technologies and Features

In addition to its new user-options and utilities, Windows 95 includes a series of new or adapted technologies designed to make it run smoother and pack it with potential for future software programmers.

Plug-and-Play

This feature allows for auto-recognition and configuration of your system hardware. When the Microsoft/Intel Plug-and-Play standard is fully supported by hardware and peripheral vendors, users will be able to install new monitors, modems, printers, and other internal system components without having to do any work to physically reconfigure the computer or its operating system.

Plug-and-play works through a combination of hardware and software. Windows 95 has many plug-and-play features that work even if you don't have plug-and-play ready hardware. With non-plug-and-play peripherals (now referred to as *legacy technology*) Windows 95 will still save you lots of time and trouble. If your printer, monitor, video card, and disk peripherals fall into the legacy category, Windows 95 may not identify them exactly, but it will make its best guess at what you've got. Your peripherals may be identified by manufacturer, if not by specific model number. Easy-to-read component lists allow you to fill in missing information. If your system has a PCI bus and peripherals or uses PCMCIA cards, Windows 95 will probably identify these components and correctly assign interrupts and port addresses even though your motherboard lacks a plug-and-play BIOS. For more information about Windows 95 plug-and-play compatibility, see Chapter 15.

32-Bit Program Support

Windows 95 includes a 32-bit file system and 32-bit disk access. This file system and disk access code was adapted directly from Windows for Workgroups 3.11. Microsoft has chosen Win32 as the single 32-bit application programming interface (API) subset to Windows NT, ending confusion over the multiple 32-bit APIs that existed previously. The 32-bit Windows applications take full advantage of the instruction set built into 80386 and higher CPUs to allow faster program execution and data handling. Applications written for previous 32-bit Windows APIs, such as Microsoft Office for Windows NT, can also be run under Windows 95.

The benefit of these various features is that the operating system is generally faster than Windows 3.*x* when performing 32-bit tasks. Under Windows 95, you can comfortably print one document while revising another and recalculating a spreadsheet. You finally get something resembling real multitasking. For more information about this subject, see Chapter 6.

Preemptive Multitasking and Multithreading

The *multitasking* feature allows for more intelligent multitasking of applications written for the 32-bit Windows API, along with the Win95 printing subsystem and DOS sessions. *Multithreading* is the capability of running independent program jobs within a single program. Multithreading communications packages allow file downloads at the same time as an upload or message transfer. The Microsoft Network, Microsoft's new online service, advertises its multithreading talents by allowing you to download files, collect messages, engage in online chat, and access online multimedia databases all concurrently.

Under Win95's preemptive multitasking, applications are less likely to become memory hogs, eating up idle CPU time and slowing down performance. The operating system itself determines when access to the CPU is granted to programs that request it.

note *16-bit applications written for the Windows 3.x environment are not preemptively multitasked. These programs are still multitasked cooperatively, determining their own priority through internal programming functions. See Chapter 6 for more details on this subject.*

Multithreading defines simultaneous activity within an application; for example, a word processor that prints in background as it allows you to repaginate a large document or run a spell check.

Messaging Application Programming Interface (MAPI)

MAPI is a technology that allows Win95 client applications to interact with multiple messaging services through a single user interface. The Microsoft Exchange mail management program supplied in Windows 95 can handle mail from The Microsoft Network, (Microsoft's new online information service), as well as CompuServe and Internet Mail, and messages sent through Microsoft's peer-to-peer network client.

Who's Buying?

With all these obvious advantages, you might assume that people would flock to Windows 95 in droves; that several months after the introduction every PC in the world would boast a Start button in the lower left corner of the screen. Truth takes a slightly different turn. The people who upgraded immediately were those who loved to tinker with their PCs and had the technical knowledge to anticipate and correct anything that may go wrong. Those who lined up at software stores at 12:00 A.M. August 24 as if Windows 95 were a new Elvis album were, let's face it, pure tech types. Everybody else has been slowly trickling in after waiting to count the casualties occurring in the front-line advance.

The bottom line is that Windows 95 is prettier and, if you have the hardware to support it, will crash less and be more useful than Windows 3.*x*. Many people in the second wave of upgrades are finding this out without learning the intricacies and exploring the nooks and crannies necessary for them to become power users. It is for this group of users that this book was largely written.

Less Documentation, More Help

One thing that you may notice about Windows 95 is the lack of printed documentation included in the package. Instead of a fat book there is a brochure and a few loose pieces of paper. But after the operating system is installed, a sophisticated set of cross-linked help files is placed on your hard disk. Much of the information that was formerly available in printed manuals must now be accessed online.

The redesigned Windows 95 Help structure will probably curtail a disk space-saving activity practiced by power users across the world: that is, deleting all files with the .HLP extension. Still accessible through the universal F1 key, Windows 95 Help staggers and organizes its material with book icons (click to open) and a tabbed interface to access different aspects. Microsoft applications have even included a module called the Answer Wizard, which allows you to type in questions and receive an instant list of all the related answers. This operates as a fairly standard text search, but the new Win95 interface is designed to make users feel as if they are relating to the computer directly and "talking" to it. As a result, pressing F1 may become the best way to get answers about a problem—sort of like a tech support line that answers at the first ring.

For users who need complete documentation of technical procedures and features, there are several options: Microsoft has placed the complete text of *The Windows 95 Resource Guide* on the installation CD. This database (in Help file format) can be opened from the Run menu accessed by pressing the Start button.

Obviously, we think the book you're currently reading is another helpful adjunct to gaining mastery over Windows 95. We've designed the book specifically to list the procedures and document the features that increase the functionality of the operating system in ways not spelled out in Microsoft's online documentation.

More Technical Details

To provide a performance balance between running applications written for the new Windows 95 API and compatibility with existing Windows 3.*x* programs, Windows 95 uses a combination of 32-bit and 16-bit code. The system design deploys 32-bit code wherever it improves performance without sacrificing application compatibility. Existing 16-bit code is retained when required to maintain compatibility with Windows 3.*x* function calls, or where 32-bit code would increase memory requirements without significantly improving performance. All of the I/O subsystems and device drivers in Windows 95, such as networking and file systems, are fully 32-bit, as are all the memory management and scheduling components (the kernel and virtual memory manager).

Win32-based applications benefit from the new operating system because they can access memory in a linear fashion, rather than being limited to the segmented memory architecture used by DOS and Windows 3.*x*. The use of a "flat" address space by the 32-bit components in Windows 95 (and by Win32 applications) allows programmers to write code without the limitations or design issues inherent in the segmented memory model used by DOS and Windows 3.*x*. For more information about Windows 95's new system architecture, see Chapter 6.

It's Compatible

One of Windows 95's most compelling features is its ability to run legacy applications, Windows 3.*x* and DOS programs that are already in use. In fact, thoroughness in this respect was the reason the operating system's release was delayed for so long. If Microsoft had chosen to sacrifice this backward compatibility, the system would have shipped a year previous to its eventual completion.

Windows 95 provides a flexible environment for running DOS-based applications. Under Windows 3.*x*, users sometimes needed to exit Windows to run DOS applications that were either ill-behaved or required direct access to system resources. Application compatibility is improved in Windows 95 to the point where almost all DOS-based programs (except for some hardware-intensive games) can run in virtual machine sessions.

Plug-and-Play Primer

The idea that you can just pop a card into a slot and it will work is exciting to anyone who has ever cracked a system case or has been irked by an IRQ. Like anything else, however, plug-and-play has several levels and degrees. Meaning, just because it is now easier it doesn't mean that it's simple.

The system's ease of use and dynamic operation depends on how many of the three main components—the operating system, system BIOS, and hardware devices—support plug-and-play.

At the lowest level, none of the components supports plug-and-play. The user needs to set card jumpers and switches manually, and load drivers from floppies.

At the next level, the operating system supports plug-and-play but the computer does not contain a plug-and-play BIOS. The computer may have a PCI bus, which assists Windows 95 in recognizing components, but it also contains non-plug-and-play (legacy) peripherals. This level is typical of many current systems. With these configurations user intervention is reduced but not completely eliminated. To aid the user in hardware setup, the operating system provides tools like the Device Wizards, the Device Manager, and the System Registry, which can install and configure drivers semi-automatically.

At the highest level, all three levels of plug-and-play support are incorporated into your system. This makes adding new devices as easy as plugging them in and turning on the power. Just plug a new printer into a parallel cable or switch video cards and Windows 95 detects the change automatically, installing appropriate drivers. Because of the plug-and-play BIOS, the system supports full dynamic operation, including hot-docking, APM 1.1 power management, automatic configuration of boot devices, and programming of motherboard devices.

The good news is that your system may already be partially plug-and-play compliant even before installing Windows 95: Many manufacturers have been shipping systems with plug-and-play BIOS for some time now. (See Chapter 15 for more information about the Microsoft-Intel Plug-and-Play standard.)

A complete plug-and-play system provides substantial benefits to both users and computer-industry vendors. The PC is easier to use, since users don't have to worry about switches, jumpers, hardware conflicts, or loading drivers manually. For example, to turn a desktop computer system into a great multimedia system, all the user has to do is plug in a plug-and-play audio card, CD-ROM drive, and SCSI adapter, turn on the system, and play a video clip.

Users will also have great mobility. For example, hot-docking stations that support the Plug-and-Play standard allow the user to remove or plug in a portable notebook while it is running. The computer automatically senses its annexation or removal from the docking station, reconfiguring itself to work with a new display, and adjusting for the new presence or absence of network cards, CD-ROM drives, and other I/O peripherals.

Win95 Limitations and Disadvantages

Windows 95 isn't a complete bed of roses. For one thing, it occupies considerably more space on your hard disk than its predecessors and it requires more memory and CPU power. In some ways, the operating system business now resembles the push by American automobile manufacturers in the '50s to turn out larger, and more expensive gas guzzlers every year. It seems as though each version of the Windows operating system contains more code, and requires more powerful hardware to sustain its minimum requirements.

In the mid-1980s a company called GeoWorks attempted to compete with Microsoft by publishing a graphic operating system that could run efficiently on 8088 machines. Compiled in assembly language, the GeoWorks Ensemble operating system featured a word processor and drawing program that consumed less than 100K on your hard disk! Although GeoWorks enjoyed brief popularity with frugal users reluctant to move into the 80286 and 80386 world, it eventually lost out to Windows for two basic reasons: 1) all of the leading application vendors were actively engaged in publishing programs designed for the Windows environment, and 2) users wanted a more powerful multitasking operating system in its own right, rather than a menuing shell (however elegant) that simply loaded on top of DOS.

The same factors that caused the success of Windows 3.0 and 3.1 will probably go a long way to ensuring the success of Windows 95.

From a Lost Episode of Star Trek: The Next Generation Recently Unearthed on the Internet (Part I)

Picard: *Mr. La Forge, have you had any success with your attempts at finding a weakness in the Borg. And Mr. Data, have you been able to access their command pathways?*

La Forge: *Yes, Captain. In fact, we found the answer by searching through our archives on late twentieth-century computing technology.*

(La Forge presses a key, and a logo appears on the computer screen.)

Riker: (looking puzzled) *What the hell is "Microsoft?"*

Data (turning to answer)**:** *Allow me to explain. We will load this ancient program, for some reason called "Windows," through the Borg command pathways. Once inside their root command unit, it will begin consuming system resources at an unstoppable rate.*

Picard: *But the Borg have the ability to adapt. Won't they alter their processing systems to increase their storage capacity?*

Data: *Yes, Captain. But once "Windows" detects this, it creates a new version of itself known as an "upgrade." The use of resources increases exponentially with each iteration. The Borg will not be able to adapt quickly enough. Eventually all of their processing ability will be taken over and none will be left for their operational functions.*

Picard: *Excellent work. This is even better than that "unsolvable geometric shape" idea.*

Hardware Hardships?

On machines that easily handle Windows 3.*x*, Windows 95 may improve the performance of your existing software. Users of marginal machines, however, may need to upgrade at least one aspect of their system. Chapters 15 and 16 provide detailed information on minimal hardware configurations necessary to run Windows 95 comfortably. If you're not sure whether your computer will do a good job with Windows 95, you may want to read those chapters first. They also provide consumer advice on shopping for a new machine and upgrading individual components. As with their cars, many people want to get as much use out of their PCs as possible. But sometimes you need to accept the fact that the old gray CPU ain't what it used to be.

Let's look at the requirements on the Windows 95 box, with a realistic eye.

386DX or Higher Processor

This is one of those "yes, it will run, but..." areas. In fact, the bottom line starting point for decent Windows 95 performance is a 486/33 processor. Anything else will require a compromise. If you are operating a similarly equipped machine you need to determine whether or not the sacrifices will be worthwhile, and if it may just be wiser to stay put.

4MB of Memory

This is the Great Lie of the 1990s. If you remember, when Windows 3.0 came out Microsoft claimed it needed 2MB of memory. This is an analogous situation, except that users are now accustomed to decent performance and memory at a fraction of 1990 prices. Consider that you can walk into just about any store with a computing department, and the clerk will tell you that 4MB is not enough.

35 to 40MB Available Disk Space

It is true that a minimal Windows 95 installation will fit into this space, but this is another area where you want to plan ahead. Reserve 30MB for each application, more if it incorporates graphics. Plan enough for a swap file (an amount at least equivalent to installed physical RAM). When you leave enough room to add supplemental Windows 95 features, and files installed by other programs, the total disk space required will probably be closer to 90MB than 40 for the Windows directory, alone.

CD-ROM Drive

This requirement, obviously, is only listed on the box of the CD-ROM version of Windows 95. Regardless, it is probably as important as anything on this list. Multimedia aside, installing software from CD-ROM is destined to become the wave of the present. Multidisk installations have become annoying, time consuming, and now unnecessary. You can even expect that floppy based software will become harder to find by the end of next year.

Pointing Device

For some bizarre reason, the Windows 95 box lists this as an option. Although it may be possible to use Windows 95 without a mouse, it is by no means desirable. You can, for instance, install the Accessibility Options and employ the numeric keypad as a pointer. It works, but not well. Face it: Windows needs a mouse or pointing device. End of story.

Modem

This is more optional than a mouse, but a PC without a modem in this new "Age of Information" is like the sound of one hand clapping. Windows 95 offers rich support for telecommunications and you will probably want to take advantage of it.

Utilities

Running Windows 95 will probably require that you update the arsenal of utility software you accumulated for DOS and Windows 3.*x*. Backup, antivirus, and disk recovery utilities that worked in previous versions of Windows and DOS retain partial functionality, at best, under Windows 95. Microsoft does provide a limited Windows 95 backup utility, but its support of tape drives is limited to the QIC40/QIC80 variety.

For information about working with older Windows/DOS utility software, see Chapter 7. Chapter 14 contains information about new packages specifically written for Windows 95.

Positive Impact of Windows 95

With perhaps 100 million Intel-based PCs actively in use throughout the world, not all users will have the time, money, or inclination to upgrade immediately—especially to a new system with such a controversial reputation. Eventually, however, Windows 95 will change personal computing in the following ways.

It Opens Up New Possibilities for Multimedia

Adding sound and CD-ROM to a PC is the most painful and troublesome operation in the world of upgrades. About 80 percent of the components may work 80 percent of the time, but there is still enough room for error to discourage all but the most technical to install multimedia in an existing machine.

Windows 95, however, will open the floodgates for multimedia creativity—both on the hardware and software levels. With plug-and-play, installing a sound card or CD-ROM drive will (theoretically) be a snap; a more hospitable software structure will encourage title development and bring Windows to parity with the superior multimedia capabilities of the Macintosh (multimedia was grafted onto Windows, just before version 3.1's release).

It Merges the Computer with the Telephone

One of the aspects of Windows 95 that was not in the first beta was its telephony module; one that will tie the PC to various voice and data functions. As phone lines become data lifelines, users need a smart way to manage all of the online and voice information. As a result, the PC will become the keystone of this communications revolution, and it will happen during Windows 95's product lifetime.

It Merges the Computer with Other Computers and with Office Devices

Windows 95 takes all the drudgery out of setting up a peer-to-peer network. And it is also the harbinger of a deeper integration between the PC, fax, copier, and related office time savers. The simple example—using the print command to send a fax–is already here. Future examples will only be limited by the needs of users and the parallel imagination of developers.

Take This Test

Let's make it clear, if you depend on your computer for your livelihood, upgrading to Windows 95 is not something you should do on the spur of the moment. The following is a short list of issues that you can use to determine whether or not you are ready for this big step.

If the following criteria apply to your situation, you should upgrade:

- You feel restricted by your current computing environment and are looking for a more flexible operating system to assist you in conveniently getting your work done.
- Features like multitasking and multithreading are important in order to accomplish daily tasks.
- You want to take advantage of the features offered by the Microsoft Network online service.
- You have access to high-end hardware—8MB of RAM, 200MB of hard disk space, and a 486 or greater processor—or have the ability to upgrade.
- You have the need for access to the most current technology; for personal or competitive purposes.

If the following criteria apply, you should probably stay put:

- Your computer is functional and useful, and accomplishes all of the tasks you assign to it.
- You are satisfied with CompuServe, America Online or a similar service, and your current Internet service connections, for all your online needs.
- Your existing hardware is functional, but not state of the art; however, a system upgrade would be inconvenient.
- The time and money that would be necessary to retrain staff and support a new operating system currently outweigh the benefits of Windows 95 that we've outlined in this chapter.

This completes our introductory chapter on the new wrinkles and benefits involved in Windows 95. The next chapter shows you what preparations you'll need to make in order to make the jump.

Printers
Settings
Find
Help
Run...
Suspend
Windows95
Start

chapter 2

Making the Jump

- Is your system powerful enough?
    - Taking inventory
- Where to find pre-installation information
- Pre-installation help
    - Third-party packages and common sense
- What to expect from old productivity applications and utilities
- Configuration changes and disk maintenance
- Migrating application settings for multiple versions of Windows

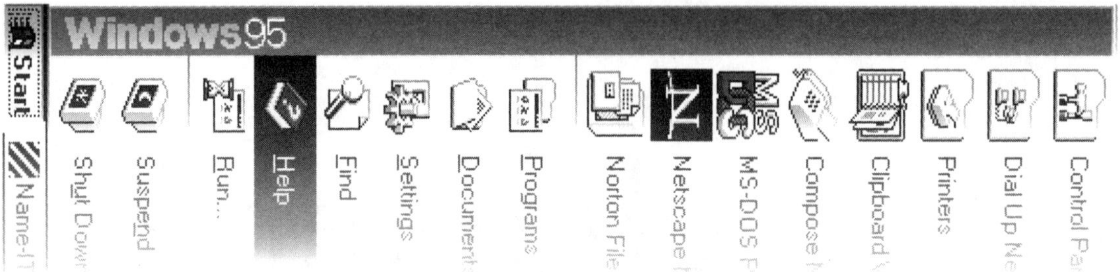

As you prepare for your jump from DOS or Windows 3.*x* to Windows 95, you may have a lot of questions on your mind. If you happen to think a product upgrade is equivalent to opening a new box of chocolates or popping a movie into a VCR, good news: Windows 95 is designed to let you get away with this attitude. However, more conservative users and MIS professionals will benefit from the pre-installation roadmap that this chapter provides. If you're the type of computer user who likes a hint of things to come, you may be concerned with one or more of the following issues:

- Is my computer powerful enough to run Windows 95 comfortably?
- Will my old software applications and utilities still work under Windows 95?
- What kind of configuration and disk maintenance preparations should I make before installing Windows 95?
- Should I install over my existing Windows or into a new directory? Do I want to keep more than one copy of Windows on my system?
- What about my network?
- What will happen to my DOS and Windows 3.1 maintenance utilities and antivirus programs?

This chapter provides answers to these questions, helping you to prepare for your Windows 95 installation. The installation process, itself, is discussed in option-by-option detail in the next chapter.

Powerful Enough? (Taking a System Inventory)

Is your system up to Windows 95? The basic requirements, as stated by Microsoft, are a 20MHz 386 with 4MB of RAM and 45MB of hard disk space. Although such a minimal system may be physically capable of running the operating system, it's bound to deliver disappointing performance. Most users will want to know what they can expect from more powerful systems that handled the last version of Windows well, but were not specifically designed to run Windows 95: Are the individual hardware peripherals compatible? Will Windows 95 provide the necessary drivers and support files for video cards, disk drives, printers, and modems?

If you have questions concerning your system's suitability as a Windows 95 hardware or software platform, start out with some reading and preparation before installing the operating system. (In a subsequent section of this chapter, we show you how to extract a bunch of useful technical documents from the Win95 CD before running Setup.) You may want to undertake one or more of the following pre-installation projects:

- Take an inventory of your system's components. Rate your system's performance with commercial or shareware benchmark packages.
- Download the Microsoft Windows 95 Support Assistant, a free information utility that contains extensive compatibility listings for both hardware and software.
- Examine the various README text files on hardware and software compatibility that Microsoft has included in the basic Windows 95 package. (You can extract and access these files before installing the new operating system.)
- Perform hardware or software upgrades based on the information you obtain from your reading and from taking a system inventory.

Several common freeware and shareware utilities can help you take your system inventory. Diagnostic programs can help you assess hardware compatibility, and benchmark results can give you a rough idea of what to expect in the way of performance efficiency. This information is particularly useful when you can compare it to diagnostic results for other widely used systems and individual hardware components.

The Windows 95 Support Assistant (see Figure 2-1) is a free information utility from Microsoft available from Microsoft's Internet FTP site, on CompuServe, GEnie, and the Microsoft Download Service BBS. It includes a set of answers to the most frequently asked support questions about Windows 95, a reference guide to available products and services, and the Windows 95 hardware and software compatibility lists. To get the files from Microsoft, log into FTP.MICROSOFT.COM, GOPHER.MICROSOFT .COM, or HTTP://WWW.MICROSOFT.COM with an appropriate Internet utility, or call the Download Service with a telecommunications program at 206-936-6735 .

The main Support Assistant module can be run under Windows 3.1 or Windows for Workgroups. It contains tutorial information on the Windows 95 interface and also addresses system configuration and post-installation hardware issues: connecting to the Internet, fixing monitor and video card refresh rate problems, configuring notebook PCMCIA cards, forcing recognition of nonstandard CD-ROM drives, and so on.

The two compatibility databases for software and hardware products may be the most useful part of the package. Compiled in Windows 3.1 Help file format, they provide detailed information on known problems with more

FIGURE 2-1 *The Microsoft Windows 95 Support Assistant*

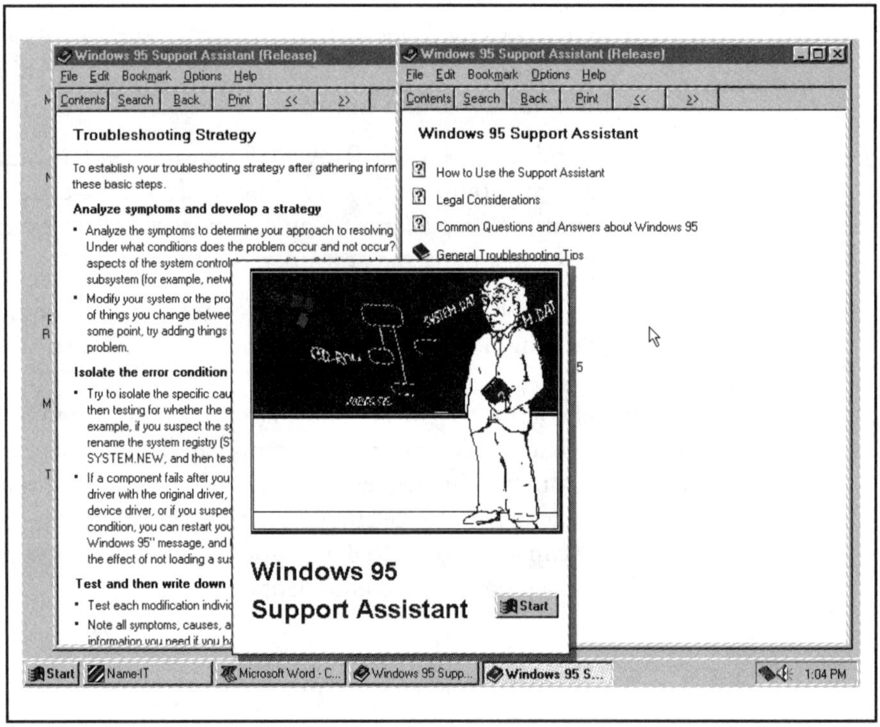

than 5000 software and hardware products. If you want to assure yourself of Win95 compatibility with particular applications or hardware components, you can look them up in these alphabetical listings.

Extracting README Files from the Windows 95 CD

The Windows 95 CD and installation disks include a number of useful documents concerning Win95 performance and compatibility. However, you won't find them, because Microsoft decided to compress these files into the Windows cabinet (.CAB) archives, rather than allowing easy access to them up front. Once you've installed the operating system, you'll find DISPLAY.TXT, EXCHANGE.TXT, EXTRA.TXT, FAQ.TXT, GENERAL.TXT, HARDWARE.TXT, PRINTERS.TXT, PROGRAMS.TXT and others are unpacked and available for browsing in your WINDOWS directory. If you want to read these documents *before* installing Windows 95, there is a way.

These files are all contained within the cabinet file called WIN95_03.CAB. The EXTRACT.EXE utility located in the root directory of the Win95 CD or on the first installation diskette can be used to unpack all of the READMEs for inspection before installing Windows 95. The easiest way to do this is to create a directory called READMES on your hard drive. If you have the WIN95 CD, log onto the CD-ROM drive and change to the WIN95 directory where EXTRACT.EXE is located. If you have the floppy diskettes, place the first one in drive A. Then use the EXTRACT command, with the following syntax for the CD version:

EXTRACT /L *C:\READMES* [D:]\WIN95\WIN95_03.CAB *.TXT

[D:] represents your Windows 95 source drive. The /L *C:\READMES* switch specifies a target directory for the text files you're unpacking. (You can use this parameter to specify any drive and directory.) For the floppy version, use this syntax:

A:\> EXTRACT /L *C:\READMES* WIN95_03.CAB *.TXT

note *There are several additional text files for Windows 95 scattered around in other cabinet archives. If you want to search the rest of the .CAB files for text files, you can modify the EXTRACT command previously described by adding the /A parameter to the command line. The command*

*EXTRACT /A /L [d:]\PATH E:\WIN95\WIN95_02.CAB *.TXT*

searches the files WIN95_02.CAB through WIN95_17.CAB, unpacking all files with the .TXT extension to the specified drive path on your hard drive.

Evaluating System Performance

Several shareware and public domain benchmark utilities can help you obtain a statistical rating of your system's performance. You may then compare the numerical rating achieved by your computer or peripherals with ratings on the same benchmark for other systems. If you're looking for benchmarks to provide you with a quick rating, download a copy of WINDSOCK, a simple, integrated utility written for Windows 3.1 (For more details about WINDSOCK, see Chapter 16).

Other freeware and shareware benchmarks are useful in testing performance aspects of individual system components. You may want to look for CORETEST.EXE, a venerable but reliable disk benchmark, SPEEDY, a video benchmark, and WINTACH, another integrated Windows benchmark. TORQUE, a video benchmark developed by Steve Gibson of SpinRite fame, is especially useful in evaluating high-performance video cards that operate in 64K and 16M color resolutions. These utilities are widely available on public bulletin board systems, and you may also find them on CompuServe, GEnie, and America Online.

WINSTONE\WINBENCH

One of the most exhaustive and widely-used benchmarks in the computer industry is the WINSTONE/WINBENCH evaluation suite. This set of utilities is distributed on a CD-ROM available from Ziff-Davis at a nominal shipping charge. Installing and running this suite takes a little time and effort, and sometimes its execution is not trouble-free. However, once you complete the tests, you'll be able to compare the results for your computer to the ratings for systems and hardware peripherals frequently reviewed in the various Ziff-Davis magazines. (Note that the IDG Corporation also markets a benchmark suite, which is used by writers for its magazines to evaluate hardware performance.)

What About My Old Applications and Utilities?

The good news is that most of your DOS and Windows 3.*x* productivity applications will work under Windows 95 with no significant problems or performance degradation. The PROGRAMS.TXT file, which you learned how to extract earlier in this chapter, and the Microsoft software compatibility list, also referenced earlier, can help you identify application problems that you may encounter.

The bad news is that a lot of the utility software you've amassed for DOS and Windows 3.*x* will become nonfunctional as soon as the new operating system is installed. Unless you own a QIC 80 tape drive, you will not be able to make effective use of Microsoft's Win95 Backup utility. Various DOS and Windows 3.*x* Backup utilities retain partial functionality, but you won't be able to use them to make reliable system backups that include the new Windows 95 long filenames and system registry information. File managers and system recovery utilities developed for DOS and Windows 3.*x* will also have to be replaced. You may be able to get along provisionally without bells and whistles like emergency disk recovery, and full-featured file management shells, but you will probably want to restore these features eventually by purchasing Windows 95-specific utility packages.

Windows 95 includes an adequate disk optimizer (the descendant of the MS-DOS DEFRAG program), and is completely compatible with the DoubleSpace/DriveSpace compression features offered in previous versions of DOS. The Win95 ScanDisk disk repair utility is little different from previous versions. It has a bare-bones capacity to repair file and directory errors, but it is not nearly as powerful as the pre-Win95 versions of Norton Disk Doctor and PC Tools DiskFix. None of the pre-Win95 disk repair utilities can be depended upon to reliably repair problems arising under the new operating system. (In a pinch, your Norton 8 Emergency Rescue disk may partially restore a trashed disk partition, but only the new Norton for Win95 version is specifically designed for the job.)

Windows 3.*x*-specific program launchers and file management shells will retain partial functionality, at best, under Windows 95. Some of them may not work at all, or may cause system compatibility problems. Users who previously enjoyed Norton Desktop for Windows version 3.0 and PC Tools for Windows version 2.0 may want to upgrade to Symantec's Norton Navigator for Windows 95 package. Norton Navigator for Windows 95 has the ability to migrate desktop configurations from both of these earlier shells.

Windows 3.*x* uninstallers (older versions of MicroHelp, Remove-It, Clean-Sweep, and so on) may be partially useful under Windows 95 for deleting unwanted applications and DLLs, but they may not reliably restore applications, since they are unaware of the changes in the new Windows Registration Database. These older packages will also be incapable of dealing with applications specifically written for Windows 95. Win95 versions of these packages are available.

Fax programs, telecommunication packages, and Internet utilities developed for DOS and Windows 3.*x* can generally be depended upon to retain their functionality under Windows 95. This is an area where upgrading to new Win95 versions will deliver feature enhancements and performance improvements, but nothing will be lost by continuing to use older applications.

Multimedia applications and CDs written for DOS and Windows 3.*x* will generally continue to work under Windows 95. Packages that specifically add Windows 3.*x* performance enhancements (like the Monty Python Complete Waste of Time CD) will lose functionality. Some Windows 3.*x* and DOS games may be incompatible. See the Microsoft software compatibility list for details.

Most real-mode DOS drivers for SCSI peripherals, CD-ROM drives, PCMCIA cards, and sound cards operate transparently under Windows 95 when loaded in CONFIG.SYS and AUTOEXEC.BAT. Many of these drivers can be replaced by Win95's protected mode support after installation is complete. See Chapter 7 for details. DOS memory managers, software drivers for Enhanced IDE controllers, and video card TSRs tend to be more problematic.

Users who depend on the peer-to-peer network connection bundled with Windows for Workgroups or connections to a Windows NT server should experience no difficulty in migrating to Windows 95's Client for Microsoft Networks. Sites that use combined Microsoft-Novell network configurations should make sure that Novell Bindery Services are enabled to use Windows 95's built-in Client for Novell NetWare.

tip *Users who depend on Microsoft's Schedule +, or some Windows 3.x groupware and network e-mail packages may want to refrain, initially, from installing the Microsoft Exchange component of Windows 95 until they are prepared to upgrade to Win95-specific schedulers and e-mail management.*

For more information about working with DOS and Windows 3.*x* software under Windows 95, see Chapter 7.

Pre-installation Preparation

Before you take the plunge and run the Windows 95 Setup program, you may want to optimize your hard disk, make some system configuration preparations, and develop an installation strategy.

Some utility packages can actually fine-tune your system to make it more receptive to Win95 installation. These programs may optimize your hard disk, and assist you in backing up, compressing, or deleting unnecessary files.

The WIN'95 Advisor

TouchStone's WIN'95 Advisor (see Figure 2-2) is a full-featured commercial package that combines a series of system performance benchmarks with installation aids written specifically to ease the transition between Windows 3.*x* and Windows 95. The WIN'95 Advisor suite conducts an inventory of all your system peripherals and rates performance in five categories: system hardware, memory, disk, multimedia, and a bonus category that evaluates your I/O ports, high-performance video, modem, and sound card. The overall results of the Advisor's tests are displayed on a colorful 100-point speedometer. If you want to know the basis of the rating assigned to your computer's performance, you can click on any individual category to bring up explanatory help screens. The Advisor is designed primarily to be run under Windows 3.*x*, but you can rerun the various tests under Windows 95 to obtain an operating system performance comparison. The tests are designed to give a low or poor rating to systems that are really Windows 95-incompatible. A 486DX4 100MHz system with 16MB of RAM, large hard disk, and CD-ROM support is likely to score above 80, with a rating of "Wow!"

The Advisor's Space Report provides both a pie-chart illustration and numerical report of the amount of space available on each of your disk

FIGURE 2-2

TouchStone's WIN'95 Advisor

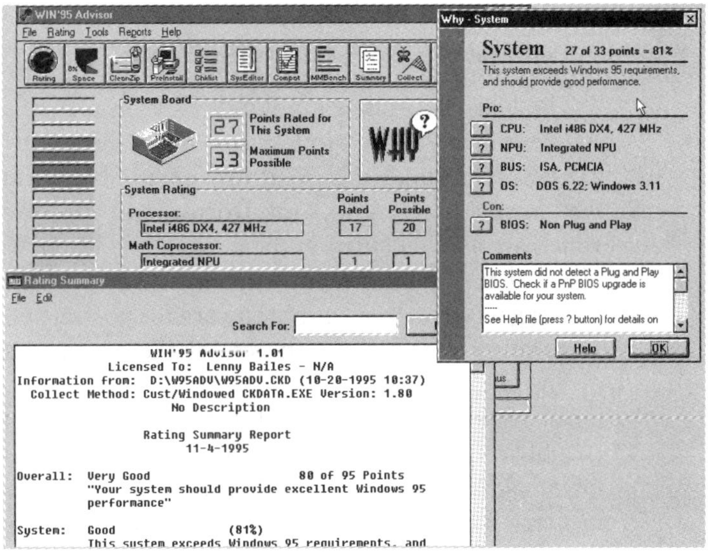

partitions versus the amount of space required for each of the four basic Windows 95 installation options. (Chapter 3 of this book also provides a thorough discussion of these installation choices.) The package also includes early versions of the Microsoft hardware and software compatibility databases, previously discussed. The lists included in the Advisor date back to June of 1995 and have been revised several times since.

Perhaps the program's most useful feature is its ability to create preconfigured Windows 95 installation scripts. While running under Windows 3.*x*, the Advisor can walk you through the various Windows 95 setup options allowing you to choose various components and features that you want to include. These choices are then compiled and saved to a script file that automates the actual Windows 95 installation. A help document produced during the system inventory provides you with an advisory checklist that suggests possible upgrade options to cover your system's weak points.

Another useful feature is a Clean and Zip module. This feature scans each of your disk partitions for files that are generally superfluous to your system's performance. The search module's default can be reconfigured with user-defined file extensions, date and time specifications, and include/exclude options for duplicate and read-only files. Any and all files in the list can be selected for global copy, delete, move, or rename operations. You can also generate a printed list that can be used in conjunction with a utility like PKZIP or LHARC to produce a compressed archive. (The package does not contain compression utilities or support for automatic file compression.)

Norton Utilities for Win95/Pre-installation TuneUp

The Norton Utilities for Windows 95 is a suite primarily designed to be run after the new operating system is installed. One disk, however, contains a Pre-installation TuneUp kit that simply batch runs MS-DOS versions of the Norton Diagnostics, Disk Doctor, and Space Wizard programs (two of which are also included in the package as 32-bit Win95 applications). The idea is that running this kit will resolve any problems with your hard disk's file structure, analyze your hardware for possible port or interrupt conflicts, and allow you to delete unnecessary files to create more disk space.

The Diagnostics and Disk Doctor modules are both excellent utilities to have around, although their functionality before installing Windows 95 is roughly equivalent to the versions included in Norton Utilities, version 8 for DOS. Ndiags provides an inventory of your system's components and memory usage, performing basic tests for interrupt conflicts, and on the integrity of your motherboard, hard disk, video card, and I/O ports. Disk Doctor is a more sophisticated disk repair utility than Microsoft's ScanDisk. It can reveal and repair problems with cross-linked files, lost clusters, the partition table, and the file allocation table. Space Wizard is a file-cleanup utility similar to the one included in TouchStone's WIN'95 Advisor. It searches for files and directories with specified extensions allowing you to delete them in bulk to create more hard disk space.

The DOS TuneUp module, while helpful, is not sufficient, in itself, to justify purchase of the Norton Utilities for Windows 95. Most of the chores performed in the tuneup can be easily duplicated by shareware utilities or previous versions of Norton, itself. However, once Windows 95 is your primary operating system, you'll probably want "Norton for 95" on your hard disk. The emergency recovery capabilities of the package can only be appreciated properly when you need to undelete crucial files, or your hard disk really develops problems. At that point, you'll wish you had it. (Norton Utilities for Windows 95 and its companion package, Norton Navigator, are discussed more fully in Chapter 14.)

Antivirus Scan

Before installing Windows 95, you would be well-advised to scan your hard disk with a recently updated antivirus utility. This is particularly true if you plan to use floppy disk media to install the new operating system. If there are any boot sector viruses lurking on your hard disk, there's a good chance that they will infect and corrupt Windows 95 floppy installation disk number 2. If you are installing from floppies, you should definitely write protect this disk, and remember to virus check your hard disk!

Preserving Useful Windows 3.x *Accessories*

If you install Windows 95 by upgrading into a Windows 3.*x* directory, several useful Windows 3.*x* productivity applets are overwritten, and others may be deleted. Some of the mini-apps bundled with Windows 3.1 contain features that are not implemented in their Windows 95 replacements. Windows 95 leaves program stubs in the upgraded directory for Write and Paintbrush, but if you double-click them, copies of the new WordPad and Paint applets are launched instead of the original programs. Windows Terminal, Recorder, and Cardfile are missing from Windows 95. The Windows 95 versions of Character Map and Calculator have less complete Help files than the older versions.

If you want to preserve some of these utilities for use in Windows 95, create a TEMP directory on your hard disk before Win95 installation. Copy both the .EXE and .HLP files for each application you want to save into the TEMP directory. After Windows 95 is installed, you can run these programs from the TEMP directory or recopy them back to your Windows directory.

(See Chapter 5 for more details on differences between Windows 3.*x* and Windows 95 mini-applications.)

Emergency Boot Disk

It's a good idea to make an emergency boot disk with your current operating system before installing Windows 95. This will allow you to restore dual boot options, if the Win95 installation process aborts before completion. More importantly, it will guarantee that you can access your CD-ROM drive or other device-driven peripherals in an emergency. Format a floppy disk with the /S system option and make sure to include the following files on it:

- Backups of your current AUTOEXEC.BAT and CONFIG.SYS
- Important system drivers for disk compression, SCSI controller, CD-ROM drive, sound card, and other I/O peripherals
- Important DOS system drivers and utilities: HIMEM.SYS, ATTRIB, CHKDSK, SCANDISK, FDISK, MEM, FORMAT, XCOPY, and so on
- An antivirus utility, such as McAfee's SCAN and VSHIELD shareware

Backup Preparations

It's not strictly necessary to back up your hard disk before installing Windows 95, but it never hurts to have a recent system backup around on tape. You may also want to back up your Windows 3.*x* configuration files to guard against the (unlikely but possible) event that they become lost or corrupted.

tip *To perform a quick backup of your Windows 3.x configuration files, make a subdirectory under your WINDOWS directory called INIS, and execute the following commands:*

```
COPY [D:]\WINDOWS\*.INI INIS
COPY [D:]\WINDOWS\*.GRP INIS
```

System Configuration Changes

Question: "Should I modify my system configuration before installing Windows 95?"

Answer: This isn't really a specific installation requirement, but making certain configuration preparations may ease the Win95 Setup process.

Modify CONFIG.SYS/AUTOEXEC.BAT to Disable DOS-Specific TSRs

The Win95 Setup program will take care of SmartDrive, MSCDEX, Setver, and other Microsoft-specific utilities, but you may want to take the additional step of disabling third-party disk caches, pop-up utilities, video and hard disk speed-up utilities, and third-party memory managers. (See Chapter 6 for more details on the compatibility of third-party memory managers with Windows 95.)

note *Don't remove commands in your AUTOEXEC.BAT that adjust the scan rate frequency for your monitor. These adjustments can be used by the Windows 95 setup routine to select the proper video card/monitor configuration.*

Clean Up the Windows 3.x System Configuration

You may want to open your Windows 3.*x* startup folder and remove icons that auto-run command shells and file utilities. If you are running Norton Desktop for Windows or PC Tools for Windows as your default desktop shell, disable them and restore the Program Manager. There is generally no need to disable third-party high-resolution video drivers. They won't interfere with Windows 95's hardware detection routines.

You may be wondering what to do with all of the DLLs and virtual drivers that have been placed in your old Windows directory by third-party applications. In general, you needn't worry about these DLLs. They probably won't interfere with the Windows 95 setup, although you can purge extraneous files with a package like Remove-It or Quarterdeck's Clean Sweep.

What About Disk Compression?

You should have no trouble installing Windows 95 on a system that has been compressed with Microsoft's DriveSpace/DoubleSpace, or Stac Electronics' Stacker 2-4.1. Some problems with SuperStor compression have been documented, and if you are running that program, you would be wise to decompress your designated Windows 95 partition before installing.

The general rule for installing on a compressed system is to make sure there is enough room for essential boot files on the uncompressed portion of your host drive. Allow at least 1.5MB of uncompressed space—more, if you want to use that partition to contain the Windows swap file. (See Chapter 3 for details about hard disk space requirements for various Windows 95 installation options.)

Planning the Installation

You will be given a choice during the Windows 95 installation of several different installation types designed to fit your productivity needs and available disk resources. For an overview of Win95 features you get automatically and those you'll need to add or install separately, see Chapters 3 and 4.

Before you actually start the Setup program, the most important decision you should make is whether to install Windows 95 in a clean directory or disk partition, or whether to do an upgrade over your current version of Windows 3.*x*. The theoretical advantage of installing Windows 95 into a clean directory is that this procedure allows you to retain your previous versions of DOS and Windows 3.*x* on your hard disk. This allows you to choose your operating system at boot time and work in either operating environment.

The disadvantage of this choice is that your Windows 3.*x* program groups and application settings are not migrated to the new environment. You're faced with the task of reinstalling many of your Windows 3.*x* programs if you want to use them under Windows 95. Furthermore, you may have to install multiple copies of some applications if you want them to work properly under both Windows 95 and Windows 3.1. This is time consuming, and it's also a waste of disk space.

The second alternative (recommended by Microsoft) is to overwrite your existing copy of Windows by installing Windows 95 in the same directory. The advantage of this choice is that your application settings and program groups will automatically be transferred to the new environment. However, you lose the ability to "dual-boot" to your previous version of DOS and you can no longer run Windows 3.*x* if you have a reason to do so.

Have Your Cake and Eat It, Too!

Fortunately, there is a third installation option, one not publicized or discussed at all by Microsoft: you can "clone" your existing Windows 3.*x* directory into another drive or directory, install Windows 95 into the clone directory and retain your old copies of Windows and DOS as well. This procedure was not specifically planned for in Microsoft's Windows 95 installation routine, but it can be carried through by using third-party utilities or manually, through a series of file manipulations.

Vertisoft Remove-It—The Easy Way

Vertisoft's Remove-It, version 2.0 is a utility package designed to uninstall, archive, and reinstall Windows 3.*x* applications. It includes the Win95 Upgrade Assistant utility (see Figure 2-3), which migrates existing Windows 3.*x* configuration information to a clean copy of Windows 95 installed in a separate directory. The Upgrade Assistant runs under Windows 3.*x*, taking a snapshot of your .INI files, program groups, and application settings. Once this snapshot is taken, you can use it at any time to migrate Windows 3.1 configuration information to a "vanilla" installation of Windows 95.

Here's how you can use this utility in the Win95 installation process:

1. Install and run Remove-It under Windows 3.*x*. The Clean-Up Coach feature can be used to archive or remove any unnecessary applications or extra files on your hard disk to free up storage space. The Upgrade Assistant component of Remove-It takes a snapshot of your Windows 3.1 system configuration.
2. After you've taken a configuration snapshot, run the Windows 95 Setup program. When prompted for an installation directory, specify a directory other than the current WINDOWS directory.
3. A clean copy of Windows 95 will be installed in the directory you specify. Your Windows 3.*x* program groups and application settings are not migrated at this point.
4. After your computer has restarted in Windows 95, open My Computer\Explorer and run the Upgrade Assistant utility again. (Open the REMOVEIT directory that was installed under Windows 3.*x* and double-click on RTUPGR.EXE.)
5. Follow the onsscreen instructions to migrate your Win 3.*x* program configuration to Windows 95.

Dual Boot with Windows 3.x App Migration—The Do-It-Yourself Method

You can keep your old copy of Windows and migrate its settings to Windows 95 manually. The procedure is a bit more tedious, but saves you the cost of purchasing the Remove-It package, which is designed primarily

FIGURE 2-3

The Upgrade Assistant

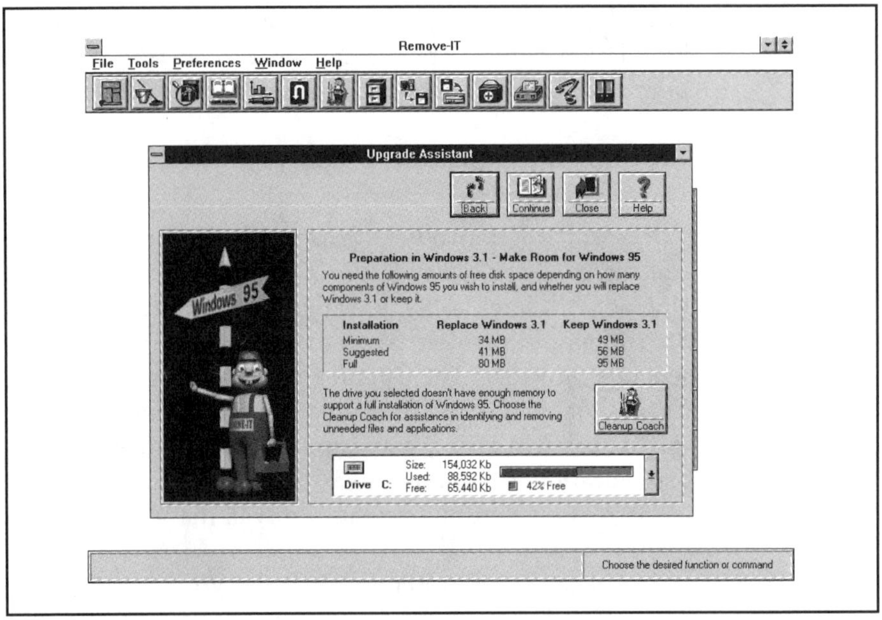

for use with Windows 3.1. (Remove-It does not support uninstalling, archiving and restoring 32-bit Windows 95 applications.) To preserve your dual boot option and application settings manually, follow these steps:

1. Exit Windows 3.*x* to a DOS command prompt. Use the DOS XCOPY command to duplicate your current WINDOWS directory on another partition or in another directory on the same partition. Here's an example:

   ```
   XCOPY C:\WINDOWS\*.* D:\WIN95\*.* /E /V
   ```

   Be sure to append the /E and /V switches to include all subdirectories.

note *You can clone your WINDOWS 3.1 directory by XCOPYing it to a new directory on the same partition, but if you have two partitions defined on your system, it will simplify things to have one version of Windows that corresponds to each drive letter.*

2. Back up your current DOS directory, since the Windows 95 installation program is going to think this is an "upgrade" install and eliminate most of its contents. For example:

   ```
   MD C:\DOSBAK
   XCOPY C:\DOS\*.* C:\DOSBAK\*.* /E /V
   ```

3. Back up your AUTOEXEC.BAT and CONFIG.SYS files. You'll need these original versions, later, when you want to dual boot to your pre-Win95 configuration. Example:

```
COPY C:\CONFIG.SYS CONFIG.W31
COPY C:\AUTOEXEC.BAT C:\AUTOEXEC.W31
```

4. Edit your AUTOEXEC.BAT and CONFIG.SYS to change all references to your current WINDOWS directory to the directory name that will be used by Windows 95. This will ensure that the Windows 95 installation routine locates and updates the proper files. Here are some examples:

   - Change DEVICE=C:\WINDOWS\IFSHLP.SYS to DEVICE=D:\WIN95\IFSHLP.SYS
   - Change PATH=C:\DOS;C:\WINDOWS to PATH=C:\DOS;D:\WIN95

5. Edit all of the files with the .INI extension in the newly cloned WIN95 directory. Change all references from your old WINDOWS directory to the drive and directory that will contain Windows 95. This is, perhaps, the trickiest step in this procedure. It is necessary so that your application settings and program groups will be migrated correctly. The following command issued from the DOS prompt or in a batch file will successively open each .INI file in the DOS text editor, allowing you to globally substitute the name of your new WIN95 directory for your old WINDOWS directory:

```
FOR %A IN (D:\WIN95\*.INI) DO EDIT %A
```

   In this example, D:\WIN95 is the name chosen for the directory that will contain Windows 95. You may substitute the drive and directory you've chosen: The DOS editor will open to the first .INI file in the directory.

6. Use the Replace function on the Search menu to enter the name of your original WINDOWS directory on the Find What line and the name of your proposed Windows 95 directory on the Replace With line. For example:

   Find What: **C:\WINDOWS**
   Replace With: **D:\WIN95**

7. When the global replacement has been made, save the file and exit the DOS editor. It will automatically restart with the next .INI file loaded. Repeat the global replace procedure until all of the .INI files have been updated.

8. Reboot your PC so that CONFIG.SYS and AUTOEXEC.BAT now point to the "cloned" WINDOWS directory. Start the "cloned" version of Windows that now resides in the WIN95 directory. You should be able to do this simply by changing to the WIN95 directory and entering **WIN** at the command prompt.

9. Inspect\Edit your Program Manager icons. This step is optional. Generally, most of the mini-apps in your Accessories folder will have Properties settings that simply list the program name with no path or directory specified. However, if you have other applications residing in the WINDOWS directory identified by drive and path, you may need to edit the properties for their icons to change the reference to your new WIN95 directory. Select the icon and click on Properties in the Program Manager File menu. Change references in the Command line and Working Directory boxes as necessary. Look for any icons that you know represent Windows applications, but which now are "MS-DOS" icons. (There may not be any, and even if there are, you can perform this step after Windows 95 has been installed if you're in a hurry.)

10. Edit the Windows System Registry to update directory references. This step is necessary so that OLE servers and clients will function properly for the various Windows 3.1 applications that will be migrated to the new operating environment. Open REGEDIT in verbose mode by entering **REGEDIT.EXE /V** in the Program Manager's File\Run screen. You will have to scroll through the database manually, searching for references to your original WINDOWS directory. When you find one, click on it with the mouse and change the reference to your new WINDOWS directory. (When you click on a key, it will appear in the Value window toward the top of the screen. You can click on the text in this window and edit it.) When you've replaced all instances of C:\WINDOWS with D:\WIN95 (or the drive/directory names that apply to your system), exit REGEDIT.

You're now ready to run the Windows 95 Setup program from the Program Manager's File\Run menu to install Windows 95. When you are prompted for an installation directory, make sure Setup is pointed to the "cloned" directory you've created. (See Chapter 3 for detailed information about the installation process.)

After Windows 95 is installed, you'll need to perform a few mop-up maneuvers to make sure that the dual-boot option works properly. (This is because the installation program now thinks that you've upgraded your only copy of Windows. It is unaware of the original copy that still resides on your hard disk.)

1. Restore your original DOS directory from the backup you made in Step 2, above.
2. Copy the pre-Win95 backups of AUTOEXEC.BAT and CONFIG.SYS that you made previously to the filenames that Windows 95 uses for its dual boot option:

   ```
   COPY C:\CONFIG.W31 C:\CONFIG.DOS
   COPYC:\AUTOEXEC.W31 C:\AUTOEXEC.DOS
   ```

3. Enable the Dual Boot option in MSDOS.SYS. From Windows 95, open a DOS command prompt and issue the command **ATTRIB -R -H C:\MSDOS.SYS.** Next, open MSDOS.SYS in a text editor (such as Notepad or the DOS Editor) and add the following command under the [Options] section of the file:

   ```
   BOOTMULTI=1.
   ```

These steps should make your migrated Windows 3.1 applications 99.5 percent compatible with the new Win95 operating environment. In order to preserve 100 percent compatibility with some applications, it may be necessary to modify registration information that the application stores in its default directory. For instance, Microsoft Word for Windows version 6 refers to a file called SETUP.STF located in the WINWORD directory (or in the MSOFFICE\SETUP directory, if you're using the complete MS Office suite).

You can open SETUP.STF in the DOS Editor and perform a global search-and-replace operation to substitute the name of your Windows 95 directory for the name of your previous Windows 3.*x* directory. If you do this, you may experience some minor problems with the OLE Server function when you run your Office applications from your original Windows 3.*x* configuration. This is usually no worse than having to open an application manually or specify path information if an OLE error message pops up when you attempt to automatically launch an application by double-clicking on an embedded OLE object.

Other Operating Systems

Windows 95 may coexist easily with Warp OS/2 or Windows NT. In the case of Warp OS/2, it is generally best to have Windows 95 and OS/2 reside on two separate disk partitions to avoid conflicts resulting from the different systems of storing long filenames. If you have OS/2 on your system before installing Windows 95, you will get some warning messages during the Win95 Setup procedure warning you that your OS/2 functionality may be lost. It is safe to ignore these messages and proceed with the installation. After Windows 95 is installed, the OS/2 Boot Manager partition is deactivated, and your primary C-drive partition is made active. If you want to restore the OS/2 Boot Manager, just run FDISK (located in the WINDOWS\COMMAND directory) from within Windows 95. You'll see that the Boot Manager Non-DOS partition is still listed. To restore Boot Manager, change the active partition from Drive C to the Boot Manager partition.

If Windows 95 is installed before Windows NT, you can simply boot to a DOS prompt and install Windows NT with the Boot-to-DOS option enabled. (Windows NT must be installed to its own directory, it cannot share the Windows 95 directory.) When you reboot the system, the Windows NT boot manager will appear. If you select the Boot-to-DOS option, this will start the system in Windows 95.

If Windows 95 is installed after Windows NT, you will need to re-enable the Windows NT Boot-to-DOS option to boot into Windows NT. See Appendix A for details.

Running Setup

This chapter has given you the necessary information you need to prepare your computer for the jump to Windows 95. The next chapter provides a step-by-step overview of the Windows 95 installation process. You may also want to take a look soon at Chapters 5, 6, 7, and 16 for supplementary information on making a smooth transition to Windows 95 from your current software and hardware configuration.

chapter 3

Installation

- Installing from different media
- Setup command-line options
- The system integrity and hardware detection phase
- Installation types and selecting components
- More of the lost *Star Trek TNG*

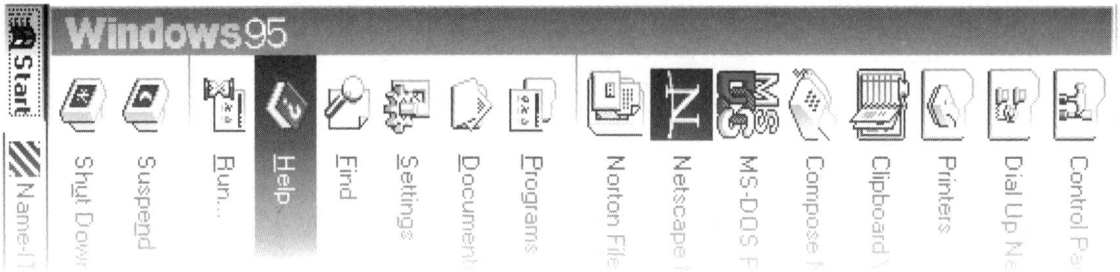

ONE of the best things about Windows 95 is that although the operating system has become more complicated, the installation process has not become correspondingly more difficult. Got a SCSI card, a CD-ROM drive, or a high-res video card? The chances are that Windows 95 will detect them automatically, eliminating the need to run third-party software and studiously append command-line parameters. This chapter walks you through the Windows 95 installation procedure. You'll find out about the different media on which Win95 is distributed, how to install from floppies, from a CD-ROM, from your hard disk, or even across a network. We take you through the installation process step by step, discussing the various screen options that pop up along the way.

Before You Begin

Microsoft has done its best to make the Windows 95 installation easy and automatic. Windows 3.*x* made it vastly easier to install new programs than under DOS, but there was still potential for chaos. One installation aspect could fail midway through, crippling the machine's ability to run either the old or the new system. Windows 95 has resolved many of these problems. For instance, if you install over an existing copy of Windows 3.1, you can ALT-TAB to different applications throughout the installation process, even escape to DOS to format a floppy disk. The new "safe recovery" feature saves aspects of your old configuration until the new one is in place.

To begin an installation simply locate the SETUP.EXE file on your CD-ROM, network, or floppy media. Setup can be executed from an

MS-DOS prompt, or from an existing copy of Windows, through the File-Run command.

note *To install Windows 95 from CD-ROM, you must boot a configuration of your previous operating system that recognizes your CD-ROM drive. Once Windows 95 has been installed on your system, you may be able to remove drivers from CONFIG.SYS and AUTOEXEC.BAT that were previously necessary. (See Chapters 6 and 8 for more details.) If you run Windows 95 Setup from a DOS command prompt, the system utilizes the SHELL=SETUP.EXE command to start the Setup program.*

Windows 95 is available as a 3.5-inch floppy product, containing 12 disks, or on a CD-ROM. If at all possible, buy the CD-ROM product. For instance, if you want to buy a Windows 95 CD-ROM and the store only has floppies, keep driving around until you find a place that has what you want. The CD-ROM version is superior for two basic reasons: speed and convenience of installation. The CD-ROM also contains extra software such as the Windows 95 Resource Kit, video animations, games, and other goodies. While you can install Windows 95 without a CD-ROM drive, anyone who lacks one may find this a good time to upgrade. As application programs grow larger and larger, they will increasingly be distributed through CD-ROMs instead of floppy disks. These CD-ROMs will include added value in the form of extra programs, utilities, clip art, and so on, as Windows 95 does. So unless you want to waste a large part of every year swapping disks, a CD-ROM will be a time saving investment.

If you have a machine without a CD-ROM drive and you don't intend to get one just now, you won't have a choice. Your floppy-based odyssey is about to begin. Consider that it could be worse: You could be stuck with a machine equipped with outdated 5.25-inch floppy drives—an acknowledged rarity, since most all machines capable of running Windows 95 now include 3.5-inch drives. If you're using an older dinosaur with a 5.25-inch drive, you have several options.

Each Windows 95 package contains a fulfillment card that allows you to acquire 5.25-inch disks by mail.

If you have access to a second machine with either a CD-ROM drive or 3.5-inch floppy drive, you may not need to send in the postcard. The installation files from the Windows 95 CD (or 3.5-inch floppy disks) can be copied to a hard disk directory. Once you've created an installation directory on one machine, Windows 95 can be installed on the second machine, directly, through a Novell or Microsoft network connection. Or, the installation files on the hard disk of the first machine can be transferred to the hard disk of the second machine through any network or local cable connection. Here's how to copy the appropriate files:

- To copy the Win95 installation files from the CD to your hard disk, simply create a directory on a hard disk partition with 35MB of available space. At the DOS command line, type **COPY E:\WIN95*.* D:\INSTALL** (where E is the CD-ROM drive and D:\INSTALL is the hard disk directory you want to use). Then simply run SETUP.EXE from the D:\INSTALL directory.
- If another machine is connected to D:\INSTALL through a Novell or Microsoft network, you can copy this directory to the client machine, or you can log on to the directory and run the installation through the network drive.

caution *This second technique will not work reliably with the current versions of LANtastic for DOS and Windows 3.x. If you're in doubt, just copy the entire installation directory from the server to the client and run SETUP.EXE locally.*

- To copy the Win95 installation files from a set of 3.5-inch floppy disks to a hard disk directory, insert each of the 12 disks in turn into the floppy drive and COPY *.* to the target directory on your hard drive.

note *If you have difficulty copying disks 2 through 12 with the DOS COPY command, then copy the EXTRACT command (found on disk 1) to your hard drive, and run it on each of the other installation diskettes using the following syntax:*

EXTRACT/C A:.* D:\INSTALL*

Once the contents of the installation disks have been copied to a hard disk directory, you can run Setup from the hard drive, or transfer the contents of the directory through a network or cable connection to a system lacking a 3.5-inch floppy drive.

If you are upgrading to Windows 95 and adding a CD-ROM drive simultaneously, it may be wiser to install Windows 95 from floppy disks before installing the CD-ROM system. Once Win95 is installed, its autodetect feature may detect and recognize the CD-ROM drive without the necessity for additional, third-party software. In this case, installing Windows 95 may be the *last* time you'll ever need to tediously swap floppies back and forth in order to install a new application program. Once you start buying 32-bit applications like the new Microsoft Office, a CD-ROM drive will look like the wisest investment you've ever made.

Getting Ready for Setup

Windows 95 tends to personify the setup process, having the operating system speak to you directly. Microsoft wants Setup to be your friend. Through screen messages, it tells you exactly what it is doing at each stage of the installation.

The Windows 95 installation process is well-designed in its ability to detect the problems and subtleties inherent in individual systems. In most cases, if trouble spots are detected, you will be warned, and the process will correct itself, automatically. The following preemptory steps may help you to prepare for the process and minimize the bumps you might encounter along the way.

1. Perhaps the most important preparation you can make for Windows 95 is to make sure that the target system is up to the task. Make sure that your computer components meet the minimum requirements for Windows 95. Chapter 2 of this book supplies information you need to know. You may also want to read SETUP.TXT, a file located on the first Windows 95 installation disk or the WIN95 directory of the CD-ROM.
2. Verify that key system files and critical data have been backed up. If your computer is a network workstation or server, make sure that the network software is running properly before beginning the installation. Windows 95 uses the settings from the existing network configuration to set up the new configuration.
3. Determine whether you will be upgrading over an existing copy of Windows 3.1 or Windows for Workgroups, or if you'll be installing Windows 95 into a clean directory. Check and defragment the partition that will contain the operating system. Have a blank, formatted floppy disk at hand to insert when Windows 95 offers to create an emergency startup disk.
4. Locate the driver disks supplied with network cards, hard drive controllers, video adapters, scanners, CD-ROM drives, and so on. These may not be needed, but it's a good idea to have them handy, in case a third-party driver disk is specifically requested during the installation.

5. Before starting Windows 95 either from DOS or Windows, remove all TSR programs and third-party memory managers, such as QEMM, NETROOM, or 386MAX. The best way to do this from within Windows 3.*x* is to load SYSEDIT and disable all references to these programs in the CONFIG.SYS and AUTOEXEC.BAT files with the REM command. (You may want to restore the Microsoft DEVICE=HIMEM.SYS statement to CONFIG.SYS if you disable your third-party memory manager.)
6. If you are installing Windows 95 from a previous version of Windows, close all applications other than the Program Manager. (If you discover that you need to create space on your hard disk, or format a floppy disk after the installation has begun, you can actually access the File Manager or open a DOS session by pressing ALT-TAB until you're back in the Program Manager.

The Voyage

When Setup begins, the opening screen informs you that the process will take from 30 to 60 minutes, depending on the number and types of selected options. This estimate might not be entirely accurate. Some sources within Microsoft estimate an installation time of 12 minutes on a fast Pentium machine, but they project that a completely outdated machine might take longer than a starship voyage to Arcturus. A long, drawn-out installation could be a harbinger of Windows 95's poor performance on outdated hardware. To spare you chagrin, we've included some tips in Chapter 16 for upgrading peripherals or choosing a computer adequate to run your new operating system.

Phase I—Hardware Detection/Component Selection

The first phase of the installation detects your hardware configuration, allows you to specify the installation type, and copies the appropriate files to the hard disk. The second phase reboots the computer in Windows 95 and finalizes desktop and other system settings. This can be a time-consuming process. If you have a fast Pentium CPU and a quad-speed CD-ROM drive, it will take only 30 minutes; a floppy installation on an outdated 386 may take an hour and a half. Most of us will be in between, within the sanctioned 30-to-60-minute estimate from Microsoft.

Starting Windows 95 Setup from Windows 3.1 or Windows for Workgroups

1. Start your computer in the usual way, and run Windows.
2. If you are installing Windows 95 from floppy disks, insert disk 1 in the drive and make it the active drive in the File Manager. If you are installing Windows 95 from CD-ROM, put the compact disc in the drive and make that the active drive. If you are installing Windows 95 from source files on a network server, connect to that server and switch to the shared network directory that contains the Windows 95 source files. If you are installing Windows 95 from files copied to a local hard disk directory, run the copy of SETUP.EXE located in that directory.

Starting Windows 95 Setup from MS-DOS

1. Start your computer in the usual way.
2. If you are installing Windows 95 from floppy disks, insert disk 1 in the drive and make that the active drive.
3. If you are installing Windows 95 from CD-ROM, put the compact disc in the drive and make that the active drive.
4. If you are installing Windows 95 from source files on a network server, connect to that server and switch to the shared network directory that contains the Windows 95 source files.
5. If you are installing Windows 95 from files copied to a local hard disk directory, change to that directory.

At the command prompt, type **SETUP**, and then press ENTER. Follow the instructions on screen, as described in the following sections of this chapter.

Starting Windows 95 Setup from a Network Computer Using a Setup Script

1. Log on to the network, running the existing network client.
2. Connect to the server that contains the Windows 95 distribution files.

3. At the command prompt, run Windows 95 Setup by specifying the batch file that contains the Setup script. Use this syntax:

   SETUP *MSBATCH*.INF

   For example, type **SETUP \\SERVER1\WIN95\SCRIPT1.INF** to run Setup using a script named SCRIPT1.INF, stored in the WIN95 directory on a server named Server1.

For detailed information about installing Windows 95 from a network server, see Appendix A.

System Integrity Check

The first thing on the agenda is a routine system check. A magnifying glass dances atop a system icon, as Windows 95 determines basic system information and confirms the location or presence of a previously installed version of Windows. If you have purchased the Windows 95 upgrade package and no previous Windows version is detected, you will be prompted to insert a floppy installation disk from Windows 3.1 or Windows for Workgroups in the floppy drive. Once a confirmation is made that you are entitled to install Windows 95, a system integrity check is performed on your hard drive subsystem with

FIGURE 3-1

After performing a system integrity check, Setup advises you of any problems that have been detected.

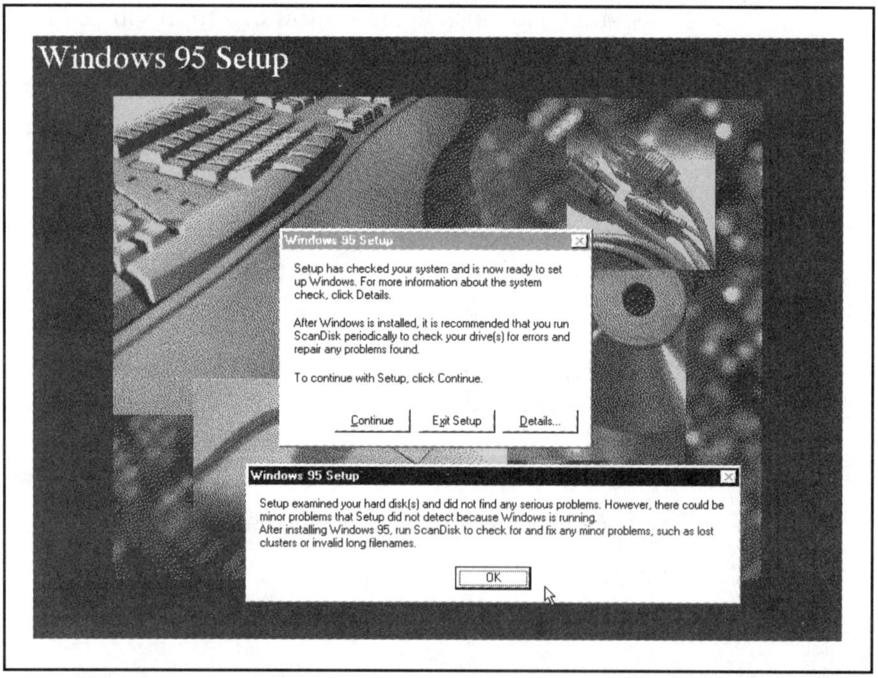

ScanDisk. ScanDisk's presence in the installation process flags and corrects the most obvious errors before the Windows 95 installation.

For one reason or another, Windows 95 may be unable to perform the system check. It may then prompt you to run ScanDisk from DOS using the command SCANDISK.EXE /ALL. After this, you may need to run SETUP /IS from within Windows to bypass the ScanDisk quick check.

note *The /ALL switch is also recommended if your system uses disk compression software other than DoubleSpace or DriveSpace.*

Other installation switches can also be employed to troubleshoot various installation problems. These include the following[1]:

Switch	Purpose
/?	Provides help for syntax and use of Setup command-line switches.
/C	Instructs Windows 95 Setup not to load the SmartDrive disk cache.
/D	Instructs Windows 95 Setup not to use the existing version of Windows for the early phases of Setup. Use this switch if you have problems starting Setup that may be due to missing or damaged supporting files for Windows.
/ID	Instructs Windows 95 Setup not to check for the minimum disk space required to install Windows 95.
/IH	Runs ScanDisk in the foreground so that you can see the results. Use this switch if the system stalls during the ScanDisk check or if an error results.
/IL	Loads the Logitech mouse driver. Use this option if you have a Logitech Series C mouse.
/IQ	Instructs Windows 95 Setup not to perform the ScanDisk quick check when running Setup from MS-DOS. You may want to use this switch if you use other compression software than DriveSpace or DoubleSpace.
/NOSTART	Instructs Windows 95 Setup to copy a minimal installation of the required Windows 3.*x* DLLs used by Windows 95 Setup, and then to exit to DOS without installing Windows 95.
/*SCRIPT_FILE*	Instructs Windows 95 Setup to use settings in the specified script to automatically install Windows 95; for example, if MSBATCH.INF is used.

If Setup determines that there is adequate space in your current Windows directory, it will proceed to the hardware detection phase. If there is insufficient space, you'll see a message like this one:

[1]From *The Windows 95 Resource Kit*. Copyright © 1995, Microsoft Corporation. Reprinted with permission of Microsoft Press. All rights reserved.

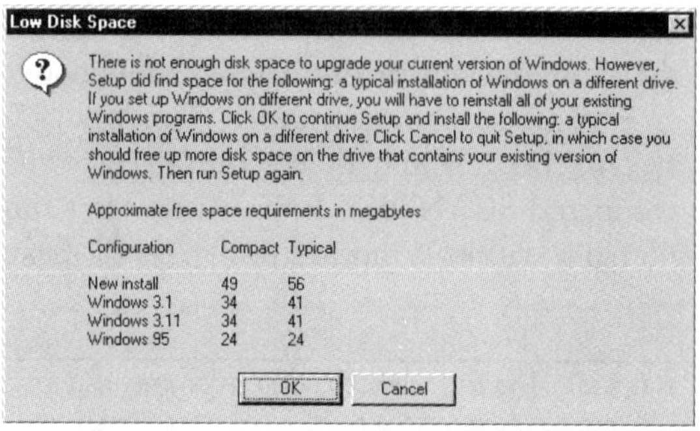

You will either need to free up space on the partition that contains your current Windows directory, or place Windows 95 in a new directory on a different drive. Miraculously, Setup actually allows you to escape to DOS or bring up the File Manager at this point, so that you can actually go into your files and create additional disk space.

tip *If you install Windows 95 in a clean directory on a different drive, your existing Windows 3.x applications will not automatically be migrated! However, you can have your cake and eat it too, by "cloning" your Windows 3.x configuration first. You can then install Windows 95 into the "clone directory," automatically migrating your old program settings and preserving the option to boot back to your previous DOS/Windows 3.x setup. For details on how to do this see Chapters 2 and 6.*

License to Compute

The next screen displays the end-user license agreement. Most people will just click OK to proceed, and in most cases this is the wisest strategy. However, some users may be curious as to exactly what they are agreeing to. You have two choices: either to accept or refuse the license terms. Actually, if you want to install the software there is only one choice; refusing to accept ends the installation process immediately.

The multilingual license agreement forbids the illegal copying of software, something with which most PC users are familiar. Aside from the inability to copy the compressed installation disks, Windows 95 is not copy protected. (If you are installing from a CD, you will be prompted to enter a serial number, located on a label pasted to the CD case.) The full version of Windows 95 can be installed on any machine running some version of the DOS operating system. The upgrade version must see files from a previously installed copy of Windows, DOS, or OS/2.

The Windows 95 license differs from the licenses that typically govern Microsoft's application software. If you buy a copy of Microsoft Word, for instance, you are within your rights to install it on every machine that you use. However, two people are *not* allowed to use the programs simultaneously. That is to say, if you've installed Word on a laptop and on a desktop machine, then you could operate both machines in the same room simultaneously. But within a strict interpretation of the license agreement, you could not lend the laptop to a friend for concurrent use in a different location.

The license agreement for Windows 95 specifies that the operating system be installed only on a single machine. So if you wish to upgrade both your laptop and your desktop machine to Windows 95, you are required to purchase two copies of the upgrade package.

Other Operating Systems

If Windows 95 detects the presence of other operating systems on your hard disk, it may display a series of warning messages, such as these:

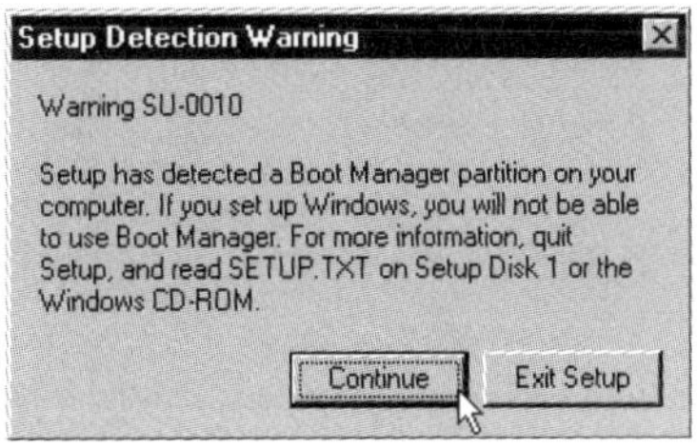

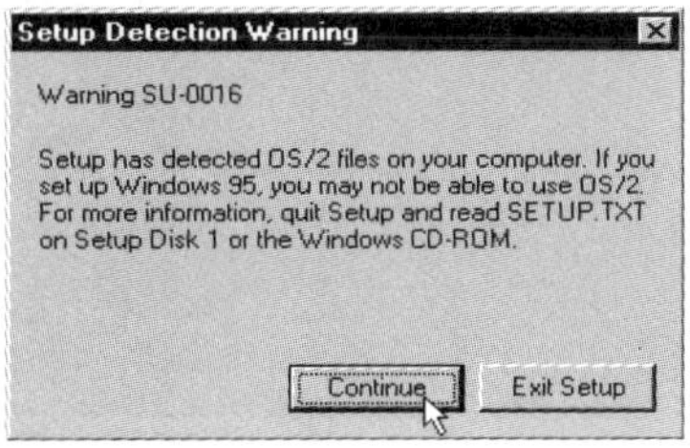

If you have been using OS/2's Boot Manager, you can safely disregard warning messages SU-0010 and SU-0016, and click OK. After Windows 95 is installed, the OS/2 Boot Manager will be temporarily disabled, but you can easily reactivate it with the DOS FDISK utility. (See Appendix A for details on dual booting to Warp OS/2 and Windows NT.)

The Windows Setup Wizard next informs us about the three parts of Setup: Collecting Information About the Computer (hardware detection phase), Copying Windows Files (file copy phase), and Restarting Your Computer (final system configuration phase). In the spirit of safety, Setup reminds you that Windows 95 will replace any versions of Windows and DOS currently on your PC. If this is unacceptable for any reason, you can cancel at this time.

note *Windows 95 is designed to notify you if there are any conflicting programs running—such as an antivirus utility or QEMM-type program—that will interfere with its installation. To accomplish this, you will need to find references to the programs in your CONFIG.SYS and AUTOEXEC.BAT files, and comment them out by placing REM in front of the appropriate statements.*

Other possible conflicts may come from laptop utilities that automatically suspend operation after a period of inactivity. You should disable these programs prior to starting the installation, or be prepared to interrupt the installation to do so.

Worst case scenario: Windows 95 tells you there is a virus protection program installed, but you can find no trace. You have no recollection of ever installing such an animal. Answer: Check to see if antivirus protection has been installed in your computer's CMOS settings. (You'll have to halt the installation process and reboot to do this. Check your computer's documentation for the hot key used on your system to bring up the CMOS options. Search for an antivirus setting, disable it, and save the new CMOS defaults. Then restart the Windows 95 installation process.)

Hardware and Software Detection

In this phase, Windows 95 analyzes basic hardware components as well as identifying the various peripherals that are available. First, Setup determines whether the PC is a "legacy" or a plug-and-play computer. With the former, Setup checks I/O ports and specific memory addresses to determine whether they are being used by known devices. If your PC has a plug-and-play BIOS, this query process is more efficient and accurate since all plug-and-play devices are registered and identified through a central registry.

Additionally, Windows measures the space on the hard disk and determines whether there is enough room to install the desired configuration. For instance, you may have selected a full install, but only have 17MB of free space on the disk. Windows will then tell you exactly how much space you need in order to complete the installation; essentially a count of how many megabytes that you need to clear from the disk.

If there isn't enough room, you have two options:

1. Select a different installation type (Laptop or Compact) or deselect components through the Custom dialog box.
2. ALT-TAB to your current shell and load the File Manager, then delete nonessential files from the hard disk. In this case, you need to be able to delete a number of kilobytes greater than the difference between your desired installation configuration and the amount of available space.

Those with older peripherals installed in their machines may be surprised how adept Windows 95 is at identifying these components. There is also the option for "cross-pollination," wherein legacy peripherals can be identified with a plug-and-play BIOS, and a standard BIOS can identify plug-and-play devices.

In the past, operating systems have plunged users into a morass of IRQ and DMA settings whenever they sought to install peripheral devices (especially multimedia cards). Under Windows 95 these settings still exist, but the burden of coordinating them has shifted from the user to the system itself.

The hardware detection module used during Win95 setup can be subsequently evoked from the Control Panel. Nevertheless, if you have new peripherals to install (like a modem or printer), it's best to plug them into your computer prior to issuing the SETUP command. Let Windows 95 do the configuration work!

note *The Hardware Installation Wizard isn't always, well, wizardly. For instance, it may inform you that you've chosen the wrong driver for your display adapter, even though you've specifically chosen the correct manufacturer's name and type from the driver list. Setup may inform you that the device is not configured properly, and, instead, select a more generic driver. Best not to argue with mom. Just resign yourself and let the system tell you what the hardware type should be. You'll have a chance to come back later and try again via the Control Panel.*

During the hardware detection phase, Windows 95 creates a system registry for the machine, which catalogs and controls all of the specific hardware connected to the PC. If anything in your system configuration throws the installation program for a loop, the installation may be aborted with a note advising you to reboot the computer and run Setup again. The second time around, you can select a special Safe Recovery mode. The information gathered on the first run-through is preserved. The Safe Recovery option causes Setup to skip over the detection of problematical hardware on the second run-through. This allows you to complete the basic Win95 installation. Later on, you can come back to the Control Panel and specify device settings that couldn't be configured automatically.

tip *If the Safe Recovery feature still produces general protection faults on the second run-through, edit your CONFIG.SYS and remove all references to third-party memory managers. Substitute Microsoft's HIMEM.SYS for any statement loading QEMM386.SYS, 386MAX.SYS, or RM386.SYS. If you are running EMM386.EXE, remark it out. (These drivers can be reinstated after Windows 95 has been installed.)*

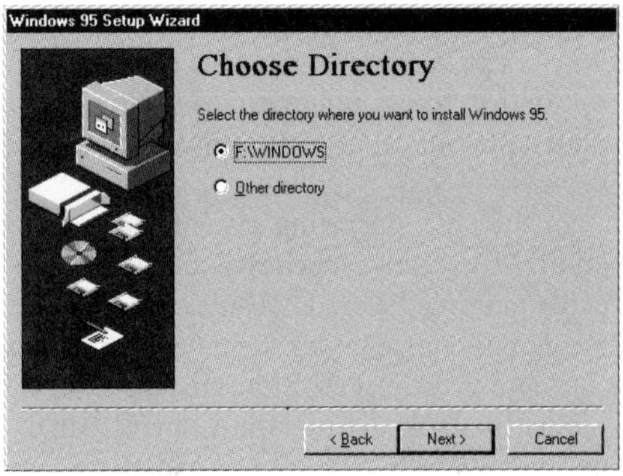

Upgrade or New Install?

The next dialog box allows you to select the default installation directory. If a previous version of Windows is present on the system, this directory (for instance, C:\WINDOWS) will show up by default. You can use the Other Directory option on this screen to specify another destination for Windows 95. If you want to preserve an existing Windows 3.1 or Windows for Workgroups 3.11 configuration, then specify a Windows directory on another partition, or install to C:\WIN95 instead of to C:\WINDOWS.

remember *If you elect to place Windows 95 in a brand new directory, a dual boot environment will be set up with your previous version of DOS and Windows 3.1. The disadvantage is that your current Windows 3.1 applications and settings will not be migrated to Windows 95.*

If you place Windows 95 in a directory that contains a previous version of Windows, an upgrade installation will be performed. Your current

FIGURE 3-2

Your old program settings will be lost if you install Windows 95 into a brand new directory.

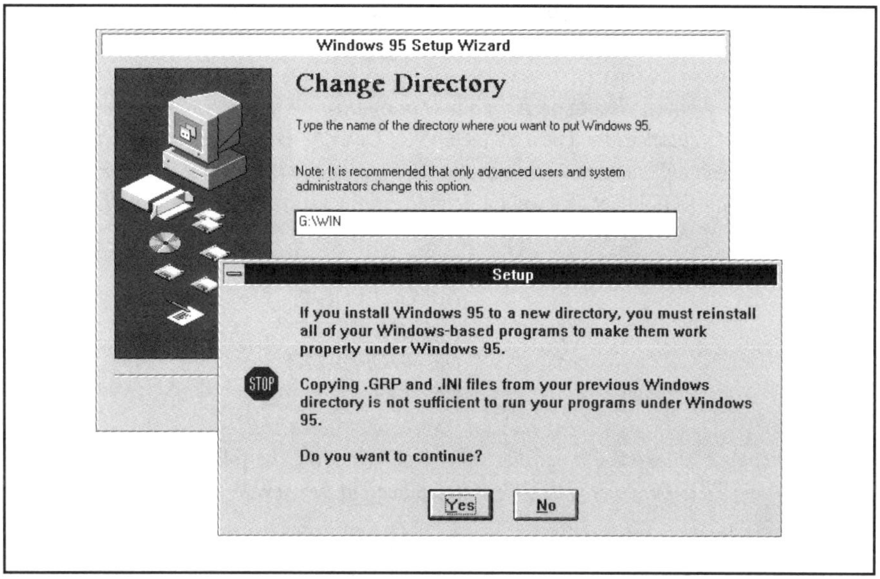

Windows program groups and application settings will be migrated to Windows 95, and the old versions of Windows and DOS will be overwritten.

note *You can choose the Save System Files option at this point to archive your current Windows and DOS files. You can use this option after Windows 95 has been installed to remove it and return to your previous Windows/DOS configuration.*

Component Selection

After you confirm the directory for Windows 95, Setup searches for already-installed components in your previous configuration and verifies that there is enough disk space on the chosen partition. The next screen offers four installation options: typical, portable, compact, and custom.

What Happens to DOS?

Whether you elect to perform a new or an upgrade installation, Windows 95 places a number of DOS utilities into a new WINDOWS\COMMAND directory on your hard disk. These utilities have been enhanced to work with the DOS command kernel that underlies Windows 95.

The following DOS utility files will be deleted from your old DOS directory if you choose to upgrade an earlier version of Windows:

DEFRAG.HLP
MWUNDEL.EXE
MWUNDEL.HLP
METWORKS.TXT
OS2.TXT

If you choose to upgrade an earlier version of Windows, the following DOS utility files will be deleted from your old DOS directory with substitutes placed in the new WINDOWS\COMMAND directory:

ANSI.SYS	EGA.CPI	MSCDEX.EXE
ATTRIB.EXE	EMM386.EXE	NLSFUNC.EXE
CHKDSK.EXE	FC.EXE	RAMDRIVE.SYS
CHOICE.COM	FDISK.EXE	README.TXT
COUNTRY.SYS	FIND.EXE	SCANDISK.EXE
DEBUG.EXE	FORMAT.COM	SCANDISK.INI
DEFRAG.EXE	KEYB.COM	SETVER.EXE
DELTREE.EXE	KEYBOARD.SYS	SHARE.EXE
DISKCOPY.COM	LABEL.EXE	SMARTDRV.EXE
DISPLAY.SYS	MEM.EXE	SORT.EXE
DOSKEY.COM	MODE.COM	SUBST.EXE
DRVSPACE.EXE	MORE.COM	SYS.COM
EDIT.COM	MOVE.EXE	XCOPY.EXE

Typical (the default option) installs the basic Windows 95 operating system and the most frequently used optional components. You should be aware that some useful features are skipped if you choose this option:

- The *Windows 95 Tour* provides a quick thumbnail view of the new features in Windows 95, and shows you how to navigate the desktop.
- The *Online User's Guide* enhances the Windows 95 help system with a series of .AVI movies illustrating various desktop functions.
- The *QuickView file filters* allows you to view documents in a number of popular formats without loading them into their source applications.

- The *Win95 disk compression tools* include an improved version of DriveSpace. This version supports larger compressed volumes than the MS-DOS 6.*x* versions of DoubleSpace and DriveSpace.
- The *Win95 Backup utility* can archive files to QIC40/QIC80 tape drives as well as to removable hard disk media and floppy disks.
- *Dial-Up Networking* can be used to establish a connection to the Internet or to dial into a local area network through a modem.
- *Direct Cable Connection* establishes a miniature peer-to-peer connection between two computers through serial or parallel port cables.

None of these features is activated in a typical install; however, you can add them to the desktop later through the Control Panel. Table 3-1 provides a complete feature-by-feature list of the components that are added or omitted under each of the installation choices.

Portable installs the basic Windows 95 operating system along with options that are specially designed for use with portable computers. In addition to the features omitted in the typical installation, this choice skips a number of desktop features, including the wallpaper, backup program, document templates, games, network tools, and applets like Calculator and Paint. You do get the Briefcase utility, used to synchronize directories and files with another computer. The Dial-Up Network and Direct Cable programs are also installed with this option.

Compact installs only the files necessary to run the basic Windows 95 operating system. This option should be used in instances when hard disk space is limited. The only auxiliary tools that are copied are disk repair utilities (Defrag and ScanDisk). This is the absolute bare bones of Windows 95. It provides only what you need to run your programs with no frills, whatsoever.

Custom allows you to select any and all components. This is the best choice for power users and for those who want diagnostic information about the internal workings of Windows 95. It is also the only choice that allows you to configure network drivers during installation. If you choose this option, Setup eventually pops up a list of all available and to-be-installed system components allowing you to select or deselect the ones you wish to include. Following this, a network configuration screen appears.

		Installation Type			Available Only	Available via Fulfillment	
Primary Setup Option	Secondary Setup Option	Typical	Portable	Compact	on CD-ROM	Diskette	Online
Accessibility Options	Accessibility Options	Yes	Yes	No	No	n/a	n/a
Accessories	Briefcase	No	Yes	No	No	n/a	n/a
	Calculator	Yes	No	No	No	n/a	n/a
	Character Map	No	No	No	Yes	Yes	Yes
	Clipboard Viewer	No	No	No	No	n/a	n/a
	Desktop Wallpaper	No	No	No	No	n/a	n/a
	Document Templates	Yes	No	No	No	n/a	n/a
	Games[1]	No	No	No	No	n/a	n/a
	Mouse Pointers	No	No	No	Yes	Yes	Yes
	Net Watcher	No	No	No	Yes	Yes	Yes
	Online User's Guide	No	No	No	Yes	Yes	Yes
	Paint	Yes	No	No	No	n/a	n/a
	QuickView	No	No	No	Yes	Yes	Yes
	Screen Savers[2]	Yes	No	No	No	n/a	n/a
	System Monitor	No	No	No	Yes	Yes	Yes
	System Resource Meter	No	No	No	No	n/a	n/a
	Windows 95 Tour	No	No	No	Yes	Yes	Yes
	WinPopup[3]	Yes	Yes	Yes	No	n/a	n/a
	WordPad	Yes	Yes	No	No	n/a	n/a
Communications	Dial-Up Networking	No	Yes	No	No	n/a	n/a
	Direct Cable Connection	No	Yes	No	No	n/a	n/a
	Hyperterminal	Yes	Yes	No	No	n/a	n/a
	Phone Dialer	Yes	Yes	No	No	n/a	n/a
Disktools	Back-up	No	No	No	No	n/a	n/a
	Disk Compression Tools[4]	No	No	No	No	n/a	n/a
	Scan Disk[5]	Yes	Yes	Yes	No	n/a	n/a
	Defrag[5]	Yes	Yes	Yes	No	n/a	n/a
Microsoft Exchange	Microsoft Exchange	No	No	No	No	n/a	n/a
	Microsoft Mail Services	No	No	No	No	n/a	n/a
Microsoft Fax	Microsoft Fax Services	No	No	No	No	n/a	n/a
	Microsoft Fax Viewer	No	No	No	No	n/a	n/a
Multilanguage Support	Multilanguage Support	No	No	No	Yes	No	Yes
Multimedia	Audio Compression[6]	No	No	No	No	n/a	n/a
	CD Player[7]	No	No	No	Yes	Yes	Yes
	Jungle Sound Scheme	No	No	No	Yes	No	Yes
	Media Player	Yes	Yes	No	No	n/a	n/a
	Musica Sound Scheme	No	No	No	Yes	No	Yes
	Robotz Sound Scheme	No	No	No	Yes	No	Yes
	Sample Sounds	No	No	No	Yes	No	Yes
	Sound Recorder[6]	No	No	No	No	n/a	n/a
	Utopia Sound Scheme	No	No	No	Yes	No	Yes
	Video Compression	Yes	Yes	No	No	n/a	n/a
	Volume Control[6]	No	No	No	No	n/a	n/a

TABLE 3-1 *Windows 95 Setup Options*

Primary Setup Option	Secondary Setup Option	Installation Type: Typical	Portable	Compact	Available Only on CD-ROM	Available via Fulfillment: Diskette	Online
The Microsoft Network	The Microsoft Network	No	No	No	No	n/a	n/a
Admin Directory	Apptools[8]	No	No	No	Yes	Yes	Yes
	NetTools[9]	No	No	No	Yes	Yes	Yes
	Resource Kit[10]	No	No	No	Yes	Yes	Yes
Microsoft Exposition	Microsoft Exposition	No	No	No	Yes	No	No
Funstuff Directory	Hover!	No	No	No	Yes	No	No
	Pictures	No	No	No	Yes	Yes	Yes
	Videos	No	No	No	Yes	No	No
DataLink Directory	DataLink	No	No	No	Yes	No	No
Other Directory	Chat	No	No	No	Yes	Yes	Yes
	Microsoft Diagnostics (MSD)	No	No	No	Yes	Yes	Yes
	Old MS DOS utilities	No	No	No	Yes	Yes	Yes
	Wordview	No	No	No	Yes	No	Yes
	Miscellaneous[11]	No	No	No	Yes	Yes	Yes
	Changecp	No	No	No	Yes	No	Yes
	Clipbook	No	No	No	Yes	Yes	Yes
	Minitel	No	No	No	Yes	No	Yes
Driver Directory	Additional Drivers	No	No	No	Yes	No	Yes
	CompuServe MAPI driver	No	No	No	Yes	No	Yes

Comments:

Data correct as of 7/12/95, based on a prefinal build of Windows 95. Information subject to change without notice.

Only Available on CD-ROM: "No" indicates availability both on floppy and CD-ROM.

Available via Fulfillment: Electronically via Microsoft Network, Internet - ftp, Internet - Worldwide Web, MSDL, CompuServe, and GEnie. Diskette fulfillment available directly from Microsoft.

[1]Includes Freecell, Hearts, Minesweeper, and Solitaire.

[2]Only Flying Windows screensaver installed in Typical install.

[3]Auto-installed if Microsoft or NetWare client is installed.

[4]Auto-installed if DoubleSpace/DriveSpace is detected.

[5]Installed by default; not exposed to user as a selectable option.

[6]Auto-installed if sound card is detected.

[7]Auto-installed if CD-ROM is detected.

[8]Includes System Policy Editor, Password List Editor, Scripting support for Dial-Up Networking, Slip, LFN back, and MS-DOS environment variables.

[9]Includes Network Monitor Agent, Network setup components, Print Agent for NetWare Networks, Remote Registry Service, RPCPP - Print Service, SNMP Agent, Help file, and Samples. Diskette fulfillment will only include Network Monitor Agent and Remote Registry Service.

[10]Includes Windows 95 Resource Kit help file, sample policy files, and sample batch setup scripts. Diskette fulfillment with Resource Kit book.

[11]Includes a number of PSS tools: Microsoft Configuration Backup Utility, Enhanced Print Troubleshooter, Emergency Recovery Utility, and Logview.

TABLE 3-1 *Windows 95 Setup Options* (continued)

Get Connected: More Hardware Detection

After giving you a chance to enter your user name and company, the Product Identification screen pops up, asking you to key in a 10-digit serial number. You can find this number on the case for your CD-ROM, or enclosed with the floppy disks.

The next screen asks you to indicate if there is either a CD-ROM drive or network adapter in the PC. Following this, a relatively lengthy analysis process takes place. If this process becomes too lengthy and there is no apparent activity for several minutes, you should turn the computer off at the power source, turn it back on, run Setup and choose Safe Recovery when prompted. Do not press CTRL-ALT-DELETE, since this may not completely clear the machine's protected mode memory. Just start Setup as you did previously, either from Windows or the DOS prompt. If you started from Windows, the machine will load that past version, from which you can run Setup again.

You must now decide whether to install Microsoft Network, Microsoft Mail, and Microsoft Fax. (You can install these features later from the Control Panel if you change your mind.) Choosing Microsoft Network or Microsoft Fax causes Setup to install and activate the Microsoft Exchange Inbox on your desktop.

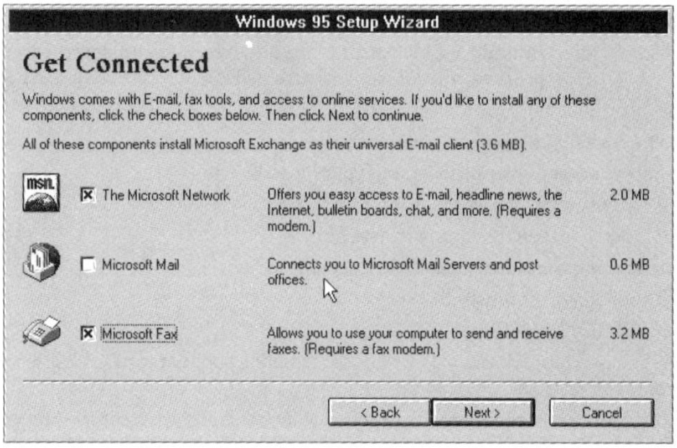

note *For many users, Microsoft Exchange will offer telecommunications features not implemented in the software they already own. Most telecommunications programs (like Procomm Plus for Windows or Delrina WinComm) will run unencumbered. Mail programs like cc:Mail or Microsoft Mail Remote may have problems with Exchange. If you depend on an older fax program (such as WinFax 3.0), you may need to make the choice between it and Exchange until an appropriate upgrade patch becomes available.*

MORE ABOUT CUSTOM INSTALLATION If you've selected the Custom Installation option, the Select Components screen follows the Get Connected screen. To get a list of what each category contains, just highlight that choice and click the Details button to select or deselect a particular component.

Keep in mind that even in a custom installation, not all of the features available under Windows 95 are automatically selected. Any category that is only partially selected will have a checkmark in a gray box. You may have to open these categories individually and place checkmarks next to the additional components you want.

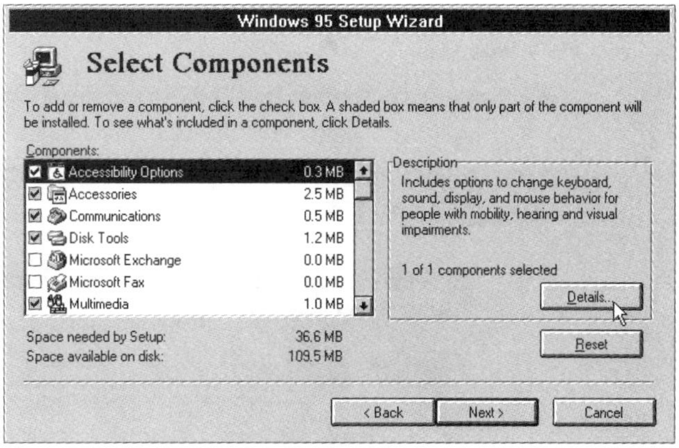

tip *To select an entire category with the fewest possible mouse clicks, deselect an existing checkmark next to a gray box and reinsert the checkmark again after it becomes blank. When you deselect a gray box, you may get a message warning you that key components will not be installed. Since you are going to immediately reselect the category, this doesn't matter.*

The different categories and their components are listed here:

Installation Category	Disk Space Needed
Accessibility Options	.3MB
Accessories:	
The Windows 95 Tour	2.4MB
The Online User's Guide	7.7MB
Communications:	
Dial-Up Networking, Direct Connection, HyperTerminal, Phone Dialer	1.3MB

Installation Category	Disk Space Needed
Disk Tools:	
Backup, Defrag, Disk Compression	2.3MB
Microsoft Exchange	4.2MB
Microsoft Fax	2.0MB
Multilanguage Support	
Special characters for Central European, Cyrillic, or Greek languages, occupying approximately 2.3MB each	7.0MB
Multimedia:	
Software connections for CD-ROM and sound cards	7.2MB

If you've selected a typical, portable, or compact installation, the Windows Components screen pops up next.

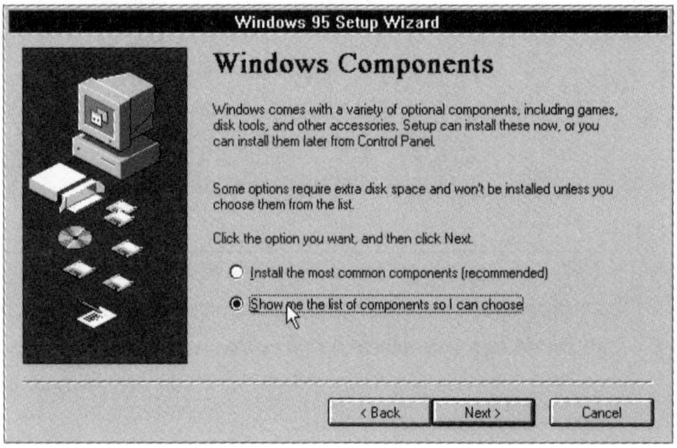

"Install the most common components" automatically selects the appropriate components shown in Table 3-1. "Show me the list" lets you sort through all components, as in the custom installation. Even if you just scan the list and click the Next button, the second option will give you a better idea of what's going to be installed and how much disk space will be consumed. In all cases, you can select the Details button to learn more about the particular component and its importance to the system.

If you are unsure about the importance or usefulness of any component, you can easily reverse the decision to install or omit a feature by clicking the Back button at the bottom of each screen.

The Windows 95 Directories

Windows 95 creates the directories listed here. (For the purpose of identification, "directories" and "folders" are the same thing.)

Windows Directory Folder	Default Contents
COMMAND	DOS commands for executing standard file functions.
CURSORS	Custom cursor programs with the suffix .ANI.
DESKTOP	Link (.LNK) files that control desktop shortcuts.
FONTS	All files for fonts installed on the system.
HELP	Help files (.HLP and .CNT) for all programs installed on the system.
INF	Information files used by Windows 95 to automatically configure hardware and plug and play devices.
MEDIA	Sound and video files that are tied to Windows 95 system commands.
PIF	Program information files used to run DOS applications under Windows.
RECENT	Links (.LNK) to the most recently used files across the system.
SENDTO	Links used for sending files to various locations on the system (floppy drivers, networks, and the Briefcase).
SPOOL	Temporary files that are sent to all installed output devices. (Such files are deleted as the command is finished.)
START MENU	Links to all of the programs listed on the Start button, presented in directory and subdirectory style. (Note that you can manipulate these files, using the Explorer or any other file manager substitute, and the changes will be reflected on the Start menu.)
SYSBCKUP	Backup versions of all .DRV and .DLL files that are installed on the system.
SYSTEM	Drivers, viewers, and I/O subsystem files.
TEMP	Temporary files created by Windows 95, many of which are automatically deleted when you quit the related application or close Windows 95.

Start Me Up

The next screen facilitates the creation of a startup disk, allowing you to boot from the floppy drive should the hard disk ever fail to initialize. This takes but a few minutes, and the difference in the setup time is imperceptible. If and when you need such a disk, however, you will be darn glad that you took the time to create it. Unsurprisingly, the reverse is also true.

remember *Windows 95 won't format a disk that it thinks contains Win95 installation files. So if you want to recycle an old beta disk, you'll need to erase or reformat it prior to its reassignment as a startup disk.*

Network Configuration

If you've chosen to install the Dial-Up Networking or Direct Cable Connection features, an identification screen appears next, allowing you to specify a name for your computer and workgroup. If you're installing Windows 95 on more than one machine, it's best to enter a unique computer name for each workstation.

If you've selected the Custom Installation option, you will see a final Network Configuration screen before the file copying process begins. This screen allows you to choose the network protocols for your client workstation or server, specify a primary network logon, and enable file and printer sharing. If you've selected either Dial-Up Networking or Direct Cable Connection in the components list, several network protocols will appear in this screen automatically. If you haven't selected either of these options, you can install your network protocols now by clicking the Add button, as shown here:

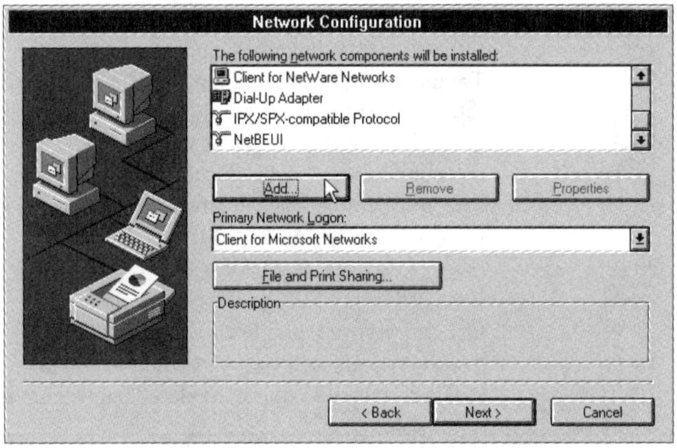

note *If you plan to use Dial-Up Networking to connect to the Internet, you can save yourself some steps later on by installing the Microsoft TCP/IP protocol now. To do this, click the Add button in the Network Configuration screen. Select Protocol, Add on the next screen, and Microsoft, TCP/IP on the following screen. (See Figure 3-3.)*

File Copy Phase

This is the lengthiest part of the installation, creating appropriate directories and installing the necessary files. Depending upon the selected components, all the files supporting a specific Windows 95 module are installed during this phase, and those you choose to omit are left on the installation disks until they are needed.

FIGURE 3-3

Choose Microsoft TCP/IP if you plan to connect to the Internet through Dial-Up Networking.

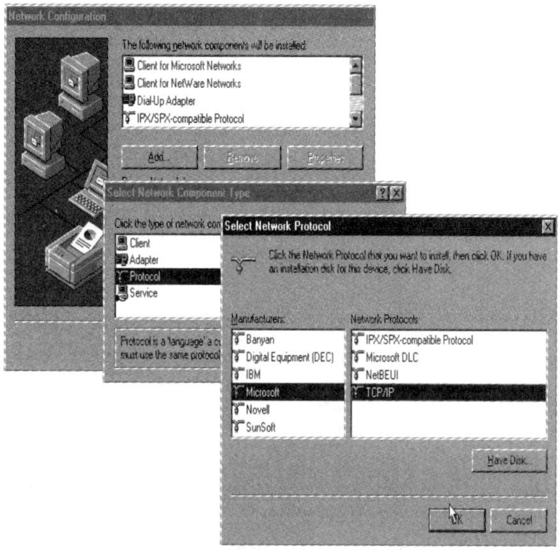

During the file copy phase, Windows 95 actually replaces the past versions of Windows and DOS with the new system, eventually rebooting the PC in Windows 95 mode.

In most cases, after the file copy sequence begins you can leave the computer and do something else for at least 20 minutes. If you choose to stay and stare at the screen during the process, you'll be treated to a set of screens presenting Windows 95 words, wit, and wisdom. These screens are designed to whet your appetite for the new operating system, delivering advertisements and information on plug and play, The Microsoft Network, and other features.

note *You can cancel the installation process at any time, by clicking the Cancel button or pressing the F3 function key. But if you wait till the file-copy phase to do this, your previous version of Windows will be unstartable. (If you've selected the option to back up your Windows 3.1 files, you can boot from a floppy disk and uninstall Windows 95 to revert to your previous configuration.)*

Final System Configuration Phase

Once the system restarts, another lengthy recognition process commences. The system reexamines the computer and its peripherals in Win95's protected mode, automatically installing any plug-and-play devices. This is accompanied by the now familiar PC-and-magnifying glass animated icon.

Next, your system configuration is migrated into the Windows 95 environment. The Control Panel is installed, old Program Manager groups are converted to the new Start Menu format, the online help system is installed, and the system asks you to set the appropriate time zone for the computer. The last step is the only one that requires user intervention.

When these steps are completed, you will see a final OK button. Clicking it will reboot the system once again, and the Windows 95 desktop will appear, ready for use.

Third-Party Memory Managers

Third-party memory managers may be one of the biggest causes of Windows 95 glitches. If you use such programs you will want to upgrade to versions for the new system as soon as possible. Until then, there is no need to panic or completely change your life, as the following help is available. See Chapter 6 for detailed information on installing Windows 95 over an existing configuration that uses an older version of 386MAX, NETROOM, or QEMM.

The CD-ROM Advantage

After installation, the Windows 95 CD-ROM continues to be of use, allowing you access to six useful features. Under Windows 95, a CD-ROM menu screen pops up automatically as soon as you pop the disk into the drive. CD-ROM features *not* included in the floppy disk kit are discussed in the following sections.

Windows 95 Tour

This is a less elaborate tutorial than the raft of third-party training packages now on the market. But the average user may find it a bit more useful. As you can see in Figure 3-4, the tour is segmented into five subtopics—Starting a Program, Exploring Your Disk, Finding a File, Switching Windows and Using Help. The tour offers a quick glance at the most significant system commands. Help topics and guidance are displayed in a box, and the Show Me button runs a quick demo. This isn't for people who expect full-blown multimedia explanations (there isn't even any sound), but is a good tool for anyone who needs basic Windows 95 training.

FIGURE 3-4

The Windows 95 Tour

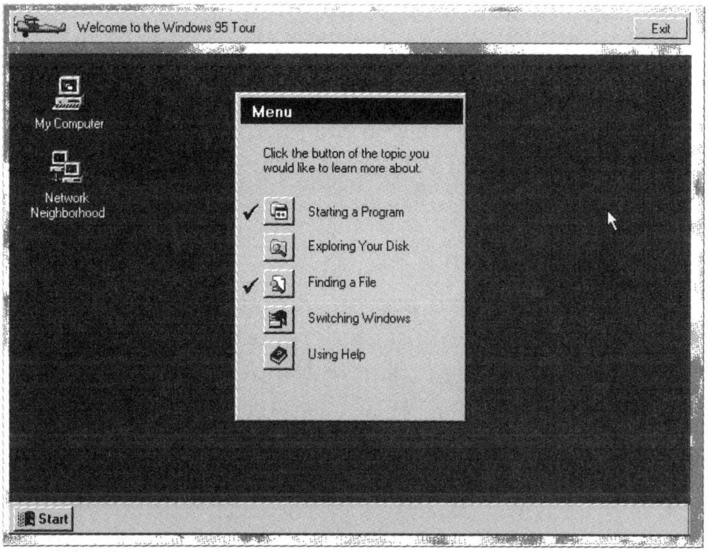

From a Lost Episode of Star Trek: The Next Generation (Part II)

Data: *Captain, we have successfully installed the "Windows" in the command unit, and as expected, it immediately consumed 85% of all resources. However, we have not received any confirmation of the expected upgrade.*

La Forge: *Our scanners have picked up an increase in Borg storage and CPU capacity to compensate, but we still have no indication of an upgrade to compensate for their increase.*

Picard: *Mr. Data, scan the history banks again, and determine if there is something we have missed.*

Data: *Sir, I believe there is a reason for the failure in the upgrade. Apparently, the Borg have circumvented it by not sending in their registration cards.*

Riker: *Captain, we have no choice. Requesting permission to begin emergency escape sequence 3F.*

La Forge (excited): *Wait, Captain! The Borg CPU capacity has suddenly dropped to 0%!*

Picard: *What do the scanners show?*

Data: *Apparently, the Borg have found the internal Windows module named Solitaire, and it has used up all CPU capacity.*

Picard: *Let's wait and see how long this Solitaire can reduce their functionality.*

—Two Hours Pass—

Riker: *Geordi, what's the status on the Borg?*

La Forge: *As expected, the Borg are attempting to compensate for increased CPU and storage demands, and so far, they have increased resources successfully. I set up our closest deep-space beacon to transmit more Windows modules from something called the "Microsoft fun-pack."*

Picard: *Heaven knows how much time that will buy us!*

Microsoft Exposition

This is Microsoft's "product catalogue of the future." It is broken into two segments: software from Microsoft and coming attractions from third-party vendors. Unsurprisingly, the Microsoft products get the star treatment, with feature lists, short demos, direct sales information, and even a little calypso music for good measure. Furthermore, an Upgrade Advisor scans your disk and determines which Microsoft applications you are qualified to purchase at the reduced rate.

The second section, covering third-party software, is somewhat less thorough, as most vendors are unveiling their plans following the release of the operating system. Additionally, the list is incomplete, omitting companies like Lotus. This is a passable reference, but by no means complete.

Hover

This arcade style game features bumper cars, 3-D mazes, colored flags....oh well, you get it. Or if you were expecting something mildly diverting to play during telephone conversations, like Windows Solitaire, you won't.

Cool Video Clips

Here, we get six short clips: Songs from Edie Brickell and Weezer, the trailer for *Rob Roy,* two artistic Windows 95-related cartoons and a flat-out advertisement. These can be used to test your video card, if for nothing else. There is also a separate folder containing the same videos for use with high performance MPEG video systems.

Browse This CD

This opens a My Computer file window on the Windows 95 CD-ROM, breaking the CD down into easily searchable components.

Add/Remove Software

This is the same as the identically named Control Panel module.

FIGURE 3-5

Microsoft Exposition, the Windows 95 Product Catalog

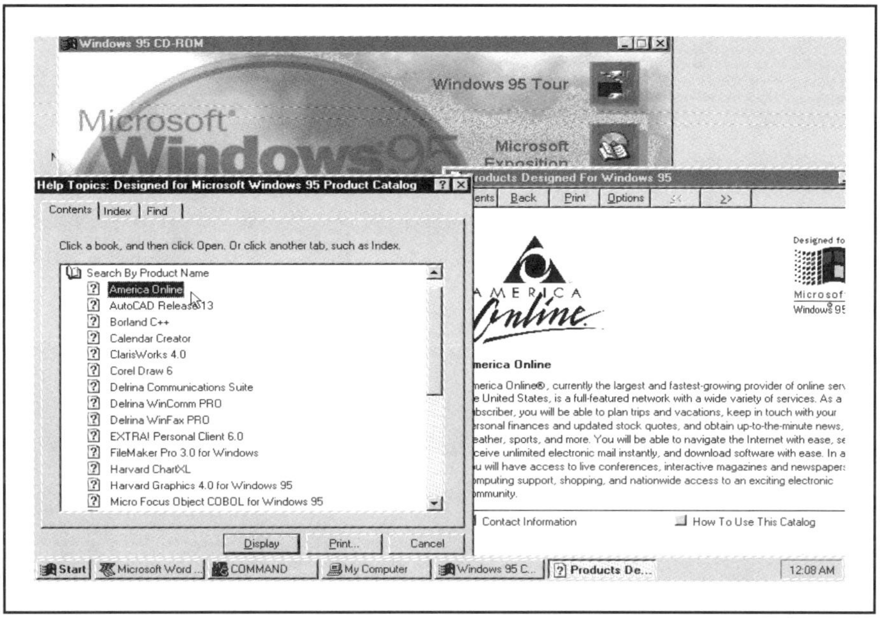

note *Owners of the floppy diskette version of Windows 95 can download most of the extra components present on the CD through the Microsoft Bulletin Board Download Service, or Microsoft's Internet sites. See Appendix C for more information.*

The Gift That Keeps On Giving

The Windows 95 operating system is one that encourages constant refinement. Some users will be comfortable installing the defaults and never looking back. The adventurous majority who comprise the readership of this book will be able to fine-tune nearly every aspect of the desktop and operating environment.

Setup, then, is only the beginning. You can select the components that you *think* are needed. Things will change (sooner than you could imagine), but Windows 95 makes it easy to add or delete different components. If space is not an issue, you can install all Windows 95 components, and learn to use them at your leisure. You can always delete the features that don't fit your productivity environment. If space *is* an issue you may add features on an as-needed basis.

Printers
Find
Help
Run...
Suspend
Windows95
Start

chapter 4

Introduction to the Interface

- What's new
- Win95 vs. Win3.1
  - Comparing the look and feel
- Desktop navigation
  - What the Win95 Tour didn't tell you
- Getting the most out of online Help
- Desktop configuration strategies
- The Explorer, My Computer, and the taskbar
  - Power tips and keyboard shortcuts
- Customizing the interface
  - Using work folders and templates

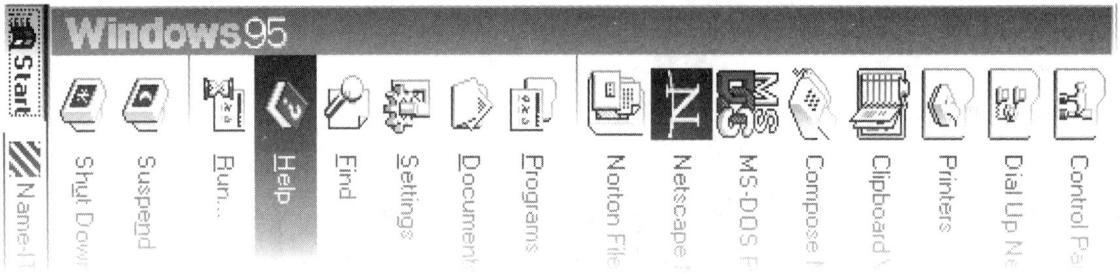

FOR many users, the new Windows 95 interface is the strongest selling point for the operating system. You get floating desktop icons, a hierarchical pop-up program menu, and easy-to-follow Wizards for installing and configuring your software. In this chapter, you'll take a brief tour of the Windows 95 interface. We enumerate the elements that have been added since Windows 3.1 and discuss critical user issues related to each element. We don't present a point-by-point tutorial on how to use the Explorer or the taskbar, because we assume you've picked up most of the basics, already. We do, however, attempt to clarify differences between the Windows 3.1 and the Windows 95 way of doing things. We show you the internal logic of the new interface and provide thumbnail sketches of key features. These sketches include the how-to-do-it and configuration information that you want, but that you can't always get from the Windows 95 Help system.

Later in the chapter, you'll learn the undocumented secrets of the Win95 Help engine, get labor-saving tips on making the most of Explorer and taskbar features, and discover useful productivity shortcuts and configuration strategies for your desktop. You'll also find a liberal sprinkling of tips and tricks that will help you avoid Windows 95 pitfalls. We'll show you that the Windows 3.1 interface and the File Manager are still here, hiding beneath the surface. Some users may want to continue using the Program Manager/File Manager combination for its greater keyboard shortcut flexibility. As you'll see, the File Manager has a number of features that are mysteriously absent in the Explorer.

What's New, in a Nutshell

The new taskbar and Explorer interface for Windows 95 creates a simpler, more interactive desktop that most users will prefer. This new interface supports long filenames and attaches convenient, context-sensitive shortcuts to the right mouse button.

On the other hand, the new interface is difficult to navigate with the keyboard alone. It may confuse some people who are used to the Windows 3.1 way of doing things. As we'll see later in this chapter, Windows 95 can easily be configured to use the old Windows 3.1 interface. If you choose to use the old interface, you'll still be able to use new productivity features such as Microsoft Exchange, My Briefcase, and Microsoft Fax. However, you'll lose access to long filenames and to the free-floating, Macintosh-like desktop. (For information on how to switch back and forth between the old and new interfaces, see "Choosing Your Win95 Shell" in this chapter.)

The Win95 Explorer and taskbar interface has a variety of features that you won't find in Windows 3.*x*:

Free-Floating Icons

Icons for programs, folders (directories), data objects, and system control options are free-floating. You can place them anywhere on the desktop. Windows 95 doesn't have the constraints imposed by separate Program Manager and File Manager windows. The Win95 Start Menu pops up to give you a bird's eye view of all your installed applications, as shown in Figure 4-1. You can also start programs and manage files from seamlessly integrated desktop folders or free-floating file icons. As with a Macintosh, you can double-click icons to start programs, position frequently accessed objects on the desktop, and open folders to display file listings. You can also make custom project folders. These can be filled with shortcut links to programs or data files hidden away in subdirectories.

Mouse-Click Convenience

The new desktop includes convenient right-click mouse options. Windows 95 borrows a good feature from IBM's Warp OS/2. You can customize icon objects simply by pointing at them and clicking the right-mouse button.

FIGURE 4-1

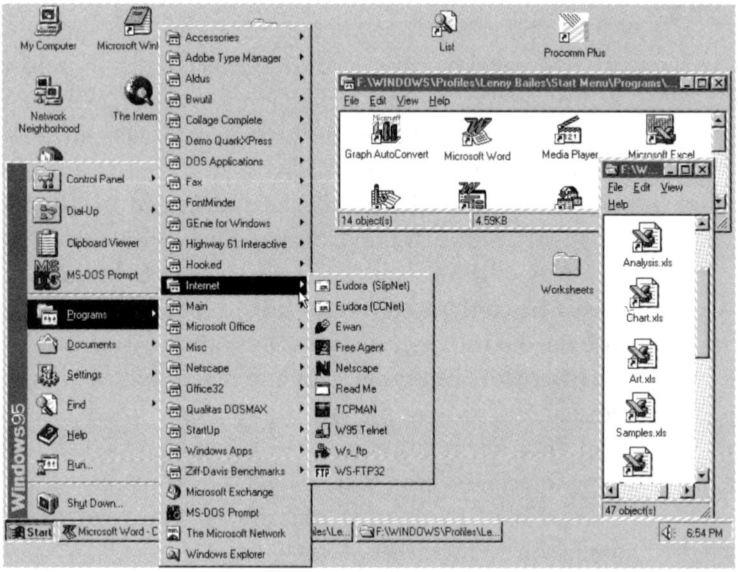

The flexible, integrated Windows 95 desktop lets you access programs and files in a number of different ways. You can float icons on the desktop, open folder windows, or use the cascading, hierarchical Start Menu.

No more searching across pull-down menus for hidden configuration options. Microsoft has streamlined Win95's nested menus with the tabbed options originally developed for Microsoft Office. Related screens and dialog boxes appear as tabbed cards that you can flip through simply by clicking on the tab at the top.

More Desktop Features

Control and connectivity features for desktop windows have also been improved. My Computer and individual folder windows contain both pull-down menus and an icon toolbar. You can select functions such as cut, copy, and paste, or set your window display options in a variety of ways. Most features can be selected from menus or the toolbar, or through keyboard shortcuts.

The My Computer object consolidates most Windows 95 system management features in one place. You can double-click this desktop icon to view file and directory listings, to run file maintenance utilities, and to format and copy disks. My Computer also provides quick access to the Dial-Up Networking feature, the Windows Control Panel, your printer settings, and other areas. Figure 4-2 shows typical objects you can access from a My Computer window.

DOS Details

Windows 95 offers added support and flexibility for DOS applications. Windowed DOS sessions now feature a toolbar that lets you conveniently cut and paste objects to the Windows Clipboard. The toolbar also lets you toggle background application execution or set the display font for the window. The Windows 3.1 PIF editor is history. Running parameters for DOS applications are now set through a pop-up Properties menu associated with each program.

FIGURE 4-2

My Computer consolidates file management and configuration options in one convenient window. The right-click context menu for each file icon adds functionality to the desktop.

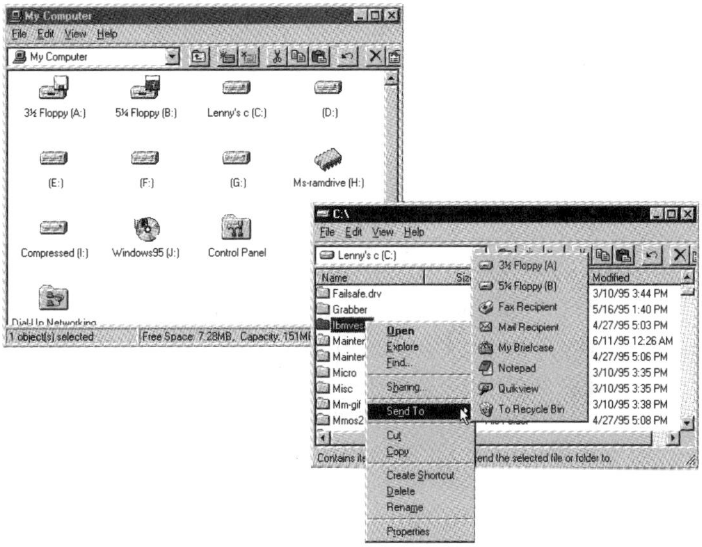

Easy-to-Use Tools

The Start Menu (shown in Figure 4-1) and the Explorer, shown here, are easy-to-use navigation tools.

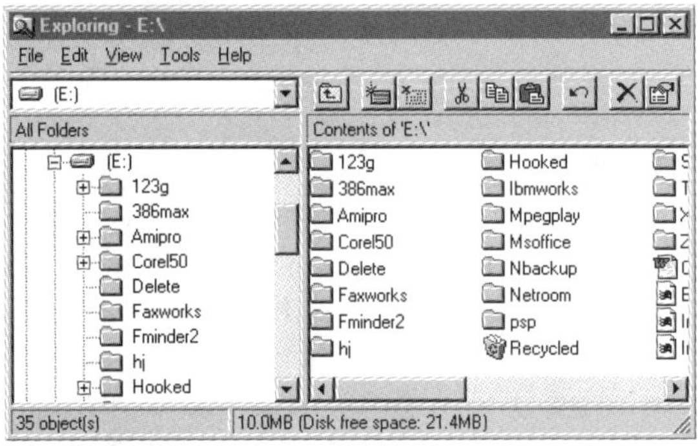

The Explorer is Win95's improved version of the File Manager. It retains the same split-screen tree display of drive and directory contents, but in the Explorer, the display is directly connected to the desktop. You can right-click any directory or file icon to bring up a set of context-sensitive menu options. The Explorer has an enhanced toolbar that contains more network, cut-and-paste, and display options. However, it does not include as many pull-down menu options as the File Manager. (For more details on these differences, see "Working with Files and Folders" later in this chapter.)

Clicking on the Start button (located on the left corner of the taskbar) rolls out the Start Menu—a hierarchical, pop-up listing of all your Windows and DOS applications—plus some internal desktop utilities. The Start Menu program list (Figure 4-1) fans out into submenus that perform the same function as Program Manager groups in Windows 3.1. Additional choices on the Start Menu let you reselect recently opened documents, open the Win95 Control Panel, or access internal system tools. (By default, access to the Control Panel is hidden under the Settings option. To find out how we put the Control Panel on the first level of the Start Menu, see the sidebar, "Making the Control Panel, Your Printers, and Dial-Up Networking More Accessible" later in this chapter.)

The Start Menu can also be used as a container for application shortcuts. This feature is analogous to the Program Manager in Windows 3.1. If you right-click the Start button and choose Open, a nested set of program folders appears, instead of the collapsible list. When the Start Menu is opened in this view, it behaves just like any other set of folders. You can drag and drop icons in and out of folders to add or remove items from either the pop-up list or the Folder view of the Start Menu.

The Windows 95 taskbar, which, by default, runs across the bottom of the desktop, is used as a pushbutton list to switch between open applications and folders. For each open window on the desktop, a corresponding button appears on the taskbar. If you click a minimized taskbar button, the window is restored to the desktop. This feature replaces the minimized icons that appeared at the bottom of the desktop in Windows 3.1. The taskbar also includes special buttons to access internal Windows 95 features. If you click the digital clock on the right side of the taskbar, up pops a calendar and an analog clock. If you pause the mouse cursor over this area, you'll see the day of the week and the date. If your system has a sound card, a speaker icon appears to the left of the clock display. Clicking on the speaker icon pops up a multimedia volume control. The right portion of the taskbar also serves as a status display for Windows 95 system events. When your fax or modem establishes a connection, a flashing icon appears in between the clock and the speaker. When you print, a busy printer icon appears. Third-party Windows 95 applications also display status messages on the taskbar, so watch that space!

Long Filenames

Like OS/2 Warp and Windows NT, Windows 95 has the ability to assign and display long filenames, both on the desktop and at a command prompt. Long filenames can contain up to 255 characters. Although MS-DOS and Windows 3.1 applications recognize only real-mode 8.3 filenames, the utilities and applications written for Windows 95 can use standard 8.3 filenames and long filenames. When files bearing long filenames are copied to floppies or displayed on an MS-DOS machine, there are no problems. On non-Win95 systems only the standard 8.3 DOS filename is used.

Making Computing Easier

Windows 95 has added a number of features designed to make computing easier and more accessible for users who have physical disabilities. You can turn on a StickyKeys feature to assist in executing multiple-key commands; create visual equivalents of system sound events; and adjust the screen for a large-font, high-contrast display. The MouseKeys feature allows you to duplicate mouse-movements and operations with keyboard equivalents. The Windows 3.1 Recorder has been replaced by a global hot key system that allows each object on the desktop to be assigned a default launch-key combination.

As we'll see shortly, however, Windows 95 has taken a few steps backward for users who prefer dedicated keyboard commands for all system operations. Tasks that you could execute with one or two keystrokes in Windows 3.1 may now require up to five or six keystrokes! You can easily configure Win95 to use either the new or the old interface, as we'll learn later on in this chapter.

New Objects, New Functionality

The Recycle Bin, Network Neighborhood, My Briefcase, the Inbox, and the Microsoft Network are additional Win95 features represented by individual control objects on the desktop. Only the Recycle Bin is installed by default. The other features can be selected during a custom Windows 95 installation, or afterwards from the Windows Control Panel. (See Chapter 3 and Chapter 8 for more details.)

The Recycle Bin is the Win95 trashcan and also a replacement for the DOS Undelete program. All objects removed from the Win95 desktop are placed in the Recycle Bin as a temporary holding area. You can delete these files, permanently, or drag them back to the desktop. The important thing to know is that the Recycle Bin doesn't store files deleted by DOS applications or in DOS command sessions.

Network Neighborhood appears on the desktop if the network support files are installed. Network Neighborhood displays the status of any computers, folders, shared files, or printers available for network use. You can use the Network Neighborhood to map drive letters to shared folders, or double-click an object within to automatically reestablish a connection. (See Chapter 12 for more details.)

My Briefcase is installed if you select the portable setup option, or choose it in a custom setup. You can also add My Briefcase to the desktop, later, through Add/Remove Programs in the Win95 Control Panel. My Briefcase lets you synchronize changes made to files located on a remote server or connected workstation. If you drag and drop items into My Briefcase, any new or edited versions can be copied back to their source locations with a single keystroke.

The Inbox (shown in Figure 4-3) is the front-end for Microsoft Exchange, an e-mail management suite that handles Microsoft Mail, CompuServe Mail, Faxes, and the Microsoft Network online service. Windows 95 includes built-in support for displaying, storing, and managing e-mail for all of these services. An additional Inbox module that handles third-party Internet Mail is available in Microsoft Plus!. Microsoft Exchange supports transmittal of binary attachments to text messages via Class I fax, MIME-compliant mail, and UUEncode/UUDecode protocols. Inbox is an optional Windows 95

FIGURE 4-3

The Inbox for Microsoft Exchange allows you to manage e-mail for Microsoft Fax, the Microsoft Network, Microsoft Mail clients, CompuServe, and the Internet.

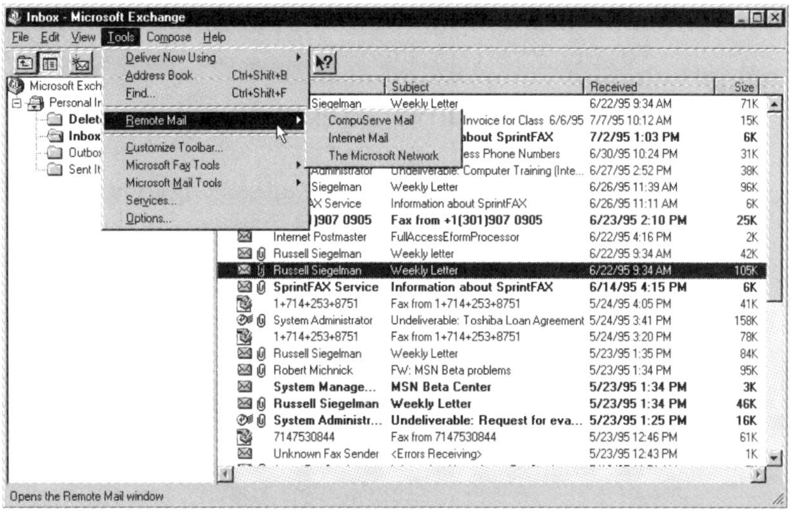

feature, installed during Setup if you choose to install Microsoft Mail, Microsoft Fax, or the Microsoft Network. You can add it to the desktop through the Control Panel after you run Setup.

The Microsoft Network, shown in Figure 4-4, is the graphic interface to Microsoft's new online service. Similar to the interface for America Online,

FIGURE 4-4

The Microsoft Network allows you to participate in online forums and access reference tools through a graphic point-and-click interface.

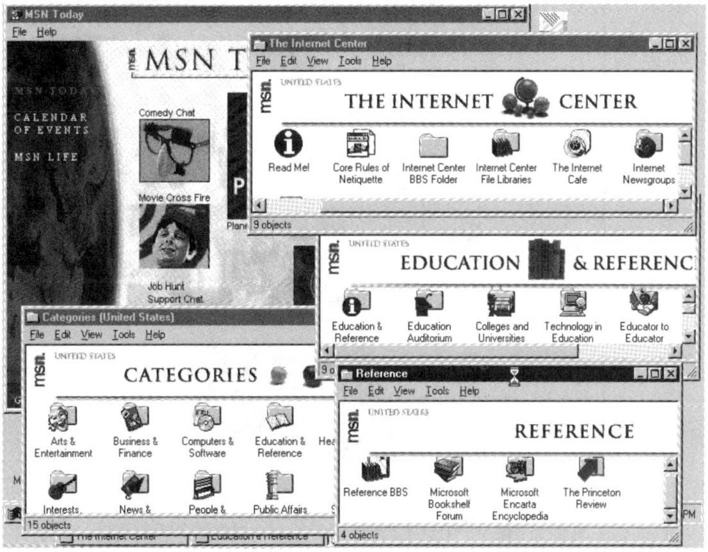

it allows for easy browsing of various Microsoft Network features, including real-time access to Microsoft's multimedia reference tools, Bookshelf, and Encarta '95.

Choosing Your Win95 Shell

If you install Windows 95 over an existing copy of Windows 3.1 or Windows for Workgroups, Setup will ask whether you want to use the new Windows 95 look and feel, or retain the look and feel of Windows 3.1.

If you decide in favor of Windows 3.1, Setup installs the Program Manager as your default startup shell, rather than the Explorer. (See Figure 4-5.) If you change your mind later and want to switch, it's very easy. If you want to boot Win95 with the new desktop, the taskbar, and the Explorer active, the following statement must appear in the [Boot] section of SYSTEM.INI:

```
[BOOT]
SHELL=EXPLORER.EXE
```

When Windows 95 boots with Program Manager as the default shell, the following replacement occurs:

```
[BOOT]
SHELL=PROGMAN.EXE
```

FIGURE 4-5

Windows 95 with the old Program Manager and File Manager interface

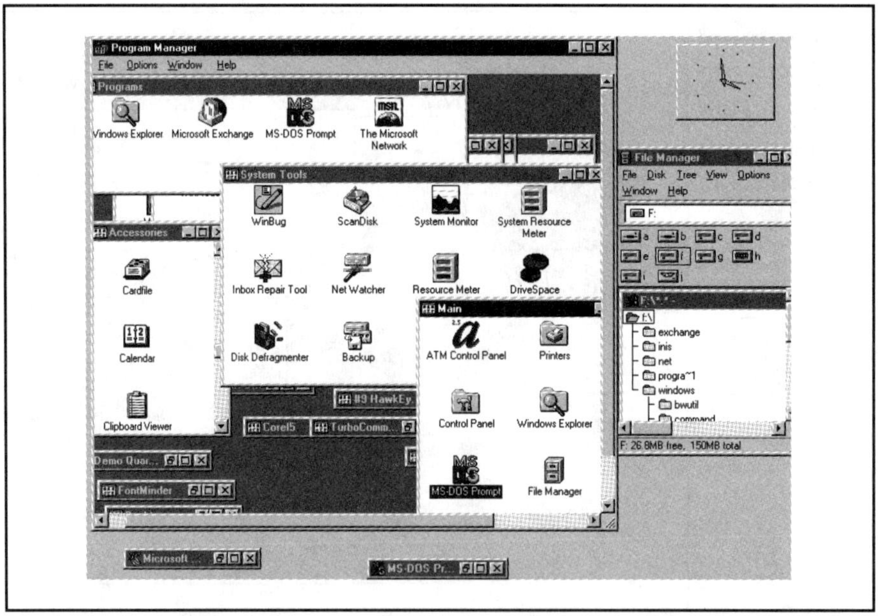

You can quickly reconfigure Windows to use either default desktop by entering the appropriate statement in SYSTEM.INI with a text editor.

Differences between the Win95 and Windows 3.1 Startup Shells

When the Explorer is your default shell, the desktop includes the taskbar, the Start Menu, My Computer, the Recycle Bin and other optional Win95 system objects. You can drag and drop free-floating objects to the desktop and access many features by right-clicking the mouse.

When the Program Manager is your default shell, the desktop will look the way it did in Windows 3.1. There is no support for free-floating drag-and-drop of programs or data files. When you minimize open windows under Program Manager, they appear at the bottom of the screen in a slightly different format from Windows 3.1 (as you can see in Figure 4-5).

note *If you choose Program Manager as your default shell, you can still run most of the new Win95 applets and setup features by launching them from program groups. The new toolbar for windowed DOS sessions will also continue to be available.*

Both the old File Manager and the new Explorer can be run within the Program Manager to maintain your file and directory structure. (See "Working with Files and Folders" later in this chapter for a comprehensive comparison of the File Manager and the Explorer.) Choosing the Program Manager as your shell also restores one other Windows 3.1 option not available in the new Win95 interface: if you double-click anywhere on the desktop, the Task Manager list appears, allowing you to switch quickly between open applications.

tip *If you choose the Explorer as your Startup shell, you can still run the Program Manager as an individual application under the new Win95 interface. (Just enter* ***PROGMAN.EXE*** *on the Start\Run menu, or create a desktop shortcut for it.) The Program Manager will behave the same way as it did under Windows 3.1, coexisting with the taskbar. But when the Program Manager is not your default shell, Win95 will not automatically create new program groups as you install new applications.*

Maintaining Up-to-Date Program Groups Simultaneously in the Program Manager and on the Start Menu

It's actually easier to transfer new program groups that have been added under the Program Manager over to the Start Menu than it is to transfer Start Menu groups to the Program Manager. A small, undocumented utility in your Windows directory can automatically add Program Manager groups to the hierarchical menu in the Start Menu. If you're familiar with Windows 3.1, you may know that the Program Manager tracks installed applications by constructing a series of binary .GRP files in the Windows directory. Each of these files contains the application's icon, its drive and path information, and the name of the program group it belongs to. When the Program Manager is the default shell, Windows 3.1 and Windows 95 both read a file called PROGMAN.INI, which contains a list of all the .GRP files. When you choose the Explorer as your Windows 95 shell, the desktop uses folders and shortcuts to applications to duplicate the original functions of the Program Manager. During installation, a utility called GRPCONV.EXE runs automatically to change Windows 3.1 Program Manager groups into Startup Menu folders. This program searches for all of the .GRP files listed in the old PROGMAN.INI file and creates shortcuts for them in the Start Menu folder. GRPCONV also searches the SETUP.INI file, creating shortcuts in the Programs folder for the Windows 95 items you select during installation.

UPDATING PROGRAM GROUPS FOR THE OLD INTERFACE When the Explorer is your default shell, Windows 95 creates no additional Win3.1 .GRP files after Setup. If you install new Windows applications under the new interface, Win95 places its shortcuts directly in the Start Menu folder. If you want to continue to use both the Program Manager and the Explorer, the following procedure will allow you to install new applications for both interfaces.

1. Switch your default shell from the Explorer to the Program Manager by modifying the [Boot] section of SYSTEM.INI (as explained in the preceding section). Restart Windows 95 so that it comes up under the Program Manager.
2. Install your new Windows application the way you did under Windows 3.1. Select File\Run from the Program Manager and run the Setup or Install module that comes with your application.

3. Most Windows applications will automatically create and install a new Program Manager group, along with individual program and README icons. If your application doesn't do this, create the groups or program icons manually, as you would have done under Windows 3.1. (Select File\New from the Program Manager and enter the necessary information.) Windows 95 will modify PROGMAN.INI appropriately, and, if you've created a new program group, a new .GRP file will appear in the Windows directory. Write down or make note of the real filename for the new program group. You can get this information by minimizing and selecting the group in the Program Manager and then selecting Properties from the File menu. (If you've installed an application into a preexisting group, then record its real filename.)
4. If you wish, you may now switch back to using the Explorer as your default shell. Modify SYSTEM.INI again and restart Win95.
5. To update the Start Menu with your new or modified program groups, open My Computer, and then your Windows folder. Select one or more of the new .GRP files to convert in the file window, right click and choose Open from the pop-up context menu. GRPCONV will run, adding these groups automatically to the Start Menu.

Desktop Ins and Outs

This section will show you how to gain control of the Windows 95 desktop interface. Microsoft designed the new desktop to be intuitive, but the transition for Windows 3.1 users may not be automatic. There are many more options hidden beneath the surface here. File manipulation with the Explorer is not exactly the same as with the File Manager. This section provides information on working with desktop windows—the Explorer, My Computer, and the File Manager—and demonstrates the capabilities of the Windows 95 online Help system.

The Windows 95 desktop is extremely flexible. You can have the Start Menu launch applications in several ways. Or, you can just place program objects and work folders in strategic locations on the desktop. The new Explorer and My Computer interface works well for simple file management chores, but a number of useful options from the Windows 3.1 File Manager were left out. Fortunately, Windows 95 also includes the File Manager, which can be used as a backup for global file maintenance when long filenames are not involved. (For power options combined with long filename support, you'll probably want to investigate some third-party utilities. See Chapter 14 for details.)

Notice that some of the default objects on the Windows 95 desktop are ordinary programs, some launch system utilities, and others open into a hierarchical file and folder display. Folders in Windows 95 have multiple purposes. For consistency of the interface some Windows 95 system objects are disguised to look like folders. The model for this in Windows 3.1 was the Control Panel, which appeared to be a program group with nested individual applications.

In Windows 95, the distinction between such system objects and "real file" folders is less evident. A Win95 system object may actually point to a hidden directory on the hard disk that contains a series of shortcut application links. As in OS/2 Warp, some of these system objects are intelligent. They can use directories as storage areas for file and program templates. Later on in this chapter you'll see how to use Win95's Find and Shortcut features to create a project-oriented object desktop.

Desktop Windows

Win95 system objects and file folders open display windows on the desktop that include four pull-down menus: File, Edit, View, and Help. These menus let you manage the appearance of the window, and also control the properties of the objects contained within. My Computer is displayed here in Detail view, and the icon toolbar is toggled on.

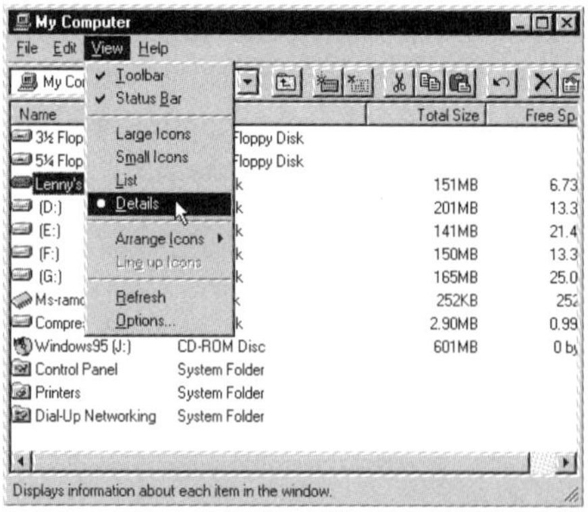

note *Many of the features on the pull-down window menus are also available when you right-click the mouse in a strategic area of the window. The icon toolbar (toggled on and off in the View menu) provides another way to manipulate the objects in the window.*

Window Behavior

Some of the display settings on the pull-down View menu are auto- matically passed down to child windows. Other settings are preserved only for the specific window that you customize. A third set of View options is passed globally to all folder windows when you change them in a single window.

You can make a child window in the display hierarchy either replace its parent on the desktop or open into a separate window. (Select View\Options\Folder on the pull-down menu for any window to toggle this browsing option.) The Browse Folder options are applied globally throughout the desktop. If you switch from "use separate windows for each" to "use a single window" in My Briefcase, then the single-window behavior will be applied to My Computer, and to all other desktop windows. The display options on the View Tab (under the View\Options menu) are also globally applied to all windows on the desktop. Changing the "hide" or "unhide" options for any desktop window unilaterally changes the display for all desktop windows:

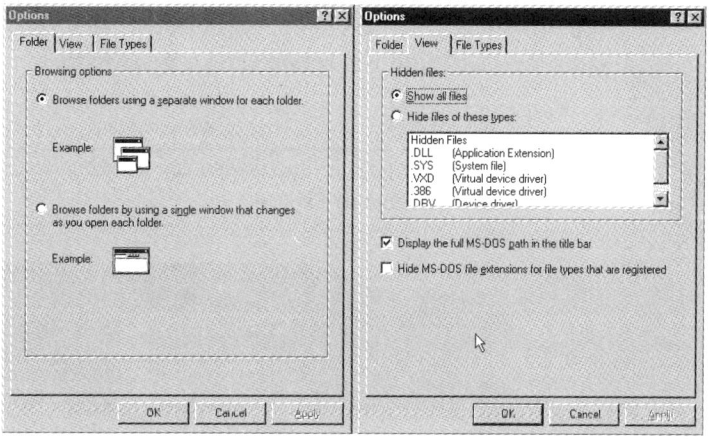

Examples of My Computer display options specifically passed down to child windows are the settings directly available in the View menu (Toolbar, Status bar, Large Icons, Small Icons, List, and Details views). Notice that these settings are passed down to child windows only if you elect to browse folders in a single window. If child folders are opened into separate windows, these View menu options are not passed down.

tip *Have your cake and eat it, too! No matter which way you choose to browse desktop windows, you can temporarily force the opposite display option. Double-click an object while holding down the* CTRL *key to reverse the default single/separate browsing behavior. For instance: with the desktop set to "Use a separate window for each folder," you can* CTRL-*double-click a folder and it will replace the parent display in the same window.*

The "Arrange icons" options (Date, Size, Type, and so on) are not passed on reliably to child windows in either single or separate browsing modes. However, changes to individual windows are preserved the next time you open that particular window.

My Computer vs. the Explorer

When you double-click My Computer, you are actually launching a special instance of the Explorer, with internally defined startup attributes. By default, the drives and directories listed in My Computer windows appear in Large Icon view. This display option can be changed from the window's View menu or toolbar. The display format for a drive or folder window is passed to its children only when set for single-window browsing mode. If you select drive C, for example, and open your Windows folder, changing the display view from Large Icons to Details causes any subdirectory of Windows that you open to appear in Details view. Folders or directories on the same level as Windows retain the Large Icon display format when opened.

tip *My Computer (or any other folder) can be opened in Explorer view by right-clicking its icon and choosing Explore.*

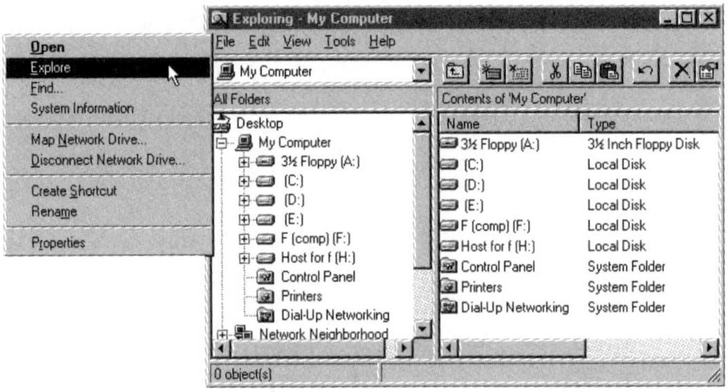

Desktop Navigation (What the Win95 Tour Forgot to Tell You)

If you own the CD version of Windows 95, you can take the Windows 95 Tour by installing it with Add\Remove Programs (which you'll find in the Accessories group), clicking the Tour button on the Welcome to Windows 95 application or by entering **TOUR** in the taskbar's Run menu. If you installed Windows 95 from floppies, the Tour is not available. You must download it separately from one of the Microsoft online resource centers. In any event, the Tour provides minimal information on navigating the Windows 95 desktop. This section of our chapter shows you some of the shortcuts, tricks, and secret options of the desktop that the Tour fails to mention.

Starting Programs

In addition to starting applications by selecting them from the Start Menu, you can also:

- Double-click any program, program shortcut, associated document, or shortcut to an associated document that resides on the desktop.
- Double-click any of these objects from within a My Computer or Explorer folder window.
- Right-click any object on the desktop or in a folder and select Open on the pop-up menu.
- Open the Run box from the Start Menu and enter the path and name of any DOS or Windows application. The Run box also lets you enter the names of Windows Help files, or data files that have been associated with specific applications. (See "Using File Associations" later in this chapter for more details on working with file associations.)
- Enter the path and filename of any application at a DOS command prompt. (Unlike Windows 3.1, Windows 95 allows you to do this with Windows as well as DOS programs.)

My Computer and Explorer

The Windows 95 Tour shows you the simplest way to examine drives, directories and files: by double-clicking successively on the icons displayed in My Computer. The Tour does not mention most of the mouse and keyboard shortcuts built into the desktop. Here are some guidelines and tips that tell you the rest of what you should know about using My Computer and Explorer.

Explorer Secrets

With command-line switches, you can start the Explorer in a number of different views in a specified drive and directory. If you just enter **EXPLORER** at the command line, the window opens to the drive and folder where Windows 95 is installed in the default display view.

As we observed earlier, the My Computer desktop object is actually a special instance of the Explorer. You can open My Computer folder windows from the command line by entering **EXPLORER /*ROOT*, [*D:*]*PATH* /N** at any DOS command prompt.

The following command-line syntax can be used to open Explorer:

EXPLORER [/N][/E][,/*ROOT*,*OBJECT*][[,/SELECT],*SUBOBJECT*]

Table 4-1 shows the parameters in more detail:

Parameter	Meaning
/N	Always open a new window (even if the specified folder is already open).
/E	Use Windows Explorer view. The default is Open view.
/ROOT,OBJECT	Specify the object in the normal namespace that will be used as the root of this Windows Explorer folder. The default is to just use the normal namespace root (the desktop).
SUBOBJECT	Specify the folder to receive the initial focus unless /SELECT is used. The default is the root.
/SELECT	Specifies that the parent folder is opened and the specified object is selected.

TABLE 4-1 *Explorer Command Line Options* ■

Windows Explorer Examples

Remember that each Explorer command switch is followed by a comma. We've already seen the syntax to launch Explorer in Open View and simulate My Computer. Here are additional statements for opening and viewing windows:

Statement	Meaning
EXPLORER [*D:\PATH*]	Open a window on a specific drive or folder.
EXPLORER /E, [*D:\PATH*]	View a window in Open view.
EXPLORER /SELECT, [*D:\PATH\FILENAME*]	View the window in Open view, with the mouse focused on a particular file.

If you're connected to a network, you can open Explorer to display a view of the server and nothing else with the following syntax:

EXPLORER /E, */ROOT*, \\[*SERVER NAME*]

The Find Utility

The Windows 95 Tour covers the basic search options that allow you to locate files on your hard disk. The tour doesn't tell you that the Date Modified tab and Advanced tab on the Find menu let you add sophisticated search filters. These filters can help you to build a series of object-oriented work folders. (See "Building Work Folders with Find" later in this chapter.) Additionally, you can make the Find utility search all of the drives and directories on your system at once. To perform a global search, select My Computer instead of an individual disk partition. You may also specify multiple search strings or file extensions in the Named dialog box to search for several file types simultaneously.

Switching Windows

The Tour tells you that you can switch between open windows on the desktop by clicking on them with the mouse, or selecting their minimized representations on the taskbar. Additionally, you can quickly switch between windows by pressing ALT-TAB. This brings up a quicklist in the center of the screen. By repeatedly pressing the TAB key, you can cycle between all open windows and applications on the desktop. Unlike Windows 3.1, pressing CTRL-ESC in Windows 95 does not bring up a window list. Instead, this keyboard shortcut pops up the Start Menu. If you press ALT-ESC, however, you will cycle between all open desktop windows, without getting the quick list in the center of the screen.

Using Help

The Windows 95 Tour provides a basic introduction to online Help, showing you how to perform a simple search for topic information. Help in Windows 95 is considerably more extensive and dynamic than it was in past versions of Windows. It is also better organized, allowing you to view topic entries instead of simple word lists. See "Exploiting the Help System" later in this chapter for a comprehensive discussion of the Win95 Help engine.

Working with Files and Folders

The strategy behind Win95's Explorer and My Computer tools is that Microsoft wants us to gradually adapt to a new *docucentric* desktop metaphor. That is, Microsoft wants to wean us away from our DOS-conditioned reflex to organize our computers by directories with large, bloated file listings. We should also avoid shuffling large groups of data files around from place to place on the hard disk. Instead, Microsoft wants us to rely on Win95's shortcut links to create an *object-oriented desktop*. If you want evidence to confirm this, notice that My Computer and the Explorer default to display settings that hide DOS file extensions. Another folder option suppresses the display of critical DOS and Windows system files (those with the extension .SYS, .DLL, .VXD, .DRV, and so on).

Microsoft's programming style guides now recommend that the file extension be dropped when a filename is displayed in an application's title bar. Even better: the title bar should display the document name before the application name. The reason for this recommendation can be seen when we minimize several open windows to the taskbar. If you open several instances of Win95's Notepad with different documents loaded, you see the document title first, so you can distinguish between various open documents. Open several instances of the Windows 3.1 version of Notepad under Win95 and minimize them. With a larger display font, all that you'll see is Notepad-[..., Notepad-[...., Notepad-[..... Contrast this with Win95's version of Notepad. You can tell the difference between the two versions by the Notepad desktop icon:

Minimized Windows 95 apps display the filename first. Minimized Windows 3.1 apps display the program name first.

Despite Microsoft's attempts to gently prod us into the future, many of us will continue to work with the habits we learned under DOS and Windows 3.1. We may find it necessary to prune and graft directories, move subdirectories from drive to drive, and occasionally inspect the contents of our hard drives, underneath the pretty Windows 95 desktop.

The Explorer and My Computer are not ideal tools for performing these functions. Those of us who've become dependent on file management shells like XTREE, Norton Desktop, or Central Point's PC Tools for Windows will miss their quick access to file browsers, unzip utilities, DOS command-line options, system information and convenient, flexible file display options. Chapter 14 of this book shows you some solutions offered by third-party utility vendors. But what about those of us who want to survive with just what's available in Windows 95?

The most obvious problems with using the Explorer and My Computer for file management involve manipulations of multiple files and directories. If you're accustomed to the Windows 3.1 File Manager (or a third-party substitute), the new Windows 95 interface can be frustrating.

The following tips show you how to get the most out of the Explorer and My Computer as file management tools. You'll also see how the old Windows 3.1 File Manager can return some missing functionality.

Drag-and-Drop Copy and Move

To drag and drop files or directory folders from one drive to a specific location on another, you must have either two instances of the Explorer open, or one instance open with display options set for multiple browsing windows.

Drag-and-drop behavior is slightly different in Windows 95 than it was in Windows 3.1:

- If you left-click an object and drag it to a folder on the same drive, the object is moved, not copied.
- If you left-click an object and drag it to a folder on a different drive, then the object is copied, with the original remaining in the source directory.

The exceptions to this rule are program files with the .EXE or .COM extension. If you left-click and drag an executable file to a new location, Windows 95 creates a shortcut link in the target folder, rather than moving or copying the file.

- To force a copy operation, you can left-click and drag the object while simultaneously holding down the CTRL key. This will produce a copy no matter what kind of file you're dragging, or where you drop it.
- To force a Move operation, left-click and drag the object while simultaneously holding down the SHIFT key. This will move the file, no matter what its extension or where you drop it.
- To force a shortcut to be created, left-click and drag the object while simultaneously holding down the CTRL and SHIFT keys. A shortcut pops up with the Create Shortcut option preselected as you release the object in the target folder. You can also pop up this option menu by dragging an object with the right mouse button held down, instead of the left button.
- If you left-click and drag a file between a folder and the desktop, it will be *moved* if the desktop is on the same drive, *copied* if the desktop is on a different drive, or a *shortcut* will be created if the file has an .EXE or .COM extension. If you right-click and drag the file, the Options menu will appear, allowing you to choose Move, Copy, or Create Shortcut.

Multiple File Operations: The SHIFT-Click Follies

You can copy or move multiple files between Explorer windows by selecting and dragging the files with the mouse or by using the Windows

Clipboard. If you left-click a file or directory while holding down the SHIFT key, all objects from the first one in the window to the object you click will be highlighted. This is sometimes annoying: Specifically, you may want to open My Computer (or an individual desktop folder) in Explorer's Pane view. The keyboard shortcut for this is SHIFT-double click. However, suppose you open or select another desktop object sometime during your session and go on working. Now, you decide you want to open My Computer and SHIFT-double click it. What may happen is that Win95 sees the first SHIFT-click, selects an entire range of desktop objects, and the second click opens all of the objects on your desktop instead of only My Computer. Microsoft thought it was adding a feature by allowing SHIFT-click to automatically select a range of objects, but in reality, it was creating a headache.

In Windows 3.1, to select a range of objects, you had to single-click the initial object in the range before SHIFT-clicking on the final object. This was less confusing than the Win95 default. To cancel the automatic range selection in Windows 95, you can left-click any object before using SHIFT-double click to open it in Explorer Pane view.

Multiple Windows in Explorer

My Computer lets you choose between browsing single-window or separate-window views of drives and folders. However, the Explorer's Pane views do not show multiple windows simultaneously. If you right-click an object in the Explorer and select Explore again, the new file window always replaces the old one. To get Explorer views of two drives at once you usually have to open two instances of Explorer. (This is one reason why you may prefer using the File Manager. Global file operations in the Explorer require more keystrokes and mouse movements than they do in the File Manager.)

Here's a shortcut that lets you open two drives in Pane views from a single instance of the Explorer:

1. Right-click an object and select Explore to open the first view.
2. Right-click any drive or folder in the tree view and select Open to produce an Open View window of the contents.
3. Right-click the folder icon (in the upper-left corner) of the second window and choose Explore.

More Explorer Esoterica

- *To use the Clipboard for global file copy operations, select a range of files (select the first in the range, then SHIFT-click the last in the range). Next press CTRL-C or CTRL-X to copy or move the files to the Clipboard (you can also use the Copy or Cut option on the Window Edit menu). Finally, open the target directory in the Explorer and press CTRL-V (or select the Paste option from the Edit menu.)*
- *To quickly bring up the Properties box for any file object, double-click the object while holding down the ALT key.*
- *To quickly close a child window and all parent windows connected with it, select the Close option on the File menu while holding down the SHIFT key.*
- *To get a quick Open View of any drive or directory, go to the Run option on the taskbar, type in the drive and pathname and click OK. (To bring up an Explorer Pane view, enter* **EXPLORER /E, [D:]\PATH** *in the Run box.)*
- *To change My Computer's default display from Open View to Explorer Pane view, open My Computer and select View\ Options\ FileTypes. Scroll down to the Folder object and click the Edit button. Click Explore in the Actions dialog box and then click Set Default.*
- *The Explorer has lost the Windows 3.1 option of sorting a list of files in a directory by their three-letter file extensions. Instead, the "Arrange Icons by Type" option sorts files by a type name in the Registration Database. This "type name" may or may not correspond to the file's three-letter extension. (See "Using File Associations" later in this chapter for more details.)*
- *To select a group of files on your hard disk by a specified filename or extension string, use the Find option under the Tools menu. Enter an appropriate filename or extension in the Named box under the Name & Location tab. Since the Explorer doesn't have a direct menu option to filter the file display in a directory, you must work with the retrieved results in the Find box instead. (For more information, see "Building Work Folders with Find" later in this chapter.)*
- *If you will be working in both the DOS and Windows environments, change your Explorer and My Computer View options to unhide Windows system files, and to display all DOS file extensions. Otherwise, you won't be able to tell the difference between a program, a batch file, or data objects that all bear the same name.*
- *If you unhide the Windows system files, you'll find some extra icons in .DLL files that would otherwise be invisible. Try inspecting MORICONS.DLL, DRVSPACE.EXE, GROUP.EXE, MPLAYER.EXE, PROGMAN.EXE, REGEDIT.EXE, and USER.EXE in addition to the default icon bank, SHELL32.DLL.*

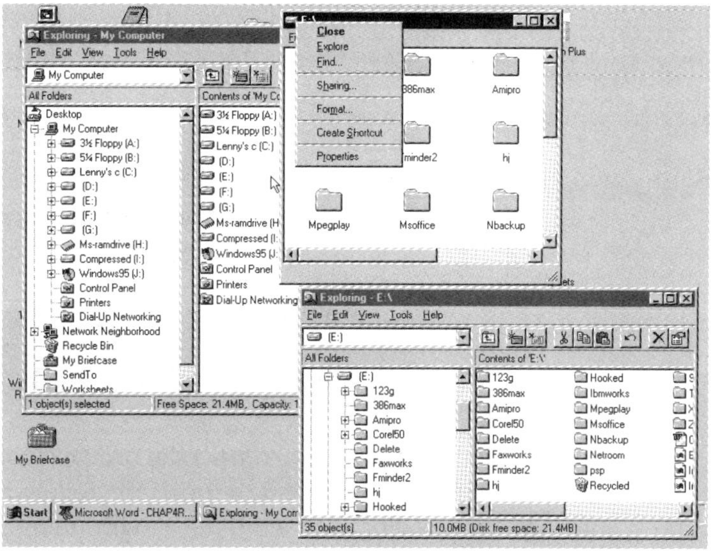

FIGURE 4-6

Open an Explorer window on a second drive by clicking the Explore option in the Large Icon view control menu.

The Explorer vs. the File Manager

Although the Explorer leaves something to be desired as a global file management tool, Win95 also includes an updated version of the Windows 3.1 File Manager (WINFILE.EXE). The File Manager gives you the following capabilities which are not available in the Explorer.

TILE FILE WINDOWS HORIZONTALLY AND VERTICALLY The File Manager can display multiple drive and file directories without launching additional instances of the program. You can arrange the windows horizontally or vertically by selecting a display option from the Windows menu.

CUSTOMIZE CONFIRMATION PREFERENCES FOR COPY, MOVE, DELETE, ETC. While the Explorer's confirmation preferences for file operations are fixed, the File Manager lets you toggle confirmation on or off for file delete, directory delete, file replace, mouse actions, format disk, or copy disk.

GLOBALLY RENAME, COPY, OR MOVE A SELECTED RANGE OF FILES The File Manager allows you to use these capabilities globally, simply by choosing the appropriate option from the File menu. (Move and Copy also have keyboard shortcuts, F7, and F8, respectively.) In addition to selecting a range of files with the mouse, you can also select files by specifying a wildcard extension in the Select Files dialog box. As you can see here, the File Manager shows file attributes in its list windows and lets you copy, move, rename, or delete a selection of files easily:

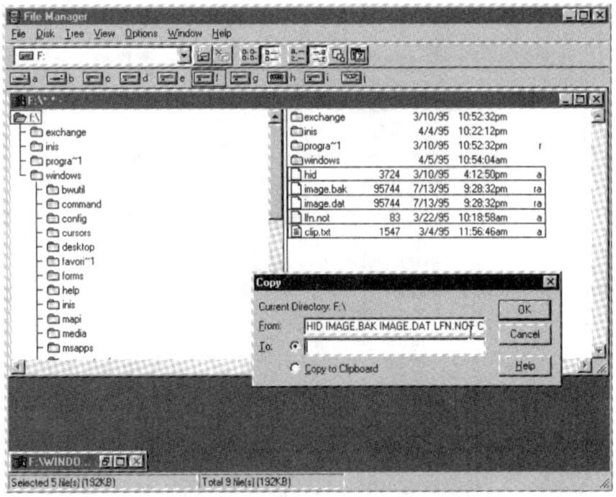

CONTROL DETAILS OF FILE INFORMATION DISPLAYED IN DIRECTORY WINDOWS

The File Manager allows you to toggle the following View options on and off: size, last modification date, last modification time, and display of file attributes. The Explorer's Details option turns all of this information on or off as a global unit.

---

tip *The File Manager has the ability to run any DOS command or batch file globally on a range of files. To do this, select the range and press F7 or F8. The filenames you've selected will appear in the pop-up dialog box. Select the contents of the dialog box with the mouse and press CTRL-C (or select Copy from the Edit menu). Next, open the File Run dialog box and type in a command or program name (for instance, PKZIP). Press CTRL-V to copy the filenames previously selected into the dialog box. Press OK to apply the command globally to the selected files:*

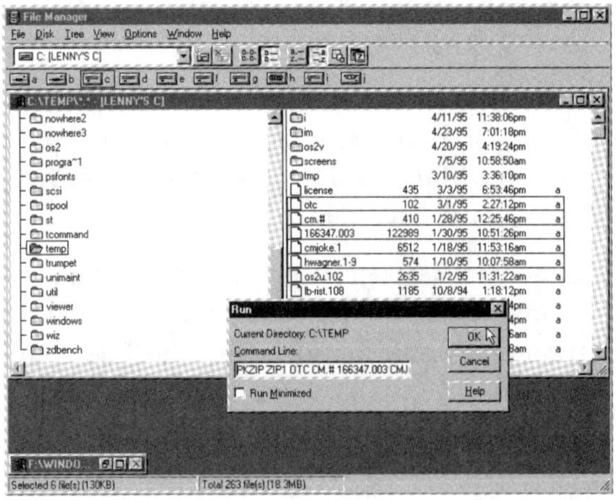

File Manager Pitfalls

If you decide to use the File Manager, keep in mind some of its limitations:

- The File Manager does not support Win95's long filenames. If you use it to move or copy files with long filenames, only the standard 8.3 filenames will be preserved in the target directory. (A work around for this involves running a special filename backup utility and restarting the system. See Chapter 7 for information on using LFNBK.) If it's important to you to preserve long filenames, then manage your files with Explorer or use a third-party package written for Windows 95. (See Chapter 14 for more information.)
- If you install Windows 95 over an existing copy of Windows 3.1 with DOS 6.*x*, the new File Manager may retain links to some useless, or obsolete features. Don't attempt to run the Windows 3.1 Undelete program from File Manager menus or from the toolbar; this will just make your system crash.

  You may find that the File Manager retains links to the old DOS and Windows 3.1 backup programs. Windows 95 usually removes these modules from your DOS directory, so that selecting Backup from the Tools menu produces a "file not found" message. Even if the old backup programs are still there, you probably won't want to use them. Windows 95 includes a new backup utility that supports long filenames and preserves system configuration information.

tip *You can, if you like, remove the associations to Undelete and Backup from File Manager's Tool menu. In a text editor, open WINFILE.INI, located in your WINDOWS directory. Remove the reference to UNDELETE.DLL in the [Settings] section and to MSTOOLS.DLL in the [AddOns] section.*

Even though the Windows 3.1 version of Undelete is unstable under Windows 95, you can use the DOS 6.x command-line version of Undelete to recover files erased in DOS sessions. To do this, you must also run the Win95 LOCK utility in a DOS session. See Chapter 7 for more details.

Instead of removing Backup from the File Manager's Tool menu, you can force File Manager to call the Win95 version of Backup rather than the old DOS version. To do this, simply copy the Win95 BACKUP.EXE and BACKUP.CFG files from the ACCESSORIES directory on the Windows boot drive to the MS-DOS directory referenced in WINFILE.INI. Then change the name of BACKUP.EXE to MWBACKUP.EXE.

Exploiting the Help System

The online help system in Win95 is more dynamic than in past versions of Windows. It is more complete and partially interactive. In addition to providing more extensive, indexed information, Win95 Help includes special tutorials and troubleshooting Wizards. These Wizards teach you an operation through animated examples, or walk you through a step-by-step system configuration process.

Each of the four main Help categories includes Wizards for a number of automated procedures. These interactive procedures are designated by small 3-D boxes containing curved arrows. When you see one of these boxes embedded in Help text, you can click it to see an animated demonstration, or get help for a specific procedure. (For instance, if you select How To\Print\Setting Up a Printer, you can click the embedded arrow to open the Install Printer Wizard.)

tip *By default, Windows Help screens are always displayed on top of other open windows on the desktop. If you need to see a complete application or folder window while a yellow Help box is on the screen, select Options\Keep Help on Top\Not on Top from the menu at the top of the Help window.*

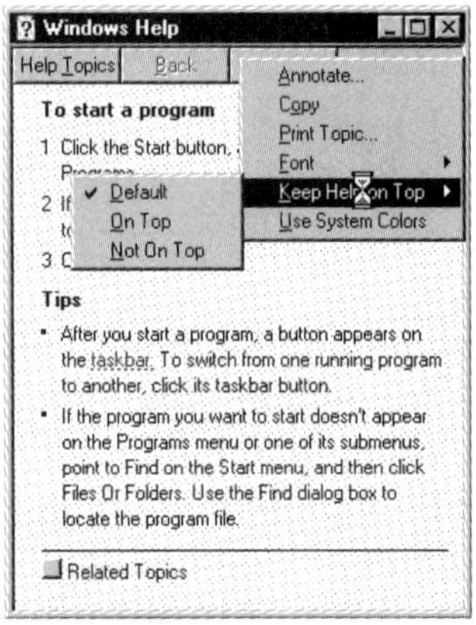

While you are in a Help text box, you can also click the right mouse button to bring up a series of options to annotate the entry, print it, copy the complete text to the Clipboard, or change Help display options.

Another useful new feature allows you to see pop-up summaries of options within dialog boxes. If you see a What's This? question mark icon in the upper-left corner of a Help box or program dialog box, you can click it once with the mouse. The mouse cursor changes into a question mark, allowing you to click any item in the window to pop up a brief information summary. In some dialog boxes, you can also right-click the mouse to bring up a rectangular What's This? box. If you right-click an option within the dialog box, and then click What's This?, you may see additional descriptive information. You can save information in a pop-up window by selecting the text you want with the mouse and pressing CTRL-C to copy it to the Clipboard. (Don't try to drag the text out of the window—use the keyboard!) You can then paste the Clipboard contents into an application, save to a file, or print it. If you right-click the mouse within any yellow Help box, another menu pops up, allowing you to copy the entire contents to the clipboard or to a printer.

Setting Up the Win95 Search Engine

The first time you access the Find tab in Windows Help (or in Help for any Windows application), a Find Setup Wizard pops up. This Wizard gives you three choices for setting up the search database. Microsoft recommends option 1, "minimize database size." This allows searches to proceed quickly and shows you entries only for essential Help topics. If you have a faster 486 or Pentium system and can spare a little disk storage space, we recommend option 2, "maximize search capabilities." This option takes a few seconds longer and writes additional index files to your hard disk.

When search capabilities are maximized, three additional Find options are activated. You'll see them if you open Windows Help, select the Find tab, and click the Options button. These options let you search for keywords in Windows Help files in the exact order you type them, and display only the topics that contain an exact match for the search string you enter, as shown here:

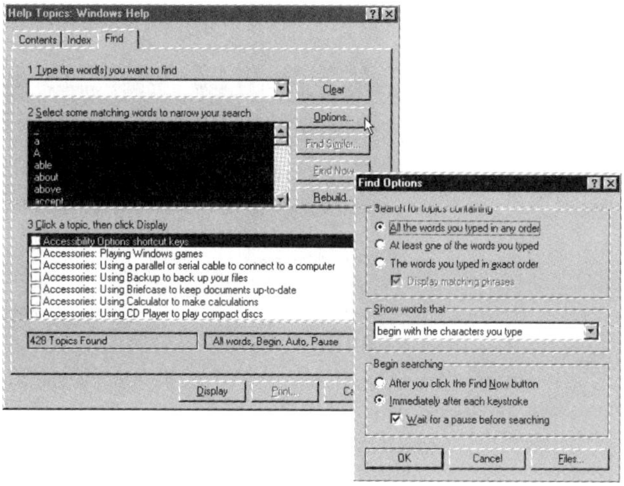

Microsoft warns that with large Help files, these options may slow down the search function. The maximize search feature works to your advantage when you are searching a large Help file for very specific information. For instance, suppose you configure Windows Help for minimized search options, select the Find tab, and enter **DELETE FILE**. The Display list in the Find dialog box will show 17 topics that you can read pertaining to this search string. If maximized search capabilities are configured and you search "for words you typed in exact order," then the text string "delete file" retrieves only four topics in the Display list.

note *Win95 searches for all alphanumeric characters in a text string you enter, including punctuation marks and upper-ASCII or foreign-language characters. White space between words in a string is minimized.*

Customize Search Capabilities

The Find Setup Wizard also displays a third option for setting the search options in Windows Help. If you select "Customize search capabilities," you can include or exclude specific Help modules (.HLP files) in building the search index. New applications written for Windows 95 include both a Help database (.HLP file) and a control file (.CNT file) for building a WinHelp table of contents. When the Wizard generates the Help index and table of contents, you can include or exclude specific Help modules listed in the .CNT file, as you see here. However, many applications include only one Help module, so this option isn't always useful.

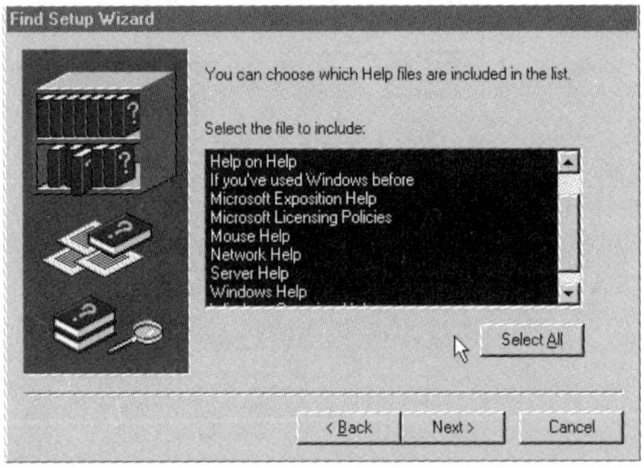

After you choose the files to be included in the index, the Find Setup Wizard asks you to include or exclude untitled Help topics in the search index. Typically, the untitled topics in the Help database are the contents of the small message boxes that pop up when you point and click What's This? If you decide to include them, then when a text string is matched, the topic list on the Find tab will show them as numbered, untitled entries.

The choices in the next setup screen pertain to the three Find options activated when you maximize search capabilities. The Help engine can search for complete phrases such as a person's first and last name. If you select "Include phrase searching," this allows you to choose the "words you typed in exact order" filter under the Find Options button. If you choose "Don't include phrase searching," then this filter remains grayed out.

The next setup choice asks whether you want the search engine to display matching phrases as you are entering a search string. If you choose this option, a checkmark is placed in the "Display matching phrases" choice under Find options (Microsoft cautions that this may slow down the search process with large Help files on slow computers).

The final setup option enables or disables the Find Similar button on the main Find tab of the Help system. See "Other Help Options" in this chapter for an explanation of this option and how it works.

The Bottom Line

The "maximize search capabilities" and "customize search capabilities" setup choices give you more extensive search capabilities at the cost of an extra few seconds of access time and some additional hard disk space. Table 4-2 shows the storage space required for the three configurations.

Help Module	Minimized Database Size	Maximized Database Size	Customized Database Size (all options enabled)
General Windows Help	697,879 bytes	1,551,383 bytes	2,847,744 bytes
Windows Resource Kit	1,132,486 bytes	4,123,590 bytes	4,123,590 bytes
Word for Windows 6.0a	961,091 bytes	3,346,688 bytes	3,592,771 bytes
Excel, version 5.0	1,115,101 bytes	4,541,197 bytes	4,907,485 bytes

TABLE 4-2 *Comparison of Storage Space Required by the Three Win95 Search Index Options*

tip *You can toggle the Find database between the minimum, maximum or custom sizes by opening Help, selecting the Find tab, and clicking on the Rebuild button.*

Other Help Options

When you bring up Help for Windows or any Windows application, you can change the way topic entries are retrieved by the search engine. By default, Win95 searches for all the words you type into a Search dialog in any order they may appear within the Help text. The Find Options button on the Find tab lets you change this behavior. You can make the topic list display entries corresponding to single words in the search string, or entries that correspond only to the complete search string in exact order.

The search algorithm can be further modified to hunt for:

- Keyword entries that begin with the characters in your search string
- Keyword entries that end with the characters in your search string
- Keyword entries that contain the characters in the string, or have the same root words as the string

These parameters can save you time in your searches. For instance, they eliminate extraneous entries in the Find topic list. If you want information about the Paste Special command, you can set Help to skip the entries on "paste," "pasting," "fast paste," or other topics that aren't relevant to your search.

USING THE FIND SIMILAR BUTTON IN EXTENDED SEARCHES If you select maximized search capabilities for your Help index, or choose to support similarity searches during a custom Setup, you enable the Find Similar button on the Find tab. When this option is active, each topic in the Display list is preceded by a small checkbox. You can extend a search by checking the boxes next to one or more topics shown in the Display list. If you check off a series of topics found through your initial search, clicking the Find Similar button causes Windows 95 to perform an extended search of the Help database. The word content of each checkmarked topic is analyzed. The search engine parses the Help database, looking for words that appear frequently in one topic or that are cross-correlated between several topics. This search produces an additional list of Help topics, as shown here, for you to browse.

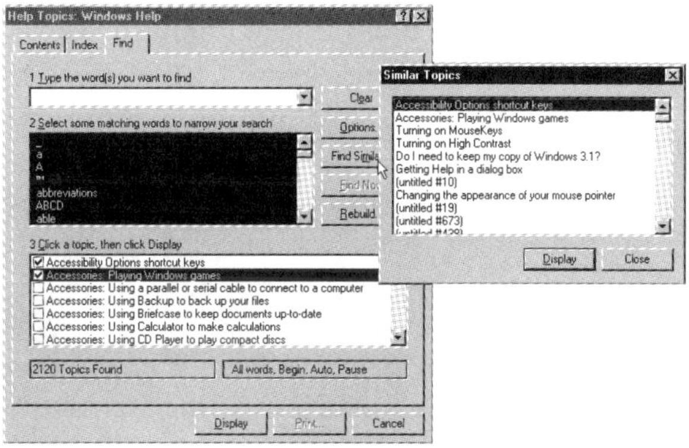

Running Windows 3.1 Help Files

Unlike Help in Windows 3.1, the Win95 Help subsystem has no menu option that allows you to open a specific Windows Help file (filename with the .HLP extension). You may occasionally want to view stand-alone Help files that were produced for the Windows 3.1 environment. Some manufacturers and organizations even compose newsletters written in the Windows 3.1 .HLP format.

You can launch a specific Win95 or Windows 3.1 .HLP file by entering it in the Run box on the Start Menu. Click the Start button, select Run and type in the path and filename for the .HLP file. You can also click the Browse button and choose All Files in the "files of type" field to browse your hard disk for .HLP files. This option is particularly useful if you've preserved the .HLP files from Windows 3.1 versions of applets like Calculator or Character Map. Both of these older Help files contain useful reference information not included in Windows 95 versions. See the sections on these applets in Chapter 5 for more details.

Desktop Strategies and Secrets

This final part of the chapter deals with solving problems related to Win95's program launching, file management, and desktop management features. The next section shows you how to create convenient program shortcuts and further customize the Start Menu. You'll find a thorough discussion of desktop configuration options: shortcut links, file associations, keyboard shortcuts, and context menu options.

Working with the Start Menu

Microsoft has made it easy for you to customize the taskbar and work with the Start Menu. You can add new programs or program folders to the Start menu in a variety of ways:

- Left-click an executable file in My Computer or Explorer file listings and drag it onto the Start Button. This creates a shortcut link on the first level of the pop-up Start Menu.
- If you want to add a program to a nested program group, right-click the Start button, select Open or Explore and open the Programs folder. Then drag the application you want to add over the appropriate program group.
- Another way to add programs to the Start Menu is to click the Start button and select Settings, Taskbar from the pop-up menu. Next, select the Start Menu Programs tab from taskbar Properties. Now you can just click the Add button, and enter a path and filename. Or, you can use the Browse button to search for applications in specified directories on your hard disk. After you choose a filename, the Select Program Folder dialog box allows you to place the entry in any existing program folder, or to create a new folder. (See Figure 4-7.) After you type in a program title, the shortcut will be added to your selected folder. If the filename you choose is listed in the Windows 95 application database, a program title and icon will be assigned to it automatically.

- If you click the Advanced button on the taskbar Start Menu Programs tab, the Start Menu will open in Explorer Tree View. You can then drag and drop a file object directly into a folder, as described earlier.
- You can also add a new program or folder by choosing New from the pull-down File menu in the Explorer or any open folder window. As described earlier, the Wizard will allow you to directly enter a filename or browse through your hard disk, then let you assign a shortcut name and icon.

The Start Menu as a Surrogate Program Manager

The Windows 95 Start Menu is a flexible tool that you can use in several different ways. You're already familiar with its standard configuration as a pop-up program launcher. You can also use the Start Menu to emulate the Windows 3.1 way of displaying programs and groups on the desktop. Some people are used to this look and feel and may prefer it to the new fold-out menus on the Start button.

To configure a desktop that looks more Program Manager-like, just right-click the Start button to open the Start Menu folder. What you see in the Start Menu window corresponds to the subdirectories and shortcut links physically stored in the Start Menu directory (WINDOWS\STARTM~1). You can drag a shortcut to the Programs folder onto the desktop, or open the folder and drag out shortcuts to any of your favorite program groups.

FIGURE 4-7

The Select Program Folder screen lets you drop your new application into an appropriate program group.

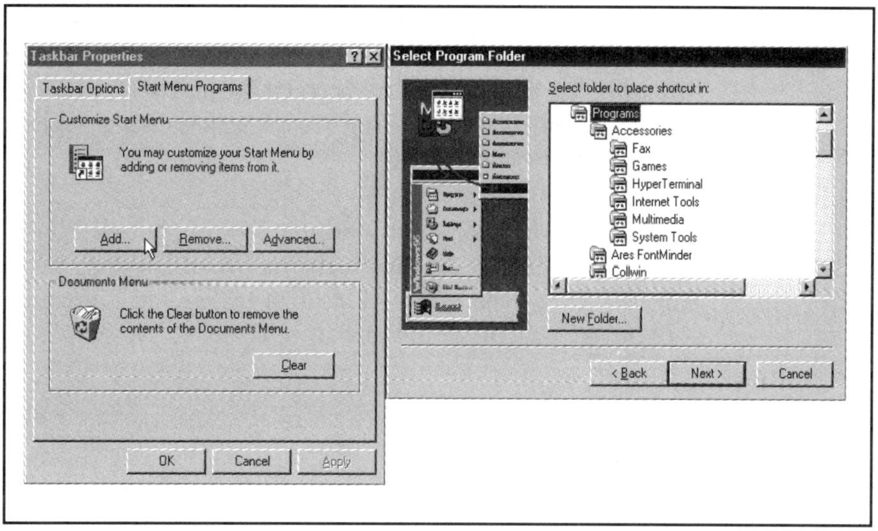

Open and size windows for all or part of your Programs group in strategic locations on the desktop. These window settings will be preserved the next time you start Windows 95. The advantage of emulating the Program Manager with group folder windows is that it's still super-easy to create new subfolders and applications or move them in and out of a group window.

If you're really a diehard Program Manager fan, you can even run the real thing concurrently with the taskbar-and-Explorer interface. Just click the Run button on the Start Menu and enter **PROGMAN.EXE**. This will allow you to retain all the advantages of the new Win95 desktop and start your applications in a variety of different ways. Most users should adapt quickly to Win95's new interface, but if there's someone in your office who's fixated on the old way of doing things, you can make them happy, as well.

Customizing the Taskbar

If you right-click the taskbar and select Properties, you'll see a number of customization options. By default, the taskbar always floats on top of other applications on the desktop. You can disable this feature, turn off the digital clock, or condense the Start Menu display to show small icons. You can also select the AutoHide option from the Properties menu to reduce the taskbar to a thin line at the bottom of your screen. If you choose this option and you want the taskbar available when you run full-screen programs, you should select both the Always On Top and AutoHide options.

tip *You can customize the color, size of the icons, and fonts on the taskbar by using the Control Panel's Display options. Either open the Display object from the Control Panel or right-click the desktop and select Properties. Choose the Appearance tab, and select Inactive Title Bar from the Item scroll list. Notice that if you click the Size box to the right of the Item list, the size of the title bars in the sample window will shrink or expand as you decrease or increase the setting. You can use the Color and Font boxes to further customize display of the taskbar.*

To move the taskbar around the desktop, left-click inside an empty area of the taskbar and drag with the mouse to the top, bottom, left, or right edges of the screen. The taskbar will realign itself along the right, left, top, or bottom margins of the screen.

FIGURE 4-8

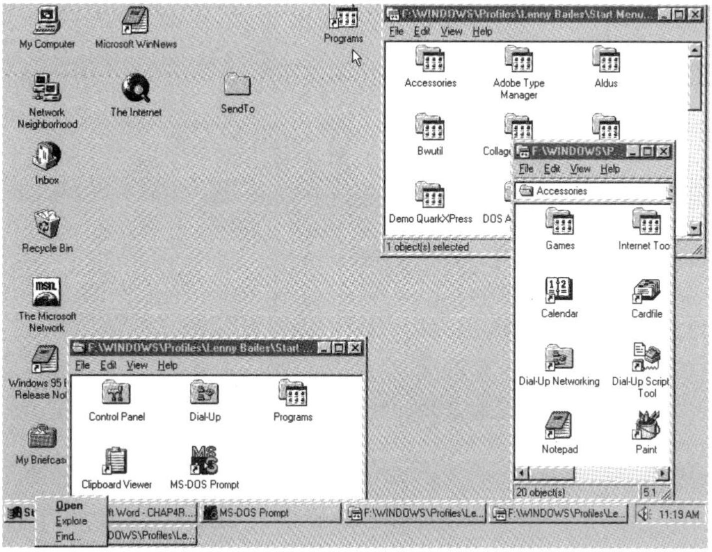

Desktop shortcuts for folders in the Start Menu emulate the look and feel of the Windows 3.1 Program Manager. ■

Tricks with the Start Menu

Normally, if you create a new folder in the Start Menu, the folder bears a program group icon. When you left-click the Start Menu, you'll see that each program group icon has a right-pointing triangle. If you pan the mouse over an icon that has one of these triangles, it opens to display a pop-up list of nested files and subfolders. An additional Start Menu option lets you create shortcuts to folders instead of physical folders. Folder shortcuts do not include triangle pointers. When you pan over one (represented by a standard yellow folder icon), it does not pop up a list of subfolders and files. Instead, when you single-click a yellow folder shortcut, the folder opens in a desktop window. This can be a useful feature, since the pop-up lists don't allow you to drag and drop objects in and out the way folder windows do.

To place shortcuts on the Start Menu that open desktop windows instead of displaying pop-up lists, open My Computer or the Explorer and select an existing folder or directory (or create a new one). Next, right-click and drag the folder to the Start button (or to an open Start Menu window). Choose Create Shortcut from the pop-up context menu.

FIGURE 4-9

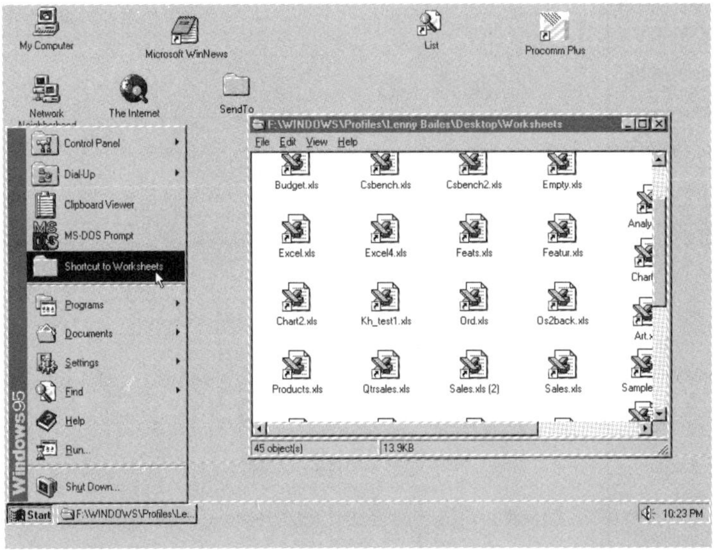

A shortcut to a folder on the Start Menu opens a desktop Window when you click it. A real folder placed on the Start Menu opens a pop-up list.

tip *If you drag any object with the mouse to a minimized window or program button on the taskbar, the minimized item reopens its window on the desktop.*

Making the Control Panel, Your Printers, and Dial-Up Networking More Accessible

The Windows Control Panel is normally three mouse-clicks away on the Start Menu. And once you get the Control Panel open, you have to point and click the settings applet that you want to run. The next tip shows you how to save time and mouse-clicks by moving the Control Panel to the first level of the Start Menu.

1. *Right-click the Start button and select Open to open the Start Menu on the desktop.*
2. *Create a new folder on the first level of the Start Menu by selecting New\Folder from the pull-down File menu.*
3. *Replace the default name, New Folder, for the object by pasting in the following information as the folder's name:*

```
Control Panel.{21EC2020-3AEA-1069-A2DD-08002B30309D}
```

4. *If you don't want to manually type in this long registry serial number, you can find it listed in the file called TIPS.TXT in your WINDOWS directory in a section called [Special Folders]. You can copy and paste it in from there with the mouse.*

If the folder is accurately renamed with this long string, it signals the Registration Database to convert the folder into a new Control Panel object. (Refer back to Figure 4-1.) The new Control Panel on the first level displays a pop-up list of its contents instead of opening a desktop folder.

This trick works because the long serial number in the folder name tells the Win95 Registration database to create a special object. You can also make special folders on the first level of the Start Menu for Dial-Up Networking and Printers. Follow the procedure just outlined and paste in the following folder names:

For Dial-Up Networking	For Printers
Dial Up Net.{992CFFA0-F557-101A-88EC-00DD010CCC48}	Printers.{2227A280-3AEA-1069-A2DE-08002B30309D}

For other commonly used features such as the Win95 Clipboard or MS-DOS prompt, there are no specific registration serial numbers. Instead, to place these features anywhere on the Start Menu, just select the original object, drag it to the location you want and choose Create Shortcut from the pop-up context menu.

For a complete discussion of how to use the Win95 Control Panel and all of its configuration options, see Chapter 8.

Default Taskbar Utilities

The digital Windows clock is installed automatically on the taskbar. Other taskbar utilities, such as Power Management, PCMCIA support, and a Volume Control are installed if your hardware supports them. Additionally, a small status area to the left of the digital clock is used to display messages from Windows 95 applications. When you use a Fax, Printer, Modem, or other Win95-aware utility, a pop-up status box appears in this message area.

The Volume Control, installed if you have a sound card, can be started in two views. A single click on the Speaker icon brings up a simple slider; a double-click brings up a more complete set of sound options.

The Battery Meter is installed on laptops, and other systems that support Advanced Power Management. It is represented by a Plug icon (see Figure 4-10).

The PCMCIA control icon appears on the taskbar if you have a computer that supports PCMCIA peripherals.

FIGURE 4-10

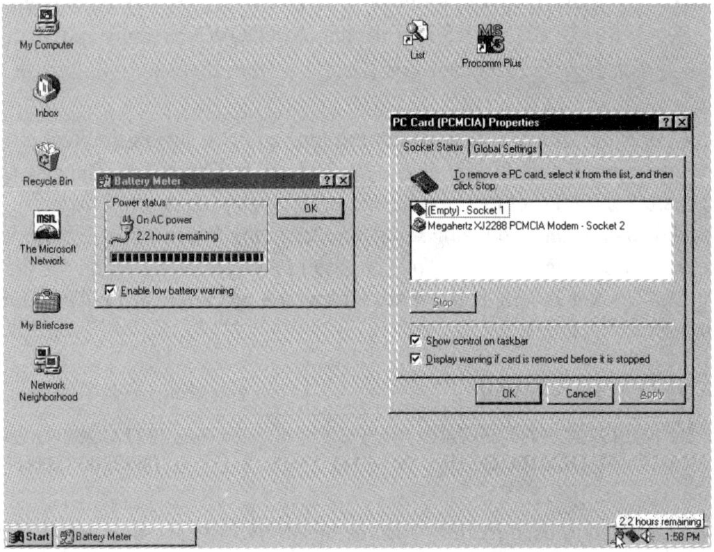

The PC Card icon on the taskbar can be opened to display information about your PCMCIA peripherals. Click or pan over the Power icon to pop up a display of time remaining in the battery.

Microsoft has reserved the status display area on the taskbar so that other applications written for Windows 95 can also use it, in the future. (If you have installed Microsoft Plus!, an icon for the System Agent appears.)

Keyboard Shortcuts

If you don't want to use a mouse, you'll find that accessing desktop features under Windows 95 is a bit more complicated than under Windows 3.1. Keyboard shortcuts to most functions do exist, but they're obscure, and you won't find all of them listed in online help. Some tasks (such as switching between objects on the desktop or selecting minimized programs on the taskbar) require a ridiculous number of keystrokes. We'll see in a subsequent section that the Windows 3.1 Recorder can help you to construct manageable shortcuts for these tasks.

Tables 4-3 through 4-10 list all the Win95 keyboard shortcuts we could find.

Customizing the Interface

Windows 95 goes a step beyond Windows 3.1 in its implementation of shortcut keys, file associations, and an object-oriented desktop. If you choose to use the Explorer/taskbar interface instead of the Program Manager/File Manager interface, a number of power-user desktop options are available.

Key or Combination	Action
F1	Activates Help
F3	Finds
F5	Refreshes the desktop
CTRL-ESC	Brings up the Start Menu and sets focus on the taskbar
CTRL-ESC, ESC	Brings up and closes the Start Menu and sets focus on the taskbar
CTRL-ESC, ESC, TAB	Lets you switch between minimized buttons on the taskbar with RIGHT ARROW and LEFT ARROW keys
CTRL-ESC, ESC, TAB, TAB	Shifts focus to the Win95 desktop so you can switch between desktop objects with the RIGHT ARROW and LEFT ARROW keys
SHIFT-F10	When focus is on desktop, brings up the context menu for the selected item
ALT-TAB	Switches between open windows and applications on the desktop
CTRL-SPACEBAR	Shifts focus from the desktop object to the desktop
CTRL-SPACEBAR, SHIFT-F10	Brings up the context menu for the desktop after shifting focus from a selected object
ALT-M	If focus is on the taskbar or the desktop, minimizes all open windows, returning focus to the desktop

TABLE 4-3 *Keyboard-Only Shortcuts for the Desktop* ■

Key or Combination	Action
F2	Renames object
F3	Brings up Find window
F4	Opens a drop-down list window
F5	Refreshes the desktop
ALT-ENTER	Brings up the properties menu for a selected object
F6	Cycles between panes in the Explorer
CTRL-G	Brings up the "Go to folder" dialog box in the Explorer
CTRL-Z	Undoes last operation
CTRL-A	Selects all objects in a window
BACKSPACE	Goes to the parent folder
SHIFT-<close> (on File menu)	On folders, closes this folder and all its parent folders
CTRL-X,C,V	Cuts, copies, pastes
DELETE	Deletes (item preserved in the Recycle Bin)
SHIFT-DELETE	Deletes object without putting it in the Recycle Bin

TABLE 4-4 *General Folder and Explorer Shortcuts* ■

Key or Combination	Action
NUM LOCK- *	Expands everything under the current selection
NUM LOCK-+	Expands the current selection
NUM LOCK--	Collapses the selection
RIGHT ARROW	Expands the selection if it's not expanded, otherwise goes to the first child folder
LEFT ARROW	Collapses the selection if it's expanded, otherwise goes to the parent folder

TABLE 4-5 *Shortcuts in the Explorer Tree* ■

Key or Combination	Action
CTRL-TAB or CTRL-SHIFT-TAB	Cycles through pages

TABLE 4-6 *Shortcuts in Property Sheets* ■

Key or Combination	Action
F4	Drops down the location list
F5	Refreshes the view
BACKSPACE	Goes to the parent folder if the focus is on the view window

TABLE 4-7 *Shortcuts in the Open\Save Common Dialog Box* ■

Keypress and Mouse Action	Action
ALT-double-click on icon	Brings up the properties menu
SHIFT-double-click	Opens Explorer view for My Computer drives, Folders, and Network Neighborhood
Hold CTRL while dragging the file to a folder	Copies the file to the folder
Hold CTRL-SHIFT while dragging the file to the desktop or a folder	Creates a shortcut to the file

TABLE 4-8 *Keyboard + Mouse Shortcuts (On the Desktop, in Folders, or in the Explorer)* ■

Key Combination	Action
WIN-R	Brings up the Run dialog box
WIN-M	Minimizes all open windows
SHIFT-WIN-M	Undoes Minimize All
WIN-F1	Activates Help
WIN-E	Activates the Explorer
WIN-F	Finds files or folders
CTRL-WIN-F	Finds Computers
WIN-TAB	Cycle through the taskbar buttons
WIN-BREAK	Microsoft Personal Systems Support Hotkey (System Properties dialog box)

TABLE 4-9 *MS Natural Keyboard Shortcuts* ■

Some of these options are not well-documented in the online Win95 Help module, but they are well worth knowing about and using. In this section you'll find a series of tips and tricks for improving productivity based on Windows 95's new, powerful desktop features.

Using Shortcut Keys

Windows 95 allows you to assign a shortcut key to launch any DOS or Windows application present on the desktop or on the Start Menu. The shortcut key option is accessed by right-clicking and selecting an object's

Shortcut	Action
Tap SHIFT five times	Toggles Accessibility StickyKeys on and off
Hold down right-SHIFT for 8 seconds	Toggles Accessibility FilterKeys on and off
Hold down NUM LOCK for 5 seconds	Toggles Accessibility ToggleKeys on and off
Left ALT-NUM LOCK/Left SHIFT-NUM LOCK	Toggles Accessibility MouseKeys on and off
Left ALT-PRINT SCREEN/Left SHIFT-PRINT SCREEN	Toggles Accessibility HighContrast on and off

TABLE 4-10 *Accessibility Shortcuts* ■

Properties menu, then selecting Shortcut Key on the Shortcut Tab (Windows applications) or the Program Tab (DOS applications). You can also assign shortcut keys to files in individual directories under Explorer or My Computer. If you assign a shortcut key to a file through the Explorer or My Computer, the key won't become active unless you also create a shortcut icon for the object on the desktop or in the Start Menu.

Shortcut key combinations for DOS programs and command-line sessions may include CTRL or ALT plus another key; for example, CTRL-Y, or CTRL-SHIFT-F1. You cannot use ESC, ENTER, TAB, SPACEBAR, PRINTSCREEN, or BACKSPACE.

For Windows applications, each shortcut key that uses an alphanumeric character (1 through 9, A through Z) must also include one of the following two-key combinations: CTRL-SHIFT, CTRL-ALT, or ALT-SHIFT. (Shortcut keys configured for DOS programs require only one special key plus an alphanumeric character.) Shortcut key combinations that use function keys (F1 through F12) do not require additional special keys, although they may include them.

No other program can use a shortcut key combination, once you assign it. If the assigned hotkey conflicts with an access key in a Windows program, the access key will not work. To deselect a shortcut key assignment, open the Program tab or Shortcut tab through the application's Properties menu, click in the Shortcut key box and press the SPACEBAR.

tip *You can also assign a shortcut key to open a folder, provided that a shortcut link to the folder has been placed on the desktop or in the Start Menu. Open the folder's or Shortcut Link's Properties menu, select the Shortcut tab, and assign a shortcut key to the folder as with program objects. When you press the assigned key, the folder pops open on the desktop.*

Using Quick View: Customizing to See More Files

Windows 95 includes a feature called Quick View that allows you to preview certain types of documents and graphic data. If you chose this option during installation, then filters for supported file types are added to the Win95 desktop. (Windows 95 recognizes file types either by their three-letter file extension, or

FIGURE 4-11

A shortcut key combination can be assigned to open any object with a corresponding shortcut link on the desktop or in the Start Menu.

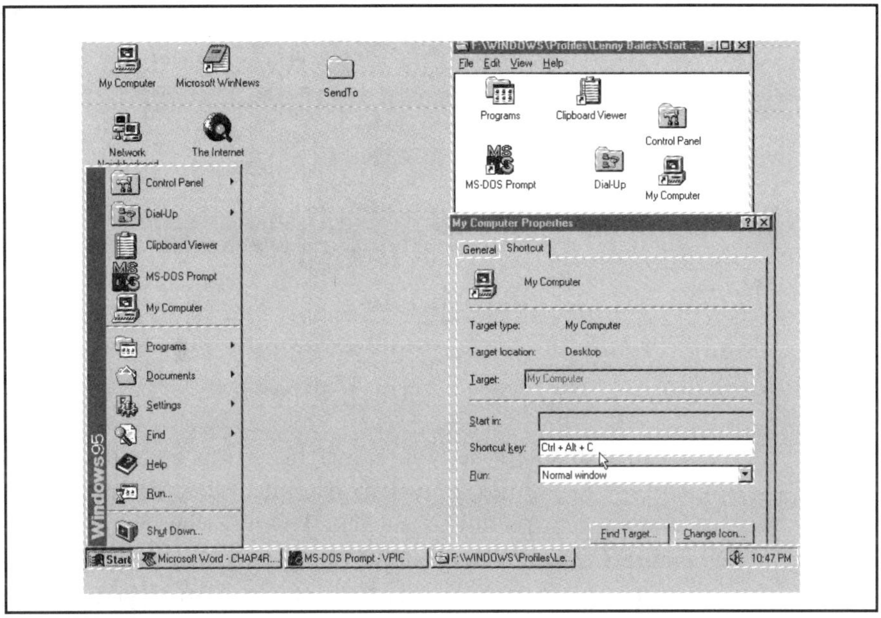

by special entries in the Registration Database. See the section called "Using File Associations" later in this chapter for more details.)

If a particular file type is supported, then a Quick View option appears when you right-click the file on the desktop or in Explorer. The filters supplied with Windows 95 allow you to view files created by Ami Pro 2-3, Microsoft Word 2-6, WordPerfect 5-6, Microsoft Works 1-2, Microsoft Excel, Quattro Pro, Microsoft PowerPoint, Lotus Freelance, and the .BMP bitmap format. But Quick View's supported formats are by no means exhaustive. If, for instance, you want to display a DOS batch file, there is no Quick View option, even though .BAT files are just ASCII text.

You can increase the flexibility of Quick View by dragging a shortcut to Quick View into Win95's SendTo folder. Open My Computer and make sure the View options are set to show all files. Open WINDOWS\SENDTO on your Win95 host drive, and open another window to the WINDOWS\SYSTEM\VIEWERS directory. Right-click QUIKVIEW.EXE in the Viewers folder and drag a shortcut into the SendTo folder, as shown next:

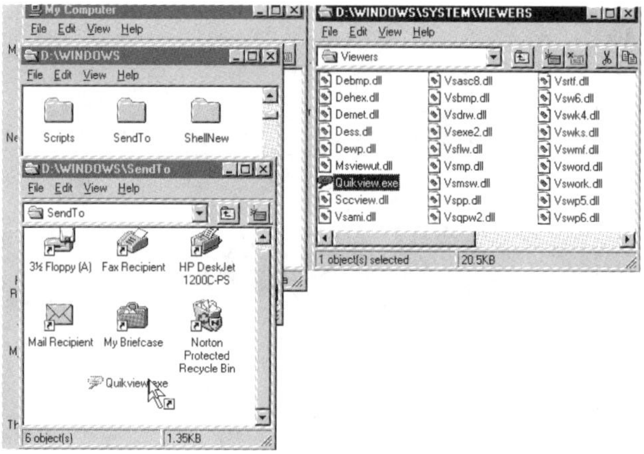

Once this is done, you can right-click a file with any file extension and attempt to "Quick View" it. If Quick View doesn't show up on the file's context menu, point to the SendTo Quikview menu option. (Refer back to Figure 4-2 for an example.) You may see a message that says "There are no viewers registered for this type of file. Would you like to try the Default Viewers?" Just answer yes. If the file is in one of Quick View's supported formats but has the wrong file extension, it will still be displayed.

See the next section for more information about how to use the SendTo folder.

Working with the SendTo Folder

The SendTo folder is a Windows 95 feature that lets you quickly drag files or programs to be faxed, printed, loaded into a program, or transferred to another drive. By default, SendTo is configured as a hidden subdirectory under the Win95 Desktop ([D:]\WINDOWS\DESKTOP\SENDTO). The destination links placed in the SendTo folder are also displayed in the Send To option found on the context menus of individual desktop objects.

tip *To make the Send To option on your system accessible and easy to work with, drag a shortcut to the SendTo folder to the desktop. Open My Computer and set its file display option to Show All Files (Select View\Options from the pull-down file menu and select the appropriate display button on the View tab.) Open the Windows folder on your Win95 host drive and drag a shortcut to the SendTo subfolder to the desktop. Now you'll easily be able to add options to the Send To menu by dragging them into the shortcut to the SendTo folder.*

To make additional options available on the Send To menu, just drag a shortcut to the appropriate object from My Computer or the Desktop to the

SendTo folder. Intelligent use of the SendTo folder lets you set up a number of convenient features:

- Right-click the mouse button and view the contents of graphics and text files by placing shortcuts to a bitmap editor and an ASCII text editor in the SendTo folder. With shortcuts to Notepad, Paint, and WordPad, you can use Send To to view the contents of many unregistered file types.
- Place shortcuts for the Inbox, Compose Fax, or My Briefcase in the SendTo folder. This allows you to quickly send e-mail, fax a file, or set up files to be synchronized with a remote computer.
- Drag shortcuts for a floppy drive, hard disk backup directory, or shared network folder to the SendTo folder. This allows you to use Send To on any file's context menu to quickly copy the file to designated locations.

tip *You can also drag a shortcut to the Recycle Bin into the SendTo folder . This allows you to quickly delete files with a single, continuous right-click motion.*

Creating Multiple Desktops with the Password, Multiuser Feature

Windows 95 allows you to create multiple desktop configurations, each assigned to a different username on a single workstation. This feature can also be used to create alternate productivity desktops for a single user. You can choose, at boot time, to log into a desktop configured for desktop publishing, telecommunications, programming, or any other productivity chore. Each alternate desktop can contain its own screen colors, wallpaper, Start Menu, open folders, and so on, prearranged for convenient use.

To enable multiple desktops, open the Password object in the Win95 Control Panel. Go to the User Profiles tab, and select "Users can customize their preferences." Also place checkmarks next to the options you want to enable under User Profile Settings. You can choose to share a common Start Menu or common desktop icons among all of your desktops, or you can make each desktop use an independent configuration.

Restart Windows 95 and enter your own name when the logon prompt is presented. (You can also, optionally, enter a password.) This will make a copy of your basic, current desktop, saving the information to a WINDOWS\PROFILE\USERNAME subdirectory on your Win95 host drive. (Some of the objects on the desktop may be set back to default positions. If so, you can readjust them to preserve the desired look and feel.)

Now, you're ready to set up a series of new desktops for different productivity scenarios. Click the Shutdown option on the Start Menu and choose "Close all programs and log on as a different user." Windows 95 quickly restarts itself and presents you with a logon prompt. To create a new desktop, choose a different username and password. Or, you can just log on with the type of desktop you're going to configure, such as DTP, or Contacts. Windows 95 restarts itself with the desktop objects set back to their default positions. (Any desktop icons you created before enabling multiple desktops will also appear.)

Next, you can arrange a "desktop publishing" desktop. Go into the Start Menu and remove extraneous program groups and objects that are not needed. (Don't worry, they'll still be there on the original desktop!) You can create a special work folder with PageMaker and CorelDRAW templates, or open other strategic folders on the desktop. For instance, you might want to create a shortcut to the Printer control panel, the Font folder, and to an image cataloging utility. If you have a program group devoted to DTP utilities, you might want to right-click the Start button and put a shortcut to that group on the desktop. When the desktop is set up the way you want it, you can shut the system down. The next time you start Windows 95 and use the DTP logon, the desktop you just created reappears. If you log on with your original username, then the original desktop appears.

If you like, you can now create another desktop called Contacts. Shut down Win95, choose "log on as a different user" and enter **CONTACTS** in the username box. Once again, you can arrange the desktop to suit you. Open windows for PIMs, project management software, and the Microsoft Exchange Inbox. (Or create shortcuts to your favorite e-mail package and Internet utilities.) When you shut down, this desktop will also be preserved. When you start Windows 95 again, you can log on with your original username to access your original desktop, or immediately log on to any of your special productivity desktops.

Using Accessibility Options

Win95's Accessibility Options, accessed through the Control Panel, are primarily designed to allow users with special needs to take advantage of features such as sticky keyboard combinations, visual pop-up warnings for sound events, and a large font/high contrast screen display. Some of the accessibility options may also be of interest to general users. For instance, the ToggleKeys option on the first tab attaches a sound tone to the pressing of the CAPS LOCK, NUM LOCK, and SCROLL LOCK keys. This is particularly useful for people who accidentally hit the CAPS LOCK key without noticing it, and become chagrined when their data entry gets messed up.

Another Accessibility Option allows you to enable a keyboard mouse simulator. If you are the type of user who prefers the keyboard to the mouse, this is an invaluable feature. Some Windows 95 functions can't be accessed through the keyboard at all, and others require a cumbersome number of keystrokes. The Accessibility MouseKeys feature cures this problem.

Using File Associations

Windows 95 makes more extensive use of file associations than Windows 3.1. By default, more than 40 individual file types are placed in the Registration Database. These file types are not all attached to specific actions or system events, but they can be. Open the Explorer or any folder window and select View\Options\File Types, and you'll see a list of all the file types registered on your system. This list also displays the file extension and icon associated with the file type and which application (if any) has been selected to open the file. If you select a file type and click the Edit button, you'll see that a number of actions can be preconfigured, as shown here:

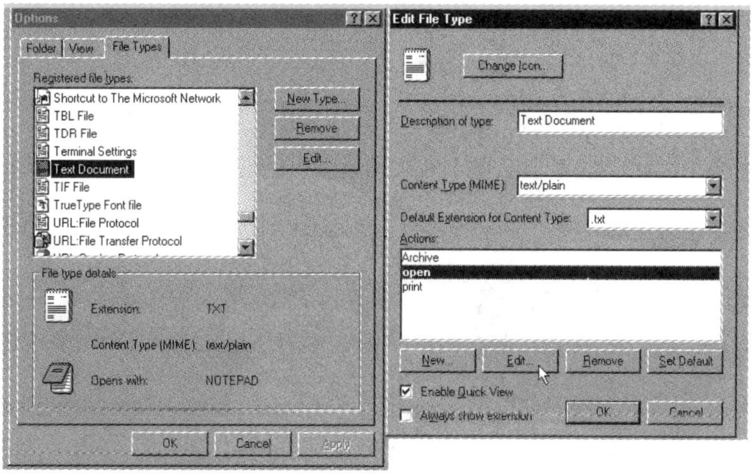

Each of the actions in this list also appears on the right-click context menu for all files of this type. Only one action (highlighted in bold) can be the default action for the file type. In most cases, the default action is simply to open a file of this type in a specified application when you double-click it.

Associating Files with Your Favorite Browsing and Editing Utilities

The View\Options\File Types tab in My Computer or the Explorer allows you to associate any Win95 registered file type with any DOS or Windows application. By default, double-clicking a file with the .TXT extension opens the file in Win95 Notepad. It's easy to change this association to another text viewer or editor. If you prefer to have your .TXT files open in WordPad or in the Write program from Windows 3.1, follow these steps:

1. Select Text Document from the alphabetical list of file types in the View\Options\File Types tab. Click the Edit button.
2. Choose Open in the Actions list on the next screen. Click the Edit button.
3. Type the name of the new "application used to perform action" in the appropriate dialog box.

Adding Options to the Context Menu

Some file types have other preconfigured options, such as Print, or Explore. These options are listed in the context menu when you right-click a file with the designated extension. Any additional options in the Actions window can also be edited, or you can create new ones. To create a new action, click the New button on the Edit File Types screen. Enter a name for the action in the Action dialog box on the next screen, and enter a DOS or Windows command or application in the "Application used to perform action" dialog box.

If you create a new action, be sure the command you specify will actually work on files of the type you've selected. Most of the Microsoft applets allow you to set up a Print action because you can simply append a /P parameter to the command line to pass a file directly to the printer. If an application has a command-line option to print or perform other operations on a file, these operations can be set up as actions associated with a particular file type.

For example, you might create actions called Unpack or View Archive associated with files that bear the .ZIP file extension. Then associate these actions to PKUNZIP.EXE, or to another archive utility. The following section shows you how to do this.

ADDING NEW FILE TYPES You can add new file types to the Windows 95 Registration Database by selecting the View\Options\File Types in any folder or Explorer window and clicking the New Type button. (See Figure 4-12.) Then enter the appropriate information for the new file type on the Add New File Type screen.

For instance, suppose you want to create an association for CompuServe .GIF files. The following procedure will create a new .GIF file type in the system registry and associate files with the .GIF extension to Paintshop Pro (a shareware image editor):

1. Open My Computer, the Explorer, or any folder window and select Options\File Types from the View menu.
2. Click the New Type button. This opens the Add New File Type dialog box. Type in **COMPUSERVE GIF** in the "Description of type" box and **.GIF** in the "Associated extension" box.
3. Under Actions, click the New button. This opens the New Action dialog box. Enter **OPEN** in the Action box and **[*D*:]*PATH*\PSP.EXE** in the "Application used to perform action" box. (You can also use the Browse button to find the path to the application.)
4. Close the dialog box.

FIGURE 4-12

A new registered file type for CompuServe GIF is created by filling out the appropriate dialog boxes on the Add New File Type screen. An Open action is added to associate the file type with Paintshop Pro (PSP.EXE).

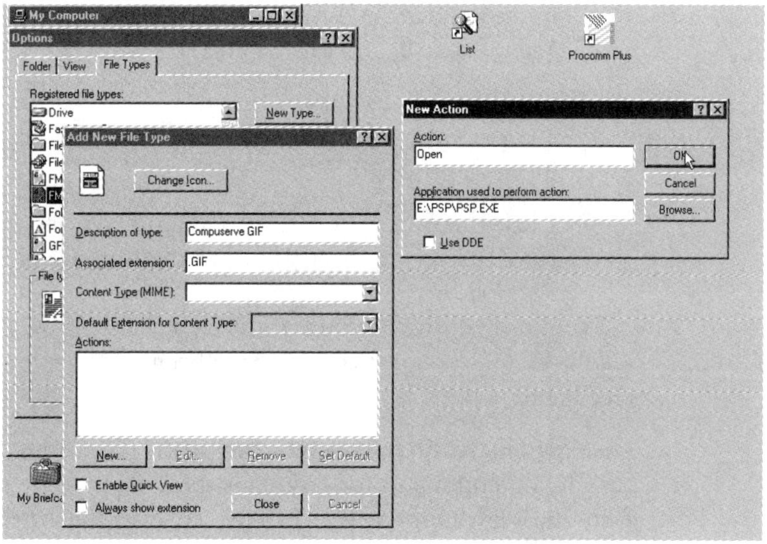

Notice that "CompuServe GIF" has appeared in the registered file types list displayed under the File Types tab. From now on, if you double-click an object with the .GIF extension, it is loaded automatically into Paintshop Pro.

Next, let's create a registered file type with the .ZIP file extension for PKZIP's compressed archives. Follow these steps:

1. Select View\Options\File Types. Click the New Type button, and enter **.ZIP** in the Associated extensions box. (This is the only box in the top half of the screen that needs to be filled in; a description of the file type is optional.)
2. Click the New button under the Actions list box. Enter the title **UNPACK** in the New Action dialog box on the next screen.
3. In the "Applications used to perform action" box, enter this command:

   ```
   [D:]\PATH\PKUNZIP.EXE -E %1
   ```

   where [*D*:]*PATH* specifies the drive and directory where PKUNZIP.EXE is stored on your hard drive.
4. Click the OK button and you'll see that UNPACK has been entered in the Actions list box on the Add New File Type screen.
5. Select Unpack with the mouse and click the Set Default button to make it the default action for handling files with the .ZIP extension.
6. For an additional View Archive action, you can click the New button under the Actions list box again, enter the description, **View Archive**, and this command:

   ```
   [D:]\PATH\PKUNZIP.EXE -V %1
   ```

   in the appropriate dialog boxes.
7. Close the Add New File Type dialog box and notice that an entry for ZIP Files has been added to the Registered File Types list.

From now on when you right-click a file with the .ZIP extension, you'll see the actions you just created have been added to the file's context menu. (See Figure 4-13.)

CREATING AN ADD TO ARCHIVE COMMAND You can create an ADD TO ARCHIVE command for any registered file type by selecting the file type from the View\Options\File Tab list, clicking the Edit button on this screen and adding another new action to the Actions list box on the next screen.

FIGURE 4-13

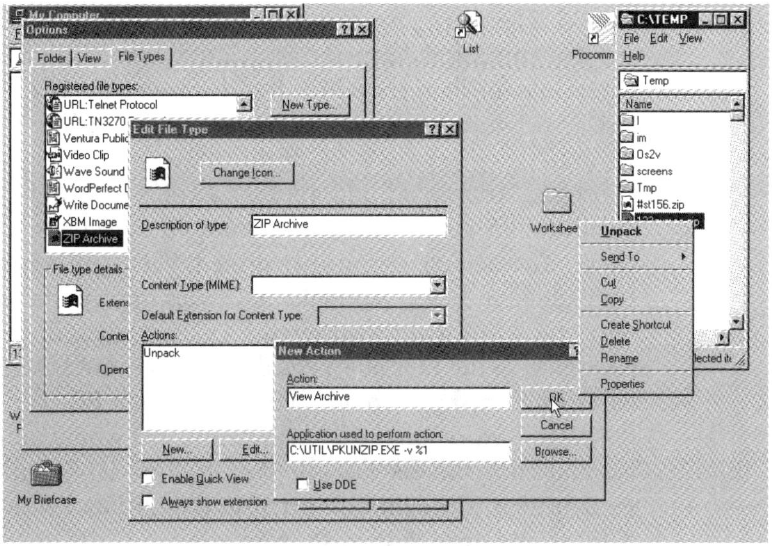

After creation of an Unpack command for files with the .ZIP extension, a View Archive command is created.

For instance, you can select the Text Document registered file type, click the Edit button, and enter the following new action:

Action:	**Add to archive**
Application used to perform it:	[*D:*\]*PATH*\PKZIP.EXE C:\ZIPFILES\MYZIP %1

This command will now appear on the context menu for files with the .TXT extension, allowing you to add them cumulatively to a ZIP archive called MYZIP.ZIP, located in the C:\ZIPFILES directory.

Using the File Manager to Reassociate File Extensions

Once a given file extension has been associated with an application in My Computer and the Explorer, Windows 95 will not allow you to edit the association to reassign the extension. This is another of Microsoft's attempts to wean users away from the habit of relying on file extensions in their work. In the Windows of the future, file extensions will be replaced by application types that will pertain specifically to only one program. In the meantime, for those of us who have Windows 3.1 applications to deal with, this "feature" can be somewhat annoying. You might, for instance, try to associate the .GIF extension with Paintshop Pro and get a message stating that you can't because the .GIF extension is already associated with Corel Systems' Corel Paint 5. There are several workarounds for this problem.

First, you could delete the association for Corel Paint entirely, and create a new one for Paintshop Pro. But this is undesirable, since you would then lose associations to Corel Paint's other registered file types (.PCX, .TIF, and so on).

Second, you could add another Action to Corel Paint's context menu. Windows 95 allows multiple actions to appear on a file object's context menu. The default action (performed when you double-click an object) is highlighted in black. To make .GIF files open in Paintshop Pro, you could select the Corel Paint registered File Type, click the Edit button, and then click New in the Edit File Type dialog. You could then set up an action that launches Paintshop Pro under the Corel Paint File Type entry. To make this the default action on the context menu, you would point to it in the Actions list and click the Set Default button. This is a cumbersome, undesirable workaround, since then all extensions associated with Corel Paint (not just .GIF) would open in Paintshop Pro.

Fortunately, there's a better solution: use the File Manager to change file extensions preassociated with an application. Let's say that you have Microsoft Office installed, but you'd like files with the .RTF extension to open automatically in WordPad, instead of in Word for Windows. As we just saw, Explorer and My Computer offer no easy way to change the .RTF association to Microsoft Word without also affecting the .DOC association.

In the File Manager, all you need to do is choose Associate from the File menu. Type in the extension .RTF, and enter the path and filename for the new association in the Associate With box. (See Figure 4-14.) If Microsoft Office is installed, you'll see that the association already points to Microsoft Word 6.0. To change this, click the Browse button, and select the path and filename to a substitute application.

If you change the .RTF association to WORDPAD.EXE, this setting is registered without affecting the association of .DOC files to Microsoft Word 6.0. The next time you open the File Type dialog box in the Explorer, you'll find that the .RTF association has been changed there, too. Using the File Manager to edit file associations bypasses error messages and avoids the complications of creating multiple actions for File Types.

Building Work Folders with Find

As an alternative to using the Start Menu or desktop program icons to run your applications, Windows 95 makes it possible for you to build an object-oriented desktop. Instead of cluttering your desktop with shortcuts to applications or open program folders, you can create a set of work folders

FIGURE 4-14

For applications with multiple file extensions, the File Manager lets you change one association without affecting the others.

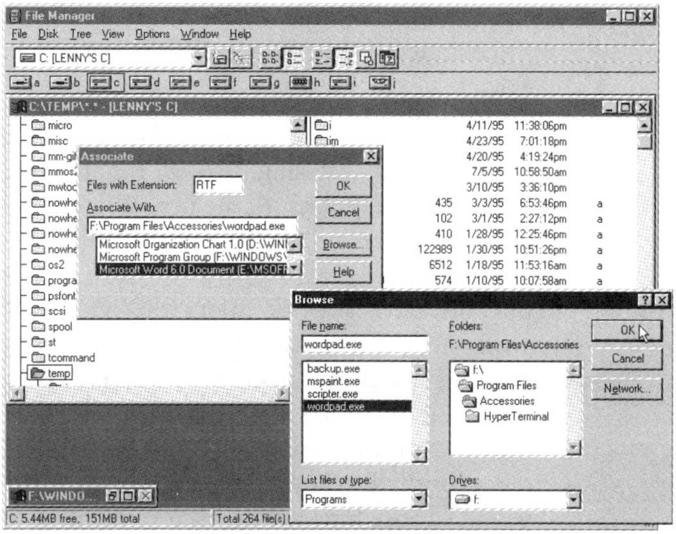

containing shortcuts to the reports, spreadsheets, and other documents you access most frequently.

For instance, you may have spreadsheets scattered over your hard disk in various disk partitions and subdirectories. Instead of launching Excel and browsing the hard disk for your real work, Windows 95 makes it easy to gather your spreadsheets into project folders that you can place on the desktop. Here's how to construct a work folder for your spreadsheets:

1. Open the Win95 Find utility by clicking on it from the taskbar or pressing F3 from the desktop.
2. Enter the string ***.XLS *.XLM** in the "Named: search" box. Select My Computer in the "Look in" box. Make sure the Include subfolders option has been selected with a checkmark.
3. Click Find Now, and Win95 searches your entire hard disk subsystem for all Excel spreadsheet and macro files. The results of your search are displayed in a list box, located below the search options dialog. (Notice that you can impose Date restrictions through the Date Modified tab in the Find File dialog box. You might, for instance, only be interested in retrieving Excel data created or modified between 3/1/95 and 6/1/95.)

4. Next create the desktop work folder. Right-click on the desktop and select New from the context menu. Create a new folder and assign it a name, such as Worksheets.
5. Return to the list box of retrieved .XLS and .XLM files. Select individual files you want to place in the work folder, or select the entire list by pressing CTRL-A). Right-click on the group of selected files and drag them to the new Worksheets folder. Choose Create Shortcut(s) Here. (See Figure 4-15.)

You now have a work folder that contains shortcuts to all of your frequently accessed spreadsheets. You can double-click any of the worksheets in this folder to quickly load it into Excel. You may further organize this folder into subfolders, for instance, worksheets created in the certain months. Or you can separate out all of the .XLM shortcuts and create a subfolder for them called Macros.

The Find procedure can be used to create work folders for a variety of different data types. You can also use Find to create project folders containing a suite of related data files. For instance, a folder called Smith Project might contain shortcuts to SMITH.XLS, SMITH.DOC, SMITH.PM5, CONTACTS.DBF, and SMITH.PPT. Win95's Long Filename feature allows you to rename these files with more descriptive titles, such as Smith Presentation—January, Smith Feasibility, Smith Contact List, and so on.

FIGURE 4-15

Use the Find tool to retrieve all of your .XLS files, select the ones you access most frequently, and copy them into a desktop work folder.

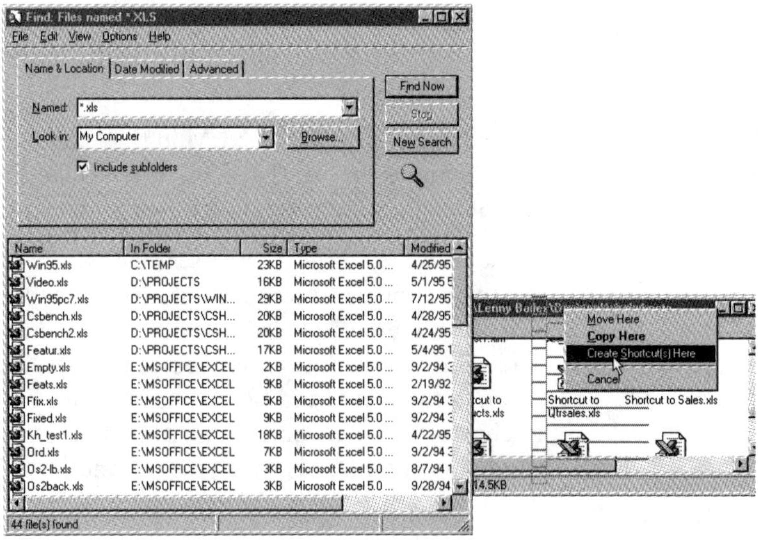

Working with Registered Templates

Windows 95 includes a convenient option to automatically create new, empty file, and folder templates on the desktop. When you double-click one of the file templates, it automatically opens a new or preformatted file in its associated application. For instance, if you know that you'll be opening a new account for Mr. Jones, you can create a Jones work folder and populate it with templates for a Jones spreadsheet, a Jones report, and a Jones database.

You can see a list of your current Win95 templates by right-clicking the mouse on an empty area on the Desktop or inside a folder and choosing the New option. The context menu will display a list of available template objects. By selecting any of the templates, you automatically create a new file object of that type on the desktop or in a folder. This feature is designed to let you plan a new work project in advance by creating a new folder, and preselecting templates for various documents.

For example, you may know that a project for your client is going to require a report, a slide presentation, and several memos. If you have Microsoft Office installed on your system, there will be template options for a Word document, a PowerPoint presentation, and an Excel spreadsheet. For novice users, this feature makes it easy to create named documents and automatically load them in the proper application. You don't have to know how to use the Start Menu and you don't need to know anything about DOS or hard disk directories. Just right-click the desktop and pan over the New option to specify a new spreadsheet or text document.

The concepts of templates and a project-oriented desktop are already well-known to users of OS/2 Warp. Warp includes almost a hundred templates used to create various types of data objects. By contrast, Windows 95 offers a very sparse set of default templates. Fortunately, you can roll your own, adding empty or preformatted templates for any DOS or Windows application.

By default, Windows 95 usually includes six or seven templates. These are created specifically by Microsoft applications, or third-party programs that exploit the Registration Database. In Appendix C, as a tutorial exercise, we show you a step-by-step procedure for registering new document templates with RegEdit. However, for users who don't want to struggle with these niceties, there is an easier way.

Among the Windows PowerToys, developed as an unofficial Win95 add-on by the Microsoft programming team, is an extremely useful utility called TweakUI. TweakUI is a Control Panel extension that includes many desktop customization options. One of its features happens to be an automatic procedure for adding new document templates to Windows 95. (See Chapter 14 for details on downloading and installing this utility.)

After TweakUI has been installed, you can turn any data file on your hard disk into a document template simply by dragging it into the TweakUI templates window. For instance, you can turn a formatted PowerPoint presentation into a formatted presentation template, as shown here:

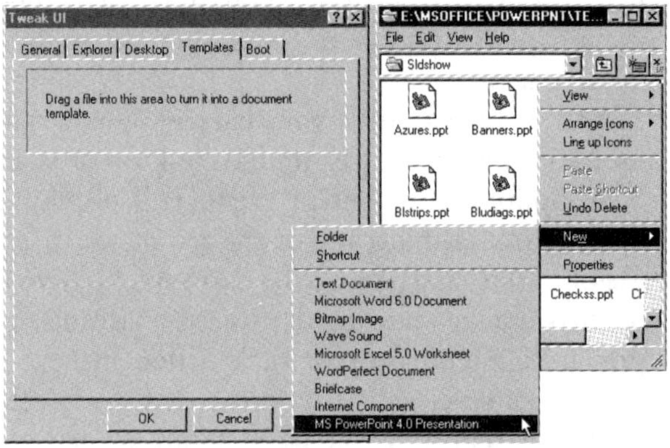

Automating Desktop Chores with Windows 3.1 Recorder

As mentioned in Chapter 2, you may want to save your copy of the Windows 3.1 Recorder. Although it is not completely functional under Win95, it can still be used to create mouse and keystroke macros to automate a number of desktop functions. Here are the main points to remember about using the Recorder under Win95:

- The recorder will not remember the CTRL-ESC keyboard combination to bring up the Start Menu. Instead, you must enable the recording of clicks and drags with the mouse and record a mouse click on the Start button if you want to work that into a macro.
- The recorder will not allow you to terminate a macro by pressing CTRL-C or CTRL-BREAK from the keyboard. Instead, when your macro is completed, you must use the mouse to click the flashing Recorder button on the taskbar.

Getting to Work

Our study of the Windows 95 interface in this chapter provided a description of the new desktop features, presented some tips for using the Explorer and the Start Menu, and outlined some of the hidden power that lurks beneath the surface of the desktop. To see how new third-party utilities complement these features, refer to Chapter 14. Next up is a discussion of the Windows 95 mini-applications that you'll find in the Accessories folder.

Printers
Programs
Settings
Find
Help
Run...
Start
Windows95

chapter 5

The Windows 95 Accessories: System Utilities and Productivity Tools

- Taming Microsoft Fax
- Quick tour of the Win95 Accessories folder
  - Add functionality to the Media Player
- Quickly setting up Internet connections
  - SLIP and PPP
- Undocumented tricks with Microsoft Backup
  - Force true differential backups
- Cheating at Solitaire and Minesweeper
- Comparing Paint and WordPad to Paintbrush and Write
  - What's new and what's gone

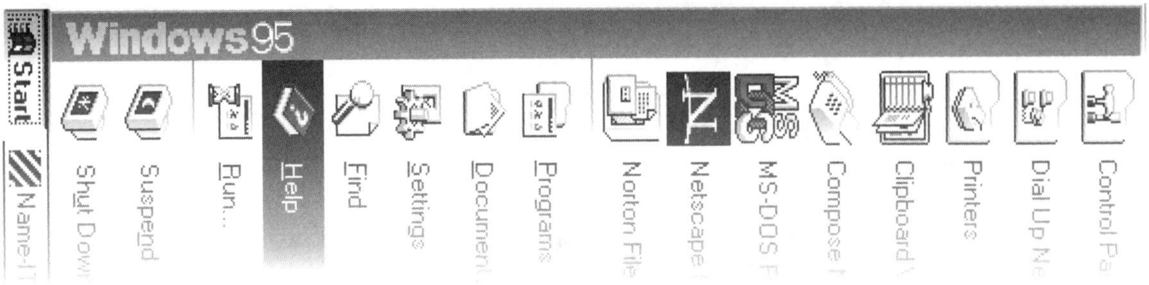

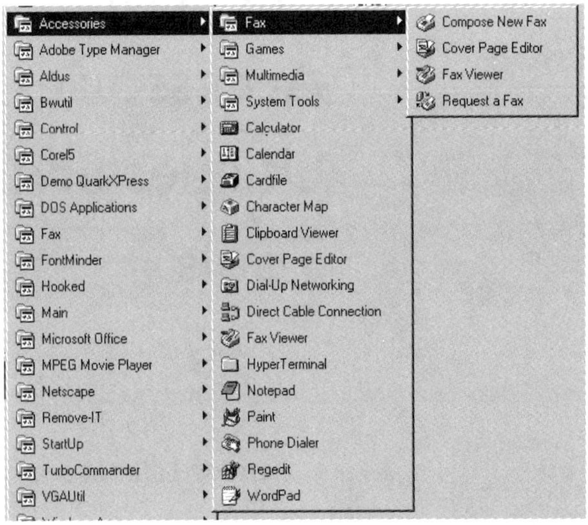

OVERALL, with the new Windows 95 accessories you gain some features and you lose some. You'll find a brand new suite of mini-applications to play with, but some of the functionality of Windows 3.1 has been left behind (or maybe it just got lost). There are definite feature improvements in the upgraded Win95 versions of old MS-DOS utilities, but you may want to keep some of the old Windows 3.1 desktop applets around—a few of the older versions have useful features and online help files that have been cut out of the new versions.

This chapter provides a series of thumbnail summaries for all of the programs that Windows 95 can place in the Accessories folder (accessed by clicking the Start button and selecting Programs\Accessories). Where appropriate, we've included "need-to-know" configuration tips and step-by-step procedures for exploiting application productivity features. For some of the applets, the interface and functionality are self-evident. Others have hidden features and tricks built into them not directly covered in Microsoft's documentation. For these programs, we've provided more extensive information. The applications are covered, here, in the order of their appearance in the Accessories folder. The Fax, Games, Multimedia, and System Tools groups each contain a set of programs related to the folder's title. The remaining mini-apps in the Accessories folder appear in alphabetical order. (For information on The Microsoft Network, Briefcase, and the other utilities placed directly on the desktop, see Chapters 4, 11, and 13.) This chapter functions as a book within a book, providing information, tips, and tricks for all of the accessories included in Windows 95.

Microsoft Fax

It's not as full featured as Delrina's WinFax Pro, but Microsoft Fax supports the basic fax features that casual users commonly need.

Here's what Microsoft Fax can do:

- Compose and send brief ASCII text memos with attached text or binary documents.
- Choose recipient(s) on-the-fly or from an Address Book.
- Request fax documents automatically from a remote server.
- Send multiple documents in a single fax transmission.
- Fax documents from within any Windows application.
- Share a fax modem over a network.
- Receive faxes in the background while other telecommunications programs are open on the desktop.

And here's what it can't do:

- Send faxes from DOS applications.
- Scan or convert bitmapped faxes to editable text.

- Sign or otherwise edit a bitmapped fax.
- Read or display view faxes in bitmapped formats produced by most third-party fax software.

Installing and Using Microsoft Fax

This section covers preparing and sending faxes using the options found on the Start Menu (Compose New Fax, Request a Fax, Edit Cover Page, and so on). For information about sending and receiving faxes through the Microsoft Exchange Inbox, see Chapter 10.

If you selected Microsoft Fax during the Win95 installation, you probably also chose a modem and filled out some configuration dialog boxes for Microsoft Exchange. If you didn't select Microsoft Fax during Win95's initial installation, you can add it to the desktop through the control panel's Add/Remove Programs option. Choose the Windows setup tab in Add/Remove Programs and place a checkmark next to Microsoft Fax in the Components list. (This automatically selects the appropriate Microsoft Exchange components that you need.)

Once you've installed Microsoft fax, you can send or receive faxes in a variety of ways—by dragging and dropping a document onto an MS Fax Printer icon on the desktop, by opening the Microsoft Exchange Inbox, from the "Compose New Fax" wizard on the Start Menu, or by "printing" to the fax driver from within a Windows application. You can't use Microsoft Fax to send a fax from a DOS application.

The Microsoft Fax Driver (located in the Printers folder) appears to your Windows applications as just another selectable printer. The Fax driver has an intricate set of configuration options best left at their default settings. On the Details tab of the Properties menu, the chosen port should be "FAX: (Unknown Local Port)" and the chosen driver should be "Microsoft Fax Driver". Change these settings at your own risk.

Faxing from the Start Menu

The Start Menu includes a Compose New Fax option under the Programs/Accessories/Fax group. When you choose this option, the Fax Wizard prompts you to type in a subject and enter text for a brief one-page memo. You can also attach a document to your fax as a binary file. Such attachments can only be received by Class I or II fax modems connected to a recipient computer. They can't be sent to a dedicated fax machine.

Faxing from Windows Apps

You can also send a formatted document to a dedicated fax machine or to a fax modem by printing directly from a Windows application. To fax from an application, use the Print command and make "Microsoft Fax on FAX" the selected printer. When you click OK in the Print dialog box, you may see a pop-up message from Microsoft Exchange asking you to select a user profile. Or, the profile may load automatically. If Microsoft Fax has been installed properly, there should be at least one preconfigured user profile called "MS Exchange Settings". If you don't find this profile the first time you fax something, you can create it by clicking the New button in the Choose Profile dialog box.

After your document is sent to the print spooler, the generic Microsoft Fax Wizard appears on the screen. This wizard also pops up when you select "Compose New Fax" from the Start Menu. The first screen of the wizard, which shows the originating location for the transmission, can be disabled. If you have a portable computer, you may want this screen to pop up each time, since you'll be dialing in from different locations.

The next screen of the wizard lets you select a recipient from the address book or type in a new name and phone number. The Address Book button opens a list of addresses and phone numbers that you use on a repeated basis. You can select an entry on the list, or create a new entry. If you choose an entry from the address book, no name and phone number appear in the fax wizard, since this information has already been stored in the address book entry.

On the next screen, you can choose to send a cover page, or skip it. Click Next> and the Subject and Note boxes on the following screen can be used as a makeshift substitute for a cover page. You can use these fields to enter the recipient's name and a quick message.

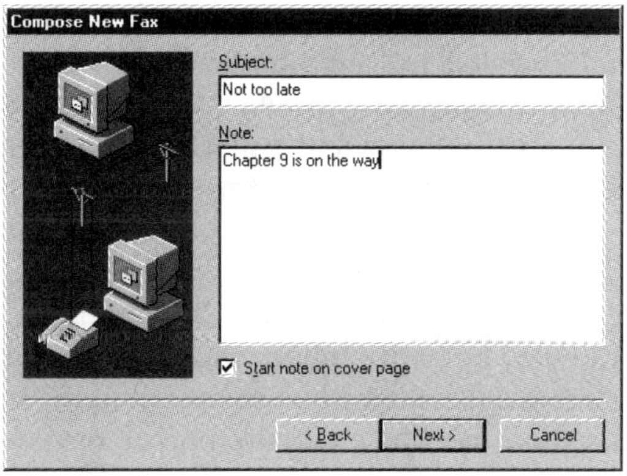

When you use Compose New Fax, the contents of the Subject and Notes fields (plus an optional cover page) are all that's sent.

When you print a fax from an application, the first page sent is the cover page (if selected) and the second page is the text you enter in the Subject and Note fields. The actual document you're printing is the third page received at the other end of the connection. If you check the "Start note on cover page" box (shown above), then the printed document becomes the second page sent.

Also note: if you're sending a fax to another fax modem instead of to a dedicated fax machine, then the cover page isn't transmitted at all. (If you like, a cover page can be sent to a Class I fax modem as a separate binary file. See the section in this chapter on using the Cover Page Editor for more details.)

Receiving Faxes in the Background

You can set up Microsoft Fax to automatically answer the telephone and receive faxes in the background. But if you didn't choose this option during the initial installation, it's hidden deep within the Exchange Inbox options. Here's how to toggle automatic answering on and off:

1. Open the Inbox with an Exchange profile that includes Microsoft Fax. (See Chapter 10 for more information on setting up Exchange profiles.) Select Tools, Microsoft Fax Tools, Options from the Inbox pull-down menus.
2. Select the Modem tab in the Microsoft Fax Properties window, choose the modem you want to answer the telephone, and click the Properties button.
3. In the Answer mode section on the next screen, you can specify the number of rings to wait before the modem answers the telephone. If you choose Manual, Microsoft Fax pops up a dialog box when a call comes in, asking if you want to receive the fax or ignore it. If you choose not to answer, you can pick up the telephone receiver, or let the call pass through to an answering machine.

To receive faxes in the background, you must first open the Inbox. You can then minimize Inbox (click the minimize button on its title bar) and let it remain dormant while you work. If the Inbox is already running, this will decrease the time it takes to pop up the Fax Wizard.

note *If an open DOS program is using your modem, you'll get a pop-up message prompting you to assign the port to either Windows or DOS. If you choose the DOS session, Windows 95 refuses COM port access to your fax program until you close the DOS communication program.*

Compatibility

Microsoft Fax in Windows 95 supports the following international standards for fax communications:

- ITU (International Telecommunications Union, formerly the CCITT) T.30 standard for Group 3 fax
- ITU V.17, V.29, and V.27 standards for high-speed fax communications (up to 14.4kbps)

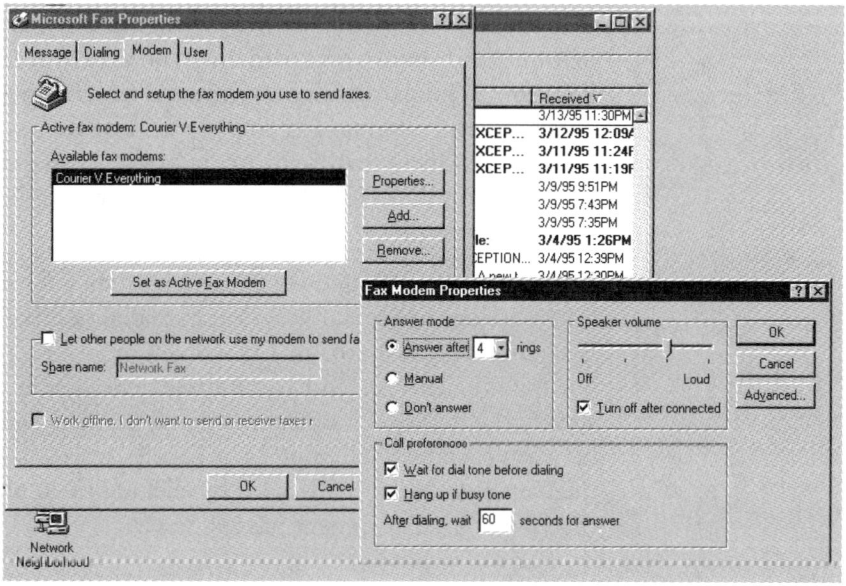

FIGURE 5-1

To activate Auto Answer mode in Microsoft Fax, open the Fax options, select the Modem tab, select your active modem, and click the Properties button.

Currently there is no support for Intel CAS modems, such as the classic SatisFAXion. The fax/modem combinations listed in Table 5-1 are also not supported by Microsoft Fax (although they may work with third-party Windows fax software).

Fax "Gotchas"

Here are some *gotchas* to watch out for:

- Inside the Fax Wizard, the F1 help key is as dead as a doornail. If you need to consult the Win95 help system about fax options, open Inbox and select Microsoft Fax from the help menu. If you want to know what some fax option like "Editable if possible" vs. "not editable" means, you can get pop-up help with the F1 option when you access the Fax Wizard through Inbox.
- By default, if an attempt to send a fax is unsuccessful, Microsoft Fax dials the intended recipient only once. If you don't get through, the fax dialog box closes and deposits the message in your Outbox folder. If you open the message in the Outbox, you'll see that the Send option is grayed out. The way to resend is to look for a System Administrator note deposited in your Inbox folder. This note reports the failure to complete transmission of a listed fax message and includes a Send Again button. Alternatively, you can right click on the original fax message in the Outbox folder and choose Forward.
- You can change the number of redial attempts on a fax transmission through another obscure dialog box. From the Exchange Tools\Microsoft Fax Tools\Options screen, select the Dialing tab. This screen has a Retries section, allowing you to specify the number of times to redial a number and the interval between each retry attempt. (The Retries screen is also available in the Compose New Fax Wizard by clicking the Options button on the "Do you want a cover page?" screen.)

Country	Manufacturer	Model
US	AT&T® Paradyne	Keep in Touch Card 3761
US	Best Communications Inc.	14496EC
Italy	BIT	MX-6, XM124S
US	Cardinal	14400 V.32bis, MB2296SR
Germany	CPV Datensysteme	F-1114HV, StarLine
Germany	CTK-Systeme	CTK V.32
US	Datatronics	Discovery 2496CX
US	DIGICOM	SNM28, SNM41PC
US	Digicom Systems, Inc.	Scout Plus
US	E-Tech Research	E1414MX
Germany	EEH GmbH	Elink 301
Germany	ELSA	MicroLink, MicroLine
US	Gateway	Telepath PM144
Japan	Hidem	14400 Fax
Germany	Kortex	KX PRO 2400
LCE	MiniModem 23	
US	Macronix, Inc.	Maxfax 9624s, VOMAX 2000
US	Megahertz	P22 Pocket Fax Modem
US	MultiTech Systems	MT932ba
Japan	National Semiconductor	TyIN 2000
Germany	Neuhaus Mikroelektronik	Fury 2400
France	PNB	TT9624
US	Practical Peripherals	PM2400 FX96SA, V.32 Pocket
QuickComm	Sprint II V.32 Fax	
US	Sysnet	SMF44 Fax
TeleJet	TeleJet 14400	
US	US Robotics	Sportster 28.8 V.FC, Sportster 9600
Germany	Woerlein GmbH	M288 Fax
US	Zoom Telephonics	FC 96/24, VFX 28.8

TABLE 5-1 *Incompatible Fax Modems* ■

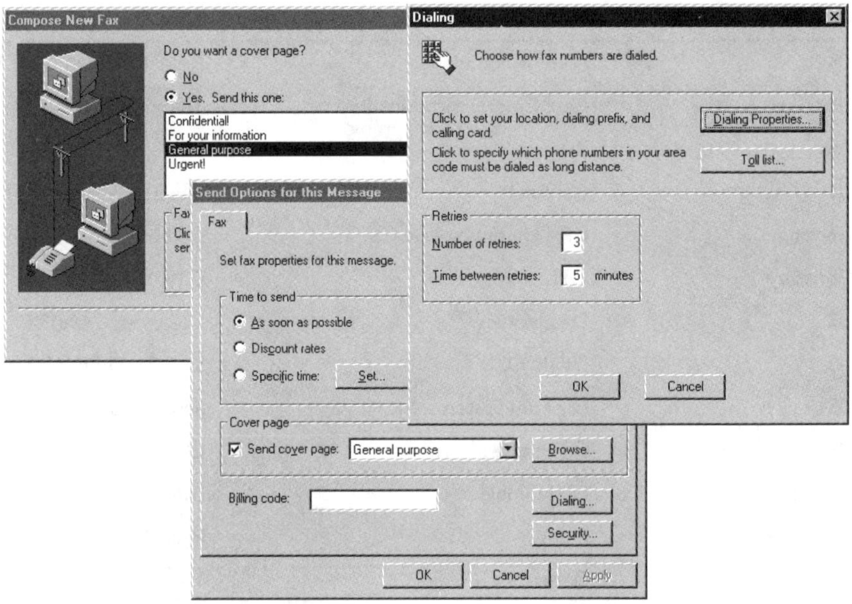

Other Microsoft Fax Bells and Whistles

If your system has a Class I fax modem, you can attach text or binary files to your fax messages. The attachments can be received by any other Class I fax modem.

You can schedule faxes to be sent at specific times of the day. From the Compose New Fax Wizard, select Fax options. (The button appears on the page that follows the Address and Phone number options.) The "Time to send" dialog has three options: "As soon as possible," "Discount rates," and "Specific time." If you select Discount rates, the Set button pops up a dialog box that lets you specify a starting and ending time for discount rates in your local phone area. This setting will be preserved for subsequent use. If you select Specific time, the Set button lets you enter a specific time to schedule the fax.

You can automatically call a Fax-Back service to request faxed information, using the Fax options in the Microsoft Exchange Inbox.

You can protect your faxes with a password. If you send a fax through the Exchange Inbox, you can also invoke the additional protection of encryption.

The Cover Page Editor

Microsoft Fax offers various predefined cover page templates that you can automatically attach to a fax. These are not humorous or particularly striking, but you can use the Cover Page Editor to enhance them if you want to add some variety to your life. The templates include sender and recipient information, useful if your recipient doesn't already know you pretty well.

The Cover Page Editor works like a drawing program, allowing different elements on the Cover Page template to be relocated and resized on the page. The Cover Page Editor also includes drawing tools for rectangles, ovals, polygons, lines, and other shapes. A wide variety of objects (Excel spreadsheets, CorelDRAW documents, PowerPoint slides, .WAV and MIDI files, and so on) can be inserted or attached to a cover page. Remember, by default, cover pages are transmitted only to a dedicated fax machine, not to a Class I or Class II fax modem.

Sending the Cover Page as an Embedded Document

You can use the cover page embedding features as an alternate way to attach a file to a fax transmission. For example, if you like, you can embed a spreadsheet, Video for Windows, or other object directly into a cover page. When this resulting cover page is attached to a fax, the embedded objects are printed out at the receiving end.

Better yet, you can embed objects in a cover page, save it, and send the resulting Cover Page Editor (CPE) file as a binary attachment: If the recipient has Win95, he or she can load the received CPE file into the Cover Page Editor—and the embedded objects are automatically linked to corresponding programs on the receiving computer. Pretty slick! You can use this trick to exchange and update Excel spreadsheets quickly, to cite one example. Or use it to collaborate on a graphic drawing project.

The Cover Page Editor can spice up fax transmissions with a wide range of added frills. If you're so inclined, you can use it as a mini-vector drawing program. You can't paste the designs you create into other applications, but you can save and print them. You can even add a series of Recipient and Sender fields to a cover page to create a mini-database that can be easily transmitted along with the body of your fax. If you don't want to bother with a full-featured database application, this is a quick way to send an address list.

tip *When you start the Cover Page Editor, you can turn on a wizard that automatically pops up a new tip for its use. If you cycle through all of the tips, you'll eventually find a list of all the Cover Page Editor* CTRL-*key shortcuts.*

The Fax Viewer

You can use the Fax Viewer to read a fax saved to disk from the Microsoft Exchange Inbox. When Microsoft Exchange receives a fax in the background, it appears as a separate item in the Inbox, but it is actually stored in a cumulative information file in the Exchange directory. (The default name for this file is MAILBOX.PST.) As a result, when you double-click a Fax message in the Inbox, it appears in the viewer window but is not present as a separate file on disk. The screen you see in the MAPI Viewer is slightly different from the one you get when you launch the Fax Viewer from the Start Menu. The MAPI Viewer can't load a fax from disk, but it can save the current fax to disk in an individual At Work Document (.AWD) file.

The MAPI Viewer and the single-file Fax Viewer have identical menu options and features, except that the MAPI Viewer only saves to disk, while the Fax Viewer only loads from disk.

tip *Once you've saved a fax to disk as an .AWD file, you can load it into the Fax Viewer from the Start Menu.*

Unfortunately, the Microsoft. AWD format is not compatible with more widely used fax formats like Intel's or Delrina's. But if you have left-over fax files in Intel's .DCX format, you may be able to load them into the Fax Viewer, since the viewer was originally programmed to accept that format. Microsoft changed the format in midstream during the Win95 development period, so you won't be able to use Intel's utilities to break a new fax into .PCX files.

Signing and Returning a Fax

Although you can't edit a fax or sign your name to it within the Fax Viewer, here's a trick to let you receive, sign, and fax back a document (such as a contract or rental agreement) without printing it out.

1. Open the received fax in either the MAPI Viewer (Microsoft Exchange Inbox) or the Fax Viewer.
2. Place a checkmark next to Select in the Edit menu.
3. Click on Copy Page.
4. Open Microsoft Paint and paste the fax in from the Clipboard. Unlike Windows 3.1's Paintbrush, the new Paint utility dynamically adjusts the screen size when you paste in an image.
5. Edit the bitmapped fax in Paint, sign your name with the mouse, and fax it back to the sender by "printing" it with the Microsoft Fax Driver selected as the output printer device.

Games

Two new games, Freecell and Hearts, now complement the Solitaire and Minesweeper games that have long been distributed with Windows. You can play Hearts against the computer on a local workstation or over a network. Freecell is a card game that lets you choose from over 32,000 canned hands.

FIGURE 5-2

To sign your name to a faxed contract, paste it from the Fax Viewer into Microsoft Paint, pan to the signature line and scrawl your signature with the mouse. ■

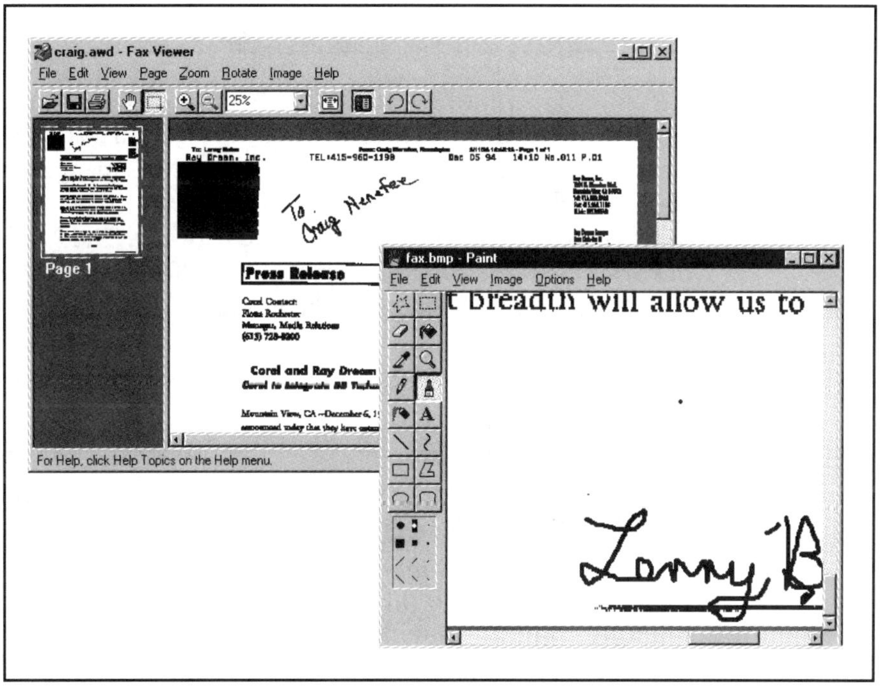

According to the Microsoft documentation, "It is believed (although not proven) that every game is winnable."

If you haven't explored the mysteries of Solitaire in Windows, keep an eye on the pattern designs on the back of some of the decks as you play. If you watch the magician's arm, you'll see an occasional Ace come out of his sleeve. In the "Palm Tree" deck, once in awhile the Sun comes up wearing dark glasses and sticks its tongue out.

In Minesweeper, you'll find that the version included in Win95 has a scantier Help file than the Windows 3.1 version. You may want to save the WINMINE.HLP file from Windows 3.1 in a spare directory. You can run the old Help file under Win95 by selecting Run from the taskbar and typing in the path to WINMINE.HLP.

How to Cheat at Solitaire

Solitaire has a hidden "cheat key" for the impatient. Just don't tell Bill Gates we revealed the secret, OK? In Solitaire, if you start a "Draw Three" game, normally you can't switch to "Draw One" to get a peek at the next card in the deck. But if you've reached the point of no return and are still determined to get at the Ace hidden under the third card, you can hold down the CTRL-ALT-SHIFT *keys at the same time and click on the deck with the mouse. As long as you hold these keys down, you can riffle through the deck one card at a time. Be aware that Solitaire now gives you three times through the deck before it declares you a loser and deals a new hand.*

Party Line/Rumor is a kind of game that you can install from the Windows 95 CD. It requires a network connection. MIS managers throughout the country will love this feature—a set of message boxes specifically designed to let people waste time over the office network. The Party Line window is one line only—you can't paste to it or use it for anything other than posting one-line messages to others on the network.

Multimedia

The Win95 Multimedia utilities include a number of significant upgrades over the Windows 3.1 version. The most noticeable new features are the stand-alone CD Player and the Volume Control. Although the Media Player doesn't look outwardly different from the Windows 3.1 version, it has been enhanced to handle long videos in Microsoft's .AVI format that formerly wouldn't play. The Multimedia Volume Control is now built into Win95. If you have a supported sound card, you can access the Volume Control directly from all of the Multimedia applets, as well as from the speaker icon on the taskbar. For more information about all of the Multimedia applications, see Chapter 13.

The CD Player

The CD Player, new to Win95, can perform all of the standard functions typical of third party CD utilities. When used in conjunction with the Win95 Sound Recorder and a supported CD-ROM drive, it lets you save CD musical selections to disk in digitized waveform format. Also, a new feature called AutoPlay lets software developers make their products easier for customers to install and run.

Here's what the CD Player can do:

- Play CD musical tracks in sequence or in user-selected order, or play samples of each track.

Here's what it can't do:

- Mark a specific section of CD track for replay.

Windows 95 can detect when a user inserts a disc into a CD-ROM drive. If the CD is Win95-aware, a designated install or menu program on the disk opens automatically upon insertion. The key to this is a file named AUTORUN.INF, which must reside in the root directory of the CD. If you want to insert a CD without activating the autorun program, hold down the SHIFT key after you place the CD in the drive.

The Media Player

Although the Win95 Media Player resembles the Windows 3.1 version on the surface, it has a number of added enhancements. The Win95 version will play full-length .AVI file-format motion pictures without generating "out of memory" messages. You can access various multimedia configuration options directly from pull-down menus, instead of having to go through the Control Panel. You can adjust volume and channel balance for sound playback (Device Menu, Volume Control), and directly control the driver and the instruments simulated in MIDI playback. (When a MIDI file is loaded, a Properties option appears on the Device menu.) .AVI video files can be played back in adjustable window sizes or in full-screen mode. However, full-screen playback still degrades video quality and sound sequencing unless you have a newer graphics card with advanced multimedia features.

Here's what the Media Player can do:

- Load and play digitized analog sound files (.WAV), digital MIDI files (.MID), CD Audio, Video for Windows (.AVI).
- Play third-party QuickTime (.MOV), AutoDesk Animation (.FLI//.FLC), and MPEG video (.MPG) when support is added manually.

Here's what it can't do:

- Play third-party digital and digitized analog sound formats (.VOC, .CMF, .MOD, and so on).
- Queue and mix multiple video or sound files.

note *Unlike Windows 3.1, Win95 does not permit you to add support for third-party video formats through the Control Panel. If you install third-party viewing software for QuickTime, AutoDesk Animation, or MPEG video, you cannot also add support for Win95's Media Player. If you have installed third-party drivers for these formats and the Media Player doesn't recognize them, you can manually modify SYSTEM.INI to add the new formats to the list of supported multimedia devices. (See Chapter 13 for more information about Win95 and third-party multimedia software.)*

To add MPEG support to the Media Player, you need third-party drivers. For instance, if you own a CD-ROM with MPEG video footage and third-party drivers, you might add MPEG support to the Media Player by copying the drivers to the WINDOWS\SYSTEM directory. If you own XINGIT, a popular shareware MPEG player, you would copy the following files:

```
MCIMPEG.DRV
MPEG320.DLL
```

and add the following parameters to SYSTEM.INI:

```
[MCI]
MCIMPEG=MCIMPEG.DRV

[Drivers]
MCIMPEG=MCIMPEG.DRV
```

```
[MCIMPEG]
MPEGDriver=MPEG320.DLL
```

The next time you open the Media Player, you'll find an MPEG playback option added to the menu. Because these are third-party Windows 3.*x* drivers, support may not be total until you get upgraded drivers. Typically, the Media Player refuses to load and play large MPEG videos. If you start experiencing GPF faults, or other erratic Media Player behavior, you should probably delete these entries from SYSTEM.INI and use third-party viewer software compatible with Win95 instead of the Media Player. Drivers for other video formats can be added to SYSTEM.INI in a similar fashion. (See Chapter 13 for details.)

The Sound Recorder

The Win95 Sound Recorder also resembles the Windows 3.*x* version on the surface, and has a number of added enhancements.

Here's what it can do:

- Load and play back digitized sound files in Windows .WAV format.
- Record and save waveform sounds: through microphone, from CD or from line input.
- Add simple effects to sounds (echo, slow down, speed up).
- Merge sounds from multiple files.
- Provide rudimentary mixing through volume control.
- Save files at several different quality and compression levels.

Here's what it can't do:

- Allow sophisticated manipulation of sound files: cut/paste segments, alter sound through graphic representation, add sophisticated special effects.
- Save files in third-party formats.

Attaching Sounds to Documents or System Events

One consequence of Win95 sound compression support is that attaching sounds to documents becomes more attractive. If your sound card is equipped with a microphone, it's easy to record a verbal description of a document, instructions for a user, lawyer jokes, or other spoken material and embed the sound into a spreadsheet, word processing document, graphic report, memo, or mash note so it can be played back with a click of the mouse.

To attach the sound, open the Sound Recorder, pick up the microphone, click on the record button (red dot) in the Sound Recorder window, and begin speaking. When you're done, click the Sound Recorder's stop button (the black rectangle) and choose Save As from the File Menu. The Format option at the bottom of the dialog box allows you to set the audio quality and degree of compression to be used when you save your .WAV file. For simple vocal recordings, you may want to choose a high-compression, monaural format to conserve disk space. For a high-fidelity message, including music, choose a stereophonic format with a higher sampling rate. See Chapter 13 for more information on working with the Sound Recorder.

You can also assign your own recorded messages or prerecorded sounds in .WAV format to Win95 events such as open and close program, exclamation, critical stop, and so forth. See Chapter 8 on Control Panel options for more details.

Volume Control

The appearance of the Win95 Volume Control depends on what type of sound card you have. With a low grade 8-bit card such as the original Creative Labs Sound Blaster, the Volume Control may not appear at all. With a 16-bit or 32-bit card, you will be able to regulate the playback and record sound level of each input and output source. There is also a balance control for each source.

What Volume Control can do:

- Control the volume level and right and left channel balance for multiple sound sources during playback and recording.

What it can't do:

- Regulate bass and treble settings of input channels.

To open Volume Control from the taskbar, double-click the speaker icon next to the digital clock. A single click will get you a simpler, slide-switch control of system sound level with a selectable mute box for occasions when you need to shut off the sound, as when a customer calls or the boss comes down the hall. The full-featured Volume Control can also be opened from the taskbar (through the Programs\Accessories\Multimedia folder) or from the Media Player's Device menu.

When you first open Volume Control, you should see a series of mixing sliders that adjust playback volume and channel balance for each multimedia source. If your system can support sound sources missing from the mixer, select Properties from the Options menu and place a checkmark next to any additional type of sound source you want to display in Volume Control.

System Tools

The System Tools subfolder in Accessories contains new, improved Windows versions of some familiar MS-DOS 6.*x* maintenance programs, plus a few completely new utilities. ScanDisk, DriveSpace, and the Disk Defragmenter now cooperate fully within the 32-bit Windows environment. You can repair or optimize a disk in the background and dynamically mount, unmount, or compress a drive without having to reboot the system to use it.

tip *For ScanDisk, the Defragmenter, and Backup, you can operate on a specific drive by double-clicking My Computer with the left mouse button, selecting the icon for the desired drive, and then clicking the right mouse button. Choose Properties, and finally select the Tools tab. You'll get the selection shown in Figure 5-3. One nifty touch: The Properties screen shows when you last performed each maintenance operation.*

ScanDisk

The new ScanDisk is present in both DOS and Windows flavors. If you start the DOS version while the Windows 95 GUI is running, it automatically launches the Windows version on the desktop. New capabilities have been added to both versions to handle Windows 95's long filenames and to repair DoubleSpace/DriveSpace compressed volumes.

Here's what ScanDisk can do:

- Check disk for FAT and directory errors.
- Repair cross-linked files.
- Report invalid long filenames and date/time signatures.
- Scan for media defects, mark bad sectors, and relocate good file clusters.
- Repair compression errors on Microsoft DoublesSpace and DriveSpace volumes.

FIGURE 5-3

Selecting a System Tool

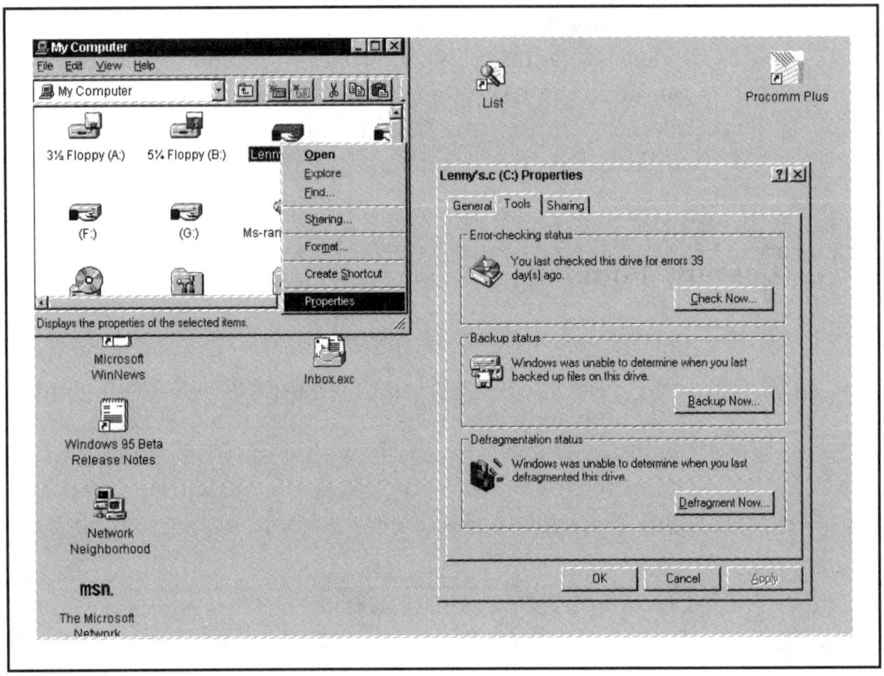

Here's what it can't do:

- Repair serious FAT or directory structure problems.
- Restore corrupted partition information.
- Repair compression errors on Stacker-compressed volumes.

When you run ScanDisk, a dialog box pops up on the desktop allowing you to set a number of default options. You can enable or disable an automatic media scan, specify which portions of the disk will be examined, enable or disable report logging, and change the way ScanDisk effects repairs.

Preserving Lost Data Clusters

To preserve lost data clusters in damaged files, change the following default ScanDisk settings:

1. Open ScanDisk from the Programs\Accessories\System Tools menu, and click on the Advanced settings button near the bottom of the window.

2. In the Cross-linked files section, select Make Copies.
3. In the Lost file fragments section, select Convert to Files.

Figure 5-4 shows advanced options you can change according to your personal preferences. You can also change the thorough (surface scan) options.

note *If you change any settings, the changes won't be preserved unless you actually run a scan on at least one drive before closing the dialog box.*

If you run ScanDisk from MS-DOS mode, there are a number of command-line options that you can tack on:

If you run ScanDisk with the "/custom" parameter, you have complete control over the repair, logging, and surface scan options. By editing parameters in the SCANDISK.INI file, located in the same directory on your hard disk as SCANDISK.EXE, you can specify any series of default operations to be run with the /CUSTOM switch.

The Disk Defragmenter

The Disk Defragmenter is a better version of the DOS 6.*x* Defrag utility. The Windows 95 Defragmenter is now almost as fast as the Norton

FIGURE 5-4

The Advanced button on the ScanDisk menu provides a number of additional options.

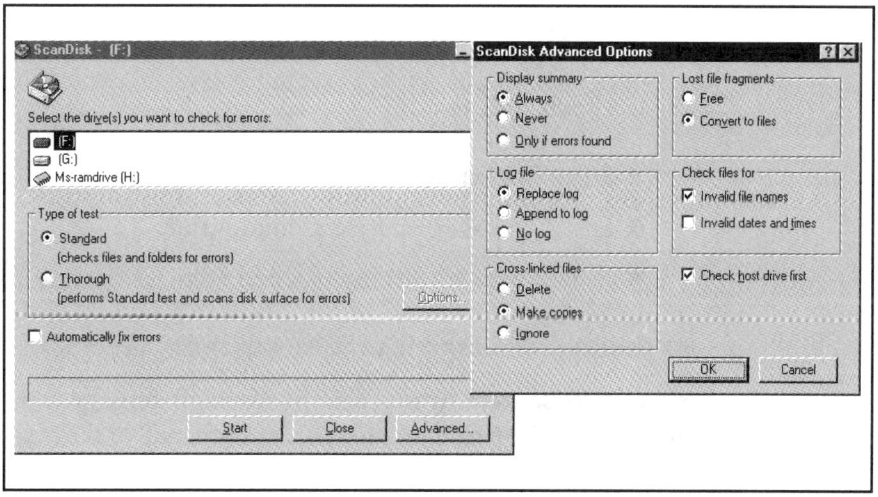

Command Option	Purpose
SCANDISK /ALL	Automatically checks and repairs all drives
SCANDISK /AUTOFIX	Makes repairs without prompting for user input
SCANDISK /CHECKONLY	Scans a drive without making repairs
SCANDISK /CUSTOM	Configures and runs ScanDisk according to SCANDISK.INI settings
SCANDISK /NOSAVE	With /AUTOFIX, deletes lost clusters rather than saving as files
SCANDISK /NOSUMMARY	With /CHECKONLY or /AUTOFIX, prevents ScanDisk from stopping at summary screens
SCANDISK /SURFACE	Performs a surface scan after other checks
SCANDISK /MONO	Configures ScanDisk for use with a monochrome display
SCANDISK /UNDO [*DRIVE*:]	Undoes previously made repairs on specified drive

TABLE 5-2 *ScanDisk command options* ■

SpeedDisk prototype which from which it was derived. Win95's Disk Defragmenter can optimize a disk in the background, and it works reliably on DoubleSpace/DriveSpace compressed volumes. The Disk Defragmenter can't be controlled to the degree that the Norton Speed Disk optimizer permits, but it does have a series of advanced options that can be configured.

Here's what the Disk Defragmenter can do:

- Report degree of file fragmentation.
- Optimize disk file structure in the foreground or background, with partial or full optimization.
- Check a drive for file allocation errors.

Here's what it can't do:

- Sort or reorder disk file structure.
- Specify sections of drive as unmovable.
- Defragment Stacker-compressed volumes.

The next sections review the various defragmentation settings available.

FULL DEFRAGMENTATION This, the default setting, will defragment files and arrange them in contiguous order so that all of the free space on the disk is at the end. This is the most efficient way to use a drive, so we recommend it even though it takes a bit longer. If you select the Show Details button, you'll see a detailed map of the drive which, as you can see here, takes the whole screen—and may even convince the boss you're being productive when you actually just needed a break.

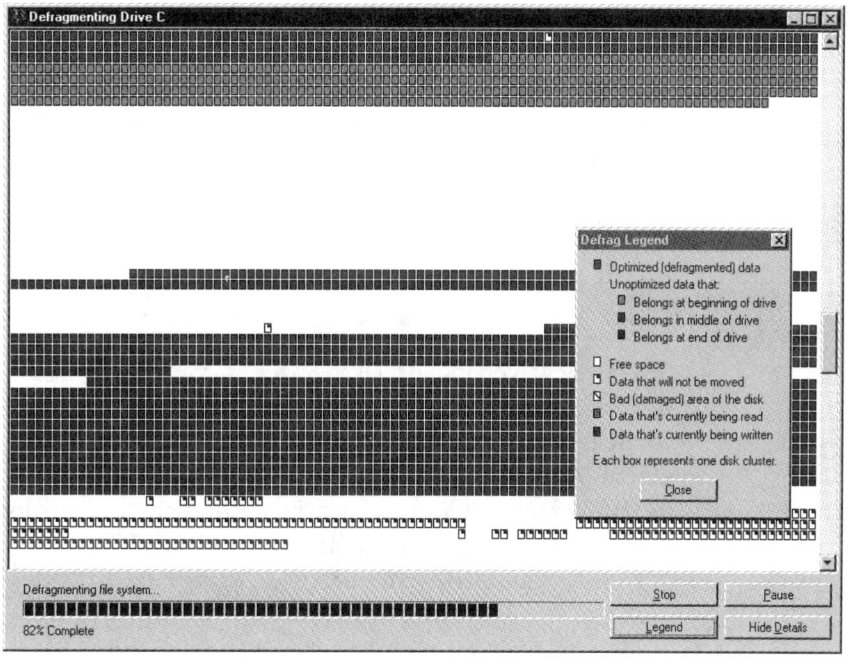

DEFRAGMENT FILES ONLY Faster than full defragmentation, this option makes sure that each individual file is a contiguous unit on the disk, but does not consolidate free space in one area. The result will be "pockets" of free space that encourage fragmentation on future file saves. Also, you may not be able to establish a large swap file on a partition with many individual pockets of free disk space instead of one large, contiguous area. So you save time but guarantee more fragmentation (and risk other problems) later.

CONSOLIDATE FREESPACE ONLY This option will consolidate all of the free space on the drive in one contiguous area so that future files will not be fragmented, but fragmented files already on the disk will stay fragmented.

CHECK DRIVE FOR ERRORS If this setting is selected, the Disk Defragmenter will scan the files and directories on the disk for errors before the optimization process starts. This option is highly recommended—if you defragment a drive that harbors disk errors, your problems can multiply drastically.

USE OPTIONS THIS TIME ONLY OR SAVE OPTIONS AND USE EVERY TIME This option lets you make temporary changes to the way the Disk Defragmenter works on your drives, or make changes permanent.

For more information, see Chapter 7 for a discussion of dual-boot options and running other operating systems with Win95. For a detailed discussion comparing Disk Defragmenter to third-party optimizing utilities, see Chapter 14.

note *There is no DOS command-line version of the Disk Defragmenter. Microsoft recommends that you not use the Defrag utility that came with earlier versions of DOS.*

DriveSpace

This new version of DriveSpace automatically recognizes compressed volumes created by previous versions of DoubleSpace or DriveSpace. These volumes will coexist with any new compressed volumes that you create from within Win95. You can even use a DriveSpace compressed volume to store the Win95 swap file, provided your software and hardware configuration supports the new protected mode DriveSpace VXD.

Here's what DriveSpace can do:

- Create and mount compressed volumes in the foreground or background.
- Mount or dismount volumes without rebooting the computer.
- Provide full 32-bit file access to compressed volumes.
- Hold Win95 swap file on a compressed volume.

Here's what it can't do:

- Coexist with Stacker 3.1/4.0 compressed volumes.
- Create compressed floppies readable on systems without DriveSpace or DoubleSpace installed.

Here's how DriveSpace works. Upon installation, Win95 automatically unloads any real-mode drivers for which it has protected-mode replacements. For example, the real-mode DBLSPACE.BIN driver from DOS 6.*x* is unloaded and the protected-mode DRVSPACE.VXD driver takes over. This is important because the protected-mode driver allows faster, 32-bit access to your compressed volumes.

tip *To determine whether a particular driver is running in real-mode or in 32-bit, protected mode, check the Performance property screen under the System object in the control panel.*

On-the-Fly Options

The big news about DriveSpace is that it will now mount, unmount, and create new compressed volumes in the background, allowing you to continue to work in another application. You'll be able to create and mount new drives in a single session, with no need to reboot the computer.

Even slicker, you can change the drive letter assigned to a compressed volume on-the-fly. If you do this, Win95 will warn you about possible problems running some DOS programs and advise you to restart the system. Don't worry about it. In reality, the only problems you're likely to encounter will be caused by missing pointers in shortcut files or in your path statement, and you'll have to update those, yourself, manually, whether you restart the system or not.

Reserving Drive Letters for Removable Media

You can reserve specific drive letters for removable media. That way, if you build a new compressed volume, the drive letter assignment won't conflict with drive letters you've already reserved for specific removable disks. Here's how to do it:

1. *In the System option in Control Panel, click the Device Manager tab.*
2. *Double-click the option in the hardware tree that represents the removable device.*
3. *Click the Settings tab.*

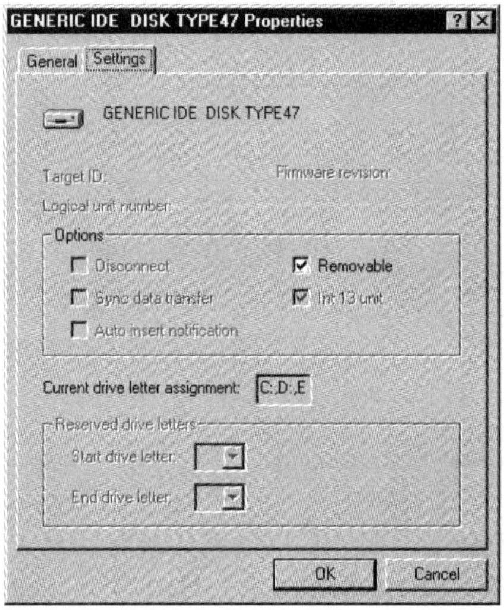

4. *Under the Reserved drive letters option, select a letter in the Start drive letter list to define the first drive to be assigned to this device. In the End drive letter list, select the last drive to be assigned to this device.*

5. *Click OK and close the System Properties sheet. Then shut down and restart the computer for the changes to take effect.*

caution *Don't recklessly switch the drive letter of a compressed volume that holds a group of OLE Windows applications. You would then also need to update the Win95 Registration Database for these programs to work properly with a new drive assignment. And that, believe us, can be a hassle.*

Why So Slow?

If DriveSpace seems to be sluggish in starting up on your system, it's probably because there are files open on one of the drives it examines during initialization. When DriveSpace runs on any drive containing open files, it has to restart the computer and run the operation under an environment that resembles earlier versions of Windows (the same subset of Windows that Windows 95 Setup uses). To do this, a directory named FAILSAVE.DRV is created that contains the system files required for this operation. If you want to avoid this, close all applications on the desktop before running DriveSpace compression.

tip *Here's a tip for swap files on compressed drives. Windows 95 allows you to store a swap file on a DriveSpace or DoubleSpace drive. DriveSpace marks the swap file as incompressible and, to reduce fragmentation, places the swap file as the last file in the CVF (compressed volume file). Locating the file at the end of the compressed volume also allows for expansion. If you change the size of the drive and DriveSpace or a defragmenting utility detects a swap file at the end of the sector heap, you'll be prompted to restart the computer.*

Avoiding Problems After Compression

Problems can occur with shortcuts after compressing the Windows 95 volume with the Stacker. If you compress your Windows 95 volume using the Stacker 3.1 or 4.0 compression program, you'll have to manually repair your desktop shortcuts. You will also need to move USER.DAT and USER.DA0 (that's a zero, not the letter "O") from the host volume to your compressed volume. When using the Stacker, do not run DriveSpace or DoubleSpace.

tip *To avoid the problem of lost desktop shortcuts, you can upgrade to Stacker 4.1 or use the LFNBK utility to back up your system's long filenames. (See Chapter 7 for details.)*

Backup

Finally, Microsoft has given us a backup utility that works with at least some tape drives. If you've got a Colorado QIC 40/80/3010 or QIC Wide drive, or a generic QIC drive that's similar to the Colorado products, the odds are that Microsoft Backup supports it. (Parallel Port Colorado Trakker 120, 250, 3010 drives are also supported.)

Here's what Backup can do:

- Create full system or partial backups to floppies, another hard disk, or QIC 40/80 tape media, and to some parallel port tape drives.

Here's what it can't do:

- Create backups on SCSI tape drives.
- Track backed-up information through the DOS archive file attribute bit.

Despite its usefulness, Microsoft Backup is not installed in Win95 by default. To add it to your Accessories folder, follow these steps:

1. Open the Win95 Control Panel, and select Add/Remove Programs.
2. Choose the Windows Setup tab.
3. Double-click on Disk Tools, and place a checkmark next to Backup in the Components list.
4. Click OK twice to exit.

The key to making Win95 Backup work is to understand how it uses individual backup sets. If you like, you can just place checkmarks next to some selected directories and drives and begin the backup process—however, if you do this, you won't be able to do a second automatic pass that grabs only new or modified files. A casual "click and run" backup will also fail to copy Win95's internal registry settings.

Win95 Backup does not use a file's DOS archive attribute to track whether it has already been backed up. Instead, Win95 Backup records archive status information in the status file used to load each individual backup set. No matter how many full or differential backups you make on your system with Win95 Backup, the actual archive attributes of your files are not altered.

To record archive information in your backups, follow these steps:

1. Open the Backup program.
2. To do a complete backup and preserve Win95 internal settings and registry information, select Open File Set from the File Menu and choose Full Backup Set. The first time you run Backup, you'll see a dialog box informing you that a "Full System Backup Set has been created." If you have a large system, the wait for Full System Backup to parse all of your files can get pretty tedious. There's a tip a bit later in this section on how to back up registry information without archiving your entire system.
3. To define a selective backup set without preserving System Registry information, don't open Full Backup Set at all. Instead, place

checkmarks next to appropriate drives, directories, and filenames in the "Select files to back up" window.

tip *If you place a checkmark in the box next to a drive icon, Backup will page through and select every file and directory on the drive. To choose files and directories selectively, double-click on the drive icon to bring up a tree-structured directory and file list. When the tree-structured list is open, place a checkmark in the box next to the drive icon to select all files in the root directory instead of paging through the entire disk. (A checkmark placed in a box next to a folder selects all files contained in that folder.)*

4. When you've selected all the files you want to back up, click the Next Step button and choose the target media from the next dialog box.
5. Important! Before starting the backup, open the File menu and save the backup set. Choose "Save" or "Save as" and enter a name for the new set in the dialog box. This is the only way Win95 Backup will preserve archive information for subsequent backups.

caution *Use "Save as" rather than "Save" to avoid accidentally overwriting a preexisting Backup Set.*

Microsoft Differential Backups

Win95 Backup includes an option to create supplementary backups of files that have changed after the last full backup. (See Figure 5-5.) Microsoft calls this feature a *differential* backup, but in reality, it is equivalent to what is commonly referred to as an *incremental* backup. (See the next section for details.) When you load a saved backup set and perform a Microsoft differential backup, all new or changed files since the last backup done with that set will be archived. These files will now be marked as backed up. When you load this backup set again and perform another differential backup, Win95 skips over the files archived in previous full, or differential, passes. This is not how a *true differential* backup works. This is what everyone else in the world calls an *incremental* backup!

FIGURE 5-5

The Backup tab of Microsoft Backup's Settings Options lets you select the type of backup you wish to perform.

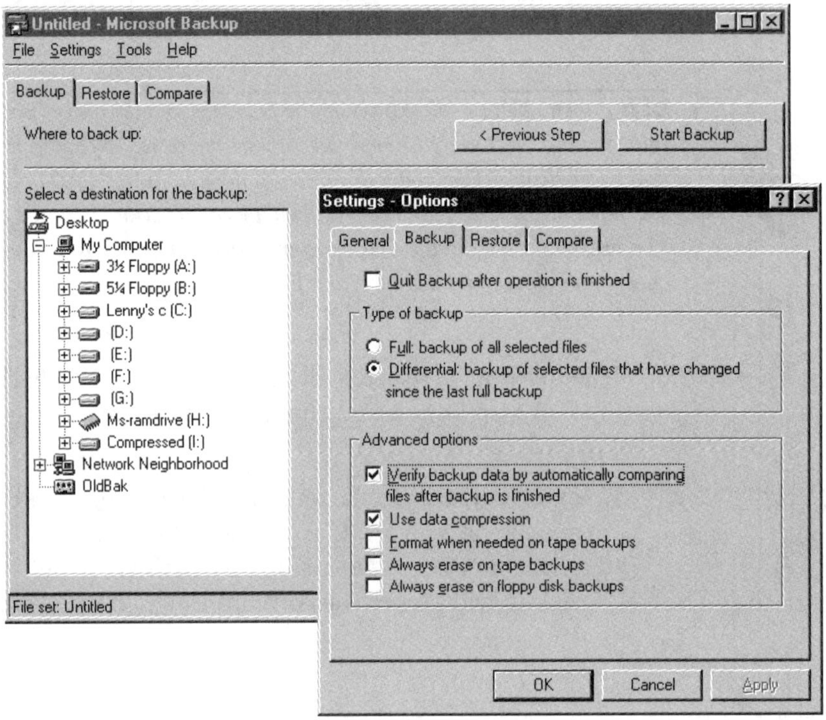

remember *Each Microsoft backup set contains an internal record of which files have been included. The external DOS archive file attributes are left untouched. If you start a backup operation with no backup set loaded, Win95 Backup just treats all files as unarchived, whether or not you select the Differential option. At Microsoft, the Windows programmers must not talk to the DOS programmers, since the archive bit was created precisely to tell you which files have been backed up.*

Why Microsoft Differential Is Really Incremental

If you're used to performing backups with programs like Central Point Backup, Norton Backup, Fastback +, and so on, you may become confused by Microsoft's terminology. The subsequent passes that Win95 Backup makes will pick up only files that have been added or modified since the last pass. This is what most companies refer to as an incremental backup.

True differential backups as implemented by companies such as Symantec repeatedly archive all files that were not included in the first full backup of your system. In other words, if you create six files in a NEWDATA directory after your full backup, then perform a differential backup, and add six more files to NEWDATA, here's how Microsoft and the other companies differ:

- *The first differential pass is the same for Win95 Backup and the third-party programs: It backs up the first six files that you create in the NEWDATA directory and ignores the old files that were archived in the full backup.*
- *The second differential pass from Win95 Backup picks up the second group of six files in the NEWDATA directory only. The six files that were archived in the first differential pass will be ignored, unless you have modified them.*
- *The second differential pass from a third-party backup product usually picks up all twelve files in the NEWDATA directory—the six that were archived in the first differential pass, plus the six new files.*

The advantage of true differential backups (as performed by third-party products) is that you can quickly find the data files you're looking for without having to rummage through an entire series of incremental backups. Each differential backup contains all of the data files that you've created since the last full backup. The disadvantage is that after awhile it takes too long to do the partial backup, since the number of old files included in each pass increases rapidly.

Forcing a True Differential Backup

You can force Win95 Backup to make true differential backups instead of the incremental differential backups it makes by default. Just do the following:

1. Define a Full Backup Set, name it, save it, and perform a full backup.
2. Open a DOS session and make this backup set read-only, using the DOS ATTRIB command. (By default, Win95 saves backup sets in the Progra~1\access~1 directory (this appears as Program Files\Accessories when you look at the long filenames from the Win95 desktop). So, if your backup set is called MYBACK.SET, then type

   ```
   ATTRIB +R [D:]\PROGRA~1\ACCESS~1\MYBACK.SET
   ```

3. You can now do as many *true* differential backups as you want by loading the read-only MYBACK.SET into Win95 Backup. Since the set is write-protected, Win95 won't overwrite it. As a result, Backup will treat each new differential backup as a true Differential instead of as a modified incremental backup.

You may be thinking at this point that working with Microsoft's backup sets instead of DOS file attributes is kind of annoying. The upside is that once you've configured a series of backup sets, you can just drag and drop them over the Backup icon to automatically perform customized backups with any set of preconfigured options that you like.

Backup Odds and Ends

Win95 Backup lets you impose date filters on backup sets and exclude specific file types, to further customize the Microsoft Differential option we've just exhumed in detail.

Microsoft wants you to know that you shouldn't use Win95 Backup to archive the physical container file for a DoubleSpace/DriveSpace or Stacker-compressed volume. Instead, you should mount the compressed volume and back up the files and directories on the drive directly, as you would with an uncompressed drive.

The good news for fans of Norton Backup and other third-party products is that most Windows 3.1 and even DOS-based backup software can run transparently in the background under Win95. These backup programs don't know about long filenames, so you'll need a few more tricks to preserve them. See Chapter 7 for details.

Saving Time on Full System Backups

If you select the Full Backup Set to preserve your System Registry settings, you may have to sit on your hands for quite awhile because Backup will parse every single file on every single hard disk partition. If you have 500MB or more of files on your system, this can take quite a long time.

To avoid going through this every time you want to back up the System Registry, select the Full Backup Set and let it copy your system settings, but then select Cancel as soon as it starts parsing individual drives and directories on your hard disk.

tip *You'll know the parsing has begun when you see a page-turning icon in the middle of the screen.*

After you've interrupted the autoscan, you can select the drives and directories you need to back up and deselect the other drives and directories. For instance, you might select only the root directory and WINDOWS directory on drive C plus the WINDOWS directory on a secondary Win95 host drive (if it isn't all installed on drive C).

You'd think Microsoft would let you save this modified system backup set, but unfortunately, if you try to do that, Backup will still try to scan every drive on your system the next time you open it. You'll just have to hit the Cancel button every time you do a system backup if you want to skip backing up the rest of your files. (Remember, this is an unauthorized shortcut, not an official Microsoft procedure.)

Net Watcher

Net Watcher is a network administration tool descended from the utilities bundled with Windows NT. Win95 Net Watcher includes more watchdog options than the administration tool supplied with Windows for Workgroups. You can use it to monitor users and shared resources on multiple servers.

Here's what Net Watcher can do:

- Add a shared network resource or stop using the resource.
- Show all shared resources, connected users, and open files.
- Close files that have been opened, disconnect a user.

Here's what it can't do:

- Automatically establish a server connection.

Net Watcher is not installed by default in Win95. To add it to your system, follow these steps:

1. Open the Win95 Control Panel, and select Add/Remove Programs.
2. Choose the Windows Setup tab.

3. Double-click on Accessories in the component list, and place a checkmark next to Net Watcher. For Net Watcher to function, you must also install File and Printer Sharing through the Network object on the control panel.
4. Click OK twice to exit.

If you've installed Windows 95 from floppy diskettes, Net Watcher must be downloaded from the Microsoft FTP Site, Web page, or bulletin board. It will not appear in Add/Remove Programs. Instead, you'll need to add it manually by following instructions in the README file that comes with the download.

When you open Net Watcher from the Programs\System Tools folder, you'll see a window with a list of users currently logged into your local workstation as a server. You can monitor other servers on the network by choosing Select Server from the Administer menu. The options on the View menu also allow you to display usage by shared drives and folders or files that are currently open on any selected server.

Using the Net Watcher tool, a network administrator can remotely monitor connections to any resource on any computer running file- and printer-sharing services, provided remote administration has been enabled on that computer. The network administrator can also disconnect users, change access rights, and administer the file system for users on a particular computer.

Using Net Watcher to Share a Resource Remotely

Here's how to share a resource remotely, using the Net Watcher utility:

1. *After connecting to the remote computer in Net Watcher, click the Show Shared Folders icon. (See Figure 5-6.)*
2. *Click the Add Share icon. (This icon is grayed out until you click the Show Shared Folders icon.)*
3. *In the Enter Path dialog box, type the drive and complete path of the resource that you want to share, and click OK.*
4. *Complete the Sharing property screen in the usual way. (See Figure 5-6.)*

FIGURE 5-6

NetWatcher monitors the shared resources on your network and allows you to reset access rights on-the-fly.

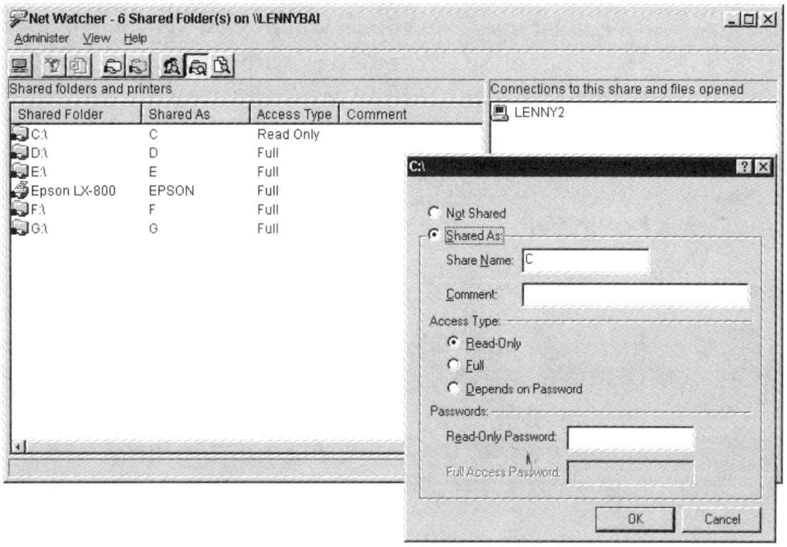

System Monitor

The System Monitor utility measures the performance of local and network disk drives, charts CPU usage, and graphs memory manager performance. If you launch it from the Programs\Accessories folder, you can leave it open on the screen to display a real-time graphic depiction of your system's performance. When you resize it—perhaps to fit in a corner of the screen—the real-time graphs are resized to fit the new window, but you'll lose some information from captions if you reduce the size too much.

The various options on the toolbar allow performance statistics to be displayed in several different graph formats. To measure performance of network drives, select the Connect option from the File menu and type in the name of the server you want to connect to.

Here's what System Monitor can do:

- Measure CPU performance, local and network disk performance, and memory manager efficiency.

Here's what it can't do:

- Measure performance through a Direct Cable Connection or perform detailed system benchmarks.

System Resource Meter

This simple TSR allows you to view the available system resources, user resources, and GDI resources without opening the Control Panel's System object. If any of these settings fall below 25 percent, you should probably close some applications and save your work to avoid a system crash.

Inbox Repair Tool

This utility performs maintenance operations on the mailbox file used by Microsoft Inbox to store your mail and fax messages and folders. (The mail file usually has a .PST extension and is located in the Exchange directory on your Windows host drive.) Occasionally, your mailbox file may grow to huge proportions, after sending or receiving complicated fax documents. Simply deleting the documents from the Inbox won't reshrink the file back to its normal size, but the Inbox Repair tool will do the job.

The Same Old C's (Calculator, Character Map, Clipboard Viewer) . . . Minus Some Departed Friends (Calendar, Cardfile, Clock)

The Cardfile, Calendar, and Clock were axed from Win95. (Maybe "C" just wasn't Bill Gates' favorite letter of the alphabet.) To learn how to preserve some of these during an upgrade, see Chapter 2.

The Calculator, Clipboard, and Character Map are all that remain of the Windows 3.1 collection of "C" utilities. They are virtually identical to their Windows 3.1 predecessors, except that some skimp a bit on their Help files. If you're upgrading from Windows 3.1, you may actually want to save copies of CALC.HLP, CLIPBRD.HLP, and CHARMAP.HLP from Windows 3.1. To do that, you can easily copy the files to a spare directory and then access them using the Run option on the Start Menu.

Here are some interesting bits on the remaining "C's".

The Calculator

The infamous Calculator bug in Windows 3.1 has been fixed in this version. You can now subtract 3.10 from 3.11 and get the correct answer of .01, instead of 0. (This flaw in the previous version of Calculator made Microsoft the butt of a series of jokes along the lines of "The difference between Windows 3.11 and 3.1 is . . . nothing. Just perform the calculation and see for yourself!")

Here's what the Calculator can do:

- Perform functions for both standard and scientific calculators, including square root, percentage and reciprocal conversions in standard view, and a variety of trigonometric and logarithmic calculations in scientific view.
- Perform numerical conversions between decimal, hexadecimal, octadecimal, and binary numbers.

Here's what it can't do:

- Perform calculations with natural logarithms, compound interest, and more complex algebraic formulas.

Other than the bug fix, the Win95 version of the Calculator is identical to the previous version. But the Help file provided with the Win 3.1 version was far more extensive, containing tutorials on converting values to other number systems, using advanced statistical functions, and other topics of interest. If you select Help from the Win95 Calculator, you'll get a skimpy set of dialog boxes that tell you to type in a number and press ENTER.

tip *To bring up the fuller Calculator Help file from Windows 3.1, select Run from the taskbar and browse or enter the path to the 3.1 version of CALC.HLP. Then click on OK. The first help menu you see will look just like the Win95 version, but once you select a subtopic, the more detailed Win 3.1 module will open instead of the Win95 version.*

The Character Map

The Win95 version of the Character Map is slightly skimpier than the Windows 3.1 version, but you're not really missing anything critical.

Here's what the Character Map can do:

- Display the character sets and numerical ASCII assignments for any installed Windows font.
- Copy selected characters into any Windows application through the Clipboard (useful for creating special effects in documents and for handling foreign language characters).

Here's what it can't do:

- Generate print samples of fonts.
- Remap the keyboard assignments for specific characters.

The main thing Character Map is useful for is to examine the upper ASCII characters of various Windows fonts to see if they contain foreign language characters, box-drawing characters, or other symbols that you need in a word processing document.

For example, suppose you're working in WordPad using Times New Roman, and you want to draw a box around a paragraph. If you open Character Map and select Times New Roman in the font window, you won't find the ASCII box-drawing characters there. However, as illustrated in Figure 5-7, you can switch the font window to Terminal Font, which does contain them. Then it's a simple matter to draw your box.

The Clipboard Viewer

The Win95 Clipboard Viewer is not much changed from the Windows 3.1 version; mostly, Microsoft gave the Display menu some extra options.

FIGURE 5-7

The Character Map can be used to paste a series of special characters into an application, such as those shown here in the "Characters to copy" box.

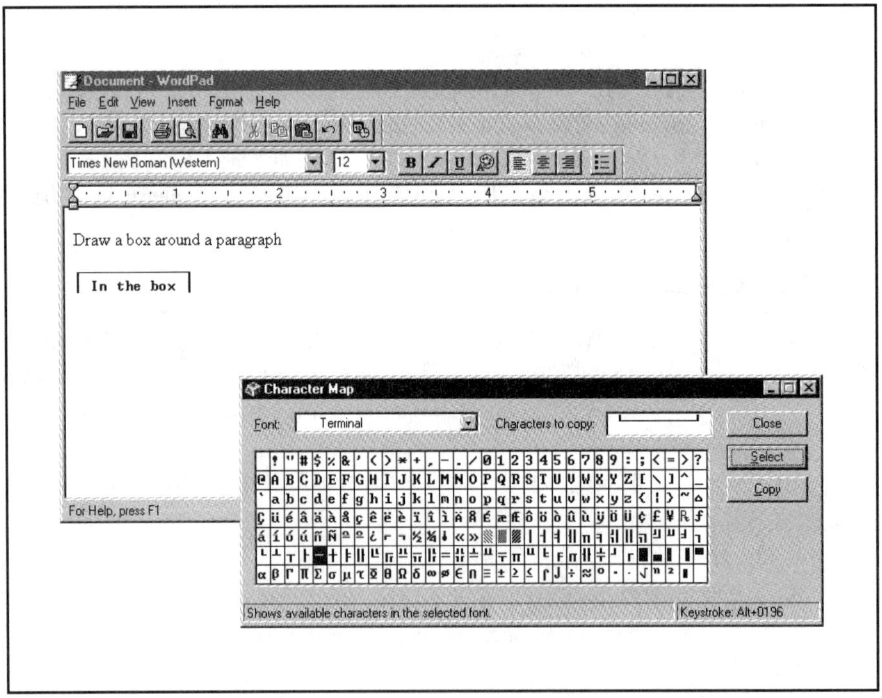

You can now render a Clipboard object in several formats in the Viewer. Depending on the source for the object, you can view it as text or a picture, and also display information about the source of OLE-linked objects.

None of these operations changes the nature of the Clipboard contents. For instance, if the source was text, you can't change it into a picture and paste it into a graphics program.

The Display menu now also allows you to view the color palette used by imported graphics. Since Win95 typically reserves some colors for internal use, this may be useful in examining the composition of a graphic, to learn whether these colors will be accurately transferred to another application.

Here's what the Clipboard Viewer can do:

- View or transfer text, graphics, and specially formatted objects between Windows applications or between Windows and DOS applications.
- Show a color pallet of graphic images.
- Save Clipboard contents in proprietary format.

Here's what it can't do:

- Save Clipboard contents in formats importable by applications.
- Transfer specially formatted objects between DOS and Windows applications.

If you've installed Windows 95 over a previous version of Windows, the old Clipboard viewer is left in the directory, and the new one won't be installed. If you don't see the Clipboard in your Accessories folder, you can add it by creating a program shortcut to CLIPBRD.EXE.

This situation is complicated by the fact that Windows for Workgroups includes a more sophisticated network Clipboard viewer than Windows 3.1. If you upgraded from Windows for Workgroups, the Clipbook feature (which allows you to view, cuts and paste contents to multiple clipboards) will still be present in your \WINDOWS directory, waiting for you to install it.

The Windows 95 CD also includes the more powerful Clipbook utility. If you've upgraded from Windows 3.1, you will probably want to install it, instead of simply reactivating the Windows 3.1 Clipboard file.

1. Open the Add/Remove Programs utility on the Control Panel and select the Windows Setup tab.

2. Click the Have Disk button, point the wizard to the Other\Clipbook folder on your Windows 95 installation CD, and click OK.
3. Place a checkmark next to ClipBook Viewer in the Components list and click the Install button.
4. The Win95 Clipbook viewer will be added to your Accessories group.

Dial-Up Networking

The Dial-Up Networking feature is not installed automatically in a standard Win95 setup, although perhaps it should be. This convenient utility allows you to connect to any Win95 supported network through a modem. As an added bonus you can use it to dial into an Internet SLIP or PPP Internet account. (See Chapter 10 for more information on setting up Dial-Up Networking Internet connections.)

Here's what Dial-Up Networking can do:

- Connect remotely to Microsoft, Novell, or other TCP/IP-based networks through your modem.
- Connect to a third-party Internet service provider (with SLIP or PPP account) through your modem.
- Configure your computer as a dial-up server to which other Win95 computers can connect by modem.

Here's what it can't do:

- Make multiple simultaneous network connections.
- Provide stand-alone mail services for third-party Internet accounts.

Before you can use Dial-Up Networking, you must install it along with your modem and several network protocols. If your modem wasn't set up in the Win95 installation, do that first by clicking on Modems from the Control Panel. See Chapters 8 and 10 for more information about modem installation.

Next, check to see whether Dial-Up Networking is in place by following these steps:

1. Open the Add/Remove Programs icon on the Control Panel.
2. Choose the Windows Setup tab and double-click on Communications (the Telephone icon) in the Components list.
3. Place a checkmark next to Dial-Up Networking in the Communications dialog box, then click OK. (If there's a checkmark already in that box, Dial-Up Networking is in place on your system and you can just close the dialog box.)
4. After Dial-Up Networking is installed for the first time, let Windows reboot and activate the new system components, as prompted.
5. To make Dial-Up Networking connect to the Internet, you'll also need to install the TCP/IP network protocol as illustrated in Figure 5-8. Double-click the Network icon from the Control Panel. You'll see the Dial-Up Adapter displayed in the Network components list, along with several network protocols. If you don't see Dial-Up Adapter there, something is wrong. You may need to return to Add/Remove Programs and reinstall it.
6. Click the Add button under the components list and double-click

FIGURE 5-8

Adding Microsoft TCP/IP Protocol

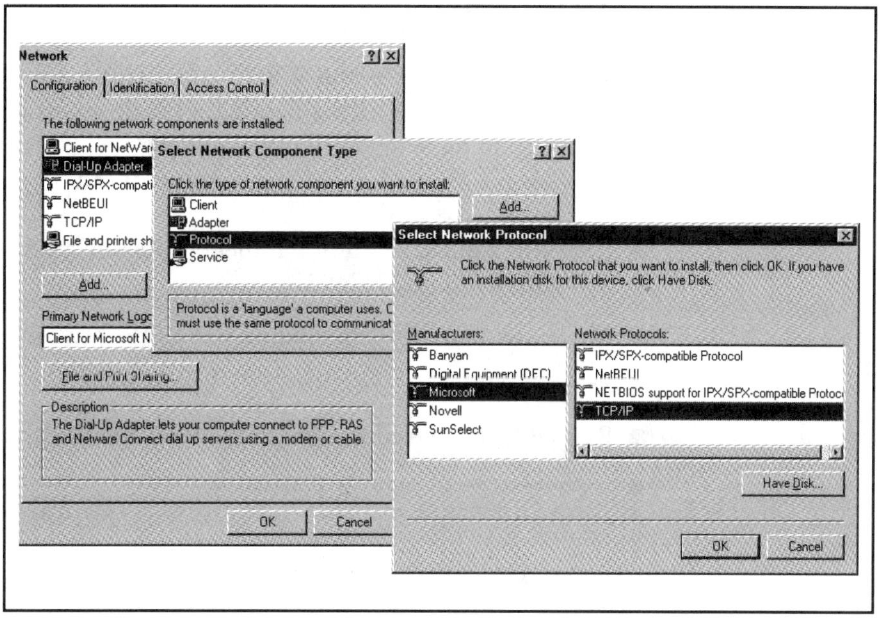

Protocol on the next screen. On the screen that follows, select Microsoft in the manufacturer's pane, and TCP/IP in the Network Protocols pane.

Other Dial-Up Networking Tricks

Dial-Up Networking can be used to dial into a Novell NetWare server. To access the Microsoft Client for NetWare, File, and Printer Services for NetWare, or IPX-SPX-compatible protocols, you'll have to install them through the Control Panel's Network object. For any such NetWare connection, specify NetWare Connect as the server type in the associated property sheet.

If you use Dial-Up Networking to access NetWare resources, you can access data remotely but you can't control another computer remotely. For that, you need Novell's NetWare Connect client software.

tip *If you use the Dial-Up Networking utility to access remote network drives, you can automatically reestablish a connection whenever you click on a network drive: Choose Settings from the Connections menu in the Dial-Up Networking folder and select "Don't Prompt to Use Dial-Up Networking."*

Direct Cable Connection

Direct Cable Connection is the Win95 replacement for the MS-DOS 6.*x* Interlink/Interserver utility. It's a handy tool for connecting two computers that are both running Win95.

Here's what the Direct Cable Connection tool can do:

- Establish a quick serial or parallel port connection between two computers running Win95.
- Mount remote drives (including CD-ROM drives) as local drives.
- Share printers.
- Run DOS and Windows programs from remote drives.
- Set user access levels on shared resources.

Here's what it can't do:

- Establish a connection to a non-Windows 95 computer.
- Maintain simultaneous cable connections while using Dial-Up Networking over a modem.

You can use Direct Cable Connection to transfer files quickly between a laptop and an office computer running Win95 or between any two Win95 machines, establishing the connection through a serial or a parallel cable. The laptop can simulate docking with the host computer, running remote programs and sharing a printer or CD-ROM drive attached to the host. Direct Cable Connection is a very nifty utility, although it can't be used on machines that aren't running Win95.

tip *You can still use the DOS 6 Interlink utility to establish a connection between a Win95 machine and a computer running DOS, Windows 3.1, Windows for Workgroups, or OS/2 Warp. Place the DEVICE=INTERLNK.EXE command in the client machine's CONFIG.SYS file, just as you would under DOS 6.x. Run a parallel or serial cable between the host and client machines, and run the Intersvr utility in the server's AUTOEXEC.BAT file. (OS/2 machines can be configured only as clients, not as servers, by loading INTERLNK.EXE into a DOS image session launched from the OS/2 desktop.)*

File transfers and remote program access generally go much faster through a parallel port, so use a parallel connection if you can. Any 4-bit parallel cable of the LapLink variety should work. Both ends of the cable should have 25-pin connectors (usually male), instead of the Centronics interface. Direct Cable Connection also supports ECP (extended capabilities port) and UCM (universal connection module) cables attached to an ECP-enabled port. These connections will produce even faster file access.

If you didn't activate the Direct Cable Connection feature during initial Win95 setup, you can install it by following these steps:

1. Open the Add/Remove Programs object from the Control Panel and select the Windows Setup tab.
2. Double-click on Communications in the Components list.
3. Place a checkmark in the box next to Direct Cable Connection in the next dialog box. This will also select the Dial-Up Networking files and appropriate network protocols needed for Direct Cable Connection.

tip *When Win95 tells you the system must be rebooted for changes to take effect, you can save time by declining the option to immediately restart the system. Instead, save your work and then select Shut Down from the taskbar. Change the Shutdown Window option to "Restart the Computer," hold down the* SHIFT *key and click Yes or press* ENTER. *The system will do a quick restart. (This trick won't work on some systems, where real-mode drivers in CONFIG.SYS or AUTOEXEC.BAT cause the system to reboot instead of simply reloading the Win95 interface.)*

The Microsoft NetBEUI protocol and File and Print Sharing for Microsoft Networks are needed to share host drives, directories, and printers with a guest computer. Generally, NETBEUI is installed automatically along with Direct Cable Connection. File and Print Sharing must be installed by clicking the File and Print Sharing button on the Network Control Panel's Configuration screen.

Some things to remember:

- When you open Direct Cable Connection, you must specify one computer as the host and the other as the guest. (See the section on Direct Cable Connection in Chapter 12 for a trick that allows you to set up a two-way peer-to-peer connection.)
- You need to assign the two computers different names. If you've run through the default Win95 installation on two separate machines, you may have assigned the same name to both of them. To change the Computer name of the host or the guest, open the Network object from the Control Panel, select the Identification tab, and enter a new name in the Computer name dialog box.
- Before the guest computer can access host drives, directories, files, or printers, they must be designated as shared resources on the host system.

tip *The simplest way to share drives, directories, and files is to open the My Computer object on the host desktop, click the right mouse button on the resource to be shared, and select the Sharing option from the pop-up menu. The type of access (Read only, Full, or Password protected) can be specified from the Properties menu.*

The first time you establish the Direct Cable Connection, a dialog box pops up on the guest system, asking for the host's name. Enter the name of the host computer without any preceding "\\" characters for the network path. That way you can map shared resources locally (see next paragraph) to have them show up automatically on the guest computer the next time you establish a direct connection.

Mapping Shared Resources Locally

Once you make a Direct Cable Connection from a guest machine, a window will open on its desktop, displaying the shared resources that have been made available on the host machine. You can map individual drives and directories on the local computer individually, or all at once. To map individually, just right-click on the drive or directory using the right mouse button. To map all at once, hold down the CTRL key and click on each disk item with the mouse. Then select Map Network Drive from the File menu in the Shared Resource window. You will be able to assign a drive letter to each disk item, in turn.

To use a shared printer, click on the printer in the Shared Resource window with the right mouse button and choose Install.

tip *If you will frequently be connecting to a host computer via Direct Cable Connection, you may want to drag a shortcut for the Direct Cable Connection object into the Win95 StartUp folder.*

Accessing the Internet and Direct Cable Connection Simultaneously

The way Microsoft has designed the Dial-Up Networking and Direct Cable Connection utilities, you can't use them simultaneously. But what if you want to remain connected by cable to another computer and log on to the Internet to collect e-mail or to surf the World Wide Web? To do this with Win95's bundled TCP/IP support, you must shut down the Direct Cable Connection before launching the Dial-Up Networking feature.

But you can have your cake and eat it too, by falling back on a third-party TCP/IP dialer such as Trumpet or Chameleon Netmanage. To make a third-party TCP/IP dialer work, you may need to temporarily rename the instance of WINSOCK.DLL that Win95 places in the Windows directory. That done, you should be able to maintain your Direct Cable Connection and dial into the Internet simultaneously. (See Chapter 10 for more information on how to pull this off.)

HyperTerminal

Still not a full-featured telecommunication program, HyperTerminal is more flexible and powerful than the old Windows Terminal. The difference is that HyperTerminal is user-friendly enough for novices to perform basic telecommunication chores. The icon toolbar and easily accessible Service Profiles should encourage beginners to log in and out of various services and even download a file or two.

Here's what HyperTerminal can do in the world of basic telecommunications:

- Connect to a bulletin board or a commercial service.
- Capture text of the session.
- Upload and download files with six standard protocols.
- Support six terminal emulations.

Here's what it can't do:

- Support automated scripts (not even to log in and enter your password).
- Support host mode.
- Support a user chat screen.
- Support keyboard mapping, macros, access to shared network modems, and other features found in more sophisticated telecommunications packages.

Though HyperTerminal's feature set will seem pretty feeble to an experienced user, the program should serve the purpose for which it was written: to demystify telecommunications and make getting online a transparent process. As soon as it's opened, HyperTerminal systematically guides you through the construction of a dial-up service profile. And once it connects you, every basic telecommunications function is accessible through icons on the toolbar.

HyperTerminal supports six standard terminal emulations, including ANSI, VT52, VT52, and VT100. The addition of fast file transfer protocols (Zmodem, Ymodem, Ymodem-G, and Kermit) actually makes it possible to use the program to do something other than read e-mail.

tip *The default terminal emulation setting for HyperTerminal is to autodetect the terminal emulation used by the host system. If you want to change this while creating a new dialing profile, click the Modify button when you get to the Connect screen. Then, from the Properties dialog box, choose the Settings tab and the Emulation scrollbox. The ASCII button in the Properties box lets you further customize your terminal emulation to echo or not echo typed characters on the screen and toggle linefeeds and carriage returns on and off.*

Notepad

The Win95 version of Notepad is identical to the Windows 3.1 version. By default, Win95 makes an association between Notepad and all files with the .TXT file extension. If the file is too long to be opened in Notepad, a dialog box pops up, asking if you want to load the file into WordPad.

Here's what Notepad can do:

- Read and write small text files in ASCII format, with or without auto-wordwrap.

Here's what it can't do:

- Perform word processing functions other than simple text-entry.
- Manage graphic elements or OLE-linked files from other applications.

If you would like to change the automatic association of .TXT files from Notepad to another text browser or word processing program, follow these steps:

1. Open Explorer or My Computer. Select View Options.
2. Choose the File Types tab and scroll down to "Text Document."
3. Click the edit button, then select the Open action in the Actions list on the next screen. Click the Edit button on this screen and enter the path to your other text browser in the "Application used to perform action" box.

The Phone Dialer

The Phone Dialer is a cute pop-up utility that lets you configure up to eight common phone numbers that you can dial at the click of a mouse. You can also paste in telephone numbers from the Clipboard, or point and click a number through touch-tone dial buttons. This little applet does quite a lot of things right, and it does what you need without getting overcomplicated.

Here's what the Phone Dialer can do:

- Digitally dial telephone numbers through numeric keypad or speed dial list.

- Maintain a log of dialed telephone numbers that can be redialed.
- Select multiple telephone devices or modems.
- Recognize the difference between local and long distance calls.
- Keep an easily editable log.
- Is flexible about the format of a phone number.
- Let you pick a number off the screen and paste it directly into the dialer for action.
- Provide easy speed dialing of often-used numbers.
- Log incoming as well as outgoing calls.
- Pluck a previously called number from a phone log.

Here's what it can't do:

- Link entries in a call log to a more complete contact management database.

Even with all its features, the Phone Dialer isn't perfect for everyone. If you make your living calling other people, you'll probably need a full-blown contact management program. But if you just call a few people regularly—or if you make a lot of calls to numbers you pluck off the screen while doing various tasks—the Phone Dialer could be all you need.

note *The Phone Dialer adds the letter "Z" to the number "9" key on the screen and the letter "Q" to the "7" key. These are typically omitted from all real telephones.*

Phone Dialer Tips

Keep these handy Phone Dialer tips in mind:

- You can switch to an alternate phone line by selecting the Connect Using option on the Tools menu.
- If eight Speed Dialer buttons won't cover your most frequently called numbers, you can use the Phone Dialer's Call Log feature.

Every time you type in a number to dial and connect, the connection information is saved as an entry in your Call Log. To redial a number, all you have to do is double-click on it in the Call Log.

- For repeated calls to just a few numbers, you can use the history list that pops up in the "Number to dial" scrollbox. It remembers the name last associated with the number and enters it into the Call Log for you.
- If you like to pluck a number off the screen and paste it into your dialer, it's easy to forget what the last number was that you copied from the screen. If you keep the Clipboard open in one corner of the screen, just big enough to show the first part of one line of text, it will tell you at a glance what number was pasted last.
- When you paste in a number copied from a source other than the log file, the dialer defaults to Unknown as the name of the person called. To enter the actual name, once you're connected, click on Talk. Then you can adjust the log entries until you finally press Hangup.

note *As with other Win95 telephony applications, you can change the default location (origin) for a call, automatically charge calls to a calling card, and control various long-distance dialing options. (See Chapter 10 for more information on these options.)*

Paint and WordPad: Mixed Blessings

Wordpad and Paint, the Windows 95 productivity applets, manage to step forward and backward at the same time in the transition from Windows 3.*x*. Both programs include new and useful options, but the Microsoft programming team also let some valuable Win 3.*x* features disappear. If you've already read our section on making the jump from Windows 3.*x* to Win95, you may remember that we recommended squirreling away copies of Paintbrush and Write. If you depend on Microsoft's bundled word processor and graphics program to handle real productivity chores, you'll appreciate having the old versions around when you hit a blank spot in their Win95 replacements. (Of course, there are a large number of commercial and shareware utilities that can fill these holes even better. See Chapter 14 for more information on some of these.)

Paint

Win95 Paint has changed in many ways from Windows 3.1 Paintbrush. Although the two applications have many features in common, there are enough differences between them to justify keeping both programs around on your hard disk. Microsoft has said that these applications were always intended more as demos than for serious use. Still, we wonder why they had to eliminate useful features in the new versions.

Here's what Paint can do:

- Construct or edit simple bitmapped graphic images with rudimentary geometric shapes, bezier curves, solid color fills, airbrush, integrated text, scale/skew images, and simple 90-degree image rotation.
- Read .BMP and .PCX bitmap files.
- Save images in Windows .BMP format.

Here's what it can't do:

- Read or save images in popular third-party formats such as .TIF and .GIF. Save images as .PCX files.
- Draw freehand curves.
- Globally replace colors, or create multicolor fills or other advanced image effects.
- Edit Win95 icons

Win Some . . .

Here are the improvements: Win95 Paint can handle 16-bit and 24-bit color images, even when running with a lower-depth display driver. The pallet of a color-rich bitmap is not destroyed when you save it under 16-color or 256-color screen resolution. And unlike Windows 3.1 Paintbrush, Paint doesn't truncate larger images when they're pasted in from the Windows Clipboard. If a Clipboard image is larger than the current file size, Paint automatically resizes its display window to accommodate the new image. You can also resize the drawing area manually, by selecting and dragging one of the eight handles on the outer border of the display window.

Paint allows you to go back and undo your last three image manipulations. The spray can now create more watercolor-like special effects, and the Win

3.1 paintbrush roller has been replaced by a more Mac-like bucket. The toolbox pallet floats, so you can click on it with the left mouse button depressed and drag it around to different positions in the editing screen. You can now use the selection tools to copy a selected portion of a drawing with an opaque or transparent background. (The area underneath the regular Toolbox icons changes with each selected drawing tool. Solid and transparent masking icons appear when you click on either selection tool (the square marquis or the cookie-cutter).

New menu features in Paint allow you to automatically send a drawing as a fax, or select the image as Win95 wallpaper. The Print Preview option on the File menu replaces the old Paintbrush Zoom Out option located on the View menu.

. . . Lose Some

Now, here's what's lost in Win95 Paint: The solid shape drawing tools are gone, replaced by an "eyedropper" color selection tool and a redundant magnifying glass.

The Color Eraser in the old Win3.1 Paintbrush program allowed you to globally replace all instances of one color in a picture with another. In Paint, the regular and color erasers have been combined into one tool that no longer offers this feature. The Paint eyedropper does allow you to pick up a color from one part of a drawing and copy it elsewhere, but you have to make your color changes in a tedious, piecemeal manner.

tip *The Win 3.1 shrink-and-grow tool has been replaced by a two-step Stretch/Skew feature under Paint's Image menu. To scale a drawing with the new menu options you must type in a horizontal increment, press ENTER, and then select the Stretch/Skew option again to type in a vertical adjustment. Instead of going through all of this, you can rescale objects with the mouse by clicking on one of the selection tools and dragging with the mouse over the screen area you want to resize. A marquis box with eight handles appears around the selected area. As you move the mouse over any of the handles, the cursor changes into a double-arrow. You can then click the left mouse button and drag the mouse to shrink or expand the selected portion of the image.*

WordPad

WordPad is another example of the Microsoft forward-and-back, two-step shuffle, at least in terms of productivity features. The design psychology makes it a tease for Microsoft's full-featured Office suite product, while subtracting several useful tools from Write for Windows 3.1.

Here's what WordPad can do:

- Perform basic word processing tasks.
- Include format ruler and toolbar, and simple paragraph styles.
- Read or save Word for Windows, Rich Text Format (.RTF), or Windows Write documents.
- Insert or link bitmap or vector graphics, spreadsheets, and other OLE objects.
- Preview full-page graphics.

Here's what it can't do:

- Import or export text and graphic files to or from an existing document (Except through the Clipboard).
- Check spelling.
- Create headers and footers.
- Insert page numbers or hard page breaks, or adjust leading (that is, the space between lines of text).

Like Word for Windows, WordPad has an icon toolbar, a format bar, and a ruler. You can easily change fonts, justify text right, left, or center, add bold or italic formatting, and so on. The stylesheet settings (from the Format menu) are equivalent to the options available on the Write Paragraph menu. The addition of automatic bullet characters in WordPad is balanced by the subtraction of a single/double/1.5-line leading option. The Ruler does let you set left and right margins, indents, and simple tab stops. Write's decimal tab option has disappeared.

The big improvements in WordPad are its ability to read and write Word 6.0 and RTF documents, and the added OLE support. Both Write and WordPad can link and embed OLE objects through the Clipboard, but WordPad can also insert files on a specified directory path directly into a document. As in other Win95-aware applets from Microsoft, the Send option on the File menu allows you to send the contents of a document through Microsoft Exchange to any configured Exchange service.

Drag 'n Drop Selected Text Right to the Desktop

WordPad's Scrap Pad option lets you select any amount of text in a document and drag it to the desktop to automatically create a new file. Just highlight the text you want to copy and hold down the left mouse button while you drag the selection to the desktop or to an open folder. This creates a Scrap Memo icon wherever you drop the text.

You can subsequently drag and drop this object back to an open document window in WordPad or Word for Windows. When you drop a Scrap Memo object into a WordPad window, it immediately reappears as a text block. If you drop the Scrap object into Word 6, it reappears as a bitmapped graphic of the original text. In other Windows 3.1 OLE-aware applications, the Scrap Memo may appear as an iconized, embedded object or be rejected as an unknown file format.

Still, the ability to park selected text temporarily as a visible object on the desktop is very handy. Eventually, Microsoft and other vendors will upgrade all of their applications to reconvert Scrap objects automatically to formatted text. Can you say "Object-oriented desktop?" IBM can, with OS/2 Warp, which is why you'll see more of this feature in Windows, as well.

More Missing WordPad Features Available in Windows Write

Besides the decimal tab and leading options mentioned above, several other Write features are missing from WordPad, including the ability to:

- Create headers and footers in a document.
- Generate page numbers or insert hard page breaks in the middle of a page.
- Move and resize embedded graphic images.

For more information on using WordPad in productivity scenarios, see the section on document templates in Appendix B.

RegEdit (The Registry Editor)

The Win95 version of RegEdit is much more powerful than the version included in Windows 3.1. In fact, it's so powerful that Microsoft doesn't really want you to use it. There's nothing about it in Win95's help files, even though Win95 stores a good deal more information about applications in the Registration Database than Windows 3.1 did.

Here's what RegEdit can do:

- Save and export the Win95 System Registry to a text file.
- Modify registry information about the desktop and specific Windows applications.

Here's what it can't do:

- Conveniently customize application performance through the entry of user-devised information.

The RegEdit utility is included primarily so that you can copy specific vendor instructions from documentation to fix problems. Although no information about RegEdit is provided in Win95's help files, the Microsoft Windows 95 Resource Kit does point out one useful RegEdit function: The entire registry can be saved or backed up using the Export Registry feature in the Registry Editor. This saves information on a specific branch or the entire registry in a text-format file. Later, you can restore the registry using the Import Registry feature. This rebuilds a branch or the entire registry from a saved, exported registry file.

If the registry is corrupted or the system no longer starts at all, you can run Registry Editor in safe mode to diagnose and correct the problem. The registry can be exported, imported, or created using Registry Editor, as shown in these command examples:

Command	Description
REGEDIT /E EXPORT.REG	Exports the entire registry to the file EXPORT.REG
REGEDIT /I EXPORT.REG	Imports the registry file EXPORT.REG
REGEDIT /C EXPORT.REG	Replaces the registry with contents of EXPORT.REG

caution *Microsoft advises that you use the REGEDIT /C option with extreme care, and only when you are sure that the .REG file specified contains a complete image of the registry. The REGEDIT /C option completely replaces the entire contents of the registry. That's dangerous if you use a partial export file as your source.*

Back Up the Registry

Because the System Registry contains many important settings that are difficult to duplicate if the file becomes corrupt, it's a good idea to preserve a backup copy for emergency use. The Windows 95 CD contains a utility called ERU designed specifically for this purpose. See Appendix A for instructions on how to use it.

note *In rare circumstances when the registry is badly corrupted, you can start the computer using the Windows 95 start-up disk. Then you can use the real-mode REGEDIT.EXE utility found on the start-up disk to import a .REG file, or to edit a .REG file in real-mode using a text editor. The Microsoft Windows 95 Resource Kit does not provide enough information to guide you through this process safely, so it is recommended that you try editing a .REG file only with guidance from your product support representative or by following a documented procedure from another trustworthy source.*

Another stopgap measure for recovery is to search the root directory of your C drive for a hidden file called SYSTEM.1ST. SYSTEM.1ST is the basic registry that Windows 95 establishes before completing installation and migrating your program groups. If you are unable to restart the Win95 desktop in any other way, you can copy the SYSTEM.1ST file into your Windows directory and rename it SYSTEM.DAT. This will return the registry to its initial state, preserving some of your desktop settings and program groups.

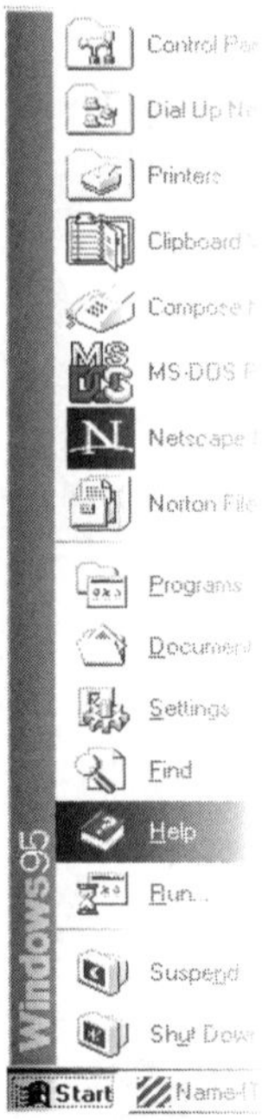
Control Pa
Dial Up N
Printers
Clipboard
Compose
MS-DOS
Netscape
Norton File
Programs
Document
Settings
Find
Help
Run...
Suspend
Shut Dow
Windows95
Start
Name-

chapter 6

Memory Management in Windows 95

- Win95 system architecture
  - 16-bit vs. 32-bit virtual machines
- Startup strategies
  - Hidden boot options
  - Working with CONFIG.SYS
  - Optimizing conventional memory
- Third-party DOS memory managers
  - Do you need them?
  - Migrating a Win3.1 configuration
  - Optimizing 386MAX, Netroom, and QEMM under Win95
- More system configuration secrets
  - Replacing real-mode drivers with protected-mode VXDs
  - Regaining 32-bit file access and 32-bit virtual memory

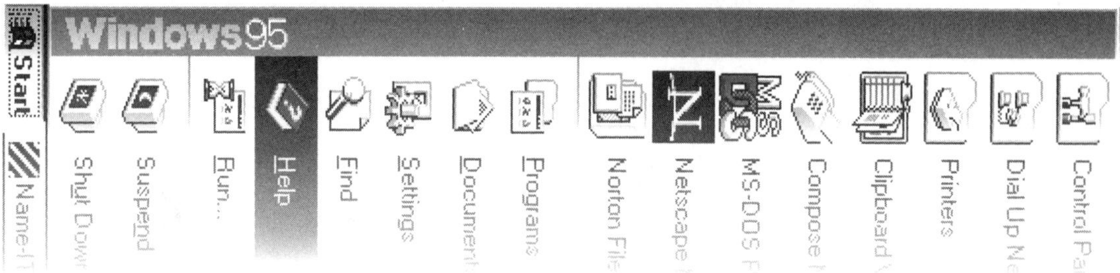

THIS chapter serves as a nuts-and-bolts tutorial of what's going on beneath Win95's desktop interface. If you must juggle DOS, Windows 3.1, and Windows 95 applications in networked environments and in complicated system configurations, read on to find both conceptual and practical material on how Windows 95 manages memory.

The first part of the chapter describes the new Windows 95 system architecture. You'll learn how 16-bit (Win3.1), 32-bit (Win95), and DOS applications are coordinated under the new operating system. This section outlines how the limits of Windows 3.1 have been redefined and stretched for Windows 95, and where they still pertain. The second part of the chapter is a tutorial on Windows 95 startup strategies. It assumes that Windows 95 is installed and you're looking at the desktop.

This chapter also provides a clinic for users who wish to integrate third-party DOS memory management software with Windows 95. You'll see the advantages and disadvantages of retaining packages like 386MAX, Netroom, and QEMM in your system configuration. Sections on each of these packages address specific configuration and migration issues.

Finally, there is a brief section on the memory management options for Windows 95 that can be specifically fine-tuned through desktop configuration settings.

New System Architecture

If we allowed ourselves to be swept away in the giddiness of Microsoft's publicity campaign, we might find ourselves echoing dramatic statements like "Windows 95 does away with DOS." And, actually, the architecture of Windows 95 makes several steps in that direction. In an ideal situation, you can run Win95 without a CONFIG.SYS or an AUTOEXEC.BAT file, and even skip loading the DOS command processor.

In a typical single-user configuration, the need for third-party memory managers, disk caches, and peripheral device drivers has been virtually eliminated in Windows 95. A new series of protected-mode virtual device drivers (VXDs) is built into the operating system to replace real-mode drivers like DBLSPACE.BIN, MOUSE.SYS, MSCDEX.EXE, and SMARTDRV.EXE. (*Protected mode* is an instruction set built into all Intel CPUs higher than the original 8088. It is used to recognize and exploit more than the original 640K to 1MB of memory available to MS-DOS.) This shift to protected-mode drivers results in smoother overall operating system performance. It can also yield more conventional memory in DOS sessions than was possible under Windows 3.1.

However, despite these enhancements, the protected-mode Win95 operating system still sits on top of a group of real-mode device drivers that must load in the first 640K of memory. Windows 95 offers more protection for 16-bit Windows and DOS applications than its predecessors, but the memory protection scheme is not bulletproof. Users will still occasionally experience annoying blue-screen protection fault errors. These protection faults can bring down not just one application, but the entire system. The widely ballyhooed 32-bit applications for Windows 95 are not wholly shielded from one another. Each 32-bit application running under Windows 95 requires a special pointer, called a *program segment prefix* (PSP). These application PSPs reside within real-mode conventional memory. The 32-bit applications are theoretically supposed to run in their own separate address spaces, using only the 32-bit Win95 kernel. In actuality, they sometimes make backward calls to the KRNL386.EXE module that manages 16-bit Windows applications. And all 16-bit applications, under KRNL386, share a common virtual machine.

On the plus side, Microsoft has added a number of enhancements to Windows 95 that are not found in Windows 3.1, as reviewed next.

Integrated 32-Bit Protected-Mode Operating System

This basic improvement eliminates the need for a separate copy of MS-DOS. Windows 95 multitasks 16-bit DOS and Windows applications as well as 32-bit Windows applications. Here's a rough summary of the way this works.

- **DOS sessions** are each executed in separate, 16-bit virtual machines, using the virtual 8086 mode feature built into all Intel CPU models 80386 and higher. While each DOS session runs in a separate address space, all share common access to certain strategic real-mode drivers, loaded in the first 640K of system memory. Because DOS applications have access to this memory, it is possible for them to bring down the system by specifically overwriting pointers established by other Win95 system functions. The probability of an individual DOS session or application doing this is small, unless you construct a DEBUG script specifically designed to corrupt the system. (Several users in the Win95 beta test program delighted in creating such scripts.) Most DOS session functions are isolated in protected, virtual machines. Additionally, Microsoft has sealed off the first 64K of conventional memory, which is where vulnerable system pointers are most likely to reside.
- **Windows 3.1 (16-bit Windows) applications** are all run in a single 16-bit virtual machine controlled by the same KRNL386 module that managed them in previous versions of Windows. Windows 3.1 apps share a common memory address space, so that malfunctioning code in one of them can also affect other currently running applications. If one of these program malfunctions while accessing system resources shared by the operating system—such as video display and disk I/O—it can still bring down all of Windows 95.
- **Windows 95 (32-bit Windows) programs** include the printing subsystem, various applets and utilities, as well as full-featured applications written to Microsoft's 32-bit application programming interface (API). These modules are loaded, almost entirely, into separate protected-mode address spaces and managed by the 32-bit system kernel. Theoretically, 32-bit applications are insulated from each other and from the operating system. However, several participants in the Win95 beta program claim to have refuted Microsoft's claim that this is so. They have produced examples of 32-bit applications making calls to the KRNL386.EXE module that manages 16-bit Windows applications. If this can happen, then a poorly programmed 32-bit application can disrupt the 16-bit Windows 3.1 virtual machine—and consequently disrupt other 32-bit programs and the overall operating system. Microsoft maintains that the statistical probability of this occurring with real 32-bit applications (instead of specially constructed test cases) is extremely low.

What's the bottom line on this in English? Well, the Windows 95 programs are theoretically each off in private 32-bit mansions on the right side of town. The DOS programs live in separate 16-bit bungalows. The Windows 3.1 applications are all lumped together in an upscale boarding house with a common dining room. The implications of what some Win95 beta testers found are that the aristocratic 32-bit apps must sometimes secretly go slumming to the Win16 boarding house to get their work done. And when the aristocrats venture into the 16-bit neighborhood, they may get mugged by disgruntled CorelDraw or WordPerfect gangsters.

Preemptive Multitasking and Multithreading Support

- **DOS sessions** under Windows 3.1, were multitasked by allocating each session a fixed, cyclical share of CPU time. This round-robin scheme (originally developed by Quarterdeck Office Systems for DESQview) simply shifted control of the CPU back and forth between the Windows virtual machine and individual DOS sessions according to a specified numerical ratio. Users could adjust this ratio through the Control Panel and PIF settings, but the system had no dynamic response to programs. If one application was configured to consume 70 percent of the available CPU time, it would do so, whether it was running idle or performing a complex calculation. There was no chance for a program allocated 30 percent of the CPU time to pipe up and say "Hey, I'm overworked here, and you're doing nothing! How about sending over a little processor time?"

  Under Windows 95, the situation is different. DOS programs can be preemptively multitasked. This means that Win95's Virtual Machine Manager monitors the activity of each individual DOS session. If WordPerfect is sitting idle, while Lotus 1-2-3 is chewing on a spreadsheet, the system can dynamically take time away from the WordPerfect session and shunt it over to the Lotus virtual machine. If you switch to WordPerfect and start a big print job, the system registers this and transfers some processor time back to WordPerfect.

- **Windows 3.1 (16-bit) programs** running under Windows 95 behave the same way as they did under previous versions of Windows. The situation is more or less a cooperative anarchy. The operating system makes no attempt to budget CPU time between competing applications. Instead, the internal structure of each program determines how much CPU time it will grab. If Microsoft Word version 6 has code that says "I'm heavy and bad; give me all of your CPU time," then a less aggressively-programmed application like Excel just hands it over, slowing concurrent spreadsheet recalculations to a crawl.

- **Windows 95 (32-bit) applications** in their separate address spaces are preemptively multitasked in the same way as DOS sessions. If you are running the Windows 95 or Windows NT versions of Word and Excel, the system monitors their individual demands on the CPU, dynamically transferring processor time from one application to the other. You'll find that two 32-bit Windows applications running concurrently can accomplish more work than two 16-bit Windows applications running concurrently. The system deals out processor time intelligently so that you can print, perform background recalculations, or run a search and replace macro without one task monopolizing the CPU.

  Additionally, Windows 95 can manage multiple processes executing concurrently within an individual 32-bit application. This feature, called multithreading, allows an application to accept keyboard input, accept or transmit data through an external port or perform other background tasks simultaneously without causing deterioration in the performance of other applications.

32-Bit Installable File Systems

The 32-bit file systems in Windows 95, VFAT for fixed disk media, CDFS for CD-ROM drives, and the internal network redirector include support for long filenames, and better performance.

32-Bit Kernel

Windows 95 has a single virtual machine (VM) called the System VM, in which all system processes run. In addition, all Win32-based and Win16-based applications run in this VM. Each DOS-based application runs in its own VM. (See Figure 6-1.)

FIGURE 6-1

Win95 architecture provides a system virtual machine that maintains separate address spaces for 32-bit applications and DOS sessions. 16-bit Windows apps share a common address space.

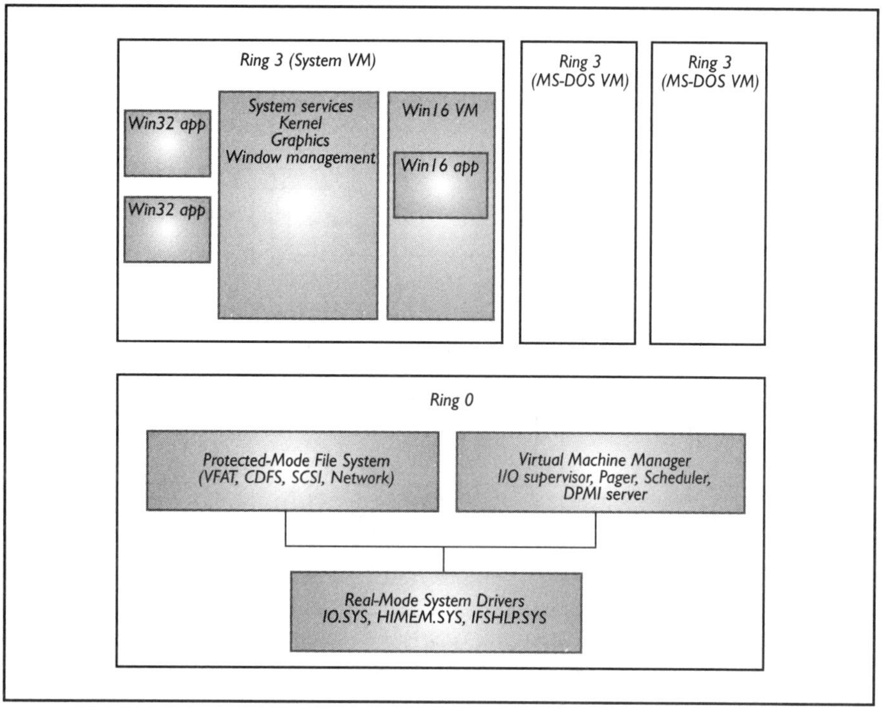

The Virtual Machine Manager provides each application with the system resources it needs. It replaces WIN386.EXE from Windows 3.1. The Virtual Machine Manager is responsible for three key areas of services:

- Process scheduling
- Memory paging
- MS-DOS mode support for DOS-based applications that must have exclusive access to system resources

Resources allocated for each Win32-based application tracked on a per-thread basis are automatically freed when the application ends. If an application stops responding, you can press CTRL-ALT-DELETE to display the Close Application dialog box, and then close the unresponsive application without affecting other running tasks. (See Figure 6-2.)

To support a 16-bit operating environment including Windows 3.1 and DOS, the Intel processor architecture uses a mechanism called *segment addressing*. Segments reference physical memory by using a 16-bit segment address and a 16-bit offset address within the segment. A segment is 64K in size, and both applications and the operating system suffer a performance penalty for accessing information across segments.

FIGURE 6-2

Windows 95 32-bit and 16-bit resource allocation[1]

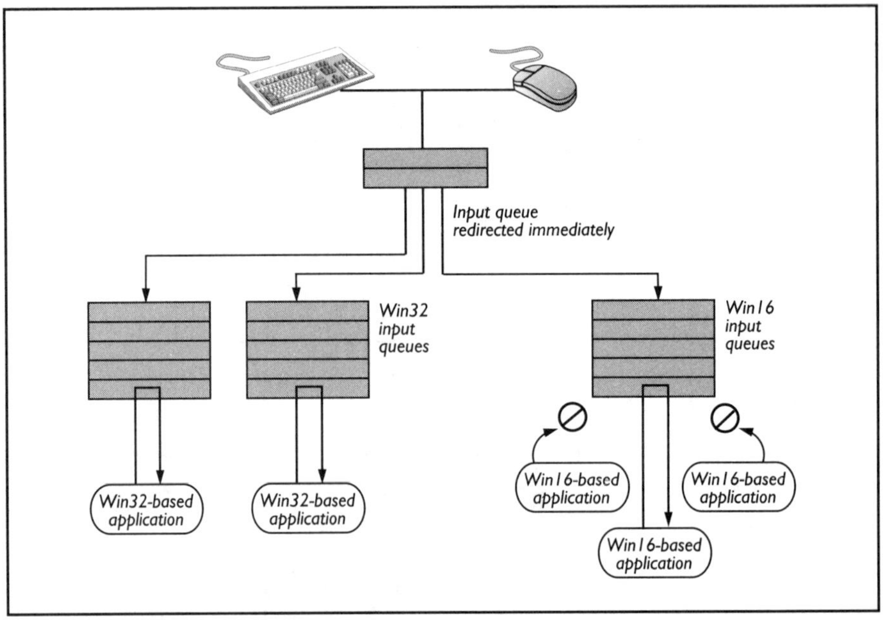

[1] From *The Windows 95 Resource Kit.* Copyright© 1995, Microsoft Corporation. Reprinted with permission of Microsoft Press. All rights reserved.

Windows 95 handles this issue by supporting a flat, linear memory model for 32-bit operating system functionality and Win32-based applications. A linear addressing model makes it easier to write applications and removes the performance limitations inherent in the segmented memory architecture. Microsoft's George Moore, the product manager and spiritual godfather for Windows 95, has this to say about Win-32 applications, memory protection, and memory paging:

> When you run a 32-bit application, the entire EXE file is divided into 'pages' of information of 4K each. When you first load the application, Windows will load the first 4K page into memory and then start executing the application's code. Pretty soon the application will execute all of the initial code in that 4K page and will attempt to make reference to another page of the program which isn't currently in memory. When this happens it is known as a *page fault* because the page isn't present in physical memory. This is a hardware interrupt that the 386 and higher processors support.

The page fault causes the virtual memory manager (VMM) to look at the required address and then calculate the offset into the executable file for the requested page. Windows then seeks into the file and loads the correct page. The app starts executing again on the new page. Eventually it will need another 4K page and the process repeats.

The beauty of this method is that the operating system only needs to load the bare minimum number of pages in order to satisfy the requests of the application. This is known as the application's *working set.* Unused (nonexecuted) pages are never loaded into memory. By running automated tools, developers can reshuffle their application's subroutines so that the most heavily used routines are on physically contiguous pages at the beginning of the file. In doing so they can reduce the working set of their application so that it uses less memory under most conditions. Less memory = faster execution because of less page faults that occur.

Windows 95 itself is page-tuned in this method. For example, the 32-bit Explorer is page tuned for the most common case of running two applications and using the taskbar to switch between the apps. Therefore, a portion of the taskbar's pages are usually in memory all the time but, for example, the shell code to deal with network browsing is located on less-used pages.

Windows 95 allows full use of the 4GB of addressable memory space for all 32-bit operating system components and applications. Each 32-bit application can access up to 2GB of addressable memory space.

Improved System Capacity

Windows 3.1 required that all protected-mode applications access a series of special resource heaps in conventional memory that were inherently limited to a maximum size of 64K. In Windows 95, system resources that were previously stored in these 16-bit heaps are stored in 32-bit heaps. This provides more storage space for data elements created by individual applications.

Table 6-1 shows the improvements that have been made.

Resource	Windows 3.1[1]	Windows 95[2]
Windows menu handles	~299	32K
Timers	32	Unlimited
COM and LPT ports	4 per type	Unlimited
Items per list box	8K	32K
Data per list box	64K	Unlimited
Data per edit control	64K	Unlimited
Regions	All in 64K segment	Unlimited
Physical pens and brushes	All in 64K segment	Unlimited
Logical pens and brushes	All in 64K segment	All in 64K segment
Logical fonts	All in 64K segment	750-800
Installed fonts	250-300 (best case)	1000
Device contexts	200 (best case)	16K

TABLE 6-1 *Windows 95 System Limits*[3] ■

[1]Limits for GDI objects in Windows 3.1 are not exact because all regions, physical objects, logical objects, device contexts (DCs), and installed fonts had to fit in a single 64K segment. Because many of these have been moved to the 32-bit heap, Windows 95 provides much more room for those remaining items, such as logical pens, brushes, and so on. The remaining items in the Windows 95 local heap are all less than 10 to 20 bytes each.

[2]System-wide resources, unless noted otherwise.

[3]From *The Windows 95 Resource Kit.* Copyright© 1995, Microsoft Corporation. Reprinted with permission of Microsoft Press. All rights reserved.

Startup Strategies

So Windows 95 is installed on your hard disk, and you're looking at the desktop. You may have a number of questions about what to do with your CONFIG.SYS, DOS memory managers, and TSR utilities:

- Do I need a CONFIG.SYS and AUTOEXEC.BAT? If I do, what device drivers and utilities should I load? Are my CD-ROM drive and SCSI devices being recognized?
- Do I have enough conventional memory for DOS sessions? What about expanded memory for DOS applications: Do I need a third-party product like QEMM?
- What if I want to dual boot back to DOS 5 or DOS 6.*x*: Will this capability be installed automatically for me?

- How is the DOS 7 part of Windows 95 different from DOS 6.*x*? Are there new commands and switches for CONFIG.SYS and AUTOEXEC.BAT?

The next sections aim to answer these questions.

Is CONFIG.SYS Necessary?

One of the bases for Microsoft's claim that Windows 95 "does away with DOS" is that the system can start up the Windows 95 interface, automatically without either a CONFIG.SYS or AUTOEXEC.BAT present in the root directory of your boot drive. How does this work? Like DOS, Windows 95 bootstraps and loads itself off two kernel files called IO.SYS and MSDOS.SYS. The difference is that the low-level machine instructions in Win95's IO.SYS are more sophisticated than in the older DOS equivalent. The system is instructed to automatically load a series of real-mode device drivers from your hard disk without reading a CONFIG.SYS file. The following drivers are loaded at boot time by IO.SYS if they can be located on your hard drive:

- HIMEM.SYS
- IFSHLP.SYS
- SETVER.EXE
- DBLSPACE.BIN or DRVSPACE.BIN

Additionally, most of the standard settings and command switches for DOS that you used to place in CONFIG.SYS are also loaded automatically by IO.SYS.

Table 6-2 lists the common entries in CONFIG.SYS that are now configured automatically in Windows 95.

To modify the default values set for Windows 95 by IO.SYS, you must place appropriate entries into a new or existing CONFIG.SYS file on your boot drive, modifying the IO.SYS defaults with the value(s) you want. If CONFIG.SYS contains switches or other parameters for any of the drivers or settings created by IO.SYS, the IO.SYS defaults are overridden. Entries for FILES=, BUFFERS=, and STACKS= must be set in CONFIG.SYS to at least the default values in IO.SYS.

Note that IO.SYS does not load EMM386.EXE. If any of your applications require expanded memory or load data into the High Memory Area,

Setting	Purpose
dos=high	Specifies that DOS should be loaded in the high memory area (HMA). Also, the UMB value is included if EMM386 is loaded from CONFIG.SYS. (IO.SYS does not load EMM386.)
HIMEM.SYS	Enables access to the HMA. This line loads and runs the real-mode Memory Manager. HIMEM.SYS is loaded by default in Windows 95.
IFSHLP.SYS	Installable File System Helper, which loads device drivers. This allows the system to make file system calls. Until this is loaded, only the minimal file system from IO.SYS is used. After this point, the full file system is available.
SETVER.EXE	Optional TSR-type device. It is included for compatibility reasons. Some DOS-based applications require a specific version of DOS to be running. This file responds to applications that query for the version number and sets the version number required.
FILES=	Specifies the number of file handle buffers to create. This is specifically for files opened using DOS calls and is not required by Windows 95. It is included for compatibility with older applications. The default value is 60.
LASTDRIVE=	Specifies the last drive letter available for assignment. This is not required for Windows 95 but is included for compatibility with older applications. If Windows 95 Setup finds this entry, it is moved to the Registry. The default value is z.
BUFFERS=	Specifies the number of file buffers to create. This is specifically for applications using IO.SYS calls and is not required by Windows 95. The default value is 30.
STACKS=	Specifies the number and size of stack frames. This is not required for Windows 95 but is included for compatibility with older applications. The default value is 9,256.
SHELL=COMMAND.COM	Indicates what command process to use. By default, the /P switch is included to indicate that the command process is permanent and should not be unloaded. If the /P switch is not specified, AUTOEXEC.BAT is not processed and the command process can be unloaded when quitting the operating system.
FCBS=	Specifies the number of file control blocks that can be open at the same time. You should use an FCBS= line in CONFIG.SYS only if you have an older program that requires such a setting. The default value is 4.

TABLE 6-2 *CONFIG.SYS Settings Incorporated in Windows 95 IO.SYS*[1] ■

[1]From *The Windows 95 Resource Kit.* Copyright© 1995, Microsoft Corporation. Reprinted with permission of Microsoft Press. All rights reserved.

EMM386 must be loaded in CONFIG.SYS. The Windows 95 IO.SYS file is automatically renamed to WINBOOT.SYS if you start the computer using your previous operating system (F4 at boot time).

The Bottom Line Here

These performance settings, now established automatically, allow you to successfully boot Windows 95 without a CONFIG.SYS file. If you want to customize the settings, for instance, add an environment parameter to the Shell statement, increase or decrease the allocation of files and buffers or load additional device drivers, then you will need a traditional CONFIG.SYS file in the root directory of your boot drive.

About MSDOS.SYS

MSDOS.SYS is the second file that Windows 95 reads at boot time. In Windows 95, this file contains ASCII text instructions instead of binary code. Like IO.SYS, MSDOS.SYS is a hidden, read-only system file in the root of the computer's boot drive. This file contains path information used to locate other Windows files, including the System Registry and device drivers. MSDOS.SYS also supports an [Options] section which is used to customize the startup process.

A typical instance of MSDOS.SYS contains the following default values:

```
[PATHS]
WINDIR=C:\WINDOWS
WINBOOTDIR=C:\WINDOWS
HOSTWINBOOTDRV=C
[OPTIONS]
BOOTGUI=1
```

The configuration instructions in MSDOS.SYS are followed by a series of dummy comment lines (;xxxxxxxxxxx) in order to round the size of the file out to 1024 bytes. Most values in the [Options] section are Boolean—(a value of 1 enables the option and a value of 0 disables it). The critical values in MSDOS.SYS are the ones we just listed above. They can be modified if you wish to transfer all of your Windows 95 files to another partition or force the system to boot to a command prompt instead of loading the Win95 interface. Other settings in MSDOS.SYS are used to enable/disable the loading of the DBLSPACE.BIN compression driver, and control the behavior of Win95's pop-up boot menu (including the use of keyboard hotkeys and the ability to boot an older version of DOS).

Table 6-3 describes all of the entries in MSDOS.SYS, with their typical default values.

Setting	Purpose
[Paths] section:	
HostWinBootDrv=c	Defines the location of the boot drive root directory.
WinBootDir=	Defines the location of the necessary startup files. The default is the directory specified during Setup; for example, C:\WINDOWS.
WinDir=	Defines the location of the Windows 95 directory as specified during Setup.
[Options] section:	
BootDelay=n	Sets the initial startup delay to n seconds. The default is 2. BootKeys=0 disables the delay. The only purpose of the delay is to give the user sufficient time to press F8 after the Starting Windows message appears.
BootFailSafe=	Enables Safe Mode for system startup. The default is 0. (This setting is enabled typically by equipment manufacturers for installation.)
BootGUI=	Enables automatic graphical startup into Windows 95. The default is 1.
BootKeys=	Enables the startup option keys (that is, F5, F6, and F8). The default is 1. Setting this value to 0 overrides the value of BootDelay=n and prevents any startup keys from functioning. This setting allows system administrators to configure more secure systems.
BootMenu=	Enables automatic display of the Windows 95 Startup menu, so that the user must press F8 to see the menu. The default is 0. Setting this value to 1 eliminates the need to press F8 to see the menu.
BootMenuDefault=#	Sets the default menu item on the Windows Startup menu; the default is 3 for a computer with no networking components, and 4 for a networked computer.
BootMenuDelay=#	Sets the number of seconds to display the Windows Startup menu before running the default menu item. The default is 30.
BootMulti=	Enables dual boot capabilities. The default is 0. Setting this value to 1 enables the ability to start DOS by pressing F4 or by pressing F8 to use the Windows Startup menu.
BootWarn=	Enables the Safe Mode startup warning. The default is 1.
BootWin=	Enables Windows 95 as the default operating system. Setting this value to 0 disables Windows 95 as the default; this is useful only with DOS version 5 or 6.*x* on the computer. The default is 1.
DblSpace=	Enables automatic loading of DBLSPACE.BIN. The default is 1.
DoubleBuffer=	Enables loading of a double-buffering driver for a SCSI controller. The default is 0. Setting this value to 1 enables double-buffering, if required by the SCSI controller.
DrvSpace=	Enables automatic loading of DRVSPACE.BIN. The default is 1.
LoadTop=	Enables loading of COMMAND.COM or DRVSPACE.BIN at the top of 640K memory. The default is 1. Set this value to 0 with Novell® NetWare® or any software that makes assumptions about what is used in specific memory areas.

TABLE 6-3 *CONFIG.SYS Settings Incorporated in Windows 95 MS-DOS.SYS*[1] ■

Setting	Purpose
Logo=	Enables display of the animated logo. The default is 1. Setting this value to 0 also avoids hooking a variety of interrupts that can create incompatibilities with certain memory managers from other vendors.
Network=	Enables Safe Mode With Networking as a menu option. The default is 1 for computers with networking installed. This value should be 0 if network software components are not installed.

TABLE 6-3 *CONFIG.SYS Settings Incorporated in Windows 95 MS-DOS.SYS*[1] (continued) ■

[1]From *The Microsoft Windows 95 Resource Kit.*

Here are uses for some of these MSDOS.SYS parameters:

- Make the Win95 Startup Menu appear at boot time. The default setting of BootMenu=0 causes the system to start directly into Windows 95 unless you press the F8 key. A setting of BootMenu=1 will display the Startup Menu on the screen automatically at boot time.
- Change the default location of Win95 system files. If your Win95 configuration is split between a small C:\WINDOWS directory and the bulk of the operating system on another drive, you can consolidate the two directories into one. You'll need to copy all the files in the C:\WINDOWS directory (including hidden/read-only system files) to the WINDOWS directory on your real Win95 host drive. Then set WinBootDir=[*D*:]\WINDOWS, with [*D*:] being the partition where Windows 95 really resides. This option can be used to make room for a separate C:\WINDOWS directory that may contain the Windows 3.1, Windows for Workgroups, or the Windows NT operating systems, should you wish to run these independently of Windows 95.
- Set another operating system as your default boot option. By default, the setting BootWin=1 is assumed in MSDOS.SYS to automatically start up Windows 95, if its files are present on your hard disk. A setting of BootWin=0 causes the computer to start the version of DOS or Windows 3.1 that was active on your hard disk before you installed Windows 95. You can also use this option to dual boot back to third-party versions of DOS such as Novell DOS 7 or IBM DOS 7. If you installed Windows 95 to upgrade a directory that contained a previous version of Windows, you may need to go to some additional trouble to restore boot options to the old operating system. (See the upcoming sidebar.)

Note that the BootWin=0 option should not be used to dual boot between Warp OS/2 and Windows 95. The best way to do this is through the OS/2 Boot Manager, or through Warp's Dual Boot feature. Windows 95 disables OS/2's Boot Manager upon installation, but this feature can be easily restored. (See Appendix A for details.)

Recovering the Dual Boot (F4) Option for Running Previous Version of DOS

If you installed Windows 95 into a new partition and directory on a system running DOS version 5 or later, the earlier version of DOS on your hard disk was preserved. If you don't see the option to boot to your earlier DOS on the Win95 boot menu (which appears when you press F8), you can turn it on by adding a command to the MSDOS.SYS text file that resides in the root directory of your boot drive. (To open this file in the Notepad, you must turn on the Explorer and My Computer display option that reveals (unhides) system files in folder lists. See Chapter 4 for details.)

Under the [Options] section in MSDOS.SYS enter the statement

```
BootMulti=1
```

This will allow you to start the earlier version of DOS by pressing F4 when the Starting Windows message appears during system startup. In order to start your previous version of DOS, Windows 95 makes the following strategic adjustments at boot time:

- *The current versions of IO.SYS, MSDOS.SYS, and COMMAND.COM are renamed WINBOOT.SYS, MSDOS.W40, and COMMAND.W40, respectively.*
- *Windows 95 searches for kernel files from your previous version of DOS in the root directory of your boot drive. IO.DOS, MSDOS.DOS, and COMMAND.DOS are renamed IO.SYS, MSDOS.SYS, and COMMAND.COM. If any of these files can't be found, then your previous version of DOS will not be booted. Instead, Windows 95 will ignore your dual-boot request and load its own system kernel.*
- *When the old version of DOS boots successfully, the Windows 95 CONFIG.SYS and AUTOEXEC.BAT files are renamed CONFIG.W40 and AUTOEXEC.W40.*
- *The system looks for two files named CONFIG.DOS and AUTOEXEC.DOS in the root directory of your boot drive. If these files are found, they are renamed to CONFIG.SYS and AUTOEXEC.BAT and then processed.*

...ou installed Windows 95 over a directory with an existing copy of Windows 3.1 or Windows for ...roups, then, by default, the dual boot option is disabled. The operating system kernel files from ...d DOS are renamed, as described earlier, but half of your previous DOS directory is deleted. Still, you can restore the dual boot option if you wish. If you've read Chapter 2, you've been forewarned about this eventuality and you may have fortified your system with a backup of your old DOS directory.

If, for some reason, your Windows 95 installation failed during the first pass, restoring the dual boot option is a little trickier. When you make your second installation attempt, Windows 95 has already renamed your DOS 6.x system files. Running Win95 Setup a second time causes the DOS 6.x kernel files to be overwritten. If this happens to you, you'll find that pressing F4 simply boots to a Win95 (MS-DOS 7) command prompt. But you can replace the missing system files from your previous operating system. All you need is a floppy boot disk formatted with your previous version of DOS. While Windows 95 is running, insert the boot disk from your previous operating system in drive A. Open a DOS command prompt within Windows 95, and perform the following operations:

1. `XCOPY A:\IO.SYS C:\IO.DOS /H`
   (If XCOPY asks you whether the target is a File or a Directory, answer **FILE**.*)*

2. `XCOPY A:\MSDOS.SYS C:\MSDOS.DOS /H`
   (If XCOPY asks you whether the target is a File or a Directory, answer **FILE**.*)*

3. `COPY A:\COMMAND.COM C:\COMMAND.DOS`

caution *Be sure to copy these files to a .DOS file extension in the target directory, or you will overwrite the Windows 95 system files, which you don't want to do!*

If you have backups of the CONFIG.SYS and AUTOEXEC.BAT files from your previous version of DOS, copy them to the root directory of drive C as CONFIG.DOS and AUTOEXEC.DOS. If necessary, you can recreate these files from scratch, or modify the Windows 95 versions, but be sure to save them in the root directory with the .DOS file extension.

Last, from inside Windows 95, open the current MSDOS.SYS file in Notepad, as described earlier, and make sure it contains the command

```
BootMulti=1
```

in the [Options] section.

Working with CONFIG.SYS and AUTOEXEC.BAT

If you decide to use CONFIG.SYS and AUTOEXEC.BAT files with Windows 95, here are some things to bear in mind.

You can retain a CONFIG.SYS but eliminate AUTOEXEC.BAT. If you need to retain DOS environment variables in Windows 95, you can enter SET statements directly in CONFIG.SYS. For instance, a SET PATH= entry can be substituted for the AUTOEXEC.BAT PATH statement. If you need to run MSCDEX.EXE for CD-ROM drives, it can be loaded in CONFIG.SYS by specifying

```
DEVICE=MSCDEX.EXE
```

(This may not actually be necessary; see the tip below. Certain other commands normally entered in AUTOEXEC.BAT can be loaded in CONFIG.SYS by using INSTALL= statements.

Note that some commands needed in CONFIG.SYS and AUTOEXEC.BAT when running DOS are removed during installation of Windows 95.

tip *Many real-mode device drivers for SCSI controllers, CD-ROM drives, sound cards, notebook PCMCIA cards, and power management are typically migrated into the CONFIG.SYS for Windows 95, even though they may not be necessary! Windows 95 auto-detects most of your hardware automatically, but does not automatically substitute protected-mode drivers for statements present in CONFIG.SYS. If you open the Add New Hardware component in the Control Panel and answer No to the Auto-detect option, you will see a list of all the devices and drivers that are built into the operating system. If your particular hardware is supported, you can tell Windows 95 to install its protected-mode drivers and remove corresponding real-mode drivers from CONFIG.SYS and AUTOEXEC.BAT. (See Chapter 8 for more information on how to add new hardware.)*

New CONFIG.SYS Commands

Table 6-4 lists optional command switches for CONFIG.SYS that have been added to the version of DOS that underlies Windows 95.

EMM386, Do You Need It?

EMM386.EXE is the DOS component that allows you to load TSR-utilities and drivers into upper memory blocks (UMBs). In Windows 95, it is also necessary if you want to provide Expanded Memory for DOS applications. Windows 3.1 and Windows for Workgroups could provide Expanded Memory for DOS applications without EMM386.EXE, but Windows 95

Command Switch	Purpose
BUFFERSHIGH	Allocates memory for a specified number of disk buffers when the computer starts. The BUFFERSHIGH form causes reserved memory to be taken out of the upper memory address. You can use these commands only in CONFIG.SYS.
FCBSHIGH	Specifies the number of FCBs that the operating system can have open at the same time. The FCBSHIGH form causes reserved memory to be taken out of the UMB. You can use these commands only in CONFIG.SYS.
FILESHIGH	Specifies the number of files that the operating system can access at one time. The FILESHIGH form causes reserved memory to be taken out of the UMB. You can use these commands only in CONFIG.SYS.
INCLUDE	Includes the contents of one configuration block within another. You can use this command only in CONFIG.SYS.
LASTDRIVEHIGH	Specifies the maximum number of drives you can access. The LASTDRIVEHIGH form causes reserved memory to be taken out of the UMB. You can use these commands only in CONFIG.SYS.
MENUCOLOR	Sets the text and background colors for the Startup menu. You can use this command only within a menu block in CONFIG.SYS.
MENUDEFAULT	Specifies the default menu item on the startup menu and sets a time-out value, if desired. You can use this command only within a menu block in CONFIG.SYS.
MENUITEM	Defines up to nine items on the Startup menu. You can use this command only within a menu block in CONFIG.SYS.
NUMLOCK	Specifies whether the NUM LOCK setting on the numeric keypad is set to ON or OFF. You can use this command only within a menu block in CONFIG.SYS.
SUBMENU	Defines an item on a Startup menu that, when selected, displays another set of choices. You can use this command only within a menu block in CONFIG.SYS.

TABLE 6-4 *New Optional Command Switches for CONFIG.SYS*[1] ■

[1]From *The Windows 95 Resource Kit.* Copyright© 1995, Microsoft Corporation. Reprinted with permission of Microsoft Press. All rights reserved.

cannot. So there are two reasons for placing a DEVICE=EMM386.EXE statement into a new or pre-existing CONFIG.SYS file:

- You want to gain more conventional memory for DOS sessions by loading some drivers into upper memory blocks.
- You want to provide Expanded Memory for DOS applications like WordPerfect 5 or 6.

EMM386.EXE under Windows 95 functions in exactly the same way as it did under DOS 6.*x*. You have a choice between two key command line parameters:

- **DEVICE=EMM386.EXE RAM** enables both expanded memory and UMB device loading.
- **DEVICE=EMM386.EXE NOEMS** enables UMB device loading, only (and the NOEMS parameter gains you a potential extra 64K of UMB space, since it disables the use of an EMS page frame).

As in DOS 6.*x*, individual drivers and executable TSRs are loaded into upper memory by substituting DEVICEHIGH= for DEVICE= in CONFIG.SYS, or by placing the word LOADHIGH (or LH) in front of the program name in AUTOEXEC.BAT. You can do this manually by editing your startup files or by running the DOS MEMMAKER program, which is included with Windows 95.

The same strategies that applied to optimizing EMM386.EXE under DOS also apply to its use in Windows 95. The bottom line is that you may be able to get the conventional memory you need for DOS sessions under Windows 95 without extensive system tweaking. You may gain enough conventional memory simply by replacing old real-mode drivers with protected-mode VXDs, as outlined in the preceding section. Still, situations may arise where you need even more conventional memory for DOS and don't have it.

- You may be running a network/LAN setup, such as an older version of Artisoft's LANtastic, which includes no built-in Windows 95 support.
- You may have a series of peripherals that insist on loading real-mode drivers under DOS.
- You may want to run a DOS-based game or multimedia program that requires a large amount of conventional memory.
- In the event that a DOS program requires you to boot to a DOS command prompt rather than running it under Windows 95, you may find your conventional memory drastically decreased. When you boot your system to a command prompt, none of Win95's protected-mode .VXDs can load. For instance, if you've created compressed volumes on your computer with Microsoft's DoubleSpace or DriveSpace, you'll see that the real-mode compression driver consumes over 100K.

Here are some common ways to increase the amount of upper memory block (UMB) space available for loading programs high:

- Add the HIGHSCAN parameter. The statement

  ```
  DEVICE=EMM386.EXE RAM HIGHSCAN
  ```

  aggressively scans the reserved memory area between 640K and 1MB for areas that can be mapped for an EMS page frame or for upper memory blocks. (On some systems, adding HIGHSCAN may cause the computer to hang or reboot constantly. If this happens to you, you'll need to remove this parameter and determine which upper memory addresses are safe to add through trial-and-error. For instance, append the parameter

  ```
  INCLUDE=F000-F7FF
  ```

  to the EMM386 command line, and see whether the system remains stable. If not, decrease the range to F400-F7FF, etc.)

- Substitute NOEMS for RAM on the DEVICE=EMM386.EXE line. If you don't require Expanded Memory, this will provide an additional 64K for use as upper memory blocks.

- Experiment with the location of the EMS page frame to obtain larger contiguous upper memory blocks. One common scenario on many systems is that EMM386.EXE defines an EMS page frame at address D000h, creating one UMB block from C800-CFFFh, and sometimes a second block from E000-EFFFh. By placing the parameter

  ```
  FRAME=C800
  ```

  on the DEVICE=EMM386.EXE line, you rearrange the UMB allocation, typically allowing a contiguous block to be created from D800h to EFFFh. This larger UMB block can contain larger DOS device drivers and TSRs that will not fit into two smaller blocks. If the entire range from D800h to EFFFh is not recognized by EMM386, you can sometimes force recognition through INCLUDE statements. Here's an example:

  ```
  DEVICE=EMM386.EXE FRAME=C800 RAM INCLUDE=D800-EFFF.
  ```

- On Notebook computers, the upper memory area reserved for video ROM often begins at address E000, instead of C000.

Hence you may want to use the following statement:

```
DEVICE=EMM386.EXE FRAME=C000 RAM INCLUDE=D000-DFFF
```

- Sometimes you can add further to the amount of available upper memory by including the range reserved for monochrome video adapters, as follows:

```
DEVICE=EMM386.EXE FRAME=C800 RAM INCLUDE=B000-B7FF
                                  INCLUDE=D800-EFFF
```

note *On some systems where network cards, disk controllers, or SCSI devices map upper memory for Adapter ROM, these tricks may not work. If the system won't start, or you experience performance anomalies, you should always remove additional INCLUDE, FRAME, and HIGHSCAN parameters from the DEVICE=EMM386.EXE line in CONFIG.SYS.*

- Use BUFFERSHIGH, FCBSHIGH, FILESHIGH, LASTDRIVEHIGH, and STACKSHIGH to ensure that memory for these system resources is allocated from the upper memory area. Note that the ability to load these resources high is new in Windows 95, and corresponds to similar features previously available in third-party memory managers like QEMM, 386MAX, and Netroom.
- Run MEMMAKER. The version included with Windows 95 is essentially unchanged from the version included in previous versions of DOS. It may be of help in gaining you additional upper memory, but will probably not optimize your system as well as you can by manually tweaking your CONFIG.SYS and AUTOEXEC.BAT files. For instance, MEMMAKER will not automatically substitute the new BUFFERSHIGH and FILESHIGH statements in CONFIG.SYS for the older commands that load resources into conventional memory.

For best results, you may want to try optimizing CONFIG.SYS manually with the tips we've just outlined, then run MEMMAKER to see if it can create additional improvements.

Working with MEMMAKER

To run MEMMAKER, first boot to a DOS command prompt, by pressing F8 and selecting Command Prompt Only from the Win95 boot menu. The

MEMMAKER utility is located in the Windows directory on your Win95 host drive. You can also run it from a DOS prompt inside of Windows 95, and the system will automatically restart itself in MS-DOS mode. After you start MEMMAKER and select Continue, you can use the first screen to choose between express and custom setups. If you choose Custom Setup, you have a chance to extract a greater amount of upper memory. If you answer No to the question about programs needing expanded memory, you will gain an additional 64K to load drivers and TSRs above 640K. In the advanced options, try choosing "Scan upper memory area aggressively" and "Use monochrome region for running programs." If these options cause problems on your system, MEMMAKER will subsequently offer to reoptimize using more conservative settings.

After you confirm the drive and path where Windows 95 is installed, MEMMAKER reboots the system several times and attempts to optimize conventional memory by establishing an EMS page frame (if you've answered yes to the EMS question), and loading device drivers and TSRs above 640K. (If you've answered no to the EMS question, no page frame is configured.) You don't have to use the F8 boot again. MEMMAKER will automatically reboot the system to a DOS prompt several times until the memory optimization process is completed.

In reality, MEMMAKER will probably not do much to increase your available conventional memory. It lacks some of the sophisticated features built into third-party products like Helix Netroom and Quarterdeck QEMM. For a discussion of how third-party memory managers can gain you additional DOS conventional memory, see the next section. In the meantime, if you want to increase conventional memory with EMM386.EXE, try using the procedures outlined in the previous section to extend the range of available upper memory.

Third-Party DOS Memory Managers

If your Windows 95 configuration requires a number of real-mode drivers for a network, or for system peripherals, a third-party memory manager will probably yield more conventional memory than Microsoft's HIMEM/EMM386 combination. And if you were using a third-party memory manager on your system prior to installing Windows 95, you may want to migrate it over to the new operating system. Generally, Windows 95 does a fairly good job of migrating a configuration with 386MAX, Netroom, or QEMM installed. There are a few specific details related to each of these packages which can make the transition smoother. This section will tell you what you need to know about migrating each of the "Big Three" DOS memory managers to Win95 from a previous configuration, or installing them under Windows 95 for the first time.

386MAX (and BLUEMAX)

386MAX and BLUEMAX, distributed by Qualitas, Inc., are the most conservative of the third-party memory managers. They are typically used by people who want more conventional memory than Microsoft can provide, but who are leery of the technical tricks used by Netroom and QEMM to provide even more memory. 386MAX is designed for use with most 80386 and higher processor computers, whereas BLUEMAX is designed specifically for IBM PS/2 systems. The two products are more or less identical as far as features and performance, except for BLUEMAX's added ability to deal with IBM's MCA bus.

386MAX, versions 7.02 and earlier, are designed for use with DOS and Windows 3.1. These versions will function under Windows 95, but some of the bells and whistles are broken. The special 386MAX PIF editor for Windows 3.1 cannot read Windows 95 shortcuts or PIF files. The DOS-MAX feature, designed to provide 700K for DOS sessions by disabling VGA video, is also broken. In 386MAX, versions 7 and 7.01, the EXTRADOS feature is broken. EXTRADOS is used to place COMMAND.COM, stacks, files, and buffers in upper memory, but since Windows 95 duplicates these features, its loss is not tragic. If you were already running 386MAX when Windows 95 was installed, the following statements should have been removed from CONFIG.SYS:

```
DEVICE=\386MAX\EXTRADOS.MAX PRO=\386MAX\EXTRADOS.PRO
INSTALL=\386MAX\EXTRADOS.MAX
```

The 386MAX Maximize utility (which corresponds to Microsoft's MEMMAKER), can be run from a DOS command prompt by pressing F8 at boot time and choosing the "Boot to command prompt only" option. If you are installing 386MAX for the first time under Windows 95, you should choose the Custom Setup option. Maximize will give you a chance to delete the lines pertaining to EXTRADOS from its proposed changes to your CONFIG.SYS. If you are running 386MAX version 7.02 or later, this is unnecessary; Qualitas has made the more recent version of EXTRADOS compatible with Windows 95.

To install 386MAX for the first time under Windows 95, press F8, choose "Boot to command prompt\Boot to command prompt only," and run the INSTALL program from the floppy diskette. Be sure to answer No to the question which asks for permission to install the QCACHE disk cache.

---

tip *The EXTRADOS feature of 386MAX can be easily duplicated by changing the FILES, BUFFERS, STACKS, and FCBS statements in CONFIG.SYS to FILESHIGH, BUFFERSHIGH, STACKSHIGH, and FCBSHIGH.*

On some systems, you may discover that 386MAX disables Windows 95's F8 boot menu option. If this happens to you, try editing the startup parameters for 386MAX. These are located in a file called 386MAX.PRO, located in the 386MAX directory on your hard disk. Open 386MAX.PRO in a text editor and add the command NOROM to the end of the file. This should correct the failure to recognize the boot menu.

If you are using a DoubleSpace/DriveSpace compressed volume, be sure to instruct Maximize to load the DRVSPACE.SYS device driver into upper memory. (This is one of the options that you have if you choose the advanced setup.) Or you can manually enter the following line in CONFIG.SYS:

```
DEVICEHIGH=[D:]\WINDOWS\DRVSPACE.SYS /MOVE
```

This line will not affect your conventional memory total in DOS sessions run under Windows 95. However, if you boot to a DOS command prompt, the line may give you up to 110K more conventional memory. (This statement requests that the real-mode DoubleSpace compression driver be loaded into upper memory.)

---

tip *If you don't already own a copy of 386MAX or BLUEMAX, there is little reason to buy or install it for use with Windows 95. It may conceivably yield 50K to 60K more upper memory than Microsoft's EMM386. This may make a difference in some configuration situations, but if you have an acute need for upper memory, you will gain much more with either Netroom or QEMM. These other memory managers also retain their ability to open 700K, text-only DOS sessions by annexing the memory area reserved for VGA graphics. It remains to be seen whether subsequent versions of 386MAX will specifically address the needs of Windows 95 users.*

Netroom

Netroom, distributed by Helix Software, is the most aggressively designed DOS memory manager. Netroom's Cloaking Technology can yield the greatest amount of conventional memory, but Netroom may take a little bit of work to fine-tune. The advanced features of this memory manager can provide more than 250K of upper memory.

Netroom versions 3.04 and later will work smoothly under Windows 95. Earlier versions are prone to system lockups when they attempt to optimize the CONFIG.SYS and AUTOEXEC.BAT files. Owners of any 3.*x* version of Netroom can upgrade to version 3.04 by downloading a patch file from the Helix bulletin board.

If Netroom was active when you installed Windows 95, you probably got a message telling you to disable the CACHECLOAK disk cache. If you have a high-performance graphic accelerator card, you may also get a message after installation that Windows 95 is incompatible with your card's high resolution modes. If you find that Windows 95 won't run in any video mode higher than 640×480×16 colors, you can fix this problem by disabling the Helix Cloaked Video BIOS. Boot to a DOS command prompt and search for a line in CONFIG.SYS that reads:

```
DEVICE=[D:\]\NETROOM\VIDCLOAK.EXE /PMBIOS
```

Remove the /PMBIOS parameter and make the following change:

```
DEVICE=[D:]\NETROOM\VIDCLOAK.EXE /CLOAK
```

This will remove Helix's generic video BIOS and will, instead, remap your video card's own BIOS into protected memory. If you still experience difficulty in using high-resolution Super VGA (SVGA) video modes, you can remove the VIDCLOAK line entirely from the CONFIG.SYS. This video anomaly is the only significant problem you're likely to encounter with Netroom and Windows 95. To optimize your CONFIG.SYS and AUTOEXEC.BAT, just boot to a DOS prompt from the Win95 boot menu and run the CUSTOMIZE.EXE utility from your NETROOM directory. This utility will reboot your system several times and automatically achieve an optimal memory configuration. When Customize asks you if any software on your system uses Super VGA modes, answer Yes. When the system reboots, it will offer to perform a video test. For most systems, you should press the ESC key to skip the video test.

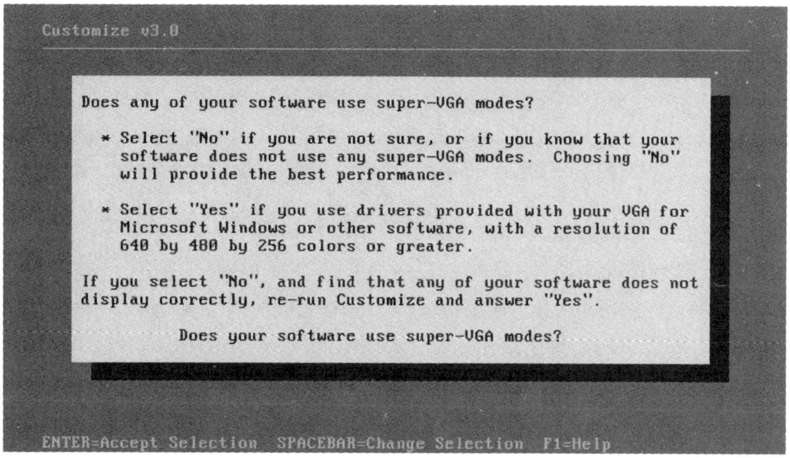

If you want Customize to test your video card for Cloaking compatibility and it fails the test, you will have to manually edit CONFIG.SYS later and remove the /PMBIOS parameter from the line that loads VIDCLOAK.EXE. If Customize says that your card has passed the video test, it will ask if you want Helix's Cloaked Video BIOS installed. Answer No to this question, unless your card uses the TSENG ET3000 or ET4000 chipset. When Customize asks for permission to modify your Windows .INI files, you can answer Yes. The changes made to SYSTEM.INI should not be detrimental to Windows 95 performance.

To install Netroom for the first time under Windows 95, boot to a DOS command prompt with F8 and run the Setup program from a floppy diskette. You will be able to pick the disk partition where Netroom is installed. Netroom automatically strips out commands placed in CONFIG.SYS and AUTOEXEC.BAT by other memory managers (including EMM386, 386MAX, and QEMM). After the necessary files are copied to the specified directory, the system will reboot, prompting you to run the Customize utility to optimize memory usage. Remember, at this point, you must be running Netroom version 3.04 or higher to prevent the computer from locking up!

After the Customize process is complete, Windows 95 will start. If you get a message about incompatible video modes, boot the system to a DOS prompt and remove the /PMBIOS parameter from the VIDCLOAK line (as described earlier). Keep in mind that you can avoid this problem by answering No when prompted for permission to use the Cloaked Helix Video BIOS. Answer Yes to this question only if you have a video card that uses the TSENG ET3000 or ET4000 chipset.

Like 386MAX, Netroom does not automatically load the real-mode DoubleSpace compression driver into upper memory. You probably won't notice this under the Windows 95 interface, since a protected-mode compression driver is substituted. However, when you boot to a DOS command prompt, you can free up to 110K of additional conventional memory by adding the following line to CONFIG.SYS:

```
DEVICEHIGH=[D:\]\WINDOWS\DRVSPACE.SYS /MOVE
```

Other Problems with Pre-Win95 Versions

Netroom's STRETCH utility, which allows you to increase conventional memory in DOS sessions up to 736K, is broken in Windows 95 versions earlier than 3.04. For a compatible version that works, check the Helix bulletin board. Additionally, 32-bit access to virtual memory may be disabled in Windows 95 due to an incompatibility in the SYSCLOAK.EXE Cloaking Device in CONFIG.SYS. Again, check the Helix bulletin board for an upgrade module that fixes this problem.

Mike Spilo's Netroom Tips

The following set of Netroom configuration tips was provided courtesy of Helix CEO Mike Spilo:

- *(Undocumented, and extremely controversial.) Your system can be made to operate faster if you change the system idle port. Use a /PORT=EC parameter on the System BIOS Cloaking command line (SYSCLOAK). Back up first, and then test the system out carefully!*
- *(Undocumented.) If you have to use EMS, use the NOLOW setting to eliminate mappable conventional memory. This will speed up many EMS-using programs, and speed up EMS inside Windows.*
- *(Undocumented.) If you can't get all of your TSRs to load high, you may do well adding the EBDALOW parameter to RM386 and recustomizing. This forces the BIOS Data Area low, and may allow a larger TSR to load high. Check Discover's System screen to see if you have an EBDA.*

Mike Spilo's Netroom Tips

- *(Undocumented.) If you are not using the Netroom Cloaked Screen Saver, remove the parameter SYSVMIN2NDBANK=FALSE from your SYSTEM.INI to speed up* ALT-TAB*bing in Windows.*
- *(Undocumented.) Even if you use Windows, don't select "optimize for Windows," as this is frequently wasteful of upper memory. Instead, load the WINMEM TSR to reserve exact amounts of memory.*
- *(Documented, but obscure.) If you are not using either the Video or System BIOS Cloaking, or you have a hard drive or SCSI BIOS in your system, you should add the ROM= (ROM=C000-C7FF, ROM=CC00-CFFF, etc.) parameter to shadow these uncloaked ROMs. Netroom does not shadow uncloaked ROMs automatically–it must be done manually.*
- *(Documented, but obscure.) If you are currently excluding the Monochrome region you can usually create a UMB there and still have it work with Windows (even if this failed with other memory managers) by installing MONOUMB2.386 which is found on the Windows 3.1 disk number 4. Use Custom mode of Netroom's Customize, select Yes to "Create upper memory in Monochrome region," and then insert the lines DEVICE=MONOUMB2.386 and MONOUMBWARNING=OFF in your SYSTEM.INI [386enh] section.*
- *(Documented, but obscure.) You may be able to save 16K of extended memory by specifying NoHighIO on the RM386 command line. (Don't do this on EISA or MCA systems).*
- *(Documented, but obscure.) Use the NOTEST and NOINIT parameters on the DEVICE=RM386.SYS line to speed up your system boot.*

tip *Netroom may add a significant amount of conventional memory to your DOS sessions if you have to load real-mode drivers for networks or peripherals.*

QEMM

Quarterdeck's QEMM has the capacity to provide almost as much upper memory as Helix's Netroom, and in some configurations may actually yield more conventional memory for DOS. The newest version of QEMM, version

8, is Windows 95-aware and resolves some problems you may encounter with earlier versions, described next:

If QEMM version 7.5 or older was running when Windows 95 was installed, then several lines should have been automatically removed from CONFIG.SYS to eliminate incompatibilities. If you are having trouble starting Windows 95 or in running QEMM's OPTIMIZE utility, check to see that the following lines have been removed:

```
DEVICE=[D:]\QEMM\DOSDATA.SYS
DEVICE=[D:]\QEMM\DOS-UP.SYS @[D:]\QEMM\DOS-UP.DAT
DEVICE=[D:]\QEMM\ST-DBL.SYS   (VERSIONS 7.01 TO 7.04 OF QEMM)
DEVICE=[D:]\QEMM\ST-DSPC.SYS  (VERSION 7.5 OF QEMM)
```

This problem has been resolved in QEMM version 8. Users of this later version need not delete the lines just cited.

QEMM version 8 can be installed from within Windows 95 or Windows 3.1, or from the DOS command prompt. If you install under Windows 95, you can select an automatic configuration or enable/disable specific memory-management features from the Tabbed QSETUP interface, shown here:

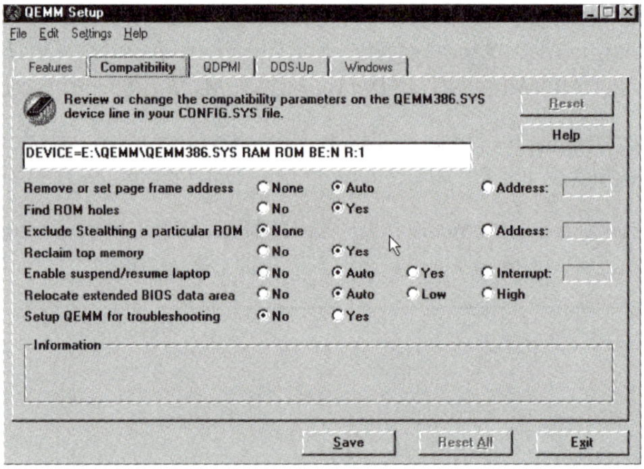

Various installation hints are available from the Hints option on the QSETUP Help menu. (A subset of these installation options will appear if you install QEMM from DOS.) Generally, you can let QEMM select the defaults for your system, with the exception that you may want to turn the QuickBoot restart feature off, since it is unreliable on some systems.

QEMM version 8 also includes a new memory compression feature called MagnaRAM. This is an interesting technological development which Quarterdeck maintains will improve your system's performance by compressing Windows code in RAM and in the swap file, creating more memory and fewer disk accesses. The limited tests that your authors performed with this feature did not yield any Win95 performance gains in actual application tasks. We suggest turning MagnaRAM off, even though your system may report additional memory present when the feature is enabled.

To install QEMM, version 7.5 for the first time on a system running Windows 95, use the F8 boot menu to boot to a DOS command prompt, insert the floppy disk into drive A and run the Install program. If you select Express Install, the QEMM files are automatically placed on drive C. A Custom install lets you choose the drive and directory. After the files have been copied, you'll be asked whether you want to review the installation. At that point, you should make sure that the Stealth D*Space and DOS-UP features have been disabled.

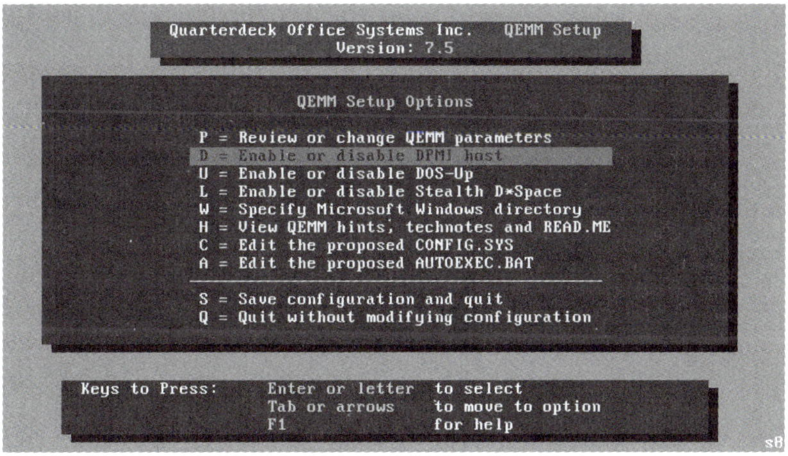

Next you'll be prompted to run the Optimize utility to arrange program loading in CONFIG.SYS and AUTOEXEC.BAT

If you select an Express Install, QEMM's advanced Stealth feature won't be activated, unless more than about 120K of driver code needs to be shoehorned into upper memory. If you select Custom Install, an Options menu lets you decide whether to invoke the Stealth feature, and whether to use the simpler Stealth F (which borrows the EMS page frame for 64K of adapter ROM) or Stealth M (which tries to mask all of the adapter and BIOS ROM on the system.)

In the course of testing for compatibility with Stealth, QEMM and OPTIMIZE may temporarily freeze your system when they reboot it. If this happens to you, flipping the power switch and restarting the boot process will usually allow OPTIMIZE to recover. You can then cancel Stealth testing at a screen prompt by hitting the ESC key. In the long run, it may be easier simply to instruct QEMM not to do any Stealth testing under Windows 95. Let OPTIMIZE place as many drivers as it can into upper memory without

Stealth, and then experiment (as with Microsoft's EMM386.EXE). This can be done by manually editing the CONFIG.SYS on a trial and error basis.

Here's a simple procedure to try that may gain you some Stealth RAM:

1. After QEMM has been installed without Stealth, edit the DEVICE=QEMM386.SYS line in CONFIG.SYS from a DOS command prompt as follows:

   ```
   DEVICE=[D:]\QEMM386.SYS FRAME=C000 ST:F RAM
   ```

   On a wide variety of systems, this simple Stealth option will place the EMS page frame over the location reserved for VGA controller ROM and allow you a continuous UMB block of 160K from address C800h to EFFFh.

   For notebook computers, the video ROM location is usually shifted upward, and you may want to try the following setting instead:

   ```
   DEVICE=[D:\]\QEMM386.SYS FRAME=E000 ST:F RAM
   ```

2. Reboot the system and determine whether Windows 95 will start properly. If it does start properly, then you can reboot to a DOS command prompt and run the OPTIMIZE utility, instructing it to retain the QEMM command line you've created.

QEMM and DoubleSpace/DriveSpace

The ST-DBL.SYS and ST-DSPC.SYS utilities included with QEMM version 7.5 do not work properly with the version of DOS bundled in Windows 95. This problem has been fixed in QEMM version 8. Like the other third-party memory managers, QEMM does not automatically load Microsoft's Win95 DoubleSpace driver into upper memory. Under the Windows 95 interface, this causes no reduction in conventional memory, because a protected-mode compression driver is substituted for the real-mode DOS driver. If you boot to a DOS command prompt from the Win95 boot menu, your conventional memory total may drop by as much as 120K if you are using DoubleSpace/DriveSpace disk compression. To regain this memory, with QEMM versions 7.5 and earlier, insert the following statement into CONFIG.SYS after the line that loads the QEMM386.SYS device driver:

```
DEVICEHIGH=[D:\]\WINDOWS\DRVSPACE.SYS /MOVE
```

You will need to have a sufficient amount of upper memory available between 640K and 1MB to force this driver to load high.

note *If you have upgraded to QEMM version 8, you can use the Quarterdeck driver and enter this command:*

```
DEVICEHIGH=[D:]\QEMM\ST-DSPC.SYS
```

Startup Problems with Stealth

QEMM's Stealth options (similar in function to Netroom's Cloaking) may also cause problems on some systems. But generally, if Stealth worked on your computer under DOS 6.*x*, it should work under Windows 95. If you are having trouble starting up and reaching the Win95 desktop, try booting to a Safe Command prompt (F8 BootMenu, usually Option 7) and manually editing CONFIG.SYS. First try replacing any ST:M parameter on the DEVICE=QEMM386.SYS line with an ST:F parameter. If this doesn't solve the problem, try removing Stealth, entirely, by deleting the ST:M parameter. Another way to remove troublesome QEMM parameters, is to run the QSETUP program found in the QEMM directory and disable DOS-UP, QuickBoot, and Stealth.

QEMM and Dual Boot

If you plan to Dual Boot back to a previous version of DOS that uses QEMM version 7.5 or earlier, you may find that the DOS-UP drivers in the DOS 6 CONFIG.SYS defeat the F4 Dual Boot option. With older versions of QEMM, after you press F4 the first time, DOS 5 or DOS 6 will start to boot, but after processing the DOS-UP statements in CONFIG.SYS, the system will again try to boot into Windows 95. To defeat this bug you have two options. Either press the F4 key twice to make the system continue booting DOS 5 or DOS 6, or remove the DEVICE=DOSDATA.SYS and DEVICE=DOS-UP.SYS statements from the CONFIG.SYS for your previous version of DOS. (When you are working in Windows 95, this file will be renamed in the root directory to CONFIG.DOS.) Note that this problem has been fixed in QEMM version 8, so that none of the Quarterdeck drivers need to be removed.

More About QEMM Stealth

The most common failures of Stealth are due to programs (or other ROMs) trying to access a portion of ROM code directly, rather than by means of an interrupt. When you use Stealth, QEMM takes control of interrupts that are reserved by the ROMs on your system. Pointers are set up to redirect these interrupts back to QEMM.

After QEMM is installed, the Optimize utility examines your system to determine which of the two Stealth modes may be supported on your hardware:

Stealth M (M = Mapping)

QEMM relocates as many ROMs as possible out of upper memory: including System BIOS, video memory, and disk adapter ROM. These ROMs are mapped out of the first megabyte, yielding 150K to 220K of usable UMB address space.

The Optimize utility in QEMM versions 7.5 and 8 performs a much more thorough test of your system than previous versions to determine whether it can implement Stealth M.

Stealth F (F= Frame)

QEMM leaves the system, video, and disk ROMs at their original addresses, but picks a 64K area that may contain a ROM and places the EMS page frame on top of it. Expanded Memory can then be mapped into the address range even though it is also reserved for peripheral ROM. (When the ROM services hidden by the page frame are requested, QEMM maps the code back into the page frame.) Under Stealth F, ROM address space can't be used to load programs high. Only the ROM code in the area under the EMS page frame is relocated. (Typically this will yield 96K to 140K of upper memory. Video or disk adapter ROM is masked, but not the system BIOS.)

All versions of QEMM since 7.0 have included a series of command-line parameters that provide various levels of exclusion and protection for specific UMB regions and DOS interrupts. In versions 7.5 and 8, if you choose the advanced install, Optimize will systematically reboot the system many times, including and excluding selected regions. If the system hangs during one of these tests, hitting the reset button allows it to automatically continue on the next reboot, trying another memory combination.

tip *QEMM is perhaps the most flexible, all-purpose memory management tool currently available for systems running Windows- and DOS-based software. The bundled VIDRAM feature that allows you to create 736K DOS sessions under Windows remains intact under Windows 95. The small amount of upper memory lost by disabling the DOS-UP feature can be regained by substituting FILESHIGH, BUFFERSHIGH and so on for the conventional FILES, BUFFERS, etc. statements in CONFIG.SYS.*

What About Stacker?

So far, in our discussion of CONFIG.SYS and DOS memory managers, we've said nothing about Stac Electronics' Stacker disk compression package. This is because the migration of Stacker compression from previous versions of DOS to Windows 95 is fairly transparent. You should have no difficulty installing Windows 95 on drives that have been compressed with Stacker 3.1 or Stacker 4.*x* for DOS, Windows or OS/2. All of your programs and operating system features will also work transparently, with the following caveats:

- You cannot place a Windows 95 swap file on a partition compressed with Stacker. The swap file must reside on an uncompressed partition. (Microsoft's DoubleSpace/DriveSpace alternative does allow you to store the swap file on compressed partitions, but you probably don't want to do it, since this will slow down performance.)
- The Windows 95 ScanDisk utility can correct file errors on a Stacker drive, but will not correct compression errors. To correct low-level compression errors, you need to run the repair utilities included with the Stacker package. This may result in the corruption of Win95 long filenames. See Chapter 7 for information on how to use the Win95 LFNBK utility to preserve long filenames with older DOS disk utilities.
- The Win95 Defrag utility will not work on drives compressed with Stacker versions 4.1 and earlier. To defragment these drives, you will have to use the internal utility supplied with the Stacker package. With Stacker versions 4.0 and earlier, this can result in the corruption of Win95 long filenames. See Chapter 7 for information on how to use the Win95 LFNBK utility to preserve long filenames with older DOS disk utilities. The most recent version of Stacker (4.1) includes support for Win95 long filenames, and a proprietary defragmenting utility that will preserve them.
- Drives compressed with Stacker 4.1 and earlier rely on real-mode compression drivers, forcing Windows 95 to access compressed partitions in MS-DOS compatibility mode rather than using the faster 32-bit file access. This does cause a degradation in hard disk access time. In our experience, the degradation is not very

significant on faster DX4 and Pentium machines equipped with a fast VESA or PCI bus or Fast-SCSI disk controllers. It may be more noticeable on older systems with slower hardware. Stacker 4.1, although still a 16-bit real-mode compression technology, is faster than previous versions, although not as fast as Microsoft's 32-bit DriveSpace.

Migrating Stacker to Windows 95

Generally, CONFIG.SYS settings from previous versions of DOS should be left untouched. With Stacker 4.*x*, the DPMS.EXE, and STACHIGH.SYS drivers should remain in CONFIG.SYS. Note that if you were running Stacker in conjunction with Helix's MultiMedia Cloaked Utilities under your previous version of DOS, Helix's CLOAKING.EXE driver was probably loaded in CONFIG.SYS instead of DPMS.EXE. Windows 95 removes CLOAKING.EXE during installation, but does not automatically install the DPMS.EXE driver. Check your Win95 CONFIG.SYS file if you are running Stacker 4.0 or 4.1 and make sure that this line is present:

```
DEVICE=[D:]\STACKER\DPMS.EXE
```

How to (Sometimes) Regain Win95's 32-Bit File Access and 32-Bit Virtual Memory

Real-mode drivers in CONFIG.SYS that are unrecognized by Windows 95 sometimes force the system to switch from 32-bit file access and virtual memory into 16-bit MS-DOS compatibility mode. You can find out whether any drivers in your configuration have this effect by opening the System object on the Control Panel and inspecting the Performance tab.

Usually, this more generic disk and file access is invoked as a safety measure to protect you against corrupted data and system crashes. Sometimes, however, a driver in CONFIG.SYS may cause an unnecessary switch to MS-DOS compatibility mode. Windows 95 maintains a list of so-called "safe" drivers that will not interfere with its 32-bit functions. (The real-mode compression drivers for Stacker are, unfortunately, definitely unsafe.) Examples of device drivers that may inadvertently force Windows 95 into compatibility mode are unrecognized SCSI or CD-ROM drivers, PCMCIA drivers, notebook power management utilities, network utilities, or fax drivers. Windows 95 maintains a list of known safe and unsafe real-mode device drivers called IOS.INI. This is an ASCII text file located in your WINDOWS directory.

If you discover that your system has been forced into MS-DOS compatibility mode, you may consider examining your CONFIG.SYS for drivers that fall into one of the categories just listed. If your device drivers are not included in IOS.INI, you may experiment with adding them to the "safe list." (Do not try this with disk compression drivers, VESA and PCI disk controller drivers, or DOS disk cache utilities.) After your drivers are added to the "safe list," Windows 95 will attempt to run with them in the faster, 32-bit access mode. If everything works, you can continue to run Windows 95 in 32-bit mode. If you experience unusual system quirks or problems, then remove your real-mode drivers from the IOS.INI safe list and drop back to MS-DOS compatibility mode.

Eventually, you should be able to obtain protected-mode drivers from third-party manufacturers or Microsoft for most of your peripheral devices. At least that's the theory. Talk to a Windows NT user, sometime, if you want to check out how well this works out in actuality.

Managing Memory from the Win95 Desktop

Having completed our survey of issues related to DOS, CONFIG.SYS, and AUTOEXEC.BAT, let's return to the Windows 95 desktop for a few final notes about Windows 95 memory that you should know.

The Win95 Swap File

The best way to ensure high swap file performance is to make sure that the disk containing the swap file has ample free space so that the swap file size can shrink and grow as needed.

The Windows 95 swap file (WIN386.SWP) is not a permanent file. By default, it will dynamically shrink and grow in response to system requests for virtual memory. Windows 95 can also use a permanent Windows 3.1 swap file. In this case, the file can't shrink below the permanent size set for it in Windows 3.1, although the file can grow bigger if required.

Under Windows 95, the swap file can reside on a compressed drive if a protected-mode driver (such as DRVSPACE.VXD) controls the compressed drive. DriveSpace marks the swap file as incompressible and places it as the last file in the sector heap. (This allows room for the swap file to grow.)

Although Microsoft advises that you keep the system defaults for the swap file, you can adjust the parameters used to define the swap file, and you can override its default location and size. A good strategy is to place the swap file on the drive or partition with the fastest performance (unless that disk is overused).

Microsoft warns that completely disabling virtual memory might cause the computer to stop operating properly.

To adjust the virtual memory swap file, follow these steps:

1. In the Control Panel's System object, click the Performance tab.
2. Click the Virtual Memory button (see Figure 6-3).
3. To specify a different partition, click Let Me Specify My Own Virtual Memory Settings. Then specify the new drive letter in the Hard Disk box. Or, type values (in kilobytes) in the Minimum or Maximum boxes. Finally, click OK.

If the maximum swap file size in the Virtual Memory dialog box is set to correspond to the total amount of free space available on a drive, Windows 95 may expand the swap file beyond that size if more free disk space becomes available. If you want to set a fixed limit on the swap file size, make sure that the limit you specify is less than the current maximum.

MS-DOS Mode vs. Virtual DOS Sessions

Most DOS applications should be able to run in virtual sessions under Windows 95. However, to accommodate ill-behaved programs and games that have problems, Windows 95 allows you to launch a true MS-DOS mode

FIGURE 6-3 Windows 95 virtual memory settings

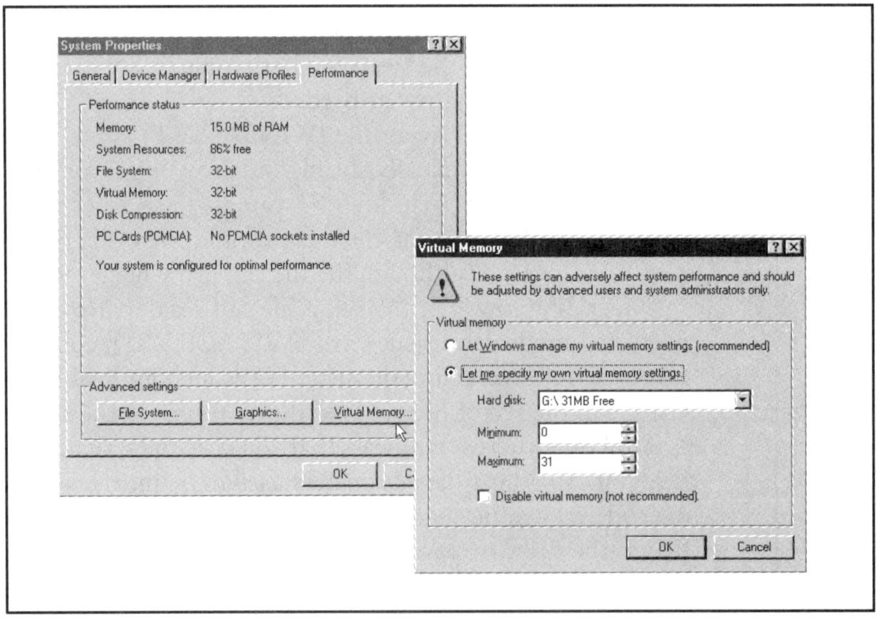

session from the desktop. Any DOS application or Shortcut to an application can be set to run in MS-DOS mode by opening its Properties menu after right-clicking to bring up the context menu. Select the Programs tab under Properties, and click the Advanced button. If you place a checkmark in the MS-DOS mode option box, three additional memory options appear. By default, when an application opens in MS-DOS mode, it uses the settings and drivers that were loaded in the original Windows 95 CONFIG.SYS. If your application requires a unique set of device drivers or TSRs, you can create a new CONFIG.SYS and AUTOEXEC.BAT for it. When an application initiates MS-DOS mode, all existing Windows utilities, applications, and desktop windows are closed. If you have information stored on a RAMdisk, the RAMdisk is preserved.

If you open an MS-DOS mode application checkmarked to "use current configuration," a special AUTOEXEC-like batch file is run before the command prompt opens. If you have a CD-ROM drive on your system, DOSSTART.BAT (located in the WINDOWS directory), will usually attempt to load MSCDEX.EXE. This command will only be successful if a real-mode CD-ROM driver was loaded in the CONFIG.SYS that originally started Windows 95. To access your CD-ROM device from the MS-DOS mode application, you will have to do one of the following:

- Reinsert real-mode SCSI or proprietary CD-ROM drivers in the CONFIG.SYS used to start Windows 95 and select "use current DOS configuration."
- Check the Specify a New MS-DOS Configuration box in the Advanced Program Options, and create new CONFIG.SYS and AUTOEXEC.BAT files that load your real-mode CD-ROM drivers. (See Figure 6-4, and refer to Chapter 7 for more details on configuring custom startup files.)

If you elect to "use current DOS configuration," you can edit DOSSTART.BAT with a text editor to add commands (such as a new PATH statement), or delete extraneous commands.

Memory Managers of the Future

As we outlined at the beginning of this chapter, Windows 95 makes a number of enhancements to Windows 3.1 in its memory management techniques. However, there's still room for improvement. Microsoft did not include rock-steady memory protection for 16-bit applications in this first release,

FIGURE 6-4

AUTOEXEC.BAT and CONFIG.SYS files customized to load real-mode SCI and CD-ROM drivers in an MS-DOS mode session

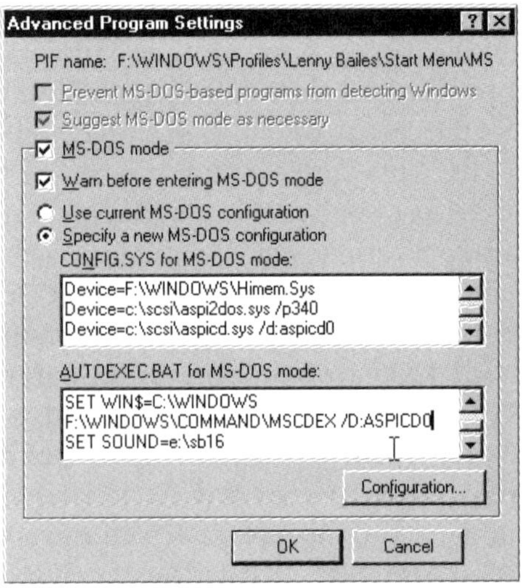

and even 32-bit applications are not completely shielded from the operating system or each other.

Helix Software and Quarterdeck Office Systems, the manufacturers of some of the memory managers discussed in this chapter, are hard at work on a new generation of products that addresses some of the things that Microsoft left out.

Helix already distributes a Windows 3.1 package called Hurricane that addresses some of these issues. The Windows 95 version of Hurricane will increase the system resources available in Windows 95, in much the same way that the older version (and Connectix Software's Ram Doubler) do in Windows 3.1 Additionally, you can expect new memory protection and memory compression techniques that allow your RAM under Windows 95 to be used more effectively.

chapter 7

In with the Old: Running DOS and Windows 3.1 Applications

- Taking stock of your software
- General migration strategies
- Working with Windows 3.*x* applications
- Backup strategies
    - Preserving long filenames
- Running DOS applications under Windows 95

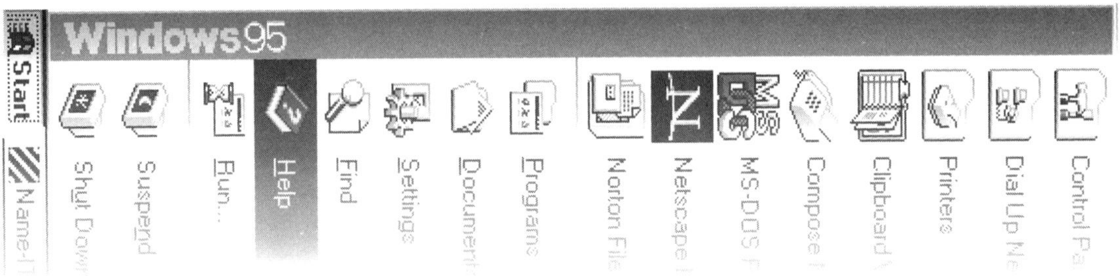

MANY applications designed specifically for Windows 95 have still yet to arrive. In the meantime, most of us are well stocked on Windows 3.1 and DOS programs. The question you face as a Windows 95 user is, "What kind of mileage can I get out of my current assortment of software?" This chapter provides an overview of application compatibility. This overview can help you decide which programs must be upgraded, which ones can be seamlessly integrated into your new working environment, and which ones can be used as stopgaps till something better comes along.

Taking Stock

Will your Windows 3.1 and DOS applications run better under Windows 95, suffer performance problems, or not run at all? The quick answer is that most of your productivity applications should run under Windows 95 with little or no difficulty. Utility programs, however, may be more problematic. If Windows 95 has enough memory and hard disk space to keep it happy, you should see no performance degradation. Some applications, tweaked for performance under Windows 3.1 may show minor display glitches in menus under Windows 95. Others may produce general protection faults when you invoke certain features. A small number of Windows 3.1 productivity applications are completely incompatible. A file called PROGRAM.TXT, located in your WINDOWS directory, provides some basic information about migrating and using some older programs.

Microsoft also maintains a software compatibility report for more than 2000 Windows 3.*x* and DOS applications (see Figure 7-1). You can download this report from CompuServe, the World Wide Web at HTTP://WWW.MICROSOFT.COM/WINDOWS/SUPPORT/MIGRATION, or via the Internet FTP at FTP.MICROSOFT.COM/PRODUCTS/WINDOWS/WINDOWS95. The list is compiled in the standard Windows Help format. To inspect the database under Windows 95, open the WIN95APP.HLP file from the Run menu on the Start button. (If you're browsing for the file, set the Browse option to display all files.)

Of the listed applications, approximately 200 entries have notations indicating minor or major problems with Windows 95. Some of the entries in the database also contain notes on how to fix specific problems. The good news is that you won't have to worry about many of your programs. In fact, you may find that Windows 95 enhances their appearance or productivity features. If you've installed Microsoft Exchange, other applications from Microsoft will have two new options on the File menu, Send and Routing Slip. These options are equivalent to what you would see running Microsoft Mail under Windows 3.1 or Windows for Workgroups.

General Migration Strategies

Perhaps the most visible difference in your applications is the new support for long filenames. However, applications not written for the 32-bit Win95 API do not recognize these long filenames. These programs can identify files only by their conventional 8.3 letter DOS filenames. If you don't have a requirement to save data files with long filenames, this is not a critical

FIGURE 7-1

The Windows 95 software compatibility report

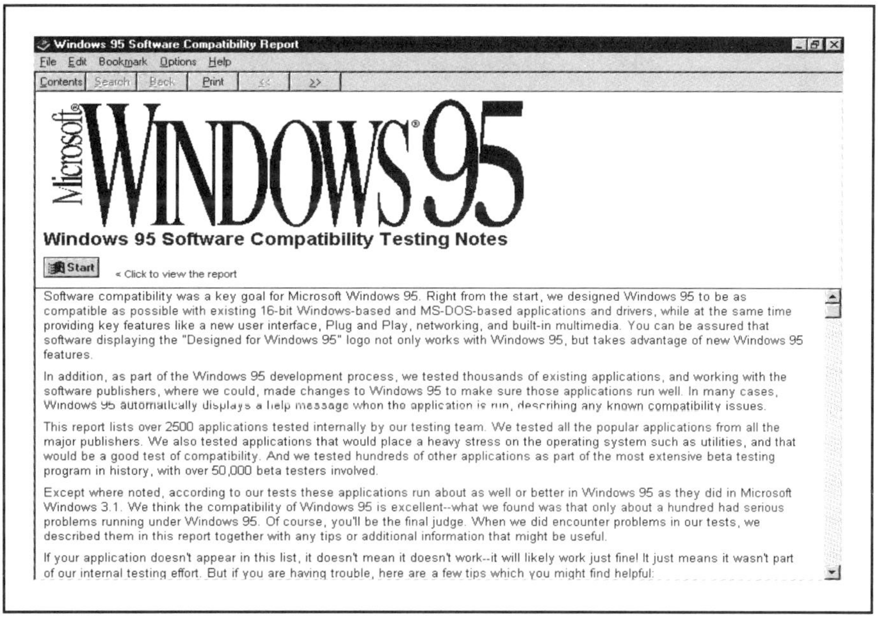

limitation (you can simply choose not to use them). But long filenames may occasionally cause problems when they are linked to automated procedures. For instance, suppose that you log on to the Microsoft Network Online Service and download information prepared in the 32-bit environment. When a data file reaches your hard disk, it may be associated with Windows 3.*x* programs (and their file viewers). If Microsoft Excel version 5 or Word 6.0 attempts to automatically load the file you've just downloaded, it won't recognize the long filename. As a result, the load process will abort with an error message.

One way to get around this problem with Word documents is to change the default association for files with the .RTF or .DOC extension from Word 6.0 to WordPad. (See Chapter 4 for details on how to do this.) Another solution is to use a third-party utility like Vertisoft's Name-It, which adds the capability to recognize long filenames to Windows 3.*x* programs. (See Chapter 14 for more information on Name-It.) Ultimately, the best solution is to upgrade to Windows 95 versions of the programs used most frequently to display and manipulate common data formats.

If you installed Windows 95 as an upgrade over a previous version of Windows, your existing applications were automatically migrated to the new operating system. Setting the issue of long filenames aside, most problems you're likely to encounter will stem from individual idiosyncrasies of a small group of programs.

Tips for Resolving Common Conflicts

If you experience general difficulty with Win 3.*x* applications after an upgrade installation, read the various .TXT files placed in your WINDOWS directory (especially PROGRAM.TXT). Open these files in Notepad or WordPad and try performing a text search for your problem application's name.

Another good strategy is to obtain a copy of the Microsoft software compatibility report, discussed earlier. Check this report to see whether your program is listed or specific problems are identified.

If you still can't identify or resolve your problem, you may want to try one of the two following strategies:

1. Back up your data files, and make backups of Win95's WIN.INI and SYSTEM.INI files. Delete the problem application from your hard disk and remove references to it in the Start Menu. Reinstall the program from your original source disks. Note that your program may attempt to replace some of Windows 95's drivers and dynamic link libraries (DLLs) with older versions. In general,

do not allow this to happen—if you're offered a choice, keep your existing Win95 drivers. Windows 95 has a partial ability to detect driver substitution and restore files from the SYSBCKUP directory. (For more details, see the sidebar, "Restoring Accidentally Overwritten Windows 95 Drivers," later in this chapter.)

2. If your problem application is vital to you, and reinstalling it doesn't cure performance problems, consider reinstalling the entire Win95 operating system in a clean directory. An upgrade over Windows 3.1 can carry over many virtual driver extensions, configuration settings, and DLLs from third-party vendors. These may conflict with one another, causing general protection faults (GPFs) and system crashes. If you experience apparently unrelated performance problems with Windows 95, a clean installation may be your best option. If you decide to take this course, you will have to reinstall all of your third-party applications from their source media or use a special third-party package like Vertisoft's Remove-It, or Quarterdeck's Clean Sweep. Remove-It and Clean Sweep for Windows 95 can take snapshots of an existing Windows configuration and transfer application information to a new, clean installation. (See Chapter 2 for more details on transferring Windows 3.1 or Windows 95 system configurations.)

A small number of Windows 3.*x* programs will not install properly under Windows 95, but they can be migrated from an existing Windows 3.*x* configuration. The Microsoft WIN95APP.HLP database flags programs that have this problem.

DOS Applications

If a DOS application doesn't work properly under Windows 95, try creating a shortcut for it, instead of launching it from a command prompt. Select File\New in My Computer or open the Start Menu to Settings\Taskbar, then click the Add button on the Start Menu tab. (See Chapter 4 for more details on adding new programs and creating shortcuts.) Windows 95 contains a special migration database of DOS applications and program settings. If the filename for your application is recognized, a shortcut may be created that resolves the performance problem. Some DOS programs (mostly disk utilities, multimedia applications, and games) will not run in ordinary Win95 DOS sessions. For these programs, you may have to either restart the system in MS-DOS mode or create custom CONFIG.SYS and

AUTOEXEC.BAT files. See the section, "Running DOS Applications Under Windows 95" later in this chapter for detailed information on how to do this and other tips on DOS program configuration.

Working with Windows 3.x Applications

Windows 95 migration issues are most likely to center around utility software: disk utilities, antivirus packages, backup programs and Windows command shells. But before we discuss these, here are a few quick notes concerning some popular productivity programs.

WordPerfect and WordPerfect Presentations

If you are a user of Novell's WordPerfect 6.0 or 6.0a for Windows, you may have difficulty pasting in text or graphics from 32-bit Win95 applications (including MS Paint and WordPad). The quick fix for this is to perform an interim copy and paste from the 32-bit application to a compatible 16-bit program (possibly Windows Write from Windows 3.*x*). Then paste from there into WordPerfect.

note *The WordPerfect 6.0 tutorial also stalls under Windows 95. In WordPerfect 6.1, the Introductory Tutorial (Coach) may not work correctly.*

WordPerfect Presentations 2.0 for Windows will not install correctly under Windows 95. However, it can be migrated from an existing Windows 3.1 configuration.

Lotus Ami Pro and Notes

Ami Pro 3.01, a Windows word processor, has a tutorial that does not run correctly under Windows 95. The problem can be corrected by setting the Windows 95 taskbar to AutoHide. (Right-click the taskbar with the mouse and select Properties, then place a checkmark in the AutoHide box.)

Lotus Notes cannot be installed from a network computer, unless a drive letter is mapped as follows:

1. Click the Start button, select Programs, and open the Windows Explorer.
2. On the Tools menu, click Map Network Drive.

3. In the Path box, type the path to the network server and click OK.
4. Click the drive you just mapped and find the Notes setup program.

When running Lotus Notes Windows Client, version 3.2, workstations running the NetBIOS interface over IPX and NetBEUI protocol stacks must configure the port for NetBIOS using the unit number that corresponds to the correct protocol. The default number for the first NetBIOS protocol is set to 0. Any additional NetBIOS interface will start at Port 7 through 1. It's likely that NetBIOS will be unit number 7 or 6 if NetBEUI is using 0. To make changes in Notes Windows Client, select the Tools menu, click Setup, and select Ports.

Aldus PageMaker

Aldus PageMaker 5.0 or 6.0 may refuse to start under Windows 95 if you've installed Novell network support and are not currently logged into the network. This is a copy-protection problem inherent in PageMaker. To make the "Unable to access network" error message go away on an unconnected workstation, either log on to the network or open the network configuration component on the Control Panel and remove the IPX protocol from the component list, as shown in Figure 7-2. (This problem apparently

FIGURE 7-2

To get rid of this error message in PageMaker or Quark Xpress, either log on to your Novell network, or delete the IPX protocol driver through the Control Panel.

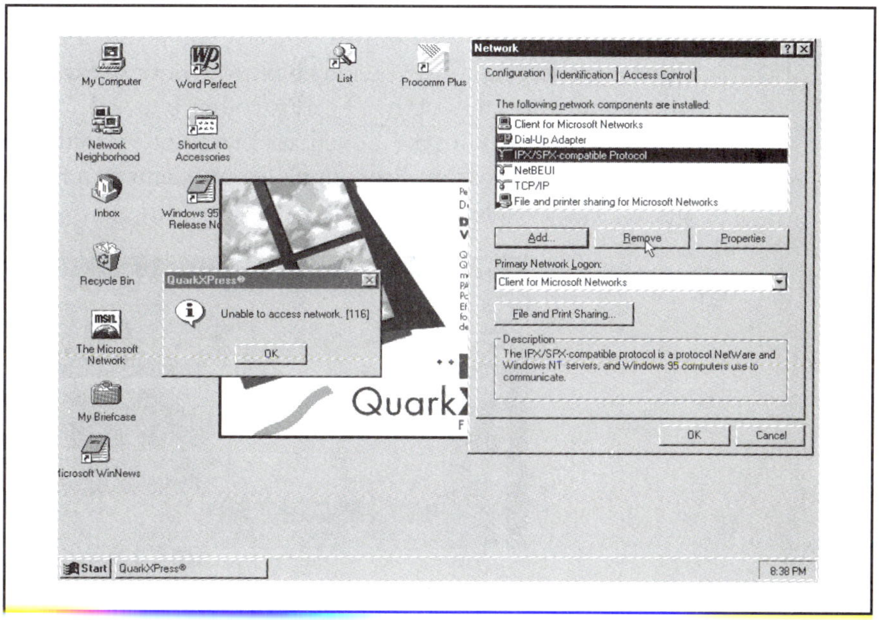

does not surface in Microsoft Network configurations using TCP/IP or NetBEUI protocols.)

Quark Xpress

Quark Xpress version 3.31 has the same network problem that PageMaker has. Quark Xpress versions 3.30 and earlier are totally incompatible with Windows 95. A patch can be obtained from Quark to update version 3.30 to version 3.31, which will run under Windows 95.

Other Applications

You may have difficulty installing certain Windows 3.*x* games and multimedia programs under Windows 95. New versions of these (as well as productivity apps that have the same problem) should be forthcoming, soon. Some of these packages will work under Windows 95, provided that they've been migrated from an existing Windows 3.*x* configuration. Before upgrading to Windows 95, you may want to download and browse the Microsoft software compatibility report referred to earlier in this chapter. It can be viewed in Windows 3.*x* as well as under Windows 95. If some of your applications are marked as "won't install but will migrate," set them up under Windows 3.*x* before upgrading to Windows 95.

Telecommunications applications written for DOS and Windows 3.*x* maintain modem and communication profiles independent of the modem settings on the Win 95 Control Panel. If you install a package that includes third-party fax support, you may have to reboot the system once, before the fax support becomes active. For Procomm Plus 2.1 for Windows, the Fax Printer object cannot be added to the Printers folder unless you select Auto-Answer\Fax from Procomm's Setup menu to activate its internal fax driver, as shown here:

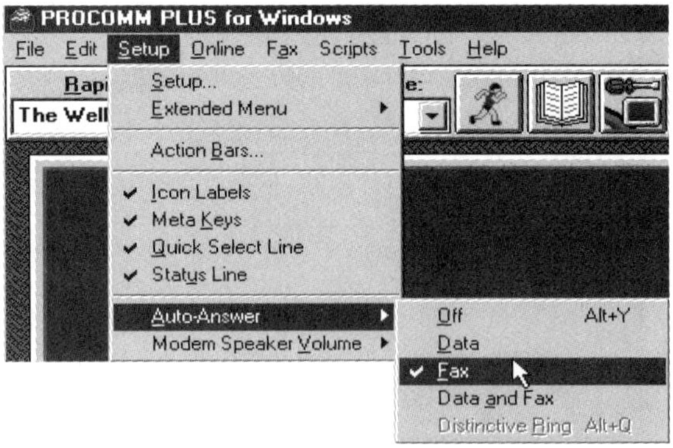

Once the Procomm fax printer has been added to the PRINTERS folder, you can turn this option off.

Working with Windows 3.x Utility Software

The best solution for working with Windows 3.*x* file managers, backup programs and antivirus utilities is to upgrade to versions specifically written for Windows 95. Chapter 14 of this book provides a survey of new third-party utility packages for Windows 95. In the interim, some DOS and Windows 3.*x* utilities can be used as stopgaps. The most problematical aspect of working with Windows 3.*x* file management and backup programs is their lack of support for long filenames. Using these older utilities can wipe out any long filenames you've created under Windows 95. Microsoft does provide a partial remedy for this problem with the LFNBK.EXE program (*LFNBK* stands for *long filename backup*) located in the ADMIN\APPTOOLS\LFNBACK directory of your Windows 95 CD. (Users with the floppy disk version of Win95 will have to download this utility from the Microsoft bulletin board or FTP site.) LFNBK is not guaranteed by Microsoft to preserve your long filenames, but it will do so in certain controlled situations that we discuss in this chapter.

The case for using older disk maintenance and antivirus utilities is even weaker. The official position of Symantec, Inc., for instance, is that using pre-Windows 95 versions of Norton Disk Doctor or Speed Disk is likely to aggravate hard disk problems rather than cure them.

Disk compression with Stac Electronics' Stacker is another touchy area. Many users will want to convert their Stacker compressed volumes to Windows 95's DriveSpace 2 format or the DriveSpace 3 format offered in Microsoft Plus!. Windows 95 does not offer an automatic procedure for this. Some users of Stacker will want to retain their old compression system because of its dual compatibility between Windows/DOS and Warp OS/2. Microsoft's disk repair and defragmenting utilities bundled with Windows 95 offer only partial support for Stacker compressed volumes. Utilities written to manage Stacker compression under older versions of DOS may be unreliable, or may not run at all under Windows 95.

In the long run you'll save yourself time and trouble by purchasing Windows 95-specific utilities to deal with system maintenance issues. In the meantime, here are some workarounds to provide stopgap solutions with pre-Windows 95 software.

Backup Programs

If your backup media and tape drive are supported by the Microsoft Backup utility in Windows 95, you should probably use it, rather than older third-party packages. Unfortunately, this is not an option for users with SCSI tape drives and other unsupported backup devices. Some Windows 3.*x* and DOS backup programs remain functional under Windows 95, with the exception that they will not record and restore long filenames. Other backup programs are partially or completely incompatible. You may need to consult the manufacturer for details on your particular software or refer to the Microsoft application compatibility list discussed earlier.

Colorado Backup for Windows (see Figure 7-3) and Norton Backup for Windows should be functional under Windows 95, except for the preservation of long filenames. The majority of DOS backup utilities will run only in MS-DOS mode. Norton Backup 2.0 for DOS is an exception that can actually run in a windowed session under the Windows 95 interface. Colorado Software has also recently issued a Windows 95 upgrade of its software that can be downloaded from the Colorado bulletin board and Web page. The new Colorado program is essentially a clone of the Microsoft Backup utility included in Windows 95. It is slightly less powerful than the

FIGURE 7-3

Colorado Backup for Windows 3.1 is functional under Windows 95, except for the ability to record and preserve long filenames.

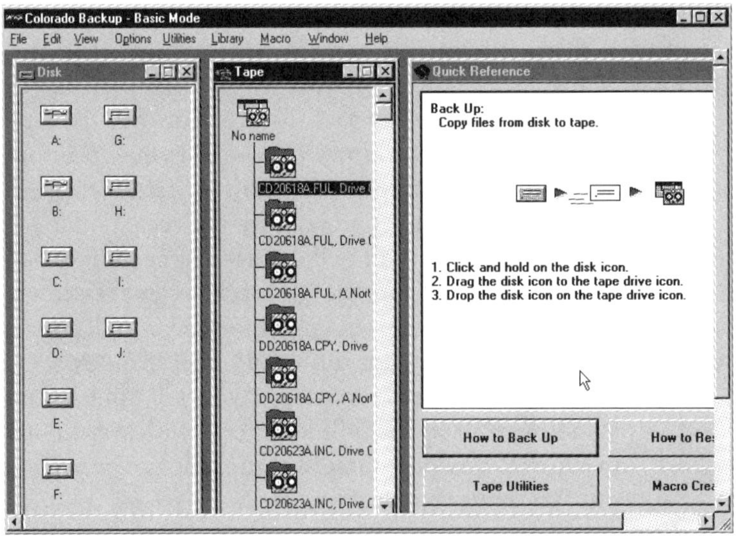

older Windows 3.*x* Colorado Backup, but it does include support for Windows 95 long filenames.

One partial solution to this problem is to establish a dual-boot configuration on your hard drive. To perform backups with older utilities, dual-boot to your previous operating system and run the backup utility from there. However, you should remember that this procedure won't preserve your Windows 95 long filenames. The LFNBK utility discussed below can solve this problem, but it isn't guaranteed by Microsoft! A prudent strategy might be to use your older backup programs to archive data directories and files not located on your Windows 95 boot drive. If you go through several iterations of backup and restore and find that LFNBK successfully preserves long filenames, then use the procedure on your boot drive, as well.

Preserving Long Filenames with LFNBK

The LFNBK utility can be used to temporarily remove all of the long filenames assigned to any hard disk partition, preserving these names in a binary data file. You can then run DOS or Windows 3.*x* backup programs, disk optimizers, and antivirus utilities on the selected partition. When the disk maintenance has been completed, you can run LFNBK again to restore the long filenames. However, there are a few limitations to this quick fix:

- Long filenames are not restored for files that are renamed, moved to different drives or directories, or stored in a renamed directory.
- LFNBK must remove and restore all long filenames on a selected partition; you can't do a partial backup and restore for specific directories.
- LFNBK might not always restore exact matches to long-filename aliases, and the related alias for individual files is not guaranteed to be the same as before running LFNBK.

One common instance when you might want to use LFNBK is to create a tape backup archive of all the files on a particular drive with a DOS or Windows 3.*x* backup utility. To do this, you would use the following procedure:

1. Turn off the Win95 feature that preserves long filenames for old programs. To do so, open the System object on the Control Panel,

click the Performance tab, and then click File System. In the File System Performance dialog box, click the Troubleshooting tab, and check the option named Disable Long Name Preservation for Old Programs.

2. Close all open applications and folders for the partition you want to back up. LFNBK cannot rename open files.
3. Copy the LFNBK.EXE utility from the ADMIN\APPTOOLS\LFNBACK directory on your Windows 95 Installation CD to the WINDOWS\COMMAND directory on your hard drive. Open a DOS command prompt and enter

   ```
   LFNBK /B [D:]
   ```

   to back up and remove long filenames, where [*D*:] is a selected drive or disk partition.
4. Restart the computer, and run your backup utility. Be sure to back up the LFNBK.DAT file that was placed in the root directory of the partition you're working on.
5. Turn long filename preservation on again, and then restart the computer.
6. Open a DOS command prompt and enter

   ```
   LFNBK /R [D:]
   ```

   to restore long filenames for drive [*D*:]

The LFNBK utility actually renames each file with a long filename to its associated alias. The filename changes are stored in the LFNBK.DAT file in the root of the drive where you are running LFNBK. This file is used to restore long filenames (when you run LFNBK with the /R switch).

note *If you run LFNBK on your Windows 95 host drive and then restart Windows 95, the default Start Menu will appear, rather than your custom Start Menu. After you run* ***LFNBK /R*** *to restore long filenames, your custom Start Menu will also be restored.*

Here is the syntax for LFNBK, followed by a complete list of its command line parameters:

LFNBK [/V] [/B | /R | /PE] [/NT] [/FORCE] [/P] [*drive*]

Parameter	Description
/V	Reports actions on the screen.
/B	Backs up and removes long filenames on the disk.
/R	Restores previously backed-up long filenames.
/PE	Extracts errors from backup database.
/NT	Does not restore backup dates and times.
/FORCE	Forces LFNBK to run, even in unsafe conditions.
/P	Finds long filenames, but does not convert them to 8.3 filename aliases. This reports the existing long filenames, along with the associated dates for file creation, last access, and last modification of the file.

File Managers

Packages like XTree Gold, Norton Desktop for Windows 3.0, PC Tools for Windows 2.0, and so on share the same limitation as the traditional Microsoft File Manager bundled in Windows 95. If you use them to create directories, rename, move, or copy files, any associated long filenames are not preserved. Unfortunately, the LFNBK utility is no help here, because it won't restore long filenames to files that have been relocated. The only real solution to Windows 95 file management is to use a Win95-specific utility that supports long filenames, or else not use long filenames at all.

Antivirus Programs

Pre-Windows 95 antivirus utilities may refuse to run at all under the Windows 95 interface. If they do run, they may be unable to distinguish between a virus and a simple difference in the operating system. If you suspect that a virus is loose on your system and you have no Win95-specific antivirus software, you can dual boot to a previous version of DOS, or boot from a floppy disk to a DOS command prompt. Antivirus utilities written for DOS 6.*x* and Windows 3.*x* may then be able to scan your system and detect the presence of a virus, but you should probably not use these utilities to disinfect your hard disk. Instead, obtain a Windows 95-specific antiviral package and use it for disinfection.

Disk Utilities

Disk Repair and defragmenting utilities written for Windows 3.*x* and DOS should not be run under Windows 95. In an emergency, you may be able to dual-boot to a previous version of DOS, or boot a DOS floppy that corresponds to a recovery utility. This may allow you to perform emergency disk maintenance, restore partitions, or repair damaged directories, but you will probably lose any Windows 95 long filenames and may find yourself unable to restart Windows 95 after such an operation. Symantec, Inc. has a new version of the Norton Utilities for Windows 95 that eliminates these problems and offers additional new features. See Chapter 14 for details.

Users of Stacker disk compression software should either convert their compressed volumes to DriveSpace or upgrade to Stacker, version 4.1, which supports long filenames.

tip *Although the Microsoft Defrag utility bundled with Windows 95 will not operate on Stacker volumes, the Windows 95 ScanDisk utility can be used to repair some FAT-related problems on Stacker volumes. If the Stacker volume has a compression problem, you will have to boot to a DOS command prompt, or restart the system in MS-DOS mode to run the repair utilities bundled with Stacker.*

Windows 95 has no built-in method to convert a Stacker compressed volume to the DriveSpace format. If you desire to do this, you should decompress the volume with Stacker's own utilities, or simply back up all the files on the compressed partition, remove the Stacker compression and restore the files from your backup.

tip *Although Windows 95 doesn't have a Stacker conversion utility, Microsoft provided one with DOS 6.x. This utility, available from Microsoft upon request, automatically changes Stacker volumes to the old DoubleSpace format. If you have a copy of this utility and wish to convert from Stacker to DriveSpace, run the conversion from MS DOS 6.x before installing Windows 95. There are no compatibility problems between Windows 95 and Stacker 4.0 with respect to storing files with conventional DOS filenames or running applications. Both Stacker 4.0 and the new Stacker 4.1 may still offer better compression ratios than DriveSpace. And the utilities bundled with the Stacker 4.1 upgrade are designed to recognize and preserve Windows 95 long filenames.*

Third-Party Font Managers

Recent versions of Adobe Type Manager 3.*x* and other font management packages such as Ares FontMinder and Font Chameleon are compatible with Windows 95. (See Chapter 9 for details.) Under the new operating system, the font information these programs write to the WIN.INI file is automatically transferred to the Windows 95 Registration Database. By default, Windows 95 stores TrueType fonts in the WINDOWS\FONTS directory instead of in the WINDOWS\SYSTEM directory, but the operating system is backwardly compatible. If you install a Windows 3.*x* application that places fonts in the old location, they will still be recognized and configured properly under Windows 95. (For more information about font management and printing, see Chapter 9.)

The WIN.INI and SYSTEM.INI Files

Under Windows 95, the WIN.INI and SYSTEM.INI files play a much less significant role than under previous versions of Windows. Most of the internal information that Windows, itself, used to write to these files is now automatically transferred to the Windows 95 System Registry. The two files remain in the WINDOWS directory in order to retain configuration information that is still necessary for some Windows 3.*x* applications.

note *All parameters for controlling mouse performance, keyboard performance, and screen and window display parameters have been removed from WIN.INI. These settings are now modified through the configuration tools on the Win95 Control Panel.*

Restoring Accidentally Overwritten Windows 95 Drivers

Some Windows 3.x programs include installation routines that copy their own DLLs and drivers into the WINDOWS\SYSTEM directory. Manufacturers are supposed to prevent more recent files from being overwritten by checking the internal version numbers of drivers as well as the file dates. Some programs check both, some do neither. If the wrong DLLs are placed in the SYSTEM directory, individual applications may generate GPF errors, or Windows 95 may even refuse to start. A partial recovery mechanism is built into the system to allow the recovery of overwritten DLLs. At boot time, if substituted drivers are detected, Windows 95 may notify you and ask for permission to restore its internal files. A set of drivers is stored in the WINDOWS\SYSBCKUP directory.

If a missing driver is not present in the backup directory, you may have to restore it manually from the Windows 95 installation media. Most of the installation drivers are stored in compressed Microsoft archives called Cabinets or .CAB files. It's possible to search for individual components in the .CAB files by using the EXTRACT.EXE utility provided in the WINDOWS directory, but this is a cumbersome process. The best way to search through the .CAB files is with a supplementary viewing filter developed by the Microsoft programming team. The CABview filter is included in a set of Win95 PowerToys available from CompuServe and the Microsoft FTP site. (See Chapter 14 for more details on finding and installing the

Windows 95 PowerToys.) Once you download and unpack the CABview filter, it's easy to install this feature. Use the following procedure:

1. *Unpack CABVIEW.EXE to any directory and open Explorer\My Computer to that directory (which should now contain the CABVIEW.INF and CABVIEW.DLL files). Right-click on the CABVIEW.INF file and choose the Install option from the context menu, as shown here:*

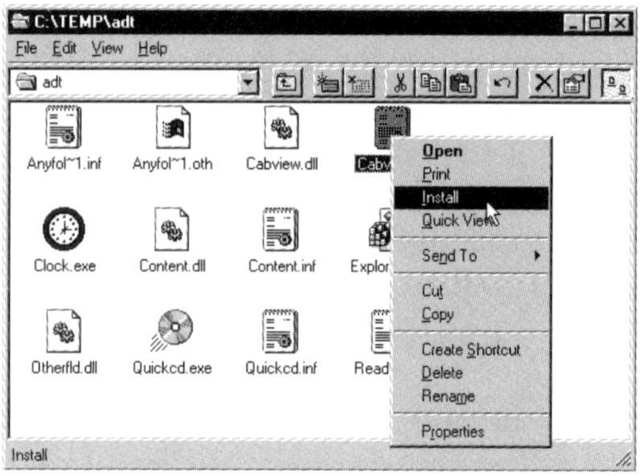

2. *Once the CABview filter is installed, open the Win95 installation CD or floppy disk in the Explorer, right-click on any file with the .CAB file extension and select View. A new window will open displaying the individual file contents of the .CAB file, as shown here:*

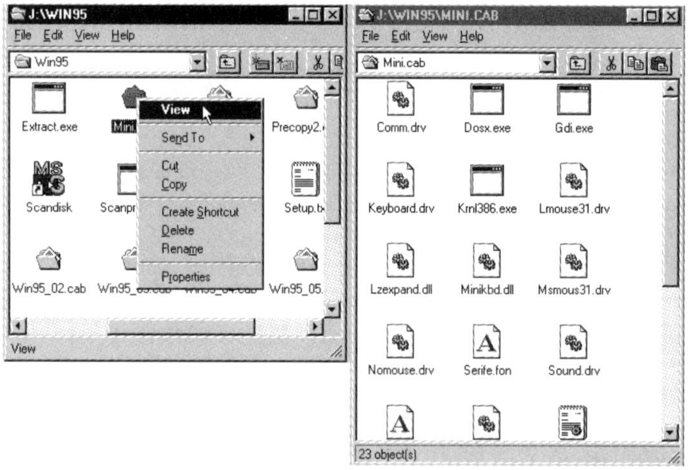

3. *The feature CAB view allows you to inspect these installation archives and drag individual files out with the mouse. If you're missing any system file that appears in the .CAB listing, drag it out of that window to the WINDOWS\SYSBCKUP directory.*

(This is necessary because you may not be able to drag the file directly to your WINDOWS\SYSTEM directory.)

4. *Select Shutdown Windows 95 on the Start Menu and choose "Restart computer in MS-DOS Mode."*
5. *Copy the system file from the SYSBCKUP directory to the WINDOWS\SYSTEM directory and restart Windows 95 by typing* ***EXIT*** *at the command prompt.*

If you're not able to obtain the PowerToy utility collection, the Extract command included with Windows 95 can be used to restore missing DLLs and drivers from the .CAB files to the WINDOWS directory. To obtain a complete listing of all the files in all of the WIN95_XX.CAB files, use the following syntax:

```
EXTRACT /A /D [D:]\WIN95\WIN95_02.CAB > CONTENTS.LST
```

Here, [D:] is the CD-ROM drive containing the Windows 95 installation CD. This will produce a file called CONTENTS.LST that contains a complete listing of the contents of WIN95_02.CAB through WIN95_17.CAB. You can now open CONTENTS.LST in Notepad and use the Find command on the Search menu to track down the name and location of your missing driver.

To view the contents of MINI.CAB, PRECOPY1.CAB, or PRECOPY2.CAB, you will have to run the Extract command individually on each of these files.

The following syntax

```
EXTRACT /D [D:]\PATH\XXX.CAB
```

displays the contents of an individual .CAB file to the screen. You can also pipe the display to an ASCII file, as we did in the first example.

The following syntax

```
EXTRACT [D:]\PATH\XXX.CAB DRIVERNAME
```

extracts a specific driver from a specific .CAB file.

For instance, suppose your missing file is MAPIU.DLL, which is not included in the SYSBCKUP directory. Open the CONTENTS.LST listing you produced earlier in Notepad, and search for the desired driver. You'll find that MAPIU.DLL is contained in the WIN95_06.CAB installation archive. To place a copy of the file on your hard disk, change to the SYSBCKUP directory and enter the following command:

```
EXTRACT [D:]\WIN95\WIN95_06.CAB MAPIU.DLL
```

Once the file has been extracted to the SYSBCKUP directory, restart the system in MS-DOS Compatibility mode and copy the file to the WINDOWS\SYSTEM directory.

Recovering from Faulty Windows 3.x Installation Programs

To recover from faulty installation of a Windows 3.*x* driver (such as a video driver), follow these steps:

1. Restart the computer. Press F8 when the "Starting Windows 95" message appears, and choose the Safe Mode option.
2. If you have a backup of the SYSTEM.INI file that was done just prior to installing the program, delete the existing SYSTEM.INI file and rename the backup file to take its place. Otherwise, open the SYSTEM.INI file in an ASCII text editor and try to determine if any modifications were added by the Windows 3.*x* driver installation. If you can spot them, remove them and resave the file.
3. Open the System component from the Control Panel and select the Device Manager tab. If the Windows 3.*x* device is listed, remove it.
4. Restart Windows 95.

Running DOS Applications under Windows 95

When you replace Windows 3.1 with Windows 95, PIFs are upgraded to the Windows 95 format. All existing settings should be preserved, but you may want to verify that they have been. When you double-click a program for the first time in a folder or in Explorer\My Computer, Windows 95 automatically creates a shortcut for the program if there wasn't one before. Windows 95 searches first for a PIF in the directory that contains the executable file you are starting. If Windows 95 cannot find a PIF there, it searches the Windows PIF directory. If there is no PIF in the Windows PIF directory, Windows 95 searches the path specified in the AUTOEXEC.BAT file. If no PIF is found, Windows 95 searches a special migration database listing of DOS applications for a match.

Windows 95 maintains a database of commonly used DOS applications. The file is called APPS.INF and is located in the WINDOWS\INF directory. When you add a DOS application through the Start Menu or File\New option in My Computer, and no file with the .PIF extension is found, Windows 95 searches the APPS.INF database. If a listing is found there, then relevant program information is copied automatically to the shortcut created for the application. A program title, an icon, and specific memory configuration parameters are read from the APPS.INF file and incorporated into the shortcut.

If Windows 95 does not find an entry for an application in the APPS.INF file, it uses default settings for the application. If you replace Windows 3.1 with Windows 95, a _DEFAULT.PIF file remains in the directory. In this case, Windows 95 uses information in the _DEFAULT.PIF file to create a PIF for the application.

If you do not have a _DEFAULT.PIF file and want to create one, you can do so by copying the DOSPRMPT.PIF to _DEFAULT.PIF.

DOS Properties and Configuration Settings

Performance options for DOS sessions are now controlled through the Properties menu, accessed by right-clicking on any program or shortcut icon and selecting Properties. This system replaces the PIF Editor that was used in Windows 3.1.

When you open the Properties menu of a DOS program or shortcut, you'll find six tabbed configuration screens that allow you to modify the program name location, assign hotkey shortcuts, and customize various screen and memory options. You probably won't need to access these screens very often, since most DOS applications will configure themselves and run automatically.

This section contains a summary of the features you will most frequently want to access. To get information on any of the Properties options from Windows 95, itself, click the Question Mark (?) icon at the top of the Properties box. Then move the mouse over the option you want explained and click the left button, as shown in this MS-DOS Prompt Properties screen:

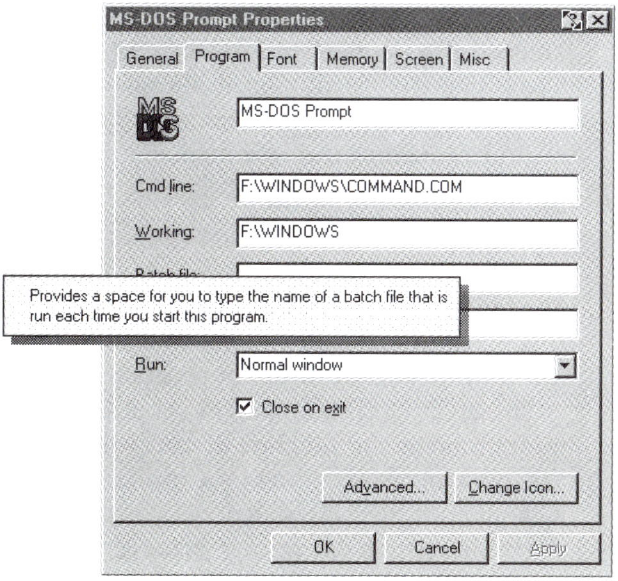

The General Tab

This screen displays the name of the program or its desktop shortcut, allowing you to change the file attribute. You can raise or lower the archive byte and make the file read-only or hidden.

The Program Tab

This screen specifies the program title, directory location of the file, and any parameters you may want to add to the startup command line. You can also assign a keyboard shortcut on the Program tab to automatically open the program without using the mouse. Finally, this screen lets you specify whether the program should appear in a minimized, normal, or maximized window on the desktop.

If you want to add command-line parameters to the program (for instance, telling it to open a specific file), these parameters are added after the path and filename in the CMD LINE box. The WORKING box lets you specify a working folder or directory for an application. This directory may contain support files or the data files that the program will access.

Here's an example. Entering the following information will cause WordPerfect 5.1 to open and automatically load a file called TEMPLATE.W51, located in a folder on drive D called TEMPLATES.

```
CMD LINE: D:\WP51\WP.EXE TEMPLATE.W51
WORKING: D:\TEMPLATES
```

You can also use the CMD LINE box to open an application from a batch file, setting DOS environment information the application may need. For instance, to open Procomm Plus for DOS, you might create a batch file called PP.BAT containing this information:

```
SET PCPLUS=D:\PCPLUS
PCPLUS.EXE
```

You would then enter **PP.BAT** in the CMD LINE box.

If the WORKING box is left blank, the program opens to the directory where the physical shortcut or program file is located.

The BATCH FILE box allows you to run an additional DOS batch file before running the program or batch file entered in the CMD LINE box. You probably won't need to use this feature, but it allows you to get fancy, without creating complicated, nested batch files for the command line. As an example, you might want to make certain preparations on your hard disk before running a specific program, e.g., creating a backup directory for your data files before starting an application. The BATCH FILE box allows you to do this, as follows:

```
BACKUP.BAT
COPY D:\WP51\*.W51 D:\BACKUPS
REN D:\BACKUPS\*.W51 *.BAK
```

To start WordPerfect for DOS, you could enter **D:\WP51\WP.EXE** in the CMD LINE box, **D:\WP51** in the WORKING box, and **BACKUP.BAT** in the BATCH FILE box.

note *If you run a shortcut or program from the Run command on the Start Menu, any parameters you specify on the Run line will override the default parameters specified in the shortcut's CMD LINE box.*

In order for an assigned shortcut key to work, the shortcut or associated program file you're configuring must be located on the Windows 95 Start Menu. (See Chapter 4 for additional information on assigning shortcut keys to applications.)

The Close on Exit button is not selected by default when you create a new shortcut. If you want an application window on the desktop to shut down when you exit the program, place a checkmark in this box.

Advanced Program Options in MS-DOS Mode

The Advanced Options button on the Properties Program tab allows you run a DOS program in exclusive MS-DOS mode. When you do this, your Windows 95 desktop and all open applications shut down and a full-screen, real-mode DOS session is opened. By default, Windows 95 is programmed to detect when certain DOS applications require this treatment. When you try to run these programs, you'll get a warning message on the screen, before the desktop shutdown. Click the Advanced button on the Program tab for options that let you place further controls and restrictions on this feature.

For example, suppose you have a DOS program that you think should be able to run under the Win95 desktop: you can place a checkmark in the box marked "Prevent MS-DOS-based programs from detecting Windows." This option should be used with caution, since it will disable any automatic interception of the program, forcing it to open under the Win95 desktop. Note that if you place a checkmark in this box for a DOS command-prompt session, Windows 95 will no longer be able to launch Windows applications from the DOS command prompt in that session.

"Suggest MS-DOS mode as necessary" is the default setting for most DOS applications. The programs will be opened under the Win95 desktop, unless specific incompatibilities are detected (in which case you'll get a dialog box suggesting that you run the application in MS-DOS mode).

If you place a checkmark in the MS-DOS Mode box in the Advanced Program Settings, this forces any DOS program to shut down the Windows 95 desktop and open in a full-screen, real-mode MS-DOS mode session. When a checkmark is placed in this box, three other options become available that apply only to running programs in MS-DOS mode:

- If you want to proceed directly to the application and skip the warning dialog, you can remove the checkmark in the "Warn before entering the MS-DOS mode" box.
- If you want to retain the real-mode settings included in your main Windows 95 startup files, select the "Use current MS-DOS configuration" option. This will pass on the real-mode device drivers, path, and environment parameters incorporated in your main CONFIG.SYS and AUTOEXEC.BAT files. Note that if your system is using Win95's protected-mode drivers for your CD-ROM drive or SCSI adapter, these peripherals won't be available in MS-DOS mode sessions. See the following section for tips on how to reactivate them.
- If you want to load custom CONFIG.SYS and AUTOEXEC.BAT for your MS-DOS mode program, select the "Specify a new MS-DOS configuration" option. This will allow you to import or type in a new set of startup files that will be loaded for your application. This option is particularly useful for loading special device drivers or settings for DOS games and multimedia programs.

Working with MS-DOS Mode

If you've opened an MS-DOS mode session with the "Use current MS-DOS configuration" option, your CD-ROM drive may not be available, even if your original CONFIG.SYS file retains real-mode drivers for it. This is because Windows 95 automatically comments out the MSCDEX command in your AUTOEXEC.BAT file. If your real-mode CD-ROM and SCSI drivers are still present in your main CONFIG.SYS file, you can restore access to

```
U.BAT
LOCK %1
[D:]\WINDOWS\COMMAND\UNDELETE %
```

3. *Save the file in the directory you usually use to store batch files.*
4. *Create a new shortcut from the File\New menu of My Computer\Explorer or through the Taskbar\Start Menu Programs\Add option on the Start Menu. Specify the directory and path to U.BAT in the CMD LINE box as follows:*

```
[D:]\PATH\U.BAT ?
```

5. *Enter **UNDELETE** as the title for the program, select an appropriate icon, and finish creating the shortcut.*

*To undelete files that have been deleted under DOS, just double-click the Undelete object you've created. The question mark you placed on the command line causes a parameters box to pop up on the desktop. You can enter a drive and directory into this box that will be passed to U.BAT. For instance, to undelete files in the DOS directory, enter **C:\DOS** in the parameters box. The LOCK.EXE utility will run first, asking you for permission to lock the directory you've specified. Then UNDELETE.EXE will run, switching the system to a full-screen window and displaying the status of the erased files in the chosen directory, as you can see here:*

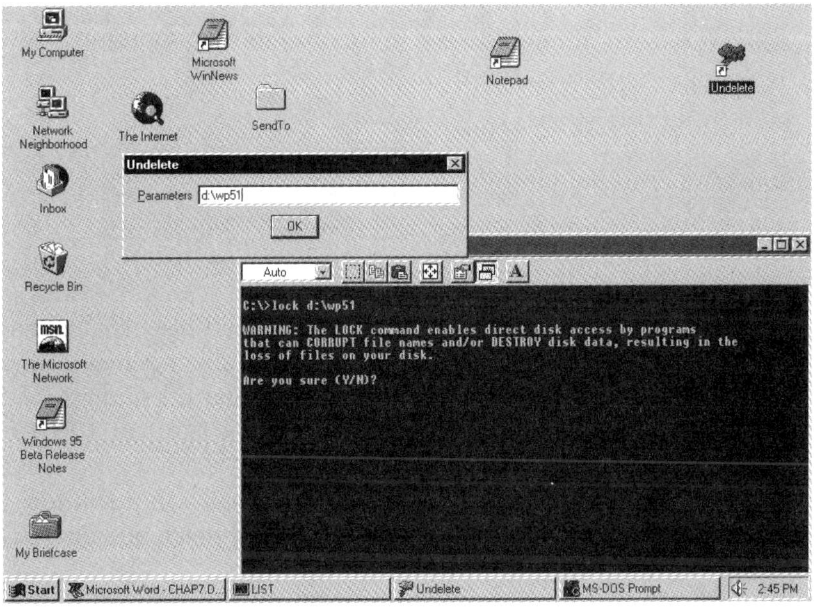

(This trick will not work on your Windows host drive, but you can use it to recover files on other disk partitions.)

The Font Tab

The Font tab is used to set the default display font for windowed DOS applications. Either the TrueType or the bitmapped display fonts can be removed from the menu. This option works the same way as the Font option on the toolbar that appears in the session's screen window.

The Memory Tab

The Memory tab allows you to control the amount of conventional, expanded (EMS), extended (XMS), and DOS protected-mode (DPMI) memory allocated to a DOS session, as illustrated here:

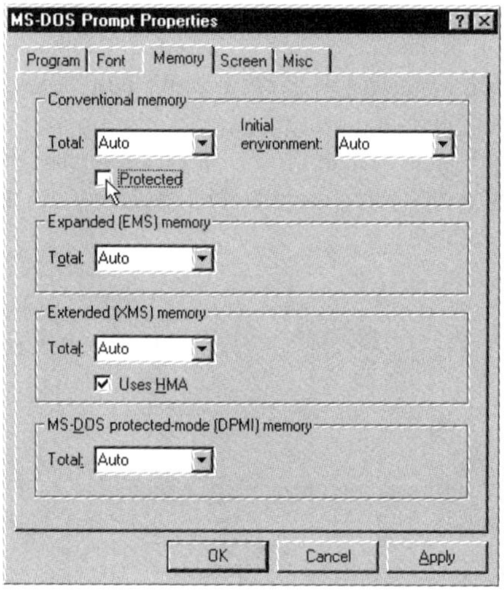

These options used to be available on the Advanced Settings screen in the Windows 3.1 PIF editor. By default these settings are determined by the values in preexisting PIF files or information contained in the APPS.INF migration database. Experience has shown that the settings specified in the migration database are not transferred to the shortcut 100 percent of the time, so you may want to examine them and make appropriate alterations. Generally, the settings can be left in the default configuration, or you can choose "Auto" to let Windows 95 decide how much of each type of memory to allocate.

The "Initial environment" list under the Conventional memory box of the Memory tab sets the number of bytes allocated to contain DOS environment strings. If "Initial environment" is set to "Auto," the amount is determined by the SHELL= setting in your CONFIG.SYS file, or set to 256 bytes if there is no SHELL= statement.

Enabling the Protected checkbox in the "Conventional memory" box may slow down application performance somewhat, but it provides additional shielding of the Win95 system machine from ill-behaved DOS programs.

The Uses HMA checkbox in the "Extended (EMS) memory" box makes the first 64K of extended memory available to individual DOS applications, provided there is no DOS=HIGH statement in your Win95 CONFIG.SYS file. Since very few DOS programs can actually use this memory, it's to your advantage to load the DOS command kernel high at boot time, and ignore this checkbox.

note *If the Expanded Memory settings on your system are grayed out, check your CONFIG.SYS file for the presence of the following statement:*

```
DEVICE=[D:]\WINDOWS\EMM386.EXE NOEMS
```

If you find such a statement, substitute the parameter "RAM" for "NOEMS."

The Screen Tab

The Screen tab, shown here, establishes the settings for the display of your DOS application on the Windows desktop.

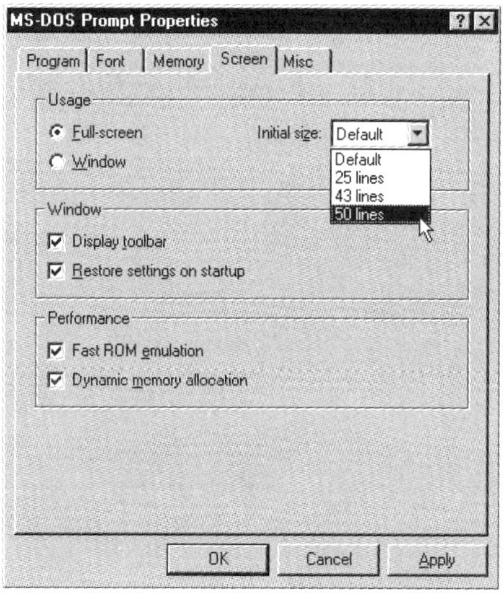

You can configure DOS sessions or programs to start in either full-screen or windowed environments, preserve the size and position of the display window on the desktop, and optimize performance parameters by enabling fast ROM emulation or dynamic memory allocation.

The "Fast ROM emulation" check box specifies whether the display driver should shadow video functions from read-only memory (ROM) to faster RAM. If you check it, screen writes should be slightly accelerated. If you experience problems with the program writing text to the screen, clear this textbox.

"Dynamic memory allocation" retrieves dormant memory assigned to an idle application and saves it for allocation to other programs. If your DOS application uses any high-resolution graphic modes, you should probably deselect this option, so that the screen will be refreshed properly.

tip *You can open a DOS command prompt to a 43- or 50-line screen display by going to the Usage box and changing the Initial size setting to 43 lines or 50 lines. When left at the default settings, an application uses its own internal configuration to determine the number of lines it will display. If your DOS program is set internally to display 43 or 50 lines, this setting may also override a Properties setting for 25-line display.*

The Misc Tab

The Misc tab has a number of useful, miscellaneous options, as shown here:

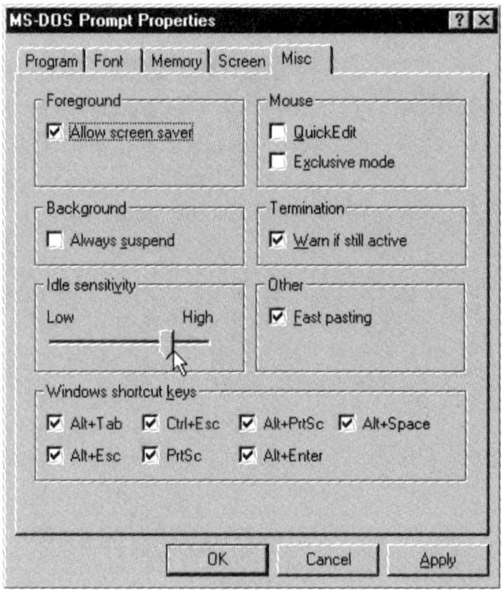

If your application is a word processor or other application that tends to remain idle in the background, the "Always suspend" checkbox in the Background box should be checked. (Don't check this option if your program has an internal print spooler and you want to print large documents in the background.) A telecommunications program should never have the "Always suspend" option selected, since this can cause online connections or file transfers to be terminated if you switch to a different desktop window.

The "Warn if still active" checkbox, if selected, causes a pop-up dialog box to warn you if you attempt to close a program window while an application is still running in it.

The Idle sensitivity slider allows you to control the extent to which Windows 95 monitors a dormant application and steals back unused CPU time. Low idle sensitivity lets a program run longer before the CPU resources allotted to it are reduced. High idle sensitivity reduces the CPU resources allotted to the program sooner. Newer DOS applications are programmed to detect the fact they are running within Windows. They automatically send a suspend message when just waiting for keystrokes. This saves Windows from having to allocate processor time to a session when the CPU time is not needed.

If a program running in the background is not getting enough CPU resources, move the Idle sensitivity slider toward Low. If the application is an older DOS program that doesn't appear to be doing anything in the background, move the slider toward High. If the application is a newer DOS application, you may want to experiment with moving the slider toward Low.

The QuickEdit option in the Mouse settings section of this screen restores the single-click cut-and-paste functionality that used to be available under Windows 3.0. If an application does not use the mouse internally, enabling QuickEdit lets you select text by simply clicking the left mouse button. (This eliminates the need to click first on the Mark option on the toolbar or Control menu.) The "Exclusive mode" checkbox disables the mouse as a standard Windows 95 pointer. You should check "Exclusive mode" if, for some reason, you see two mouse pointers on the screen when you're working in a mouse-aware DOS application.

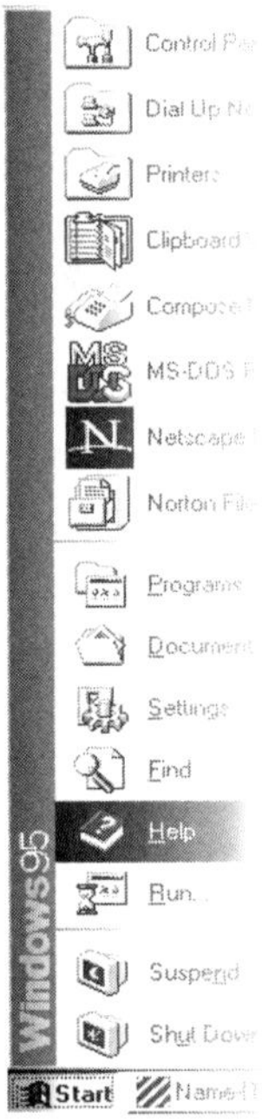
Control
Dial Up
Clipboard
MS-DOS
Netscape
Norton
Programs
Settings
Find
Help
Run...
Suspend
Start
Windows95

chapter 8

Tweaking the System: The Windows Control Panel

- Overview of the Control Panel
- Fast access to Control Panel features
- Fine-tuning performance settings
- Useful features omitted by Setup

  What to configure and turn on
- Obscure and secret options

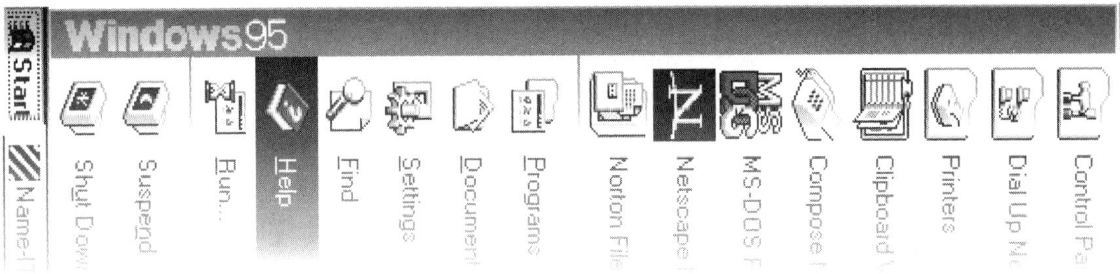

THIS chapter gives you a guided tour through the Windows 95 Control Panel. You'll see how to get fast access to the most common setup and customization features. You'll also find detailed explanations of more obscure features: including pertinent tips on fine-tuning the interface and obtaining diagnostic information.

The Control Panel in Windows 95 lets you manage all of your system's performance settings from one centrally located folder. A set of approximately 20 utilities govern various aspects of the Win95 operating environment. These utilities range from desktop customization menus to software and hardware installation components, controlling every physical, visual, and operational detail of the system. After being placed on your hard disk, Windows 95 assigns system defaults that will be good enough for many users. But, you can also delve into the minutiae and modify every last screen detail.

By default, the Control Panel appears in two places: on the Start button (as a submenu under Settings, as shown in Figure 8-1), and as an icon in the My Computer folder. When you double-click Control Panel in either location, it opens up like any other Windows 95 folder: displaying a desktop window with a series of icons. Each icon in the Control Panel folder represents a configuration option for a corresponding component of the Windows 95 interface.

During installation, Windows 95 determines the options that will appear in the Control Panel folder. These options depend partly on the individual components of your system: if you have a PCMCIA slot, a corresponding PCMCIA object is installed. If your system supports Advanced Power Management, a Power icon appears. Microsoft Mail, Mail and Fax, Multi-

FIGURE 8-1

The Windows 95 Control Panel

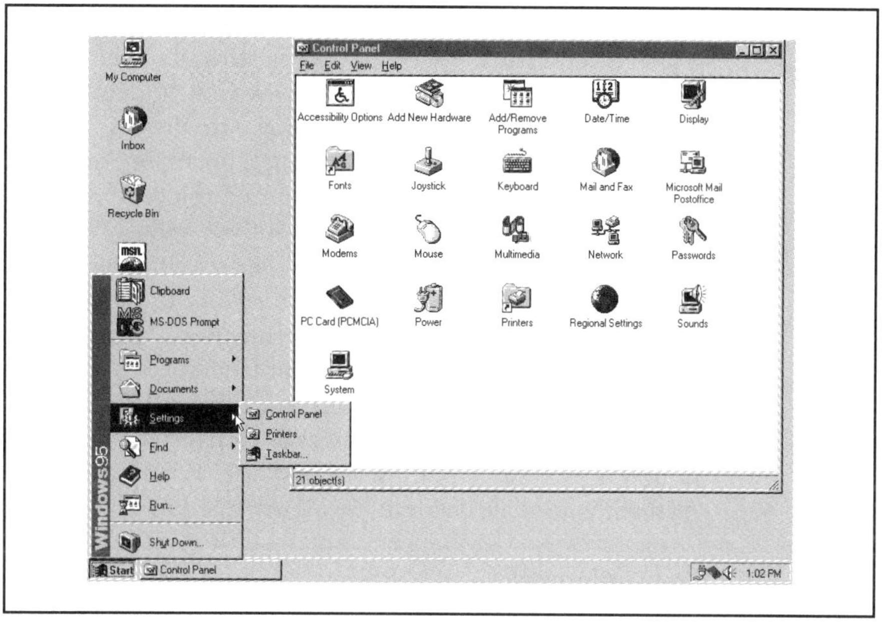

media, and Network Management appear if you've selected corresponding software features during Win95 Setup.

The Control Panel is a fixed object. You can't drag new shortcuts into it or delete the existing applets. However, when you add or remove new hardware and software, discarded features may disappear and additional objects will be installed. The important point to remember is that although you can't drag programs or shortcuts into the Control Panel, you can drag shortcuts for its individual components out. Shortcuts to Control Panel items can be placed on the desktop or in any program group or file folder. You can also create custom Control Panel shortcuts on the Start Menu containing only those features you use most frequently.

Customizing Control Panel Access

There are some utilities on the Control Panel that you will use all of the time and others that you can completely ignore. When Windows 3.0 was released, some users spent hours fine-tuning color schemes, but never touched the mouse module. It worked well enough, so why bother?

The Windows 95 Control Panel, however, is more complicated than its predecessors. You can modify the parts that are important to you, and leave the rest at their default settings. In Windows 95, you can access Control Panel components in several ways to streamline the customization process.

The most obvious way to get quick Control Panel access is to place one or more of its internal applets directly onto the desktop. For instance, if you want to have access to Display settings, open the Control Panel and drag the Display icon onto the desktop or into a folder, then click Create Shortcut Here. You can modify the name of the new object from "Shortcut to Display" to plain old "Display." This technique is probably best as a temporary solution: at first, you may use the Control Panel application repeatedly to fine-tune an aspect of system performance. When you're satisfied, you can delete the shortcut from the desktop.

A more permanent way to bring a Control Panel component closer is to place it onto the Start button menu. Perhaps you frequently need to access four Control Panel objects: for instance, Printers, Fonts, MultiMedia, and System. You would do the following to make these components more accessible:

1. Open the Control Panel.
2. Right-click the Start button, and select Open.
3. Select FILE\NEW\FOLDER. Type a name (such as **Control**) into the new folder.
4. Select and drag the desired Control Panel components into the new folder. Windows won't copy or move these components, but will offer to create shortcuts to each. Click Yes, then shorten the names if desired.

This procedure creates an abbreviated Control Panel at the top of the Start Menu for quick access. Place the mouse cursor over this new Start Menu entry, and a menu will fan open to show the applets you've dragged in.

tip *If you make shortcuts by dragging one or two physical file objects out of an Explorer window and keep shortening the filenames, eventually Windows 95 stops adding the words "Shortcut To" to the filenames. This doesn't work if you drag out Control Panel objects from a simple folder view. Instead, open an Explorer Panes view by right-clicking the Start button or the My Computer icon and selecting Explore. Drag a physical file from a real directory to the desktop and manually delete the words "Shortcut To." The second or third time you do this, Windows 95 catches on and transfers only the filename to the shortcut. You can then go into the Control Panel and drag out shortcuts to components without the annoying "Shortcut To" prefix.*

The Windows 95 Power Toys (which you can download from the Microsoft Internet sites, the Microsoft BBS and CompuServe) add a special option to the Control Panel that can automatically eliminate the Shortcut To prefix from new desktop shortcuts. See Chapter 12 for more details.

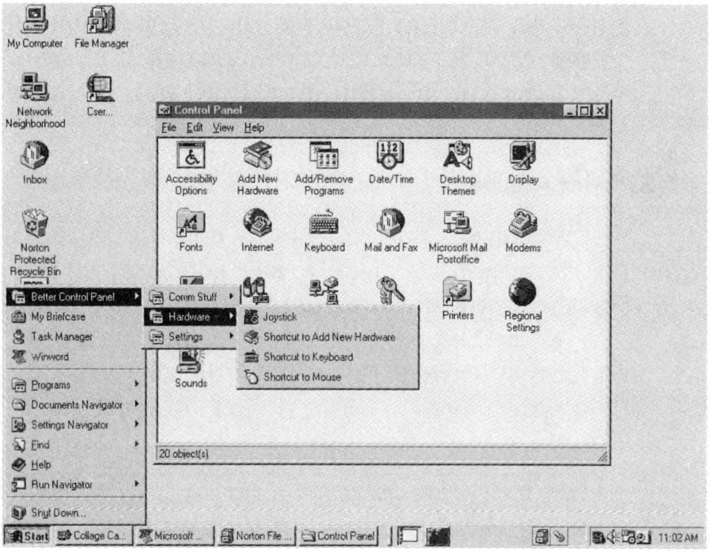

FIGURE 8-2

A smart way to build an organized Control Panel

Another desktop strategy you can use is to make a series of Control Panel subfolders grouping utilities into function-related categories. This may be more efficient than always opening the entire collection.

Here's another way to build a better Control Panel:

1. Create category folders on the desktop (right-click New\Folder), grouping the applications. For instance, a Hardware group could have Add New Hardware, Mouse, Joystick, Keyboard, Modems, and Printers. A configuration group would contain Display, Accessibility, Regional Settings and Passwords. And so on.
2. Right-click on the Start button, and select Explore.
3. Select File\New\Folder and type **Better Control Panel** on the label.
4. Drag the category folders from the desktop onto the new folder within the Explorer. The results are shown in Figure 8-2.

Working with Control Panel Objects

The Control Panel in Windows 95 carries on a Windows tradition: It is a potpourri of various checks and balances, fine-tuning system aspects from the cosmetic to the cosmic. Like other parts of Windows 95, the Control

Panel can be approached by users with a wide range of technical sophistication. No matter who you are, you'll probably find utilities here that you may never need. At the same time, a remarkable range of useful system controls are hidden within the Control Panel's vast, well-lighted caverns.

Dis Playing Around

Windows is praised by many users for its appearance as much as for its performance. The ability to look good has a lot to do with how people relate to the system and, consequently, with how much they can accomplish with it. So the Display component might therefore be considered one of the primary Control Panel utilities. You will probably want to use it to fine-tune the system for your own custom look and feel.

tip *If you're like the authors of this book, the first thing you'll want to do after Windows 95 appears on your screen is to get rid of the ugly blue Setup wallpaper. Open the Display object to the Background tab, pan up in the Wallpaper list and select none. We also suggest changing the default electric blue or green background of the desktop to a lighter, more sedate color. You can select the Appearance tab in the Display object, click on the Color box, and select the white or light gray backgrounds to create an uncluttered, Macintosh-like look. (Or maybe you really prefer psychedelic colors and wallpaper. The choice is up to you!)*

The Display Properties dialog box is one of the rare Windows 95 components that lags behind the Windows 3.*x* version. Those who know the old Control Panel will notice that the new module combines two related utilities, Color and Desktop. Now, you can select color schemes, select wallpaper, control screen savers, and adjust interface subtleties from a single set of menus. But you may not be able to escape the feeling that portions of the old Control Panel were just a little easier.

The most obvious example of this is the color selection feature. Previously, the color utility was the first thing you saw when you opened the Control Panel. Some desktop programs even allowed you to drag the color icon onto the desktop (for those who had trouble committing to a single scheme or pattern). If it was often hard to find an original color combination, this utility at least allowed you to learn the various parts of the interface and see how they could be customized.

But even experienced users may have difficulty modifying the Windows 95's color scheme. Used to be, you could just double-click on the Color icon and do your thing. Now, you need to follow two steps: Select the Display icon, and the Appearance tab to find the color control facility. Oddly, the word "color" is nowhere to be found during that particular sequence. And Windows 95 was supposed to be easy!

note *You can also access the entire Display Properties dialog box by clicking the desktop and selecting Properties.*

Once you get there, however, selecting colors for your Windows environment is a pretty straightforward process. The Appearance option, it turns out, contains more than just color selection. Fonts and other interface aspects are controlled from this panel. So we can almost forgive Microsoft for excluding the word "color" from the title.

"Almost," because the procedure still isn't as simple and straightforward as it could be. The top section is a representation of all of the interface parts. Below this representation, there are three drop-down list boxes:

- The Scheme box loads a preconfigured desktop color scheme. Windows 95 gives you a couple dozen of these out of the box, displaying various themed patterns. "Wheat," for instance, pops up an odd light yellow. These schemes range from innocuous to obnoxious, but are generally the former. They are best used as starting points for developing your own custom color scheme, offering a reasonably clear idea of the possibilities. By the way, Microsoft Plus! offers a series of additional schemes that include more than just color changes. The Microsoft Plus! themes include changes of font and wallpaper as well as new screen savers, sounds for system events, icons, and mouse pointers. These Plus! schemes are selected through the Desktop Themes object on the Control Panel if Plus! has been installed. (For more information on this and other Microsoft Plus! features, see Chapter 14.)

  Two buttons manipulate schemes in the Win95 Display object. Save As gives your new scheme a name, while Delete removes superfluous schemes (and saves you a little disk space).

- The Item drop-down list box (see Figure 8-3) lets you edit 18 aspects of the desktop's appearance. When you highlight one, you can then modify applicable font and color settings. The Desktop item, for instance, only allows you to select the color. Menu, on the other hand, allows you to select background color as well as font style and size, and foreground color. This gives you a serious personalization quotient, even allowing you to use a bold italic symbol font for your menu titles, if that's what you want. Each attribute on the list has different applicable properties. Icon Spacing (Vertical), for instance, gives you a point size (default is 43) that can be adjusted accordingly.

- Font is the third drop-down list. It only becomes active when the highlighted window aspect uses text.

When you modify an attribute, each change is immediately reflected on the interface replica that comprises the top half of the display window. You can always cancel changes by clicking Cancel, the center button on the bottom. The other button choices are Apply (temporarily shows the changes in the Display window), and OK (saves the change to the desktop). Be sure to give the scheme a name and save it if you want to preserve it for posterity.

The one aspect of the interface that you can't change on the Display Properties\Appearance tab is Window Text (shown as a terminal font in the pictorial mock-up of the desktop). The font used for ordinary display text in a window is usually determined by the application running in the window.

FIGURE 8-3

The Display Properties screen lets you adjust the size and color of most desktop components.

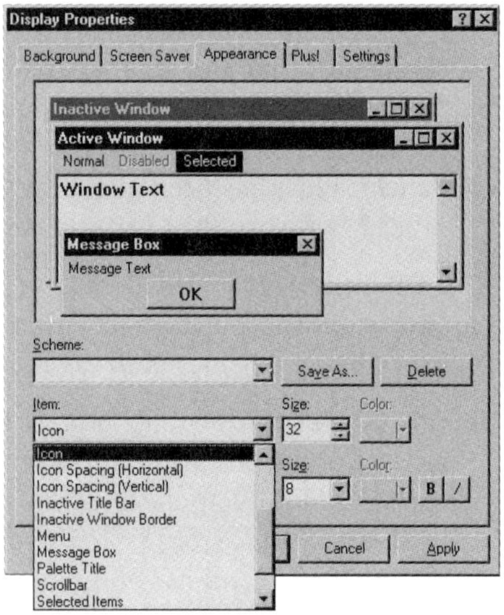

Selecting a Scheme

As we mentioned, most of the schemes are pretty lame, if you judge them for aesthetic and artistic qualities. Perhaps that's not the point. You want your screens to look nice, with colors you enjoy that make your PC your own. At the same time, you probably want to keep the whole thing fairly understated, and avoid the more outrageous choices—assuming that your priority is to actually get some work done.

Consider the preconfigured Windows color schemes: All of them use white as the background for the main window. This doesn't represent a Microsoft effort to stifle individuality or make us all work alike. In fact, most of the paper we use in the office and home is white. The PC screen needs to reflect this, quite simply because black type on a white background is the easiest scheme for the eye to comprehend. And while installing a cyan or light yellow background made some sense in the EGA years, when the whites were awfully harsh, the Windows soft white is now more appealing as the desktop background.

As for menus and other aspects, there are all kinds of possibilities. We hate to say it, but the Microsoft defaults of light gray and an occasional highlight color are the most hospitable for the purpose. Bottom line: If you are going to be looking at this stuff all of the time, it shouldn't be too outrageous or disturbing.

Other Display Properties Tabs

The Display Properties box has three other tabs, aside from Appearance: Background, Screen Saver, and Settings. If you've installed Microsoft Plus!, an additional "Plus" tab also appears.

BACKGROUND This module overrides the default desktop color in one of two ways. The Pattern list pops up designs like "Daisies" or "Diamonds," giving the desktop a faux texture. Wallpapers are a little more interesting, with backgrounds that resemble bricks, rivets, blue sky, or marble.

You can also install your own wallpaper by copying a new bitmap into the list. The default location for such bitmaps is the Windows directory, but you can also add bitmaps from any directory or across the network for this purpose. The simplest way to do this is to select the bitmap title in My Computer and drag it to the area above the Wallpaper list box with the mouse. This will add the bitmap title to the available patterns. New bitmaps can also be added with the Browse button.

You can tile or center wallpaper, depending upon the individual bitmap.

SCREEN SAVER Like Background and Appearance, the Screen Saver module, illustrated in Figure 8-4, shows a preview of a proposed change before it is actually implemented. Or at least it tries to. You might get active mini-representations of some of the included screen savers, while other, third-party programs just display a static image. Still, this is one of the simplest customization aspects of Windows 95: a drop-down list of all available screen savers, with a button to control settings, and a preview button to the right of the list.

Settings are specific to each screen saver, and usually encompass things like the number and speed of the various flying objects. Preview runs the saver in full screen mode instead of on the mini-monitor.

Any time you install a screen saver into the Windows 95 environment, it appears in this drop-down list. A handful of savers is included in the Windows 95 System folder. These are not resource intensive and also not especially compelling. If they have a generic look and feel, they at least get the job done; providing moderate graphical entertainment, screen privacy, and password protection.

note *Third-party screen saver manufacturers will approach the Control Panel interface one of two ways: they will install savers directly into the Display module, or they may install savers directly into an application group, outside of the Control Panel. The After Dark family from Berkeley Systems is an example of the second implementation, since the complicated controls of the After Dark family don't easily fit into the Display object's tabbed settings screens.*

FIGURE 8-4

Windows 95 built-in screen savers

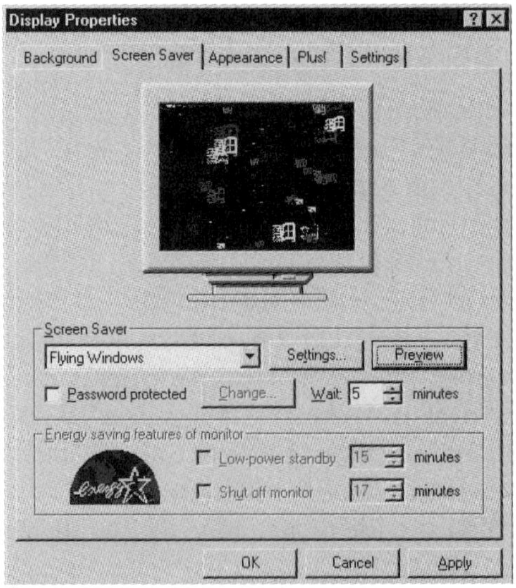

What's the use of screen savers? They offer another way for you to personalize the system. They are, in fact, now misnamed. Back when most people were using monochrome display monitors, screen savers prevented high-contrast text from being permanently burned into the CRT display. With VGA monitors, it's highly unlikely that any image would be "burned in," even if you left it there for weeks. Those looking for any intrinsic value for screen savers can use them for privacy and password protection, although you don't actually need flying appliances to accomplish this.

The bottom line: The screen saver that makes the most sense is Blank Screen, which intercepts all signals and makes it appear as if the monitor is off. Touch the keyboard or the mouse and it comes back to life. This module is *really* unexciting, but it works—and with no drain on memory, resources, or hard disk space.

SETTINGS This final Display Properties screen allows you to change screen resolution on-the-fly; for instance from 640 × 480 pixels to 800 × 600 pixels and beyond. This is a feature borrowed from some of the higher-end video cards currently available for the Windows 3.*x* environment. You can also change Win95's supported color-depth, but this change won't be implemented on-the-fly. When the color-depth is changed, you'll see a message telling you to restart the system.

Any new screen resolution or color-depth must, of course, be supported by both your video card and monitor. If the hardware won't support it, then your change won't take, and the system will retain the original settings. This is a big improvement from the way video setup behaved in past versions of Windows. In the old days, you might inadvertently (or 'vertently) choose improper video options and end up with incomprehensible garbage on screen. If you didn't have a smart set of drivers, the only way out was to fiddle endlessly with .INI files through a DOS text editor.

Adding (and Removing) Programs

The Add/Remove Programs object is one of the most helpful new additions to the Control Panel for Windows 95. It should be easy to add or delete an application from the Windows environment, but in practice your Windows environment probably contains hundreds of extraneous files; the dregs of programs that were deleted long ago. The Add/Remove Programs object can install, track, and uninstall applications written for the Windows 95 environment, removing all trace of them from hard disk directories and .INI files. Additionally, the Install button universalizes the installation procedure for older Windows 3.1 programs, obviating the need for hundreds of separate, proprietary setup schemes.

The Install/Uninstall Tab

Installing and uninstalling programs in Windows 3.*x* was a random process that belonged on the wild frontier. If you got a new program, there would probably be a file on the first disk called "install" or setup" that, when executed, would probably walk you through the installation process with a minimum of manual irritation. Conversely, getting rid of a program might involve finding its directory with the File Manager and executing a File\Delete command.

This process was unscientific and far from thorough. In order for each program to work under Windows, it may often deposit files in odd places, like the WINDOWS or WINDOWS\SYSTEM directory These files were untracked and unrecorded by Balkanized third-party setup utilities. So one day you might get a "disk full" message, and discover that your Windows directory was jammed with .DLL files from 1993.

The Install/Uninstall tab helps you to manage your hard disk by tracking the .DLL files and program files of Windows 95 applications. This feature is so simple as to be insulting to computer geek consultants and writers trying to make a living. To install a new program from a floppy disk or CD-ROM, click Install, insert the disk, and the Wizard will walk you through. Below this dialog, a list of installed programs is displayed. Click on your choice, select Add/Remove, and you can modify system components or remove a program—and its renegade files—from the disk altogether.

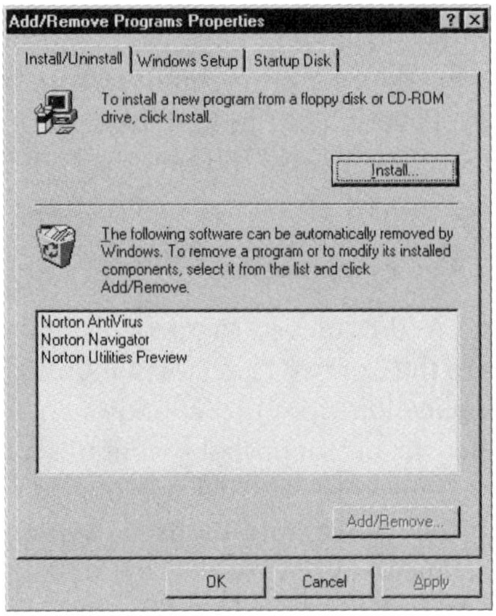

note *Windows 3.1 programs installed through Add/Remove Programs utility will not necessarily appear in the Uninstall list. This feature was designed for programs written to the Win95 API. Windows 95 is flexible. You can still do things the old way, if you want, even if it won't be to your best advantage. In this way Windows is like parents to a grown child: They can't make you do things their way, only make suggestions. But in some cases the suggestions make sense.*

Experienced users will probably have the tendency to install programs the old fashioned way. But this is a habit that you may want to break. Typing **RUN A:\SETUP.EXE** still works fine. But if you install a program this way, it won't show up on the registry list for Uninstall. As a result, you can't easily remove it.

In the time-honored Windows tradition, the Add/Remove Programs module qualifies as an "applet." That is to say, it meets minimum requirements to get the job done, but if you seriously want to use the feature, you may want a third-party solution. Vertisoft's Remove-It, popular in its Windows 3.1 version, now offers limited Windows 95 support. It includes an archiving feature and the ability to move programs and their components. This feature works well with Windows 95's connectivity options. For instance, you may only use an accounting package four times a year. By compressing the software and moving it to a dark corner of a network drive, you save the local disk space for day-to-day functions. When it is needed you just move it back. (For more information about Vertisoft Remove-It, see Chapter 14.)

FIGURE 8-5

If you click the Install button on the Add/Remove Programs screen, a built-in Win95 Installation Wizard appears.

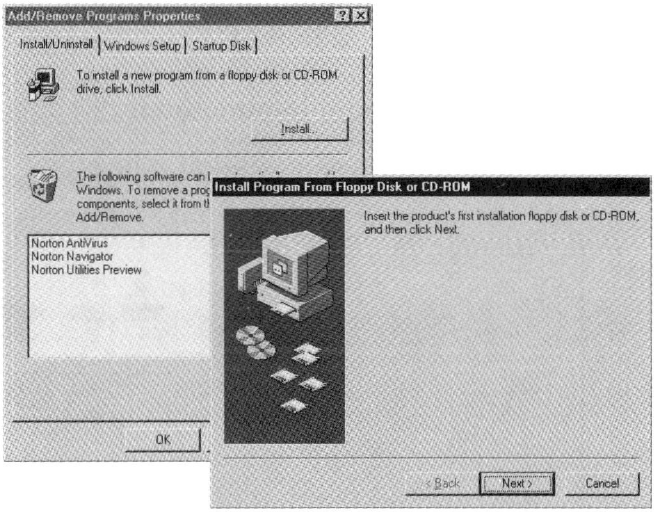

note *There's a difference between the Control Panel's Install/Uninstall feature and the generic option to uninstall the entire Windows 95 operating system. The tab in Add/Remove Programs works for specific Win95-aware applications. If you checkmarked the Windows 3.x archive option when installing Windows 95, you can restore your previous operating system and remove Windows 95 entirely. You probably won't want to do this unless you're pretty unhappy, and it is accomplished with a DOS UNINSTALL.BAT file that's placed in the root directory of your boot drive.*

The Windows Setup Tab

Windows Setup maintains a record of internal Windows components and accessories. In the days of Windows 3.1, veteran installers would try to save space by skipping over unneeded stuff like the Recorder and Microsoft Write. Later, if these components were needed, you'd have to perform a complicated and annoying disk swap process. In Windows 95, all of the ancillary features can be added or removed from a handy check box list, which shows the size of the selected components compared to the amount of available disk space. When you examine the components listed under the Windows Setup tab, you'll find that uninstalled categories have no checkmarks in the boxes that precede their names. Partially installed categories have checkmarks inside darker gray boxes. You can double-click on any component or click on the Details button to break down the category. For instance, Accessories allows you to select Calculator, Games, and Mouse Pointers among other choices.

FIGURE 8-6 *The Windows Setup tab of Add/Remove Programs shows you the features and programs that have and haven't been installed.*

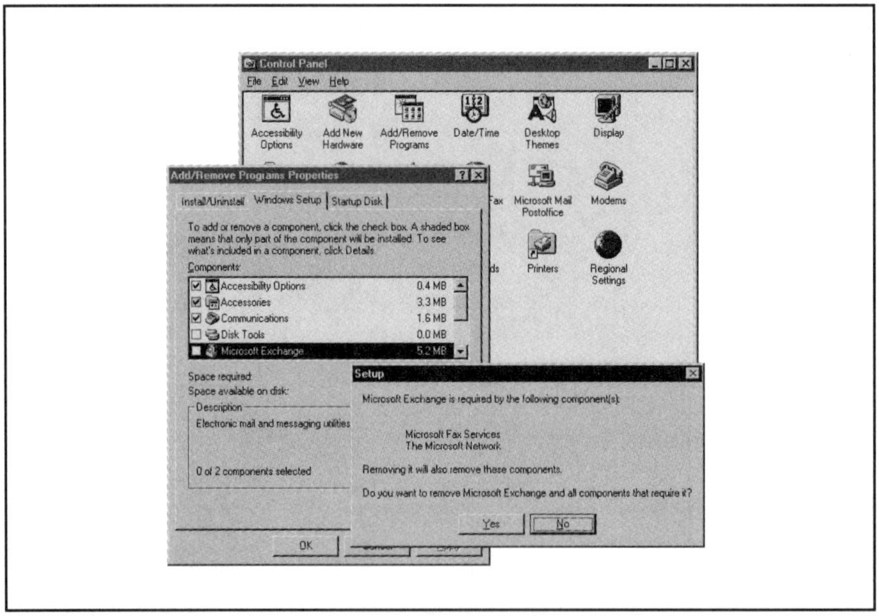

The Most Popular Missing Features That You Really Want

If you selected the typical, portable, or compact installation options when you placed Windows 95 on your hard disk, a number of features and accessory applications were probably not installed. These installation options are omitted in the interest of saving time and disk space, but you may find that you really want some of the missing features.

The Win95 Clipboard Viewer is not automatically installed on the desktop! You'll find it listed in the Accessories group along with some handy programs that you may want to add: Character Map is a useful utility that allows you to identify the upper-ASCII characters in any Windows font and paste them into documents. QuickView is a file viewer and set of filters that let you quickly browse documents and bitmap graphics in desktop windows. The Online User's Guide is a major portion of the Windows 95 hypertext help system. Backup and DriveSpace are two utilities found in the Disktools section, but installed in the System Tools subfolder under Accessories.

The most common use for Add/Remove Programs will probably be to add Microsoft Exchange and The Microsoft Network (MSN) to your desktop. Here, there is a safety net to protect naive users from themselves. Windows 95 won't allow you to install MSN without having Exchange on the disk as well. Similarly, if one program depends upon the presence of another, Windows 95 will remind you of the relationship before allowing the installation.

Win95 has a separate screen during installation that asks you whether Microsoft Fax, The Microsoft Network, and Microsoft Mail should be installed

note *If you select The Microsoft Network, then some features of Exchange are installed automatically, but not Fax or Microsoft Mail–you must select these components specifically if you want to use them.*

If you've opted for a typical or a portable installation and Windows 95 didn't detect a network card, you may also want to go into the Communications group of Add/Remove Programs and select Dial-Up Networking or Direct Cable Connection. Even without a network adapter in your computer, these options are useful: allowing you to dial into the Internet with a modem or to connect two computers via serial or parallel cable. (See Chapters 5, 10, and 12 for more detailed information on configuring Dial-Up Networking and Direct Cable Connection.)

The Windows 95 Tour is an interactive tutorial that introduces you to Win95's basic features. Again, you may want to select this and install it if you have the hard disk space to spare.

If Windows 95 detects a CD-ROM drive or sound card, then the appropriate multimedia applications are automatically installed. Windows 95 also has an assortment of sound schemes for system events. These are not installed unless you select them manually.

For a complete list of Windows 95 components that are added by each of the initial Setup options, see Chapter 3.

The Startup Disk Tab

Startup Disk is roughly equivalent of **FORMAT A:\S**, the process of creating a bootable system diskette. If you choose this option, Windows 95 also copies must-have system utilities to the diskette (ATTRIB, CHKDSK, FDISK, FORMAT, SYS, and so on). Having such a disk is a good idea, in case something goes wrong with the hard disk and it fails to boot. Microsoft offers the option of creating a floppy startup disk during Win95 installation. If you've ignored this option, it's available in Add/Remove Programs. So create a Startup disk now and put it in a safe place, or you'll be sorry.

Adding New Hardware

Add New Hardware is the twin-sibling of the Add/Remove Programs module. This is the heart of the plug-and-play facility that has become one of the biggest selling points of Windows 95. Theoretically, plug-and-play automatically senses any hardware component and installs it into the Windows environment without requiring any troublesome user intervention.

That's the theory. In this case, the theory is pretty darn close to the actual practice. The result of the protracted Windows 95 development process has made plug-and-play actually work in the majority of cases. It's not perfect, but chances are that Win 95's Hardware Wizard magic will be potent enough to recognize whatever hardware is in your system and make it work. (See sections later in this chapter and in Chapters 6, 7, and 9 for information about recognizing stubborn SCSI cards, sound cards, and PCMCIA devices.)

Not everything will work. Some installation instances may require the time-honored ritual of calls to hardware vendors, consuming hours on hold with technical support specialists for obscure system peripherals.

The Add New Hardware Wizard is another example of the simplified Windows 95 interface: There aren't very many choices here, and the options you do find are free of ambiguity.

You have a choice when adding new hardware; you can ask Windows to automatically detect and configure the hardware, or pick and choose peripherals and drivers yourself. (See Figure 8-7.) If you select "Yes, let Windows search for your new hardware," the process takes "several" minutes, and pops up a list of the found peripherals at the end. If you select No, and click the Next button, the Setup Wizard pops up a Hardware types dialog box containing a list of various adapters, controllers, modems, and other peripherals, allowing you to effect a more specific (and in some cases more rapid) installation process.

The Add New Hardware dialog does a fair job of recognizing old hardware (now referred to by industry insiders as "Legacy Technology"). It recognized a pair of ancient cards in one of our test machines: the Media Vision 16 Soundcard, and Intel's SatisFAXion Classic (although it refused to designate the latter as a fax board, since the Classic Intel fax modems use a proprietary CAS protocol). In the not-too-distant future, all new hardware worth using will be designed to accommodate the Intel/Microsoft plug-and-play standard. So the days of spending hours installing a particularly stubborn multimedia upgrade kit are due to fade, soon, into the dusty memories of grizzled user-group veterans.

At least that's the theory.

Things may go wrong, of course. If Windows 95 doesn't recognize your hardware, you may need to install third-party drivers through the Have Disk button. This can come from either direction on the time line: You may be attempting to install an old board that you bought at a garage sale, or something so new that the drivers haven't arrived in the Windows 95 system. In addition, Windows 95 has several optional modules available in .INF profiles, stashed in strategic directories on the installation CD-ROM. In any of these cases, you click the Have Disk button and point Windows to the floppy diskette, hard disk, or CD-ROM directory where your hardware device drivers are stashed.

FIGURE 8-7 *The Add New Hardware Wizard can automatically detect and configure many peripherals when you drop them into your system after Windows 95 is installed.*

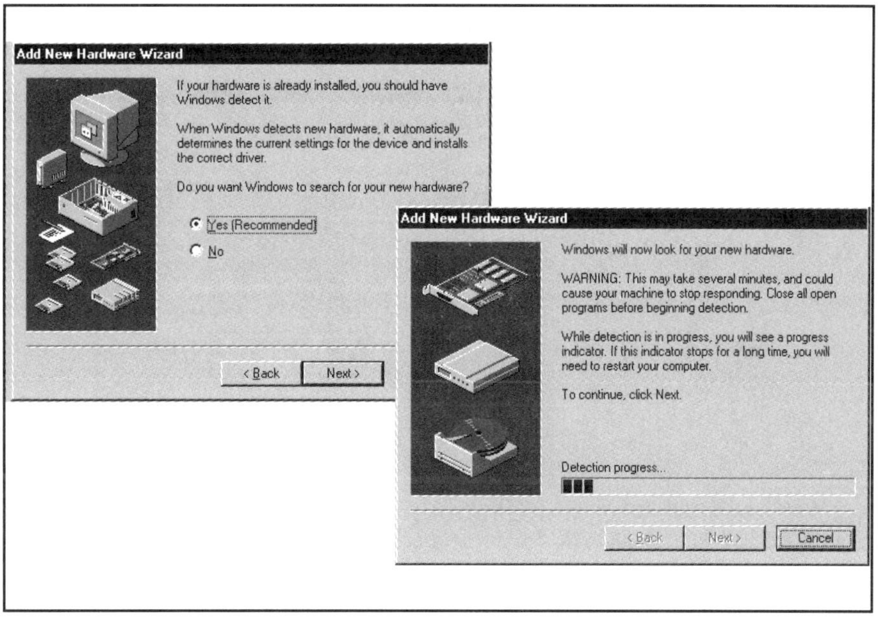

Gain Performance Efficiency by Replacing the "Real" with the "Virtual"

If you had a PCMCIA device, Power Management, Sound Card, CD-ROM, or SCSI device attached to your system before installing Windows 95, a series of real-mode DOS device drivers may be loading unnecessarily in your new CONFIG.SYS file. Windows 95 is smart enough to comment out lines in AUTOEXEC.BAT that load MSCDEX.EXE or SmartDrive; these hardware, multimedia, and disk-related drivers are usually untouched when you migrate to Windows 95. The drivers occupy DOS conventional or upper memory, and can be eliminated if Win95 has VXD equivalents. For instance, select Add New Hardware and choose No for the peripheral search, but if you have a Creative Labs Sound Blaster or Adaptec SCSI card, you can select these from the device list, as shown here:

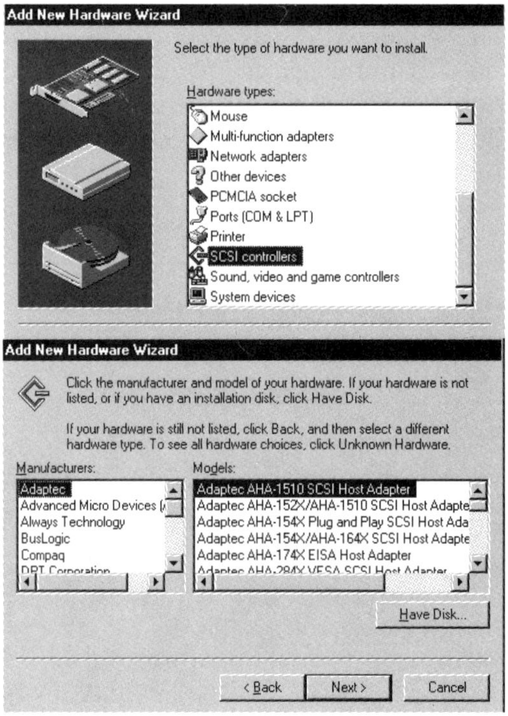

Win95 will install its own drivers for these peripherals, allowing you to remove the real-mode drivers left by DOS in the CONFIG.SYS. The same procedure can be used to recognize a PC card (PCMCIA), or install Win95's internal power management support for portable computers.

Several optional hardware options can be added from .INF files located on the CD-ROM. For instance, you can add support for the Internet SLIP protocol by selecting the Have Disk option and pointing it to the appropriate directory on the CD-ROM. The Have Disk option is also used for third-party video drivers not specifically included in Win95.

The System Object—Win95's Central Nervous System

The System object works in conjunction with the Add New Hardware component. It bears an icon that resembles the old Windows Terminal program. "System" is really the brain of the Windows Control Panel. It has four tabs that let users delve into the guts of a computer's hardware configuration and inspect Win95's built-in performance settings. Useful things you can do here:

- Confirm that all of your computer's peripherals are properly recognized and in working order.
- Display or print diagnostics about low-level system settings.
- Edit and troubleshoot system settings.
- Adjust Win95 features like File System Access, hard disk caching, graphics acceleration, and Virtual Memory (the Win95 swap file).

The General Tab

The General tab shows you the version of Windows 95 you are running, as well as any incremental beta or revision number. It also displays your registration information, computer CPU-type, and amount of RAM installed in the system.

The Device Manager Tab

The Device Manager tab contains a representation of the system and its components, presented in a convenient outline structure:

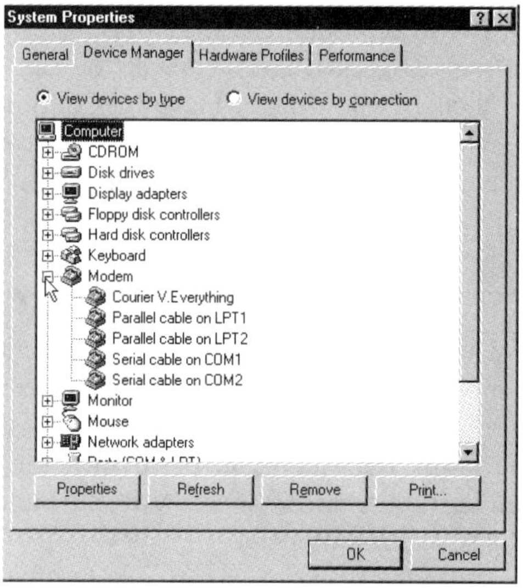

For instance, you can click on ports for a tree display of all the printer and communications ports available. The Device Manager doesn't allow you to install components; rather it is the best way to make sure that everything is connected. You can run this utility immediately after installation, to make sure all of your modems, network connections, and multimedia hardware are in place and working properly.

For instance, if you double-click the modem object on the outline, you'll see a list of all the modems which the system currently recognizes (You can also single-click the "+" box in front of any item on the tree to expand it.) If you select an installed modem and click the Properties button, this will open a three-tabbed examination of modem details. (This information screen is also available through the modems object elsewhere on the Control Panel. One of the nice things about Windows 95 is the redundancy that allows you to access system information through a number of different routes.) Through the tree-based Device Manager list you can proactively examine every aspect of the system. For instance, you can view the input/output range of the system speaker by selecting System Devices\System Speaker\Properties.

tip *To get a more complete diagnostic dump of your system's configuration than you've probably ever seen before, select the Computer icon at the top of the Device Manager tree and click on the Properties button. You'll see that you can display a system interrupt list, examine all of the port addresses assigned in conventional memory, show a list of DMA channels used by peripherals or browse a segment-by-segment list of all reserved memory addresses. You can also print this diagnostic information by highlighting the My*

Computer icon and clicking the Print button. It's actually a good idea to do a printout of all of this information shortly after installing Windows 95. Some of this stuff may look pretty weird and useless to you. But if you discover that there are things on your system that don't work, the list will be invaluable to your consultant or support technician who has to figure out what's wrong.

The Device Manager Properties dialogs can also help you perform diagnostic tests on the internals of your system and let you change low-level system settings. For instance, if you open the Port properties for a Serial Port, you'll see that the Port Settings tab allows you to set the initial internal connection rate for the port. (See Figure 8-8.) This is analogous to what you used to have to do in DOS with the MODE command. The Advanced Properties button allows you to regulate the Receive and Transmit buffers for a high-speed 16550 serial port. If there is an address conflict or other hardware conflict on your system, you'll see it described in the Device Status box on the General tab. For some devices, you can actually change the system driver and reassign a port address or IRQ to resolve system conflicts or improve performance. For instance, you might have a high-speed, serial port installed with a low-speed driver, or a high-speed ECP Printer Port assigned to a standard parallel port driver. The Driver and Resources tabs under Properties allow you to edit the system configuration when appropriate.

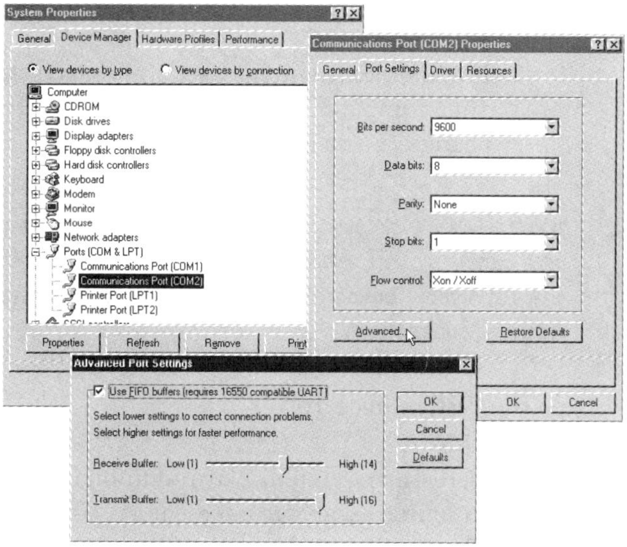

FIGURE 8-8

The configuration of some installed hardware devices can be modified by selecting the component in the Device Manager listing and clicking the Properties button. Here you see the settings for a high-speed serial port. ■

The Hardware Profiles Tab

The Hardware Profiles tab allows you to create multiple system configurations that you can choose from at startup. For instance, you may be expecting to use a portable computer with several different monitors, or in both stand-alone and docked productivity situations. When you create multiple Startup profiles, you are prompted to select the hardware profile in which to start Windows. Windows loads only the device drivers for those hardware devices included in the profile you select.

tip *If you have a hardware profile with the same name as an MS-DOS multiple configuration menu item, the corresponding menu item will be run automatically when you start in that hardware profile.*

You can also use the Device Manager to enable or disable individual elements of a hardware profile on-the-fly. Here's how:

1. Click on the plus sign next to the hardware type and then double-click the hardware.
2. In the Device Usage area, place a checkmark next to each hardware profile in which you want the specific component to be enabled. Clear the check box to disable the component for that hardware profile.
3. If you do this, you may see a message prompting you to restart your computer. Click Yes to do so and activate the hardware change you've just made.

note *If you discover a resource conflict with a component that is no longer being used on your system, select the component on the main Device Manager display and click the Remove button. With newer plug-and-play hardware, Windows 95 will clear resources automatically.*

The Performance Tab

The Performance tab displays additional information about memory and system resource usage, virtual memory, disk compression, and whether the 32-bit file system is active.

The numerical percent listed for System Resources is analogous to the display you used to see in the old "About Program Manager" box in

Windows 3.1. Basically, a number between 75 and 100 percent is good, and indicates that you have plenty of resources to spare. If you are working with multiple applications, System Resources may sometimes drop below 50 percent, in which case you should proceed with caution. If the number drops below 30 percent, you should immediately close all unnecessary windows and applications and be sure to save your work. In the beta-test days of Windows 95 there was a lot of controversy and static about The Microsoft Network and 32-bit versions of Microsoft Office programs causing a drastic resource drain. As a result, Microsoft implemented some changes that make this kind of resource drop less common.

tip *You don't have to open the System object and waste keystrokes to check available System Resources. Instead, just make sure the Win95 Resource Meter has been installed on the desktop. Open Resource Meter, and you have a permanent, floating display available on the taskbar.*

The File System setting tells you whether Windows 95 is providing 32-bit access to your files or whether one or more hard disk partitions are operating in MS-DOS compatibility mode. The 32-bit file system of Windows 95 is similar to the feature first provided in Windows for Workgroups version 3.1. It makes a significant improvement in the speed with which programs are launched, files are loaded and saved, and in other disk-related operations. There are several configuration issues that may bump this setting down to MS-DOS compatibility mode:

- You are using an older disk compression package like Stacker 3.1/4.*x* on one or more partitions.
- There are real-mode device drivers in your CONFIG.SYS file that conflict with 32-bit file access. Examples of these are drivers for certain IDE and SCSI controllers, and some drivers for CD-ROM devices, scanners, and other "Legacy Technology" (old hardware) peripherals.
- Third-party .VXD drivers designed for Windows 3.1 have been migrated to your Win95 SYSTEM.INI file.

In some cases, removing these drivers from CONFIG.SYS or SYSTEM.INI may restore 32-bit file access to your system. In the case of real-mode compression drivers, you will need to upgrade to a version of Stacker or DriveSpace that is specifically written to accommodate Windows 95. In the case of real-mode drivers for controllers and CD-ROM devices, the first thing you should attempt is to run the Add New Hardware component, discussed previously, and see whether Windows 95 has a protected mode driver for your peripheral. In some cases, Windows 95 can be told to recognize specific real-mode drivers as "safe" and restore 32-bit file access. This involves making an entry in the IOS.INI file located in your Windows directory.

FINE-TUNING PERFORMANCE SETTINGS Three buttons at the bottom of the Performance tab allow you to fine-tune Win95's internal settings. The File System button allows you to adjust caching for your hard drives and CD-ROM drive. The Graphics button controls the relationship between Windows 95 and your video adapter, and the Virtual Memory button lets you control the size and location of the Win95 swap file.

tip *Be sure to check the File System settings for CD-ROM drives after installing Windows 95. The default on many systems is to configure Windows 95 with a small cache for single-speed drives. This default is set even if a double or triple-speed drive is installed on your computer.*

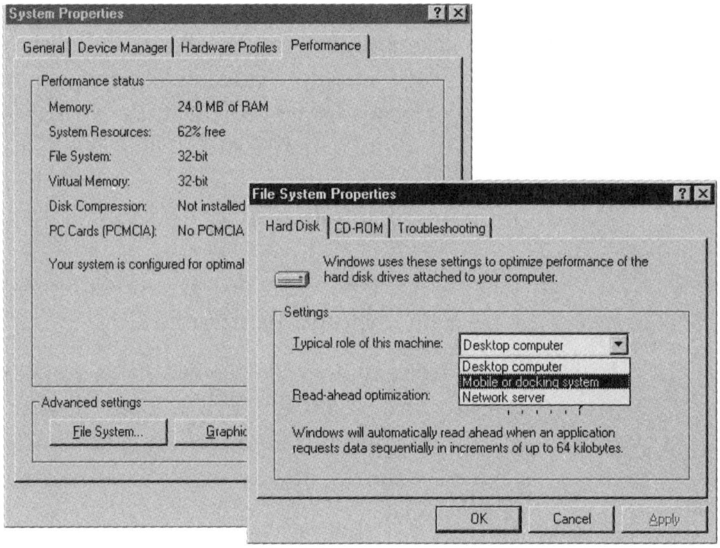

The Troubleshooting tab under the File System button will disable a series of advanced Win95 options that may cause problems on older computers. You can disable the locking of individual disk partitions, write-behind operations for the disk cache, and protected mode/32-bit handling of the hard drive. The time when you want to use these options is when your system is not performing properly. Disabling various features on this tab may clear up performance problems and allow you to isolate hardware conflicts.

The Graphics button allows you to minimize or maximize the extent to which Win95 uses accelerator functions built into your graphics card. Virtual Memory allows you to reassign the location of the swap file to another location other than the default on the Win95 host partition.

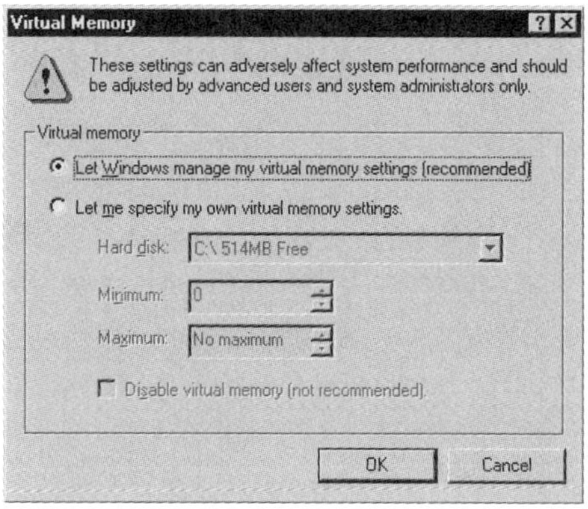

You can also establish a minimum and maximum size for the swap file, if you have disk storage limitations. Generally, it's best to allow Windows 95 to regulate the swap file, since it can dynamically expand or shrink the file depending on the need for additional virtual memory. It does no harm to reassign the physical partition where the swap file resides. This is a useful option when you run out of disk space on the original Win95 host drive. If Win95 is installed on drive C, and you have 20 or 30MB of free space on drive D, then relocating the swap file to the freer drive is a good, logical move.

Other Hardware-Related Components

Other hardware-related aspects of the Control Panel include:

The Mouse

Using the Mouse object, you can select the buttons for right or left handed use. You can adjust click and pointer speed, add or remove "trails," (helpful in finding the cursor), and select different pointer shapes and styles. All actions are so easy that they do not have to be explained. With this component, Microsoft has shown some consideration for other viewpoints. The company has always supported the two-button mouse (no surprise, they manufacture the market leader in that category), but Windows 95 supplies driver options to support Logitech and others that offer devices with a third button (which many people find useful). Nevertheless, you can expect this to be an area where you may need to install drivers if your pointing device is not one of the top five.

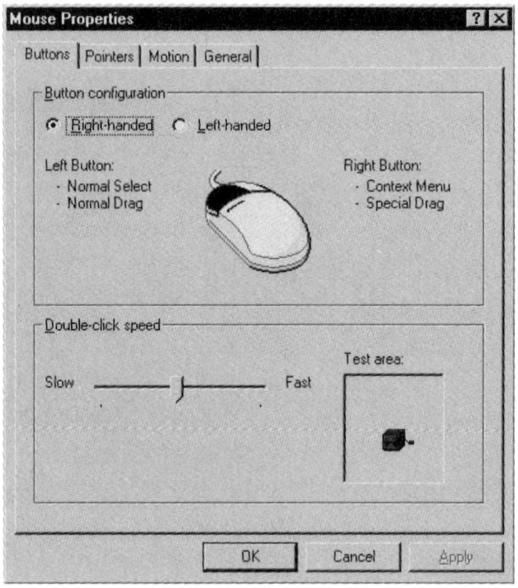

There is, however, a disappointing omission: Later versions of the Microsoft mouse driver offer a "wrap-around" feature that allows you to slide the cursor off one edge of the screen and emerge in the corresponding opposite space. This feature—which either you love or you hate—is unavailable in the Windows 95 system.

The Keyboard

The Keyboard object controls character repeat rate, delay interval, and cursor blink rate. It also allows you to select different languages, or install "alternative" keyboards. If you have a Microsoft Natural Keyboard, a separate Control Panel object may be installed, which will override the generic control. (See Chapter 4 for a detailed list of keyboard shortcuts that allow you to control the desktop without a mouse.)

tip *To choose languages other than English on the Language tab, you need to install multi-language support with the Add/Remove Programs object. Under each choice on the Language tab, you can also select individual keyboard layouts.*

The Joystick

Microsoft wants to be your game company; the Joystick feature is an important part of that strategy. Most "normal" Windows 95 users will ignore this, and the component connects to other Control Panel aspects in that it is recognized at installation, can be automatically installed at a later time by plug-and-play, and turns up on the Device Manager. Hardware permitting, you can install up to 16 different joysticks of 17 different modes.

Joysticks may not seem important now, to the average Windows user. This will change. Microsoft is giving Windows 95 the big game push, and doesn't want to be caught short in the joystick support department. Once the game software appears, more people will realize that the mouse isn't enough.

Joysticks also could find other "non-game" uses as graphical software becomes more sophisticated. This will meet with the typical backlash, but think of it this way—In 1989, most "serious" PC users sneered at the mouse.

tip *On some systems, if you don't have a joystick attached to the game port during installation, the Joystick control component won't appear on the Control Panel. To add the Joystick controls after installation, open Add New Hardware, and answer No, to the question about automatically searching for new hardware. Click the Next button and choose Sound, video and game controllers from the hardware list. In the next screen, choose Microsoft from the manufacturer's list on the left, and Gameport Controllers from the Models list on the right. Click the Next and Finish buttons, and the Joystick component will be placed on the Control Panel.*

Talk Talk (Communications and Connectivity)

Many people believe that the greatest advantage Windows 95 has over its predecessors and competitors is a set of well-integrated connectivity features. To implement these features, you'll find a series of communications-centric aspects on the Control Panel.

The Modem Control Panel utility allows you to automatically detect and configure one or more modems attached to your system. This is one of the more impressive of Win95's plug-and-play features. When you click the Add button, the Setup Wizard actually goes out through your serial and parallel ports (or PC Card slots), interrogating any attached devices. The Wizard does a fairly good job of detecting and identifying individual brands and modem types automatically. As more and more peripherals are programmed to adhere to the Microsoft/Intel plug-and-play standard, this Wizard will do an even better job. After Win95 does its best to detect your individual modem type, you can adjust the settings from a list of hundreds of different manufacturers and modems. What actually happens when a particular type is selected is that a preconfigured set of initialization strings and settings are automatically copied to the System Registry. You have the ability to modify or add to these settings through the Modem Properties configuration options.

The General tab under Modem Properties lists all of the modems currently installed on the system and the default dialing location. A series of buttons for each modem type lets you inspect or reconfigure their port assignment, maximum speed, and speaker volume. The Modem component also controls data bits, stop bits and parity, along with "Call Preferences." You can wait for a tone before dialing, cancel the call if not connected in 60 seconds, and disconnect a call if the line is idle for a proscribed time. The first feature will be handy for those who use a line for voice and data, and will prevent annoying tonal interruptions if someone is on the extension. (These options are accessed on the Connection tab under Properties for each individual modem.)

The Dialing Properties option contains options to select tone or pulse, use a calling card, disable call waiting, or dial any other special access codes.

Advanced settings govern flow control, error control, modulation type and any extra settings. This box also has a checkbox to create a log file to measure all modem activity.

The Diagnostics Tab under Modem Properties lets you see your port and configuration information. Select the port your modem is attached to and click the More Info button to run a set of diagnostic tests.

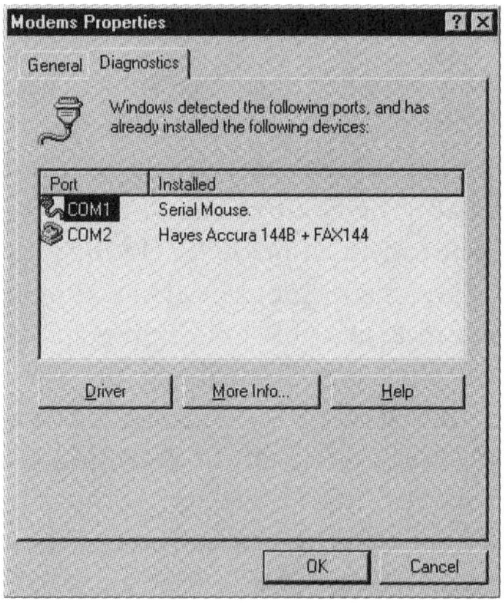

tip *If the installed modem isn't working, you can use the Modems object to de-install the modem and install a generic (Standard Modem Types) driver. If your modem isn't automatically detected, you can also scroll through the list of manufacturers and try selecting an alternate modem type from the same vendor. If worst comes to worst, you can add a custom initialization string to one of the Standard Modem types: select Properties\Connections and click the Advanced button. You can enter additional Hayes modem commands in the Extra Settings box: &C2 to enable carrier detection, &K1 to enable high-speed compression, or &F to reset the modem to its factory defaults. Consult your modem manual for the specific Hayes commands that apply to your modem.*

The Network Component

The Network object allows you to install, remove, or verify any of four basic networking components—Client, Adapter, Protocol, or Service. Like many other Windows 95 aspects, this provides the second or third line of attack to connecting these aspects. If you are installing a card or signing on to a service, the process will be handled through other avenues—like plug-and-play, Hardware Detection, or a third-party installation program. Nevertheless, this object is a handy troubleshooting tool that allows you to make sure that everything is connected properly, and that you are speaking the same language as the connected client or server.

note *The most common uses you will have for the Network component are to enable file and printer sharing for a direct cable connection or to install the TCP/IP protocol for Dial-Up Networking to the Internet. Windows 95 does not install these features during Setup unless you choose them specifically.*

To install File and Printer Sharing, click the File and Print Sharing button on the Configuration tab. To install the TCP/IP protocol (if it doesn't already appear in the Network Components list), choose Add\Protocol (double-click Add), Microsoft\TCP/IP as shown in Figure 8-9. Refer to the sections on Direct Cable Connection and Dial-Up Networking section in Chapter 5 for more information on how to configure these features.

The Identification tab displays the Computer Name and Workgroup for this individual computer. In order to establish a network or direct cable connection, each workstation must be assigned a distinct, individual Computer Name.

Access Control allows you to control individual user access to shared resources. Each drive, directory, printer, and so on, can be password protected or restricted to use by individual users or workgroups.

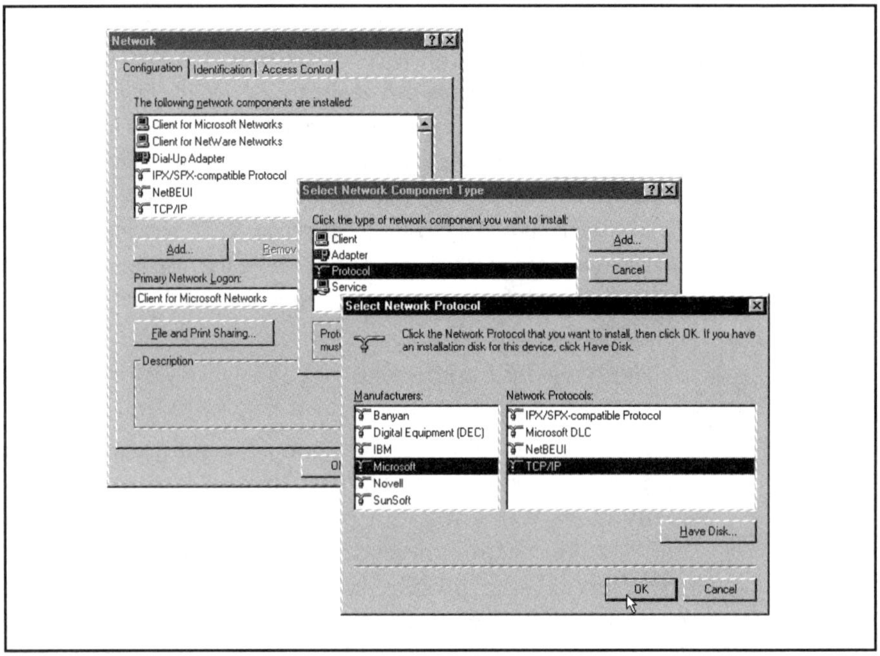

FIGURE 8-9 *You can install the Microsoft TCP/IP protocol (necessary for Dial-Up Internet Connections) through the Network Configuration tab by clicking the Add button and selecting Protocol\Microsoft\TCP/IP.*

Microsoft Mail

The Microsoft Mail Postoffice object browses the network for individual Microsoft Mail post office boxes. Once located, the post office box on your network server will know automatically where to send your electronic mail. You may find when installing The Microsoft Network and Mail and Fax profiles that no post office box for you exists. In this case, you can use the Microsoft Mail component to create a post office box for you on your local machine.

Mail and Fax

The Mail and Fax object provides the configuration information for Microsoft Exchange, which is one of Win 95's major new conveniences. The trouble with electronic mail, as it has developed, is how people are compelled to subscribe to e-mail through several different sources. Even the Internet, with its universal "@" addressing system, has failed to centralize the process. Typically users will have to use one mail program to log into CompuServe, another mail program for Internet accounts, and a third package for the office network. Microsoft Exchange is designed to transmit and receive mail from a single source, making it transparent to the user which service is being used. The comparison is to regular mail delivery, where it all arrives in the same box whether it comes from Tucson, Tucumcari, Tehatchapi, or Tonopah.

The Mail and Fax object allows you to inspect or edit user profiles for all of the information services supported by the Microsoft Exchange Inbox. Currently, the services supported out-of-the-box in Windows 95 are the Microsoft Network (you'll have to sign up and subscribe to use it), dedicated Fax transmissions, and Microsoft Mail. The Microsoft Mail protocol is supported over a Dial-Up Connection, Direct Connection, or Local Area Network.

The universal Exchange Inbox/Outbox has the intelligence to track who gets which message through what service. You finish work on a file and select File\Send. The recipient's address book listing determines if it is sent as a fax, through a LAN, through an online service, or as a message over a beeper.

The Personal Address Book contains not only e-mail addresses, but names, phone/fax numbers, mailing addresses, and other personal contact information. Through the open MAPI interfaces, the Personal Address Book is accessible from a wide variety of applications, and through the use of MAPI drivers, it is also the user interface for corporate e-mail and information services directories. The Personal Address Book can store addresses for multiple e-mail systems at the same time. The Personal Address Book and Personal Information Store are kept in two files, MAILBOX.PAB and MAILBOX.PST, stored in the Exchange directory on your Win95 host drive. You also have the option of configuring alternate .PAB and .PST files for Exchange with different sets of addresses and e-mail logs.

remember *If you have to subsequently reinstall Win95, be sure to back up and save the .PAB and .PST files to preserve your e-mail records.*

While a certain amount of competition exists between online service providers, it is likely that cooperation will prevail with regard to the Windows 95 universal Inbox. Drivers for CompuServe and the Internet will be readily available, from Microsoft or elsewhere, for free. These drivers will load through the Services\Add dialog box, and will require that the user have an account with that particular provider. For instance, the CompuServe driver will allow the seamless transfer of mail and files on CompuServe, but will not provide access to other online services. You might prepare a message for delivery to a CompuServe recipient and hit Send for a seamless transaction. To log on to a forum, however, you'll still need to use WinCIM, TAPCIS, or a standard telecommunications program.

Mail and Fax can be used to configure several different services on the same user profile when you open the Inbox. If you decide to do this, each of the installed services can be contacted in succession to transmit and receive e-mail. Each of the individual Service profiles can be edited by selecting it on the Services tab and clicking the Properties button. Services can be added or deleted from an individual profile with the Add and Remove buttons.

---

tip *To set the delivery order for the Services configured in a user profile, open Mail and Fax and click the Show Profiles button. Select the Profile you want to adjust and click the Properties button. This will open a three-tabbed menu of settings properties. Select the Delivery tab. The bottom portion of the window displays the configured services in the order that they will be accessed when Inbox is active. The up and down arrow boxes to the right of the list can be used to rearrange the delivery order.*

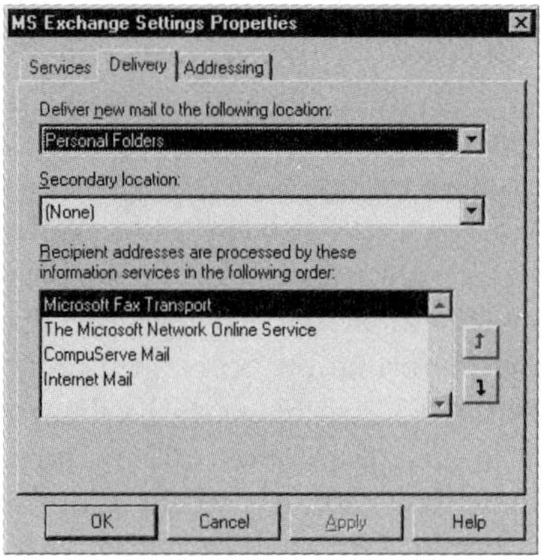

After you click the Show Profiles button on the MS Exchange Settings Properties screen, the Microsoft Exchange Profiles screen appears. The option at the bottom of the General tab on this screen lets you select a default service profile. This service profile will be loaded automatically when you open Inbox. You can also configure the Inbox to prompt you for the correct service profile each time you open it. Unfortunately, the "prompt on open" option can't be selected under the Mail and Fax Control Panel component. You would think it should be there, but it isn't. To make Microsoft Exchange prompt you for a service profile, you must first open the Inbox with the default profile. Then select Options from the Inbox Tool menu. You'll find a set of radio buttons on this screen to toggle "Prompt for a profile" on or off. (For more complete information about configuring and working with Inbox/MS Exchange, refer to Chapter 10.)

note *If Fax Services is installed in a profile, a variety of Fax options are buried in the Message and Modem tabs under the Fax Properties screen.*

The Password Is "Swordfish"

Microsoft has a program called Bob, a "social interface" environment that anyone who has ever used a PC before loves to hate. Advanced users take special pleasure in scorning its simplistic interface. Windows 95, however, retains Bob's sole redeeming feature, universal password protection and the ability for separate users to create different environments on the same PC. This feature is controlled through the Passwords object on the Control Panel.

Password protection has become more necessary, as data security needs have increased. While the machines themselves have become more expensive, powerful, and sophisticated, their real value has to do with the data on the hard drive. For this reason, you want to take steps to protect this data. A password then becomes the equivalent of a lock on your door, and will be especially important in the cubicle culture that has taken over modern corporations. Even if you are just trying to keep the kids off of your PC, this is a handy feature.

The User Profiles tab allows you to select a single password configuration for the machine, or customize preferences and desktop settings for each user. This level of customization extends to desktop icons and network connections and Start Menu settings and program groups. While the level of security isn't complete and thorough, these settings allow several people in the same family to share a computer with a moderate level of privacy.

The Change Password screen allows you to change one or more of these passwords by typing in the old sequence and then typing in the new sequence twice:

When the Passwords option is activated with multiple users, the Shut Down command adds another option; that to shut down and log on as another user.

Multiple Desktops for Individuals or Workgroups

The Password object has a nifty, hidden feature. It allows you to set up alternate desktops for multiple users. See the section on multiple desktops in Chapter 4 for details on how to make it work.

Sight and Sound

Sound can add a lot to the computing experience. Specifically, the PC's incorporation of multimedia aspects will evolve into the world of the talking computer. Like Scotty on "Star Trek," we will one day carry on meaningful dialogues with our PCs.

On a simpler level, Windows 95 contains a way to provide sound cues, little squawks and beeps that are tied to simple system functions. Can you do without this? Absolutely. Anyone who has ever participated in a focus group about PC productivity has no doubt failed to mention the need to assign odd sound clips to different activities.

Now that they are here, however, these cues provide a small step toward usability. The Sounds object of the Control Panel ties such squawks to about 40 different system functions. You won't memorize them all, and won't consciously associate a certain blip to a specific action. After a while, however, you will learn to recognize the various sounds, to the point where it seems that you are carrying on a conversation with your PC. It may not be especially profound, and is on the level of your cat telling you to change the litterbox—a furious sound that may signify nothing.

Sound *schemes*, where certain themes are explored, will gain popularity. Several of these are included as options in Windows 95, and even more are present in Microsoft Plus!.

In the spirit of personalization, you may want to create your own sound schemes. To do so, follow these steps:

1. Open the Sounds object and select the item to assign the sound to.
2. The sound currently assigned to that function will appear in the box below the function list. Hit the Browse button to select a sound, then select the > key to preview that sound.
3. When you've finished selecting all the sounds, select Save As and give the new scheme an appropriate name, as shown here:

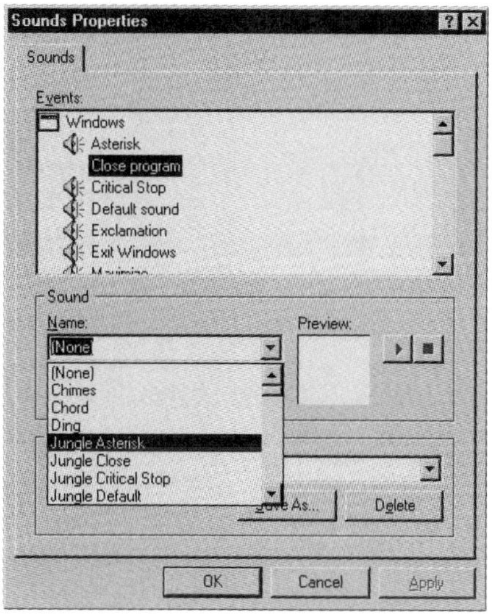

This process opens the door to rampant creativity, providing the opportunity to attach the most compelling sounds in history to simple commands. With sound compression technology, large hard disks, and enough time, you can blast out "Louie, Louie" every time Windows starts and hear Nixon's resignation speech at system close.

On the other hand, taste and restraint are as applicable here as in the selection of screen colors. Spending too much time developing a complex sound scheme represents a wasted effort. Sound cues should be brief and innocuous. It will help if they have some relation to the assigned function, but not necessary. Like screen colors, any aspect that demands too much attention here will detract from rather than enhance the computing experience.

Power users know how to record complex .WAV files and attach them to system functions. But the reason they are "power" users is they don't waste electricity doing so.

Sound schemes, as they appear here, have nothing to do with multimedia CD-ROM titles. The sound capacity of a commercial title will operate independently of these sound cues. Which is to say, if one works, it doesn't mean that the other will; or will not.

The Multimedia Properties Dialog Box

The Multimedia Properties dialog box contains several tabs that let you fine-tune sound and video effects.

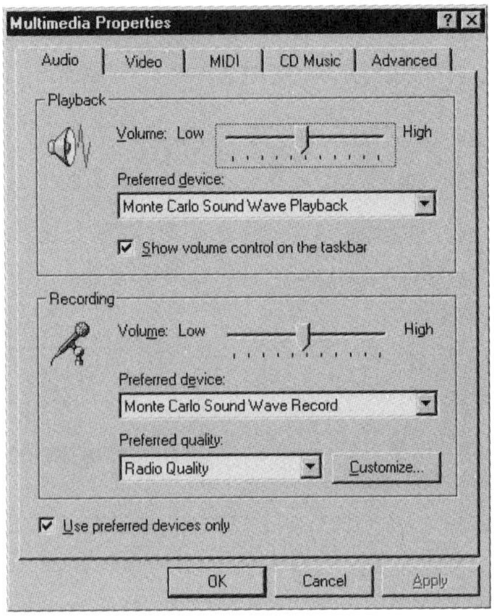

- The Audio tab lets you set various options for sound compression as well as making rough-and-ready adjustments to sound playback and recording volume. (The full-powered volume control on the taskbar allows you to make more refined adjustments.) .WAV files can be recorded with a number of different compression and sound quality settings. The Preferred Quality list box at the bottom of the Audio tab presents three basic recording qualities. If you hit the Customize button for any of these, another dialog box opens up, allowing you to toggle mono and stereo recording, select a particular compression format, and control the sound sample rate. See Chapters 5 and 11 for more information about how these options work.
- The Video tab allows you to select between Full screen and window for video playback, with the window options being original size, double original size, 1/2, 1/4 and 1/16 screen size. The Advanced tab displays all multimedia-related drivers, in outline form.
- The MIDI tab lists the installed drivers, and contains a button to install a new instrument. Like most Windows 95 installation procedures, the Wizard walks you through the process. This option is similar to the MIDIMAP utility that you used to see in Windows 3.1
- The CD Music tab shows the letter of the CD-ROM drive that is being used to play music, along with the volume control for the headphones that output directly from the drive. This is a handy

tool if your drive doesn't have an independent volume control (usually a little wheel on the drive face).

note *Unlike the Windows 3.1 Drivers applet, Win95's Multimedia component does not let you install direct support for third-party sound and animation schemes like Quicktime and MPEG. However, if you are clever with SYSTEM.INI parameters, you can still do so. See Chapter 5 for details.*

The Cut Curb (Accessibility) Options

The Accessibility Options module, a new addition to the Control Panel for Windows 95, is designed to meet the special needs of Windows users who have some sort of physical disability. While these services may make the difference between PC use and PC uselessness to some people, the aspects can also be helpful for the so-called able-bodied user. Consider that the motivation behind the mouse, now a universal pointing device, was to give disabled users a means to control the computer. Another real world example: Cities have installed "cut curbs" in sidewalks ostensibly to make it possible for wheelchairs to travel downtown. This has become a convenience for everyone; bicyclists, merchants and others who want to avoid tripping over a "normal" curb.

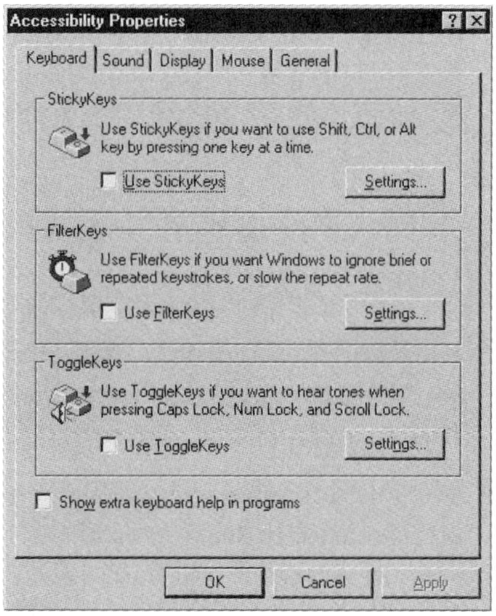

The Windows 95 Accessibility Properties box, shown here, is separated into five sections:

- The Keyboard tab allows the use of StickyKeys, FilterKeys, and ToggleKeys.

  StickyKeys sensitizes the CTRL, ALT, and SHIFT keys and keeps them active until you press a key other than one of those keys. This is meant to help people who have trouble pressing two keys simultaneously to execute multiple key commands used by some applications. It can also help "lazy" typists, or those who feel that multiple key commands are confusing or require too complicated hand configurations.

  FilterKeys disables repeated keystrokes. For instance, an unsure-fingered typist might hold the "s" key down too long and end up with sssss. This module also adjusts the keyboard repeat rate, which can also minimize such mistakes for the less than skilled touch typist.

  ToggleKeys provide an audio/visual cue for the CAPS LOCK, NUM LOCK and SCROLL LOCK keys, beeping when they are toggled on or off. This is about two-thirds useful: The SCROLL LOCK key doesn't have very many real uses. With the others, it may be helpful to know when the features are active or disabled. This feature raises the interactivity feature of the PC just a notch.

- The Sound tab complements system alerts with visual cues, to help the hearing impaired or the visually inclined.

  SoundSentry allows you to configure parts of the interface to flash in conjunction with various system warning sounds and beeps. There are three categories: Windowed programs, full-screen text programs, and full-screen graphics programs. For instance, you can set the active window bar to flash along with system error messages. This will of course help the hearing impaired, but will also make the system's response a little more interesting than a plain old beep.

  ShowSounds is a little like closed captioning, common to television. Here, programs display captions corresponding with the sounds they make. The developers of such programs, however, need to preconfigure the software to include the feature.

- The Display tab toggles a high contrast mode, that makes the screen easier to see and read.

  This screen mode flattens out all of the graphics and raises the contrast, as shown in Figure 8-10. The best explanation is that it makes Windows 95 look like Windows 2.0, removing all of the character, excitement, and polish from the interface. Another way to look at it would be to picture the removal of VGA components and replacing them with EGA.

This generic environment is actually easier to see. All of the menus are triple size, and the taskbar explanations are replaced with rudimentary icons. The screen is reproportioned to make everything clear and unambiguous, even if it is, well, ugly by Windows 95 standards.

At the same time, this mode may be useful in situations where flash means little and light is scarce—like on a dark plane. Along the same lines, this high-contrast low graphics mode may help extend battery life in those really crucial situations. (You'll also need to set your default color resolution to 16 colors or less through the Control Panel Display utility to conserve power.)

- The Mouse tab configures the numeric keypad to act as a pointing device.

  This ability was first seen in the ergonomically sensitive Microsoft Natural Keyboard, and is the coolest Accessibility feature for the so-called able bodied user. When the Mouse option is activated, the cursor control aspects of the numeric keypad are disabled; instead, these keys move the cursor in the general direction of the key. This is to say that it does not reflect the subtlety of movement of a mouse or trackball, but it does get where it's

FIGURE 8-10

The Accessibility high-contrast screen settings present a Win95 desktop designed for easy reading.

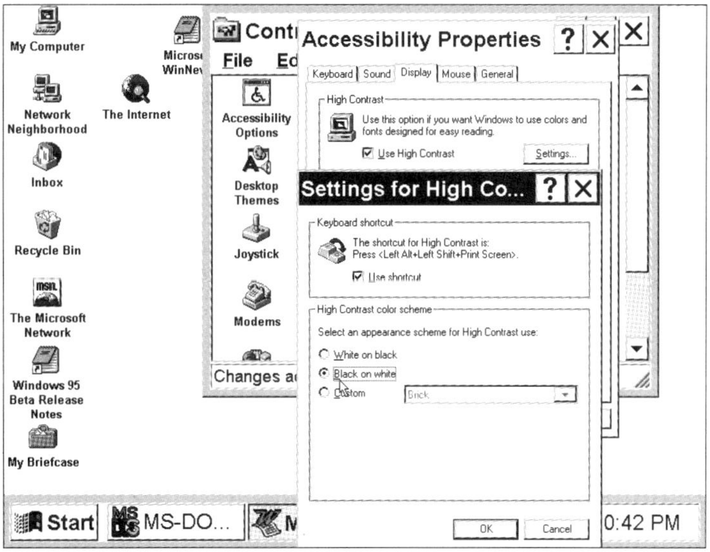

supposed to go. And once you arrive, a double-tap motion on the numeric 5 key is the same thing as a double-click on the mouse.

When this feature is enabled, it is indicated by a mouse symbol on the lower right-hand portion of the taskbar. When the feature is installed but turned off, it is covered by a standard circle-with-a-slash symbol (as in No Smoking).

This capability is handy for disabled and so-called able bodied users alike, as it provides yet another way to get things done under Windows. Unfortunately, the component is somewhat limited, as it has no option to select the right-hand mouse button, which is of increasing importance in Windows

tip *If you use this feature, you'll probably want to push the speed up to at least the second to the highest notch or it will be unbearably slow.*

- The General tab controls user notification of accessibility features, and provides a way to turn off these features after a period of inactivity.

If you have a disability that corresponds with these modules, then you may find some help here. At the same time, a disabled person attempting to get any real use out of the PC will probably find these aspects rather shallow—in the same way that a writer won't really be thrilled by Windows 95's resident "word processor," WordPad. True productivity for users with serious disabilities will come from third parties.

In the meantime, the Accessibility Options of the Control Panel provide the first steps toward supporting users with disabilities. This is a little like supplying room for a handicapped parking space, widening the doors, or installing ramps. It shows some effort, but the real work is still required by the person who has the disability.

Ultimately, these cut-curb options can make the Windows 95 PC just a little easier, for users with or without any disabilities; representing little ways to polish, personalize and improve the interface.

ODBC 'Ya Later

The ODBC component allows you to add, modify, or delete ODBC drivers and data sources. ODBC drivers are specific .DLL files that applications like Excel, Access, or Quattro Pro can use to gain access to a particular data source.

Like other universal protocols, Open Database Connectivity (ODBC) is an open, programmable gateway development tool that continuously brokers requests between client applications and a variety of back-end data sources—including relational and nonrelational databases, real-time data feeds, electronic mail and scheduling, and more. In order to plug in here, users need to be speaking the same language, which is controlled by the Control Panel's ODBC object.

The object's default types—dBase, FoxPro, Access, and Paradox—provide a basic who's who for the category; chances are any database on the market will read and write to at least one of these types.

Should developers of other database types—old or new—wish to interface directly with ODBC they will supply the appropriate driver. In these cases, the object also allows you to easily set up, delete, or add all ODBC drivers on the system. Additionally, the options button allows you to select a log file for the tracing of ODBC calls.

To the Letter (Printer/Font Options)

While printers and fonts are discussed in detail elsewhere in this book (see Chapter 9), the road to typographical bliss begins on the Control Panel. Printers and Fonts are represented by folders shown in the default Control Panel, offering a clear way to manage installation and option settings.

The Fonts Folder

Under Windows 3.*x*, it was easy to inadvertently fill your disk with extra fonts and one day wake up to find there was no space left. The Win95 Fonts folder provides a faster path to cataloguing exactly which fonts are on the system; adding and deleting them as the need arises. The Fonts folder displays icons for all bitmap, Microsoft Vector, and TrueType fonts that are active under Windows 95. To manage Adobe Type 1 Postscript fonts, you need to use the third-party Adobe Type Manager utility. Postscript fonts are not displayed here. You can display the fonts that are listed alphabetically or by typeface similarity by selecting the appropriate option on the View menu.

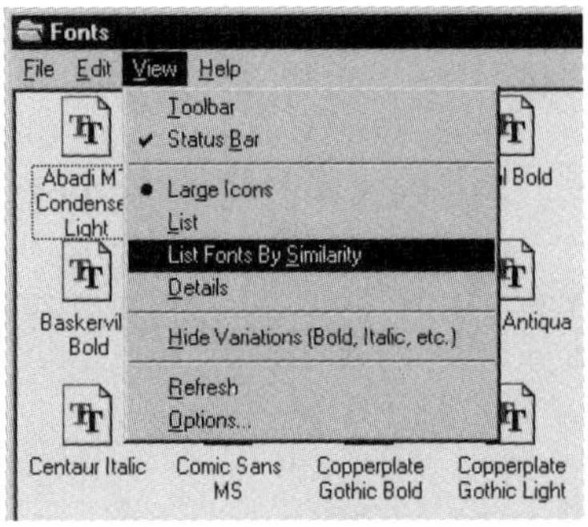

Located in the Windows\Fonts folder, any installed font will also be listed and displayed in the Font selection menu of Windows applications. Each font is its own object. A right click on that object allows you to delete it, show font properties, or open the object for a sample of the font, itself. So if you're uncertain about whether you'll ever need "Lucida Sans Unicode" you can display the font by double-clicking on it in the Fonts folder. In this way, you can inspect various installed fonts before deciding to delete them from the system. Offered in several sizes and styles, the font samples can also be dumped to a printer.

Inside the Fonts folder, fonts are shown with a "TT" or an "A" label, corresponding to TrueType or internal Windows system fonts. With the View menu, you can group similar fonts, or show the details for each font file. The "hide variations" view simplifies the list somewhat, as it weeds out stylistic variations of the same font. You can further streamline the list by checking the TrueType box in the View\Options menu, which removes any non-TrueType fonts from the list (although it does not remove these fonts from the disk).

The Fonts folder also contains a toolbar, which includes the same choices as the View menu.

note *If you have PostScript fonts installed on your system in the Adobe Type 1 format, these will not be displayed in the Win95 Fonts folder. The best way to view and manipulate PostScript fonts is through Adobe Type Manager. (See Chapter 9 for more information.)*

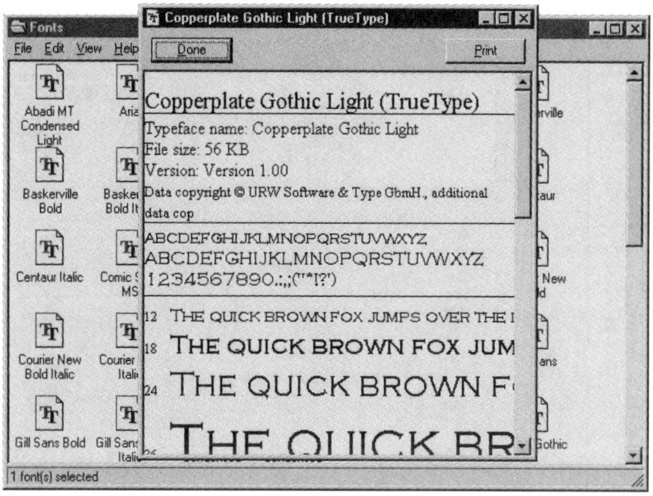

FIGURE 8-11

If you double-click any TrueType font that appears in the Fonts folder, a second display sample window will open.

The Printers Folder

The Printers folder looks like the Fonts folder, with the multiple views and different icon options. It appears in both the Control Panel and on the Start Menu under Settings.

If you double click on the Add Printer icon, the Add Printer Wizard is activated. This Wizard leads you through the process of selecting local or network printers, make and model, port, and name. (You can rename "HP DeskJet" with something more exciting, if you like). After a new printer has been installed, you have the option to immediately print a test page. You can do this at any time by right-clicking the Printer object's Properties menu and selecting the Print Test Page button.

Each installed printer is an individual object in the Printer folder. When you right-click on a Printer, a series of options come up on its context menu. In addition to the standard Create Shortcut/Delete/Rename opportunities, you can set the object as the default printer, pause current print jobs, or purge them completely. Additionally, you can activate printer sharing over a network.

As you can see in Figure 8-12, if you click on Open (or just double-click on the Printer icon), a print queue box pops up, showing a list of all the current and pending jobs. (This is similar to the bygone Windows 3.1 Print

FIGURE 8-12

The Properties dialog for each printer allows you to configure and control device-specific performance settings.

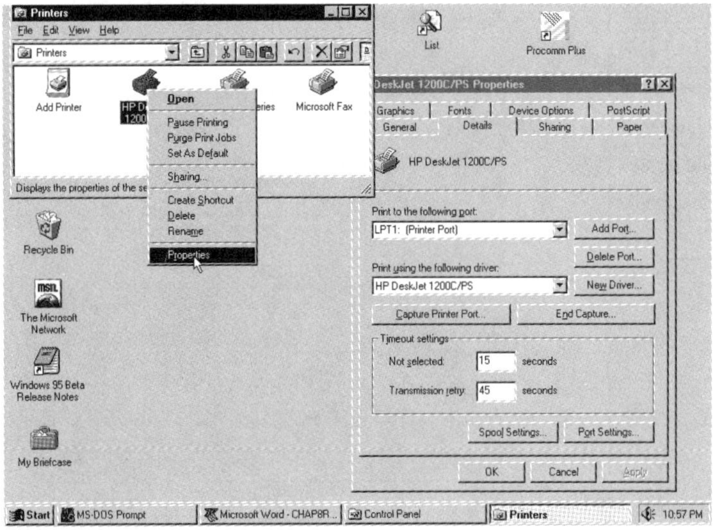

Manager.) The print queue information window includes the document name, current status of all print jobs, the owner (originating application), and a live readout of its current status. The pulldown menus contain the same set of Default/Purge/Pause options as the right-click context menu.

The Properties dialog box can be opened either from the print queue Printer menu or by right-clicking the Printer object's context menu. The Properties dialog box contains printer information and features in six categories:

Category	**Purpose**
General	Printing a test page
Details	For port, driver, and spool settings
Paper	For size and orientation
Graphics	For resolution, intensity and color settings
Fonts	Showing typefaces available to the specific printer
Device Options	Displaying or configuring available printer memory and print quality

If you are planning to access these printer options on a frequent basis, you may get tired of burrowing into the recesses of the Control Panel each time you want to change the configuration. Instead, you can create a shortcut to any Printer object simply by dragging it to the desktop. You can right-click on a desktop Printer shortcut to place all of its control features at your fingertips.

Some Handy Things to Remember

- *In Windows 3.1, you edited the font mapping associations between Adobe Type 1 and TrueType fonts within the Printer driver's Setup options. In Windows 95, you'll find these options in the Properties dialog for each printer under the Fonts tab.*
- *The scaling and resolution options for PostScript printers are found in the Properties dialog under the Graphics tab. For color printers, a series of color calibration options is also located under this tab.*
- *Print Quality options are found under the Properties\Device Option tab.*
- *If you want to print to a file, you'll find this option under the Properties\Details tab. Print spooler controls are also under the Details tab.*
- *To share a printer across a network or Direct Cable Connection, sharing is enabled under the Properties\Sharing tab.*

note *In Chapter 4, you'll learn a trick that will let you re-create the Printers folder as a fan-open menu on the first level of the Start Menu.*

For more information about controlling and working with printers, see Chapter 9.

Are We There Yet? (Date/Time and Regional Settings)

Windows 95 automatically configures the computer in terms of time and location. Reading from the existing system clock, it will select your time zone and, conveniently, automatically change the clock between standard and daylight savings (and notifying you at the next login). The Date/Time Properties dialog box, shown in Figure 8-13, lets you select either, along with a graphical representation of the world from which you can select the time zone.

note *You can also reach the Date/Time Properties dialog box with a right click on the taskbar's digital time readout.*

FIGURE 8-13

Windows 95 Regional Settings and Date/Time Properties

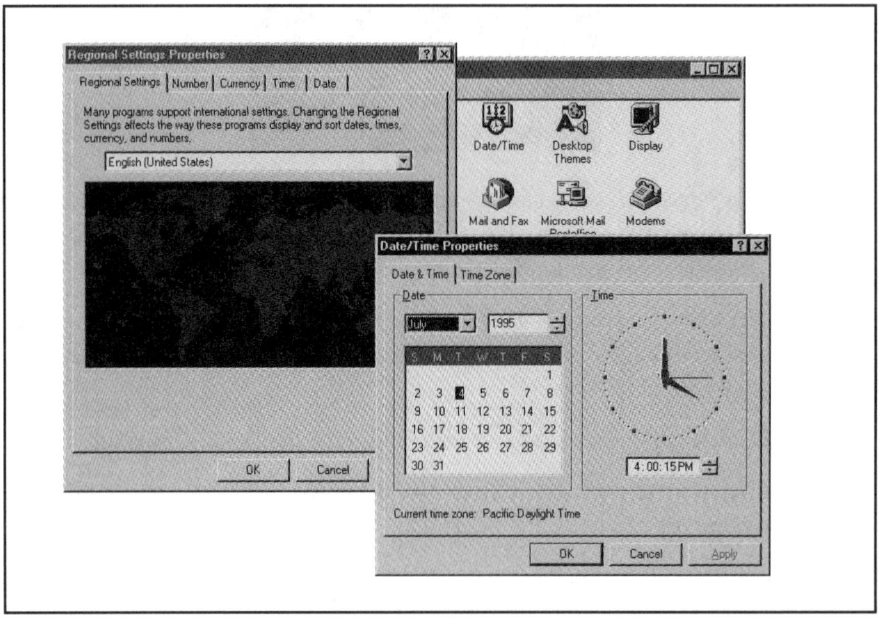

Regional Settings gives Windows 95 an international feel. You can choose a language, from Afrikaans to Swedish. Currency symbols and date styles can also be modified—for instance to accommodate the British "15 March" structure.

note *Some aspects can be changed individually, but changing the Regional settings automatically changes the settings on the Currency, Time and Date tabs to match the local customs. The Number, Currency, Time, and Date tabs allow you to edit the formats for individual display components.*

Additional Components

If you have a computer with Advanced Power Management or PC Card (PCMCIA) sockets installed, some additional options will appear on the Control Panel.

The PC Card (PCMCIA) component allows you to install new peripherals added to PC Card sockets and display the status of each individual socket. Options on the Socket Status tab allow you to display or disable the PC Card status icon on the taskbar. If Win95's automatic configuration of a PC Card causes memory conflicts, the Global Settings tab allows you to specify a specific range in upper memory (640K to 1MB) to be used as a shared memory resource.

The Power Management component allows you to toggle Advanced, Standard, and disabled power management features. For notebook computers, the Power status window displays the amount of battery time you have left, and allows you to place the Power Status monitor on the taskbar. The Suspend options allow you to determine when your computer's Suspend mode features will be activated.

Stay in Control

Have we missed anything? Here's a review summary of the most common things you'll want to do on the Control Panel after installing Windows 95:

- Add useful programs not included in a typical installation with Add/Remove Programs.
- Make a Startup disk if you didn't make one during installation. (Add New Programs, Startup Disk).
- Adjust video resolution above 640 × 480; change or remove wallpaper. Adjust the background color of the desktop (Display).
- Install/Configure Microsoft Exchange if you need it to manage faxes or e-mail (Mail/Fax).
- Install your modem if it wasn't detected during initial installation (Modems).
- Install network protocols you intend to connect to another computer via Direct Cable Connection, or Dial-Up Networking connection. Also set up TCP/IP for Internet and File Sharing (Network component).
- Install your printer if it was missed in the initial Win95 installation (Printers).
- Install the Joystick component if it wasn't added automatically (Add/Remove Programs, Soundcard, Microsoft, Gameport).
- Change CD-ROM speed settings if Win95 has a configured default of 1X CDROM (System Object, Performance, File System, CDROM—you may also want to adjust cache size and hard disk settings).
- Make a shortcut to the Control Panel on the Start Menu (see the first section of this chapter).

Ultimately, the Windows 95 Control Panel carries on a Windows tradition: It is a potpourri of various system checks and balances that allow you to fine-tune system aspects from the cosmetic to the cosmic. Like other aspects of Windows 95, it can be approached by users with a wide range of technical sophistication and needs. No matter who you are, there is stuff here that you will probably never use. At the same time, a remarkable range of system controls is accessible here in the vast, well-lighted caverns of Fingal's Cave. Next up, the wonderful world of Windows fonts and printing.

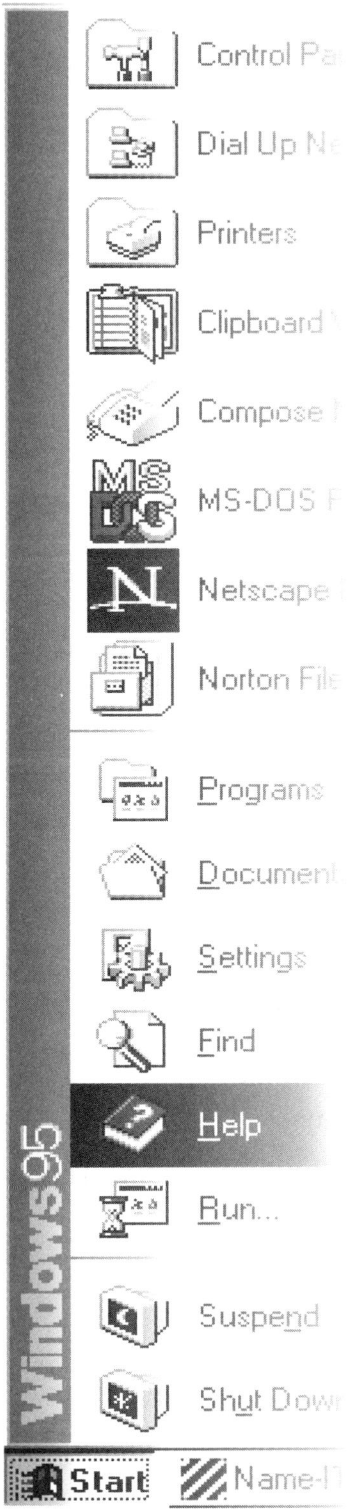

chapter 9

Fonts and Printing

- New printing and font management features
- Extending drag-and-drop printing support
- Plug-and-play printers
- Deferred printing
- Windows 95 font management
- Working with PostScript and Adobe Type Manager
- Optimizing printer performance
- Configuring print properties
- Network printing issues
- Third-party font utilities

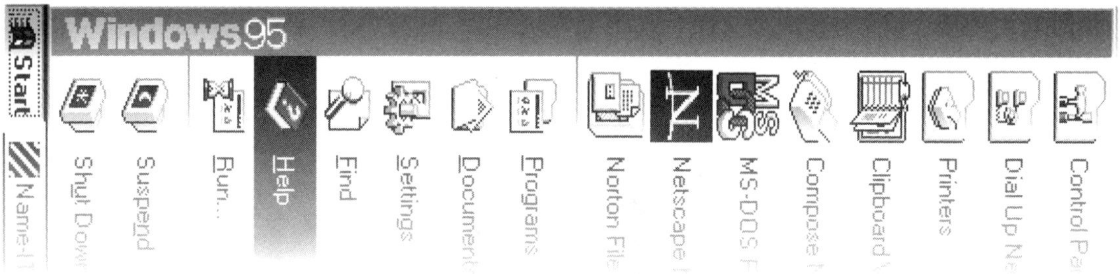

THIS chapter tells you what you need to know about font management and printing under Windows 95. Thanks to changes made to the Win95 printing subsystem, your documents will print much faster, TrueType fonts are easier to install and manipulate, and the operating system bundles many new printer drivers with sophisticated features. About the only down side to printing with Windows 95 is that some of your Windows 3.*x* font management utilities may now be obsolete and require an upgrade. Most important among these is Adobe Type Manager, if you use it in conjunction with Hewlett-Packard's PCL printers. See "Working with PostScript Fonts" later in this chapter for details.

What's New

The Windows 95 printing subsystem features an array of improvements:

- Easy access to multiple printers through the desktop
- Faster printing through the 32-bit multithreading subsystem
- New Enhanced Metafile (EMF) print spooling, resulting in quicker "return-to-application" time
- Drag-and-drop printing by dragging documents over a Printer shortcut icon or using right-click context menu options

- Improved printer drivers built into the operating system: support for printing at higher 600×300 dpi resolutions and Image Color Matching support (licensed from Eastman Kodak) that synchronizes the colors of images displayed on the screen to printer output
- Network printer management features: elimination of logical port redirection; no need to store multiple printer drivers on a local workstation; deferred printing; adding software to turn a Windows 95 computer into a network print management station; and Microsoft Print Services for NetWare, which allows you to direct print jobs from a NetWare server to printers attached to computers running Windows 95.

About New Desktop Printing Options

Printer settings are accessed through individual icons for each output device in the Printers folder (located under Settings on the Start Menu). As in Warp OS/2, you can also create shortcuts for any printer directly on the desktop for more convenient access. Just open the Printers folder, right-click, and drag out the printer you want.

Other options that appear when you right-click a printer icon replace the Windows 3.*x* Print Manager and Printer settings. You can pause printing, purge print jobs, or fine-tune the printer's performance by selecting Properties. Double-clicking on a printer icon opens a queue that lists the documents waiting to be printed, as shown in Figure 9-1.

Drag-and-Drop Printing

Drag-and-drop printing allows you to print documents conveniently from the Win95 desktop. Assuming that you don't need to edit a file, you can simply drag its icon out of a folder and drop it onto your printer icon (located either in the Printers folder or on the desktop). You can also print many document types by right-clicking their file icons or (desktop shortcuts) and selecting Print from the pop-up context menu.

The default printer used by Windows applications (both older 3.*x* and newer, Win95-specific programs) can be switched simply by dragging and dropping a file you want to print on the appropriate output device icon. Or, you can right-click on any printer icon and choose the "Set as default" option.

Drag-and-drop printing works for file types associated to certain Windows and DOS applications. These applications are written to allow a pass-through print option on startup. All of Microsoft's applications and accessories written for Windows 3.*x* and Windows 95 have this feature.

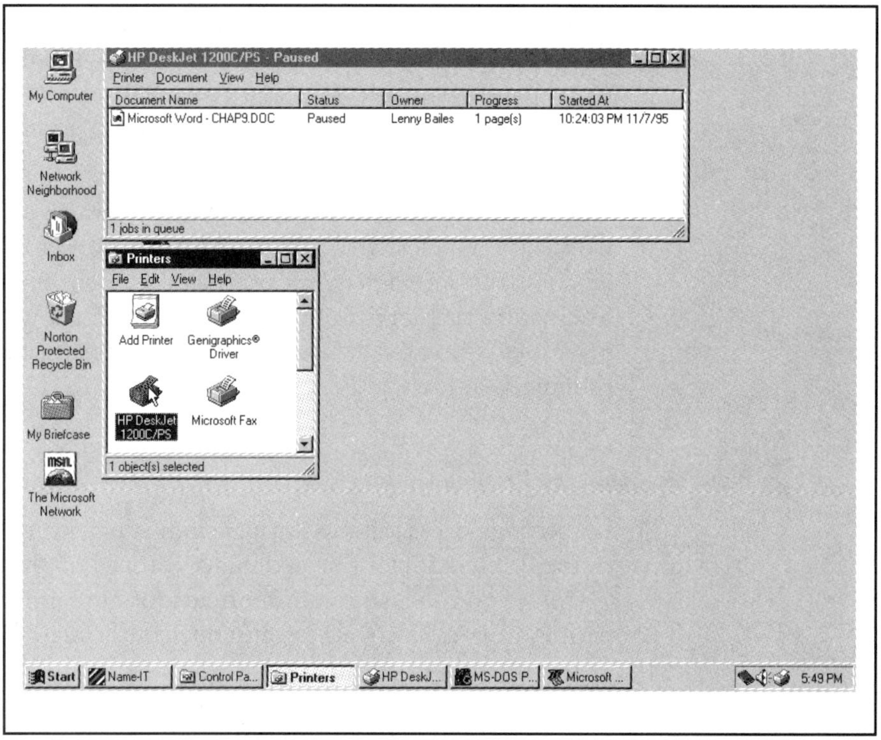

FIGURE 9-1

Double-click any printer icon under Windows 95 to open a list of documents waiting in the queue for that printer.

Many third-party programs also include it. Support for drag-and-drop printing is usually added to the System Registry when a new application is installed: Microsoft Excel adds printing support for .XLS documents, Word adds support for .DOC documents, and so on.

If you have a Windows or DOS program that supports a pass-through command-line print option, you can manually add drag-and-drop print support for specific file types. This is done by associating a file extension to the application through the View\Options\File Types dialog box under My Computer. The file association is then edited to add a drag-and-drop print command.

This procedure is similar to adding an Open command to the right-click context menu options, as described in Chapter 4. For a good example of how to add a Print command, open the View\Options\File Types option in My Computer for the text document file type. Click the Edit button and select the Print command (click the Edit button again). This will show you the preconfigured Print command for text files (.TXT extension), associated to the Notepad. For Microsoft applications, the pass-through print command is created by appending a /P switch to the command line, as in NOTEPAD.EXE /P, or EXCEL.EXE /P.

Extending Drag-and-Drop Printing with the SendTo Folder

If you drag a nonsupported file type over a printer icon, Windows 95 displays a message stating that there is no associated application configured to print it. If you right-click the file icon, there is no Print command on the context menu. You may recall that in Chapter 4 we discussed a similar problem relating to Win95's QuickView file filters. In that case, there was no View option on the context menu. We solved the problem by dragging a copy of QUIKVIEW.EXE to the SendTo folder to provide viewing access for nonregistered file types.

A similar procedure provides a way for you to set up drag-and-drop print options for nonregistered file types. Here's how to do it:

1. Create the following batch file with Notepad or any other ASCII text editor:

   ```
   TEXTPRNT.BAT
   NOTEPAD /P %1
   ```

2. Save the file in your WINDOWS directory.
3. Open the Windows\SendTo folder in My Computer or the Explorer. Drag in a shortcut to the TEXTPRNT.BAT file you've just created.

From now on, you can print any ASCII file, regardless of its three-letter file extension. Just right-click the file, select the Send To option on the context menu, and drag the file over the Textprnt option (see Figure 9-2).

This technique will allow you to print any file that can be loaded into the Windows Notepad application. You may wish to extend the technique by creating "Send To" shortcuts to other, more powerful applications that support the /P switch for pass-through printing. For instance, you could create a WORDPRN batch file:

```
WORDPRN.BAT
[D:\]\MSOFFICE\WINWORD.EXE /P %1
```

Placing this batch file to the SendTo folder would allow drag-and-drop printing of files in all of Microsoft Word's supported formats (Excel, Windows Write, RTF, WordPerfect, etc.), regardless of their three-letter file extension.

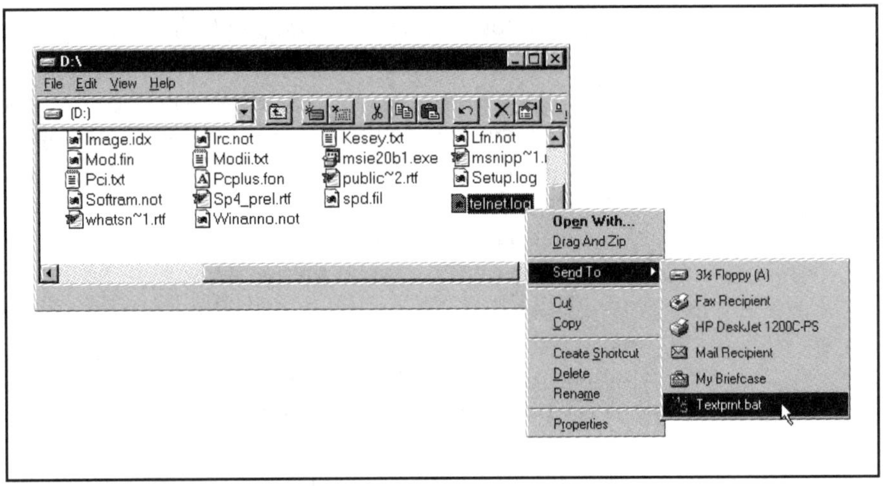

FIGURE 9-2 *More generalized drag-and-drop printing through the SEND TO folder*

Drag-and-Drop Limitations

You might be tempted to use Win95's desktop printing features to select a whole folder full of files with the mouse and drag them to the printer. The operating system permits you to do this, but be advised: if you drag-and-drop a large number of files onto a printer, you may exceed your computer's memory capacity. Windows 95 opens a new instance of the parent application for every file you drop to print.

About Faster Printing

Windows 95 has a new 32-bit print spooler that supports DOS as well as Windows applications. The new spooler provides smoother background printing by using multithreaded background processing. Data is passed to the printer only when the printer is ready to receive more information.

Under the Windows 3.*x* Print Manager, the operating system did a lot of processing through the printer driver before returning control of an application to you. This meant that you would often wind up staring at an hour glass, unable to continue your work until the print spooler relinquished control. Under Windows 95, the Enhanced Metafile (EMF) spooler works more quickly. The spooler generates an intermediate data file, processing data faster than the printer driver alone. The EMF data file is generated by the Win95 graphical device interface (GDI). Control is returned quickly to the source application while the print processing continues in the background. So you can get back to work that much sooner—a real asset, assuming that working is what you really want to be doing.

DOS applications can now print directly to the 32-bit Windows spooler; however, they don't benefit from EMF spooling. (For more details on EMF spooling, see "Working with Printer Options" later in this chapter.)

IEEE-1284 Parallel Port Standard Support

Another important speed-optimization in Windows 95 printing is the operating system's built-in support for the new IEEE-1284 parallel port standard. This is the standard being adopted by Microsoft, Hewlett-Packard, Xircom, Zenith Data Systems, and many other computer and peripheral manufacturers.

The IEEE-1284 standard is actually a combination of two separate proposed standards for the PC parallel port: EPP (Enhanced Parallel Port) and ECP (Enhanced Capabilities Port). The original idea was to provide two important capabilities: a) increase the basic data transmission speed of the parallel port, and b) allow for true bi-directional data communications.

Although the speed of the original (Centronics) parallel port is generally sufficient for simple printing processes, parallel ports are now being shared between a much more diverse variety of peripherals like external disk drives, tape drives, Ethernet interface adapters, sound adapters, and SCSI ports. As such, higher data throughput is becoming more and more of a necessity.

Initially, the EPP standard was developed by Xircom Inc., a manufacturer of Ethernet adapters. Using Intel's 82360 chip, they were able to increase the speed of the parallel port from about 150 Kbytes per second to about 2 Mbytes per second! Additionally, the new chip supports asymmetrical, bidirectional data transfer. So using EPP, it is possible to have fast two-way data transfer between the computer and any peripheral that supports the EPP standard.

At about the same time, Hewlett-Packard was developing an improved parallel port nick-named "Zippy" that was designed to increase the performance of their laser printers through faster data transmission through the parallel port. Zippy also provides high-speed, bidirectional data transmission.

Windows 95 fully supports the IEEE-1284 standard. If your computer has the hardware necessary for supporting this standard, Windows 95 can auto-detect and configure any new output device that you plug into your parallel port.

The following components are necessary for Windows 95 to auto-detect your printer:

- A built-in chipset or I/O card that supports the new, faster parallel ports
- An Intel/Microsoft Plug-and-Play BIOS
- A printer cable that supports the IEEE-1284 standard
- Plug-and-play support built into your printer

If your computer doesn't have all these features, don't worry. You can still install your printers the old-fashioned way by double-clicking the Add Printer icon in the Printers folder.

Deferred Printing

If you have both desktop and portable computers, you probably know that when you're on the road, you generally can't print anything. The trouble is that if you are working on a number of projects, you'll have to open them all up again when you get home so you can print them.

With Windows 95, you can tell your computer to print any files you want, whether your computer is connected to a printer or not. The process is called *deferred printing*. Here's how it works. If you are printing offline to a network printer, right-click it in the Printers folder and select the Work Offline option. If you are printing to a local printer that is not currently connected to your computer, right-click it in the Printers folder and check the Pause Printing option. When you tell any application in Windows 95 to print, the output will be stored in a queue for the selected output device. Once you reconnect to your network, or plug your local printer back into your notebook, a dialog box will pop up on the screen asking you whether to print the files waiting in the queue. (If you print while connected and the printer is busy, the job is also put into a queue and prints as soon as the printer is available.)

Device Independence

The Win95 printing subsystem is very powerful and flexible. It allows you to set printer properties for each individual printer rather than requiring global properties, as in Windows 3.*x*. For example, each printer can have a different separator page, and each can be set to print jobs directly or to place them in a queue.

About Windows Fonts

Windows 95 is bundled with three different categories of fonts: raster, vector, and TrueType.

Raster fonts, also known as *bitmapped* fonts, are a carryover from Windows 3.*x*. MS Sans Serif, Serif, Courier, and Symbol are examples of raster fonts. These fonts generate simple bitmapped images of a character set to the screen. A separate file is required for each individual point size. Raster fonts display correctly only in the specific sizes available on disk—they can't be scaled or rotated, and they may not print on a laser or an inkjet printer.

Vector fonts—also called *stick*, *stroke*, or *plotter* fonts—are simple outlines drawn on the screen by mathematical algorithms, in the same way you would generate a circle in algebra by graphing the equation $X^2 + Y^2 = R^2$. With vector fonts, only one physical file is needed for all point sizes. These fonts can be scaled or rotated, but they don't look very nice as body text for documents. Vector fonts are intended primarily for use with pen plotters to produce schematics and engineering diagrams. Modern and Roman are examples of vector fonts.

The third built-in font technology for Windows is TrueType. TrueType fonts are scaleable typefaces for both the screen and printer. One outline file supplies any requested point size. TrueType fonts can be printed on any output device from dot matrix to PostScript printers. The Windows printer driver for the output device controls the manner in which the TrueType font outlines are converted for output. On dot matrix printers, a bitmapped image of each page is created at the specified printer resolution (which may vary from 75 to 300 or more dpi). On Hewlett-Packard PCL printers, a translator called a *font rasterizer* downloads bitmapped representations of the TrueType fonts for output in the specified point sizes. With PostScript printers, the user has a choice between sending bitmapped representations of the font characters to the printer for output, downloading an outline version of the TrueType font to the printer, or substituting an Adobe PostScript Type 1 font, which prints instead of the TrueType version. (For a more detailed discussion of PCL and PostScript printing, see Chapter 15.)

A fourth font type commonly used by Windows applications is Adobe PostScript font outlines. PostScript fonts may be *resident* (built into the ROM of your printer) or *downloadable* (soft font files that reside on your hard disk). Like TrueType fonts, each individual PostScript font outline can supply type in any requested point size. Windows 95 has marginal built-in support for PostScript fonts. By itself, Windows can recognize resident fonts in a PostScript printer or download soft PostScript outlines to a compatible printer, but working with these fonts is cumbersome. You don't see what they look like on the screen, you may have to manually edit your WIN.INI file to install them, and they don't print on Hewlett-Packard PCL or ordinary dot matrix printers.

For Windows to effectively manage PostScript soft fonts, you really need Adobe's third-party utility, Adobe Type Manager. Adobe Type Manager lets you install and remove PostScript soft fonts from your Windows configuration with a couple of mouse clicks. But more importantly, ATM rasterizes PostScript fonts so that they display correctly on the screen and can be printed on Hewlett-Packard laser and inkjet models as well as older dot matrix printers. With Adobe Type Manager installed, Windows is equally versatile in handling TrueType and PostScript font outlines.

Changes in Windows 95 Font Handling

In earlier versions of Windows, if you wanted to have a large number of fonts at your disposal, you'd have to load them when you started Windows. This caused several problems. First, it used a lot of memory. Second, it could make starting Windows a pretty tedious experience since all of the fonts had to be loaded before you could start doing anything. And third, having a lot of fonts could even impact the overall performance of your computer.

Windows 95 has a different approach to handling fonts than previous versions of the operating system. Instead of loading all fonts into memory upon startup, Windows 95 loads only a list of font names (so that your applications know they're there). The physical font data for display and printing is paged from the hard disk on an as-needed basis. More physical fonts can be installed in the operating system and over 1000 fonts can be used in one document.

Windows 95 also includes an enhanced rasterizer for more accurate rendering and generation of TrueType fonts.

caution *Although Win95 specifications indicate that you can use as many as 1000 different fonts in a single document, you should probably exercise some restraint rather than testing out this feature. Not only would a document with that many fonts look pretty ugly, it would also impose a memory and performance tax on your system.*

How Fonts Are Stored

The bitmap, vector, and TrueType fonts included in the Windows 95 package are no longer listed in the WIN.INI file, as they were under Windows 3.*x*. Instead, the names and characteristics of these fonts are stored in the System Registry, a database maintained by Windows 95 to track system resources. The Registry now holds a wide variety of information that was formerly stored in WIN.INI and SYSTEM.INI. If you perform an upgrade installation of Windows 95 over a previous version of Windows, the font list that used to be maintained in WIN.INI is automatically transferred to the Registry. Physical font files are now stored in the WINDOWS\FONTS directory. In order to maintain compatibility with Windows 3.*x* applications and utilities, fonts stored in the WINDOWS\SYSTEM directory are still recognized.

Every time Windows 95 starts, the [Fonts] section of WIN.INI is examined and any font information written there by older applications is transferred to the System Registry. TrueType fonts installed in the WINDOWS\SYSTEM directory are migrated to the WINDOWS\FONTS directory the next time you boot Windows 95. The bottom line of this routine is that you don't have to worry about the avalanche of TrueType fonts installed by Win 3.*x* packages like CorelDraw version 5 or WordPerfect for Windows. Migration to the Windows 95 environment is handled automatically.

Installing and Managing TrueType Fonts

As stated earlier, when you upgrade from an older version of Windows to Windows 95, all of the TrueType fonts that were previously installed in your system automatically move to Windows 95. Additionally, standard Adobe PostScript fonts that were installed before the upgrade will still be available afterwards.

The Fonts folder is a new component in Windows 95. It holds the Microsoft bitmap, vector, and TrueType fonts discussed in the previous section. When you open the Fonts folder, you'll see a list of all fonts of these types that are currently installed. The Fonts folder does not display, store, or manage PostScript fonts, Type 1, 2, or 3 (for more information, see "Working with PostScript Fonts" later in this chapter).

The FONTS folder is much more than just another window on your desktop. It's closer to a mini-application that allows you to inspect and control your fonts. To use the Fonts folder, click the Start button, and then choose Settings\Control Panel. Once the Control Panel window is open, double-click the Fonts icon. The Fonts folder will open, as you can see here:

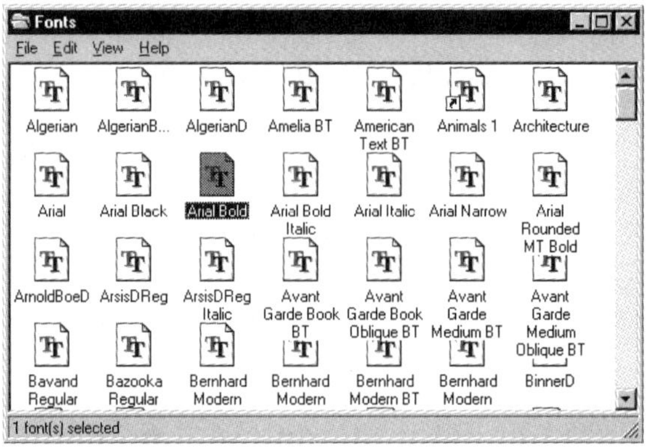

To add a TrueType font to your system, all you have to do is drag it into the Fonts folder from another hard disk directory, floppy diskette, or CD-ROM. To delete one, right-click its icon in the Fonts folder and select delete from the pop-up context menu. Simple? You bet!

tip *Although you can effectively delete a font by just dragging its icon out of the Fonts folder, this isn't the best way to do it, since Windows 95 won't update your application menus until you restart the system. If you want to delete a group of fonts, select them in the Fonts folder with the mouse and select the Delete option from the folder's pull-down File menu.*

You can install new fonts into Windows 95 en masse by choosing the Install New Fonts option on the pull-down File menu. The next dialog box lets you point to a specific directory on your local computer or network. A list of fonts available for installation in that directory will appear. You can select all of them or choose the ones you want to make active. To select multiple fonts individually, hold down the CTRL key as you left-click on the font names in the list that you want to install.

DISPLAYING AND PRINTING FONT SAMPLES If you want to see what one of the fonts in the FONTS folder looks like, double-click the font's icon. Windows 95 then opens a window that contains samples of the font in various point sizes (see Figure 9-3). To print the font sample, double-click the Print button in the upper-right portion of the window.

Some programs can interfere with some Fonts folder functions. For example, older versions of Corel's Gallery redirect the font display function to Gallery 2's Font Master program. While this program can also display the fonts, they won't appear as in the font window shown in Figure 9-3.

In Windows 95, information in the System Registry points to a single .TTF file for each TrueType font. The .FOT description files that were used in Windows 3.*x* are no longer needed (and are deleted from your hard disk).

FIGURE 9-3

Viewing a font within the Fonts folder

Windows 95 includes a hidden file in the WINDOWS\FONTS directory named TTFCACHE. This file now contains the FOT type data for TrueType fonts to ensure backward compatibility with Windows 3.1.

Working with PostScript Fonts

Although Windows 95 doesn't have built-in support for PostScript fonts as it does for TrueType fonts, adding Adobe's ATM (Adobe Type Manager) to your system will make managing PostScript fonts nearly as easy as using the FONTS folder.

To make ATM work properly with Windows 95, you should upgrade to version 3.02 or higher. This isn't hard to do since Adobe includes ATM with quite a few of its products, including many of their font packages. You can also upgrade ATM version 3.0 or 3.01 to the current version through a patch file available on America Online (AOL), CompuServe, the Microsoft Network, and Adobe's BBS and World Wide Web site. On AOL, use the keyword "Adobe," then select Adobe Online\File Library\PC Library. On

FIGURE 9-4 *The Adobe Type Manager (ATM) Control Panel*

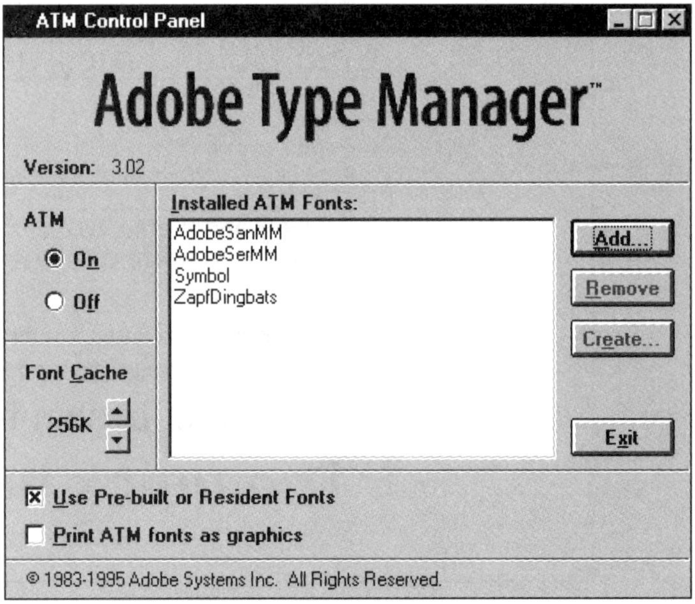

CompuServe go to ADOBEAP\ATM/Windows File Library. On the Microsoft Network, go to the Desktop Publishing Forum\DTP File Libraries\Patches and Updates. Adobe's BBS can be reached at 206-623-6984. Their web site address is

HTTP://WWW.ADOBE.COM/SOFTWARE.HTM

Registered users of ATM 3.*x* can also receive the upgrade on floppy disk for $9.95 by calling 1-800-833-6687. Upgrades from earlier versions of ATM are slightly more expensive.

To determine which version of ATM you have, all you need to do is look at the ATM Control Panel's version box; the version number will displayed there.

Using Adobe Type Manager (ATM) 3.02

To install a new font using ATM, double-click the ATM icon (usually located in a program group called Main or Adobe Type Manager to open the ATM window, shown in Figure 9-4.

Initially this window displays the currently installed PostScript fonts in the center box and displays the status of some ATM options around the box. To add a font, click the Add button to open the Add ATM Fonts window:

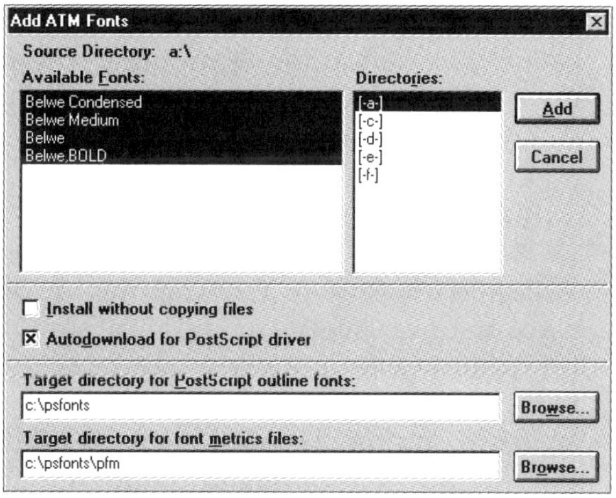

As you can see, a number of fonts were found on drive A. They are all selected and are ready to be added to the system. In fact though, when you open this window, you'll probably find no fonts in the Available Fonts box until you point to a directory that contains some. In most cases, new fonts are supplied on either CD-ROM or on 3.5-inch floppy disk.

Once you have selected the right drive and directory, the names of the available fonts will appear in the large, left-hand box in the Add ATM Fonts window. ATM recognizes these fonts through a series of short Windows description files that bear the .PFM file extension. So if you see a PFM directory on the drive you're browsing, that's usually the one you should choose.

To select a font, click it with the mouse. If you want to select multiple fonts, hold down the CTRL key while you click the font names you want to select. To select a whole block of fonts, click the top font in the list, hold down the SHIFT key, and then click the name of the font at the bottom of the list. This will select all of the fonts between your two selections as well.

To deselect one or more fonts, hold down the CTRL key and click the selected fonts to remove the highlight.

If you are installing your fonts from a floppy disk or CD-ROM drive, make sure the box marked "Install without copying files" is not selected, since you do want to copy the font files to your hard disk.

The Autodownload for PostScript driver box should also usually be selected. This tells Adobe Type Manager to download the font to the printer on-the-fly, each time the font is requested by a document. Fonts downloaded in this way do not set up permanent residence in the printer, conserving use of printer memory. If you choose to pre-download your PostScript soft fonts to the printer before starting Windows 95, then the Autodownload option should be deselected.

The PSFONTS Directory

The default path for PostScript fonts in Windows 95 is the PSFONTS directory. Using this path, you can install up to 900 fonts. You should be aware, however, that a few limitations make it unwise to install that many PostScript fonts. First, Windows 95 imposes a 64K limit on the size of the .INI files. To be properly loaded, all PostScript fonts need to be installed in the ATM.INI and WIN.INI files. Additionally, many applications can display a maximum of 200 fonts. This includes both PostScript and TrueType fonts.

PostScript fonts generally have two parts: the outline of the font and a small file called the font metrics. The Type 1 font outline file always has the three-letter suffix .PFB. The outline files are stored in a directory called PSFONTS. The file contains the actual shape of each character in the font.

The font metrics file ends with .PFM and contains information about how the font should be spaced when printed, and how it should be scaled as it is made larger and smaller.

The other kind of PostScript font is the *multiple master font*. While Type 1 PostScript fonts have fixed outlines, multiple master fonts can be modified to make them bolder, wider, thinner, or whatever you want. The names of multiple master font outline files end in .PFB, just like standard PostScript fonts. The metrics files for these fonts, however, use the .MMM extension. To use multiple master fonts, you need to create *instances* of the font. This is accomplished by clicking the Create button on the main ATM Control Panel. The Font Creator dialog box opens up (see Figure 9-5), showing you all of the multiple master outlines currently installed. You can use this box to vary the weight, width, and typeface style of your chosen font or to generate new, individual fonts.

Once created, instances of multiple master fonts work just like standard PostScript fonts. ATM creates two additional files for each font instance. The stub file (using the .PSS file extension) contains all of the user-configured data for this instance of the multiple master font.

WHAT'S NEW IN ATM 3.02? The most important new feature of ATM 3.02 is that it supports Windows 95 properly. Although ATM 3.01 works with

FIGURE 9-5

Adobe Type Manager's Font Creator dialog box

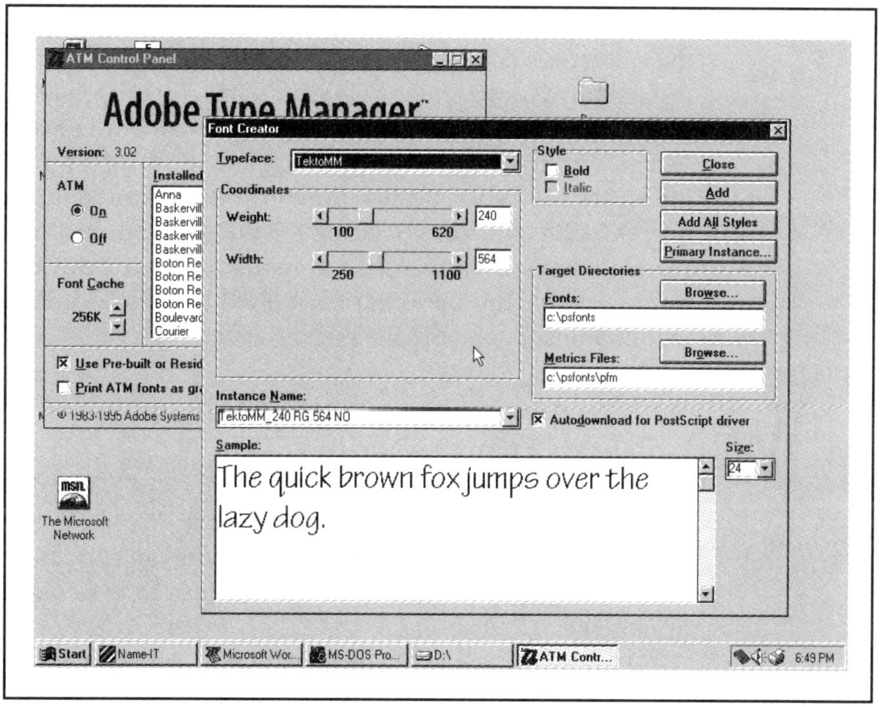

Windows 95, ATM 3.02 adds some features that make it better for some applications. For example, ATM 3.02 supports the Universal Naming Convention (UNC). In older versions of ATM, fonts added to UNC network printers would not recognize fonts sent to them from client systems. ATM 3.02 allows you to send fonts to network printers with UNC designations.

Additionally, ATM 3.02 supports Windows 95 soft font printing on PCL (HP-compatible) printers. Previous versions of ATM have a problem with Windows 95, so that PostScript fonts are printed as graphic bitmaps on PCL. While this still works, it drastically slows down print processing time.

ATM CONTROL OPTIONS Adobe Type Manager can be toggled on or off by selecting the On or Off button on the main ATM Control Panel. When ATM is disabled, the PostScript fonts it controls will not appear on your application font menus.

The Font Cache setting on the ATM Control Panel sets aside a portion of RAM to be used as a buffer for speeding up printing and screen display. A setting of 384K is usually sufficient for managing up to 25 typefaces. If you regularly work with a larger number of PostScript fonts, you may want to increase the cache setting.

The Use Pre-built or Resident Fonts checkbox toward the bottom of the ATM control panel tells Windows 95 to use fonts that are resident in your printer, rather than downloading soft fonts from the hard disk. Most Apple-compatible PostScript printers contain built-in versions of common typefaces like Helvetica, Times, Bookman, and so on. If this box is checked, the printer-resident versions of those fonts are used, rather than the ones installed by Adobe Type Manager. This generally speeds up the printing process.

The "Print ATM fonts as graphics" box forces ATM to send font information to your printer in the form of bitmap graphics, rather than downloading soft fonts or using the built-in font rasterizer. If a document that contains mixed type and graphics does not print correctly, you may want to enable this option. It must also be enabled for certain PCL printers that do not support ATM's font rasterizer.

Working with Printer Options

Depending upon which printer(s) you have, Windows 95 lets you control the way your printer prints. Although results can vary, the following section shows many of the features you can expect to have available with your own printer(s).

To begin examining or changing printer settings, you need to open your printer's property window. To do this, first choose Printers from the Settings option in the Start Menu. Now right-click the icon for the printer you want to examine. From here, choose Properties from the pull-down context menu:

This opens the Properties window for the printer, as shown in Figure 9-6.

The number and type of tabbed settings that appear on the Properties menu will vary from printer to printer. Most printers will contain tabs marked General and Details. Most printer drivers directly installed from the Windows 95 CD will also contain tabs for Paper and Graphics settings. More sophisticated printers will contain tabs for Fonts, Device Options, and (if applicable) PostScript options.

FIGURE 9-6

The Properties window for the HP DeskJet 1200C/PS includes a number of configuration tabs.

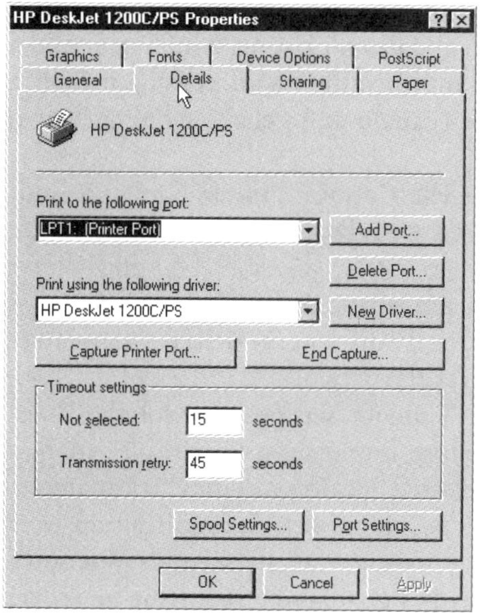

The General Tab

The General tab under Printer Properties allows you to enter a specific comment about the printer and to choose a separator page. The separator page option allows you to divide your print jobs by inserting a special page between each finished document. Separator pages may consist of text, graphics, or a combination of the two. The built-in options allow you to choose a simple (text) page or a full (graphics) page. You can also define your own custom separator page, by clicking the Browse button and selecting an appropriate one-page document in the Windows Metafile (.WMF) format.

The Details Tab

The Details tab under Printer Properties contains most of the primary configuration options that were formerly set through the Windows 3.*x* Control Panel.

The "Print to the following port" option allows you to select a physical I/O port on your local computer, select a network connection, use the Microsoft fax driver, or print to a disk file. Network paths and additional ports are added to the option list by clicking the Add Port button to the right of the dialog box. The Delete button lets you delete a port from the option list.

The "Print to the following driver" option should generally be left alone. This setting usually corresponds to the printer model and manufacturer you selected on installation. In the case of printers not directly supported by Windows 95, this dialog box is used to integrate an OEM-specific driver into a more general Win95 printer control shell. This option can also be used to update an existing Win95 printer driver with a later, OEM version. If you want to configure an existing printer control icon with a new OEM driver, you can do so, by clicking on the New Driver button to the right of the dialog box.

The Capture Printer Port and End Capture buttons are designed to be used with DOS applications and with network devices that don't support Microsoft's Universal Naming Convention (UNC) printer protocol. For instance, you can route access to a non-UNC network printer by defining a virtual port that the driver will use to capture output and transmit print data over the network.

Timeout settings control the time interval that applications will wait before reporting a "time out" inability to access your printer. The "Not selected" option specifies how many seconds Windows will wait for a printer to be online before reporting an error. The "Transmission retry" option specifies how many seconds Windows will wait for a printer to generate a ready signal before reporting an error.

tip *For PostScript devices, increase the transmission retry interval if you frequently receive timeout errors while printing large jobs.*

Spool Settings control the printer's use of Win95's EMF spool files and allow you to enable or disable bi-directional printing support.

Disabling EMF Spool Options

Some applications are not compatible with Enhanced Metafile spooling. If you run into a program that gives you some trouble printing with EMF, you can disable EMF by following these steps:

1. Choose Printers from the Settings option of the Start Menu.
2. Right-click the icon for the printer you are using and choose Properties from the context menu.
3. From here, click the Details tab to reveal the Spool Settings button (see Figure 9-6).
4. Click the button, and the Spool Settings dialog box appears.
5. Choose RAW in the "Spool data format" box to disable EMF:

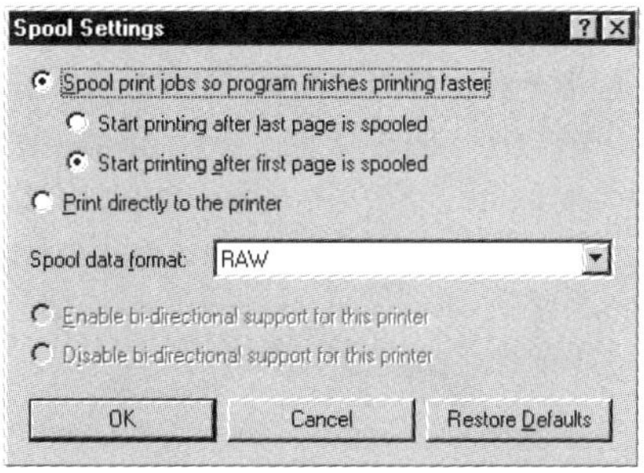

Close all of the windows and you're done.

Other Tabs

If your printer has been configured with a special OEM driver that has been migrated to Windows 95, some of the options for paper, graphics, fonts, and output quality may be hidden away on submenus, accessible from a Setup button on the Details tab, as shown in Figure 9-7.

FIGURE 9-7

The Details tab for the Lexmark 1020 printer

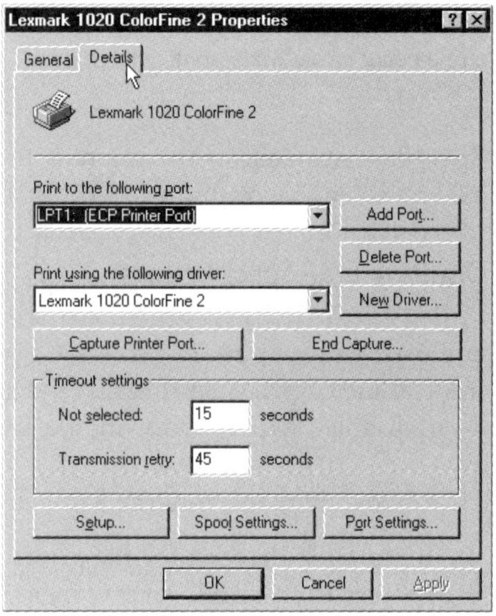

The Lexmark 1020 printer is such an example. Its driver is not directly present on the Windows 95 CD, although the operating system can autodetect it and migrate settings from an OEM diskette. To change the printer settings for the Lexmark 1020, choose the Setup button near the bottom of the Details tab. This opens a variety of printer-specific output options, as shown in Figure 9-8. The Paper and Image Settings tabs for this printer are analogous to the Paper, Graphics, and Device Option tabs that appear in other printer drivers. Notice that, like most Windows 95 control windows, this one also looks like a stack of index cards. Each tab has one category of controls for the printer.

Document Type/Color

The one that's on top in Figure 9-8, Document Type/Color, lets you optimize the printer for different kinds of documents. Let's explore these options in more detail.

AUTOMATIC The first option is Automatic. This option uses the computer's logic to determine what kind of image you're producing. For most jobs, using the Automatic setting works fine, but if you're setting up to do a long print run or are using expensive stock (some of the special plastic stock for making

FIGURE 9-8 *Document Type/Color and other settings for the Lexmark 1020*

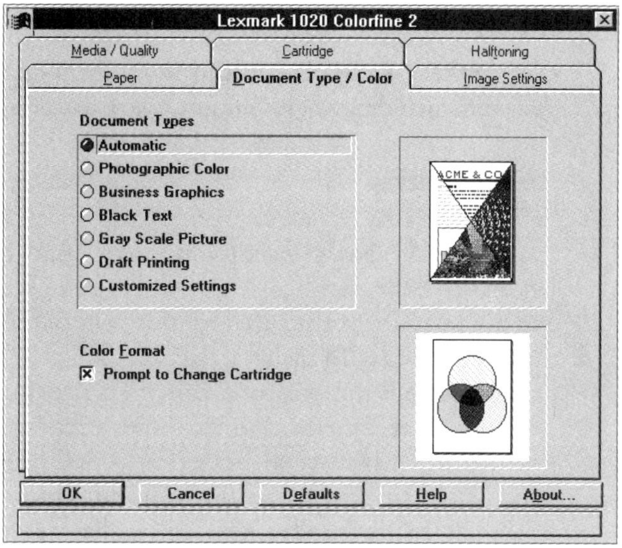

high-quality color images can run more than a dollar a page) you should probably review and select one of the other settings.

PHOTOGRAPHIC COLOR When you click this option, the image on the right changes to a full-color image to indicate that the printer is optimized for high-quality color output with the best shading the printer can produce. The images look great, but a single page uses a lot of ink and can take as much as 10 minutes or more to print on this printer.

BUSINESS GRAPHICS In this mode, the printer is optimized to print a combination of color or black-and-white charts and graphs (high-contrast for best visibility) and sharp, black text. If the page has both color and black images, the black will be produced using a composite of the three inks in the color cartridge.

BLACK TEXT In this mode, the printer uses a black cartridge only. It's optimized for black, high-resolution text.

GRAY SCALE PICTURE Gray scale images use the black cartridge, have generally lower contrast than text images, and are very high resolution, for this printer 600×600 dpi. In fact, this mode is very much like photographic color mode, using dithering (unless you deselect it).

DRAFT PRINTING This mode produces the lowest-quality images. The purpose of this mode is simple: SPEED. The pages fly out at the maximum speed the printer can produce, which although relatively fast, will always be dependent on the nature of the image(s) on the page.

CUSTOMIZED SETTINGS In this mode, you can choose exactly the settings you want including the resolution, color, dithering pattern, contrast and so on.

Paper Settings

Figure 9-9 shows the options you'll find under the Paper tab in the Lexmark 1020's settings. This tab lets you optimize the printer for the size and kind of paper being used for this printout. Paper size for this printer can range from 8½ × 14 inches (legal size) to 3 × 5 inches (index card size). This printer also has options for a variety of sizes and kinds of envelopes.

The printer also lets you choose either portrait mode (vertical page orientation) or landscape mode (horizontal page orientation). You also can select paper thickness and the order in which the pages are printed. This feature is really handy. You can collate several copies of a multipage document automatically and also print pages from the back of the document

FIGURE 9-9

Lexmark 1020 Paper options

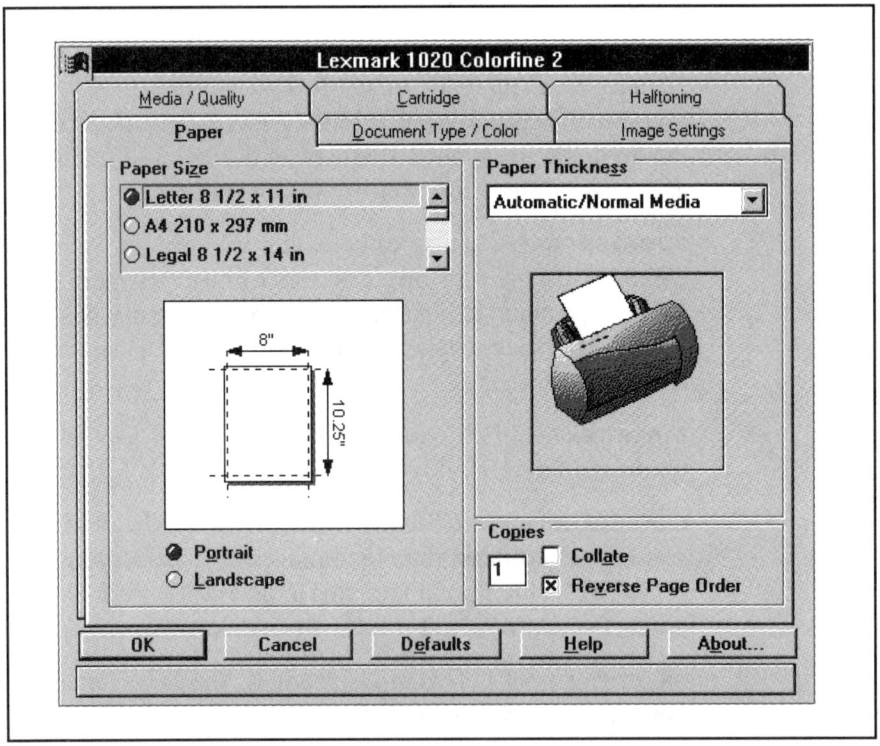

to the front, which—although it sounds backwards—actually puts the pages in the correct order when they're done printing.

Media/Quality

This tab lets you control the kind of output material used, the print quality, and the resolution. Clicking this tab opens the window shown in Figure 9-10.

MEDIA TYPE This setting lets you choose the kind of paper or plastic you'll be printing on. Depending upon the kind of target media the printer is using, the printer adjusts ink flow to get the best image quality. Transparencies, for example, need more ink density so they can be viewed on a projector. Paper, on the other hand, requires less ink. This is done for two reasons. First, plain paper will bleed if it gets a lot of ink density. And second, since the paper is white, the image will automatically appear denser because of the opaque background.

PRINT QUALITY This setting determines the density of the dots put down on the page. Presentation quality puts down the greatest density of dots,

FIGURE 9-10

Lexmark 1020 Media/Quality options

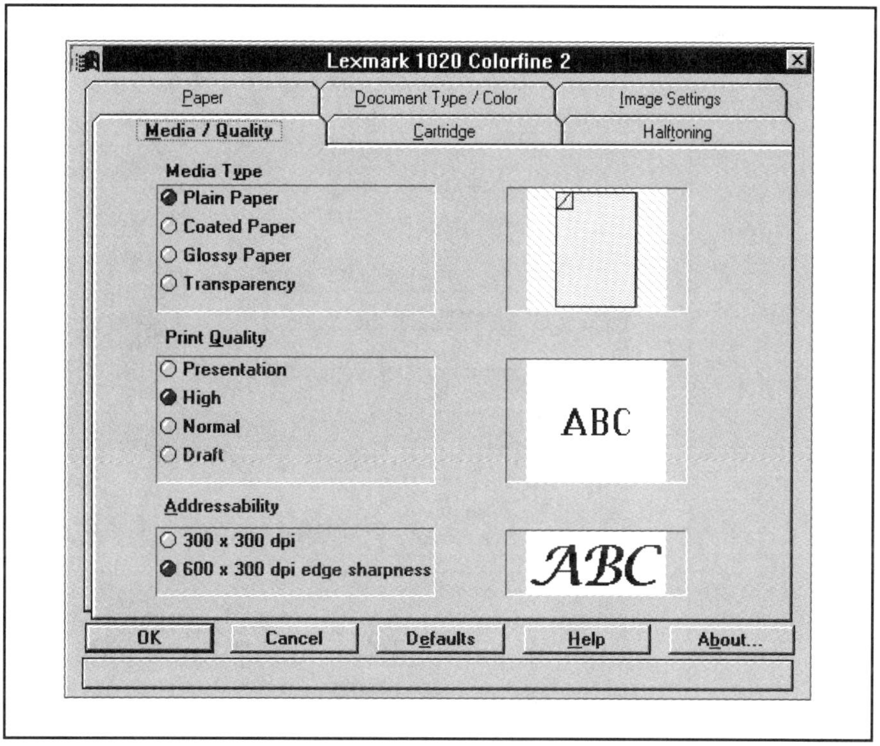

while draft output is more open. If you're just printing a page to get a feel for what you're doing, print in draft mode to get greater speed and use less ink.

ADDRESSABILITY This setting determines the actual resolution of the printer. This printer has two options: 300×300 and 600×300 with enhanced edge sharpness. Once again, the higher the resolution and sharpness, the slower the printer prints. So the better mode should be reserved for final printouts.

Cartridge

The settings in the Cartridge tab (see Figure 9-11) are primarily maintenance functions.

CARTRIDGE OPTIONS The Cartridge Options buttons, for example, are used to install a new cartridge, clean the nozzles of a clogged cartridge, and align the colors on the cartridge.

FIGURE 9-11

Lexmark 1020 Cartridge options

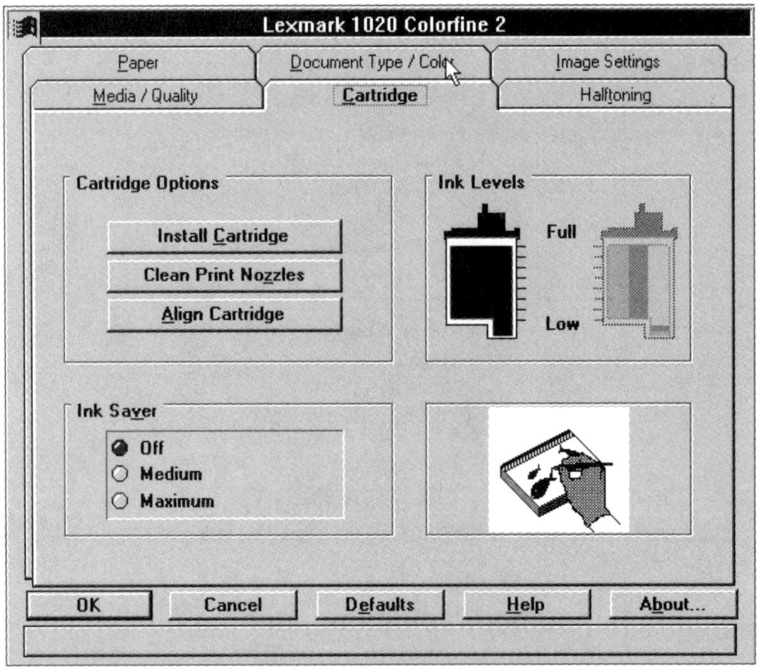

FIGURE 9-12

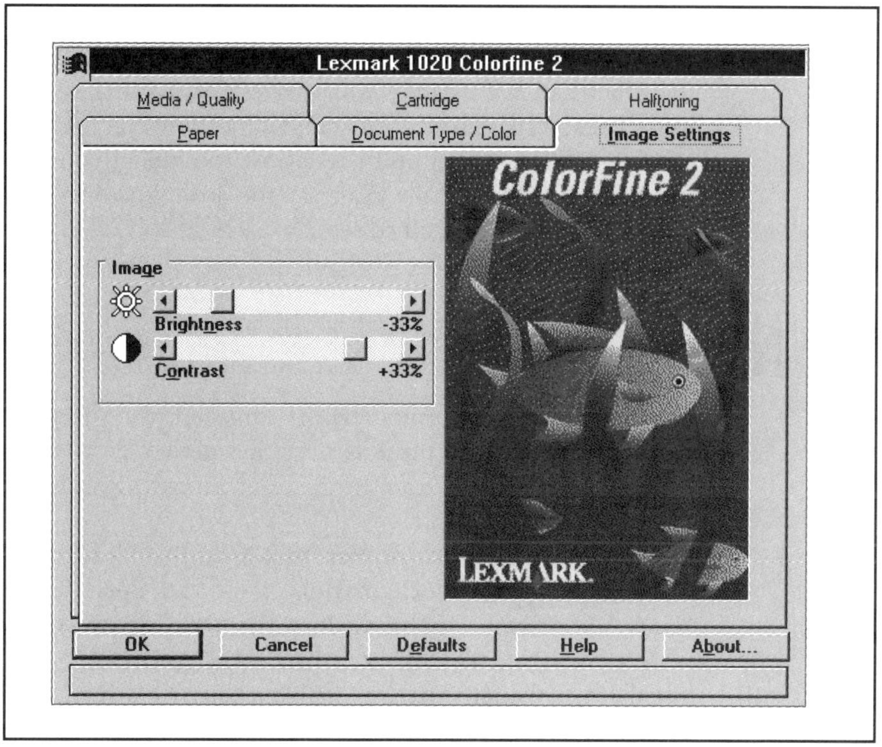

Lexmark 1020 Brightness and Contrast controls

INK SAVER The ink saver determines the overall density of the ink used to produce images. If you're running a lot of draft pages, you can use this option to preserve your ink.

INK LEVELS This is not actually an option. This box shows a graphical representation of the amount of ink left in both the color and the black cartridges.

note *The ink level information is updated as the cartridges are used. Even though the printer can only accommodate one cartridge at a time, the software maintains data on both cartridges all of the time.*

Image Settings

The image settings control the brightness and the contrast of the printed image. Figure 9-12 shows the controls found on this window tab. One thing that is often difficult for computer users is seeing the difference between contrast and brightness. And in fact, the differences can be subtle in a way. Brightness controls the level of all of the shades in your image. Contrast, on the other hand, changes the brightness of the image, based upon what it looks like. Increase the contrast and dark things get darker while light things get lighter. If you turn up the contrast too much, your image is harsh and lacks detail. Turning the contrast too low, however, makes your image appear hazy and difficult to see.

Network Print Issues

When Windows 95 computers are attached to a properly configured network, they can share printers over that network. Additionally, computers running Windows 95 can act as print servers for any printers connected through a local I/O port.

To access a network printer, you must install a token network printer control icon on your local machine. To do so, open the Printers folder and select Add Printer. Double-clicking the Add Printer icon starts the Wizard, which takes you through the process, step-by-step. When you're asked whether you want to install a local or a network printer, choose the Network printer option. In the next dialog box, enter the path to your network printer, and its name on the network, for example, \\LENNY3\BIGIRON. In some cases, when you are already logged on, this information appears automatically.

If you intend to print from DOS applications, select the appropriate button near the bottom of the Add Printer setup box.

If you are not currently connected to the printer you specified, you'll get a message informing you that you can work offline until you establish your network connection. Click Next> and the next dialog box asks you to select the printer type. Specify the manufacturer and model number of the printer you'll be sharing. In general, when the system prompts you for the printer driver diskette, you will find the driver software on the host computer's drive.

The final dialog box gives you the opportunity to change the default name for your printer, and asks whether you want to make it the default printer for Windows applications. Click the Finish button to complete the installation. From now on, when your applications print to this printer, the output will be either spooled over the network when you're connected, or stored in the offline queue for this printer when the printer is unavailable.

If your applications don't support Microsoft's UNC naming convention, the network printer you've just created may not appear as an output option when you issue a print command. You can still print over the network with these problem applications. Here's how:

1. Use the Add Printer dialog box to set up a local printer with a driver type that matches the network printer.
2. Configure this new local printer to use a specific local port address. (If LPT1 is already in use, choose LPT2 or LPT3.)
3. Enter the following commands either from the Run box on the Start Menu or at a DOS command prompt:

   NET USE LPT2: *SERVER**PRINTER*

   example: `\\LENNY\BIGIRON\CAPTURE LPT2:`

The first command maps LPT2 to the network printer you designate for Windows applications. The second command captures output to LPT2 for DOS applications. You can now print from problem applications to the "local" printer for LPT2; Windows 95 will intercept the output and route it to the network printer.

Point and Print

Point and print is a new Windows 95 option that allows you to quickly install a printer over a network. The user points to a print server by opening a shared resource in the Network Neighborhood folder. Or you can open a print server's queue by typing its path name in the Run dialog box on the Start Menu.

JetAdmin

Hewlett-Packard's JetAdmin utility is a network and printer administration program. It allows you to install, remove and configure any Hewlett-Packard printers connected to the network. Although JetAdmin is a Windows utility, it works in Novell NetWare environments as well. To install the JetAdmin utility, open the Control Panel from the Start Menu and double-click the Networks icon. This opens the Network Configuration dialog box:

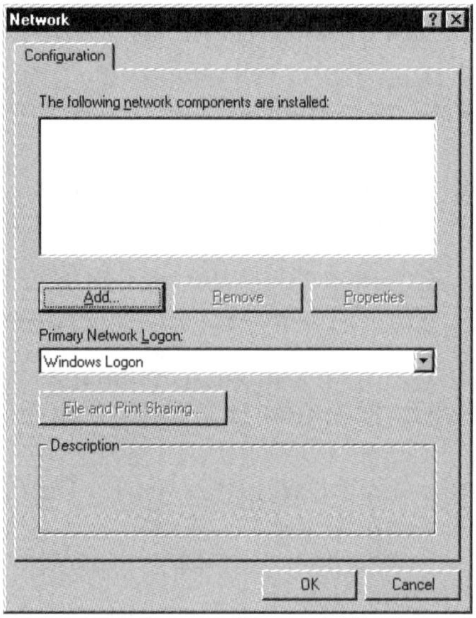

From here, choose Add to open the Select Network Component Type dialog box shown in Figure 9-13. Double-click Service and then choose Hewlett-Packard to open the JetAdmin options. You can choose either HP

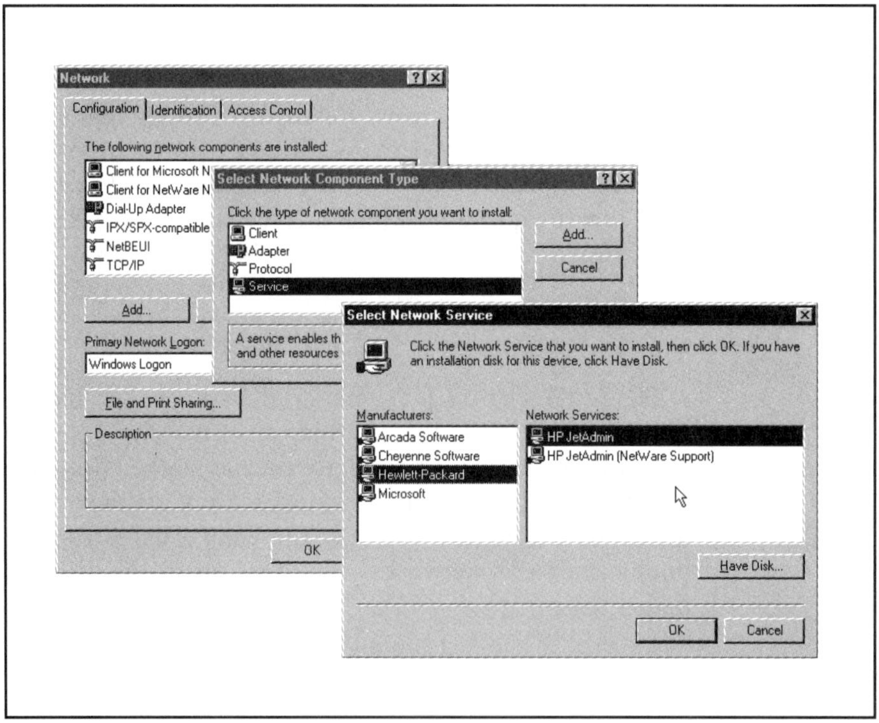

FIGURE 9-13

Installing the HP JetAdmin network component

JetAdmin or HP JetAdmin (NetWare Support), depending on what's in your system.

Once you have selected the correct driver, the system prompts you to either install the diskette or gets the file from your Windows 95 CD-ROM.

Microsoft Print Services for NetWare

If you are running Windows 95 on a NetWare network, you can use Microsoft Print Services for NetWare to control the print jobs of other computers using your printer on the network. This utility operates more or less like NetWare's PSERVER utility, but is a true, Windows 95 32-bit utility. The host computer (the PSERVER itself) must be a dedicated computer. This is because the Windows 95 clients that are running Microsoft Print Services for NetWare require the full support of the network host to run the utilities.

Installing Microsoft Print Services for NetWare is pretty much the same as installing HP's JetAdmin software. But instead of choosing Hewlett-Packard, choose Microsoft, and from that menu choose "Microsoft Print Services for NetWare."

Optimizing Print Performance

Printing to a shared network printer produces different speed results, depending on the server's operating system. If you print to a server running Windows 95, the rendering from the EMF format to the printer-specific language happens on the server. This means that less work is performed on the client computer, giving the user better performance.

When you print to NetWare or Windows NT servers, the rendering from EMF to the printer-specific format happens on the client computer. Although this happens in the background, it still means more work is performed on the client computer. Printing to a printer attached locally causes both the EMF rendering and the device-specific rendering to happen on the computer. To optimize network print performance, you need to decide on the trade-off between disk use and return-to-application time when configuring printing in Windows 95.

To define spool settings for print performance, follow these steps:

1. Open the Printers folder, select a printer, right-click, and choose Properties.
2. Select the Details tab, and then click Spool Settings to display this dialog box:

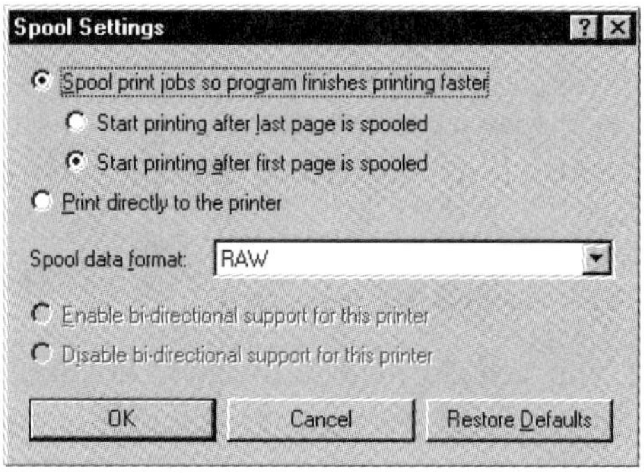

3. Select "Spool print jobs so program finishes printing faster," and then click one of the following options:

   - Click "Start printing after last page is spooled" if you want the return-to-application time to be faster. This requires more disk space and increases the total print time. The second rendering does not start until the entire file is written to the EMF file, which decreases the amount of work performed on the computer as you print but increases the disk space because the entire file has to be written before the second rendering starts.
   - Click "Start printing after first page is spooled" if you want the second rendering to take place simultaneously with the writing of the EMF file. This reduces the total print time and disk space required, but it increases the return-to-application time.

Third-Party Font Utilities

Even with built-in support for TrueType and the addition of Adobe Type Manager, Windows 95 is less flexible than many users might like in its management and handling of fonts. Literally thousands of TrueType and PostScript fonts can be installed into Windows by zealous application vendors. Between WordPerfect for Windows, Corel Systems' CorelDraw, and Microsoft's own TrueType fontpacks, users may become lost in a maze of duplicated typefaces. Arial, Helvetica, Helvetica Narrow, Swiss, Times, Times Roman, New Times Roman—in both TrueType and PostScript versions—may all be present on the system at the same time. Font menus bulge at the seams, applications take longer to load, and system resources are decreased. Besides, take a look at Figure 9-14. Who can remember which font is which?

Under Windows 3.*x*, commercial and shareware font management packages made life considerably easier for people actively involved in desktop

FIGURE 9-14

Too many fonts!

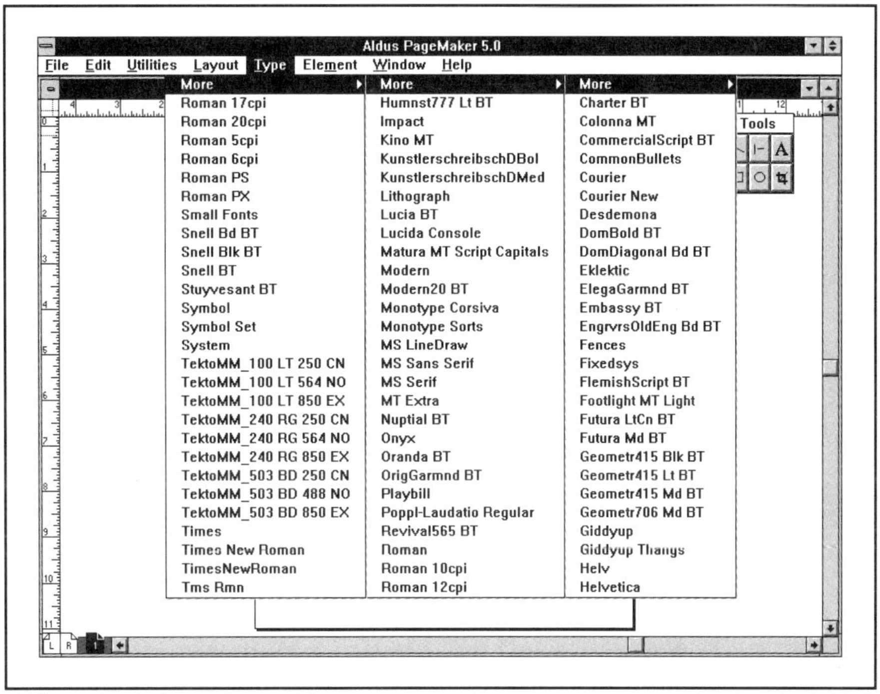

publishing. These third-party packages give you a number of powerful ways to deal with Windows font glut. If two fonts from different sources have the same name, you can assign one of them another name and font ID on your application font menus. Display viewers let you see what each font on the system looks like in a variety of point sizes, or dump font lists, sample paragraphs, and character sets to your printer.

But the key element of a good font manager is that it can create custom fontpacks for Windows that contain only the typefaces you most want to see on the menu. With a custom fontpack, if you want to work in Microsoft Word, you can eliminate the 500 display fonts installed by CorelDraw from your font menu. Then, if you want to switch to PageMaker, you can call in a different font platoon. By setting up only 25 to 50 typefaces as the Windows default, you avoid the slow loading time and resource drain that results from trying to handle 500+ fonts every time you start a Windows session.

Incompatibilities with Windows 95

After whetting your appetite for better font management with the forego-ing pitch, we need to tell you that most of the utilities designed to accomplish this under Windows 3.*x* do not work properly under Windows 95. Notable among these are Microsoft's own Font Assistant, which is distributed with Microsoft TrueType Pack #2, and Ares FontMinder, versions 1.0 to 2.51. The problem is that these applications don't recognize Win95's new way of storing font information in the System Registry instead of in WIN.INI.

At present, there's no upgrade for Microsoft Font Assistant, but fortunately, Ares has recently issued FontMinder, version 3.0. This newest version of FontMinder is completely compatible with Windows 95.

About Ares Font Products

FontMinder version 3.0 is a powerful, sophisticated font manager (see Figure 9-15). It manages both TrueType and Adobe PostScript fonts, allowing you to generate fontpacks that can be loaded on-the-fly, without quitting and restarting your Windows session. FontMinder coexists with Adobe Type Manager and the Win95 Fonts folder, automatically intercepting and modifying the information based on your fontpack configuration choices.

Each fontpack can contain a custom selection of the most appropriate typefaces suitable for a particular production task. FontMinder lets you choose the contents of a fontpack from a general list of all the fonts on your hard disk, or you can create custom fontpacks by a series of predefined

FIGURE 9-15

Ares FontMinder version 3.0

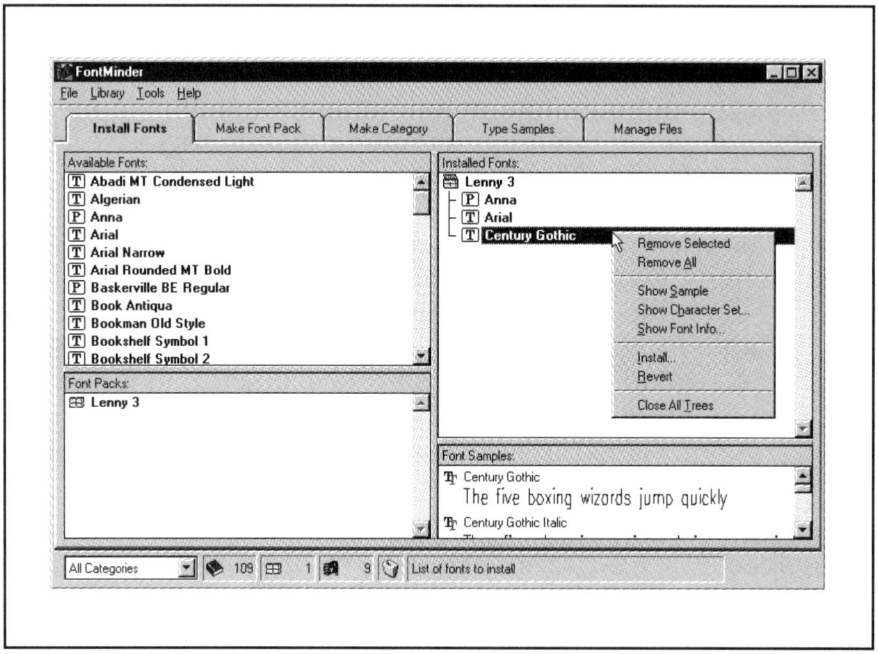

categories. This feature exploits the fact that each TrueType and PostScript font includes a family name, and style classification information in its file header. FontMinder can automatically create fontpacks sorted by typestyle: sans serif, serif, script, decorative, monospace, and so on. The monospace option is particularly useful when you need to sort through 500 fonts to choose a monospaced typeface for spreadsheets or other tabular documents.

Individual FontMinder fontpacks can be associated with a specific Windows application or document. When you create an icon for a fontpack, double-clicking it automatically makes those fonts active in Windows 95, loading an associated document or program.

Finally, FontMinder allows you to organize your TrueType and PostScript fonts by moving or copying them to specified directories on your hard drive. Unused fonts can be automatically packed into compressed file archives.

FontMonger and FontChameleon, two other well-known Ares font utilities, do not require a specific upgrade to work under Windows 95. FontMonger is a conversion utility, used to translate various flavors of PostScript fonts from different manufacturers into the common Adobe Type 1 format, or to export them as Microsoft TrueType files. FontChameleon allows your system to mimic the appearance of fonts that are not actually installed, allowing you to read and create documents that retain their original look and feel.

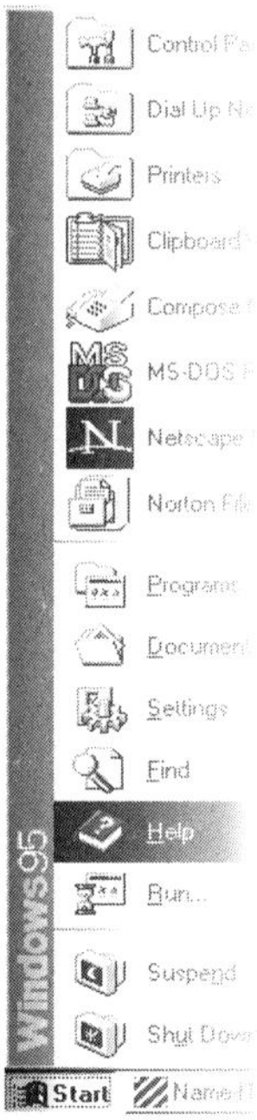
Printers
Settings
Find
Help
Run...
Suspend
Windows95
Start

chapter 10

Telecommunications and Connectivity

- New online support features in Windows 95
- Modem configuration tips
- HyperTerminal and Windows 3.*x* Terminal
- What about DOS and Windows 3.*x* telecomm packages?
- Setting up and working with the Microsoft Exchange Inbox
- Dial-Up Networking

  Your new gateway to the Internet

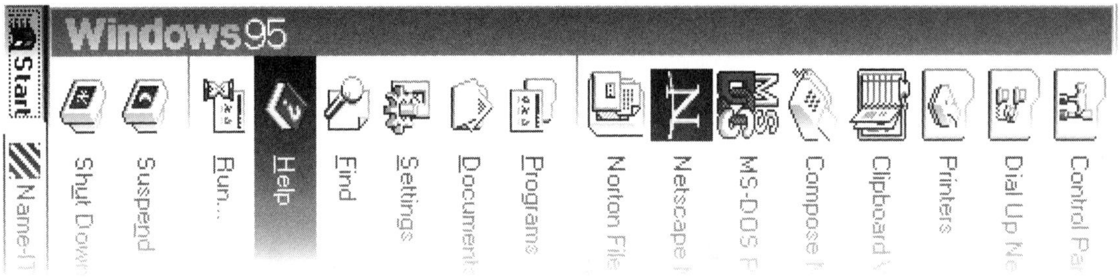

THIS chapter provides you with all the technical information you need to install and configure your modem, and to use the two principle telecommunications components of Windows 95: the Microsoft Exchange Inbox and the Dial-Up Networking Adapter.

You'll find step-by-step instructions that cover each phase of the setup and use of these features. You can skim the topic headings to get basic information, or delve into each section as deeply as you wish for more technical information. But first, let's take a quick look at Windows 95 telecommunications from the air, sketching in the broad changes in Microsoft's operating system flight-path.

One of Microsoft's goals with Windows 95 has been to thoroughly integrate online communication features into the basic operating system. Older versions of Windows offered very little in this area: a bare-bones terminal program, and substandard communications drivers that couldn't exploit a high-speed serial port.

While Windows 95 was in the early beta testing stage, IBM seized a strategic advantage by bundling an Internet connectivity kit with its Warp OS/2 package. This turned out to be a shrewd move, as the World Wide Web, a graphically enhanced Internet subsystem, was rapidly exploding. In less than a year, the Web would become an international craze that redefined the shape of personal computing.

The inclusion in IBM's operating system of Internet dial-up software, e-mail management, a Web browser, and other online access tools, acted as a spur to Microsoft's developers. Exponentially expanding user interest in online services effectively piqued Microsoft into developing its own Microsoft Network to compete with established giants like CompuServe and

America Online. In addition, not to be outdone by IBM, they added an Internet dialer and an enhanced mail client to Windows 95. Microsoft's World Wide Web browser is not directly bundled on the Win95 installation CD, but it can be downloaded at no charge, or added through Microsoft Plus!, an inexpensive supplementary collection of Windows 95 utilities.

New and Improved

The good news about Windows 95 is that you can expect it to deliver better online performance than any of its predecessors. The following new features are built into the operating system.

Modem or Fax Auto-Detection and Configuration

Windows 95 includes support for hundreds of manufacturers and model numbers, establishing unique initialization codes for manufacturers' variants of the Hayes command set. Even modems with no built-in plug-and-play features can often be identified by manufacturer, requiring a minimum of user effort to install them. Microsoft's Telephony Applications Programming Interface (TAPI) is a universal modem driver.

note *Windows 95 has a dual strategy for managing older DOS/Win 3.x and Windows 95 communication programs. Older programs use their internal command settings to operate the modem, whereas 32-bit Windows 95 applications pass control of the modem directly to the operating system.*

The 32-bit Win95 applications are fine-tuned and controlled through a series of options available through the Win95 Control Panel. (HyperTerminal and Dial-Up Networking, which Microsoft includes on the installation CD, are two such applications.) Through the Control Panel Modems object, you can set internal and external connect rates, establish custom dialing strings, toggle flow control, and data compression settings for multiple modems (see Figure 10-1).

Improved Serial Port Management

Win95's VCOMM is a new protected-mode communications driver that takes advantage of the new plug-and-play services in Windows 95. The VCOMM communications driver supports the high-speed serial ports necessary for smooth data transfer with high-speed modems.

FIGURE 10-1 *The Modem Properties windows*

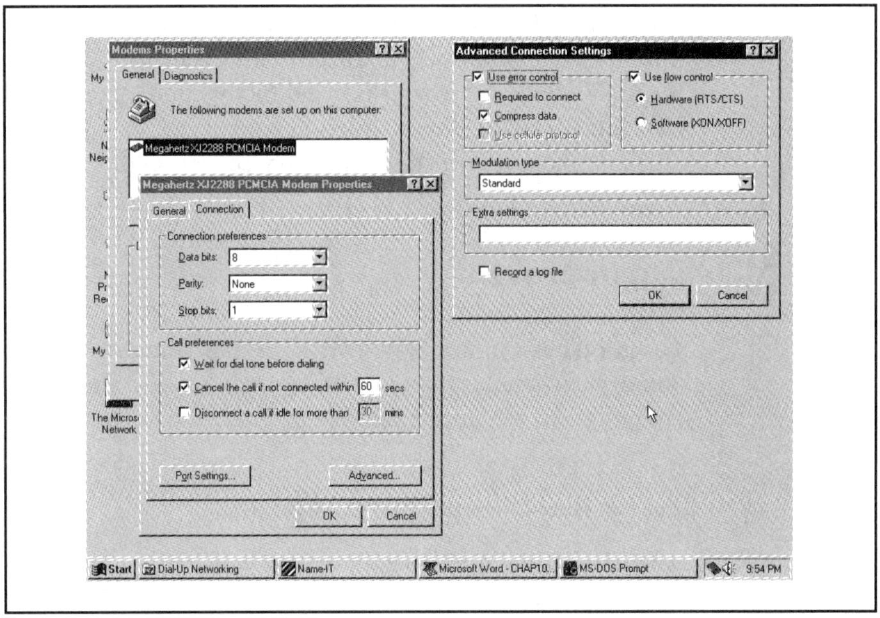

Windows 95 allows you to regulate both the receive and transmit data buffers built into ports that use the NS16550 UART. VCOMM also improves the operating system's arbitration of serial port access. If two open applications both try to use the same serial port, the system won't crash, as often occurred in previous versions of Windows. Instead, Windows 95 is reliable about awarding the port to one program and suspending the other program's access until the port is free. (If you attempt to send a fax while another program is open on the same port, the fax is placed in a queue. When the port becomes available, the fax is sent.)

If you open a Win95 communications program configured for the same port as the open Inbox utility, Inbox access to the modem is temporarily disabled. The second program takes over the port, returning control to Inbox when you close it. When a Windows 3.*x* program tries to access a serial port in active use, it receives a system message that the port is currently unavailable. Finally, if there is a port conflict between a DOS session and a Windows application, a pop-up message appears to let you choose which application program gains control of the port, as shown here.

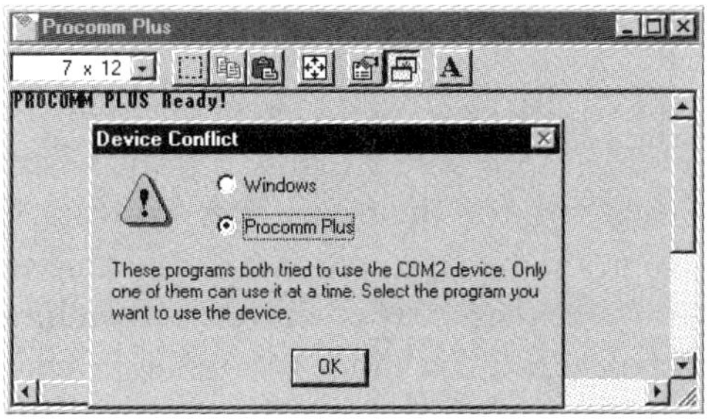

note *Windows 95 does not provide the sophisticated port arbitration offered by some third-party communications packages. For instance, it does not allow fax auto-answering to remain active while a second communications program is open. The operating system also lacks drivers that support Hayes ESP, NS16750, and other high-speed I/O devices. See the section later in this chapter for a description of how third-party utilities address these issues.*

HyperTerminal Communications Program

Windows 95 includes a less-than-full-featured telecommunications program called HyperTerminal. This is a modified, licensed version of a more powerful product put out by Hilgraeve, Inc. Microsoft's version of Hyper Terminal lacks a scrollback screen buffer, but it does include improved setup of online service profiles, a full complement of file transfer protocols, and better terminal emulation than its Windows 3.*x* predecessor.

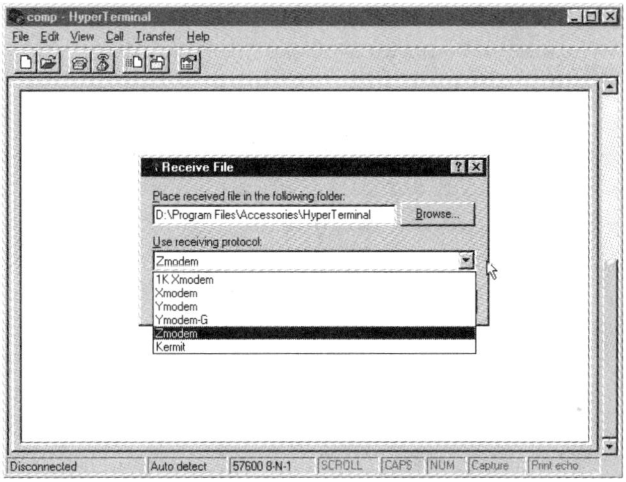

Built-In Fax Tools

Microsoft Fax is an elementary fax management application built into Win95's Microsoft Exchange Mail Client. It allows you to compose fax messages on-the-fly, print faxes from any Windows application, and receive faxes in the background with any standard Class I or Class II fax modem. (Binary files can be transmitted as attachments to Class I fax modems, only.) The Microsoft Exchange Inbox, described next, allows you to keep a simple fax address book and stores received and transmitted documents.

note *Microsoft Fax does not contain an optical character reading translation feature, nor does it permit you to edit received documents.*

Microsoft Exchange—Built-In Mail Client

Microsoft Exchange (represented by the Inbox icon on the desktop) is a multi-service mail management program. Designed primarily to handle mail sent through a Microsoft mail server or through the Microsoft Network online information service, Exchange can also manage e-mail for the CompuServe online information service, and for standard Internet Simple Mail Transfer Protocol (SMTP) or Post Office Protocol (POP) mail addresses.

Exchange maintains a Personal Address Book that can contain separate name and address listings for individual information services. Sent and received e-mail messages (including fax transmissions) are stored in an aggregate file on the hard disk called a Personal Information Store. (It's possible to set up multiple information stores, if you want to track messages from different sources in separate listings.)

Exchange can send formatted documents as embedded binary files over the Internet through two widely used mail protocols: MIME and UUEncode. You can use it to log on automatically and download your mail for all configured services, or as a preview utility, scanning a server for new mail and retrieving it selectively.

The mail management interface for Inbox is fairly straightforward. It allows you to create and display individual message folders. The e-mail contents of the folders can be sorted through a number of filters: by date, sender, recipient, subject header, message priority, or file size. Messages can be dragged and dropped between folders, resaved in separate disk files, or placed in a Deleted Items folder that can be purged on a regular basis. Right-clicking on any e-mail message brings up a set of options that allow you to read it, forward it to another recipient, or reply to the original message sender.

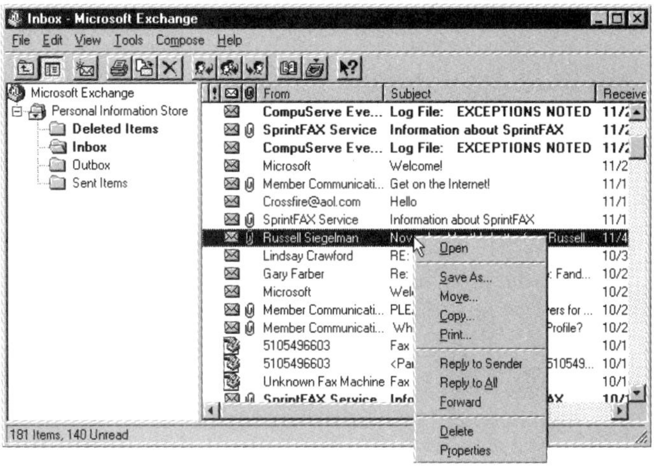

The Compose New Mail option brings up a message editor to prepare outgoing e-mail for fax transmittal, or any of the installed online services. Support for multiple information services can be combined in a single Microsoft Exchange profile, or separate profiles can be configured for each individual service. See the section on working with Exchange later in this chapter for more details.

Dial-Up Networking—Internet Connectivity

Win95's Dial-Up Networking utility frees you from the need to use third-party Transmission Control Protocol/Internet Protocol dialers (TCP/IP) to connect to the Internet. Dial-Up Networking also allows you to connect to a dedicated cable network by dialing into the server or any workstation on the network through a modem.

The Dial-Up Networking folder contains a Setup Wizard that will walk you through the creation of various dial-up service protocols. If you have Internet connections through multiple service providers, you can create individual profiles for each service. Each connection profile that you establish can contain individual modem and port settings, network protocol information, Internet Protocol (IP) addresses, and login and password information. By specifying IP information (name server addresses, etc.) in each individual service profile, you can avoid conflicts with TCP/IP settings for a dedicated network. Dial-Up Networking can be used to connect to non-Windows 95 computers running operating systems, such as Novell NetWare, Windows for Workgroups 3.*x*, or Windows NT.

Dial-Up Networking makes use of a 32-bit TCP/IP protocol that allows you to use application software specifically designed for the Win32 API. 32-bit Internet applications like the Microsoft Web Browser, Telnet, and File Transfer Protocol (FTP) utilities, Netscape for Windows 95, and Delrina's CyberJack require a 32-bit connection in order to function. These programs download, display, and write information to your hard disk faster than their older 16-bit counterparts.

To automate connections to Internet service providers that require non-standard login procedures, a Dial-Up Scripting utility is provided on the Win95 installation CD. Among the included sample scripts is one that allows CompuServe users to establish a direct point-to-point protocol (PPP) Internet connection. If you have the floppy disk version of Windows 95, this enhancement can be downloaded from the Microsoft Bulletin Board, or via its Internet FTP and World Wide Web sites.

Phone Dialer

This small Windows 95 applet allows you to set up a quick database of addresses and telephone numbers that you can point to with the mouse and dial directly through your modem. See Chapter 5 for some tips and information about using Phone Dialer.

Supplementary Online Bells and Whistles

Here's more information about additional features you'll find useful.

Client Interface for the Microsoft Network

The Microsoft Network (MSN) is a graphic-based online information service that Microsoft hopes will offer tough competition to CompuServe, America Online, and other information resources. You don't get a free membership just because you've purchased Windows 95, but you do get the elegant front-end for the service that allows you to subscribe at a small monthly rate. The Microsoft Network boasts the most well-designed, useful interface of any large commercial information service. (Right now, it runs only under Windows 95.) Microsoft is currently in the process of filling MSN with content from various corporate and hobbyist sources. A number of computer software and hardware companies have established a presence in

MSN's support forums, although CompuServe and AOL still offer more support resources.

One of the unique facets of MSN is the access it provides to Microsoft multimedia reference tools. MSN members can access fully functional versions of Microsoft Bookshelf, Encarta, and the TechNet Database online through their modems. MSN also offers near-complete access to Internet news groups through an attractive, easy-to-use, built-in news reader.

Microsoft Internet Explorer

Like CompuServe, the Microsoft Network can also provide complete access to the Internet through a PPP dial-up connection. In order to establish a PPP connection, MSN users must either purchase the Microsoft Plus! package or download and install the free Microsoft Internet Access Kit. (Details are provided in Chapter 11.) The Microsoft Internet Explorer kit consists of a sophisticated Web browser with full drag-and-drop desktop features, and an Internet Setup Wizard that adds PPP capability to the existing Win95 MSN client interface.

Communicating Through Windows 95

Setting up telecommunications software has always been one of the thornier aspects of personal computing. Under Windows 95, this task can range from being an automated no-brainer to an epic treasure-hunt through twisty, hidden setup screens. It pretty much depends on how far away you stray from generic software programmed for Windows 95 to (sometimes more useful) third-party applications written for DOS and Windows 3.*x*.

Modem Setup

To detect or install a new modem under Windows 95, open the Modems component from the Control Panel, open the General tab, and click the Add button. On the next screen, you can specify either a PCMCIA (Personal Computer Memory Card International Association) modem or other type. PCMCIA modems—now referred to by Microsoft as *PC cards*—are plug-in modules that slide in and out of special slots on a portable computer. (Some desktop units may also include PCMCIA slots, but this isn't typical.) For all other modem types, both internal and external, select the Other option. Supported PC cards will be recognized and installed automatically by Windows 95. For other modem types, you can ask the system to attempt an automatic installation, or bypass the detection routine and select the manufacturer and model directly from a component list. If you choose the modem this way, you'll also have to manually specify the port it's connected to.

Typically the Win95 Modem Installation Wizard may detect the manufacturer of your modem (this information is built into the modem's ROM and is usually available via a Hayes dialing command), but it may not always detect the specific model number. For instance, you may have a USR HST Dual Standard modem that Windows 95 sees as a Courier. In the case of popular manufacturers, it's easy to fine-tune the modem selection by scrolling up or down in the list of units to select the correct model number. If your particular model number does not appear in the list, you can select one that is close to it, or scroll up the list to Standard Modem Types and select one at the appropriate connect rate. You can add custom performance parameters later through the Advanced button on the Modem Properties Connections tab.

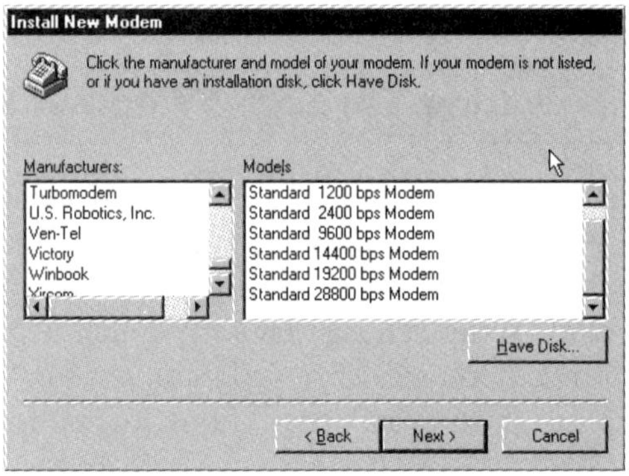

When your modem is first installed, you'll also be given an opportunity to specify the area code for your calling region and whether your telephone line uses a tone or pulse dialing connection. These options can be changed later by pressing the Dialing Properties button on the Modem Properties General tab, to reveal the My Locations section.

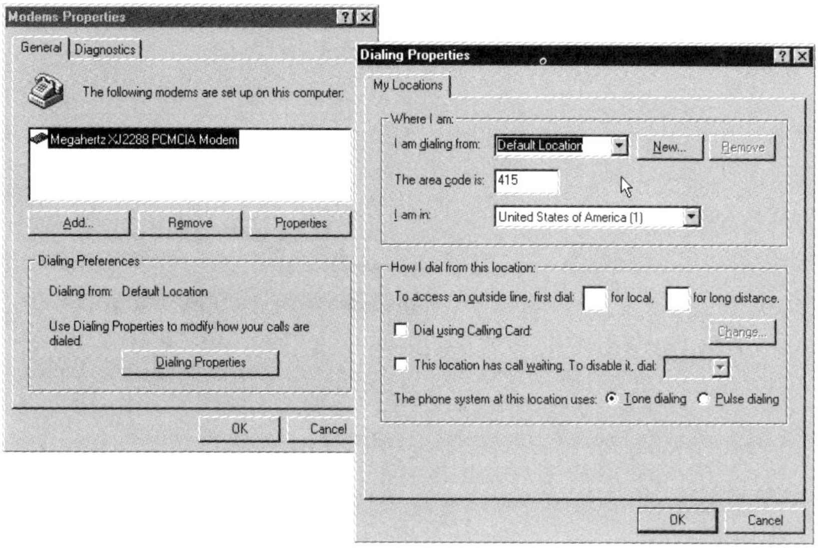

Working with Dialing Properties

The My Locations section of Dialing Properties allows you to set a default area code and line access options for a particular site. For numbers in this area, the three-digit area code will automatically be omitted.

If you are dialing through a switchboard or device that requires other dialing code prefixes, you can enter them in the lower portion of the My Locations properties screen. If you're taking a notebook computer on the road with you, just click the New button to set up an alternate calling area location.

Both the Win95 Dial-Up Networking Adapter and the Phone Dialer utility allow you to make credit card calls or specify a calling card for a particular long distance carrier. Just place a checkmark in the Dial Using Calling Card box located in the lower portion of the Dialing Properties\My Location screen. This will bring up a menu of American and International telephone access providers. If your carrier is on the list, select it as shown here. If necessary, enter your calling card number in the Calling Card Number field below the carrier field.

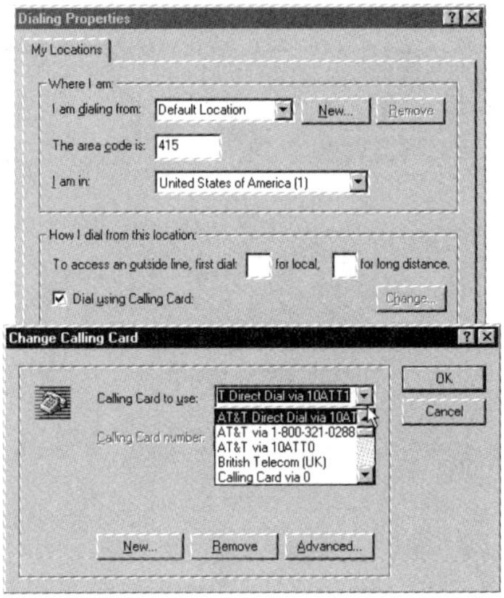

This number will then be entered automatically for you when you use one of Windows 95's built-in dialing accessories.

If your long distance carrier is not included in the default list, you can define a custom long distance carrier by clicking on the New button in the Change Calling Card dialog box. Enter a name for the carrier and click the OK button. Next click the Advanced button in the Change Calling Card dialog box to bring up the Dialing Rules box. In the three fields for the Dialing Rules box, you must enter the access number of your long distance carrier, and any additional instruction codes necessary for dialing out. If your custom service resembles one of the default long distance carriers, you can use its dialing rules as a template by clicking the Copy From button.

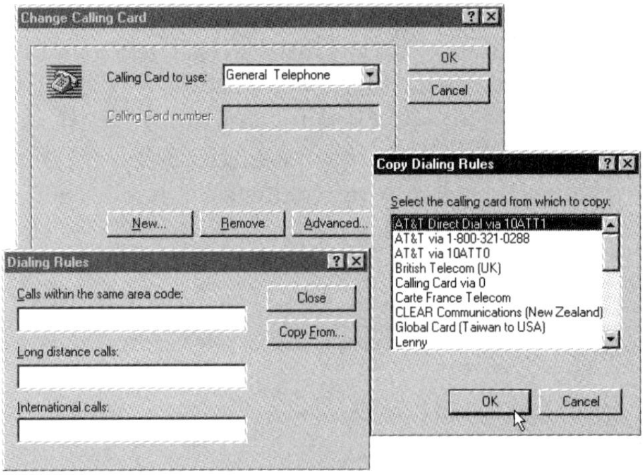

Modem Diagnostics

You can perform a simple test to see whether your modem is physically recognized by Windows 95 by opening the Modems Properties screen and selecting the Diagnostics tab. The Diagnostics box displays a list of serial ports and installed modems. For more information, select a serial port and modem combination and click the More Info button. Windows 95 will interrogate the modem and deliver a diagnostic information dump.

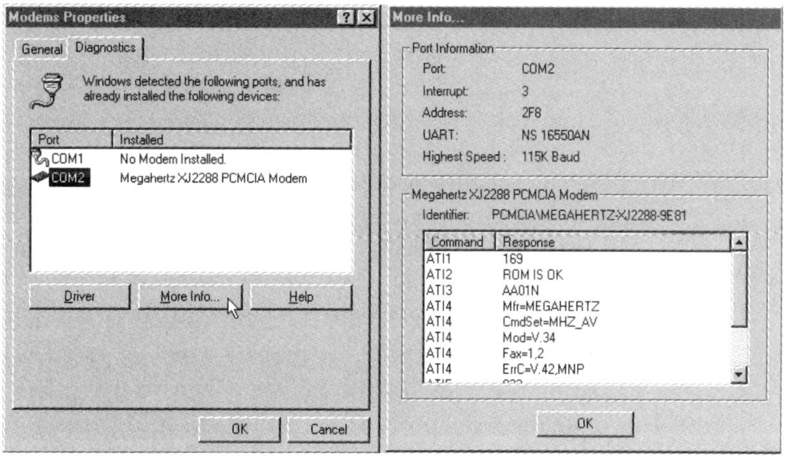

Adjusting Modem Properties

The performance settings for any installed modem in your computer can be customized by opening the Modem component of the Control Panel, selecting the modem on the General tab, and clicking on the Properties button.

THE GENERAL TAB The General tab of Modem Properties chooses the communications port, speaker volume, and maximum connect speed for the serial port. For PCMCIA and internal modems, the communications port generally can't be changed, since it is fixed, internally. An external modem can be switched to an alternate serial port, if one is available.

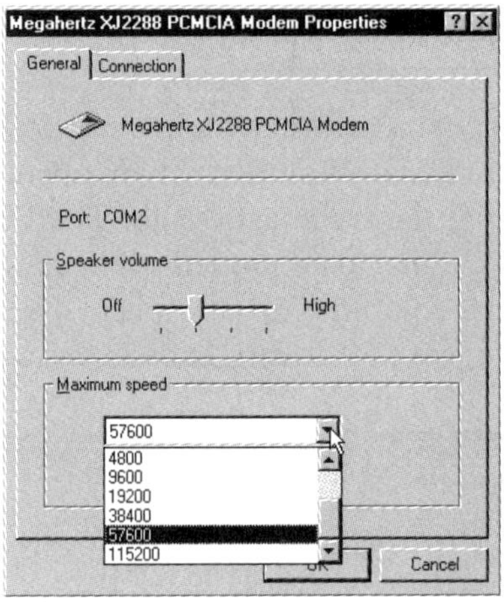

These settings are used only by Windows 95 applications that access the operating system through the TAPI interface. DOS and Windows 3.*x* programs continue to set these parameters through their individual internal setup menus.

Maximum connect speed is sometimes referred to as Data Terminal Equipment (DTE) speed, or *internal connect speed*. This number (in bytes per second) represents the rate at which your modem passes received data through the serial port to the CPU. This setting does not necessarily represent the maximum external connection rate between two modems, which is usually considerably lower. The best strategy for setting the maximum connect speed is to make it as high as your serial port and modem permit to avoid file transmission errors:

- For older, low speed serial ports with 8250 or 16450 UART (Universal Asynchronous Receiver/Transmitters), the setting should be no greater than 38,400. (In some cases, if you experience transmission difficulties, you may have to decrease it to 19,200.)
- For newer, high-speed serial ports equipped with NS16550 UARTs or better, the maximum connect speed should be set to 115,200. On some systems, you may need to drop it back down to 38,400 or 57,600. Generally, the box marked "Only connect at this speed" should be left unchecked. Selecting this option prohibits your modem from establishing connections at speeds lower than the specified maximum rate.

tip *If you're unsure what kind of serial port your modem is using, open the Modems component of the Control Panel and click open the Diagnostics tab. Select the serial port you want to test and click the More Info button toward the center of the screen. If the UART entry under Port Information reads* NS16550AN, *then you have a high-speed serial port. If it reads* 8250 *or* NS16450, *then you have an older, lower-speed serial port.*

Some proprietary I/O devices like the Hayes ESP board and the Turbo Express Card, which is discussed later in this chapter, are capable of higher DTE connect rates than 115,200 bps. To get the connect rates these cards are designed for, you must install manufacturer-supplied drivers.

Also note that some newer PCMCIA and internal modems are now being shipped with upgraded interfaces that allow serial port connect rates higher than 115,200 bps. For these modems, the Windows 95 setting should be set to 115,200, and the modem's ROM will automatically handle the higher internal connect rate.

THE CONNECTION TAB The Connection tab of Modems Properties sets the initial connection preferences that will be used by the Windows 95 Terminal and the Dial-Up Networking Adapter. These settings, as well as the Call preferences listed immediately below them, can be overridden by dialing profiles for individual information services. For most information services and bulletin boards, you will want to set these preferences to 8, None, and 1 (8 data-bit transmission, no parity, and 1 stop bit). One notable exception to this is CompuServe, which requests initial settings of 7, Even, and 1 (7 data-bit transmission, even parity, and 1 stop bit) in order to connect to its user interface through a common terminal program.

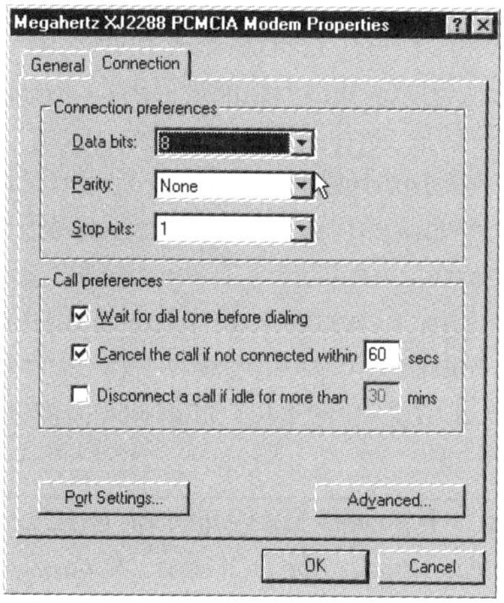

The Call preferences dialog lets you toggle the option to make your modem wait for a dial tone before dialing. Outside of the United States, this option should be deselected. This section also lets you specify initial connect and call-in-progress time thresholds for your modem to disconnect if the host modem does not respond.

The two buttons at the bottom of the Connection tab set advanced communication options that are applied globally to all information service profiles configured to use that modem. Port Settings allow you to enable and fine-tune the first in, first out (FIFO) data buffer present in high-speed serial ports driven by the NS16550 UART. This screen is self-explanatory: the sliders can be moved to the left to correct connection and file transfer problems and to the right to speed up modem performance.

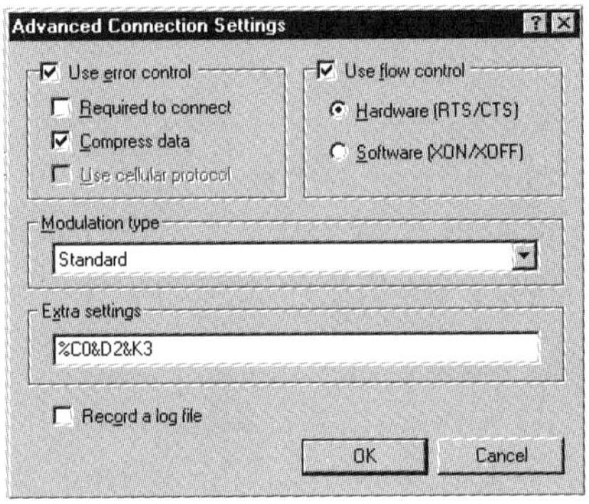

The Advanced Connection Settings dialog box shown above lets you toggle error-correction, data compression, and flow-control options for your modem. Generally, these options can be left at the default setting, but if you experience connection or data transfer difficulties, you may want to modify them.

Selecting or deselecting one of the checkbox options in the upper portion of the dialog box causes an appropriate Hayes command string to be sent to your modem when a Windows 95 communication program is opened. The particular Hayes commands sent to the modem to enable checkbox options are determined by the manufacturer and model you've selected. You can monitor the strings sent to your modem during initialization by selecting the "Record a log file" checkbox at the bottom of the dialog box.

note *The checkbox settings on this box don't affect the Hayes initialization strings sent to your modem by DOS and Windows 3.x communication programs. These applications usually send their own individual modem initialization strings when you launch them.*

The Modulation type option in the center of the Advanced Connections Settings dialog box allows you to choose between the standard modulation used by most other modems and the nonstandard HST modulation used by some U.S. Robotics modems.

The Extra Settings option toward the bottom of the dialog box allows you to fine-tune your modem's performance by adding additional Hayes commands to be sent to your modem when you open a Windows 95 communications utility. This field is particularly useful if you have a modem that is not properly initialized by Windows 95. The commands you enter here are passed to the modem after Windows 95's preconfigured Hayes string and before dialing a telephone number. A simple, common addition would be to enter the string &F in this box. This has the effect of automatically returning your modem to its factory defaults before dialing, no matter what Windows 95 sends to it.

Using a Modem Log File to Troubleshoot

As mentioned earlier, if you're having problems connecting to a particular information service through a particular modem or serial port, you can monitor the modem's activity by placing a checkmark in the Record a logfile box. This causes all commands transmitted and received by the modem to be recorded to a file called MODEMLOG.TXT in your WINDOWS directory. To track communications problems, enable log recording and attempt to dial into a service with your Windows 95 communications utility.

Afterwards, you can open MODEMLOG.TXT for a blow-by-blow description of what Windows 95 said to your modem, what your modem sent to the host, and what the host modem said in reply. This can help you to isolate the exact point at which a connection failure occurred. For instance, one common connection problem may be caused by your modem's attempt to set up a data compression or error-correction protocol not supported on the host being called. If your inspection of the log file confirms this, you can use the Extra Settings option, discussed previously, to modify modem performance. You can enter Hayes commands that enable or disable v.42 BIS or MNP protocols, or you can enter specific Hayes S-Register commands that change the communications handshake. (Consult your modem's manual for troubleshooting modifications suggested by the manufacturer.)

Third-Party Support for High-Speed Communications

Despite the telecommunications improvements that have been added to Windows 95, there are still some limitations that may cramp the style of users with state-of-the-art hardware.

NO BUILT-IN SUPPORT FOR DTE SPEEDS ABOVE 115,200 BPS

Some v.34 modem manufacturers now include special DTE-doubling firmware that supports a DTE rate of 230,000 bps. Super-high-speed modems capable of faster connection rates than the v.34 modem standard, and 16550 UART, can support are also beginning to appear. One of several competing ISDN (Integrated Services Digital Network) standards, for instance, features Hayes-compatible modems capable of supporting DCE (Data Communication Equipment or modem-to-modem) connect rates higher than 115,200 bps and DTE rates of 500,000 bps or more. High-speed I/O ports to accommodate these devices, now use newer 16650 and 16750 UARTs that are not directly supported by Windows 95's communication drivers.

One company, Pacific Commware of Portland, Oregon, is already well-known for its Windows 3.x port management package, Turbo Commander. At this writing, Pacific Commware's Turbo-Express I/O card and Turbo Commander for Windows 95 are wrapping up their beta-test cycle. The Turbo-Express card, designed for ISDN modems like the IBM Windsurfer and Motorola Bitsurfer, uses a 16,750 UART with twin-64 byte FIFO buffers. It is capable of supporting DTE rates of 1,121,600 bps with Turbo Commander's Win95 communications drivers. Turbo Commander includes a module that replaces the standard Win95 serial port options, allowing you to fine-tune the performance of I/O ports with all standard UART types. A desktop display panel is used to control your modem and serial port settings and show the status of a current online connection.

NO SMART MANAGEMENT OF SHARED SERIAL PORTS

As mentioned previously, control of a shared serial port can be awarded to only one open application. Although the system no longer crashes when two applications compete for the same serial port, it is not typically possible for the modem to receive a fax in the background while a second communication program is open. Delrina, Inc., the manufacturer of the popular Communications Suite that contains WinComm and WinFax Pro, offers a partial solution to this problem. Both the Windows 3.x and Windows 95 versions of WinComm (the terminal communications part of the suite) are programmed not to demand access to a serial port unless the user actively initiates a dialing procedure. The result is that WinFax Pro (or Windows 95's Inbox) can be loaded in the background and retain access to the serial port while WinComm is open in the foreground. If you've just logged off a bulletin board, you can keep the WinComm terminal window open for cutting and pasting, or viewing a captured session while the fax software remains alert and active in the background, ready to answer the telephone.

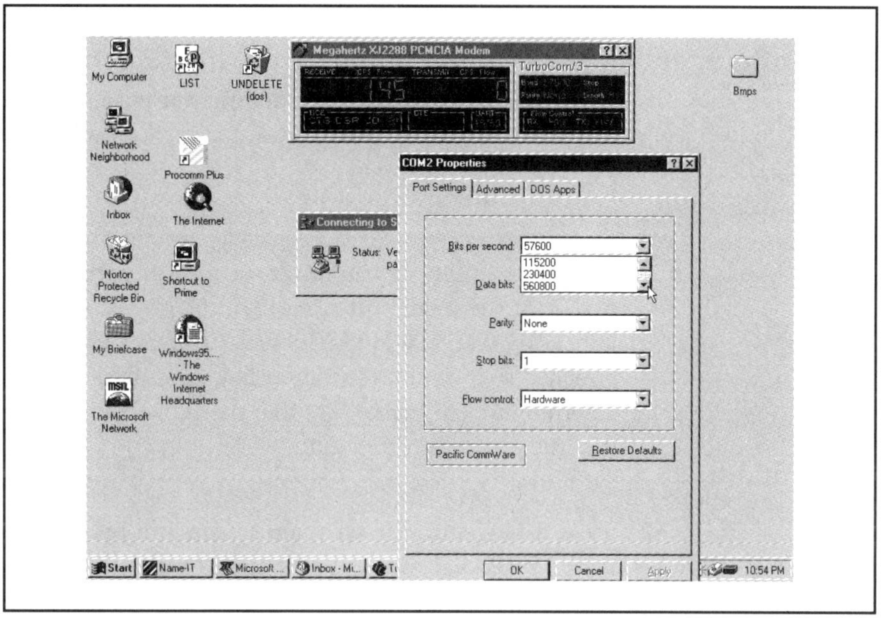

FIGURE 10-2 *Turbo Commander offers advanced configuration options for high-speed I/O ports.*

Telecomm Applications

Windows 3.*x* and DOS telecommunications applications work transparently under Windows 95. Until the 32-bit versions of your favorite packages appear, you can continue quite comfortably with older versions of Procomm Plus, QModem, the Delrina Communications Suite, and others. DOS standbys like Telix, Telemate, and Procomm Plus for DOS are also still quite useful tools. These packages ignore most of the Control Panel's communications settings for TAPI applications. They continue to use their own configuration menus to initialize the modem, set data connect rates, and so on.

The Win95 settings that really affect these older packages are those that directly control the serial port: port address, IRQ, and advanced settings for high-speed port FIFO buffers. With these settings determined by the operating system, WinComm, Procomm Plus for Windows, QModem for Windows, and most other Windows 3.*x* telecommunication programs continue to be fully functional under Windows 95. If you want to make adjustments that affect data compression, flow control, and other modem initialization settings while using these programs, make them through the program's internal setup options as under Windows 3.*x*.

More Troubleshooting Tips

If you're experiencing difficulty dialing out with a DOS or Windows 3.*x* communication program, you may want to try following these troubleshooting steps:

1. Open your communications package to a terminal screen. Type **AT** and press ENTER. If you don't see an OK prompt, check to make sure that the serial port selected in the program corresponds to a port appearing on the Win95 Modems Control Panel that has a modem attached to it. If not, try reinstalling your modem. If you have an external modem, make sure that the cable connection is correct and that the power is turned on.

2. Type **ATDT** into the terminal screen and press ENTER. You should hear a brief dial tone. (If you have a pulse-dial telephone system, type **ATDP** instead.) If you don't hear a dial tone, try locating and turning up the volume on your modem's speaker. If you still don't get a dial tone, check to make sure the cable from the telephone jack is properly plugged into the modem. If you have a switchboard device attached to the line, try removing it and connecting the modem directly to the wall socket to see if the problem disappears. If problems persist, your serial port or modem may not be configured correctly, or there may be a conflict with another peripheral on your system.

3. Open the System component of the Control Panel and select the Device Manager tab. If you have a PCMCIA or an internal modem, expand the modem listing (click the + sign on the folder) and select the modem you want to test. If you have an external modem, expand the Ports listing instead, and select the port the modem is connected to.

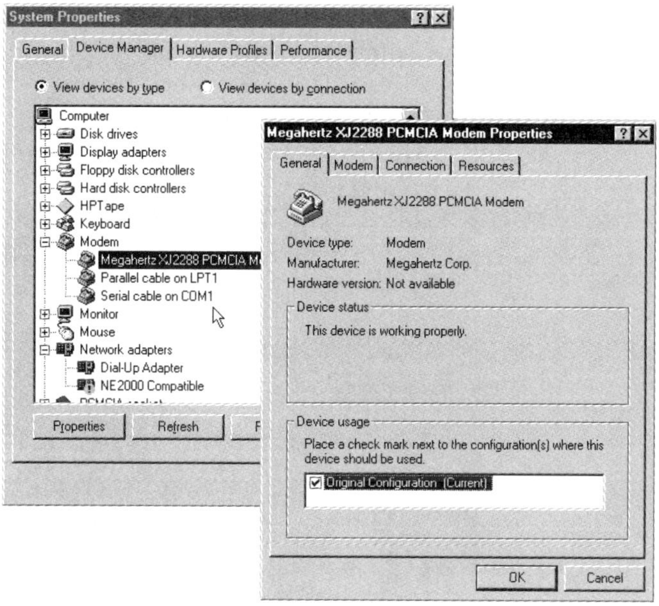

4. Click the Properties button near the bottom of the dialog box. The General tab should contain a Device status message that says whether the modem (or port) is working properly. Select the Resources tab to display information on the port address and IRQ used by the modem.

If the modem (or port) has been assigned a conflicting address or IRQ, you can change it. A typical problem with modems configured for COM3 or COM4 occurs when the port is assigned an exotic system interrupt (such as IRQ 10 or IRQ 12). Windows 95 TAPI applications may work with this nonstandard IRQ, but your DOS and Windows 3.*x* programs will refuse to dial out. If this is the case, you can try changing the interrupt used by the modem to a more common configuration like IRQ 3 or IRQ 5 that your older programs can recognize.

1. On the Resources tab, deselect the box marked "Use automatic settings."

2. Highlight the Interrupt Request resource type and click the Change Settings button, as shown here:

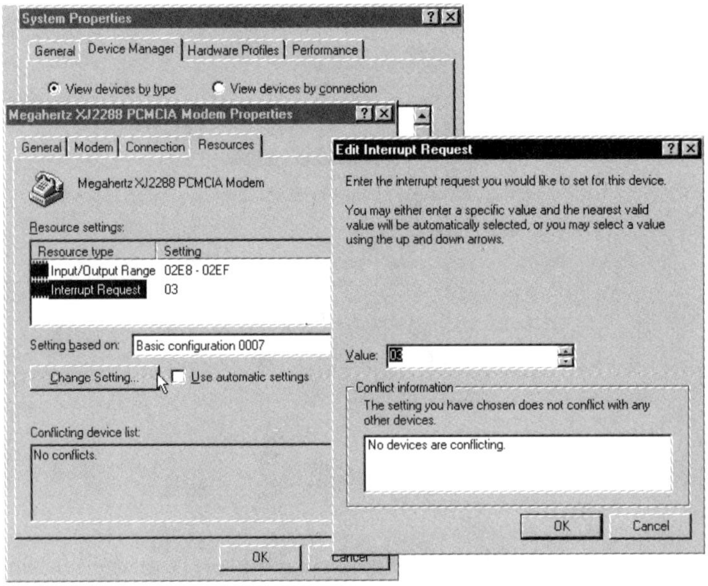

3. If, when you click the Change Settings button, you get a message stating that the resource setting can't be modified, try selecting a different basic configuration in the "Setting based on" scroll list, and click the Change Settings button again.

4. Select an appropriate interrupt value on the Edit Interrupt Request dialog box. The Conflicting device list on that screen will tell you whether the interrupt is available.

5. Click OK to close that screen and click OK again on the Resources tab dialog box to save the configuration.

If you want to change the port address instead of the IRQ, follow the procedure just outlined, selecting Input/Output Range in the "Resource settings" area of the Resources tab instead of Interrupt Request. To get an internal modem or a serial I/O card to cooperate, you may also need to open up your computer's "chassis" and change the jumper settings on the card.

tip *If a DOS telecommunications application slows down or freezes up when you run it in the background, open its Properties settings (right-click the icon and select Properties from the context menu) and select the Misc tab. Make sure that the "Always Suspend" Background option is not selected, and move the Idle Sensitivity slider on this screen all the way toward Low on the left. Click OK to save the new settings.*

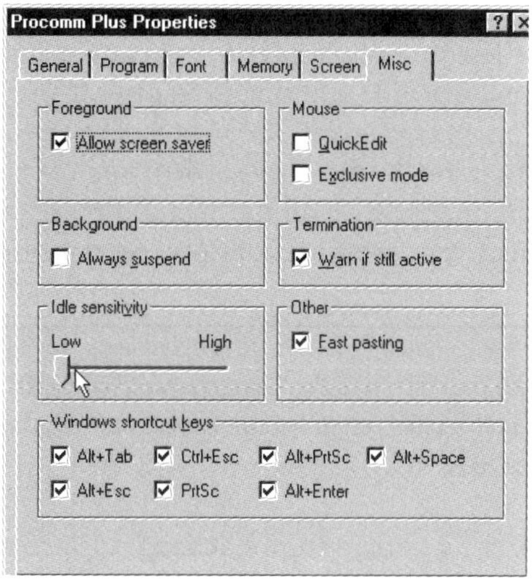

Working with Microsoft Exchange

Microsoft Exchange (which is activated via the Inbox icon on your desktop) is an optional component of Windows 95 that will be installed if you select any of the various Windows 95 features that require it. If you've chosen to install Microsoft Fax, the Microsoft Network, or Microsoft Mail Services during the initial Windows 95 setup, the Inbox also appears on your desktop.

If there is no Inbox on your desktop, and you want to take advantage of Exchange's fax and e-mail management, you can install it by opening the Add/Remove Programs icon on the Control Panel to the Windows Setup tab, and then selecting MS-Exchange in the components list.

Exchange is a memory- and disk-intensive application. If you plan to use it, your system should have a minimum of 8MB of RAM and 20MB free on disk for Windows 95's dynamic swap file.

Exchange Profiles

When you first install Exchange, the Setup Wizard steps you through the creation of a default profile. This profile contains a listing of all the information services you want Exchange to manage, and the administrative information (login, password, telephone numbers, and so on) that applies to each one. Later, after Exchange is installed, you can configure additional profiles. You don't have to select every information service for inclusion in the main profile (although you can). If you prefer to set up individual profiles for fax management, the Microsoft Network, and Microsoft Mail, you have that option. In the future, when you open the Inbox, you'll have the option to automatically load the default profile, load a custom profile, or bring up a menu that prompts you to select a profile. (See Figure 10-3.)

note *Although Exchange is capable of managing e-mail from third-party Internet service providers and the CompuServe information service, these options do not appear during the initial setup. Information on how to install these features is provided later on in this section.*

During initial setup, Exchange also creates a Personal Information Store that will be used to track your e-mail messages and a Personal Address Book used to store the names and e-mail addresses of frequent message recipients.

FIGURE 10-3

The Inbox can be configured to prompt you for a startup profile.

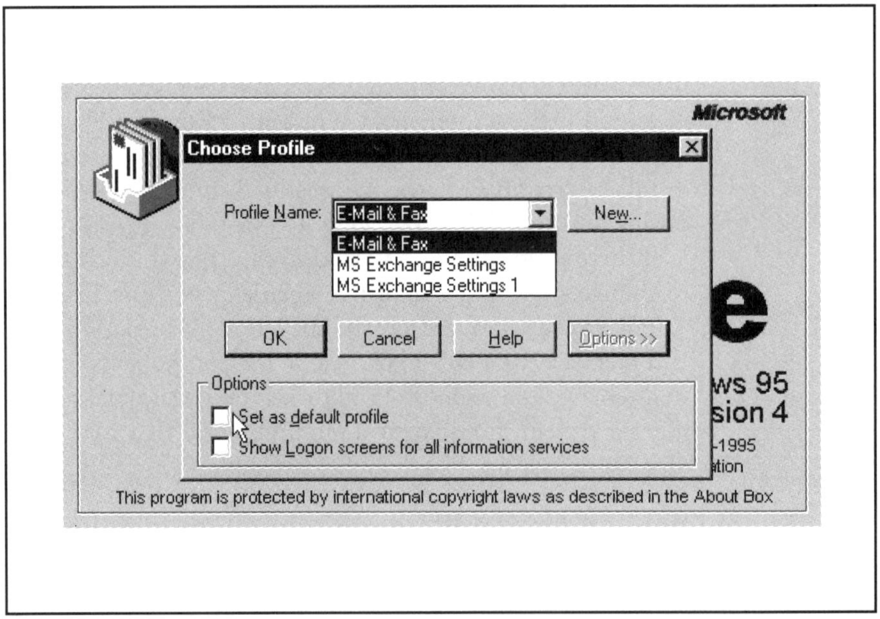

As with the profiles, you can create additional versions of the address book and the information store, later on. If there are multiple users on your system, each user can have a separate information store and address book, or you may choose to set up one information store to record fax transactions, another one for Microsoft Mail messages, and so on.

Choosing a Startup Profile

The default behavior of the Inbox when you double-click on it is to open the MS-Exchange Settings profile that you created during installation. If you have created other Exchange profiles, any of them can be set as the default, or you can configure the Inbox to prompt you for a profile every time you open it.

To set Inbox to prompt you for a profile, you must first let it open with the default settings you've created. From the open Inbox, select Options from the Tools menu.

The section of the Options screen labeled "When starting Microsoft Exchange" lets you choose between being prompted for a profile on startup or automatically loading the profile selected in the "Always use this profile" drop-down list.

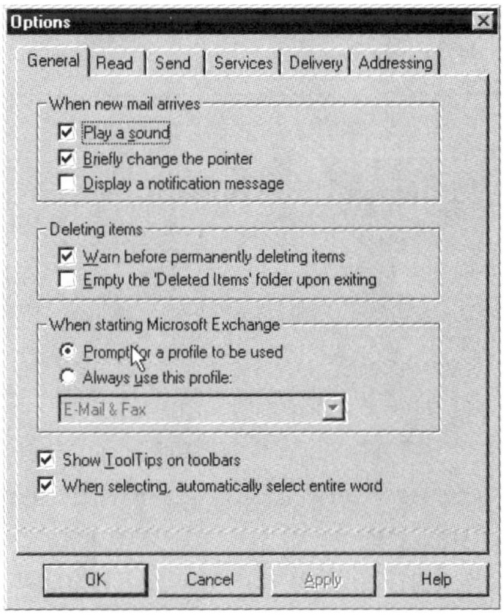

You can also change the default startup profile without opening the Inbox. Right-click the Inbox icon on the desktop and select Properties from the context menu. The first part of the General screen that follows displays the current list of Exchange profiles. (You can create a new one by clicking

Adding Third-Party Information Services to Microsoft Exchange

The files necessary to add the CompuServe information service to Microsoft Exchange are located in the DRIVERS\OTHER\EXCHANGE\COMPUSRV directory of your Windows 95 installation CD. To install them, just run the SETUP.EXE program in that directory. That's all there is to it. If you installed Windows 95 over a network or from floppy diskettes, you'll need to download a file called CISMAIL.EXE, available on CompuServe, the Microsoft Bulletin Board, and the Microsoft Internet site. (See Appendix C for Internet addresses and telephone numbers.) CISMAIL.EXE is an archive that contains the same drivers found on the CD.

There are two ways to add support for Internet Mail to Microsoft Exchange. The first is to purchase and install Microsoft Plus!, the CD of supplemental utilities that Microsoft sells to enhance Windows 95. Currently, you can also add Internet support by downloading and installing the beta version of the Internet Explorer that Microsoft has made available. At present, you can find the Internet Explorer beta in the usual places: in the Microsoft Products section of The Microsoft Network (see the section on navigating MSN for details on how to find it), at the Microsoft Internet Web and FTP sites, on the Microsoft Bulletin Board Downloading Service, and on CompuServe in the Windows 95 and WinNews forums. The filename will be something like MSIE20B3.EXE. Once you've downloaded it to disk, all you need to do is run it from a DOS command-session inside Windows 95. The Microsoft Web Browser and Microsoft Exchange Internet components will install themselves. The Internet Explorer version 2.0 is also included as part of Microsoft's first Service Pack Upgrade for Windows 95.

the Add button.) The bottom part of the screen allows you to change the default startup profile by selecting a different one from the drop-down list. (See Figure 10-3.)

Creating Exchange Profiles

To create a new Exchange Profile, right-click on the Inbox icon with the mouse and choose Properties from the pop-up context menu. Click the Show Profiles button toward the bottom of the screen to display the existing Exchange profiles. Click the Add button, as shown on the following page, to create a new profile.

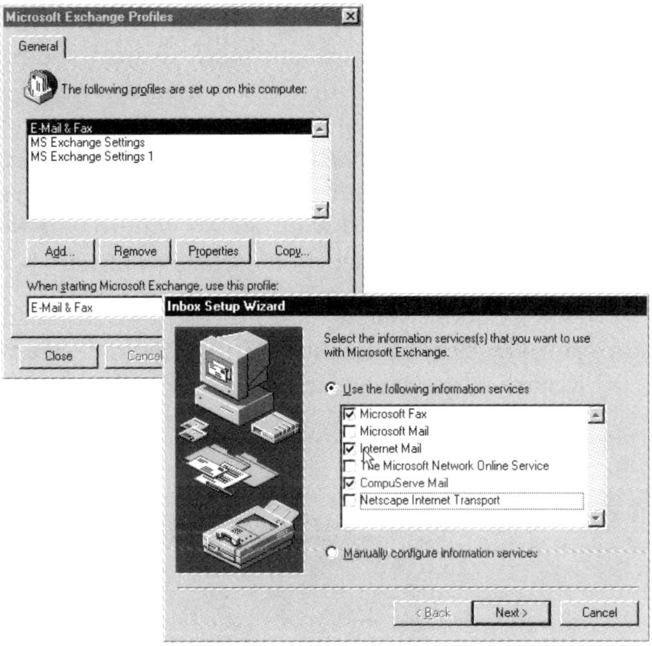

This opens the Inbox Exchange Wizard, which displays a list of the information services that can be made available within the profile. (This is the same screen that appears when Inbox creates the default Exchange profile.)

Place checkmarks next to the information services you want to include in the profile. (If Internet Mail and/or CompuServe Mail do not appear in the list, see the sidebar a few paragraphs back to learn about adding third-party services to Exchange.)

A good selection strategy is to check the services you'll use most commonly for your default profile, and create additional ones for the services you'll access less frequently. Your default profile should probably include Microsoft Mail and the Microsoft Network, if you plan to use it as a frequently accessed maildrop. You may want to create a separate profile exclusively for Microsoft Fax, and configure the Inbox to let you select this profile whenever you open the Inbox to send or receive fax mail. The same may apply to CompuServe Mail or Internet Mail; whatever pattern best suits your mail-collecting habits.

You can include all of the information services in one profile, but this will cause Exchange to consume more memory and possibly run a bit slower.

After you choose the information services to include in your new Exchange profile, you'll be prompted to enter a profile name. You may want to specify a name that's descriptive of the profile contents, such as "E-Mail and Fax," "Microsoft Network," or "CompuServe."

The Setup Wizard will now ask you to enter configuration information for each of the services you decided to install:

FAX Choose a modem. If no modem is installed, you can add one at this point by clicking the Add button. Next, decide whether you want the fax modem to answer all incoming calls while Inbox is open on the desktop. On the final screen for this option, enter your name, calling area information, and telephone number.

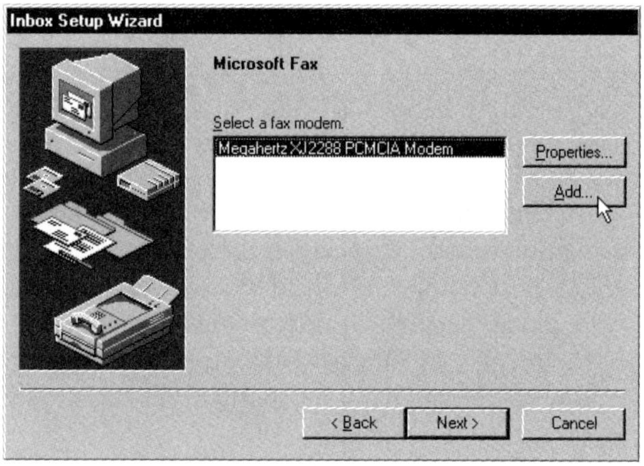

MICROSOFT MAIL The first screen asks you for the location of your Microsoft Mail Post Office. If you don't know, or haven't installed one, you must still enter something in this box. If you don't have a Post Office, enter the path to your WINDOWS directory and click the Next button. The next screen will tell you there's no Post Office in that directory, but you can ignore this and click Next, again, to continue.

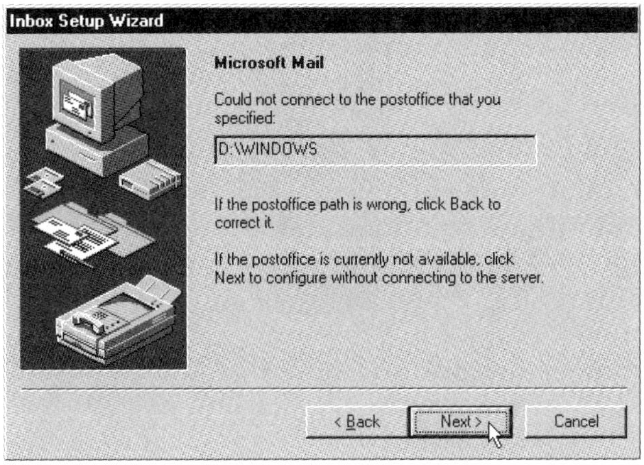

The next screen requests the name of your mailbox and your password. This information should be available from your network administrator. If you don't know, or are just testing this feature, enter your own name and the word **PASSWORD**. You can change this later.

INTERNET MAIL The first screen asks whether you want to connect to the Internet through a modem or over a direct TCP/IP network connection. For dial-up Internet access, choose the Modem option. For connection through a dedicated network, choose the Network option.

If you choose the Modem option, you'll be asked to specify a dial-up connection for your Internet service provider. Select a Dial-Up Networking connection profile that you've previously created. If you are using the Microsoft Network as your Internet service provider, choose that connection. (If you haven't already configured an Internet connection profile under Dial-Up Networking, you can do so now, by clicking the New button. See the sections on Dial-Up Networking in this chapter and in Chapter 5 for information on how to do this.)

The next screen asks you for the name of your Internet mail server. You can enter this as a site and domain name, or as an IP address. Consult your Internet service provider to obtain this information. Some examples are Mail.Compuserve.Com or 149.174.211.5.

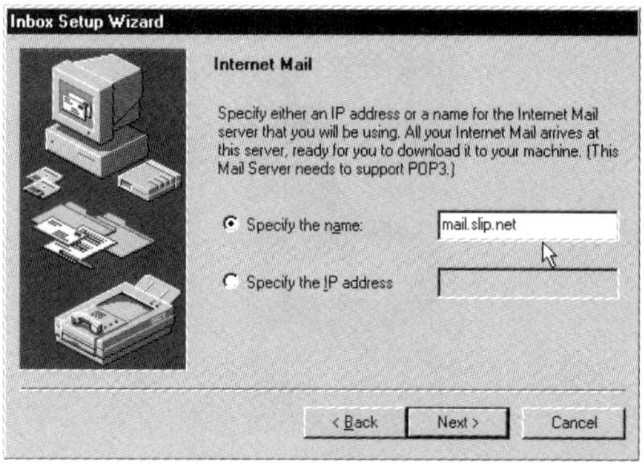

Next, decide whether you want to preview your Internet mail offline before downloading it or automatically download all of your Internet mail to the Inbox. Click Next again, and enter your name and e-mail address on the next screen.

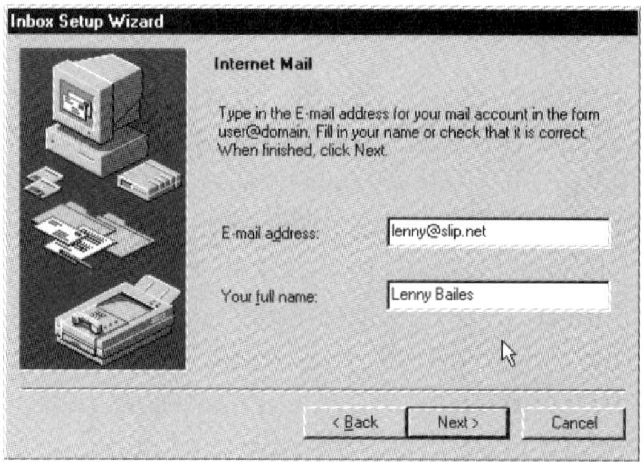

Finally, enter your mailbox name and mail password. (With many service providers this information duplicates your login ID and password.)

THE MICROSOFT NETWORK Click Next at the introductory screen. Installation is automatic.

COMPUSERVE MAIL The first screen asks you to specify a path to a common CompuServe directory that other CompuServe applications can share. Usually, if other CompuServe programs have been installed previously, this directory is called CSERVE. If you don't already have a CSERVE directory, you can specify your Windows directory instead, or else open My Computer, create a CSERVE directory, and return to the Inbox Setup Wizard, specifying the directory you've just created with the Browse button. Click Next to go on to the next screen.

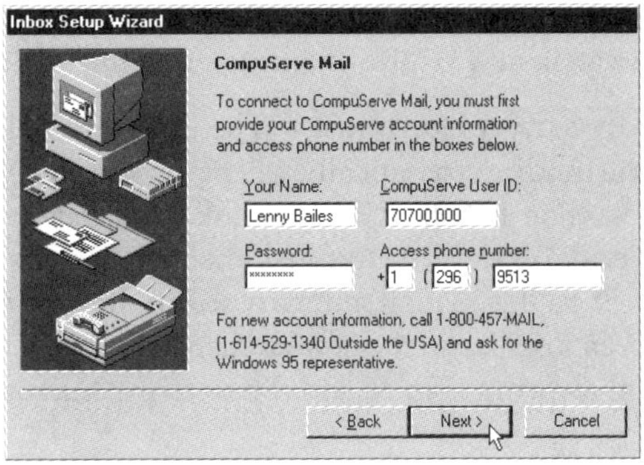

Enter your name, CompuServe User ID, Password, and the local access number you use to connect to CompuServe. Click Next to go on to the next screen.

The next page allows you to set some default CompuServe Mail options. You can elect to create a session activity log and decide whether to delete messages after download or accept Postage Due messages. Click Next to go on to the next screen.

YOUR PERSONAL ADDRESS BOOK This screen allows you to specify the name of the file for your Personal Address Book. (MAILBOX.PAB is the shared default.) You can use another address book already present on your hard disk, or create a new one with a different name. Click Next to continue.

YOUR PERSONAL FOLDER

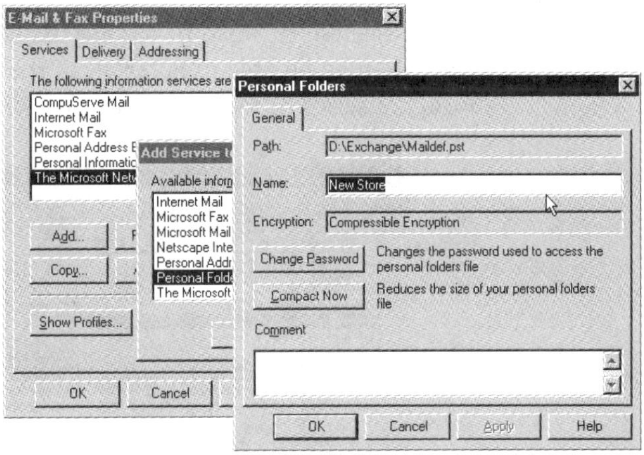

This screen allows you to specify the name of the file for your Personal Information Store (MAILBOX.PST is the shared default.) You can use another Personal Information Store already present on your hard disk, or create a new one with a different name. Click Next to continue.

AUTOSTART EXCHANGE The final option lets you decide whether to open the Inbox automatically whenever you start Windows 95. If your system has less than 16MB of RAM, think twice before enabling this feature. After you decide, click Next to finish the installation.

You'll see a final summary screen showing the information services that have been installed in the new Exchange Profile. Click the Finish button to close the Inbox Setup Wizard and return to the Microsoft Exchange Profiles screen.

Modifying Existing Exchange Profiles

Instead of creating new Exchange profiles, you can also modify existing profiles to add, remove or edit information services in an existing Exchange profile.

1. Right-click on the Inbox icon and select Properties from the pop-up context menu.
2. The General tab shows the information services installed in the default Exchange profile. If you wish to edit a different profile, click the Show Profiles button, select another Exchange profile, and click the Properties button.
3. To delete an information service, select it, and click the Remove button. To add an information service, click the Add button, and follow the steps outlined in the previous section for the service you've selected. (Instead of having to click Next after filling in each field, you may be able to enter all of the information for the service through a series of tabbed screens.)

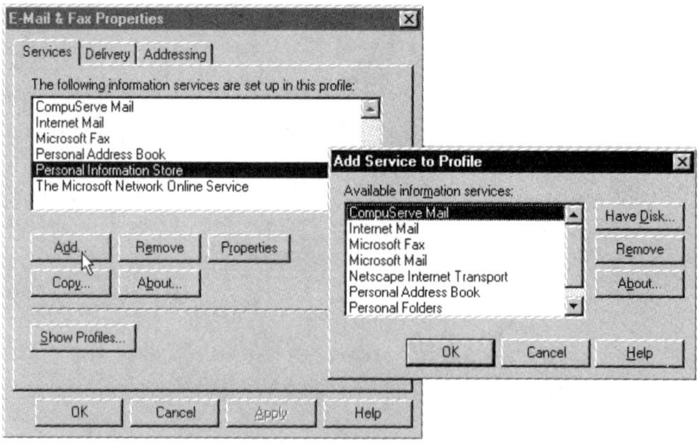

4. To change the connection information for an information service, select it, and click the Properties button.

OTHER EXCHANGE PROFILE PROPERTIES In addition to the properties for the information services within a profile, you can also modify some general defaults for the profile. When you select an Exchange profile (as described in the last two sections) and click the Properties button, you'll see three tabs: the Services tab, the Delivery tab, and the Addressing tab. (When the profile properties are accessed through the Inbox pull-down menus, three additional tabs appear: General, Read and Send.)

- The Services tab simply lists the information services installed in the profile.
- The Delivery tab allows you to set some e-mail delivery options. The first section on this tab allows you to switch mail delivery to a second Message Store configured for this information profile. (Exchange profiles can include as many Message Stores as you like. See the next sidebar for more details.) The second portion of the Delivery tab specifies the order in which the Inbox checks the information services in the profile for new mail and posts new messages that you've composed. For instance, in the next illustration, if you want to change the delivery options to log onto CompuServe before calling the Microsoft Network, highlight CompuServe and click the up arrow to move it to the top.

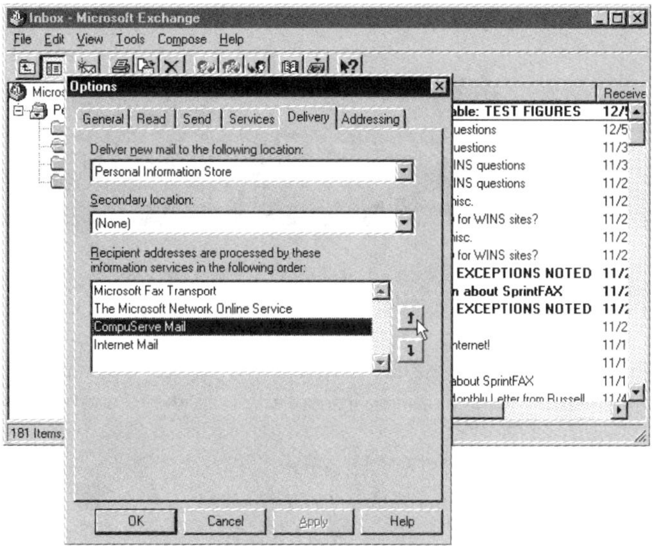

- The Addressing tab allows you to specify the Personal Address Book that will be checked first when you want to look up an e-mail recipient. In the second portion of the screen, you can change the order in which Exchange checks the address books in the same way you changed the service delivery options described in the previous paragraph.

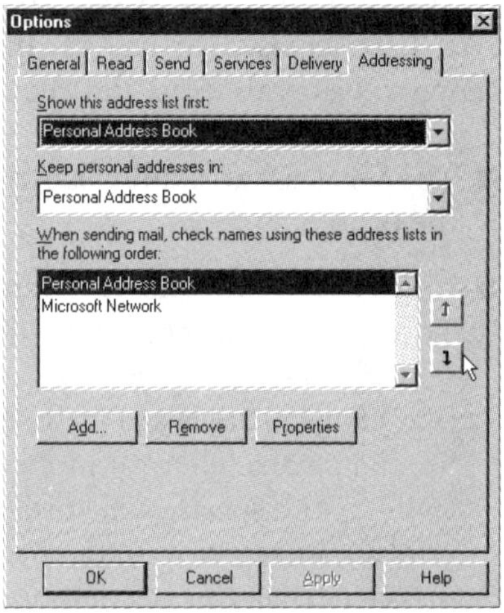

- The General, Read, and Send tabs that appear when profile properties are accessed through the Inbox are specific to the display of mail messages in the Inbox folder windows.

Transferring Personal Address Books and Message Stores between Workstations

If you are using Windows 95 on several different computers, you may want to transfer an address book or e-mail message database from one machine to another. The name of the default address book which Exchange configures is MAILBOX.PAB. The name of the e-mail message store is MAILBOX.PST. These files are located in the EXCHANGE directory of your Windows 95 host drive. To transfer the contents to another machine running Windows 95, use the following procedure.

1. *Copy the MAILBOX.PAB and MAILBOX.PST files in the EXCHANGE directory on the original computer to new files called MAIL1.PAB and MAIL1.PST.*

2. *Transfer the new MAIL1.PAB and MAIL1.PST files to the EXCHANGE directory on the destination machine. You can do this by establishing a direct cable connection between the two machines, or by copying the files first to a floppy disk as a portable transfer medium.*

3. *On the destination machine, right-click the Inbox, select Properties, and select the Personal Address Book. (If you want to change the address book in a nondefault Exchange profile, then click the Show Profiles button on the first screen, select the Exchange profile you want to modify, click Properties, and then select the Personal Address Book for the profile you've chosen.)*

4. *Click Properties for the Personal Address Book. On the next screen change the filename for the address book to [D:]EXCHANGE\MAIL1.PAB (where [D:] is your Windows host drive), as shown here:*

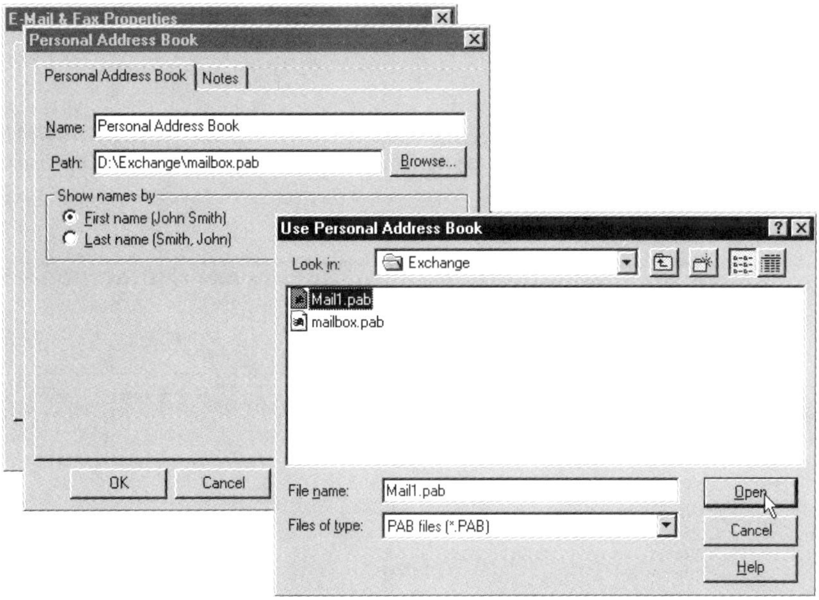

Don't worry—your old address book file won't be deleted, and you can always switch back to it later.

5. *Click OK to return to the Profile Properties screen. Click the Add Button, select Personal Folders from the list of available information services, and click OK.*

6. *In the next Create/Open Personal Folders file list, go to the Exchange directory and select the MAIL1.PST file that you copied from the original machine. Assign a new name to this message store (for instance, New Message Store) in the Name field. Click OK to return to the Profile Properties screen. There you should see the new Personal Information Store listed with the name you've entered. Click OK and then back out of the Exchange profile setup screens.*

7. *Double-click the Inbox and open it with the Exchange profile you've just modified. (If you modified the default profile, this is automatic.) Select Options from the Tools menu, and click the Delivery tab.*

8. *Open the "Deliver new mail to the following location" drop-down list and select the New Message Store option. (You can always go back and change this setting again, later, if you want to return to the original Personal Information Store.) Finally, click OK to close out the dialog box.*

With the Inbox View Folders option selected, you'll see that Inbox has two message stores, as shown here. The New Message Store you've just configured contains all of the message transactions stored on your other Windows 95 workstation.

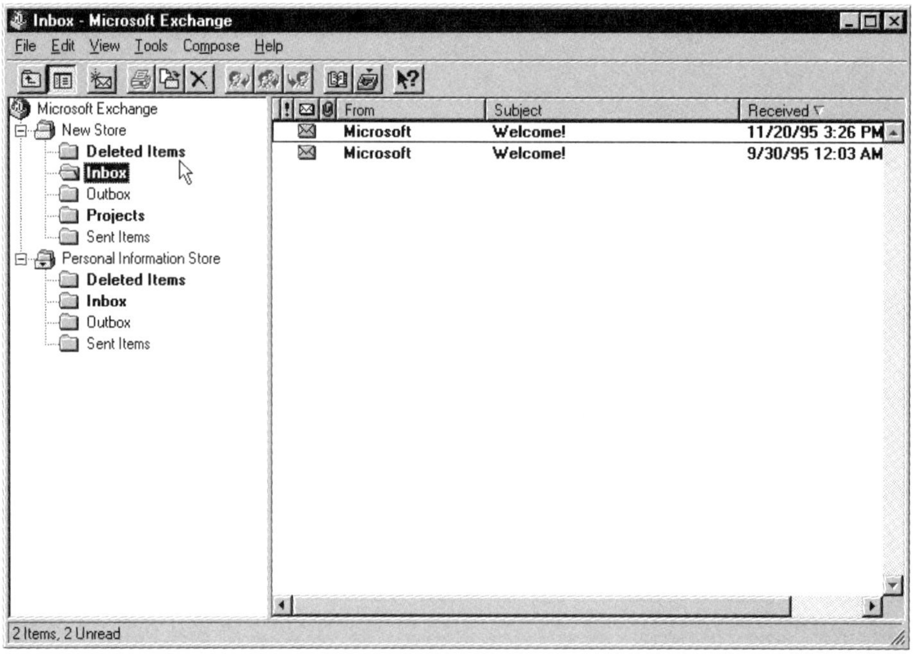

You can display the messages in any of the folders in either information store by expanding and clicking in the folders pane. Any mail you retrieve and compose from now on will be recorded in the information store you've just made the default.

To switch the Inbox back to using the original information store, select Options from the Tools menu, click the Delivery tab, and select the information store you want the mail to be stored in. To restore the original Personal Address Book, click the Services tab (also under Tools\Options), highlight the Personal Address Book, and use the Properties dialog to return to the original MAILBOX.PAB file.

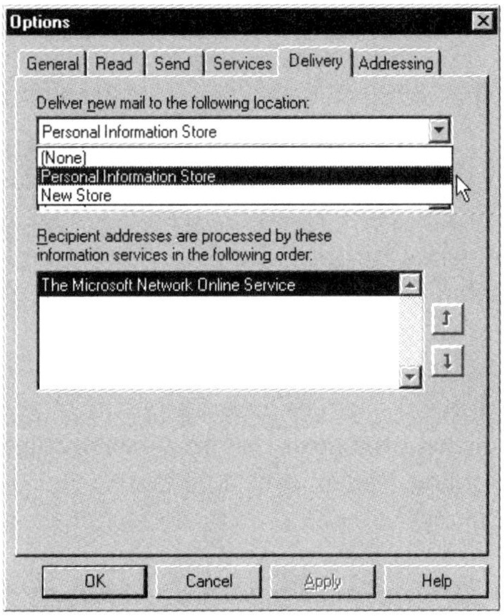

MIGRATING MAIL FROM WINDOWS FOR WORKGROUPS When you upgrade a Windows for Workgroups installation to Windows 95, the Workgroups Mail or Microsoft Mail 3.2 message file (.MMF) is automatically converted into a Windows 95 Personal Information Store if the file is located in the WINDOWS or MSMAIL directory. After Windows 95 is installed, you can manually upgrade .MMF mail files to the new format by using the Import option located on the File menu in the Inbox. This option can also be used to upgrade a Windows for Workgroups Personal Address Book.

About the Inbox Interface

Initially, when you double-click the Inbox, Microsoft Exchange opens into a single display window, showing all of the messages and faxes stored in the Inbox subfolder of your Personal Information Store. To see the rest of the folders in the Personal Information Store, select the Folders option on the Inbox View menu. By default, the Personal Information Store contains four subfolders: Inbox, Outbox, Sent Items, and Deleted Items. The Outbox contains the messages or faxes you've composed that have not yet been delivered. These messages are transferred to the Sent folder after you go online and Exchange transmits them. The Deleted Items folder serves as an interim trashcan for messages deleted from the other folders. You can transfer a message from one folder to another by left-clicking on it with the mouse and dragging. Multiple messages can be selected by holding down the SHIFT or CTRL keys while you click, as in My Computer\Explorer.

The message queue shown in the right-hand Inbox pane—or the only pane, if the View Folders option is disabled—can be sorted by a number of criteria. There are 37 column fields that can be used to differentiate messages. Six of them are configured by default. The exclamation point indicates priority messages. The envelope icon indicates the message type: e-mail, fax transmission, or other file type. The paper clip indicates that a message or fax includes a binary attachment. From, Subject, Received, and Size are self-explanatory.

Messages in the queue can be sorted by any of the selected criteria. You can do this by selecting Sort from the View menu (as shown here), or by right-clicking the mouse directly in the column header for any of the fields. More column fields can be added to the display queue through the View Column option on the menu.

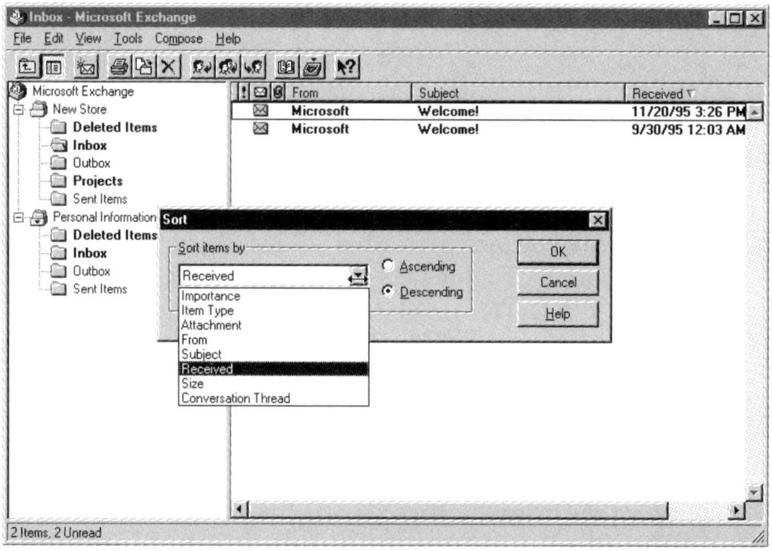

Note that the Inbox is not limited to displaying your e-mail and fax messages. You can drag and drop any file or document you like into an Inbox folder from the desktop or My Computer\Explorer. The additional column options can be used to build a file directory database that you can sort by application name, author, edit time, or a number of other column fields, as you can see here:

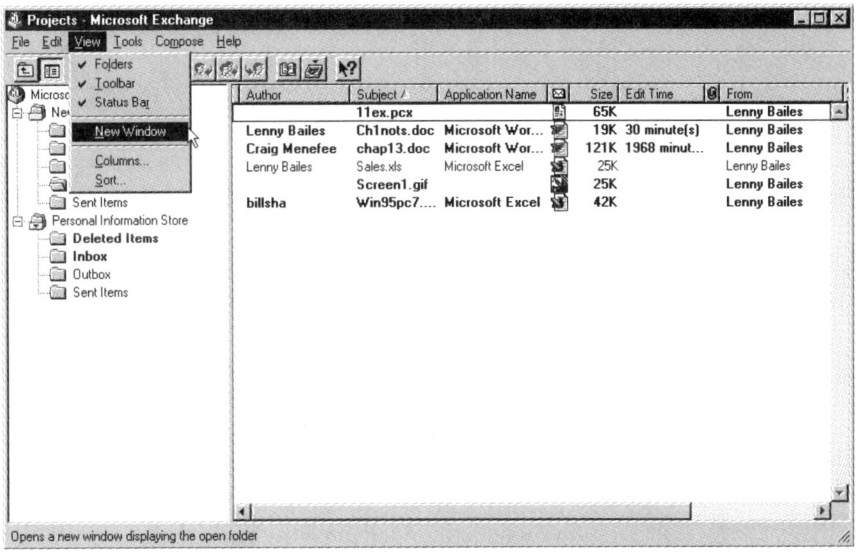

You can create multiple windows on the same information store by selecting the View\New Window option from the Inbox menus and then sort each window by different display criteria.

If you right-click on any message or document shown in the display queue, a pop-up context menu appears, allowing you to conveniently view, edit, or forward it via any of the configured Exchange information services. To compose new mail, select the appropriate option under Compose on the pull-down file menu. Messages can be sent, either through the File Send command on the editor's menus, or through the Deliver Now option on the Inbox Tools menu.

tip *If you conduct a lot of message traffic through the Inbox, you may find that the .PST message file on your hard disk grows to occupy an excessive amount of hard disk space. You can reduce the size of the message store in two ways. First, open the Deleted Items folder, select all of the messages in it (CTRL-A), right-click and delete them permanently from the Message Store. Or, compact the Message Store by selecting it from the list of services in your Exchange profile (right-click Inbox on the desktop and open the Properties Sheet or select Options\Services from the Tools menu in the open Inbox). Open the Properties Sheet for the Personal Information Store, and click the Compact Now button.*

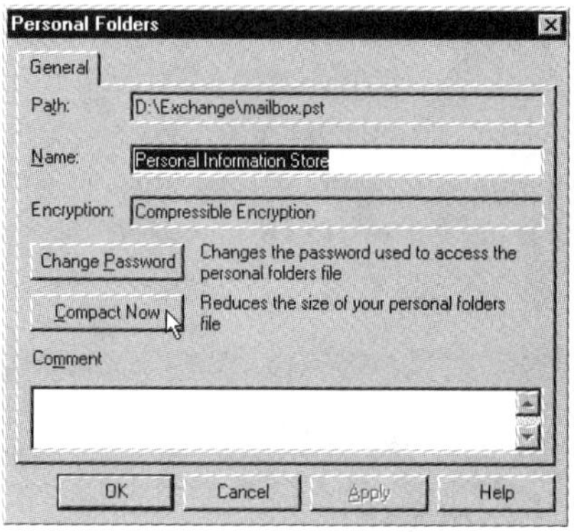

Using Remote Mail

The Inbox will not automatically log onto the Microsoft Network online information service or CompuServe when you launch it, even though these options are still buried in setup menus left over from the beta test period. Instead, to collect mail for one of these services, you need to select the Remote Mail option on the Tools menu. This opens a temporary mail queue for the information service you've selected. To log on and collect your mail, choose the Tools\Connect option from the Remote Mail pull-down menus. You can also log on by selecting Deliver Now from the Inbox Tools menu. If messages in the Outbox are waiting to be sent, they will be delivered.

For MSN, if the option to download new mail upon connection is enabled, your incoming mail will be transmitted. This option is in the Properties for the Microsoft Network Online Service on the Transport tab. If this feature is disabled, your outgoing mail will be sent, and you have the option of previewing your incoming mail through the Tools\Remote Mail \Tools\Connect and Update Headers option.

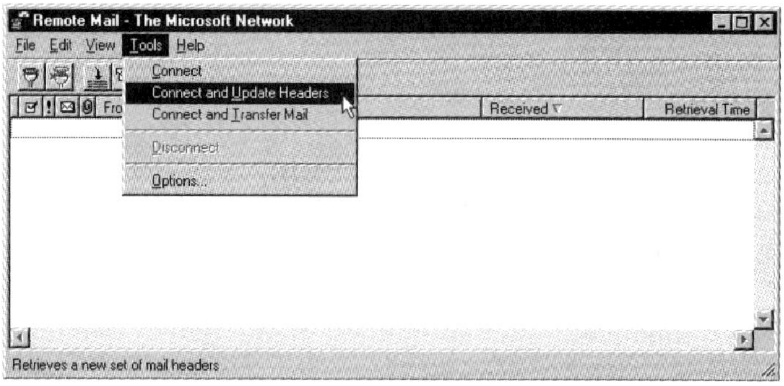

For CompuServe, you must collect your incoming mail by selecting the Tools\Remote Mail\Tools\ Connect and Transfer Mail option. If you simply want a preview of the messages waiting for you, use the Remote Mail\Tools\ Connect and Update Headers option.

For Internet Mail, you have a choice between automatically logging onto your Internet Service Provider when Inbox is launched, or using the same Remote Mail feature available for CompuServe and MSN. This option is toggled in the Properties for Internet Mail on the Connect tab, as shown here. When "Work offline and use Remote Mail" is deselected, opening Inbox logs you into your Internet provider and transfers your mail, as well.

note *If you select the Microsoft Network online information service as your Internet service provider, then double-clicking Inbox also logs you onto MSN.*

If you have Microsoft Fax in an Exchange Profile along with Internet Mail, you probably want to keep the Internet "Work Offline" option enabled. Otherwise, when you attempt to send a fax, Exchange may dial into the Internet service provider first.

To change the sequence in which Exchange accesses the information services, open the Tools\Options\Delivery tab. Note that this screen is identical to the one accessed by right-clicking the Inbox icon on the desktop and opening the Profile Properties dialog box. Some of the Inbox options are deliberately designed for redundant access through a number of routes.

Configuring and Using Dial-Up Networking

The Windows 95 Dial-Up Networking Adapter is your gateway to the Internet and other network connections through your modem. It replaces the complicated Internet connection schemes that you had to resort to under Windows 3.*x*. Although you can still use Trumpet Winsock, Chameleon NetManage, CompuServe NetLauncher, the Netscape Personal Internet Kit, and other third-party dialers under Windows 95, you don't have to. Once you connect to the Internet through the built-in Windows 95 dialer, you can freely run most Internet applications, such as Web browsers, FTP utilities, and Telnet, written for Windows 3.*x*.

The Windows 95 Dial-Up Networking Adapter uses a 32-bit version of the WINSOCK.DLL required to manage a TCP/IP Internet connection. Most of the third-party dialers written for Windows 3.*x* use a 16-bit version of this file. Consequently, newer, 32-bit Internet applications written for Windows 95 don't work under Internet connections established by older Windows 3.*x* dialing programs. It is true that many users have configured packages like Netscape's Personal Navigator, or Spry's Internet-in-a-Box under Windows 3.*x*. When these people upgrade to Windows 95, they may be chagrined if their Internet connectivity isn't migrated automatically.

In Chapter 11, we provide some tips and information on using Windows 3.*x* dialers under Windows 95. But in the meantime, we encourage you to get acquainted with the Dial-Up Networking feature of your new operating system. In the long run, you will probably prefer it.

Installing the Dial-Up Networking Adapter

In order to use the Dial-Up Networking Adapter, you have to install it. If the Dial-Up Networking folder wasn't placed in your Programs\Accessories group during the initial Windows 95 setup, you can install it with the Add\Remove Programs utility from the Control Panel. This procedure is discussed in more detail in the section on setting up Dial-Up Networking in Chapter 5.

Dial-Up Networking also requires the Microsoft TCP/IP network protocol to establish an Internet connection. Microsoft TCP/IP is not added automatically with the Dial-Up Network Adapter. To determine whether this network protocol is present, open the Network Control Panel object and inspect the components list. If you don't see Microsoft TCP/IP, click the Add button on the Configuration tab, highlight the Protocol icon on the

Select Network Component Type dialog, and click Add again. On the next screen, scroll down to Microsoft in the manufacturer's list on the left, and select TCP/IP in the network protocols list on the right. Click OK and OK again to close the Network object. You'll see a message that Windows 95 has to be restarted to activate TCP/IP support.

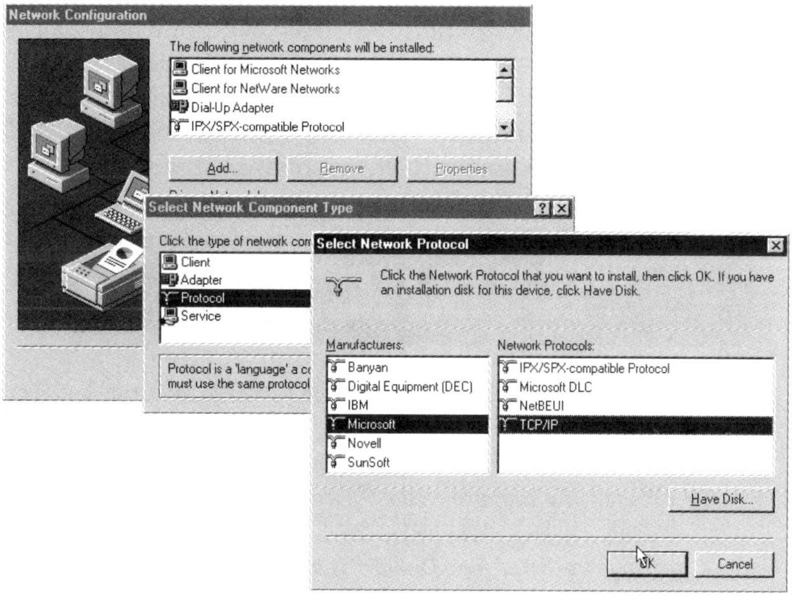

Setting Up SLIP and PPP Dialing Profiles

Once the Dial-Up Networking folder is installed in your Accessories group, you can open it and create connection profiles that will allow you to dial into the Internet or connect to a dedicated LAN through your modem. You can also use Dial-Up Networking to connect to the shared drives, printers, or other resources of a remote computer over the Internet. Details on how to do this are provided in Chapter 11.

note *If you purchase and install Microsoft Plus! or download and install the Microsoft Internet Explorer kit, an Internet Setup Wizard will be installed in your Programs\Accessories folder. You can run this Wizard to automatically establish an Internet connection through the Microsoft Network online information service. To use a third-party Internet service provider, instead of Microsoft, follow the procedures outlined in the next section.*

Creating a Connection Profile

Most Internet accounts currently available from service providers make use of a special connection protocol called Point-to-Point Protocol (PPP). Support for this connection type is built into Windows 95. Some service providers offer accounts through the older Serial Line Internet Protocol (SLIP) connection type. To use Dial-Up Networking with a SLIP account, you must take the additional step of installing SLIP support from the Windows 95 installation CD. You may want to install this option even if you have a PPP Internet account, since it includes a Dial-Up Scripting utility that can be used with either connection type.

Setting up Slip/Dial-up Scripting Support

1. Open Add/Remove Programs, select the Windows Setup tab, and click the Have Disk button.

2. SLIP support is available on the Windows 95 CD in the ADMIN\APPTOOLS\DSCRIPT directory in a file called RNAPLUS.INF. Select this directory and file by using the Browse button in the Install from Disk dialog box.

You may get a message telling you to reboot the system to make the SLIP protocol available.

If you've installed Windows 95 from floppies rather than CD, and you want to set up a SLIP connection, you'll need to download a file called RNAPLUS.ZIP. RNAPLUS.ZIP is available on CompuServe and on the Microsoft BBS download service. It unpacks into RNAPLUS.INF and a small README that explains how to install it.

To dial into the Internet, you must create a connection profile for Dial-Up Networking.

1. Open Dial-Up Networking by selecting it from the Start Menu in the Accessories folder.

2. After the Dial-Up Networking folder opens, double-click the Make New Connection icon or select Make New Connection from the Connections pull-down menu.

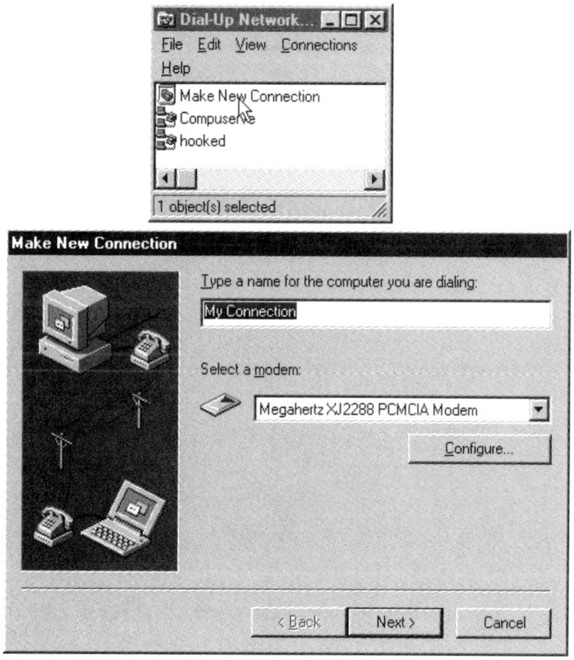

3. Choose a modem to use, type a name for the connection, and click the Next button. If no modem is currently installed, the Modem Installation Wizard will start automatically and allow you to configure one.
4. On the next screen, enter the area code and telephone number for your Internet service provider. If you're setting up a dial-in connection to a network server, enter the appropriate telephone number to connect to that computer. Click Next.
5. Click the Finish button. A new connection profile icon will appear in the Dial-Up Networking folder.

6. Click on the connection profile icon with the right mouse button and select Properties to open the profile's connection options.
7. Click on the Server Type button toward the bottom of the General Properties tab, as shown next.

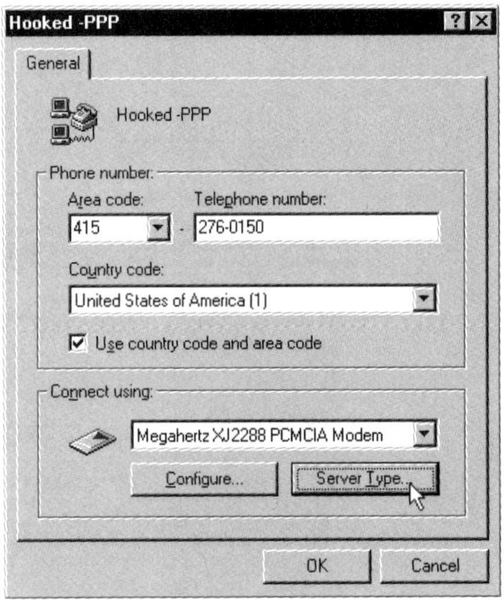

8. In the Server Types setup screen, choose PPP or SLIP Unix Connection as appropriate for your Internet account. Toward the bottom of the dialog box, under Allowed Network Protocols, make sure that TCP/IP is checkmarked.
9. Click the TCP/IP Settings button toward the bottom of the Server Types dialog box. This opens the TCP/IP Settings box. Fill in the information in this box with the appropriate information supplied by your Internet Service provider. Typically, you'll want to select "Server assigned IP address" and "Specify name server address." In the "Specify name server" section, enter at least the IP address for the name server supplied by your Internet provider. Note that you can configure more than one connection profile, specifying different DNS and WINS addresses in each. (DNS=Domain Naming System, WINS=Windows Internet Naming Service.)
10. Click OK twice to close the dialog box and once more to close the configuration window.

Now you're ready to double-click the connection profile and dial into the Internet.

SETTING NETWORK OPTIONS If you plan to connect to the Internet through a modem, you should probably not tamper with the TCP/IP options through the Network object on the control panel. Some Windows 95 users make the mistake of entering Internet IP information into this series of dialog boxes. While entering Internet service provider (ISP) information through the Network Control Panel object does allow you to connect, this feature was not intended to contain dial-up Internet information. It was actually designed to contain TCP/IP information for a dedicated TCP/IP network.

Entering ISP information directly through the Network object may interfere with a connection to a dedicated local area network (LAN). It also slows up the performance of Inbox, which will pause on opening for as much as

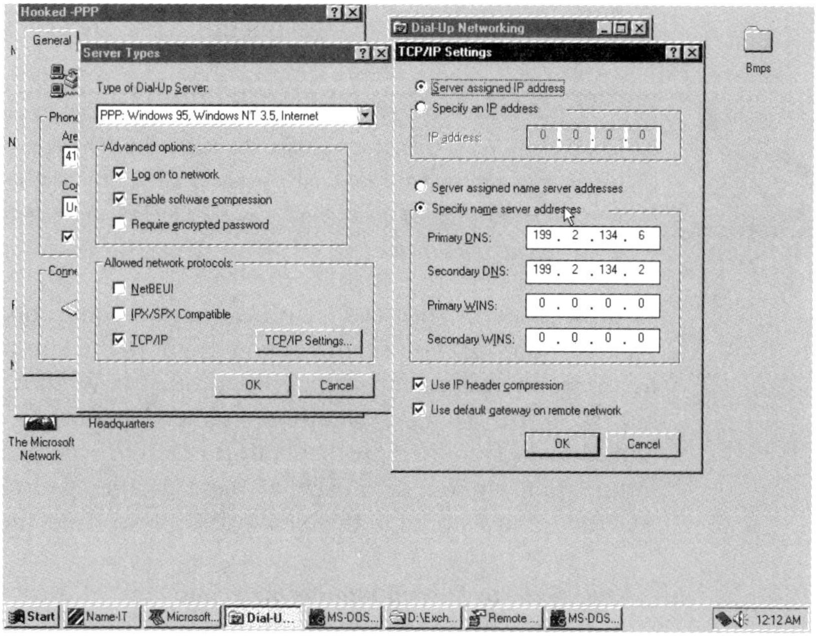

FIGURE 10-4 The Server Type and TCP/IP buttons in each connection profile let you specify server information for that individual connection. Place the server information here for dial-up connections. Reserve the Network/TCP/IP dialog box on the Control Panel for direct network connections.

two to three minutes searching for a non-existent TCP/IP cable connection. Additionally, ISP information in the Network settings from one vendor may be wiped out by the setup program of another vendor. (The Internet Setup Wizard for Microsoft Plus! is guilty of this crime—see Chapter 11 for details.) The bottom line is that if you're not using TCP/IP to connect through a network adapter, you should enter all of your Internet configuration information through the individual Dial-Up Networking service profiles, as just outlined.

Making the Connection

To make the connection, double-click the connection profile you just created (in the Dial-Up Networking folder). Make sure your Internet username, password and telephone number are correct (in the Connect To dialog box). Click the Connect button, sit back, and listen to your modem.

At this point, the Dial-Up Networking Adapter will call your service provider. If the login succeeds, you'll see a small dialog box showing the speed of your connection. You can then run any third-party Internet tool, such as Netscape, Eudora, or WS_FTP. For more information on setting up and using third-party Windows Internet tools, see Chapter 11.

tip *Enable automatic redial with Win95 Dial-Up Adapter. By default, when you open a Dial-Up Networking connection profile, the telephone number is dialed only once. To enable an automatic redial after a busy signal or missed connection, open the Dial-Up Networking folder (located under the Accessories folder), and select "Settings" from the pull-down Connections menu.*

MULTIPLE SERVICE PROFILES You can set up connection profiles for more than one service. For example, you might want one for a Windows NT network, one for an Internet account, one for Windows for Workgroups, and so forth. To make multiple connection profiles work, add the IP addresses and required protocol information to each individual profile. The information entered into each of these profiles will override the default TCP/IP settings stored in the Network Control Panel module.

Logging In to Special Internet Accounts

Some Internet service providers do not support the standard password authentication protocol (PAP) that allows for an automatic connection through Dial-Up Networking. The CompuServe Information Service is one such example. Accounts from these providers may require special login commands before a connection can be established.

Windows 95 allows you to bring up a terminal window to enter custom login commands. You also have the option of entering these commands through a simple dial-up scripting tool described in the next section.

To allow for manual entry of login commands, do the following:

1. After choosing your modem (step 3 in "Creating a Connection Profile"), click the Configure button next to the modem list. If you've already created your connection profile, right-click it with the mouse and select Properties to access the Configure button.
2. Select the Options tab in the Properties dialog box.
3. Place a checkmark in the box labeled Bring up terminal window after dialing.

Now, after Dial-Up Networking connects to your service provider, a terminal window pops up, allowing you to type in your username, password, and any additional necessary information. For instance, some service providers may require that you invoke the TIA (Internet Adapter), a special UNIX utility that converts a terminal connection into a SLIP connection.

After entering all necessary login information, click the Continue button in the Terminal window to let the connection procedure continue.

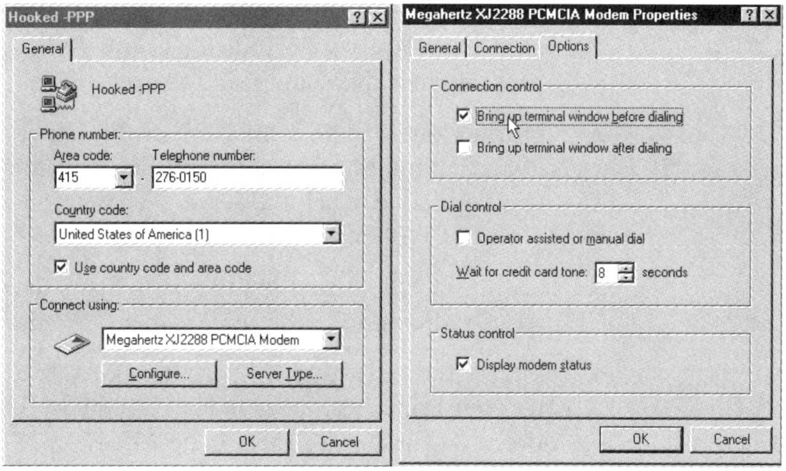

FIGURE 10-5

The Configure button in the connection profile allows you to open a terminal screen before or after dialing into a service. This option allows you to issue login commands before invoking a SLIP or PPP emulator.

Dial-Up Scripting

The Dial-Up Scripting utility can automate login procedures for third-party service providers. This utility is installed when you enable SLIP support for Dial-Up Networking. Refer back to the sidebar, "Setting Up SLIP/Dial-Up Scripting Support."

Dial-Up Scripting includes a number of sample login scripts, including one for PPP access to CompuServe. To associate a login script with a Dial-Up Networking connection profile, open the Scripting utility, located in the Programs\Accessories folder. The left pane of the Scripting Tool window displays a list of the currently available connection profiles. The right pane allows you to associate an existing login script with a connection profile or to create a new one. Highlight the connection profile on the left, enter a filename in the dialog box on the right (the three-letter extension should be .SCP), and click the Edit button to create a new script in Notepad. Or use the browse button to open an existing script that you can modify for this connection.

Setting Up and Automating a CompuServe PPP Connection

If you have a CompuServe account, you can use it for PPP access to the Internet without downloading CompuServe's NetLauncher connection kit. Once connected, you can use the CompuServe Web browser or other third-party Internet browsers simply by opening them.

1. Set up the CompuServe connection profile. Open the Dial-Up Networking folder and double-click the Make New Connection icon to create a service profile for CompuServe. (Enter the appropriate telephone number and area code.)
2. After the CompuServe connection profile appears in the Dial-Up Networking folder, right-click on it with the mouse and open the Properties dialog. Click the Server Type button and make sure the PPP and TCP/IP options are selected in the next dialog box.
3. Click the TCP/IP button in the Server Types dialog box and make sure the radio button for Server assigned IP address is selected.
4. Select the radio button for "Specify name server addresses" and enter your Primary and Secondary CompuServe DNS Server IP addresses. (These will probably be 149.174.211.5 and 149.174.213.5.) Click OK three times to close the connection profile's configuration settings.

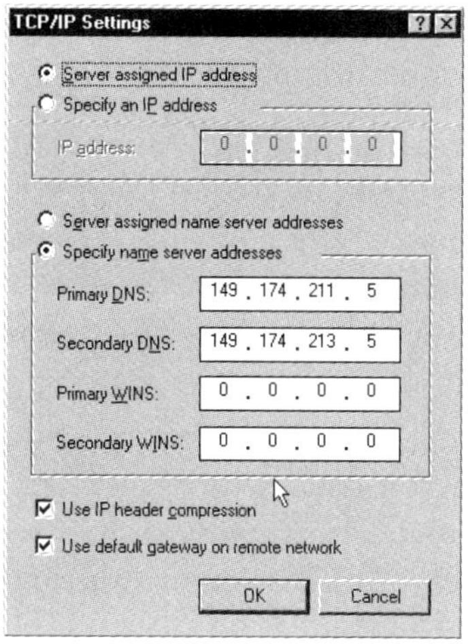

5. Open the Dial-Up Scripting tool, which should now be installed in the Accessories Folder. If not, install Win95 SLIP support through Add\Remove Programs, as described earlier in this chapter.
6. Select the CompuServe connection profile in the left pane of the Scripting Tools window. Then click the Browse button in the right pane under the filename field. The file listing should open to the Accessories folder, where a number of script files have been installed. Select CIS.SCP and click the Open button.

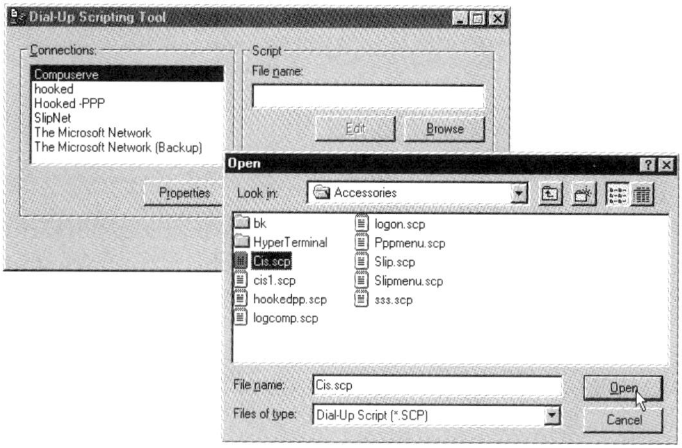

7. You should now be returned to the Dial-Up Scripting Tool screen. The entry in the filename box should read "[d:]\Program Files\Accessories\CIS.SCP."

8. Click the Close button to associate this script with the CompuServe connection profile.
9. Double-click the CompuServe connection profile in the Dial-Up Networking folder. Enter your username and password in the appropriate boxes and click the Connect button.

Working with the Script Language

The CompuServe script outlined above is probably the simplest one that you can construct with the scripting tool. You can also modify existing scripts or create new ones to execute more complicated Internet login procedures. To see a complete listing of the commands in the script language, click the Help button on the main Dial-Up Scripting screen, click the Creating a Script button in the pop-up help screen, and then click the Scripting commands button at the bottom of the next Help screen.

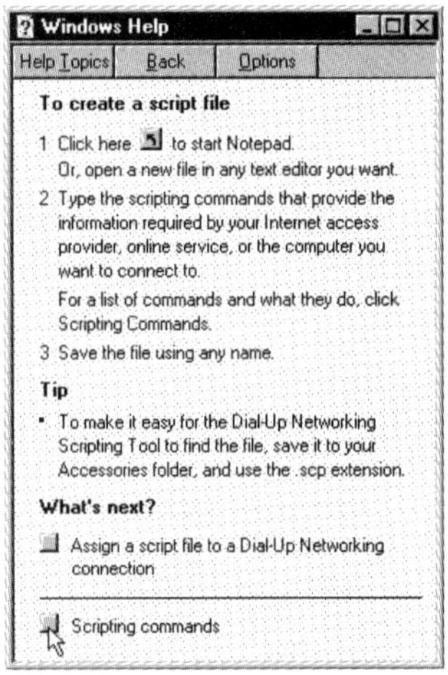

The following is an example of a quick script that will automatically log on to an Internet account. The account requires the use of TIA emulation software to establish a SLIP connection.

```
proc main
 transmit "^M"
 delay 2
 waitfor "login:"
 transmit $USERID
 transmit "^M"
 waitfor "Password:"
 transmit $PASSWORD
```

```
 transmit "^M"
 waitfor ">"
 transmit "tia^m"
endproc
```

Other Dial-Up Networking Tricks

Dial-Up Networking can be used to dial into a Novell NetWare or Windows NT server. (Keep in mind that if you use Dial-Up Networking to access NetWare resources, you can access data remotely but not control another computer remotely. For that, you need Novell's NetWare Connect client software.)

To access the Microsoft client for NetWare, file and printer services for NetWare, or IPX-SPX-compatible protocols, you'll have to install them through the Network object on the Control Panel. (See Chapter 5 for details.) Specify the appropriate server type by opening the connection profile's property sheet, clicking the Server Type button and choosing the correct type from the Dial-Up Server Type drop-down list.

tip *If you use the Dial-Up utility to access remote network drives, you can automatically reestablish a connection whenever you click on a network drive: Choose Settings from the Connections menu in the Dial-Up Networking folder and select "Don't Prompt to Use Dial-Up Networking."*

Putting the Tools to Work

We now have some grounding in the use of Windows 95's basic telecommunications tools. In the next chapter, we'll see how to wax our electronic surfboards in search of that perfect online wave.

Printers
Find
Help
Windows95
Start

chapter 11

Windows 95 and Online Access: Waxing Your Internet Surfboard

- What does the Microsoft Network mean to me?
- An Internet primer
- Connectivity clinic

    Connecting with third-party software

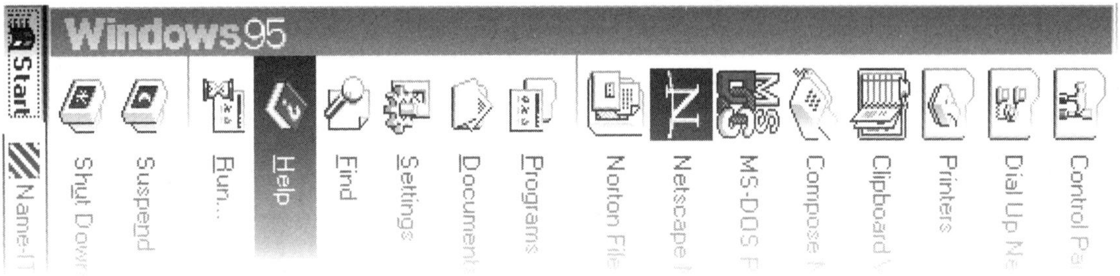

THE experience of going online in the '90s is changing rapidly, and Windows 95 is contributing to some of the most exciting improvements. The days of hunting for DOS utilities on small local BBSs are rapidly fading, along with the practice of keeping a single e-mail account on one of the Big Three commercial information services.

The thing that you'll probably notice most about Windows 95's contribution to the online experience is the sense of connectedness it brings. Browse a forum on the Microsoft Network, and you may find a hot link to a World Wide Web site. And while you read the news, your e-mail is being collected for you automatically. See something interesting in your Web browser and you can right-click to save it, or drag the item directly to the desktop. The Microsoft Network online information service was designed to be a seamless extension of the Windows 95 desktop.

This chapter shows you the ins and outs of the online experience with Windows 95. You'll see what you can do with Microsoft's new online service, and get all the information you need on working with old and new Internet tools for maximum convenience and productivity.

The Microsoft Network

Microsoft is now the household symbol for an unbeatable market controller, and everyone assumed the competition at America Online (AOL), Prodigy, and CompuServe would panic. After all, with a Microsoft information service built into the new version of Windows, how could anyone compete? Actually Microsoft was including only the client software for its online service, but many people—including the United States Justice Department—were unclear on this issue up until the operating system was actually released.

Not long after Windows 95 came on the market, AOL exceeded a record 4 million member mark, and people forgot about the panic that never existed. But still, the entry of the Redmond giant into information servicing and Internet access changed the game. Microsoft pledged to limit early membership to 500,000—partly to quell the doubts of federal antitrust authorities, and partly because Microsoft feared they might be inundated with users. Recently, however, Microsoft has removed the upper cap on the membership limit, making the Microsoft Network (MSN) information service open to all. Still more recently, Microsoft has made arrangements with its content providers on MSN to allow free access to some resources directly over the Internet through the World Wide Web. Although currently you can only connect to MSN through a Microsoft dial-up account, this is expected to change by second quarter of 1996.

Some Good MSN Touches

The MSN online information service has surprised many of Microsoft's critics by avoiding the "bigger is better" bloat trap. It is a very economically designed, quick-acting system. In a world where the size of graphics files seems to stay just slightly ahead of the comfort curve for the fastest available modems, MSN is carefully set up to be just fast enough not to demand too much of systems equipped with 14.4 K or even slower modems.

That's good because currently, all you can access is 14.4 K access numbers unless you purchase Microsoft Plus! or download the free Internet Explorer kit. When you add Internet connectivity to MSN, a series of 28.8K access nodes miraculously appears on the list of available phone connections.

The fast-loading design makes MSN's performance comfortable for people who have modems slower than 28.8 Kbps. The system accomplishes this trick in two ways: first, MSN limits the size of any graphics that load without having been specifically requested. It's a trick the best Internet sites use—when you keep the graphics small, people don't snort with impatience and leave before they see the whole page. Second, and every bit as important, MSN loads the *text first*—until all the text is available, you only see little graphics markers that tell you where a picture will appear.

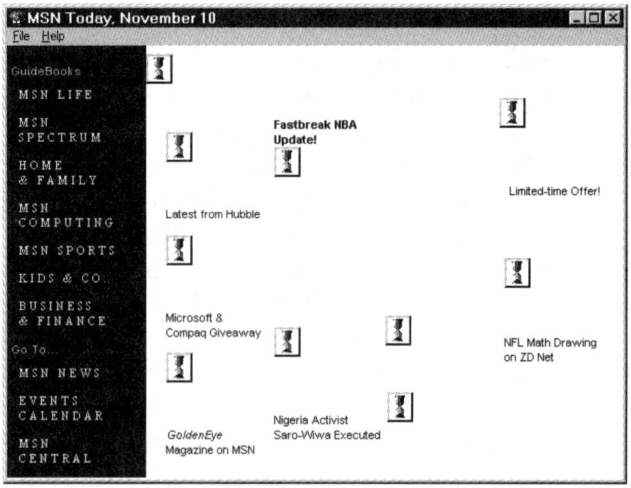

The effect is that if you see a destination where you want to go next, you can leave without waiting for graphics files to finish downloading. You just click on outta there.

If you're connected at 9600 Kbps or less—perhaps on a laptop, or with your older home or business desktop system—it's a blessing to be able to stop the data feed and just read the text, or to read the text at leisure while small graphics gradually appear in the background.

The Familiar Interface

Another "designer touch" on MSN is its familiarity. If you know how to use Windows 95—or even Windows 3.1—you'll have no trouble navigating through MSN from day one. Microsoft has set up the network to look like a Windows 95 application, with sortable icons and everything else you'd associate with working in a Windows application.

Because of this thoughtful touch, you won't have to learn to use a brand new program to access the service, the way you do with competing information services. Figure 11-1 shows the initial entry screen. To go into an area of interest in the network, you just double-click the appropriate icon or highlight it and press ENTER.

Signing Up for MSN

To join MSN, you need to add its icon to the desktop, if you didn't select it during the initial Windows 95 setup procedure. Open the Add/Remove Programs object in the Control Panel to the Windows Setup tab and place a checkmark next to the Microsoft Network in the Components list. You may have to restart Windows 95 to get the MSN icon to appear.

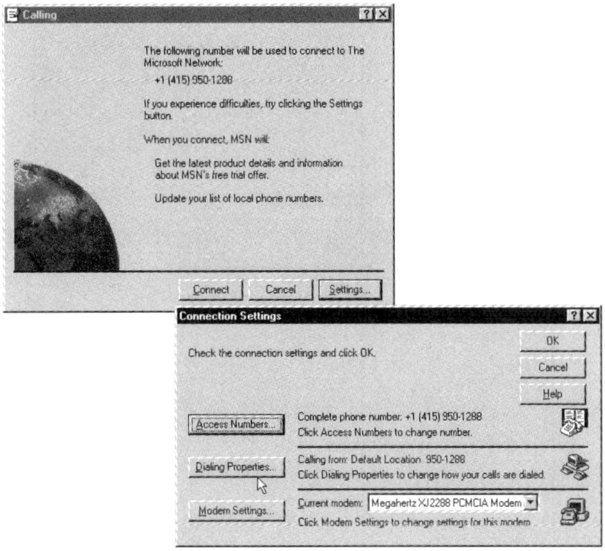

FIGURE 11-1 *Click on settings set from the Calling screen to modify telephone options and connection settings.*

Once the MSN icon has been placed on the desktop, you can sign up simply by double-clicking it open. The first sign-up screen asks whether you already have an MSN membership. If you got one during the beta test period, place a checkmark in this box, and you can enter your name and password in the MSN sign-on screen. To modify any of the default settings, including the access telephone number and the modem settings, you can click the Settings button.

If you're signing up for MSN for the first time, click the OK button and enter your area code and first three digits of your telephone number on the next screen. This allows the Setup Wizard to locate the nearest access number in your calling area. It then displays the telephone number that will be used to sign you up for MSN access. To change settings, you can click the Settings button on the first MSN sign-on screen to reach the Connection Settings dialog. Then click the Modem Settings button to change the modem that will be used, the Dialing Properties button to change how your calls are dialed, and the Access Numbers button to change the access number. (See Figure 11-1 again.)

When you're ready to dial in, click the Connect button on the Calling screen. As soon as the connection is established, a current list of telephone access numbers will be downloaded to your system and the modem will disconnect. The MSN Registration screen then appears on the desktop. (See Figure 11-2.) Click the first icon to fill in your personal information, such as street address and telephone number, and click the second icon to fill in

FIGURE 11-2

The Microsoft Network enrollment screens

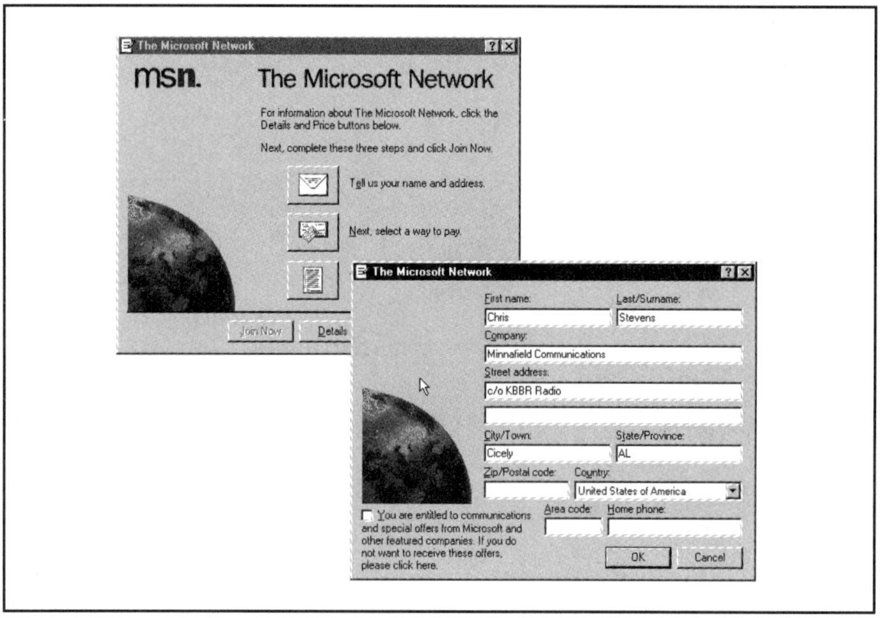

a credit card number for billing. You can click the Price button at the bottom of the first screen to find out about the charges. As of this writing, MSN allows you a 10-hour free trial membership, during your first 30 days, free of charge. The third icon in the middle of the screen lists the rules of MSN membership, which you must read (or at least open) before the signup process can continue.

For more information about MSN services and features, you can click the Details button at the bottom of the signup screen, or browse a little bit further into this chapter. When all three buttons in the center of the enrollment screen have been opened, the Join Now button will be activated. The Access Numbers screen will once again display the proposed primary and backup telephone numbers to dial into MSN. Click the Change button to choose other access numbers. (As we mentioned before, if you're looking for a 28.8K access node, you'll have to install the Microsoft Internet Explorer. Information on how to do this is presented later in this chapter.) When you click Connect again, MSN will ask you to select a user ID and password to complete the sign-in process.

Navigating the Microsoft Network

The trick to using MSN effectively is to spend a bit of time at first getting to know the lay of the land. You can find out where the areas of your interest are and how best to get there by using the general navigation tools built into

MSN's opening screens. Start at one of the two main screens that appear when you sign onto the system—MSN Central, or the MSN Today screen shown here:

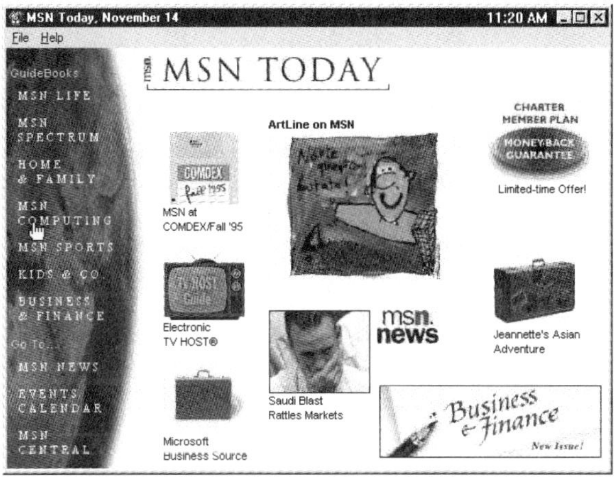

MSN Today contains hot links to many of the stories and events that it advertises. For instance, if you double-click one of the guidebooks on the left side of the window, an appropriate hypertext link is opened.

Figure 11-3 shows the end of one computing article with a link to a more complete article selected. Such articles can become a major source of up-to-the-minute information on changes in new versions of Windows 95, MSN, and the MSN Internet browser.

FIGURE 11-3

The MSN Computing Guidebook page

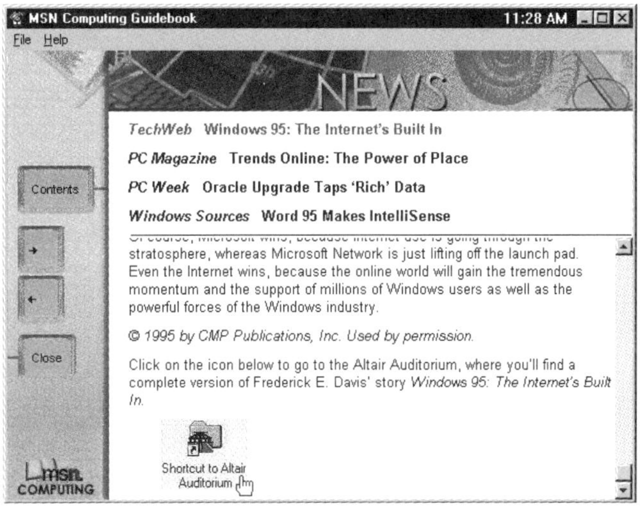

FIGURE 11-4

Some of MSN's forums and reference resources

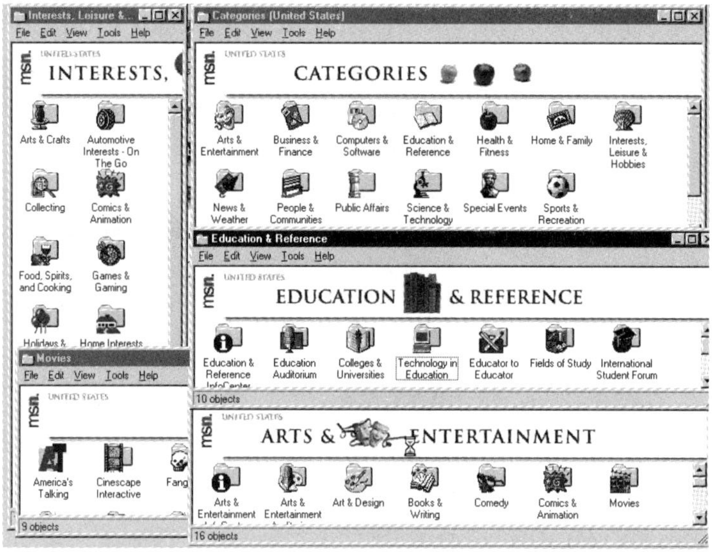

tip If you know you won't be browsing MSN Today in a given session, you can keep MSN from downloading the screen to you by clicking the Close button in the upper-right corner of the window. The MSN Today feed takes time even though it is done in the background, and aborting the download can speed your access to other sites.

When you select an area from the Categories screen, MSN displays a new window (or replaces the existing one). You can toggle MSN's new window replacement window feature in My Computer, by selecting View Options, and clicking the Folder tab.

Figure 11-4 reflects a sampling of general MSN content, but bear in mind that MSN content changes constantly. When you select an area from the Categories screen, MSN opens a window with icons representing forums, bulletin boards, chat rooms, or downloadable documents.

Finally, you'll run into a ubiquitous SiteSeeing Guide symbolized by a pair of binoculars. The binoculars icon opens a preconfigured selection of sponsored sites on the system. The SiteSeeing Guide can be a useful way to find support for various products, or information about participating companies.

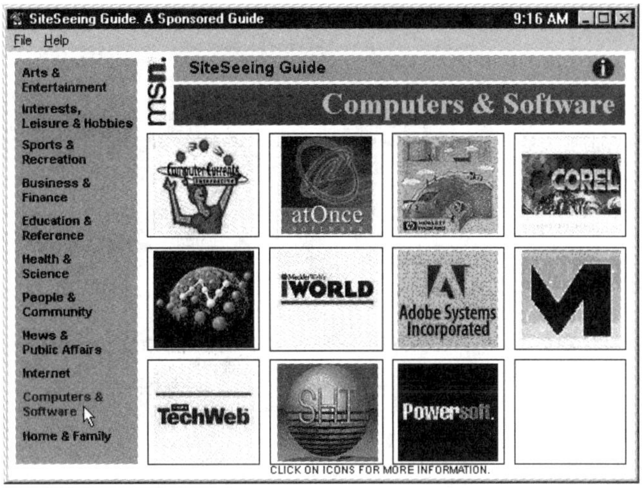

About MSN Forums

MSN Forums offer a variety of different features. The traditional message bulletin boards and real-time conference areas are the common glue that unite the system. However MSN's Win95 interface includes a number of other attractive features. Forums may contain hot links to Internet discussion groups and World Wide Web pages. MSN's built-in message browser treats Internet news groups and MSN's message boards transparently under a single easy-to-use interface. If Microsoft's Web browser and Internet support are installed, you can move automatically from a link in an MSN forum directly to the World Wide Web.

Most forums also include icons representing formatted documents: technical reference material, frequently asked question (FAQ) lists for newsgroups, photos, and so on. Clicking on one of these icons automatically downloads the associated document, opening it on the desktop in an associated application. This is a two-sided feature. If you own Microsoft Office, for example, double clicking on an MSN file with a (hidden) .RTF file extension keeps the MSN clock running, while Microsoft Word starts up to display the document. What's worse, some of these documents have long filenames and may refuse to open in versions of Word designed for Windows 3.*x*.

tip *You can speed up the display of most downloaded documents (and eliminate the older Word's long filename problems) by making sure that the .RTF file extension is assigned to Win95 WordPad instead of Word. See the section on file associations in Chapter 4 for details on how to do this.*

FIGURE 11-5

The Microsoft Windows 95 Support forum

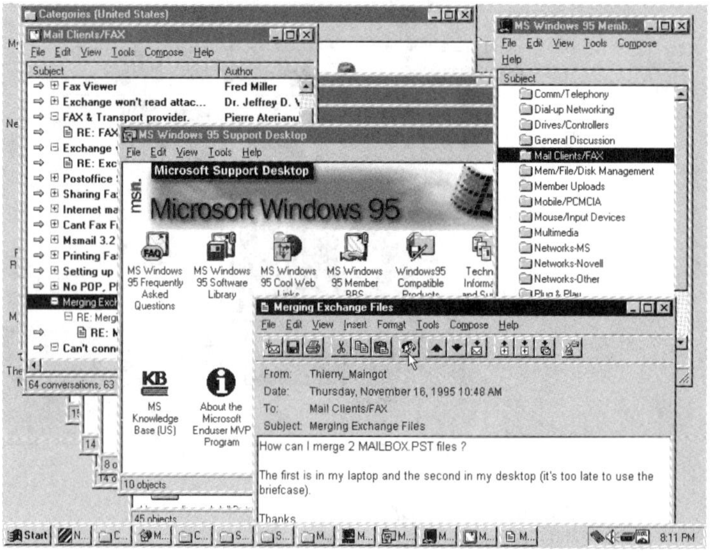

Figure 11-5 shows the resources available in the Microsoft Windows 95 Support forum, located under the Microsoft products group in the Computers & Software category. The screen full of folders on the upper right shows the various support topic categories in the Windows 95 message forum. Double-clicking on one of these folders opens a user-posted message database like the one shown on the upper-left screen. You can scroll through the various threads in the topic until you find a message you want to read. The message reader shown in the center of the screen resembles the e-mail composition tool included in Microsoft Exchange. You can use it to read messages, mark and copy sections to a disk file, compose new messages, send e-mail, or post a reply on the original message forum.

Multimedia Reference Tools

Users who don't mind running up their online service bills may find the online versions of Microsoft's multimedia reference tools to be the gems of the Microsoft Network. Microsoft Encarta, Bookshelf (see Figure 11-6), and the Microsoft Knowledge Database are available on MSN in real time without requiring a CD player. The versions included in the MSN Reference category are not as full-featured as the commercial CDs, but they can be run on non-multimedia PCs.

FIGURE 11-6

Microsoft Bookshelf's world atlas on MSN

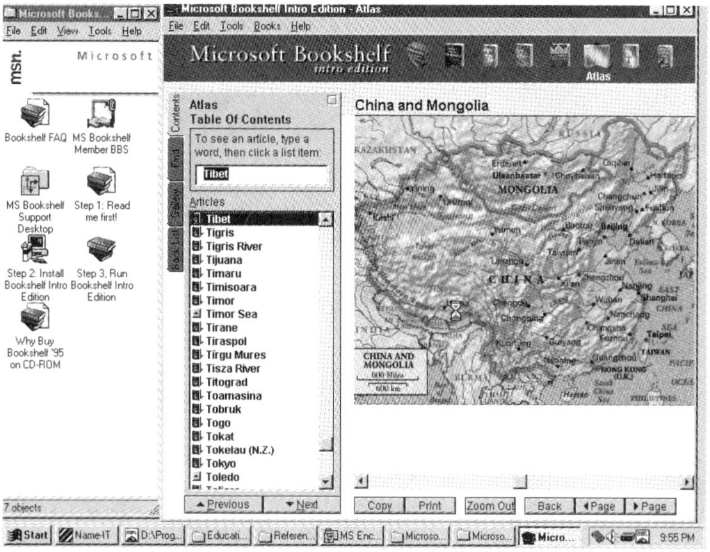

The following table shows the differences between the CD and MSN versions of Bookshelf and Encarta.

Feature	On MSN	On CD
Bookshelf 95		
Seven Reference Books	Yes	Yes
Quickshelf Toolbar	No	Yes
United States Zip Codes	No	Yes
Video Clips	No	Yes
Animation Clips	No	Yes
5hrs of Sound	No	Yes
Year in Review	No	Yes
Encarta 96		
26,000 articles	Yes	Yes
Content updated for 1996 (7000 revised articles)	No	Yes
Photos	5000+	8000+
Audio	No	Yes
Video	No	Yes
Animation	No	Yes

Feature	On MSN	On CD
***Encarta 96* (Continued)**		
Media Gallery	No	Yes
New Guided Tours	No	Yes
New Yearbook Builder	No	Yes
Interactivities	No	Yes
Timeline	No	Yes
Atlas	No (Atlas available in MSN Bookshelf)	Yes
MindMaze	No	Yes

E-mail and Chats

One of the most valuable uses for any information service is its ability to act as a forum in which you can interact with others—at this point in the technology, by exchanging e-mail and by entering "chat rooms," where people exchange messages to each other in real time. On MSN, the e-mail function is handled through Microsoft Exchange. If there is new mail waiting when you log in, a screen prompt lets you start the Inbox, which will automatically download it.

remember *To ensure that you get your MSN mail, make sure that your default Inbox Exchange Profile includes the Microsoft Network information service, or configure Inbox to let you choose a profile on-the-fly that contains MSN. (See Chapter 10 for more details.)*

Sending e-mail to MSN users is easy. Select Compose\New Message from the Inbox pull-down menus and enter the login ID of the recipient on the "To:" line.

MSN also lets you send e-mail over the Internet, even if you have not configured the Internet Mail service for Inbox. Just enter the recipient's Internet address on the "To:" line, in the standard Internet *user@domain* format. (See the "Internet Primer" later in this chapter for more details.)

Internet users can also reach you at MSN by addressing your mail to *username@msn.com*, where *username* is your MSN login ID.

MSN Chat

The ability to chat with others in real time is standard now on commercial information services, but some of them implement it more smoothly than others. On AOL, for example, you can only type in one short line at a time. If you expect to say anything even as long as this sentence, you have to expect to type in a short line, hit ENTER, and type in another line. In a busy chat room, your separate line entries can wind up separated by many lines of other people's text. It makes for a very chaotic experience. To reduce that tendency, many chats are *moderated*—that is, a moderator gives the floor to one participant until that person is finished and then passes it on to someone else. A bit of structure helps communication.

MSN implements the function much more smoothly. It allows you to type in multiple lines and send them all at once by pressing ENTER.

MSN includes a category called ChatWorld, which includes general discussion groups and private chat rooms that can be occupied by two, four, or more users. Most MSN forums also include an auditorium where moderated conferences take place, and chat rooms where forum participants can conduct unmoderated chats.

Personalizing the Service

Once you know MSN fairly well, you can avoid the necessity of clicking through screen after screen of folders to get where you want to go. MSN provides two good ways to bypass the search through hierarchical windows. First, you can add most locations to your personal Favorites folder. Second, you can create a desktop shortcut that signs onto the service and takes you directly to your destination.

Adding Places to Your Favorites Folder

When you find yourself at a location you know you will want to revisit, you can usually add it to your Favorites folder. To do this, click File\Add to Favorite Places.

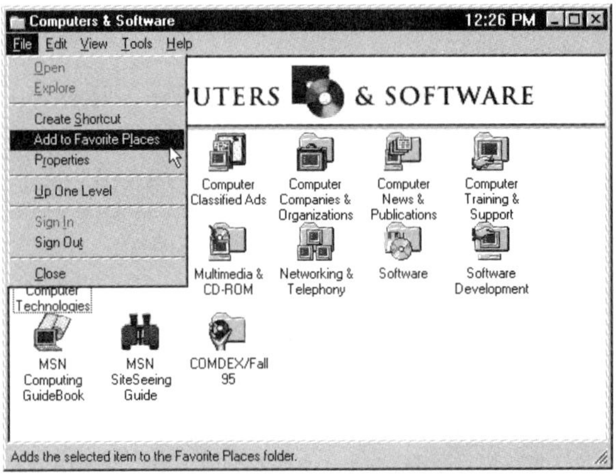

Next time you sign on, click Favorites in the MSN Central opening screen, and you'll find direct shortcuts to the places you want to go. Double-click an icon to go directly to your destination.

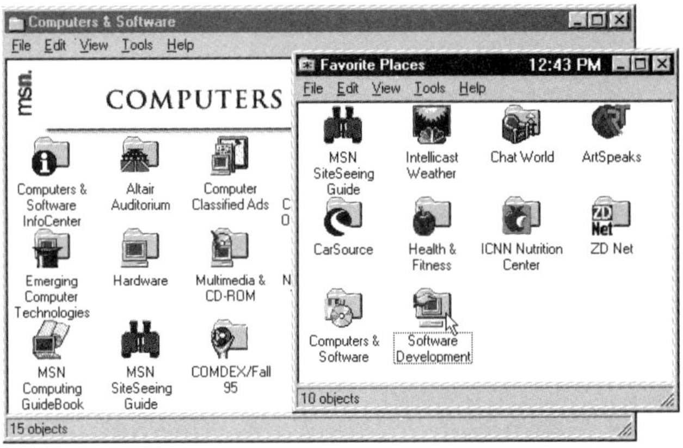

tip *Each window you open in MSN uses additional resources, to the extent that you can actually run out of resources even on systems with 16MB or more of RAM. To avoid this problem, hold down the* CTRL *key when you click a new icon, to avoid opening a succession of new windows. To backtrack into previous windows, simply press the backspace key; there's no need to keep multiple MSN windows open at once.*

Creating Desktop Shortcuts

The other good way to access a destination directly is to create a desktop shortcut, as shown here:

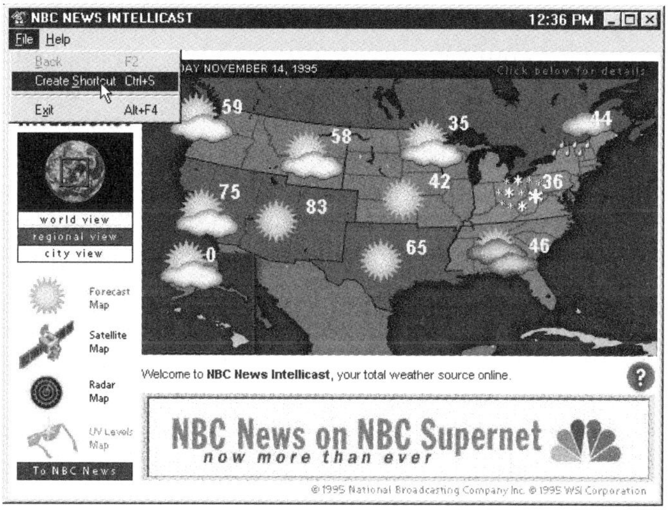

By default, Windows 95 asks for confirmation whenever you create a shortcut. You can turn this confirmation off, but this dialog box can be useful, since it tells you exactly what the shortcut is named—you can change the saved name to something more intuitive later, if you like. For example, you might prefer a shortcut named Weather Map to one named Shortcut to NBC News Intellicast.

caution *When renaming MSN shortcut icons, be sure to retain the .MCC extension or Windows 95 won't recognize it as an MSN shortcut.*

Once you've created an MSN shortcut, you may want to move it into an MSN Shortcuts folder on your desktop to reduce clutter and to put all the shortcuts in one place. Just right-click on the desktop, select New\File Folder, and name it MSN Shortcuts or something similar.

tip *If you "lose" your MSN Central screen, you can get it back by closing all MSN windows at once. A prompt will appear asking if it's okay to hang up. Click No, and then double-click the Microsoft Network desktop icon. MSN Central will come right up on the screen.*

Updating Your MSN Access Numbers and Adding MSN Internet Support

The simplest way to set the access number for MSN the first time is to sign on using the default number. MSN automatically sends you a list of access numbers. You can expect these to change rapidly in the first couple of years, as MSN expands and adds new access points.

As numbers change or get added, you can update your list automatically for your local area code by signing on and using this procedure:

1. At MSN Central, open the Tools menu and click Connections settings.
2. Click the Access Numbers button.
3. Click the Change button.

If there are any new access numbers in your area code, MSN will automatically update your on-disk list. The program uses the area code entry under the Dialing Properties button in the MSN Connection Settings dialog to determine your location. Not updating the whole list saves space on your hard disk and limits the time you lose downloading unneeded numbers as MSN expands.

Getting the Internet Explorer

As mentioned, you don't absolutely need to use Microsoft's World Wide Web browser, but it is a good one that keeps being improved, and it works well with MSN. If you want 28.8 Kbps access through MSN, or just want the nationwide Internet access that MSN provides, you'll want to install the Microsoft Internet Explorer into Windows 95. The easiest way to do this is to buy Microsoft Plus! and use its automated installation routine. Microsoft Plus! includes other useful Windows 95 utilities in addition to its enhanced MSN support. (See Chapter 14 for details.)

If you don't want to spend the extra money, you can easily download the Microsoft Internet Explorer directly from MSN. Currently, the Internet Explorer version 2.0 is an icon that you can select after opening the Internet Center category. Here's another way to find whatever may be the latest version and learn how to use one of MSN's information retrieval tools:

1. Sign on to MSN using your regular access number.
2. From the main page (Microsoft Central) choose Tools\Find\On the Microsoft Network.

3. In the Containing field of the resulting dialog box, type **Internet explorer.**
4. In the Of type field, select all services of the Microsoft Network.
5. Click Find Now.

The resulting search field will contain a list of available Internet Explorer-related files. You can expect the version numbers to change occasionally as Microsoft continues to upgrade the programs.

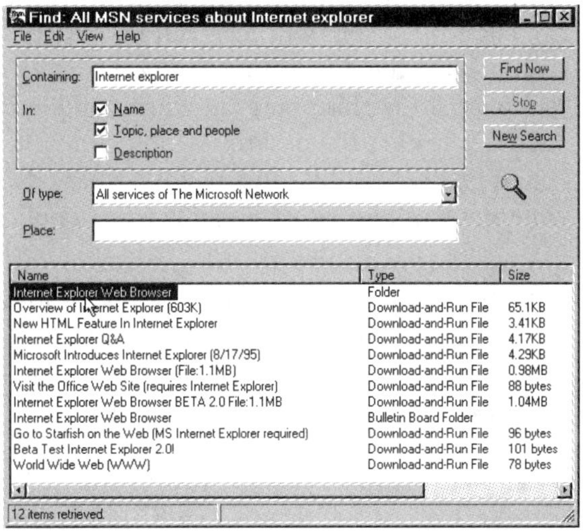

Once you have the version of Internet Explorer you want, locate the downloaded file on your system, double-click it, and follow the onscreen directions to install it onto your system. If you're the old-fashioned type, you can simply open a DOS command prompt, go to the directory where the file was downloaded, and run the executable from the C: prompt.

note *The version of the Microsoft Web browser that you download from MSN will almost certainly be newer and have more features than the one included on the Microsoft Plus! CD. So even if you own Microsoft Plus!, you may want to download the new version. It is also available in the first Windows 95 Service Pack. (See Appendix A for details.)*

Installing Internet Support

The next step after running the downloaded executable file is to run the Internet Setup Wizard, placed in the Programs\Accessories\Internet group on your Start Menu.

THE EASY SCENARIO If you plan to use the Microsoft Network as your dial-up Internet service provider (ISP), and have no other third-party dial-up profiles configured, the installation will proceed automatically. The Internet Setup Wizard will quickly create a MSN Dial-Up Networking profile and complete the setup. You will be asked whether you are already a member of the Microsoft Network or if you wish to sign up.

If you're signing up for the first time, see the section earlier in this chapter about filling in enrollment screens. If you're already a member (and check the appropriate box), you'll be prompted again to enter your area code and first three digits of your telephone number.

The MSN client will then call in, update your telephone access list, and reconfigure the connection for both the Microsoft Network and Internet support. From this point on, when you log into the Microsoft Network by double-clicking the desktop MSN icon, you will also establish a point-to-point protocol (PPP) Internet connection so that you can run the Microsoft Internet Explorer or any other Internet applications while logged into MSN.

note *Late-breaking news! The problems discussed in the following sections have been resolved in the final version of Microsoft's Internet Explorer. If you have already upgraded from the version in Microsoft Plus!, you can skip the next few pages. Your Network TCP/IP settings will not be overwritten.*

A SLIGHTLY TRICKIER SCENARIO If you have an existing third-party dial-up profile, but not a dedicated TCP/IP local area network (LAN), you may need to take some precautions to ensure that the Internet protocol (IP) and DNS information is not lost when you install Microsoft Plus!. Be sure to check the TCP/IP property settings for the Dial-Up Networking Adapter in the Network Control Panel object before running the Internet Setup Wizard. Copy down all IP and DNS information and transfer it to the individual third-party connection profile.

1. Right-click the connection profile in the Dial-Up Networking folder, and open the Properties menu.
2. Click the Server Type button in the Connection Properties dialog.
3. Make sure the TCP/IP protocol is selected on the next screen. Click the TCP/IP Settings button and transfer the IP and DNS information that you copied into the third setup screen.

You can now run the Internet Setup Wizard and select the Microsoft Network as your primary Internet connection. You will also retain your previous dial-up connection profile through a third-party ISP.

AN OUT-AND-OUT MESS If you want to preserve a dedicated LAN connection to the Internet, you are probably better off not running the Microsoft Internet Setup Wizard at all.

Unless you specifically want to use Inbox to collect your Internet mail, you can simply keep your current ISP or LAN connection to the Internet, using third-party mail management. The Microsoft Web browser, placed on your desktop as "The Internet", will be functional with your existing third-party Internet connection.

If you do want to use Inbox with a LAN or a third-party ISP Internet connection, you'll have to go through a messy configuration scenario. If you select either of these options in the Microsoft Internet Setup Wizard, you'll be prompted to re-enter all relevant login, IP, and DNS information on a series of successive screens. The information you enter will be written directly into the Dial-Up Networking Adapter TCP/IP properties under the Network Control Panel object, overwriting any information that was there before. The IP address information will also be transferred to the TCP/IP settings for any dedicated network card in your system. This doesn't make a lot of sense, but it's the way Microsoft programmed it.

If you want to keep existing third-party ISP information from being overwritten, you'll need to follow the procedure described here to record TCP/IP properties settings and then transfer them to a separate connection profile.

If you want to keep your existing TCP/IP LAN connection, you'll need to jot down the IP information for your network adapter card before running the Internet Setup Wizard:

1. Open the Network Control Panel object, highlight the TCP/IP protocol for your network adapter, and copy down all information entered on all of the setup tabs.
2. If you have any third-party ISP dial-up connections, highlight the TCP/IP protocol for the Dial-Up Adapter and copy down all the information entered on all of the setup tabs. Then transfer the information to a separate Dial-Up Networking connection profile as described in the preceding subsection.
3. Close the Network object and run the Microsoft Internet Setup Wizard. Select either the "Connect using my phone line" or the "Connect using my local network" option.
4. Fill in all of the subsequent setup screens, entering appropriate TCP/IP IP and Internet information for your ISP or your dedicated LAN. Answer yes to the question about using Microsoft Exchange to send and receive your mail.

5. When the setup procedure is complete, open the Network Control Panel object again. Compare the new properties for your Network Adapter's TCP/IP protocol to the ones you wrote down. If they are the same, you will be able to continue using your LAN and send Internet Mail through the Inbox. If they are different, you will have to choose between the two configurations. Test to see whether your Network and Inbox are both functional with the new settings. If you can no longer connect to your LAN, restore the original TCP/IP settings through the Control Panel and see by trial-and-error whether the Inbox Internet Mail feature remains operational.

Changing Your MSN Access Number

If you're going out of town and plan to use the Microsoft Network, you'll want to change the access telephone number to a node at your destination. Here's how to do it:

1. Right-click the Microsoft Network desktop icon.
2. Click Connection Settings.
3. Click Access Numbers.
4. Select Internet and the Microsoft Network.
5. Click the Change button next to Primary Access Numbers, and select a new access node by country, state, and city.
6. Click the Change button next to Secondary Access Numbers, and select a new access node by country, state, and city.
7. Click OK twice to close the dialog box.

The Internet and You

There is so much hype about the Internet these days that it can be hard to separate fact from fiction. No, the Internet won't toast your bread in the morning, though if you have a digital camera, it can send images of your toaster onto the Net so you can tell in London when the toast pops up in Sydney. The Net won't do your work for you, but it can be an incomparable

Want to Explore?

If you like the way Windows Explorer works, you can access MSN in the same frame of reference. Instead of double-clicking on the MSN desktop icon, right-click and select Explore. Here you can see the result at MSN Central, with the categories part of the Explorer tree (left-hand window) expanded:

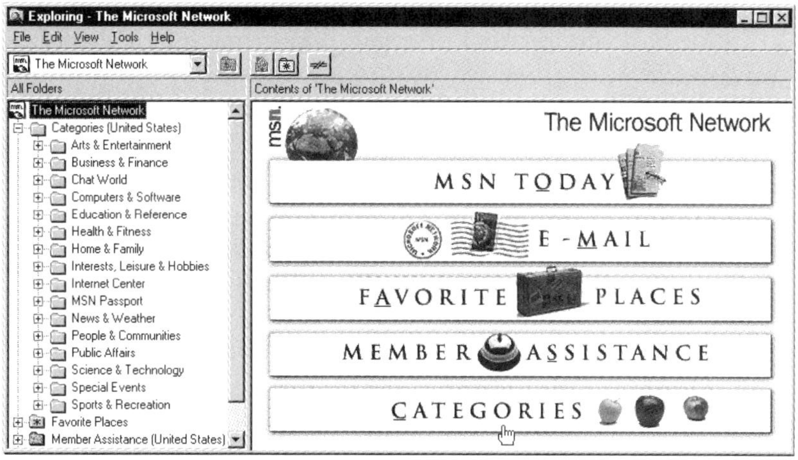

We like this method of browsing MSN because the tree provides a useful sense of context. You can keep only one window open at a time—this saves your machine resources—and still navigate rapidly around the system, using the tree.

source of information about almost any topic. And it won't solve your life's problems, though it can point the way to an amazing variety of possible solutions for almost any problem.

The Internet makes a certain type of politician extremely uneasy, because it's too sprawling and international to control. No particular authority is fully in charge. If you don't trust people to pretty much take care of their own business, or if you think people need to be controlled most of the time for their own good, a system like the Internet may give you ulcers. On the other hand, if you enjoy the yeasty feeling of roaming through an incredibly rich, often banal, just as often surprising, and completely unrestricted "virtual universe," the Internet may be the yogurt dessert you're looking for.

Connecting Through Windows 95

Windows 95 has built-in support for Internet connections. You simply have to set up a dial-up connection to a service provider, or subscribe to the Microsoft Network and install the enhanced Internet support discussed in the previous section. In this section you'll read about how to use the Internet once you're connected, and you'll find descriptions of Windows 95's bundled Internet utilities with some guidelines on how to use them. We also provide some basic information on using third-party Internet software with Windows 95.

When you visit any of the sites mentioned in this section, bear in mind that an Internet server is under no one's control but that of the person or company maintaining it, and a site's Internet address can change for a variety of reasons. If an address we mention is out of date, you may find a forwarding address at the old site location. If you don't, it's possible the page is simply gone, having evaporated from the unending froth of the Net. It happens all the time.

An Internet Primer

As you probably know by now, the *Internet* is a global network of computers maintained by universities, scientific research institutes, non-profit organizations, and commercial corporations. In order to connect to these resources, you must have a registered account with an Internet service provider, also known as an ISP.

When you delve into the Internet it helps to know what you're dealing with. A wealth of Internet books offer detailed descriptions of the basic services, so here we'll limit ourselves to a brief summary of the most important things you need to know. Many people typically start their Internet voyaging wanting only to browse the World Wide Web. For that, you really only need a standard browser like Netscape, Mosaic, or Windows 95's own Internet Explorer. As you get more familiar or adventurous, you may decide to experiment with the lesser known Internet features.

This section provides thumbnail descriptions of the various tools you'll need to take advantage of all of the Internet's capabilities. (Yes, the Web browsers are here, too. We saved the best for last and you can skip directly to that part of the chapter if you can't wait.) First, let's review the basic Internet services that can be exploited through Windows 95.

E-mail

You can send electronic messages to users in almost any part of the world through the Internet's array of networked computers. If you share the same computer host as your message recipient, the mail can be addressed simply by a designator: a "nickname" that designates the user, such as lennyb, cmenefee, or cbermant, to pick some contributors to this book. Some information services (CompuServe and MCI) use numerical designations for their customers rather than alphabetical ones. On most of the newer access providers, however, you can pretty much pick your own nickname.

When you send e-mail over the Internet, you are dispatching messages to users at different computer hosts. The Internet has developed a computer equivalent to the post office's area codes to identify different hosts all over the world. These host names are referred to as *domains*. A standard Internet e-mail address consists of a username followed by a domain name; for instance: lennyb@hooked.net. The domain name may be divided into several parts, and the username may refer to a group mailbox rather than an individual, as in this example:

```
TEACHERS@SPACEMET.PHAST.UMASS.EDU.
```

As you may know or may have guessed, this last one is an address located on a server at the University of Massachusetts. The first part of an Internet domain name may be entirely arbitrary, and Internet users being what they are, you're likely to encounter some pretty bizarre and arcane hostnames. The last part of the domain name obeys a convention; the three-letter extension identifying the organization type:

.EDU—AN EDUCATIONAL INSTITUTION
.COM—A COMMERCIAL ORGANIZATION
.GOV—A GOVERNMENT ORGANIZATION
.MIL—A MILITARY ORGANIZATION
.NET—A LARGE NETWORK PROVIDER
.ORG—A NON-PROFIT ORGANIZATION

In the days before the Internet became popular, e-mail messages were mostly limited to ASCII text transmissions, but in the last several years, a number of protocols have become popular that allow transmission of binary files as attachments to text messages. There are several ways to decode these attachments when a message shows up in your mailbox. The principal ones are called MIME and UUEncode Fortunately, Windows 95's Inbox supports both of these protocols, so that messages you receive are automatically decoded and displayed as text plus icons for attached files. To add an attachment to an e-mail message with Inbox, all you have to do is drag the icon out of My Computer and drop it into the message window. Similarly, to detach a binary attachment from a received message, all you have to do is drag it out of the message window to the desktop or into a folder.

Although the Microsoft Exchange Inbox is a powerful mail management tool, it contains many hidden configuration options, and requires a large amount of RAM to run at speeds faster than a snail's pace. For this reason, some people prefer simpler, light-weight alternatives. One of the most popular third-party mail management packages for Windows is Eudora.

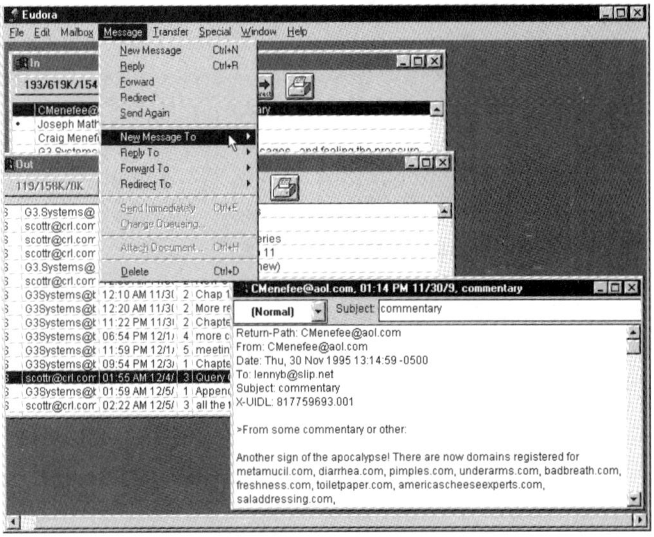

This easy-to-use program is available in a freeware version through the World Wide Web, FTP, and CompuServe. (See Appendix C for specific vendor contact information about the more full-featured commercial version.)

Remote Server Access Tools

Another popular, common use for the Internet is to establish connections to remote computers, for the purposes of obtaining stored information, downloading software, or taking advantage of specific program services offered on the remote computer. With so many public servers connected to the Internet, indexing and search systems have been developed in order to help you locate information. Before the advent of the popular World Wide Web, there was a simple text-based menuing system called *gopher*. The Internet also has its own built in file transfer protocol designed to let you transfer binary files from a remote server to your local computer. A third important remote access feature allows you to log into a server and run programs installed on it as though they were present on your own local machine. (This is called Telnet.)

DIGGING AROUND IN GOPHERSPACE Gopher is the typically cute and indirect Internet name for a menu-driven system developed at the University of Minnesota. Gopher utilities are tools for browsing the contents menus of Internet sites throughout the world, burrowing through systems in search of interesting information.

Millions of subjects included in Internet-connected bodies of information can be found simply by starting at the top-level gopher item—typically, a menu entry reading "all the gophers in the world"—and burrowing ever deeper in the direction of the information you want. The entire system of interconnected menus is known as *gopherspace*.

You can use gopher client software to search for news, research databases, get software files, read electronic books, participate in discussion groups, view directories, and access just about any other text-based Internet resource. The results show up in a hierarchical display window like the folder/file view in My Computer (except that the names of things can be much longer than 256 characters).

Windows 95 does not include a gopher browsing utility, but you can use the Telnet client to log into a server that does offer a gopher browser. Usually, such a browser can be activated on the remote server by entering the command "gopher (or "!gopher") at a UNIX command prompt.

If you have installed the Microsoft Internet Explorer, however, you do have a rough-and-ready gopher browser on your system. Internet Explorer handles gopherspace quite well. If you're familiar with browsing the Web, gopherspace will not feel mysterious at all. It's character-based instead of graphical in nature, but its interconnected nature will make you feel right at home.

Also, unless you're seeking something very specific (in which case, see the upcoming descriptions of Archie and Veronica), the best place to start is anyplace that provides general listings of gophers devoted to more specific information for links to specific servers. Here you see one of our favorite gopher starting places, the Gopher Jewels World Wide Web page at HTTP://GALAXY.EINET.NET/GJ/INDEX.HTML

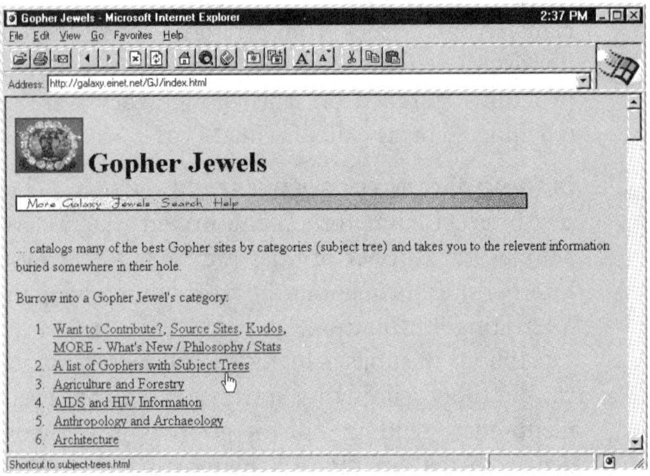

You can also go directly to the true character-based Gopher Jewels site through the University of Southern California at this rather daunting address:

```
GOPHER://CWIS.USC.EDU/11/OTHER_GOPHERS_AND_INFORMATION_RESOURCE
S/GOPHER-JEWELS
```

tip *Microsoft Internet Explorer accepts gopher space addresses of the form GOPHER://SITENAME—note the similarity to World Wide Web HTTP:// addresses.*

Another good place to start is at Rice University's gopher server accessed at GOPHER://RICEINFO.RICE.EDU/11. Like Gopher Jewels, this server has both live gopher and linked Web pages, so you can work with the system of your choice. The Rice location features a very well-organized menu by topic, plus links to several other types of organized servers.

tip *If you start your gopher dig at either Gopher Jewels or Rice University, you should be able eventually to find just about anything you might look for. When you find a site you expect to visit often, you can save the gopher address in your Internet Explorer personal Favorites folder just as you would a World Wide Web page. Just click the Favorites icon.*

ARCHIE *Archie* helps find publicly available files by searching through file databases. Archie servers regularly scan thousands of Internet systems and build a database of files that are available to the public. When you do an archie search for a subject, you get back a list of sites that have files available that fit your search criteria. All files in an Archie search are available to anyone, which means you can sign on with FTP using the user ID "anonymous" and automatically have access to the files; no special passwords are required.

FINGER *Finger* is a tool for getting information about users of systems connected to the Internet. If you simply finger a particular system, you'll get a list of all users of that system. Or you can finger a specific user and get back user-specific information, usually including the target user's e-mail address—a handy feature. Or you can use Finger to find information about a specific server's contents. Finally, you can use Finger to request the status of a given resource followed on the Internet, such as a hurricane, papal election, political campaign, rock tour, or other natural or unnatural event.

note *Not all systems support Finger because of its potential to give unauthorized users access to private information about authorized users. You may want to check with your service provider to see if it supports Finger or, if so, whether it maintains a member directory that Finger can search, and then take steps to control the information it contains about you accordingly.*

VERONICA *Veronica* is a tool to make gopher searches faster and more efficient. Using Veronica, you can automate your gopher search for resources that contain the keywords you specify. Instead of browsing through gopherspace, Veronica looks for your keyword through all the gopher menus and reports back with a temporary, customized gopher menu that contains all the items that matched your query. This lets you directly select appropriate items instead of branching around in a haphazard search.

WHOIS Whois (pronounced "who is") is a tool that finds information about users of a specific network. Whois information is stored in a specific system database that is sometimes called the "white pages" because it resembles a phone book's alphabetical listing. The Whois database is often limited to people who have something to do with the workings of the Internet in some way and so is less useful than Finger to most Internet users.

FTP

FTP (file transfer protocol) is the Internet's universal method for transferring binary files between sites on the Internet directly to your local computer. FTP utilities, which run through a serial line Internet protocol (SLIP) connection or point-to-point protocol (PPP) Internet connection, let you avoid the chore of transferring files first to the host computer of your Internet service provider, and then downloading them through a protocol like ZMODEM, which is what people used to do. When a file is available to the public at large, you download it using what is called "anonymous FTP" because you sign onto the remote system using the ID "anonymous." The remote system doesn't know—or care—who you are; it just uses the FTP protocol to send you any publicly available files you request.

Windows 95 includes a simple text-based FTP utility that requires you to learn some UNIX commands in order to download files. If you have no other FTP utility, probably the only thing you'll want to use this for is to go online to a server and download a better FTP utility. If you dread using command-line utilities, and have a World Wide Web browser, you'll be pleased to know that Web browsers can also be used to connect to FTP sites. (Compared to dedicated FTP utilities, Web browsers have very limited file management and file transfer features, but they're better than the command line Win95 program.)

tip *Microsoft Internet Explorer (and most other Web browsers) accept FTP addresses of the format FTP://SITENAME.*

Readers who are secretly UNIX and DOS command-line junkies may actually like the relatively simple command set of Win95's text-based FTP. You can enter FTP at the DOS command-line, and type a question mark at the ftp> prompt to see the complete list of available commands. For more command information, you can type **HELP** followed by the command. Here's an example:

```
ftp> HELP OPEN
CONNECT TO REMOTE FTP
```

To open a remote FTP site while you're connected to the Internet, you can just enter the word FTP followed by the site name at the DOS command prompt. If you have the AutoDial feature of Microsoft's Internet Explorer turned on, then entering this command automatically brings up a dial-up networking connection profile to establish your Internet connection.

After you connect to an anonymous FTP server, you must go through a login procedure. Traditionally, you enter *anonymous* as your user ID and use your real e-mail address as a password. (The inclusion of your e-mail address is a courtesy so that the administrator of the FTP site has some idea of who has been using it.) If you connect using Microsoft's text-based FTP utility, you'll have to enter all this information manually. It's a lot easier to connect to an FTP site through a World Wide Web browser, which will enter the necessary login information for you automatically. Figure 11-7 shows

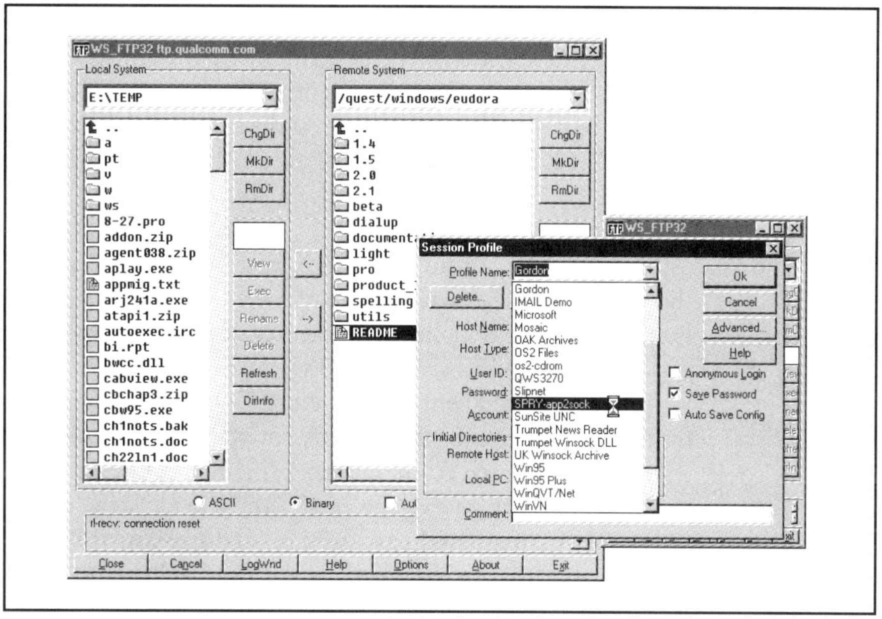

FIGURE 11-7

WSFTP, a dedicated FTP utility, makes it easy to manage multiple file transfer operations.

the popular WSFTP shareware package, which is a dedicated file transfer utility written for the Windows interface. WSFTP makes it extremely convenient to log onto multiple servers and manage your file directories. WSFTP is available via the Web, FTP, and CompuServe. (See Appendix C for specific vendor contact information.)

Telnet

A telnet terminal package lets you log onto a remote Internet site and act as if you were dialing into it directly. Telnet allows you to access all the commands available on the remote server as though you were running them on your local computer. For instance, you can telnet into an information service like CompuServe or the Well over the Internet, read messages and participate in conferences, just as though you had dialed in through a communication package like Procomm Plus. In fact, a new trend in some information services is not to offer dial-up telephone access at all, but to allow connections only through the Internet.

If you have an advanced telnet terminal program, you can also use it to upload and download server files, and run server-based programs. (One common use of telnet is to use the Internet instead of long distance lines to access BBSs in distant cities, thus avoiding long-distance charges.)

Windows 95 includes a basic Telnet utility that runs on the desktop and is capable of several different terminal emulations. Microsoft says nothing about this application in its documentation, and Win95 Telnet will not be installed in a program group unless you do it yourself. (You'll find TELNET.EXE in your main Windows 95 directory. You can open it from the DOS command line, or create a shortcut to it on the Start Menu or on the desktop. See Chapter 4 for details on how to do this.)

Connecting to an Internet server through Telnet is an easy task. Just click the Connect pull-down menu and select Remote System. In the next dialog box enter the host name for the server you want to connect with, as in these examples: COMPUSERVE.COM; WELL.COM, CS-PUB.BU.EDU. The port setting should generally be left at TELNET, and you can select whatever terminal emulation is appropriate for the site you want to reach. If you are currently connected to the Internet through a PPP or SLIP connection, you will reach the site you've specified after you click the Connect button. If the site requires a login and password procedure, you will see this on the screen. After you've connected to a site once, it will be added to the list on the pull-down Connect menu. To reach the site again, just select it from this list.

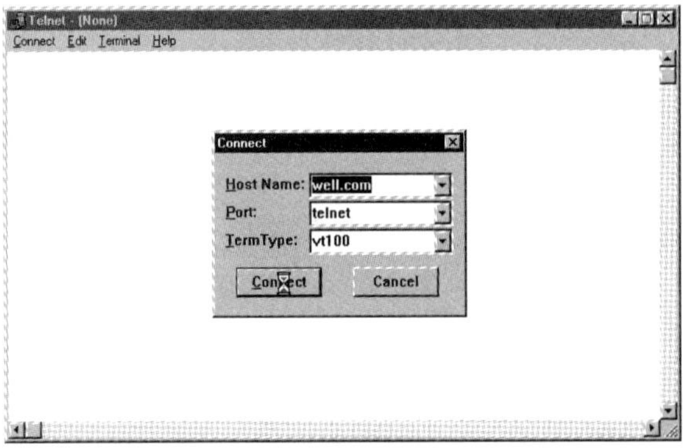

Unfortunately, Win95's Telnet utility does not support Internet file transfers. If you're serious about Telnet, you probably want a more powerful Telnet client, such as the one shown in Figure 11-8. NetTerm is a full-featured terminal program that can establish either dial-up modem connections or Internet Telnet connections. It includes a Telnet phone directory, supports FTP, ASCII, KERMIT and ZMODEM file transfers over a SLIP or PPP Internet connection, and has most of the sophisticated terminal emulation features of other telecommunications applications. NetTerm is a shareware program available through the World Wide Web, FTP, and CompuServe. (See Appendix C for specific vendor contact information.)

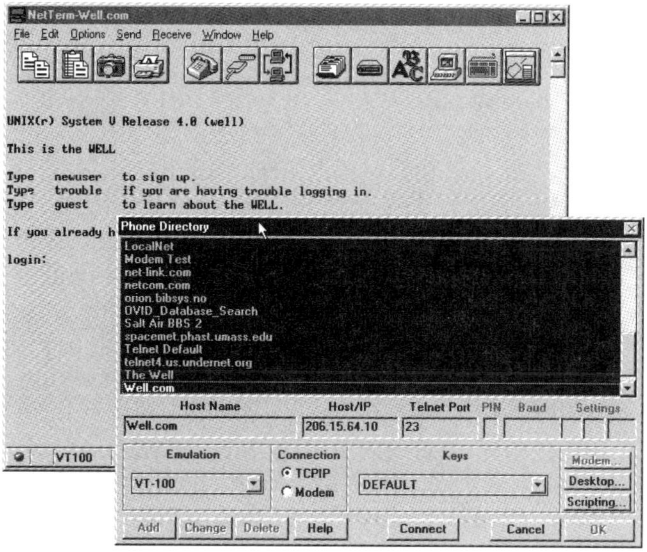

FIGURE 11-8 *The NetTerm telnet utility is also a full-featured terminal program.*

Internet Relay Chat

Internet Relay Chat (or IRC) is the citizen's band radio and traveling street circus of the Internet. It consists of a series of text-based discussion channels that can be accessed by anyone who is logged into an Internet IRC server. Typically, IRC is a late-night pastime for college students all over the world cooped up in dormitories with their free Internet access accounts. (Although, in national emergencies, such as earthquakes and armed coups in third-world countries, IRC has also proved to be a surprisingly useful resource for getting information out of troubled areas into the hands of people who can help.) IRC has an intricate set of customs and byways, with a truly science fictional argot of the English language. You may never know whether the people you're talking to are postmodern poets, pizza delivery workers, or *'bots*—computer programs that participate in IRC discussion channels as though they were live human beings.

To join IRC, you need a well-designed Telnet utility or a dedicated IRC client program. In a pinch, the Windows 95 Telnet utility can be used for Internet Relay Chat. You can Telnet to a dedicated IRC server that allows public access, and set your terminal emulation for VT-100. The port connection may also have to be reset from the standard Telnet configuration to a number like 6667, or 6677. Several commercial and shareware vendors, however, make chatting access a lot easier through dedicated Windows IRC clients. Figure 11-9 shows the IRC client in Delrina's Windows 95 Cyberjack Internet toolkit.

Newsgroups

Newsgroups are the chief joy of the Internet for people who love electronic correspondence and online debates. These groups are collections of messages and replies posted by computer users all over the world. Most Internet newsgroups are distributed to servers through a subsidiary network called Usenet. Usenet contains literally thousands of newsgroups, and they change from day to day. Any message posted in a newsgroup is available for all members to read and post replies to. Not all Internet access providers carry all newsgroups, but most will add a newsgroup if you ask.

There's a Usenet newsgroup out there on just about any subject you can think of and hundreds you wouldn't have thought of in years. Usenet is a welter of fact and opinion, and anyone who wants to join in is welcome.

So just what is a newsgroup? It's really just a bulletin board on which anyone is invited to post messages. People trade facts, opinions, and occasionally *flames*—angry tirades—about everything imaginable. There are some consensual rules which you can learn by reading a newsgroup's associated FAQ (Frequently Asked Questions). Break the rules and someone is likely to issue you a friendly reminder or (if you get unlucky) a flame against your ancestors, progeny, and rightful place in the universe. News-

FIGURE 11-9

Cyberjack Internet Relay Chat

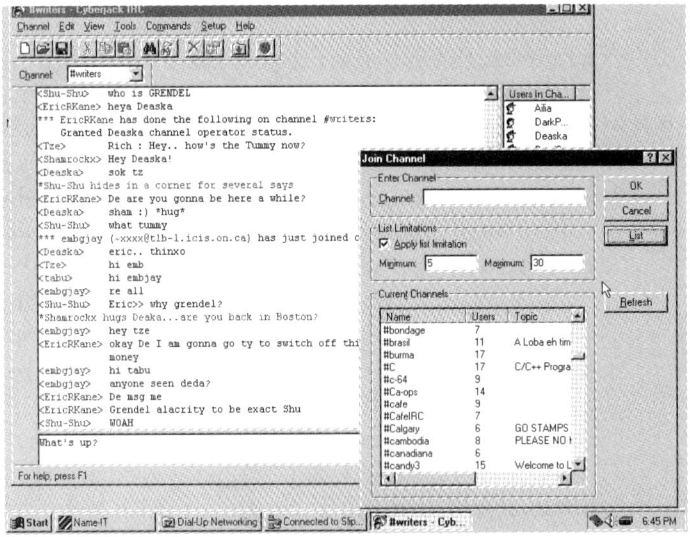

groups can be great places to practice vituperation, and many do, but if that bores or upsets you, you're always free to sign off a given newsgroup and join another.

---

tip *Some offline news readers and mail programs have "bozo filters" that let you ignore messages from specific senders or with specific keywords in the subject line. Got a bozo on your back? Filter 'em out!*

Usenet is not always about politics and raging hormones. If you pick your newsgroups thoughtfully, the possibilities for broadening your knowledge are enormous. One of this book's authors was diagnosed with late-onset diabetes. A doctor said "do as I say and, if you want to know more, read a book." As an experiment, the patient used an Internet search engine to look for the topic "diabetes." From that search came a connection to the Usenet newsgroup at misc.health.diabetes and, on the Web, the Diabetes Knowledgebase at HTTP://WWW.BIOSTAT.WISC.EDU/DIAKNOW/INDEX.HTM, plus the home page of the American Diabetes Association at HTTP://WWW.DIABETES.ORG/.

Between the organized knowledge available through the two World Wide Web sites and the give-and-take of the diabetes newsgroup, the author soon had the equivalent of a crash course in living with and managing diabetes. Similar resources are available for victims of spousal abuse, people in recovery from alcohol or drug abuse, families of Alzheimer's victims, and just about any other health-related topic imaginable.

Types of Newsgroups

Usenet newsgroups are subdivided into a number of categories and subcategories. Table 11-1 shows the basic divisions, along with some sample newsgroups in each category.

In order to participate in reading Usenet news and posting messages to newsgroups, you need a news reader utility. The Microsoft Network online service has a well-designed news reader built into its interface (see Figure 11-10). On MSN, you can participate in Usenet simply by double-clicking the Internet Center Category and then opening the Usenet subcategory.

Most Internet service providers include simple text-based newsreaders that can be read from a UNIX command prompt, but you don't have to struggle with these if you don't want to. Usually, your service provider will have a collection of downloadable shareware and freeware that includes a Windows newsreader or two. In a pinch, you can also access newsgroups through your World Wide Web browser. Web browsers vary in the degree

Prefix	Subjects In This Category	Example Newsgroups
alt	Alternative lifestyle	ALT.CALIFORNIA, ALT.FAN.TOLKIEN, ALT.FOLKLORE, ALT.SEX, ALT.SOC.ETHICS
biz	Business	BIZ.COMP.SERVICES, BIZ.JOBS.OFFERED, BIZ.MISC
comp	Computers	COMP.GRAPHICS, COMP.HOME.MISC, COMP.OS.MSWINDOWS.APPS
misc.	Miscellaneous subjects	MISC.HEALTH.DIABETES
news	Current events/USENET info	NEWS.ADMIN.POLICY, NEWS.ANNOUNCE.IMPORTANT
rec	Recreation	REC.ARTS.CINEMA, REC.GARDEN.ROSES, REC.HUMOR
sci	Science	SCI.MED, SCI.PHYSICS, SCI.SPACE.NEWS
soc	Society	SOC.ORG.NONPROFIT, SOC.POLITICS, SOC.NET-PEOPLE

TABLE 11-1 *Categories of USENET Newsgroups*

FIGURE 11-10 *Using Usenet through MSN*

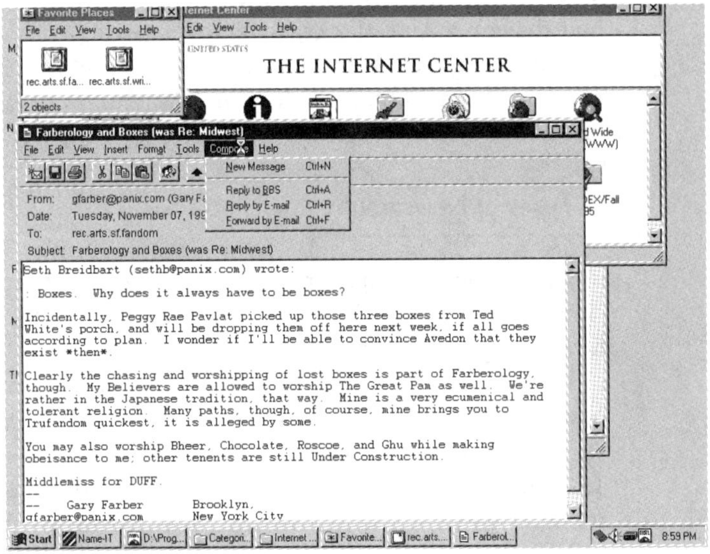

of support they offer for participating in Usenet. The Microsoft Internet Explorer has a limited capacity to display newsgroup threads (no sorting or other bells and whistles), and it also allows you to compose and post newsgroup messages. This capability came along only in the version 2.0 beta program, so if you got your Internet Explorer from the Microsoft Plus! CD-ROM, you may want to go to the Microsoft Internet site and download a newer version, as explained earlier in this chapter.

note *You can't use a World Wide Web browser to read newsgroups through a connection to the Microsoft Network online service. MSN has no public Internet news server. Instead, MSN users must access newsgroups through the MSN client software.*

OFFLINE NEWSREADERS Many active Usenet participants firmly believe in using *offline readers*: programs that log on, post messages that you've composed offline, download new message headers to selected newsgroups, and log off again. You can pick what you want to read offline; the newsreader logs on again, downloads only the messages and newsgroups you've selected, and logs off. If you're paying for connect time, such readers let you reply at your leisure without breaking your bank.

Free Agent is one of the more full-featured offline newsreaders for the Windows environment:

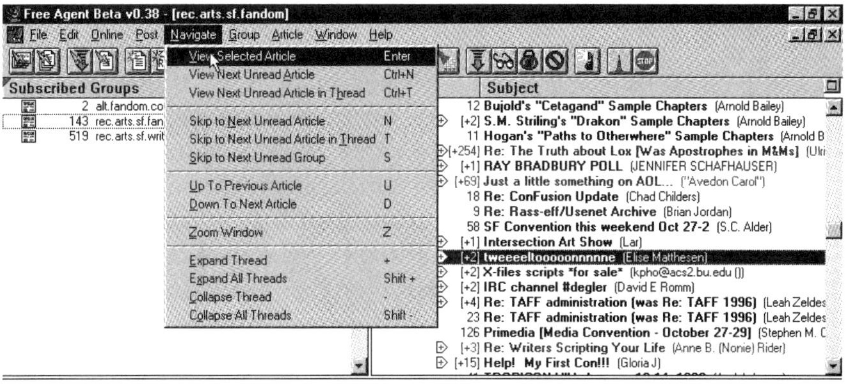

It has many display, group subscription, message sorting, and message composition options. Free Agent is available via the World Wide Web. See Appendix C for vendor contact information.

The World Wide Web

The World Wide Web is the fastest growing part of the Internet, and now well-known even to people who don't own personal computers. Originally the invention of nuclear physicists in Switzerland, the World Wide Web allows users to create documents that can contain formatted text, graphic images, real-time video, and sound. The Hypertext Markup Language (HTML), used to transmit Web pages over the Internet, also allows hypertext links to be embedded within Web documents. This makes it easy to link Web pages to one another or to downloadable files that may contain programs, recorded sounds, or video animations. The effect of this technology over the past four years has transformed the Web from the domain of scientists and software junkies, into a populist, multimedia phenomenon. The original concept of using the Web as a repository for text and pictorial research documents, was gradually expanded to make it a place where personal collages and artistic statements could be published. That concept is now being expanded to include corporate advertising and commercial entertainment. On the current Web, you can browse through pages devoted to old-time radio and television and listen to Groucho Marx, you can subscribe to live rock-and-roll concerts, or leaf through amateur and commercial magazines. The recent development of additional Web programming languages has also made it possible to log into interactive databases and other computer applications without purchasing them and installing them on your hard drive.

And the Web's other important aspect is that it can effectively serve as a superset of most of the Internet services that we've previously discussed in this chapter. A well-written Web browser can serve as a single master interface that supports e-mail, gopher, archie, ftp, and Usenet newsgroups. Links for additional services such as telnet and IRC can be embedded in World Wide Web pages so that the click of a mouse in your Web browser launches a helper application that handles anything the Web browser can't do by itself.

Making Web Browsers Do Triple Duty

Web browsers vary in their features and functionality, but most of them can also do overtime duty browsing other parts of the Internet. You can use your Web browser as gopher tool or FTP utility, or even to read Usenet newsgroups. For the first two chores, any Web browser will do. For Usenet newsgroups, the current versions of Microsoft's Internet Explorer and Netscape Communications' Netscape include both read and response capability. Other Web browsers can be used simply to skim through messages.

FIGURE 11-11 *Radio Yesteryear presents the Adventures of Sherlock Holmes (with Realaudio sound).*

USING GOPHER RESOURCES Accessing a gopher archive through a Web browser is probably the most transparent function. Gophers are really just nested text menus, anyway, with the bottom layers executing UNIX commands to perform text searches, or transmit files to you. (In fact, some Web browsers may have gopher sites already entered on their default hotlists of places to visit.) As you begin to visit various Web pages, you'll notice jump buttons that take you to gopher archives are intermingled with the buttons that take you to other graphical Web pages.

You can jump to a gopher site directly in a Web browser simply by entering its location in the Open URL box. Just as Web pages are all addressed with the string HTTP://, gopher sites are located with the string GOPHER://. Some sites also include "gopher" in their domain name. For instance to log into the Well (Whole Earth 'Lectronic 'Link), you would enter **GOPHER://GOPHER.WELL.COM**. To log into the main gopher at University of Minnesota, just enter **GOPHER://UMN.EDU**.

This procedure is the same whether you're using Netscape, NCSA Mosaic, IBM Web Explorer, Pipeline, Spry Air Mosaic, or some other Web browser. If your browser can save site locations to a hotlist, you can make bookmarks to gopher sites just as you would for Web pages.

FTP WITH WEB BROWSERS If you can use a Web browser to go gopher-hopping, you might guess that it's just as easy to use one for anonymous FTP file transfers. And, generally, it is. Just as long as you've set up your browser's configuration with your username and e-mail address, you can use it to go file-hunting at any anonymous FTP server site. All you need to do is open the URL dialog box and type in **FTP://** followed by the address of the server you want to contact. The individual locations may or may not include the string "ftp" in their domain names. Here are some examples:

```
FTP://FTP.MICROSOFT.COM

FTP://SUNSITE.UNC.EDU
```

Your Web browser will establish a connection to the server you name, and automatically log you on for anonymous file transfers. Usually when you log on to an FTP site, you'll see a series of buttons or folder icons representing various file directories. To download files, just click open the directory you want to browse, and select a file. Your Web browser may then pop open a dialog box asking you for a directory to store the file in. Some browsers simply grab and stash files in a default directory.

tip *Some anonymous FTP sites also have pages set up on the World Wide Web. If you know the FTP address for a site, you can see if it also has a Web page. Open the URL dialog box and enter* ***HTTP://*** *followed by the domain name. Browsing and selecting files from a Web page tends to be easier and more fun than scrolling through descriptionless directory listings.*

YOUR WEB BROWSER AND USENET NEWS Reading Usenet newsgroups with a Web browser is slightly more problematical than obtaining gopher or FTP access. To gain access to newsgroups through your browser, you must first make sure that the name of your news server is specified in the browser's configuration options. Often, the name of the news server is simply NEWS.*XXXXX.XXX*, where *XXXXX.XXX* is the same domain name as in your e-mail address. If you don't know the official name of your news server, then call up your Internet provider and ask.

If your browser is Netscape Navigator version 1 or 2, or the Microsoft Internet Explorer version 2, all you need to do is select the Go To Newsgroups option (on the Window menu in the current Netscape Navigator and on the Go menu in Internet Explorer). Your Internet service provider will then generally log you onto an introductory page where you can select the newsgroups that you want to subscribe to. Just click the newsgroup you want and the screen will shift to display a series of posted articles.

The disadvantage of reading newsgroups over the Web is you can't sort the messages by date, author, or topic thread. The best that you can do with browsers that don't directly support Usenet is to log into a particular newsgroup and scroll through messages without the ability to post your own replies. To accomplish this, open the URL dialog box and enter **NEWS:** followed by the name of the newsgroup that you want to read. For example:

```
NEWS:REC.ARTS.SF.WRITTEN
```

Setting Up Microsoft Internet Explorer for Usenet

Use these steps to be able to monitor your choice of Usenet newsgroups using Microsoft Internet Explorer:

1. Install Internet Explorer version 2.0 or later. If you don't have it yet, you can get it from the MSN home page at HTTP://WWW.MSN.COM/ among many other places. Download it using your current version of Internet Explorer (or any other Web browser) and install it on your system, as we discussed in a previous section of this chapter.
2. Start the Internet Explorer.
3. Under View\Options, select the News tab.
4. Make sure the "Use Internet Explorer to read Internet newsgroups" box is checked.
5. Enter the news server settings appropriate for your Internet access provider. The news server address will usually begin with "NEWS" followed by the domain name of your ISP. Here's an example:

   ```
   NEWS.COMPUSERVE.COM.
   ```

Keep in mind that MSN does not have a news server that can be accessed in this way. If your Internet connection is through MSN, you'll have to read your newsgroups through the MSN interface, not through a Web browser (unless you can locate an alternative public news server).

tip *If you have trouble accessing news on your Internet provider's server, try checking or unchecking the "requires password" box in the Settings dialog.*

Microsoft's Internet Explorer Browser

The Microsoft Internet Explorer is constantly changing, so the version you got on CD-ROM or on a disk set may not be the most recent one. The

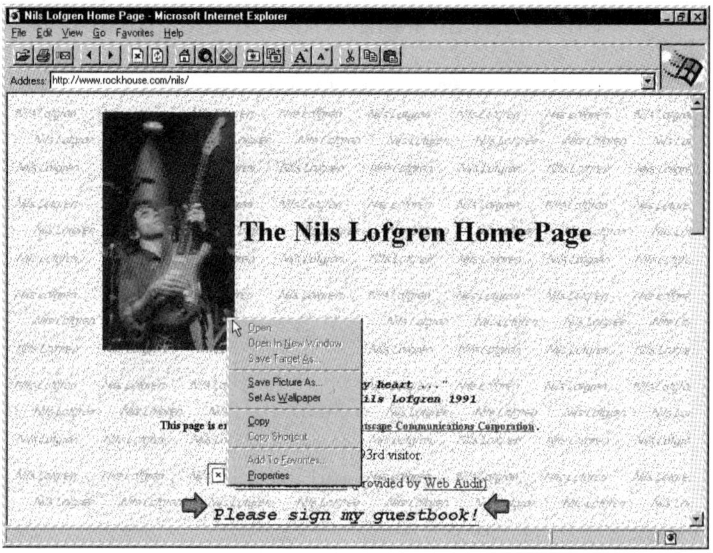

FIGURE 11-12 *Right-click in Internet Explorer to pop up the context menu.*

current release, as of this writing, includes the Realaudio sound player, and also has a built-in capacity to play MIDI files embedded in Web pages. Internet Explorer version 2 has also been updated to support most of the new page display features implemented in the HTML version 3 page description language (colored page backgrounds, tables, and so on). Performance has also been improved; text and graphics display is much snappier in version 2 than it was before. Internet Explorer even has some features that you won't find in Netscape. You save embedded objects in Web pages simply by clicking on them and dragging them to the desktop! Right-click any area in a Web page and a series of open, save, and copy options appear in a pop-up context menu.

USING THE INTERNET AUTODIAL OPTION If you right-click the Internet globe icon on the desktop and select Properties, you'll see an option called AutoDial. When the Use AutoDial box is selected, you'll find that opening any 32-bit Windows 95 application when you're offline automatically launches the Dial-Up Networking connection profile for your default Internet Service Provider. The default Dial-Up Networking connection is shown in the drop-down list in the middle of the screen:

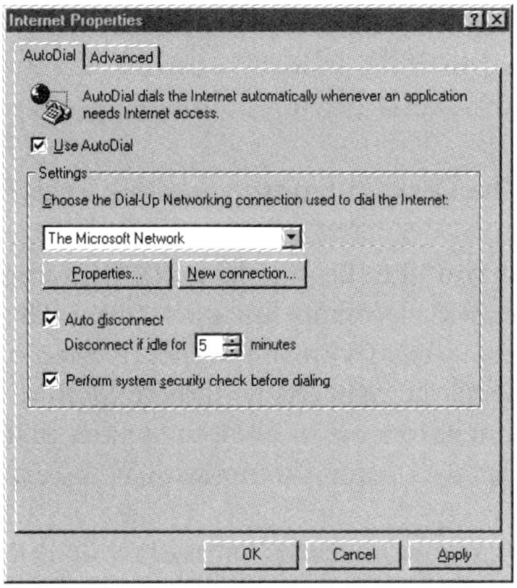

Some people have complained about this feature. They install the Microsoft Internet Explorer and inadvertently choose the option that makes the Microsoft Network the default Internet service provider. They may not actually have accounts on MSN, and may find that the MSN login screen comes up even when they open third-party Internet applications from a different service provider. This situation can be easily remedied by choosing a different Dial-Up Networking profile to connect with, or by deselecting the AutoDial option entirely.

Netscape Navigator for Windows 95

Netscape Communication Corporation is generally considered to be the industry leader in the field of personal World Wide Web browsers. The current implementation of their Windows 95 product has an impressive set of support features. If you don't like Windows 95's built-in e-mail management, or you're just looking for a change, you can establish your own e-mail database within the Netscape browser. Dash off messages on-the-fly, without expending RAM to load the Inbox. Netscape's support for browsing newsgroups is also slightly better than Internet Explorer's. A three-pane window makes it easy for you to view newsgroup listings, message threads, and individual posts simultaneously.

The Windows 95 version of Netscape Navigator has its own installation program, similar to the one for Internet Explorer. Netscape adds its own information service profile to Microsoft Exchange. This allows you to redirect mail from the Inbox to Netscape Navigator by filling in the appropriate Properties information. (The Netscape Transport service is not automatically installed into any Exchange Profile. To implement this feature, you must open the Inbox Properties, select the Exchange Profile you want to modify, click the Add button, and select Netscape Internet Transport.)

The Desktop Emissary Internet Tool

If you like the Windows 95 Explorer, you'll feel comfortable from the start with Desktop Emissary, from The Wollongong Group. It opens to double panes, with an Internet tree analogy on the left and an active display pane on the right. As with the Explorer, you can click a plus symbol on the left, next to a major area, to expand that area into selections. Figure 11-13 shows the opening screen with Web Surfing entry expanded to the Directories entry.

Desktop Emissary supports full drag-and-drop, which makes it and extremely good tool for surfing either the Web or gopherspace. In the Web, once you have linked to a location, the item labeled Current Wave changes to the name of the selected page. You can then simply drag its icon down and drop it on any of the displayed folders to add it to one of the hot link pages. You can do the same thing through menus by selecting Surf\Add to Link Page, but once you get accustomed to drag-and-drop, you probably won't bother much with the menu system.

FIGURE 11-13 *Desktop Emissary with Web Surfing expanded*

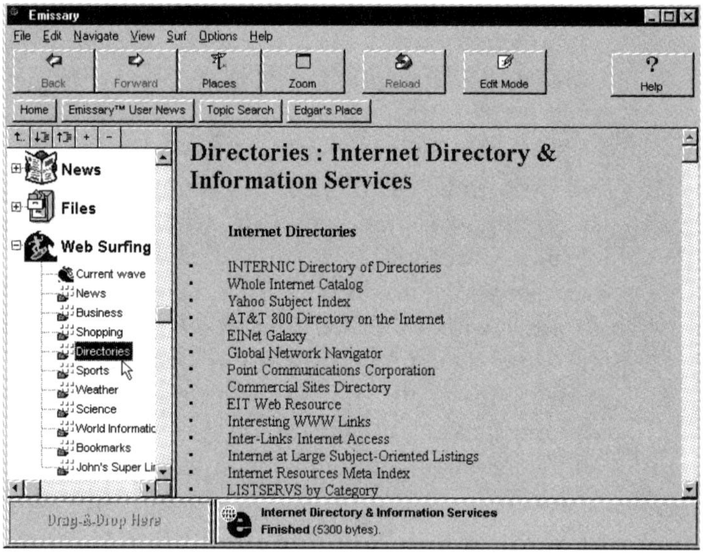

AN HTML WYSIWYG EDITOR, AND MORE On the very positive side, Desktop Emissary was the only browser we came across that could double as a What You See Is What You Get file editor for Web pages. It has a small "editing mode" on the upper right that lets you edit, and save locally, any Web page displayed in the righthand pane. It's great for annotating saved Web pages and, since you can add all commonly used tags (not to mention many Microsoft Internet Explorer tags and most of the Netscape "Mozillisms"), you can use it to author complete pages. Newer versions will handle all of HTML 3.0 features, Wollongong says, which should place this WYSIWYG program well in the forefront of Web editors.

Desktop Emissary's FTP capability is fully drag-and-drop capable. To open a session you select Files in the lefthand pane, then click the Connect button to bring up an address entry window. That means you can simply click a remote file and drag its icon to the file directory of choice on your local system—a tremendous convenience. But it gets better. You can start multiple FTP sessions and freely drag and drop files from one remote site to another, and the transfers will be made directly between the remote systems. It's as if both systems are fully networked extensions of your own system.

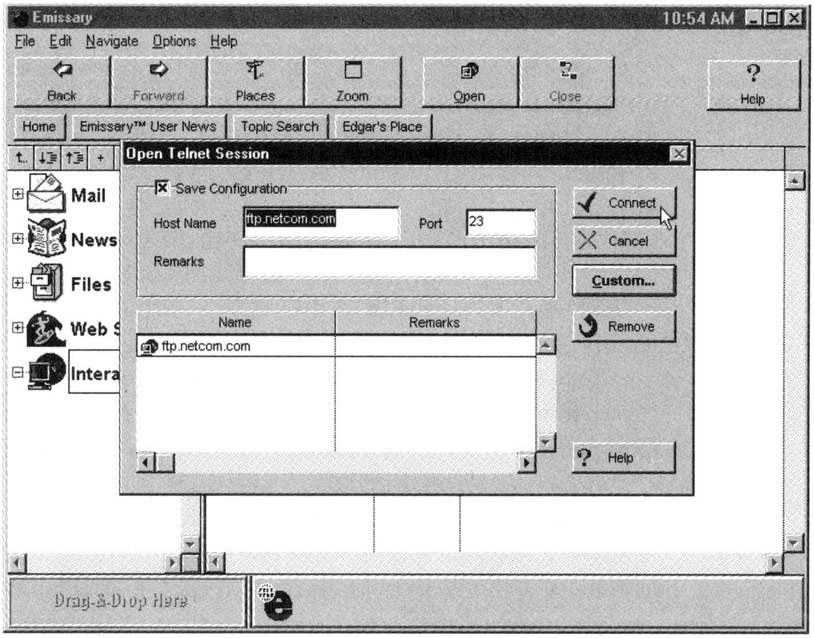

Internet Connectivity Clinic

Although it's certainly fun to stay up-to-date with the latest and greatest 32-bit Windows 95 applications, a great many people have made a substantial investment in Internet tools written for the Windows 3.*x* environment. Users with Internet accounts from third-party service providers have often installed dial-up utilities and browsers under Windows 3.*x*, and they may be reluctant to abandon software that they've already mastered.

The following are a few known problems with using Windows 3.x Internet applications under Windows 95, and some suggested solutions.

Windows 95 Disables Third-Party Internet Dialers

Users of Netscape's Personal Navigator, Eudora, and other browsing utilities were accustomed, under Windows 3.*x*, to having a third-party TCP/IP dialer load whenever these programs were opened to access the Internet. Windows 95's replacement of third-party WINSOCK drivers with its own WINSOCK.DLL disables the third-party Internet dialers distributed by CompuServe, Netcom, and Spry. The popular Trumpet Winsock dialer can also be affected.

CompuServe users can download a utility from the CompuServe Internet forum specifically designed to resolve Win95 problems with older versions of Netlauncher. WinCIM version 2.0.1, and all later versions, resolve the problem automatically by installing WINSOCK directly into the Compuserve application directories. The manual solution to the problem for older versions of Netlauncher is to check the WINDOWS\SYSTEM directory for the presence of Microsoft's WINSOCK.DLL, which will have a file date of 7/11/95. The user should then search each of the directories that contain CompuServe Internet applications for a file called WINSOCK.OLD or WINSOCK.001. This file should be renamed to WINSOCK.DLL. If the file is not found, then the original WINSOCK.DLL should be copied off the CompuServe Internet installation diskette to each directory that contains CompuServe applications.

The same procedure can resolve problems with other third-party Win 3.*x* dialing utilities, such as NetCom's NetCruiser. Users of Trumpet Winsock should leave the Win95 version of WINSOCK.DLL alone, provided that the Trumpet WINSOCK.DLL is copied to each directory that contains an application which will pre-launch Trumpet. Trumpet users should note that a 32-bit Win95 upgrade for Trumpet Winsock is now available and can be downloaded from the Trumpet FTP site.

32-bit Internet Applications Don't Work

Some people download new, Windows 95 Internet utilities (Netscape Navigator, Delrina's Cyberjack, and so on) in good faith, only to find that when they connect to the Internet in their usual way, these applications refuse to work. The problem here is that the Internet connection is probably being established by an older 16-bit Windows 3.*x* dialing utility. These older dialers do not support 32-bit Windows applications. (The Microsoft Internet Explorer, Win95 Telnet utility and FTP utility won't work, either.)

Either obtain a third-party Internet dialer that supports 32-bit applications, or use Windows 95's Dial-Up Networking to establish your Internet connections. (See Chapter 10 for detailed instructions on setting up Dial-Up Networking Internet Connection profiles.)

Installing Microsoft Plus! Wipes Out Existing Win95 LAN or Internet IP Information

See the discussion of this issue under "Installing Internet Support" in the MSN section of this chapter. As much as possible, try to refrain from entering Internet IP information through the Network Control Panel object. Upgrade to Microsoft Internet Explorer, version 2.0 if you own Microsoft Plus!

After Microsoft Plus! Installation, the MSN Connection Screen Comes up on Internet Application Launch, Regardless of the Internet Service Provider

This problem was also discussed in the MSN section of this chapter. Change or disable the Microsoft Internet AutoDial option to resolve it.

Users Experience Problems with Older Versions of Netscape Navigator

Users of Netscape Navigator Personal Edition version 1.1 have found that the TCP/IP protocols installed in their 16-bit package are incompatible with Microsoft's TCP/IP protocol bundled with Windows 95. A selective reinstallation of Netscape Navigator Personal Edition can solve this problem. Install only the application portion of Netscape Navigator Personal Edition; don't install the TCP/IP support or the Internet dialer.

For those who insist on using the TCP/IP dialer supplied with the package, Netscape has a 9-step procedure posted on their technical support Web page that involves uninstalling Windows 95's TCP/IP support to retain use of the Navigator Personal Edition dialer.

Desktop Shortcuts to Web Pages Launch the Wrong Browser

File associations to the .HTM file type are transferred to the last Web browser you install. To restore the association to a previously installed browser, Open the View\Options\File Type options in My Computer. Select the Internet Shortcut file type, click the Edit button, and highlight the Open command on the next screen. Click the Edit button on this screen and change the associated application back to the Web browser you want to open your shortcuts.

note *If you open Microsoft's Internet Explorer version 2 after another browser has been associated to Internet shortcuts, a dialog box pops up, asking whether you want to make Internet Explorer the default browser again.*

Help on the Web

If you're experiencing Internet configuration problems, you should be aware of the fact that a number of World Wide Web sites have been established to provide tutorial material and help you to troubleshoot. Of course, to take advantage of this, you have to be able to establish an Internet connection to access the Help pages. Microsoft itself has a Windows 95 Technical Support page that can be reached from the MSN Home Page by clicking the To Windows 95 icon followed by the Tech Support screwdriver icon on the next linked page. The direct address is http://www.microsoft.com/support/products/windows95/windows95.htm.

An even more impressive resource has been established unofficially by a group of dedicated Windows 95 users and master-class HTML programmers. If you make just one visit to Steve Jenkins' WINDOWS95.COM, you'll probably find yourself returning frequently. The first thing you'll notice is that visiting this Web page is almost like opening an extra, magic folder on your desktop, full of enticing icon options. WINDOWS95.COM offers extensive support in all things relating to TCP/IP connectivity (see Figure 11-14). You'll find step-by-step instructions for peer-to-peer networking, setting up PPP and SLIP connections, Dial-Up Networking profiles, using

FIGURE 11-14

WINDOWS95.COM, the most sophisticated technical support system on the Internet

third-party dialers from major online services, as well as live chat, discussion forums, and an excellent collection of 32-bit Windows 95 shareware. Set your Web browser to HTTP://WWW.WINDOWS95.COM and you won't be sorry.

Printers
Programs
Settings
Find
Help
Run...
Windows95
Start

chapter 12

Networking with Windows 95

- Setting up network support
- Sharing network resources

  Drives, folders, printers, modems, and fonts

- Peer-to-peer connections over the Internet

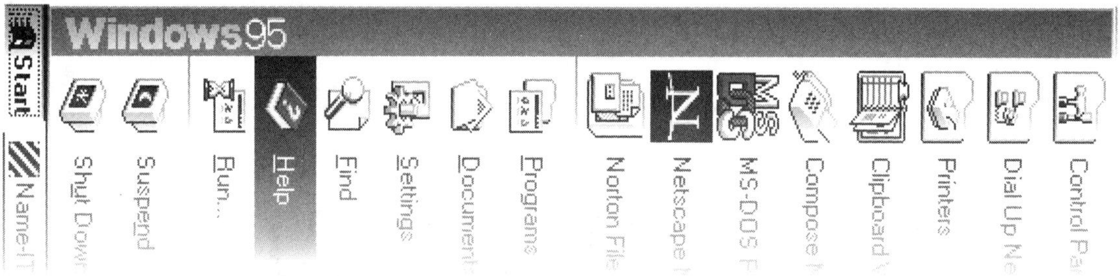

WINDOWS 95 is a much more versatile platform for networking than its predecessors. In addition to improving the built-in peer-to-peer network services of Windows for Workgroups, it contains protected-mode support that allows semiautomatic connections to a Windows NT or Novell NetWare server. The Microsoft peer-to-peer and dedicated server connections can exist simultaneously, so that one workstation connected to a dedicated server allows any other peer workstation to access the server through the Microsoft client protocols.

In addition to providing network e-mail support and allowing folders, drives, and programs to be shared, Windows 95 networking lets you share printers, fonts, or a fax modem.

Any computer running Windows 95 can also establish a quick-and-dirty connection to a dedicated network through a modem, a parallel cable, or a serial cable. In this way, portable machines that lack network adapters can get full or partial access to shared drives, programs, printers, and other resources through a dial-up or direct cable connection.

Setting Up Network Support

If you installed Windows 95 over a previous version of Windows on a computer networked to a Microsoft peer-to-peer network, Windows NT server, or Novell server, your network connection may have been updated automatically. In some cases, depending on the choices you make during Setup, a few additional steps may be necessary to restore the connection.

If you had a network adapter in your system when you installed Windows 95, it was probably detected automatically. You probably saw a network configuration screen that allowed you to select the protocols for your network and confirm the hardware settings for your adapter card. You can view the current network resources available to any Windows 95 machine by double-clicking the Network Neighborhood icon on the desktop.

If there is no Network Neighborhood icon, this indicates that your network adapter card and connection protocols have not yet been configured by Windows 95. To confirm this, open the Network object in the Windows 95 Control Panel. If you see no network adapter or protocols listed on the configuration tab, you must install them.

To install the network adapter, confirm that it is physically in place in your computer. Before starting Windows 95, it may be necessary to configure jumpers or run DOS-based setup software to set the port address and IRQ that the card will use. (You can boot to a DOS command prompt by pressing F8 at boot time and selecting "Boot to Command Prompt" from the Win95 Boot menu.)

Start Windows 95. You may see a message that the network card has been detected and set up automatically. After the desktop appears, open the Network object in the Control Panel and inspect the component list on the Configuration tab. If your network card has been detected, it will be listed along with Microsoft's basic IPX/SPX-compatible and NetBEUI network protocols.

If your network adapter was not detected automatically, you can add it manually by clicking the Add button on the Network Configuration screen and double-clicking Adapter on the next screen, Select Network Component Type. A list of manufacturers and models will appear. Scroll through the manufacturers in the left pane and select a model number in the right pane. (If your network adapter is not in the list, and you have a driver disk from the vendor, you can click the Have Disk option to install third-party network drivers.)

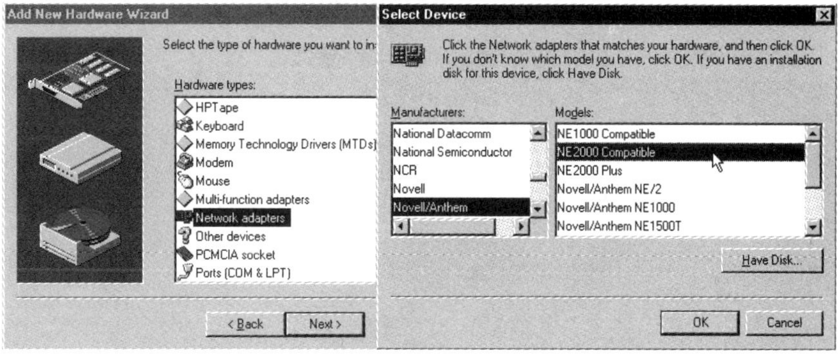

If you're uncertain about the manufacturer and model of your network adapter, you can try installing it by opening the Add New Hardware object in the Control Panel, clicking the Next button, and selecting the option to let Windows 95 search for your hardware. Clicking the No option eventually brings up the list of manufacturers and models.

note *If you install the network adapter through the Add New Hardware object, Windows 95 will attempt to assign a currently available port address and interrupt. This may not correspond to the jumper settings or flash ROM configuration for the adapter. If you install the network adapter through the Network\Add Adapter dialog box, the default port address and IRQ suggested by the manufacturer will be used. In either case, you may need to change these settings, as described in this section.*

After you select your network adapter and close the Setup Wizard, Windows 95 copies the appropriate files to your hard disk and asks you to restart the computer. (Make sure your Win95 CD or installation diskettes are handy.) When the system restarts, you may see a warning message if the network card is configured incorrectly.

If you see no error message, proceed to the next step. If a network error message was displayed, open the Network Control Panel object again to the list of installed components. Select the network adapter in the list, click the Properties button and select the Resource tab. Check the port address and IRQ in the current configuration to see that they match the hardware settings of your adapter. If they don't, you can reconfigure the settings by clicking the Configuration Type drop-down list and selecting another configuration. Click OK and restart Windows 95. When you've selected an available port and IRQ configuration that conforms to the adapter's physical settings, the error message should disappear.

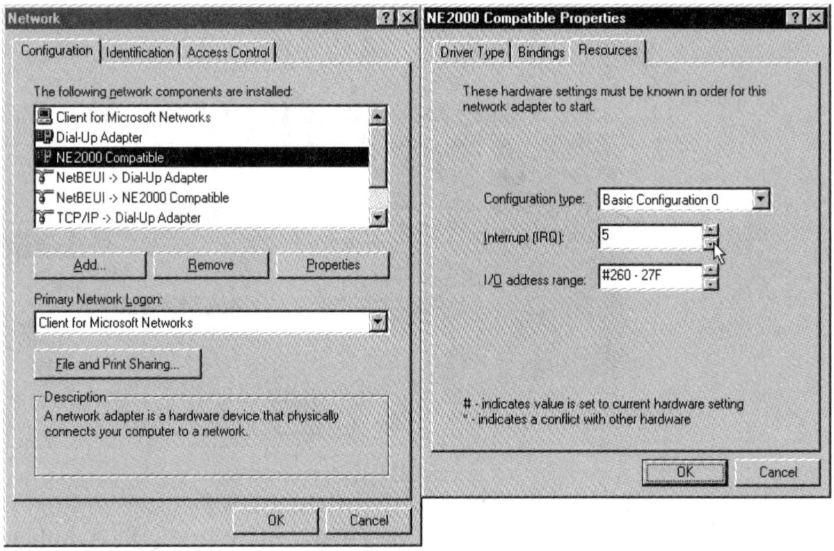

Double-click the Network Neighborhood icon, which should now appear on your desktop. If your Microsoft peer-to-peer network has been configured to share any resources, they should now be visible in the Network Neighborhood status window.

Primary Network Login

When you install a network adapter, the default network login is set for a Microsoft peer-to-peer network. A dialog box will pop up when Windows 95 starts requesting you to enter your name and password (if any) to access the network. The login dialog for the Novell server will appear after you've logged into the peer-to-peer network.

tip *If there is a Novell NetWare server on your network and you have the same username and password for both networks, you can change the default login to allow simultaneous connection to both the peer-to-peer network and the server. Just open the Control Panel Network object, click the Primary Network Login drop-down box and select "Client for NetWare Networks" as your default network login.*

If you have an account on a Novell NetWare server, and the Novell login does not appear, you may need to change the frame buffer setting for your IPX/SPX connection protocol. Open the Network object, highlight "IPX/SPX-compatible protocol," click the Properties button, and select the Advanced tab on the next screen. Highlight Frame Type in the Property list on the left and select a value other than Auto on the right. Older Novell 3.11 networks are often configured to use an Ethernet 802.3 Frame Type, whereas Novell 3.12 and later versions use the 802.2 Frame Type, as shown here:

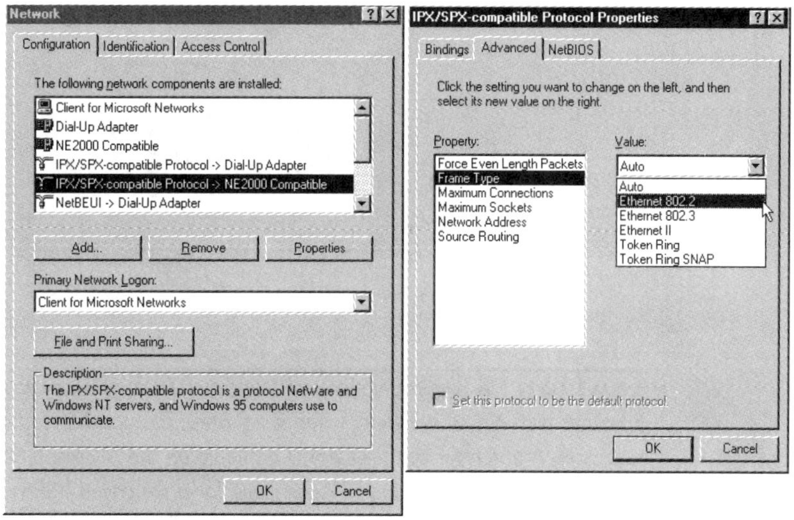

About the Network Control Tabs

As we've seen, the Configuration tab in the Network Control Panel object lists the network components that are currently installed under Windows 95. The Identification tab lists the name of your computer and the workgroup that will be recognized on the network.

tip *To avoid login problems, assign a different computer name to every workstation on your network.*

The Access Control tab, shown here, sets the security level for resources on your computer that you make available as shared resources. You can set individual passwords for each individual resource, such as folders and printers, or you can set user-level access control that grants a particular user or workgroup blanket access to all shared resources on your computer.

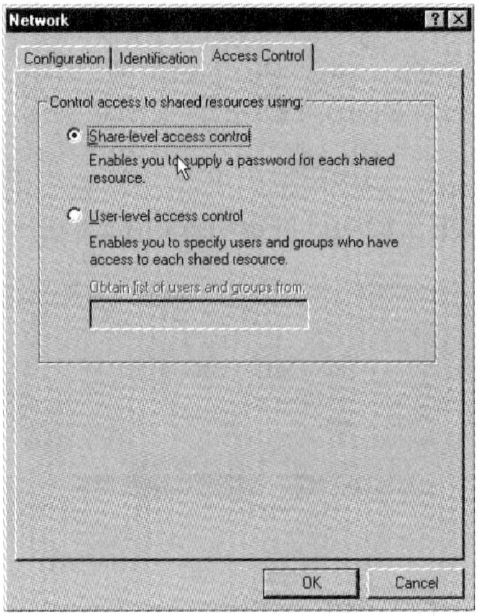

caution *A bug in the shipping Windows 95 code may cause network security breaches with Novell networks when users attempt unauthorized access to shared resources. A patch for this problem is available on the Microsoft BBS Download service, World Wide Web page, and FTP site. Look for a file called VSERVUPD.EXE. (This patch is also available in the first Windows 95 Service Pack update.)*

Sharing Network Resources

To see the shared resources available on other computers in your network, open the Network Neighborhood icon. You can double-click the name of any computer listed in the Network Neighborhood window to display a list of its shared drives, printers, and so on. You may be required to enter a password. After the connection window for the server you've selected appears on the desktop, you can right-click any listed resource to display a context menu of access options.

tip *If you know the path to a server resource, you can log into it directly from the Run button on the Start Menu. Left-click the Start Menu, click Run, and enter the network path to the resource you want to access as shown in Figure 12-1. Then click OK to open the resource on the desktop.*

Mapping a Network Drive

You can use the Map Network Drive option to map a remote network

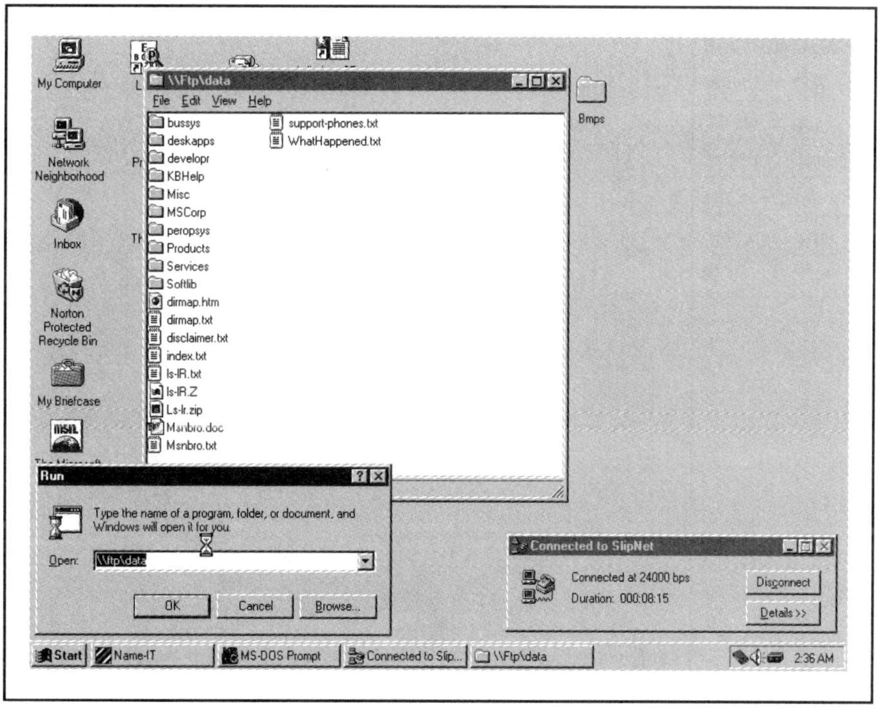

FIGURE 12-1 *Logging onto a network resource directly by clicking the Run button on the Start Menu*

drive or folder to a local drive letter on your computer.

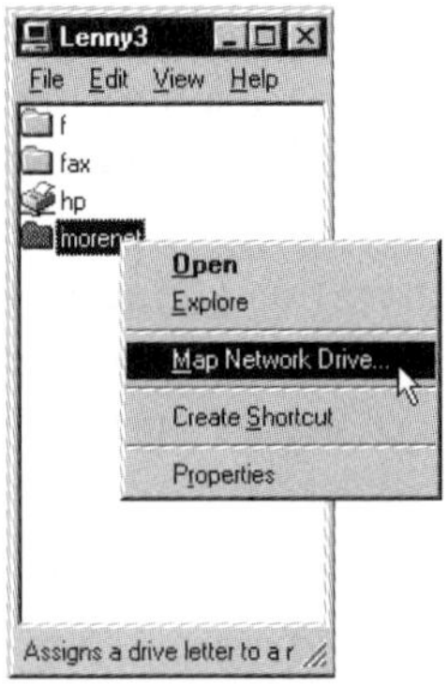

When you select this option, a dialog box appears on the desktop, displaying the available local drive letters and the path to the network connection. You may be required to enter a password after you click OK. Checking the "Reconnect at Logon" box (see Figure 12-2) automatically remaps the drive the next time you log into the network, assuming the server is still available.

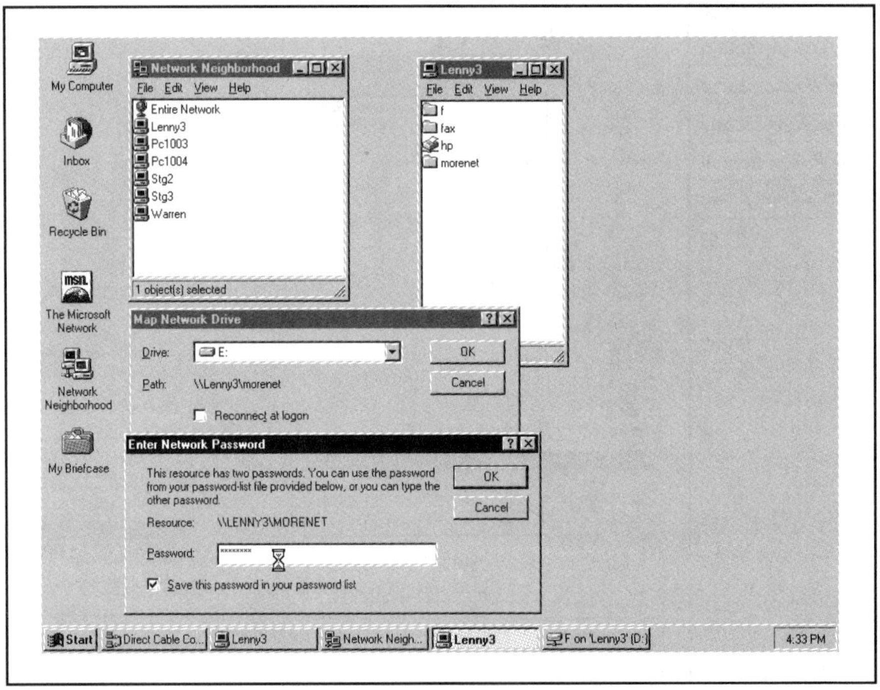

FIGURE 12-2 *The Morenet folder shared on the network is mapped to drive E on the local computer.*

Designating Local Shared Resources

To make resources on your local computer available on a peer-to-peer network or over the Internet, you must enable file and printer sharing. Open the Network Control Panel object, click the "File and Print Sharing" button, and place checkmarks next to the resource types you want to publish. Performing this operation has the effect of adding a binding to file and printer sharing to all of the network protocols currently installed in the component list. In order to conserve resources and avoid performance slowdown, you may want to examine the properties for each protocol and deselect the file and printer binding from the superfluous ones, as shown here:

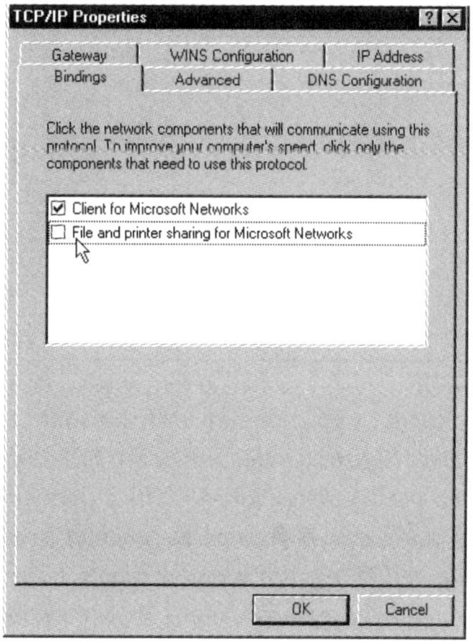

Here's some background on various configuration options:

- NetBEUI is used for file and printer sharing over Microsoft peer-to-peer networks.
- IPX\SPX-compatible can be used for file and printer sharing with a Novell NetWare or Windows NT 3.5*x* server or any NetBIOS-compatible network.
- TCP/IP is used for file and printer sharing on a TCP/IP LAN or over the Internet.

After enabling file and printer sharing, you can make local resources available over your network by right-clicking on a drive, folder, or printer, selecting the Sharing option on the context menu, and opening the Sharing tab. Selecting the Shared button on the Shared Properties tab allows you to enter a name for the resource you want to publish and a password. For drives and folders, the type of access—read only, full access, or password protected—can also be specified.

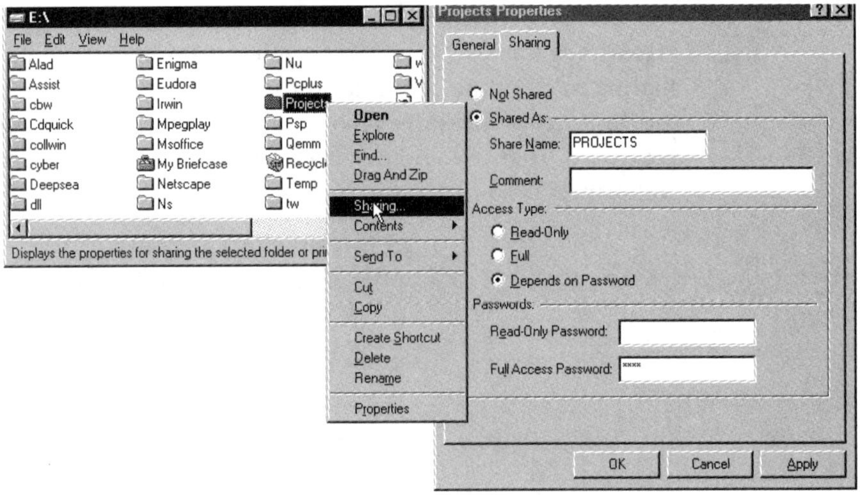

caution *As mentioned in the "About Network Control Tabs" section, a bug in the shipping Windows 95 code can nullify password protection. If you have enabled the WINS Server Registration feature of the Microsoft TCP/IP protocol, be sure to download the Win95 patch called VSERVUPD.EXE from one of the Microsoft file sites. If you don't have this patch, then anyone on the Internet who knows how may establish root access to your computer! (The patch is also available in the first Windows 95 Service Pack.) If you plan to share local resources in any large, networked environment, be sure to password protect them—especially if you are on a LAN that includes a dedicated or dial-up TCP/IP connection to the Internet.*

Sharing a Fax Modem

To make a fax/modem on a local computer available to other computers on the network, follow these steps:

1. Make sure the fax/modem and Microsoft Fax support have been previously installed.
2. Start up the Inbox with the appropriate Exchange Profile.
3. Open the Microsoft Fax Tools\Options screen from the Tools menu and click the Modem tab.

4. Select the modem you want to share in the Available Fax Modems list. Click the Set as Active Fax Modem button and then place a checkmark in the "Let other people on the network use my modem" box toward the bottom of the screen. A dialog box may open up, requesting you to designate which drive the network fax service will use. Select your Windows host drive.
5. Click the Properties button to the right of the checkbox you enabled in the last step and assign access rights and a password, as appropriate.
6. Click OK and back out of the Microsoft Fax Tools setup screen.

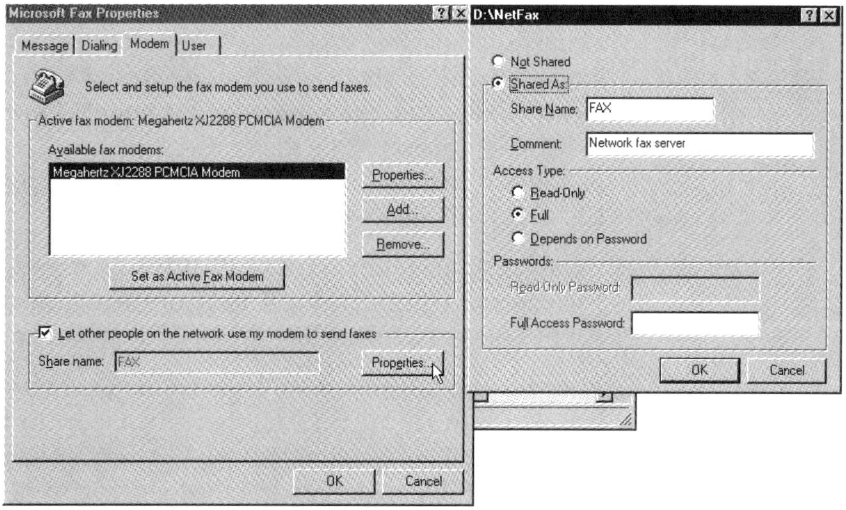

To enable access to the shared fax/modem on another computer, make sure that computer is logged into the network.

1. Open the Inbox on the remote computer and select Microsoft Fax Tools\Options from the Tools menu.
2. Select the Modem tab on the Microsoft Fax Properties screen and click the Add button to the right of the Available modems list.
3. Choose the network fax server from the "Add a Fax Modem" list.
4. In the next dialog box, enter the network name of the computer and fax modem you'll be sharing. You can find this by opening the appropriate server in the Network Neighborhood window (\\Lenny\Fax, for example) and examining its resources.
5. Click OK to close this setup dialog.

6. Select the shared modem you've just configured on the Microsoft Fax Properties Modem tab and click the Set As Active Fax/Modem button.
7. Click OK to return to the Inbox.

Sharing Fonts over the Network

If you have a large number of fonts installed on one computer in the network and your licensing agreement permits, it is possible to share those fonts with all other computers on the network.

1. Create a net directory for shared fonts (C:\NETFONT, for example) on the host computer. Copy all of the font files for the fonts you wish to share into that directory. For TrueType, copy the files with the .TTF extension found in your WINDOWS\FONTS or WINDOWS\SYSTEM directory. For PostScript, copy the contents of both the PSFONTS and PSFONTS\PFM directory into the C:\NETFONT directory.
2. Open the Fonts folder on the server. If any of the TrueType fonts you copied to the NETFONT directory are currently installed, remove them. (See Chapter 9 for details on how to do this.)
3. You will now reinstall those fonts on the server from the instances you copied to the NETFONT directory. Open the Fonts folder, choose Install New Fonts from the File menu, and open the C:\NETFONT directory. Select the fonts you want to install and make sure the "Copy Fonts to Fonts Folder" option is deselected.
4. The TrueType fonts you've selected will be installed by creating shortcuts in the server's Fonts folder.
5. Click OK and close the font installation dialog.
6. Open My Computer\Explorer to the drive where you've created the shared fonts folder (in this case C:\NETFONT) and share that folder over the network. (See the previous section for details on how to share a folder over the network.)

To install the fonts on another computer in the network:

1. Select the font server in the Network Neighborhood window, right-click the Netfont folder, and map it to a local drive letter. (Select Map Network Drive from the context menu as previously

described.) Select the Reconnect at login option toward the bottom of the Map Network Drive dialog box.

2. Open the Fonts folder on the client computer, select Install New Fonts from the File menu and browse to the mapped network drive that you've just created. Select the fonts you want, and deselect the Copy fonts to Fonts folder checkbox.
3. Click OK to install the shared fonts on the client computer.

tip *If you know the path to the shared font directory on the server, you can skip step 1 above and map the folder to a local drive letter by clicking the Network button in the Install Fonts dialog. (For instance, enter **\\SERVER\NETFONT** in the Path field.)*

To share PostScript fonts over the network, share the PSFonts folder on the server, map the folder to a local drive letter on the client, then open Adobe Type Manager on the client. Click the Add button and browse to the mapped drive for a list of the available shared fonts. If you only plan to access the fonts while connected to the network, check the Install without copying checkbox.

For more detailed information about the font installation procedures for TrueType and PostScript, refer to Chapter 9.

Establishing a Peer-to-Peer Connection over the Internet

One of the more exciting networking features built into Windows 95 is its ability to establish a peer-to-peer connection over the Internet (see Figure 12-3). It is possible to share and access drives, folders, and printers, or run programs from a remote server. You can even map the entire Microsoft FTP site to a local drive letter on your computer! We'll show you how to do this in a minute, but first, try reading through the technical explanation of how it works. This is an extremely powerful connectivity feature, and it should be used carefully.

Win95's peer-to-peer Internet connections are made possible through Microsoft's Windows Internet Name Service (WINS) built into the TCP/IP connection protocol. In order to make it work, you must establish a point-to-point protocol (PPP) connection to a server configured to offer the WINS lookup service. Unfortunately, WINS doesn't work with serial line Internet protocol (SLIP) Internet connections. WINS is a service that runs

FIGURE 12-3

A peer-to-peer connection through the Internet

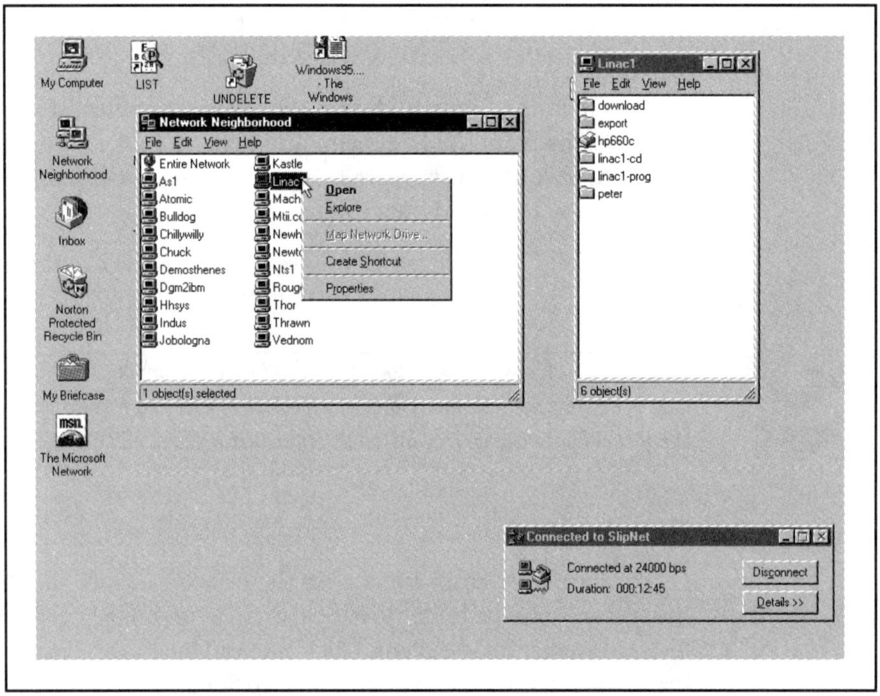

on Windows NT 3.5*x* file servers. A Windows 95 or Novell machine cannot be a WINS server. WINS clients, however, can be machines running Windows for Workgroups (with Microsoft's Win32s support), Windows 95, or Windows NT 3.5*x* servers and workstations.

When a WINS client connects to the Internet, its NetBIOS names (machine, workgroup, and user) and IP address are automatically registered with the WINS server. This makes it possible for anyone connected to that server through the Internet to achieve a direct peer-to-peer connection with any other registered computer. WINS is capable of recognizing your local computer, even if your Internet service provider assigns you a dynamic Internet protocol (IP) address that changes every time you log in.

Finding a WINS Server

If you do not have local area network (LAN) access to a Windows NT WINS server, you can take advantage of one of the public WINS servers available on the Internet. Currently, a number of Internet sites offer this service, and a number of additional sites offer their file directories and hard disk storage space, either as free resources or as a commercial service that you can subscribe to.

The best place, as of this writing, to look for a WINS server is through the WINDOWS95.COM World Wide Web page, which we discussed in Chapter 11. The author of this page has included extensive links to other Web pages that provide detailed, step-by-step solutions to a number of TCP/IP and Internet problems. You might also look for a WINS server through one of the World Wide Web search pages. (Yahoo at HTTP://WWW.YAHOO.COM is one of the most popular search sites.)

Once you locate a public WINS server, familiarize yourself with the terms under which access is granted and make a note of the server's IP address.

Installing WINS Services

To add the WINS lookup services, you must first have a dedicated cable or dial-up TCP/IP connection configured. You may want to review the first part of this chapter, and the section on Dial-Up Networking in Chapter 10 for instructions on how to do this. (If the Microsoft Network is your Internet Service Provider, see Chapter 11 for details.)

After your Internet connection has been set up, open the Network Control Panel object. Select the network adapter that's used for your TCP/IP connection (either a network card, or the Microsoft Dial-Up Adapter), click the Properties button, and select the Bindings tab. Confirm that the network adapter is bound to the TCP/IP network protocol. (If not, then enable the TCP/IP binding on that screen and click OK.)

Next select the TCP/IP protocol for your network adapter in the Components list, and select Properties. You'll see a screen with a number of tabs.

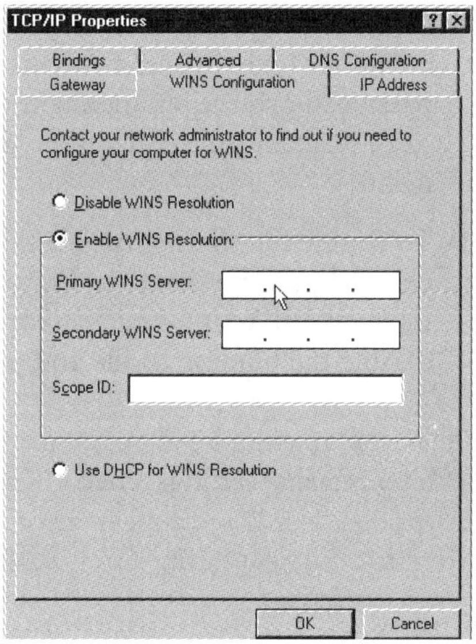

Click the Bindings tab and make sure that the Client for Microsoft Networks option appears with a checkmark next to it.

The next step is the key. Select the WINS Configuration tab and click the Enable WINS Resolution option button. In the dialog below this, enter the IP address (a four-part numerical value, separated by periods) for the primary and secondary (if there is one) WINS servers on your network. You may enter the IP addresses here for a public WINS server that publishes its resources over the Internet. Click OK to close this dialog and return to the Network Configuration tab.

File and Printer Sharing

This is an issue of great importance if you intend to establish peer-to-peer networking connections over the Internet. If you want to be able to share the resources of other computers but do not want to allow people to access your own computer, then the safest procedure is simply not to install the "File and Printer Sharing" option on the local machine. This is not always a practical solution, because you may want to make resources available to other computers on a local network. If you want to allow file sharing with other locally networked machines, but prohibit anyone on the Internet from zeroing in on you, there are several strategies you can take:

- Password protect all the files and resources that you share on your local machine. You can use the Netwatcher utility in the Programs\Accessories\System Tools group on the Start Menu to do this. Open Netwatcher and select "View by Shared Folders" from the View menu. A list of all public resources on your local computer will appear in the shared folder window. To check for password protection, highlight each resource in turn and press ALT-ENTER,or select Shared Folder Properties from the Administer menu.

- To enable file sharing on a local Microsoft peer-to-peer or Novell network, but not over the Internet, open the TCP/IP protocol for the Dial-Up Adapter or Network card, click the Bindings tab, and disable the binding to file and printer sharing.

When you've completed customizing the WINS Configuration and File and Printer Sharing settings, click OK and back out of the Network Control Panel options. You'll see a message on the screen that Windows 95 must be restarted for the new settings to take effect.

tip *You can render shared drives or folders on the network invisible in the Network Neighborhood window. To do this, simply append a dollar sign ($) to the resource's "Share Name" in the Sharing dialog box. Example, assign drive C on USER1 the share name "C$". When a network user opens the Network Neighborhood and double-clicks the USER1 computer, drive C will not be visible. However, if someone has been told that the drive is available, they can log into it directly by entering \\USER1\C$ in the Run box on the Start Menu.*

Dialing In

To finalize the settings for your peer-to-peer Internet connection, open the Dial-Up Networking folder (in the Programs\Accessories group on the Start Menu) and right-click the connection profile that you will use to dial in. (If you connect to the Internet through the Microsoft Network online service, then open the connection called The Microsoft Network in the Dial-Up Networking folder.) Open the Properties settings and click the Server Types button on the first option screen. On the Server Types option screen, place a checkmark next to the Log on to Network option. It is not necessary to enter the WINS IP addresses here, since they have already been entered through the Network Control Panel object.

Dial into the Internet. If you use the desktop Microsoft Network icon, Windows 95 is thoughtful enough to perform a security check for you and warn you when file and printer sharing is bound to the TCP/IP protocol. If you log in through a third-party ISP, this security check is not performed.

Once you connect to the Internet, your peer-to-peer networking services will be enabled. To test them, click the Run option on the Start Menu and enter **\\FTP\DATA**. This is the NetBIOS address for the Microsoft FTP server. If the WINS lookup service is working, a file window should soon open on your desktop listing all of the folders and files available on the Microsoft server. (Refer back to Figure 12-1.)

tip *If the Microsoft Network online service is your Internet provider, you'll have to compensate for an annoying bug/feature if you want to take advantage of WINS services. The Log on to Network option in the MSN Dial-Up connection profile is automatically turned off by Windows 95 every time you open up the MSN client interface. This means that you'll have to open up the Microsoft Network connection profile in the Dial-Up Networking folder and reenable this option every time you start MSN to keep WINS services active. If you want to avoid this, then don't open the MSN desktop icon to make your connection. Instead, click directly on the Microsoft Network connection profile in the Dial-Up Networking folder to gain Internet access without opening the MSN client interface.*

WINS Share Sites on the Internet

A number of people have set up public sites on the Internet: testing sites, public file archives, disk storage space, and other services. For more information and a list of currently available sites, fire up your Web browser and log on to HTTP://WWW.WINSERVE.COM.

Sharing Resources with a Friend on the Internet

If you are logged into the Internet with WINS services enabled, you can connect directly to any other computer logged in, if you know its NetBIOS name on the network. Usually, the NetBIOS name is the name of your computer found under Network Control Panel properties on the Identification tab.

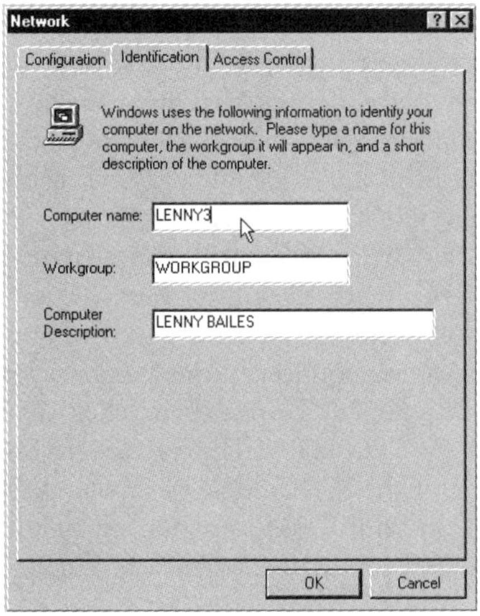

Just open the Run box on the Start Menu and type in the name of the computer you want to connect to, as in these examples:

```
\\TED
\\STARGATE\PUBLIC
```

The Network Neighborhood

If you're ready for an awe-inspiring experience with WINS, double-click your Network Neighborhood icon after establishing your Internet connection. If you've configured your system for a popular public WINS server, you'll find the computers currently logged onto your workgroup. Click the Entire Neighborhood icon and you may see the screen filled with hundreds of workgroups (see Figure 12-4). To see the shared resources available for any of the computers in your workgroup, highlight it, and double-click it. If the site administrator is on the job, you'll have to enter a password before the resource window opens on your desktop.

note *If you open Network Neighborhood and see no workgroups listed, or get a message that the network is unavailable, check with the administrator of your WINS server. You may have to change the name of the workgroup for your local computer.*

Network Neighborhood Behavior

You may be somewhat puzzled as to the behavior of the Network Neighborhood. At times, you may be connected to other computers through direct cable or on the Internet, and those machines will not appear in the

FIGURE 12-4

Click the Entire Network icon to see all workgroups connected to your WINS server.

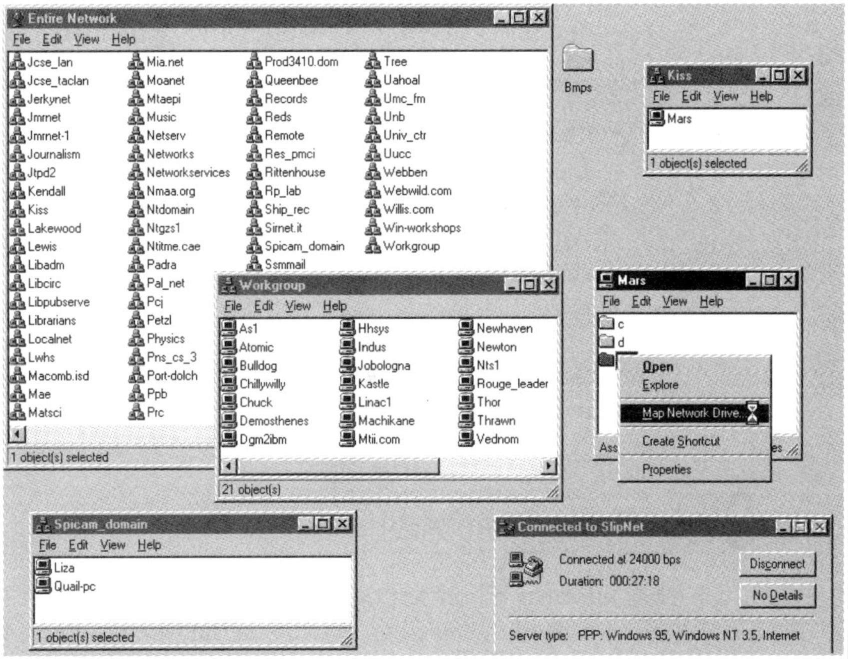

window. The rules are basically as follows:

- For a direct cable connection to show up in the Network Neighborhood window, your local computer must be a guest dialing into a dedicated network, or as the host, must also have a dedicated network adapter card.
- For your computer to appear in the Network Neighborhood for a TCP/IP Internet connection, you must have enabled "File and Printer sharing," and you must have enabled the advanced option that turns your machine into a Browse Master for the network. Our advice is *not* to enable this option, unless you want everyone on the Internet who uses your WINS server to see your computer listed in their Network Neighborhood windows!

Mapping Network Resources to a Local Drive

The procedure for mapping a folder shared over the Internet to a local drive letter is the same as for any other network connection.

1. Log into the server through the Run menu or open it in Network Neighborhood.
2. Right-click the resource you want to add to your local computer and select the Map Network Drive option from the context menu.
3. Enter the password to the resource, if one is required, and click OK.
4. The Map Network Drive dialog box will pop up (refer back to Figure 12-2). Choose an available drive letter and click OK. If you want to reassign this resource to the same drive letter whenever you log onto the network, check the Reconnect at Logon option at the bottom of the dialog box.

The drive or folder you've mapped will now be accessible in My Computer\Explorer and in the File\Open and File\Save windows of your Windows and DOS applications.

Direct Cable Connections

For information on setting up and using the Microsoft Direct Cable Connection option, refer to the section on the Direct Cable Connection utility in Chapter 5.

Converting Direct Cable Connection into a Two-Way, Peer-to-Peer Network

Normally, when you use Win95's Direct Cable Connection, one machine is designated the guest and the other machine is designated the host. The host user does not have access to shared resources on the guest computer, although local work can continue while the guest uses shared resources in the background.

An undocumented feature (or bug) in Direct Cable Connection allows the host machine to access resources on the guest anyway, establishing a true peer-to-peer network connection. Here's how to exploit this quirk.

1. Set up a Direct Cable Connection with one machine as the guest and the other as the host.
2. Share appropriate folders and other resources on the host computer (see the early part of this chapter), then log into this machine through the guest computer. (Open Direct Cable Connection in the Accessories group, and click the Connect button.)
3. After the connection is established, Click View Host in the guest computer's Direct Cable Connection window, to make all shared resources appear on the desktop.
4. Log the guest computer off the direct cable connection without closing the shared resources on the desktop.
5. On the guest machine, share the resources or folders that you want to make available to the other computer.
6. Now, here's the trick: reconfigure Direct Cable Connection to reverse the host/guest settings. Turn the guest machine into the host, close Direct Cable Connection on the old host machine, and reconfigure it as the guest.
7. Log into the new host from the new guest machine. The folders and resources you've shared will appear, as expected, when you click the View Host button.

The machine which is now the host will still show the shared resources on its desktop that were found when this machine was the guest. When you double-click one of these leftover resources, you'll get a message that it is no longer available on the network. Windows 95 will offer to use the Dial-Up Networking feature to connect to the resource through a modem. Answer

No in this dialog box, and you'll find that the old shared resource becomes available again through the Direct Cable Connection. Thus, either machine on the cable connection may access resources on the other.

chapter 13

Multimedia Under Windows 95

- What's new in Windows 95 support for multimedia
- Necessary hardware
- Installing multimedia peripherals
- Using Windows 95's multimedia utilities
- Hot multimedia titles
- ...and more

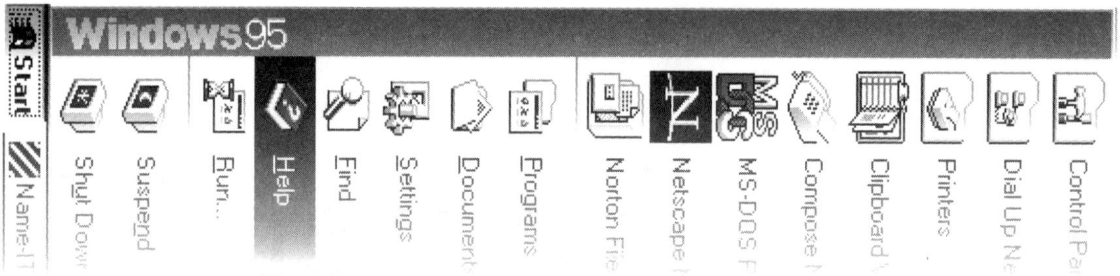

As you may know, *multimedia* is the use of integrated text, graphics, animation, audio and video in an integrated single computer environment. Windows 95 was specifically designed to make multimedia applications more accessible than previous PC operating systems did. Multimedia greatly expands the personal element of computing, giving you new ways to assimilate and distribute information.

Behaviorists tell us that we are more likely to remember things that are spelled out and demonstrated. The multimedia capabilities of Windows 95 allow us to watch movies, listen to accompanying narrative, and link our eyes and ears to the learning process. Multimedia discs are likely to change how we assimilate information. They won't replace books, but they will make the contained information come alive. At the same time, multimedia provides the opportunity for "ordinary" people to create compound documents that contain sound, pictures and, animation, all embedded within the text to ultimately enhance the message.

Windows officially recognized multimedia with version 3.1, released in 1992. Since then, Windows multimedia users have often traveled a long, dark path. Adding necessary hardware was often a nightmare, as most users had never even opened the PC case. Getting software to operate correctly was a dice toss; users often needed to reconfigure their systems to suit each individual title. If you got the hardware and the software to work—and work together—the program could be unbearably slow. Some people contended that driving to the library and looking up something by hand provided a faster path to the information than using a Windows-based Multimedia encyclopedia. Throughout, there was the reality that multimedia software looked sharper and performed better in the Macintosh environment.

Windows 95 provides dramatic improvements, and offers a platform for new entertainment opportunities, with its more intelligent integration of multimedia. The 32-bit architecture allows larger slices of digital video and audio to run faster, yet occupy less storage space.

In previous versions of Windows, game programmers were limited by the necessity of routing all video functions through a 16-bit graphics device interface (GDI). Under DOS, programmers have long been able to write directly to video hardware, squeezing better performance and more impressive effects out of their products. In Windows 95, an interface called Direct Draw will eventually provide similar fast access to video hardware. This application program interface (API) is not included in the first version of Windows 95, but right now Direct Draw functionality can be embedded into individual applications through the Win95 Game Software Developer's Kit. (The Hover game included on the Windows 95 CD is an example.) You'll read more about Direct Draw later in this chapter.

Windows 95 Advantages

Windows 95 supports many new multimedia features, including enhanced support for digital video, sound, and CD-ROM control. There's an AutoPlay feature for music CDs, easy recognition of hardware through plug-and-play, new APIs for better multimedia performance, and APIs for 3-D image rendering. Let's look at these features in more detail.

Enhanced Support for Digital Video

In the past, Microsoft's Video for Windows was a separate technology from the Windows operating system. The Microsoft Media Player under Windows 3.*x* was also limited in its playback functionality by the physical size of Audio-Visual Interleave (.AVI) files. In Windows 95, full-length .AVI movies can be played without using third-party players and drivers. In earlier versions of Windows, digital video display depended on 16-bit drivers for reading, decompressing, and displaying data on the screen. Windows 95 allows larger video segments at deeper color depths to play smoothly. The Win95 Media Control Interface allows all Windows applications to manipulate multimedia devices (including CD-ROM drives, sound cards, and animation players). These devices can be run in concert or independently. Windows 95 makes it easy to embed or link video clips to documents or attach them to system events. Portions of full-length movies can also be captured and saved to disk. With the addition of appropriate video hardware, input can be directly captured from or recorded to an ordinary VCR.

Enhanced Support for Sound and MIDI

In Windows 95, a number of audio compression and decompression schemes (referred to as *codecs*) have been incorporated to pack more waveform sound information into smaller files on your hard disk. Enhanced support is also included for the Musical Instrumental Digital Interface (MIDI) used to record, encode and play back poly-voiced instrumental music. Windows 95 includes a number of recorded MIDI compositions as part of its desktop sound schemes feature. In addition to supporting the General MIDI Standard, which is an industry standard, Windows 95 includes a new technology called *MIDI streams*. This technology allows a MIDI-compatible sound card to play complex MIDI sequences with minimal CPU usage.

Enhanced CD-ROM Support

Windows 95 includes a built-in CD-ROM file system (CDFS) with internal caching to improve the read/playback speed of CD data. CDFS is a 32-bit file system designed to read files from CD-ROM drives as quickly and efficiently as possible. The dedicated CD Player, which you'll find in the Multimedia folder, has a sophisticated feature set that includes random play, programmable playback order, and the ability to save program lists that you define. Windows 95 also supports the new Sony/Phillips enhanced CD format. This format supports CDs that mix data, audio, and video that can be played on standard stereo CD units as well as on computer CD-ROM drives. Windows 95 also includes extended support for CD-ROM drives that read Kodak PhotoCDs and video CDs.

AutoPlay

The AutoPlay feature lets users insert a Win95-aware compact disc in the CD-ROM drive and have it automatically run a specified program or start playing music automatically. When a disk is inserted in a CD-ROM drive, Windows 95 automatically searches it for a file called AUTORUN.INF. If this file exists, Windows 95 opens it and follows configuration instructions. This improvement makes the setup of multimedia applications and games much easier. CD vendors may set up an auto-installation routine that bypasses the need for locating specific directories or launching programs manually. (See Figure 13-1.)

FIGURE 13-1 Windows 95-aware CDs automatically play a vendor-specified menu or startup program whenever they are inserted into a CD-ROM drive. ■

Plug-and-Play Hardware Support

Plug-and-play hardware support in Windows 95 lets you install and upgrade sound and CD-ROM components simply by putting cards into slots and connecting cables. For many supported devices, it's no longer necessary to set jumpers, worry about address conflicts, or install third-party device management software. Windows 95 automatically detects and configures your hardware. The magic of Win95's plug-and-play support extends not only to newer machines with plug-and-play BIOS and PCI peripherals, but also to older motherboards running ordinary 8-bit and 16-bit ISA peripherals. The Device Manager included in the Windows 95 control panel presents a birds-eye view of the configuration for all your peripheral devices, allowing you to troubleshoot and reconfigure hardware that escapes the built-in auto-configuration. (See Chapter 15 for more information on Windows 95 support for plug-and-play hardware.)

New APIs for Better Multimedia Performance

Windows 95 includes a new graphic display architecture that provides high performance levels for game animation, rendering of 2-D and 3-D graphics, and for video playback. The new architecture consists of a series of APIs tuned to exploit hardware acceleration features built into high-end video cards. These APIs also provide software emulation of acceleration features on lower-end cards. Some of these API features are integrated directly into the shipping code of the first Windows 95 release. Other features are implemented through Win95 development kits, and specifications for third-party video drivers. Win95's 32-bit multitasking and multithreading features facilitate the simultaneous presentation of high-quality sound and video.

APIs for 3-D Image Rendering

For rendering 3-D images under Windows 95, Microsoft has licensed two APIs called Reality Lab and Open GL. The Hover game located on the Windows 95 CD, and 3-D Pinball, included in Microsoft Plus!, are examples of games that use this technology. The advanced APIs allow games to display crisp 3-D graphics on current video hardware. Future Windows 95 applications that make use of 3-D Direct Draw, Reality Lab and Open GL will be more efficient at executing 3-D rotation and image translation than older Windows 3.*x* programs.

What About Movies?

The software support for MPEG video playback technology, which was to be implemented in DCI, is expected in a future Windows 95 version. This feature, analogous to the Media Player's capability to handle .AVI video, will allow movies encoded in the MPEG format to play back on standard VESA and PCI video cards in large screen windows at 24 frames per second with 11KHz audio. This high performance may only be obtained on machines with 90MHz Pentium CPUs or better. The current shipping version of Windows 95 can use Windows 3.*x* software to play back movies encoded in the MPEG format or Apple's QuickTime at lower performance rates. See later in this chapter for more information on playing back MPEG, AutoDesk FLI/FLC, and Apple QuickTime video.

DCI vs. Direct Draw—What's Happening to the Multimedia Interface?

Microsoft's original plans for multimedia and Windows 95 included an API called the Display Control Interface (DCI). DCI was to include integrated hardware and software support for the MPEG video standard. It was also to include acceleration routines for rendering 2-D and 3-D graphics, and a series of game-oriented programming libraries (referred to as *WinG*). In the later stages of the Win95 beta test, it became apparent that DCI was not going to provide the kind of direct access to video hardware necessary for DOS-like graphics performance. Consequently, DCI was replaced by a new Windows 95 display architecture.

The new graphic subsystem that was actually included in Windows 95 has several separate components that address the requirements of Windows applications. The GDI that controlled screen display in Windows 3.*x* has been enhanced to include 32-bit support for rendering and manipulating two-dimensional bitmap images. This subsystem is now referred to as the *graphics device interface-device driver interface*, or GDI-DDI. To complement it, Microsoft has developed a method of addressing video hardware directly called Direct Draw.

The Direct Draw API allows games and digital video players to write 2-D display information directly to a video card's frame buffer. Microsoft refers to Direct Draw as the future composition engine for 2-D and 3-D video display. It allows applications to manipulate video memory easily, taking full advantage of the page flipping, blitting, transparency, and color-and-space conversion capabilities of display hardware. Direct Draw also lets digital-video playback take advantage of hardware features included on advanced graphics adapters. Most notably, .AVI animation playbacks can be scaled and enlarged on the screen without degradation.

For an application to bypass the GDI-DDI layer and make use of Direct Draw, your video card must use a display driver that supports the Direct Draw API. Currently, there are few driver sets available that include Direct Draw support. Added driver support is expected for many graphic cards in the first maintenance release of Windows 95 (now being referred to as the Windows 95 Service Pack).

Your application or game must be programmed to make calls supported by the Direct Draw API. This support is included in the Windows 95 Game SDK (Software Development Kit) shipped to game manufacturers in September 1995. The API support will also be directly incorporated into the shipping code of Windows 95 beginning with the first maintenance release.

Shopping for a Multimedia PC

Here are Microsoft's recommendations and requirements for a multimedia PC:

- CD-ROM drive: double-speed or better.
- Sound card: 16-bit with MIDI support, at the minimum.
- Video card: support for 800×600 display, 16-bit color depth, and 32-bit VESA or PCI bus. PCI is preferable.
- Monitor: support for 800×600 display, 24-bit color depth.

To this list, the authors of this book would add the following:

- Motherboard/CPU: 486DX/2 66MHz CPU at the minimum, with VESA local bus or PCI support (to take advantage of high-speed sound, SCSI, and video compression).
- Hard disk/hard disk controller: EIDE 32-bit VESA local bus or PCI disk controller/hard disk, or SCSI-2 controller and hard disk. These combinations are capable of sustaining data transfer rates of 8000KB per second or higher. (EIDE drives of this type are sometimes referred to as *PIO Mode 3 capable*. PCI SCSI-2 and SCSI-3 drives can achieve even faster data transfer rates.)
- Speakers and headphones.

Microsoft recommends that you "balance" your multimedia PC, even at the expense of horsepower. Playback places heavy demands on many parts of the computer, from the CD-ROM (for reading data), to the hard disk (for writing data), to the CPU (for decompressing), and to the video and audio subsystems (for playing). A fast CPU does not guarantee a great playback system. A chain (or computer system) is only as good as its weakest link.

A double-speed CD-ROM is the minimum you'll want to use for multimedia. Your drive should be capable of a data transfer rate no less than 300KB per second. Your CD-ROM should also support the multisession Kodak PhotoCD format, which means that it will read disks with photos added on a cumulative basis. Most current multimedia titles assume a 2× data rate. At present, most multimedia programs don't exploit the capabilities of quad-speed and 6× drives, but programming standards are changing.

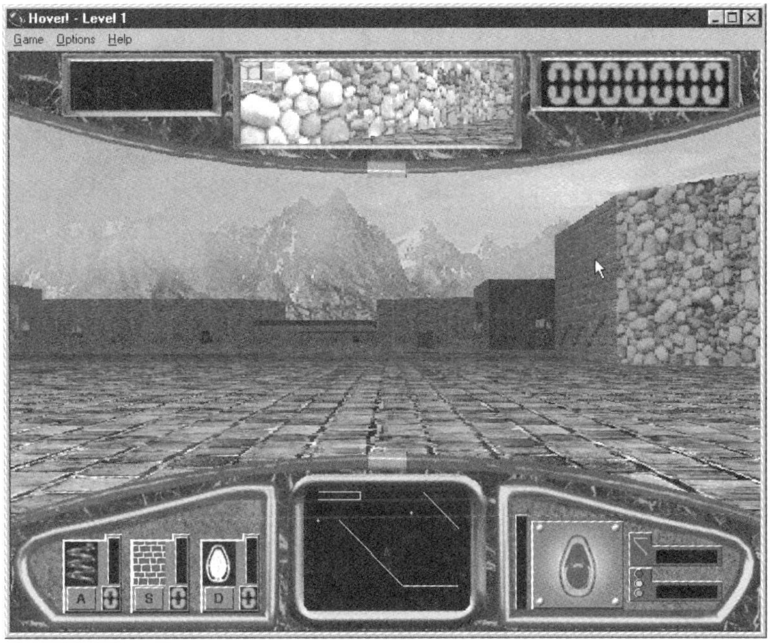

FIGURE 13-2 *Microsoft's Hover illustrates the new Direct Draw 3-D API. For maximum performance benefits you'll need to install the Direct Draw-aware video driver supplied by your video card vendor or bundled in the first Windows 95 maintenance release.*

You can expect to see packages that benefit significantly from 4× and 6× data rate hardware in next year's crop of software.

The 16-bit audio and MIDI capabilities should be a feature of any sound card that you consider. Although an 8-bit sound card works on Windows 95, the quality isn't great. Instead, choose a sound card with a 16-bit digital-to-analog converter (DAC) for playback, and for developers, a 16-bit analog-to-digital converter (ADC) for recording.

Microsoft also recommends a system that supports stereo sound and 8, 11, 22, and 44KHz waveforms. CD-quality sound uses 44KHz. The 11 and 22KHz waveforms are sampled less frequently. The low sample-rate is often used for compressed waveforms that save CPU processing time and hard disk space. The 8KHz waveform is used for a new capability in Windows 95 called *Truespeech compression*. The Truespeech format is meant primarily to reproduce voice messages attached to system events or documents. For best results with sounds recorded at the 44KHz sampling rate, you should use a system that has a 486DX2/66 CPU or better. (In a pinch, a 486DX/33 CPU can also provide acceptable performance.)

Features to Look for in Sound Cards

SUPPORT FOR GENERAL MIDI FORMAT

This means that the MIDI files you play and record will be universally compatible with other systems.

INCLUSION OF SAMPLE SOUNDS

Sound cards imitate musical instruments either by simple 16-bit emulation programmed into a chip, a 32-bit process known as wave table synthesis, or by including actual sample sounds from real musical instruments. This last method is the best way to obtain real musical fidelity.

A STANDARD MIDI PORT

This is a 15-pin connector that allows you to plug in a keyboard or other MIDI recording device.

SUPPORT FOR MIDI STREAMS

This is a new Windows 95 feature that allows your card to play back without consuming large quantities of CPU time. The result is better multimedia performance.

WAVE TABLE SYNTHESIS

This feature, found in newer Sound Cards allows more faithful simulation of the true sound of musical instruments.

The performance of a computer with local bus or PCI video is about ten times better than one without a local bus, assuming everything else on the computers is equal. Without local bus video, the display of video data in current multimedia titles and games is sluggish and unsatisfactory. (See Chapter 15 for more information on PC bus issues.)

A video card with 1MB of RAM can support a color depth of 64,000 colors (16-bit display) at a screen resolution of 800×600. In this color depth, photographs and paintings display with a higher degree of realism than the standard 256-color palette supported by an ordinary VGA card. There are many games and CDs programmed to display themselves in 32,000 and 64,000 color modes. However, for compatibility with the high-end industry standard called TrueColor, you must use a video card capable of a 24-bit (16 million color) display. Also make sure that your video card is capable of rendering high-resolution screen displays in a non-interlaced format. Non-interlaced display modes avoid the annoying screen flicker common in older EGA and VGA monitors. (See Chapters 15 and 16 for more information on compatible video hardware for Windows 95.)

A 24-bit display monitor is necessary for TrueColor support, and will offer far better video reproduction than a simple VGA monitor. Your monitor should accommodate a screen resolution of 800×600 pixels or higher and be capable of a non-interlaced screen display. The display font should also be crisp and readable in high-resolution modes. Generally, these monitor capabilities are tied in to three performance specifications called *horizontal scan rate, vertical scan rate,* and *dot pitch*. Minimal specifications for Windows 95 are horizontal scan rate, 30 to 35KHz; vertical scan rate, 60Hz; and dot pitch, .28mm. (You can do better than this—see Chapter 16 for details.)

You need speakers to use multimedia effectively, unless you don't mind wearing headphones while using the computer. (This tends to preclude using the telephone or carrying on conversations during the multimedia experience.) Many people go out and purchase tinny plastic speakers with built-in preamplifiers. We recommend avoiding the low-end on this item. If you want to economize, you can probably find a pair of wooden 15 to 25-watt stereo speakers in a thrift shop that give you better sound than the cut-rate multimedia specials you find at swap meets. The rated, unamplified capacity of a Creative Labs Sound Blaster 16 is only 4 watts, but in our experience, this seems to satisfactorily drive a pair of 20-watt, 4-ohm speakers.

Installing Multimedia Peripherals

To add multimedia peripherals such as a CD-ROM drive, CD-ROM controller, sound card, or video capture board before installing Windows 95, simply place the peripherals into the appropriate slots and drive bays in your computer and connect the appropriate cables.

For a CD-ROM drive and/or controller card, if Windows 95 has not yet been installed, boot your current version of DOS, and run the appropriate configuration software supplied by the vendor. (See Chapters 4 and 7 for information on how to switch your CD-ROM drive from using real-mode DOS drivers to protected-mode drivers after Windows 95 has been installed.)

For other peripherals, it may not be necessary to run third-party software intended for Windows 3.*x*. Simply place them in the machine and proceed to the installation of Windows 95. If your peripherals are not recognized and supported automatically, then you may wish to run third-party installation software. (See Chapters 4 and 7 for more details.)

In the case of your sound card, if you haven't already installed the manufacturer's software, you can install Windows 95 first. Your sound card may be detected automatically during the operating system installation. After Windows 95 is up and running, if the sound card has not been recognized, open the Add New Hardware component of the Control Panel, answer No to the prompt for Windows 95 to perform an automatic hardware search, select "Sound, video, and game controllers" from the Hardware types list, and click the Next button. If your card appears on the manufacturer's list on the next screen, Windows 95 will install protected-mode drivers for it. (See Chapter 4 for more details on installing peripherals with the Add New Hardware utility.)

Finally, you can install the third-party software that comes with your sound card in order to take advantage of any bundled multimedia utilities.

caution *Be on guard during third-party installation procedures that newer Win95 versions of multimedia drivers are not overwritten by older ones. Recent versions of software from Creative Labs and other vendors will warn you before replacing a newer driver in the WINDOWS\SYSTEM directory with an older one, as shown here:*

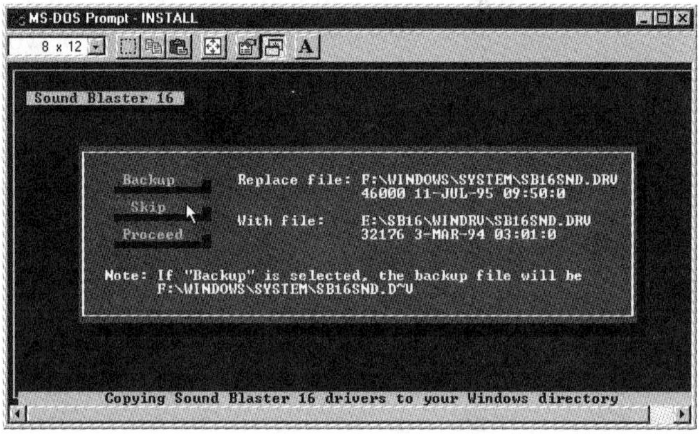

If your third-party software overwrites drivers in this directory, it may be necessary for you to use the Win95 Add New Hardware utility again, to restore Windows 95's built-in multimedia support.

Using Your Headphones and Speakers

If you decide to use headphones, make sure to plug them into the sound card itself and not the front of the CD-ROM drive if you want to get the sound from a multimedia program. The front jack on the CD-ROM drive is fine for listening to audio CDs, but won't reproduce MIDI or .WAV files.

If you don't get any sound from an audio CD when the headphones or speakers are plugged into your sound card, then a tiny patch cable used to route output from the CD-ROM drive to the sound card may be missing. If adjusting the CD-slider in the Volume Control doesn't work, this confirms the problem. Internal CD-ROM units may use a variety of proprietary cables and plugs to channel their output to a sound card. Sometimes this cable connection is omitted during installation. External CD-ROM players are often configured to route audio CD sound through the line-in channel instead of the CD-slider. A stereo cable is run from the line-out jacks on the CD-ROM unit to the tiny plug line-in jack on the sound card. If adjusting the CD-slider in the Win95 Volume Control does not produce output from an audio CD, try adjusting the Line-In slider. (See the "Volume Control" section later in this chapter for detailed information.)

Other Connections

Some notebook computers are shipped with an accompanying docking station that contains a CD-ROM drive. Plugging the computer into the docking station usually activates a series of ports and other I/O devices mounted on the rear of the docking station. With these systems, CD-ROM audio through the docking station output jack may not be enabled. The following procedure may allow you to control or mix CD audio on such a system.

1. Purchase a stereo male-to-male tiny plug (1/8-inch) cable at an electronics supply store.
2. Plug your notebook computer into its docking station. Connect one end of the male-to-male tiny plug cable to the external headphone jack on your CD-ROM drive. Connect the other end of the tiny male-to-male plug cable to the line-in jack that is physically located on your notebook computer.
3. Connect your speakers or headphones to the output jack mounted on the back or side of the docking station.
4. Play an audio CD and experiment with the settings of the external volume control located on your CD-ROM drive. Use the line-in slider of the Windows 95 Volume Control to mix output to your speakers or headphone.

This same procedure can be used to connect the output of an internal CD-ROM drive in a desktop computer to the line-in jack of its sound card, but you'll need a longer cable. You can use this procedure on a desktop machine if it's inconvenient to open the case and install the proprietary CD cable.

Working with Sound

Windows 95 reproduces sound for several supported formats: MIDI sequencer (.MID and .RMI), waveform (.WAV), and CD audio. In addition, you can still play third-party sound formats that were developed for DOS PCs and for other computing platforms. We'll see later on in the chapter how third-party utilities let you work with sounds in DOS formats like .CMF and .VOC, Macintosh .SND and .MOV files, and Amiga .MOD files.

CD Audio

The audio CD Player is part of Windows 95, and can serve as a replacement playback unit with your CD-ROM drive, if your regular stereo is in the shop.

To use the audio CD Player, follow these steps:

1. Place the CD in the CD-ROM drive.
2. From the Start Menu, open the CD Player, located under Programs\Accessories\Multimedia.
3. To start playing the first track, click the right-arrow Play button in the top row of CD Player controls.

note *If the Win95 Autoplay feature is enabled, the CD Player will start automatically when a music CD is inserted into the drive. The CD Player shows an LED display of elapsed play time in its status window. The two rows of buttons to the right are a standard series of CD controls, as shown in Figure 13-3.*

The Artist and Title areas allow you to enter information for a program of tracks that you create. Other options include Continuous Play, Random Play, and an Intro Play preview feature. These features are available on the Options menu. If you select Intro Play, the CD cycles through the first few bars of each song. When you hear something you want to play all the way through, simply deselect the Intro Play button. (You can adjust the length of the intro clip from one to fifteen seconds through the preferences box under the Options menu.)

Here's how to define a play list for your CD:

1. From the Disc menu, select Edit Play List.
2. Use the Add and Remove buttons to specify the play list.

FIGURE 13-3

CD Player buttons and settings. Select Edit Play List from the Disc menu of the CD Player to define a play list.

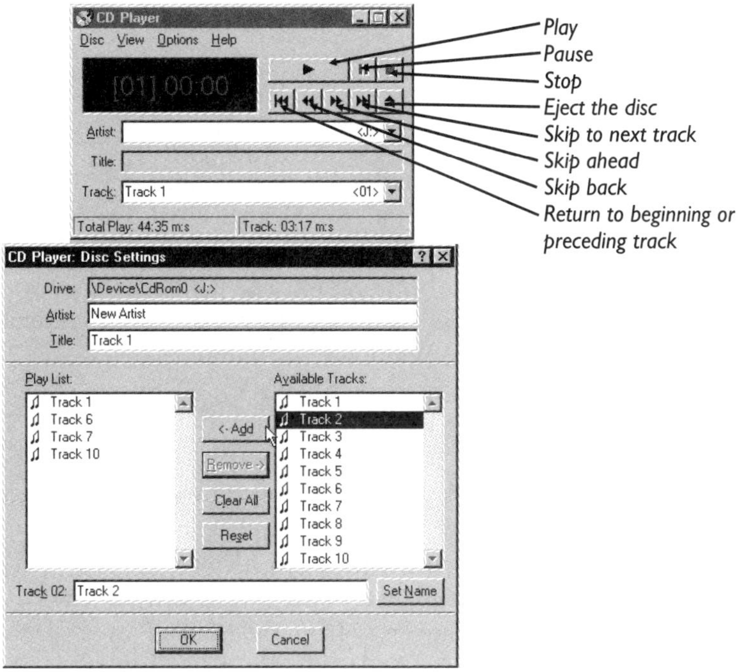

The volume of CD playback can be adjusted by selecting Volume Control from the View menu. Your CD output may be controlled through either the CD-slider or the Line-In slider. (Refer to the previous section for a discussion of how to determine which slider to use.)

The CD Player can be set to terminate play when you close the program, or continue to play tracks sequentially. This option is toggled from the Options\Preferences menu.

You can essentially "multitask" with the CD Player, using different applications as you listen to music. You can format a disk, print a document, or perform any other task that doesn't require a CD-ROM drive. If you have tied system functions to sounds, these will play concurrently with the CD.

The Media Player

The Media Player is located in the Programs\Accessories\Multimedia group on the Start Menu. It is a simple playback device that looks like this:

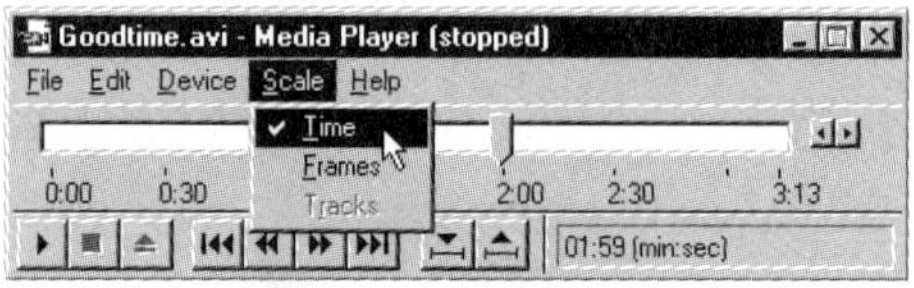

The Media Player has a simple, rectangular interface outfitted with VCR-like controls: Start/Pause, Stop, Eject, Skip to Previous Mark, Skip to Next Mark, Rewind, and Fast Forward. The two buttons to the right of these controls let you mark the beginning and end of a selection to be played or copied to another program. The sliding timer shows where you are in selected tracks (for CD), frames (for video), or time increments.

By default, Windows 95 configures the Media Player to handle three file types: waveform sound (.WAV), Microsoft audio-video interleave (.AVI), and MIDI sequencer (.MID, .RMI). If you have a CD-ROM drive, CD audio is added as a fourth type.

The Media Player can control most of the multimedia devices on your system used to play sound or video recordings. (Exceptions and instructions for working with third-party formats are provided later in this chapter.) To play a multimedia file or activate a device (such as a videodisc player), choose the appropriate entry from the Media Player's Device menu. To install new devices use the Add New Hardware option in the Control Panel to add appropriate drivers.

Multiple copies of the Media Player can be opened to play back more than one file simultaneously. Two sound files in the same format can't be played concurrently, but you can play CD audio, a MIDI selection and a .WAV file simultaneously. Multiple video files can be opened and played concurrently, but only one clip at a time will be accompanied by sound (the one in the active display window).

MIDI Support

MIDI is a widely recognized interface standard that allows music synthesizers and musical instruments to be connected to your computer. MIDI is both a hardware and a software standard. It condenses input into a special digitized file that contains an encoded description of music and sounds. MIDI, as a musician's tool, is widely supported by all advanced musical equipment, from pianos to piccolos.

To play a MIDI sound file, follow these steps:

1. Open the Media Player.
2. From the Device menu, select MIDI Sequencer.

3. From the dialog box that appears, choose the file you want to play.
4. Click the Play button.

In Windows 3.*x*, the mapping of MIDI instruments to particular recording channels was accomplished through a Control Panel applet called Midimap. In Windows 95, this feature is accessed by loading a particular MIDI file into the Media Player and selecting Properties from the Device menu. (You can also access this screen by opening the Multimedia object in the Control Panel and selecting the MIDI tab.) The MIDI Properties screen allows you to select an existing map of MIDI instruments and channels, or to design your own custom map. In order to do this, you may need updated third-party MIDI software containing instrument profiles written in the new Windows 95 format. The default drivers Microsoft includes for standard sound card devices are not as flexible as the Midimap configurations that were supplied in Windows 3.*x*.

tip *If you plan to create a custom MIDI instrument configuration, first back up the default map configured for your sound card. From the MIDI Properties screen, select Custom Configuration and click the Configure button. On the next screen, click the Save As button and type in a new name for this copy of your default MIDI profile.*

Videotape Support

Windows 95 includes built-in support for common multimedia authoring devices such as laser discs and videocassette recorders (VCRs). This makes it easy to set up a computer for single-frame or frame-by-frame capture, a process in which the author captures digital video data one frame at a time, usually to be compressed later. This is a slow process, but it is absolutely the best way to get the best possible quality of digital video.

Frame-accurate control of the VCR is also important for recording broadcast-quality special effects to use in commercials, movies, television programs, music videos, and so on.

Windows 95 provides VCR control services through the MCI VISCA device driver, which is based on the MCI command set for VCRs. This device driver is used with a video capture or overlay card to control SONY® VISCA-compatible videotape recorders, such as the CVD-1000 VDECK. The VISCA-compatible driver controls the parts of the VCR, including the tape transport, channel tuners, and VCR input and output channels.

note *The specs on the VDECK show it to be accurate to about +/– one frame. In reality, the authors have found it is accurate, at best, to +/– three frames. With cheap tape, the accuracy may even drop to plus or minus 1/2 second.*

To play the contents of a videotape on your computer, you must connect the video and audio outputs from your VCR to the video capture or overlay card of your computer, and to the audio inputs of your computer. You might also need to install an MCI digital-video device driver. The Advanced tab for Multimedia settings in the Control Panel shows a number of devices. Double-click the Media Control Devices icon, select a listed device and click on Properties to enable Win95's built-in support for a listed MCI peripheral. (See Figure 13-4.)

Inserting and Linking Multimedia to Documents

The Media Player allows you to use OLE to insert multimedia files in a document. To do this, load a file or mark a selection in the Media Player, and select Copy Object (CTRL-C) from the Edit menu. To insert the file in another application, choose Paste or Paste Special from the application's Edit

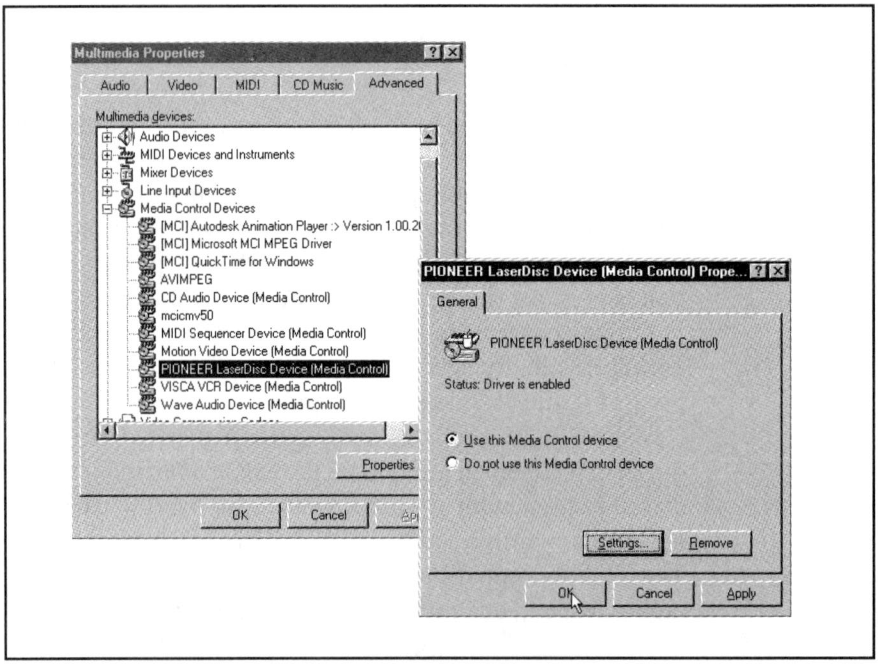

FIGURE 13-4 *Media Control devices can be activated from a list on the Advanced tab of the Control Panel's Multimedia settings.*

menu. Microsoft's Media Control Interface (MCI) pops up a control bar to play back the file when you double-click it in the target application. This feature can be toggled on and off by selecting Edit\Options in the Media Player and selecting the "Control Bar on Placement" button. If this option is checked at the time you copy the selection to the Clipboard, the control bar will appear in the target application. This option can also be used to assign a caption to the inserted multimedia file in the target document.

Playing Back System Sounds without an Audio Card

Although you generally can't use the Media Player without a sound card, a simple trick allows you to reroute the playback of Windows 95 system events to your PC's built-in speaker. This will allow you to hear the opening and closing sounds for Windows 95, exclamations, mail notifications, warning messages, and so on. To reroute the playback of .WAV files for system events to your internal PC speaker, you must download a Windows 3.1 utility called SPEAKER.DRV. This utility can be found on CompuServe, and most common bulletin boards as part of a file called SPEAKER.ZIP. In Windows 3.1, you could install this driver directly through the Control Panel. In Windows 95, you must install it manually:

1. Unpack SPEAKER.ZIP and copy the file SPEAKER.DRV into your WINDOWS\SYSTEM directory.
2. Verify that the Sound Recorder, Volume Control, Sample Sounds, and one or more Sound Schemes have been installed through the Add/Remove Programs utility in the Control Panel. Install these files even if your system does not have an attached sound card. (See Chapter 4 for more details on using the Add/Remove Programs utility.)
3. To activate the Win 3.1 speaker driver, open SYSTEM.INI in Notepad or another text editor and add or verify the following entries:

```
[DRIVERS]

WAVEMAPPER=*.DRV

MSACM.IMAADPCM=*.ACM

MSACM.MSADPCM=*.ACM

WAVE=SPEAKER.DRV
```

Reboot the system, and you should hear the opening chime for Windows 95 through the speaker. Use the Sound utility in the Control Panel to customize the playback of system events.

The Sound Recorder

The Sound Recorder is used to record, play, and embed sound files in the wave (.WAV) format. It has five buttons—Go to the Beginning of the Clip, Go to the End, Play, Stop, and Record, shown here from left to right:

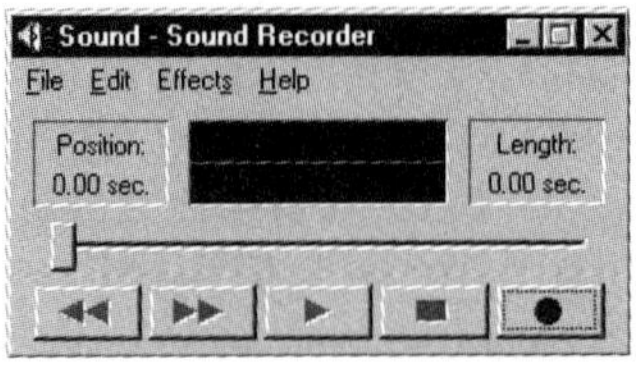

You can use the Sound Recorder to open, create and save .WAV files. You can also create a compound sound effect by inserting one file within another. To do this, use the Insert File option on the Sound Recorder's Edit menu, or open the Media Player and use the Clipboard to cut and paste captured sound information into the Sound Recorder. A series of special effects are available on the Sound Recorder's Effects menu. You may add echo or make the file play in reverse. You can also increase or decrease the volume of a sound in 25-percent increments, and double or halve the playback speed.

Here's another handy tip: use the Sound Recorder to increase or decrease the default playback volume of Windows 95 System Events. This is useful, for example, if you like music and multimedia to play back at one level, and system messages to announce themselves at a different level. For instance, to change the volume of the "Critical Stop" error message, do this:

1. Open the Sound component of the Control Panel and determine which .WAV file is attached to the Critical Stop event. The default is CHORD.WAV.
2. Start the Sound Recorder and open the CHORD.WAV file, located in the WINDOWS\MEDIA directory.
3. From the Sound Recorder's Effects menu, select Increase Volume or Decrease Volume. Play back the file as often as necessary to adjust the volume as desired.
4. Save the file and close the Sound Recorder.

Win95 Sound Compression

The big difference in the Win95 Sound Recorder from previous versions is a new series of compression options in the Save As menu. Using compression can condense an existing sound or record a new one at a variety of different quality levels.

Uncompressed stereo audio contains a lot of data—about 150K for every second of sound—which is why an audio CD only holds a bit more than one hour of music. Win95 includes both music- and voice-oriented sound compression codecs. Music-oriented codecs (such as IMA ADPCM or Microsoft ADPCM) allow not-quite-CD-quality sound at about one-quarter of its uncompressed size. Voice-oriented codecs (such as Truespeech or GSM) allow even more efficient sound compression. Table 13-1 shows the Win95 sound codecs and descriptions.

The Sound Recorder's Audio Properties option (located on the Edit menu) lets you customize playback options and switch between multiple sound devices. You no longer need to open the Control Panel to set an output device, and the Audio Properties menu also lets you set the volume and preferred quality for new recorded sounds.

To expand or compress an existing .WAV file using another compression algorithm, open the file into the Sound Recorder, then select Properties from the File menu. The Format Conversion scroll box lets you choose among the compression formats listed in Table 13-1.

Recording and Capturing New Sounds or Spoken Messages

You can use the Sound Recorder to capture sound from an internal source, like a CD-ROM drive, or an existing .WAV file. You can also create your own sound for manipulation, although this requires that a microphone be plugged into the sound card.

Here's how to record sound from a microphone:

1. From the Start button, choose Programs\Accessories\Multimedia, and then click Sound Recorder.
2. Click the Microphone button and record.
3. Click the Stop button to end recording.
4. From the File menu, click Save As and type a filename for this .WAV file.

Windows 95 Sound Codec	Description
DSP Group, Inc. Truespeech	Offers good compression for voice-oriented sound, but is not a good option for sound other than voice. Truespeech offers a better data rate than GSM, the other voice-oriented codec provided with Windows 95. This makes Truespeech a good option for users who want to record notes in their documents or spreadsheets, store voice mail on their computers, and so on. Truespeech does not offer real-time compression rates, but does offer real-time decompression rates, making this codec a good alternative for use with modems and networks.
Microsoft GSM 6.10 Audio	Offers real-time compression (so long as the hardware is fast enough to support it), making this codec a good option for recording voice with the Sound Recorder. GSM conforms to the European Telecommunications Standards Institute—Groupe Spécial Mobile recommendation 6.10. GSM also allows you to select from among a range of sampling rates.
Microsoft CCITT G.711 A-Law and U-Law	Provided for compatibility with telephony standards for Europe and North America. This codec is supported by many hardware configurations and offers a 2-to-1 compression ratio (from 16- to 8-bits per sample).
IMA ADPCM	Defined by the Interactive Multimedia Association for multiple hardware platforms; similar to Microsoft ADPCM. Offers real-time compression.
Microsoft ADPCM	Offers both real-time and non-real-time compression. When authors choose the latter option, the compression process takes longer but authors can create better-sounding audio files. Microsoft ADPCM is the codec used for Microsoft Encarta multimedia encyclopedia and other CD-based publications.
Microsoft PCM converter	Included for use with Sound Blaster and other 8-bit sound cards. With this codec, 8-bit cards can play 16-bit samples by reducing the quality of the audio produced to match the card's capabilities. Similarly, you can use this converter to play a sample at one Kilohertz rate on a card that supports another rate.

TABLE 13-1 *Win95 Sound Compression Codecs*[1] ■

[1] *From The Windows 95 Resource Kit. Copyright © 1995, Microsoft Corporation. Reprinted with permission Microsoft Press. All rights reserved.*

You can also record sound from a standard CD player or other component that you connect to your sound card's line-in. To do so, follow these steps:

1. Use the Volume Control tool to turn on Line-In and turn off the microphone input. (See the following section for information on how to do this.)
2. From the Sound Recorder, click the Microphone button and record.

Volume Control

Volume Control governs the input and output audio levels for all of your multimedia devices. When Windows 95 installs drivers for a particular device, a sliding control for that device may be placed in the Volume Control. You can control speaker or headphone output level, left/right channel balance, and mute (which cuts off that channel when selected).

When you first open the Volume Control, you should see a series of mixing sliders. These adjust playback volume and channel balance for each multimedia source. If your system can support sound sources not shown in the mixer, you can activate them by selecting Properties from the Options menu and placing a checkmark next to each additional sound source.

The Volume Control's mixing sliders can be toggled back and forth between Playback and Recording settings by selecting either the Playback or the Record buttons in the Options\Properties menu. When the Volume Control is set for Playback, a series of Mute boxes appears underneath each slider. A checkmark placed in the Mute box turns off the playback for that source. When the Volume Control is set for Recording Control, the box under each input source becomes a Select box. The checkmark function for Recording is reversed—a checkmark in the Select box turns the control for that source *on*. Removing the checkmark turns that recording source *off*.

You can record a new waveform sound (.WAV file) from multiple input sources by setting both the output playback level and the record input level for each source. Here's how to do it:

1. From Start, choose Programs\Accessories\Multimedia, and then click Volume Control.
2. If only the master control (Vol) is displayed, right-click the icon in the upper-left corner of the Volume Control window and select Expand.
3. Check the check boxes for the audio input lines from which you want to receive sound; clear the others.
4. Adjust the volume and balance on each input line that you have checked.

tip *In recording sounds from multiple input sources, you can monitor playback and record levels simultaneously by opening two copies of the Volume Control, as shown in Figure 13-5. Just double-click the Speaker icon on the right side of the taskbar to bring up another instance.*

FIGURE 13-5

Monitor playback and record levels simultaneously by opening two copies of the Volume Control.

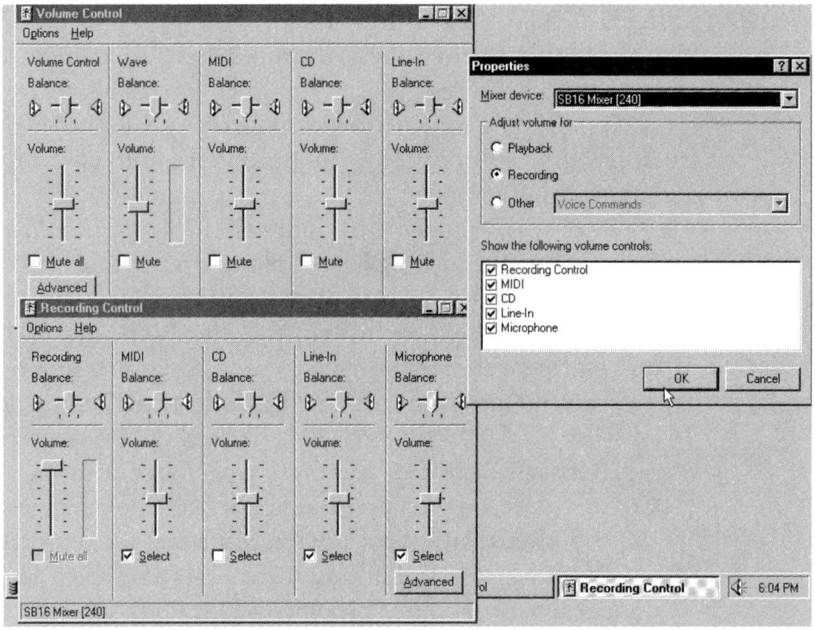

Capturing a CD Audio Sample to a .WAV File

The CD Player and Sound Recorder can work in conjunction to let you capture a selection from an audio CD and save it as a waveform (.WAV) file. Once you've extracted a sample from the CD, it can be played in the Media Player, dropped into an OLE-compliant application or used as a sound for a system event. Here's how to do it:

1. Open the CD Player and the Volume Control. Confirm that CD audio is recognized by either the CD or Line-In slider of the Volume Control. (See the preceding section for details.)
2. Open a second copy of the Volume Control. Set one copy to monitor playback levels and the other to monitor recording levels, as described in the previous section. Set an appropriate playback level for the CD audio selection. Duplicate the setting for this slider on the Recording Control slider. (After you run through this process several times, you may want to customize the input level for this slider.)

3. Insert the source CD into the CD-ROM drive, and find the selection to be captured. Stop audio playback immediately before the selection is due to play.
4. Open the Sound Recorder. Choose a recording format by selecting File\Properties. The Details menu shows you the default Audio Format for your recording. To customize this format, choose Recording Formats from the Format Conversion menu and click the Convert Now button.
5. The Sound Selection dialog allows you to choose the recording quality, compression format and sampling rate for the selection you are about to capture. To record a stereo selection from the CD, you will probably want to change the default from mono to stereo. Set the quality (radio, CD, and so on), bandwidth (8, 16, or 32-bit), and sampling rate (22Hz, 44Hz, and so on) to accommodate your CPU type and available disk storage space.
6. Click the Round record button on the right end of the Sound Recorder controls to begin recording. Now, quickly click the Play button in the CD Player to resume CD audio output. When the passage you want is through, click the square Stop button to the left of the Record button.

FIGURE 13-6

Capturing a sound sample from a CD audio track

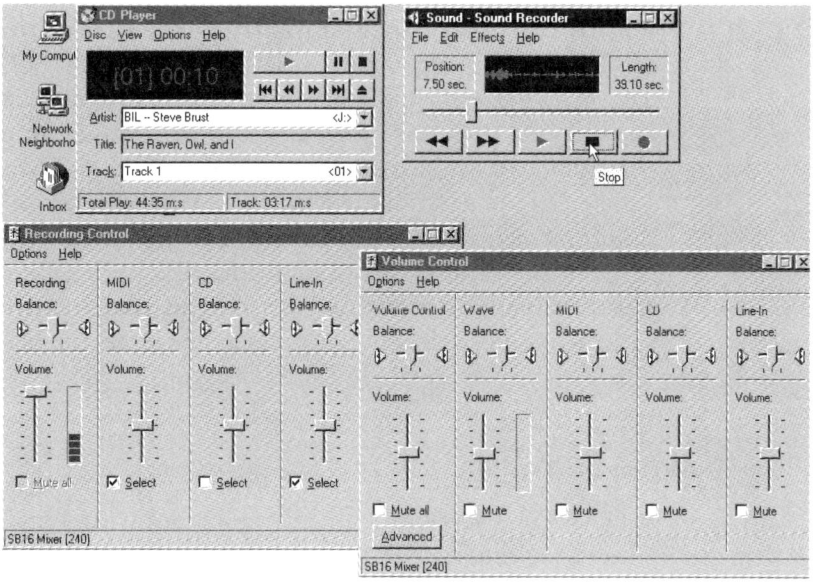

7. You can listen to the selection before saving it by clicking the Seek to Start button in the Sound Recorder, followed by the Play button.
8. If you're satisfied with the way the sample sounds, select File\Save in the Sound Recorder and enter a descriptive name for the clip.

If you want to edit the file, open the Media Player and load the clip you've created. You can cut unwanted material from the beginning or end of the file by marking a position with the slider control and using the Start Selection and End Selection buttons to mark the portion you want to save. Press CTRL-C to copy the marked portion of the file to the Clipboard, then paste it back into the Sound Recorder and save it again.

note *A similar procedure can be used to capture a selection of a MIDI file by substituting the Media Player for the CD Player. Portions of CD-Audio, .WAV files and MIDI files can also be played concurrently and captured to build a collage, or layered effect.*

The .WAV files you create with this procedure can be embedded into a word processor, spreadsheet, data base, presentation, or any other appropriate application.

QuickTime, MPEG, and Other Third-Party Multimedia

Windows 95 can be used to display multimedia presentations in formats developed for other computing platforms. Support is not explicitly built into the Media Player or the other bundled Win95 applets, but there are many freeware and shareware programs that you can use for this purpose.

In Windows 3.*x*, installing a shareware viewer or a Multimedia CD would also register a new multimedia format for display in the Media Player. Unfortunately, some of this support has been removed from Windows 95. However, most third-party multimedia viewers that ran under Windows 3.*x* are still compatible with Windows 95. This section provides information on packages you can download from CompuServe, the Internet, or your local BBS.

QuickTime (.MOV, .PIC)

QuickTime support is added automatically to Windows 95, when you install a multimedia CD that is programmed to be compatible with both the PC and Macintosh environments. However, some of these programs use

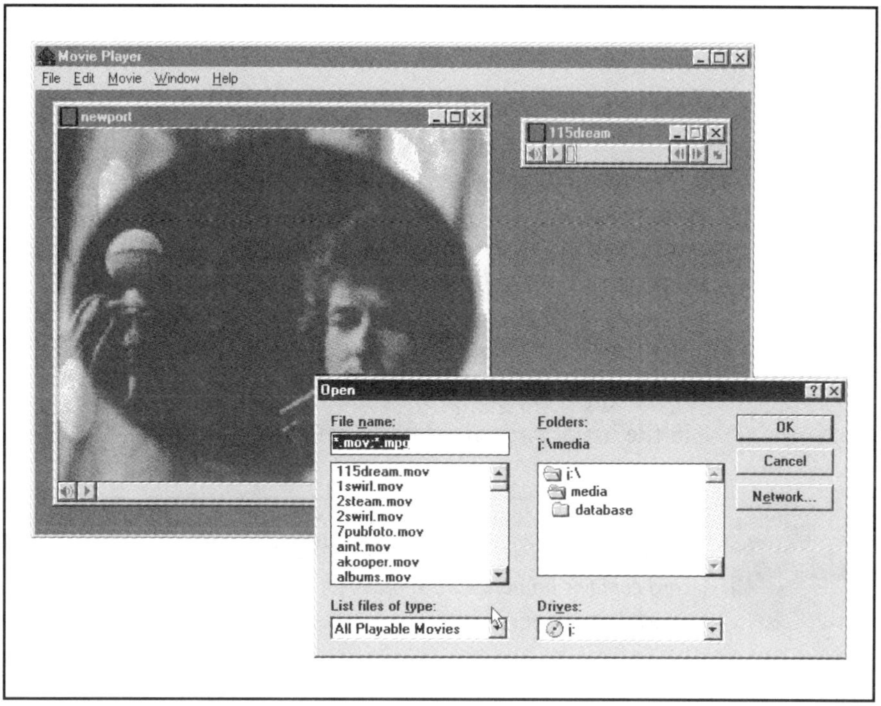

FIGURE 13-7 The Apple Movie Player for Windows plays QuickTime video and sound clips.

older versions of Apple's QuickTime extensions, which may cause general protection faults (GPFs) under Windows 95.

If you have access to the Internet, one easy solution to this problem is to download the current Apple QuickTime for Windows package from their World Wide Web site at HTTP://WWW.APPLE.COM. Click on the Apple QuickTime subheading and download the file called QTINSTAL.EXE. The QuickTime extensions are also available on CompuServe, but the most recent versions are always posted to the Apple site first.

The self-extracting QTINSTAL.EXE file can be run from a DOS command prompt or through the RUN command on the Windows 95 Start Menu. When you run it, the program offers to search for and replace previous versions of QuickTime on your hard disk. An Apple QuickTime folder is created that contains a Movie Player and Picture Viewer. The Movie Player (see Figure 13-7) shows QuickTime movies (sound and video clips bearing the .MOV file extension). The Picture Viewer displays bitmap images in the Macintosh (.PIC) and compressed JPEG (.JPG) formats.

By default, Windows 95 disables support for the QuickTime video format in Microsoft's Media Player. If QuickTime extensions have been installed for third-party applications, the Media Player's support for QuickTime can be reactivated by following these steps:

1. Open WIN.INI (found in the WINDOWS directory) in an ASCII text editor.
2. Search for the following string in the [MCI Compatibility] section of WIN.INI, and comment it out with a semicolon or REM statement:

```
[MCICOMPATIBILITY]
QTWVIDEO=0X0001
```

3. Restart Windows 95.

The next time you open the Media Player, QuickTime video will appear in the list of supported file formats.

---

note *The Movie Player bundled with QuickTime version 2.0.3 has an option on its menu to play movies in the MPEG (.MPG) format. This option may not work if your video card contains no hardware support for MPEG. See the next entry for more information on working with this video format.*

MPEG Video

The original Microsoft plan was to include support for the MPEG (Motion Pictures Experts Group) video format in Win95's Media Player. This feature didn't make the deadline for the first version of Windows 95; It will be included in a subsequent release.

In the meantime, it's easy to add MPEG support to your system by installing drivers through a third-party CD-ROM or shareware package. One of the most common packages is the Xingit! MPEG Player. (Look for XINGITXX.ZIP or MPEGVXX.ZIP on CompuServe or your local bulletin board.)

Xingit!'s MPEG Player plays MPEG videos in either a 160×120 pixel or 320×240 pixel window. On a Super-VGA system, these windows are a bit small, so that you may want to switch back to a 640×480 screen resolution for Windows 95, if you're serious about your movie watching. One of the side-effects of installing Xingit! is that limited MPEG support is also installed for the Windows 95 Media Player. MPEG videos opened in the Media Player can be scaled to any screen size, but the results and rendering may be somewhat less than ideal. Under the Media Player, there is also a file size limit to the MPEG format. Really large MPEG video clips may refuse to load. You can view full-length movies in the Xingit! program in its smaller default screen windows. For more powerful MPEG support, you'll need to wait till Microsoft's new software standards are implemented in a subsequent version of Windows 95, or else purchase a special video adapter with built-in hardware support for full-screen MPEG.

AutoDesk FLI/FLC and Other Formats

To play AutoDesk FLI/FLC animations, you should be aware of another Windows 3.*x* shareware package called VIDVUE. In addition to running AutoDesk Animations, VIDVUE also runs Microsoft .AVI videos, Apple QuickTime movies, and plays Microsoft .WAV and MIDI files. (For VIDVUE to handle QuickTime files, Apple's QuickTime for Windows support must be installed separately. See the earlier section on QuickTime in this chapter for details.)

A larger number of display and editing options are available in this program than in any of the other utilities we've discussed. It's easy to resize display windows on-the-fly, and adjust various playback options, such as the display rate for video frames, the brightness, contrast and gamma-color settings for your monitor.

FIGURE 13-8

The VIDVUE Multimedia Player supports a number of movie and sound formats.[1]

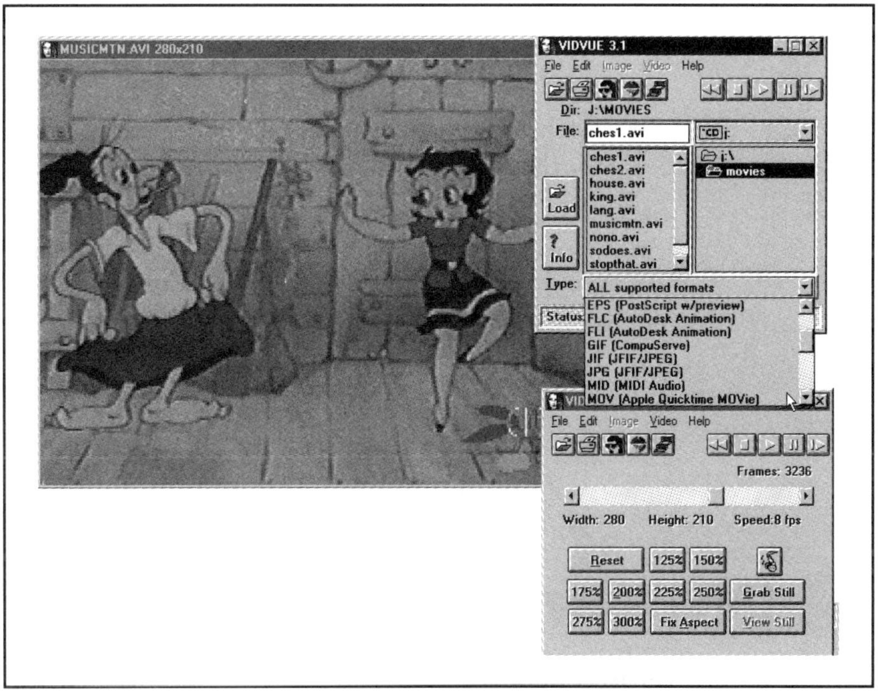

[1] Betty Boop cartoon from the Chestnut Classic series, courtesy CDRP, Inc.

VIDVUE is also a dedicated picture viewer, supporting .EPS, .TIF, Auto-Cad .DCX, Kodak PhotoCD, and several other bitmap formats.

Multimedia Troubleshooting

Reliable multimedia performance can be one of the most problematic areas in personal computing. The multimedia display process is hardware intensive. Individual pieces of software may use independent standards and techniques to display animation and sound. If you're having difficulty playing a particular multimedia file, you may want to check the following basic points:

- Make sure your multimedia peripherals have been installed, the power is turned on, and the appropriate cables have been connected.
- Make sure that microphones, speakers, and line-in devices are plugged into the proper jacks on your sound card.
- If you don't hear any sound, check the volume controls, both on your hardware and in software mixing controls.
- Make sure that microphones, speakers, and line-in devices are plugged into the proper jacks on your sound card.
- Use the Add/Remove Programs utility in the Control Panel to make sure that all relevant Windows 95 multimedia components have been installed.
- Open the System utility in the Control Panel to the Device Manager tab. Expand the entry for sound, video and game controllers. Examine the settings for your sound card and determine whether Windows 95 reports any device conflicts. If a device conflict is reported, refer to the troubleshooting section on the contents page of Windows 95's online Help. Open the entry titled "If you have a hardware conflict." The Win95 Hardware Troubleshooter Wizard may help you to resolve the problem.

Thirteen Hot Titles

PC-based multimedia is about five years old. During this time we've seen some inspiring and some downright terrible applications of multimedia technology. Sometimes both have appeared on the same disc! There are certain "must have" discs of long standing, however. Many of them, unsurprisingly, are from Microsoft. Both Microsoft Bookshelf (see Figure 13-9) and Beethoven were early discs that still have value today. Bookshelf, after several upgrades, is now the "must have" reference tool that belongs on every... well...bookshelf.

Encarta 96 (Microsoft)

Previous editions of Encarta have won dozens of industry awards. The newest version of this multimedia encyclopedia has a new feature that allows you to build a scrapbook of relevant data. It also provides a direct connection to the Microsoft Network, so that you can access late-breaking information on a variety of subjects (see Figure 13-10).

Technet CD (Microsoft)

One of the coolest discs manufactured by Microsoft has nothing to do with multimedia and contains no sound or video. TechNet, a monthly

FIGURE 13-9

Microsoft Bookshelf

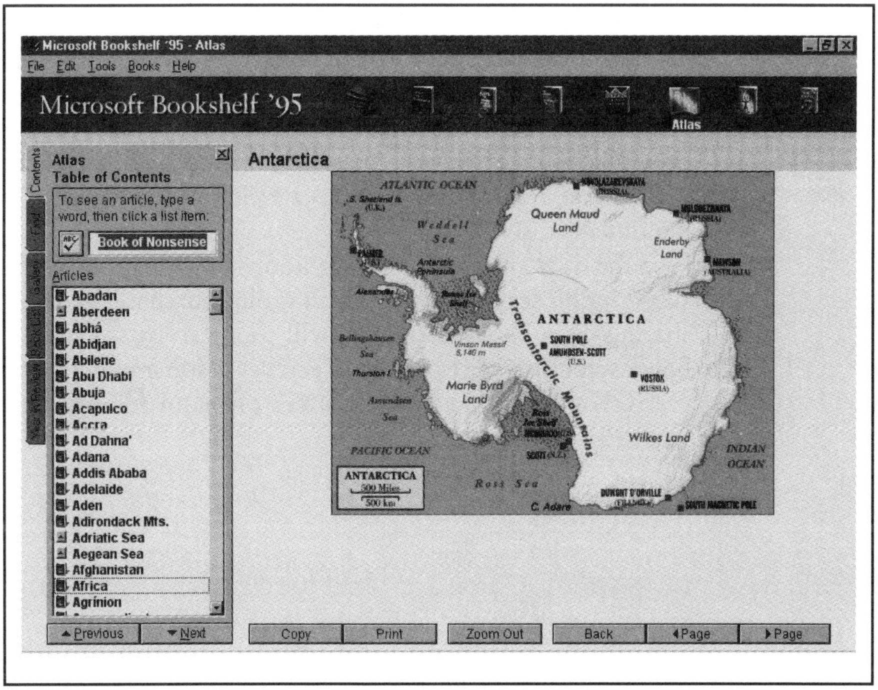

FIGURE 13-10

Encarta 96

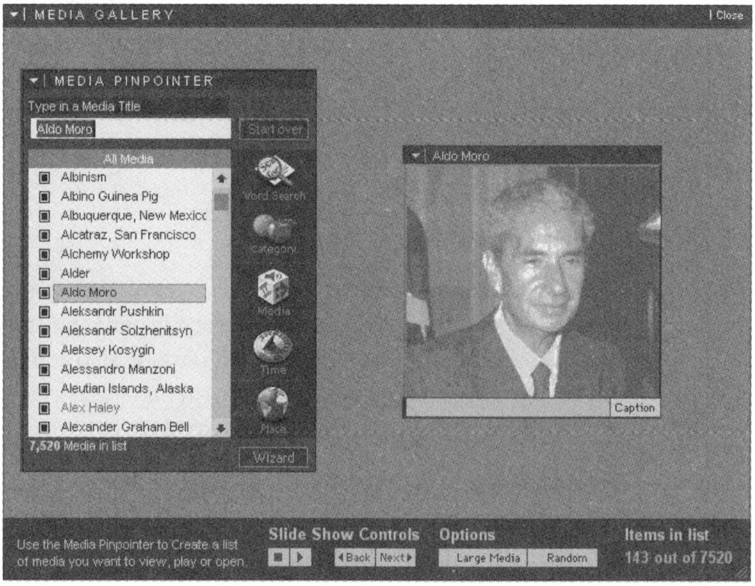

compendium of technical documents, questions and answers, and miscellaneous information, is designed as a technical support tool for anyone who needs to answer specific questions about Microsoft products. In fact, it will fascinate anyone who takes any flavor of Windows really seriously, by providing a searchable database of the most arcane technical information.

TechNet also represents a greater initial investment than your average multimedia disc. A subscription service, TechNet costs about $300 a year to keep the discs coming. The temptation, as with any "overpriced" CD-ROM subscription service, is to make a group purchase: Alternating months and sharing discs between friends, will soon fall by the wayside when you see how useful these discs can be. TechNet is something that you'll want to use every month, and keep back issues on hand for reference purposes. (See Figure 13-11.)

FIGURE 13-11

Microsoft TechNet CD

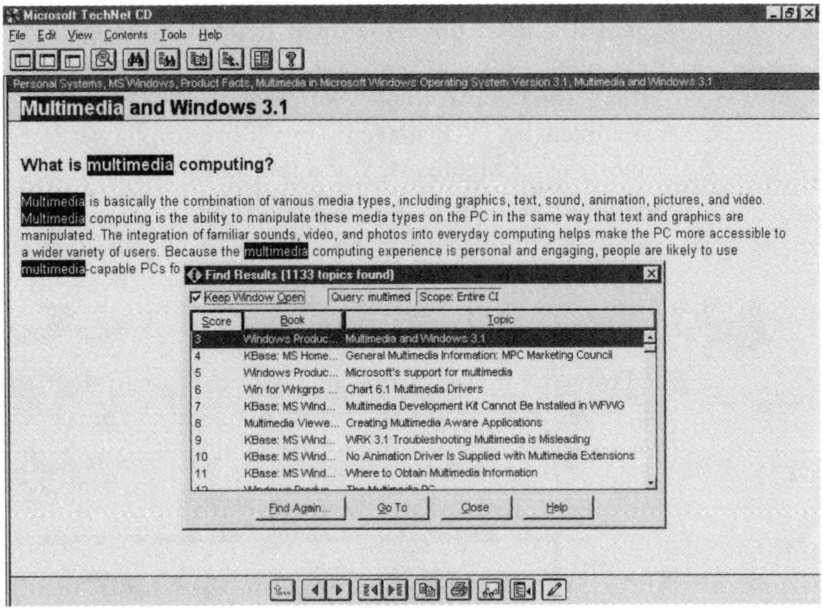

Haight Ashbury in the Sixties (Rockument)

Another disc that deserves a special mention is *Haight Ashbury in the Sixties* (Rockument). Here's a sample to help you remember that groovy scene:

You can put this disc on autoplay and get eight hours of sound, video and light shows from one of our most potent cultural periods. Or you can "grow your own" and select the clips, text (including the complete San Francisco *Oracle*), and music, to provide a kinetic portrait of the period. This disk was assembled by DTP maven Tony Bove, and *Oracle* editor Allen Cohen. Among other highlights, you'll find Janis with Big Brother and the Holding Company singing "I Know You Rider," and the famous Grateful Dead concert from the back of a pickup truck on Haight Street.

Songs from The Gypsy (Boiled in Lead/Steven Brust—Omnium Recordings)

From the music of the '60s, you can go straight to the '90s if you're interested in reading a great story of magic and music, with a soundtrack by America's most famous underground Celtic punk rock 'n roll band, as headlined here:

This CD includes the complete text of *The Gypsy*, a psychological fantasy adventure by Steven Brust and Megan Lindholm. It also includes the *Songs from The Gypsy* album with words by Steven Brust and music by Boiled in Lead. The album can be played as an ordinary music CD, or you can browse through the story and click the lyrics to play the songs.

A Passion for Art (Corbis Publishing)

This disc is a true original, offering both structure and content that is unavailable anywhere else. It tells the story of Dr. David Barnes, a collector of impressionist art, who built an unprecedented personal gallery which has never been open to the public. That is, until now. The disc takes us through the gallery, room by room, and offers background about each artist and each piece. This is an extraordinary title, not only for the content but for its presentation: Those who don't know or don't care about art will be fascinated by the story and the presentation and get a little culture in the bargain.

Highway 61 Interactive (Graphix Zone)

For the majority of the public, watching Bob Dylan has often been like one of his most famous lyrics, here taken out of context: "There's something going on here, but you don't know what it is." The Dylan CD-ROM, called *Highway 61 Interactive,* provides a reasonable explanation. Its potpourri of collected sounds, images, and clips show what he has done and, ultimately, why you should care. The *Highway 61 Revisited* Collage allows you to explore Bob Dylan's career by clicking on strategically placed objects:

This is the antithesis of the CD-ROM products that feel it is their function to immediately startle your senses as they stretch technological limits. The technology in this CD-ROM is certainly up to snuff, but it is the content that makes it outstanding. In this respect, *Highway 61 Interactive* strikes a balance between the interests of a fan and a Dylan newbie. Someone who knows there's something going on but doesn't know what it is can take digestible bites of the legend, and enthusiasts can find a variety of minutiae and collectibles.

Stephen Hawking's *A Brief History of Time* (Blasterware)

Stephen Hawking's book managed to explain complicated scientific concepts to normal people. The CD-ROM goes a few steps further. Instead of having to read the book, you now feel as if you were attending a lecture or presentation. Hawking's computer-generated voice is either spooky or compelling, depending on your point of view. If you like, you can also skip around from one topic to another, exploring areas of specific interest (simulating the act of asking questions at the lecture). Trained physicists might look askance at some of the simplified explanations this CD provides, but the disc offers a pleasant means for the rest of us to gain some basic knowledge of the nature of time and the universe. Hawking has proven that such concepts can be explained, and the disc version serves to further democratize this knowledge.

Bullwinkle Screen Saver (Asymetrix Entertainment)

This screen savers takes a lot of resources (requiring more than 100MB of host data for the entire program) and its animations take up who knows how much RAM. As a CD-ROM-based version of one of TV's coolest cartoons, however, this is a valuable document. You can watch these absurd playlets for hours (which is probably the point). And it's not all that hard to make your PC scream out "Hey, Rocky! Watch me pull a rabbit out of my hat!" every time Windows starts. It should go without saying that the disc is for fans of Moose and Squirrel only.

A Hard Day's Night (Voyager)

This frame by frame dissection of the first Beatles movie has some cool tricks. You can jump from scene to scene, or follow along with the script (this is especially helpful, as some of us Yanks still find their accents incomprehensible). Since this is a documentary, it doesn't really follow a linear plot line and as a result lends itself well to this format. Given its structure, you can jump in at any point and not really lose anything. The video window is too small, but this complements the unpolished, spontaneous character of the film itself.

VidGrid (Geffen)

It seems natural that the two most mindless modern trends—rock video and computer games—would eventually merge. By rights, the results shouldn't be this much fun. This game challenges you to piece together videos in a manner similar to the popular sliding hand puzzles. Finish with all of the clips and the next level starts.

You will probably tire of the videos before you get sick of the game—they emphasize modern heavy metal, although Jimi Hendrix and Peter Gabriel's classic "Sledgehammer" are included (perhaps for variety's sake). In any case, this is one example of how the sum of the parts can equal a greater whole, and it perhaps predicts how interactive TV may look in the future.

Windows 95 for the Technically Challenged (Graphix Zone)

This disc adds a heavy dose of levity to the training process. Set in the Improv comedy club, you click on a laptop that is located on a front table and select the level of lessons that you want to access. Its warped sense of humor differentiates the program. If you think that training is a serious business and should be taken literally, this disc is not for you. The easily offended might also pass. One sequence is an East Indian stereotype that segues into a multi-armed goddess holding an assortment of Windows 95 components.

The jokes are fast enough so you don't mind the repetition, as you might not get it all the first time. There is also a "humor filter," where you can just get the straight information without the jokes. This might be wise, once you've heard this stuff two or three times. At the same time, humor is the key to this program's effectiveness: As you learn the jokes through repetition you learn Windows 95 procedures at the same time.

Cinemania 95 (Microsoft)

Cinemania 95 allows you to hypertext through the world of film fact and trivia, restricted only by your imagination. This latest revision adds a new interface, expanded criticism, and a greater breadth of clips. These new features neither enhance nor detract from the original ability to filter specifics, for instance to list all of the 1987 movies that included Cher and John Mahoney.

Cinemania—or something like it—is an indispensable part of anyone's CD-ROM collection. Few aspects of modern life are certain, but it's more than likely that anyone who owns a multimedia PC also owns a VCR, and could use some help choosing movies. This disc is easy enough to manage and understand, and with populist critics like Roger Ebert and Leonard Maltin, within the reach of most superficially inclined viewers.

The *Playboy* Interviews—Three Decades

The multimedia elements in The *Playboy* Interviews are limited, but this doesn't stop the disc from being one of the most compelling reference CD-ROMs available. *Playboy*'s subjects get the full treatment, allowing you a (presumably) unvarnished view of each. Even if these 15-hour interviews are edited by the writer, they still seek to present the subject's true voice. With more than 300 interviews (some subjects have sat more than once), you get a fair cross-section of the people who have made the past three decades interesting. The subjects generally hail from the political, entertainment, or sports arena, but an occasional scientist adds to the perspective.

You can't read a 1976 session with O.J. Simpson or a 1984 piece on David Letterman without thinking about what they mean today. And even if there are omissions—Richard Nixon and Frank Zappa are conspicuous absentees—this disc allows you to take in some modern history a bite at a time.

Multimedia Is Flexible

With a sound card and a CD-ROM, you can expand the horizons of your PC. It can be one byte at a time: For instance, with a single speed CD-ROM and no sound card at all, you can enjoy all of the benefits of the aforementioned TechNet CD. For this, you may only need a 386/40. If "multi" only translates to mean "more than one," the concept can shrink to fit.

At the same time, multimedia will suck up as much power as you can throw at it. The *Haight Ashbury* CD-ROM will look better, as you throw more hardware power at the disk. With a 100+ MHz Pentium and 24-bit TrueColor, everything will look more realistic. It may remind you of an old dialog, about money: "How much do you need? Well, how much do you *have?*"

chapter 14

Enhancing Windows 95: Microsoft Applications and Third-Party Utilities

- The Norton family of Win95 products
- Microsoft products
    - Office 95, Works, Microsoft Plus!
- Lotus Word Pro
- Vertisoft Name-It
- Freeware and shareware for Windows 95

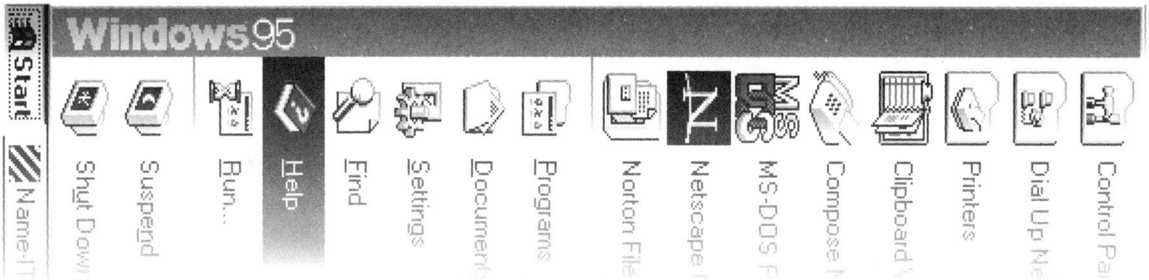

THE Windows 95 software market is expanding rapidly, as more and more companies upgrade the Windows 3.*x* versions of their products. The freeware and shareware programmers who enhanced previous versions of Windows with their innovative utilities are also beginning to write for the new operating system. You can already find shell and file management programs that surpass the Explorer, and other programs that improve the functionality of Win95's built-in desktop utilities.

The Norton Family

Peter Norton has been the foremost developer of operating system utilities for Intel-based PCs ever since IBM marketed the first one in 1981. Although in recent years, Norton has done very little programming himself, his company—now owned and operated by Symantec, Inc.—has continued to issue useful utility suites for each new version of DOS and Windows. The technology in the Norton Utilities is regarded highly; Microsoft has licensed and included key elements in each version of DOS since 5.0. The ScanDisk and Defrag system utilities in Windows 95 are based on Symantec's code.

For Windows 95, there are three members of the Norton Family:

- Norton Utilities offer disk maintenance and system diagnostics.
- Norton AntiVirus offers protection from digital germs.
- Norton Navigator provides file management and desktop enhancements, similar to the features formerly offered in products like Norton Desktop and PC Tools for Windows.

Microsoft and Symantec have both streamlined their Windows 95 utility features, eliminating some useful programs that used to be thrown in for free. Windows 95, for instance, does not include the antivirus, FAT table recovery, and Windows-based Undelete utilities that Microsoft shipped with MS-DOS 6.*x*.

Symantec, no longer faced with the necessity of engaging in "features wars" with arch-rival Central Point Software, has divided its Norton Desktop for Windows package into three smaller utility suites. Following the marketing idea that users really want core functionality in a utility suite, a number of bells and whistles have disappeared in the Windows 95 family of Norton products.

Norton Utilities for Windows 95

The heart of the new Norton Utilities is the System Doctor (see Figure 14-1). This is a pop-up panel of gauges and status icons that makes the desktop look like a submarine. System Doctor has meters for everything from battery power to Windows uptime. You can configure the display to show what you think are the important components. The default includes CPU

FIGURE 14-1

The Norton Utilities System Doctor

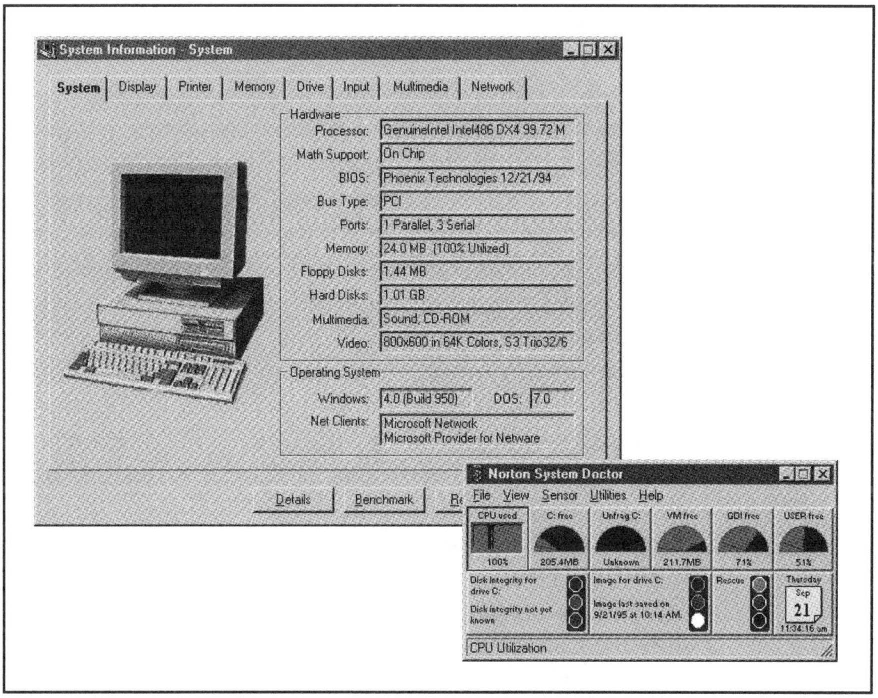

power used, disk space free, disk space defragmented, and virtual, user, and GDI resource memory.

To customize the "submarine" you right-click anywhere on the status screen and select the Add menu. System Doctor includes a number of internal alarm features that you can set to watchdog the integrity of your hard disk. By default, the System Doctor sensors warn you when the free space on your disk partitions falls below a user-configurable threshold. Sensors also alert you when there are lost file clusters on a disk, and trigger Speed Disk (the defragmenting utility) when the fragmentation on a disk partition exceeds 10 percent.

You can customize the alarm settings or other defaults for any of the sensors installed in the System Doctor display by right-clicking its icon and selecting Properties from the pop-up context menu.

tip *If you think System Doctor occupies too much space on your desktop, you can enable its autohide docking feature. This is similar to the autohide feature of the Windows 95 Taskbar. Right-click anywhere in the System Doctor display, select the pulldown View menu and place a checkmark next to the Dock option. System Doctor will disappear from the desktop unless you move the mouse cursor to the edge of the screen (top, bottom, right, or left, depending on how you've set the display properties). As soon as the cursor hits the edge of the screen, System Doctor reappears.*

Strategic Recovery Utilities

The most important features in these Norton Utilities (as in the past) are Norton Disk Doctor and UnErase. Symantec provides both DOS and Windows-based versions of these utilities. The Windows 95 version of Disk Doctor is very similar to the version shipped in Norton Utilities, version 8. The important difference is that it has been tweaked to work properly with Windows 95's long filenames, and to recognize the subtle differences in the File Allocation Table and other disk structures that have been programmed into the new operating system.

Symantec recommends very strongly, and the authors of this book tend to agree, that you should not try repairing a Windows 95 disk with any previous version of Norton Disk Doctor. (In a case where FDISK does not recognize your disk partitions at all, older versions of Disk Doctor may restore partial access, but your entire Windows 95 installation is likely to be trashed in the process.)

Norton Disk Doctor includes a number of features not included in Microsoft's ScanDisk (which is included in the basic Win95 operating system). Disk Doctor is much better at disaster recovery, with a superior ability to reconstruct damaged directories and preserve file information. The Windows 95 version of Disk Doctor also has an improved ability to run in the background. You no longer have to worry about conflicts with open files on a drive. Although we don't recommend this, you can even keep using your word processor, saving documents to a drive that Disk Doctor is repairing in the background.

The Norton UnErase Wizard for Windows 95 is programmed to integrate itself with Microsoft's Recycle Bin, which is already installed on the desktop. The difference is that once Norton UnErase Protection is installed, files deleted within DOS sessions or from applications are protected along with the files you drop into the Recycle Bin from the desktop. The Norton enhancement to the Recycle Bin adds many useful features, such as the ability to search for deleted files by name, location, registered file type, or embedded text strings, but several features of the old DOS "UnErase" are no longer implemented. You can no longer search the erased or unused portion of a hard disk for text strings, or specific file types. And there is no manual unerase feature for emergency recovery on partitions where the Norton protection features have not been turned on. The good news is that these features are still available in the DOS UnErase that comes with the package. The bad news is that (as with previous versions of Windows) DOS UnErase works only when you boot to a true DOS command prompt.

Emergency Rescue Disk

Another handy Norton Utility feature is the rescue disk: a bootable floppy that will bail you out in the case of an irreparable crash. The Norton Setup Wizard offers to create such a disk when you first install the package. Afterward, the System Doctor lets you know whether changes to the system have made the disk obsolete. With this in place, you can restore the system to its exact state, if and when the crash occurs.

This is a real improvement over crash-protection utilities in older versions of Norton. When disk disasters occur, people have become accustomed to restoring partial system data and reconstructing or reinstalling the missing parts. With an up-to-date rescue disk, you may never need to reconstruct a system again. The only question is whether or not you take the time to update the rescue disk each time System Doctor tells you this is necessary.

Norton Navigator

Norton Navigator is a collection of desktop enhancement utilities. It includes a sophisticated file manager with important features that Microsoft left out of Win95's Explorer. Also included is a taskbar enhancer. You can drag your own program icons or folders to the taskbar for easy launch access or open an entirely new "virtual desktop."

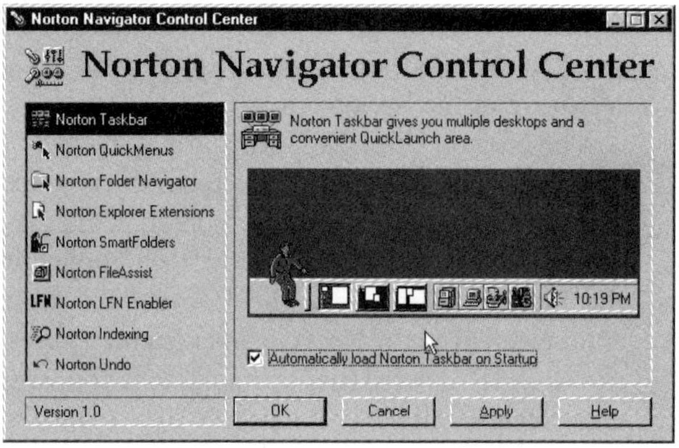

The virtual screen concept allows you to build independent desktops, each with an independent set of icons and its own Start Menu. If you use your computer for a variety of different tasks, you can set up one desktop for word processing and database work, another desktop for Internet browsing and telecommunications, and so forth. Icon buttons on the taskbar let you switch back and forth between desktops on-the-fly. This feature is derived from Norton Desktop and PC Tools for Windows. In fact, a special utility allows you to import desktops created for these two interfaces into Windows 95.

The crown jewel of the package is the Explorer/File Manager replacement. It only takes serious Windows users about 5 seconds to determine that the Windows 95 Explorer is vastly underpowered. The Explorer has none of the sophisticated file management capabilities that have spoiled the users of XTree Gold and PC Tools for Windows. Navigator returns some of these desktop tools: multiple drive and directory windows, built-in file compression, menu-accessible print, file run, and file compare options, and even a built-in FTP client for the Internet. Navigator's file management windows also allow you to selectively display and tag files through specified file extensions. The file display can be sorted on two levels by DOS file extension, creation date, last access date, compression ratio, or file attribute in addition to the four sort options offered by the Explorer. In its default configuration, Navigator shows all available data sources on the left with a file and folder list on the right. As in the Explorer, you can right-click any object in the list to pop up a context menu of additional options, including the bundled Norton Zip and UnZip programs.

Additionally, the Norton File Manager has a customizable toolbar (you can add buttons for your own programs or create alternate toolbar sets). For

Windows 3.*x* File Manager fans, the tabs at the bottom of the screen allow you to select a "classic" display interface.

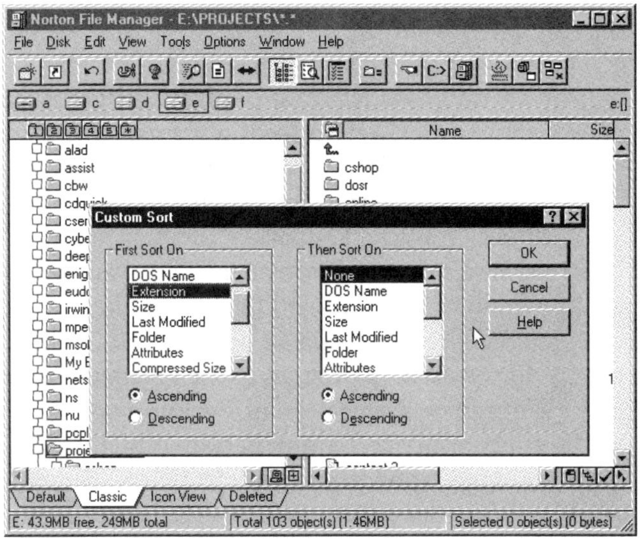

Other Bells and Whistles

Navigator features a series of Norton QuickMenus that make the Win95 Start Menu faster and easier to use. You can add a cascaded history list to the Run menu and Documents menu, so that programs or documents can be reopened with a single mouse-click. The Control Panel QuickMenu opens a cascaded list on which you can place the Control Panel applets that you access most frequently. (Chapters 4 and 8 of this book provide tips that show you how to do this without Norton's assistance.)

Norton Explorer Extensions can add a number of additional command options to the right-click context menus of files, folders, and drives. These include Norton Copy and Norton Move, which make it easier to manipulate a large number of files in a single operation.

Norton SmartFolders allow you to create desktop links to applications or documents that, unlike Windows 95's own shortcuts, do not get broken when the source files are shuffled to different directories or disk partitions.

Navigator also provides limited long filename support for some Windows 3.*x* applications. Programs that use the standard Windows 3.1 File menu Open/Save dialog box (specified in the Win3.1 API) gain the ability to load and save files with long filenames. This feature does not work properly for many popular applications (including Microsoft Word and Excel), but it does work for some programs. (For more information about adding long filename support to Windows 3.*x* programs, see the section on Vertisoft's Name-It later in this chapter.)

Limitations

With all its features, Norton Navigator lacks some popular and useful features that were present in Symantec/Central Point/Norton products for previous versions of Windows. Norton Desktop for Windows featured almost 100 file view filters that allowed you to display data from almost any application on the market. These file viewers are gone from Navigator. Instead, you can automatically view any of the 19 data types supported by Windows 95's built-in QuickView filters.

A more important utility, the loss of which may be keenly felt, is the Norton Backup program. When Symantec and Central Point were separate companies, Central Point Backup was regarded as the Windows backup utility of choice. Norton Backup for DOS was also an outstanding, well-programmed application. The fact that Symantec has discontinued both of these packages leaves a large hole in the backup utilities market that has not been filled at the time of this writing.

Norton AntiVirus

Norton AntiVirus does a thorough scan of your computer's RAM and hard disk partitions before installing itself to avoid contamination by existing computer viruses. It offers three levels of protection: an auto-protect startup scan that examines the total contents of your system, a selective scan of critical system files, or a schedule that allows drives to be scanned at specified intervals.

When a potential virus is detected, you have the choice of repairing the infected file, deleting it, excluding it (to avoid false alarms with files that are really clean), or inoculating (recording the signature of the file in its present version, so that you will be alerted later, if the signature is changed).

Monthly updates for the antivirus database are available on Symantec's bulletin board, through CompuServe and at the Symantec World Wide Web site. The in-the-box version, for instance, does not have the ability to clean and protect Microsoft Word templates that have been infected by the "Prank Macros (Payload)" virus, but you can download an updated version that will.

Microsoft Applications

As the creator of Windows 95, Microsoft also offers both application suites and operating system enhancements designed to exploit the new operating system.

Microsoft Office

Microsoft Office 95 is an astounding product and an astounding deal, demonstrating in a single stroke how far software has evolved over the last few years.

The Office 95 lineup reflects some realignment. Previously, Office consisted of Word, Excel, PowerPoint, and Mail. Now that Mail is part of the Windows 95 system itself, Office 95 incorporates Schedule +, which was formerly an applet in the Windows for Workgroups environment. The Office 95 Professional package also includes Microsoft Access, a popular database application.

Within Office 95, toolbars are important within and outside of applications. Through the same right-click switching process, system toolbars can take over a strip at screen right and offer fast access to every application on the system. You can toggle between preconfigured bars, or design your own. The Desktop toolbar, for instance, is a convenient way to access all of the floating icons on your Windows 95 desktop. The Office toolbar provides a direct link to certain Schedule + functions, like adding a task, an appointment, or a contact.

If you prefer the Office 95 Toolbar to Win95's built-in taskbar, you can use it as your principle program selector and avoid the taskbar, by setting it to Auto Hide through its right-click Properties menu. You can take this concept one step further and select the Auto Hide option on the toolbar, creating two "hot" areas of the screen that pop up control menus when touched by the mouse.

Word for Windows Version 7

Winword 7 represents an incremental rather than a substantial improvement over its predecessor. Consider that Winword 6 had a few jaw-dropping features, like unlimited undo, that made a real workstyle improvement.

Writers and word processing veterans may find Word 7's refinements to be minor, but cumulatively they yield a better program.

- Tip Wizards can be toggled to monitor your document preparation. If you're taking the long way around to invoke a feature, pop-up dialog boxes appear to suggest shortcuts.
- The new AutoFormat feature allows you to create bulleted lists and borders as you type.
- The AutoCorrect feature learns your personal preferences for capitalization and spelling as you type. Special shortcuts let you insert non-alphanumeric characters like arrows, section marks, and copyright symbols.
- An address book makes it easier to manage distribution of faxes, memos, and letters. Documents can now be shared electronically with a built-in e-mail editor.

Excel Version 7

The emphasis in Excel version 7 is to make spreadsheets smarter, to perform appropriate cell-formatting and calculations without making you manually choose menu options or enter formulas. Excel version 7 allows you to save keystrokes when entering data in lists or databases with its new AutoComplete feature. This is an extension of the AutoFill feature that was available in previous versions.

Like the other Office 95 products, Excel has a Smart Template Wizard that allows you to quickly set up the formatting for various document types, such as invoices, expense tracking, business planning, and personal budgeting. New link features with Microsoft Access allow you to easily collect information or distribute it across a network between spreadsheets and database files.

PowerPoint

Recognizing the increasing importance of desktop presentations in the business environment, the new PowerPoint has received the greatest feature boost and the most significant upgrade of the dynamic Office trio. Among the new features are the Slide Navigator and the Meeting Minder. The Slide Navigator allows you to jump to different points in the presentation to answer audience questions, and the Meeting Minder lets you to take appropriate notes during a presentation.

In PowerPoint's slideshow view, you can now right-click anywhere on the screen and select Meeting Minder from the pop-up context menu. You can make notes in three different formats: Notes Pages, Meeting Minutes, and

Action Items. These free-form notes can later be cut and pasted into a word processor or another part of a presentation.

PowerPoint qualifies as the best package for presentation newbies due to its easy-to-use outline feature, which debuted a few versions back. Here, you can build a presentation as a text outline, switch views, and everything comes up as slides. Or you can import a Winword outline, with the same effect.

Schedule +

Schedule + includes an interesting module that belies Microsoft's reputed lowest-common-denominator attitude toward software development. The Seven Habits Wizard is a mini-course on getting organized; asking you questions about values, priorities, and those aspects that may be thwarting your potential. This is a bit more "new age" than most users may expect, especially as its purpose is to develop a "personal mission statement."

Binder

Binder is another handy Office 95 tool. A natural outgrowth of increased integration, it allows you to situate files and charts from different programs into the same place. This is a very obvious and well-executed idea. You add the files, charts, presentations, or excerpts to the binder, with each represented by an icon across the left margin. Click the icon and the file appears at right, with the host application loaded and in an editable form. A toggle button in the upper-left suppresses the binder icons, in case you want to work with a full screen.

MS Access

MS Access, a relational database program included only in the Professional version of Office 95, has the following new features:

- New Template Wizards for creating tables, reports, forms, and queries
- A Table Analyzer Wizard that can convert flat-file databases into relational tables
- Links to the AutoCorrect, Format Painter, and Spell Checker used by other Office 95 applications
- A new filter by selection feature that allows you to query a database by any selected field or through specific forms

- Improved file import and export capabilities
- Better integration with Excel

Microsoft Works

It was once easy to ridicule Microsoft Works as the lowest common denominator of PC software. Works, which began life on the Apple platform, was designed as a foundation for various integrated applications: word processing, spreadsheet, database, graphics, and sometimes communications, all for a convenient, low price. Problem was, since the individual modules were designed to meet the needs of "basic" users, they were way too simplistic for anyone who actually wanted to get anything done.

The lowest common denominator now isn't what it used to be. The new Microsoft Works, which is preloaded on many new Windows 95 machines, is a versatile tool. It can usefully fill the holes in your stockpile of applications. For instance, you might choose Microsoft Word or WordPerfect as a heavy-duty word processor, but employ Works to handle spreadsheets and telecommunications, which may be less critical to you.

FIGURE 14-2 *An Office Binder example integrating information from different programs*

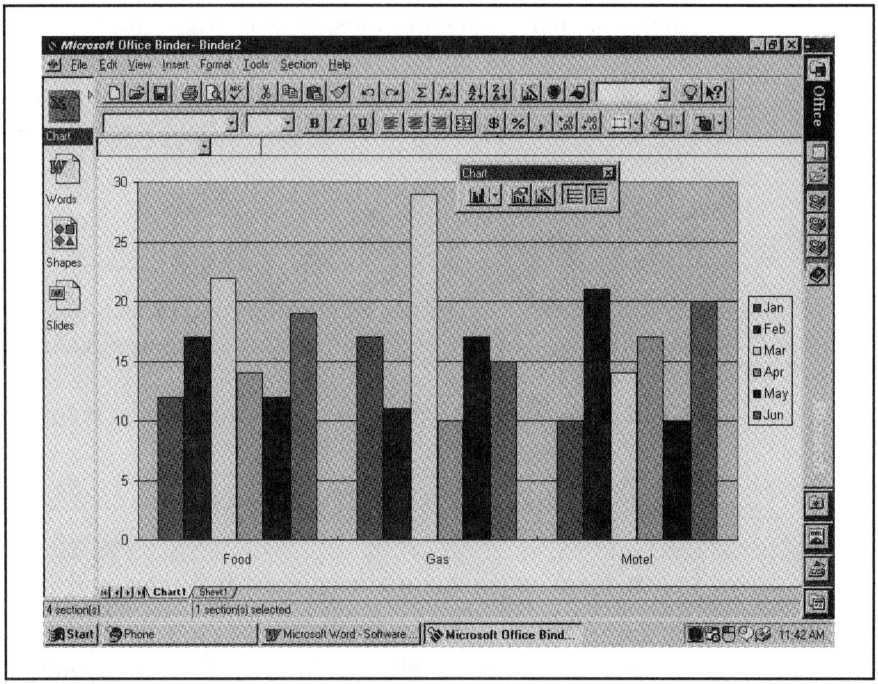

Like Office, Works has a consistent interface across all of its modules. Additionally, it relies on Wizards to create many of its documents. Works, however, is more specific and thorough in its use of Wizards. Computer novices may use them as the default method of creating a new Works document. The File\New dialog calls up a tabbed interface that can select a document creation Wizard or open existing documents in the word processing, spreadsheet, database, and telecommunications modes (the fifth Works component, graphics, can be added as needed to any of the other modules).

Works has several very cool, exclusive features. Easy Text allows the insertion of boilerplate text and commonly used expressions. You can type a sequence, such as your address, once. The entry then appears on the Easy Text menu, from which you can insert it at a keystroke.

The Works communications module is a better low-end terminal program than Windows 95's resident HyperTerminal—if only because you can customize the toolbar. As in Office 95, the ability to customize the toolbar reaches across the Works modules.

Works is more limited than Office 95 in that it won't let you create macros and assign buttons on the toolbar to other applications.

As an added sweetener, Works is currently packaged with the Microsoft Bookshelf reference tool.

Microsoft Plus!

Many users may buy Microsoft Plus! simply because it's cheap, or because it is out there. This Microsoft companion package to Windows 95 contains some useful operating system enhancements. However, at this writing, the most important Plus! feature, enhanced support for MSN and the Internet, can be installed in Windows 95 simply by downloading a free upgrade module from Microsoft. (See Chapter 11 for details.).

Here's a closer look at the features available in Microsoft Plus!

Enhanced Microsoft Network and the Internet Explorer

The enhanced network interface provided in Microsoft Plus! allows you to subscribe to the Microsoft Network (MSN) online service through a point-to-point protocol (PPP) Internet Connection. Without this enhancement, MSN is only a stand-alone information service. With the Internet Explorer kit installed, your MSN connection gives you access to the entire Internet as well as to events and conferences offered on MSN. You can surf the World Wide Web, using Microsoft's bundled Internet Explorer or your favorite third-party Internet tools, such as Netscape, NSCA Mosaic, or Eudora. Win95's bundled Telnet and FTP utilities also allow you to establish text-based connections to any site on the Internet. Also included in Microsoft Plus! is a set of drivers that allow you to manage Internet mail through Win95's Exchange Inbox, or turn your computer into a Dial-Up Networking server. (For information on using the Internet Setup Wizard to enhance your MSN connection refer to Chapter 11.)

Enhanced DriveSpace Disk Compression

The DriveSpace utility included in the basic Windows 95 package is substantially identical to the one offered in MS-DOS 6.*x*. Compressed volumes are limited in size to 512MB, and the file compression ratio is less than 2 to 1. Microsoft Plus! includes DriveSpace 3.0, which can manage volumes up to 2GB in size and achieve better compression ratios. The new DriveSpace contains a variety of compression options. The Hipack and Ultrapack settings may obtain ratios of better than 3:1. (Microsoft recommends reserving the Ultrapack option for use with Pentium machines, because it does slow down performance.)

Additionally, DriveSpace 3 lets you fine tune compression options, turning high compression on or off for files accessed within a specified number of days. Or you can set the compression algorithm to change when available disk space falls below a specified threshold.

System Agent

System Agent is a terminate-stay-resident (TSR) watchdog utility that you can use to automatically run any DOS or Windows application at specified times and dates. Programs can be scheduled to run hourly, daily, weekly, monthly, at Windows startup, or during Windows idle time, when the CPU isn't busy.

By default, System Agent schedules several system maintenance utilities. ScanDisk and Defrag are programmed to run on a periodic basis to check the integrity of your hard drives. System Agent also notifies you when the available file space on each disk partition falls below a specified threshold.

tip *If you are annoyed by screens popping up to warn you that your disk space is low, or that it's time for a disk check, you can disable System Agent. Here's how: Double-click the System Agent icon on the taskbar to open it on the desktop. Select Stop Using System Agent from the Advanced menu. To reactivate System Agent later, open it from the System Tools group under Program\Accessories on the Start Menu.*

Scheduling Daily Disk Defrag

If you like the idea of a watchdog popping up to take care of things you'd otherwise forget, here is an example of System Agent's usefulness. You can schedule a daily defragmentation of your hard disk partitions. Defragging a hard disk increases the likelihood of data recovery in emergencies and also improves system performance. Use the following procedure:

1. *Double-click the System Agent icon on the right of the taskbar.*
2. *Select Program/Schedule a New Program.*
3. *Click the down arrow on the Program box, and select Disk Defragmenter.*
4. *Click "When to Run," select the daily button, and enter a convenient time in the Start At field.*
5. *Click OK and back out of the configuration options.*

Desktop Themes

The basic Windows 95 package includes a complement of color schemes for the desktop along with bitmaps suitable for wallpaper. These are mostly 16- and 256- color palettes that are not much different from similar options provided with Windows 3.1. The Desktop Themes component of Microsoft

FIGURE 14-3

Microsoft Plus! provides dramatic high-color wallpaper and a convenient application-scheduling utility.

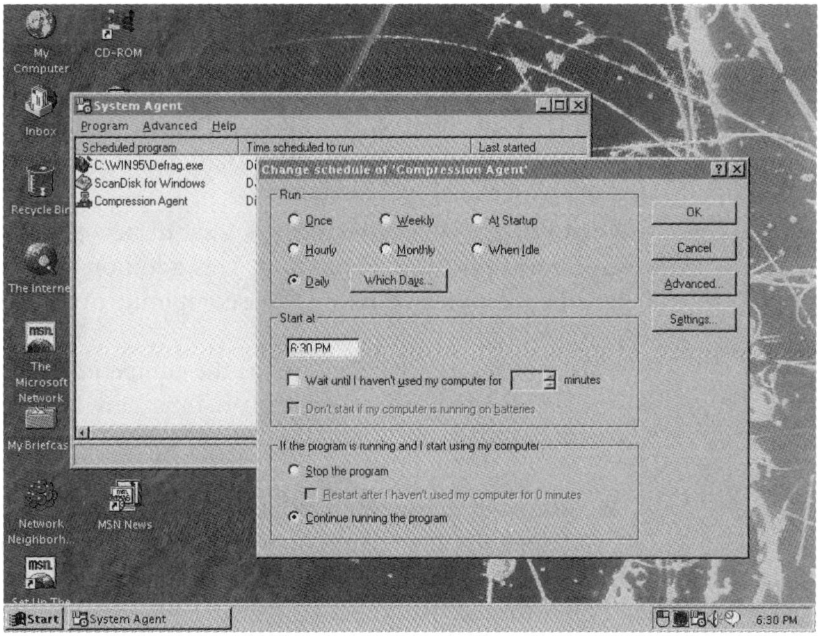

Plus! installs a number of integrated high-color schemes, each with coordinated wallpaper, icons, screen saver, system sounds, cursors, and fonts related to the scheme.

This feature is designed to appear to the escapist or to the interior decorator who lurks in the heart of some Windows users. You can select themes that are either beautiful or garish with titles like The '60s, Nature, Science, Sports, and others. Each theme has its own set of animated cursors, icons, desktop fonts, and system sounds, in addition to wallpaper that stretches to cover the entire desktop. The animated cursors and hi-res wallpaper are fun to look at, but loading them may cause a noticeable slowdown in system performance.

3-D Pinball

This three-dimensional arcade game is also included in Microsoft Plus! If and when your system includes a video card and drivers that support Microsoft's DirectDraw 3-D graphics API, you may be amazed at the performance of this utility in a low-memory configuration. For most current systems, it performs adequately with 8MB of RAM.

Microsoft Plus! occupies 10 to 35MB on your hard disk, depending on which features you elect to install. Its retail price is around $50.

Lotus Word Pro

Lotus' SmartSuite is currently the third most popular suite package, after Microsoft's Office and Novell's PerfectOffice combination. Some of the suite (Lotus 1-2-3, Freelance, and Approach) has not emerged in Windows 95 versions at this writing,

Word Pro's greatest advantage is a set of new groupware-style features, which Lotus calls *team computing*. This addition may not be important to single-computer users, but for Office computing over a network it may make a significant impact.

Word Pro has as many features as the competition, but has a much more streamlined look. Here's a review of some new features that make word processing easier:

- Instead of multilevel dialogs, a right mouse click pops up a single, tabbed box that gives you entree to all text controls. Just click the fonts, margins, justification, or style tabs, and the appropriate controls are front and center, at your beck and call.

- Word Pro can zip through a document, then present a list of misspelled words. You don't have to hop from word to word as you do in other word processors. Click to correct the words that need it.
- Word Pro takes templates into a whole new realm. For example, you can specify a "click here" area of the screen that guides a user in placing text in a document. Crafting one of these SmartMaster templates takes some doing, but the time-saving potential is unlimited.
- The concept of divider tabs first appeared in Quattro Pro and now, finally, it's in a word processor. Positioned across the top of the screen, the divider tabs let you instantly access different files, templates, or even different parts of the same document, such as a table of contents or different chapters.

Inso's Quick View Plus

If you find the Windows 95's built-in Quick View feature useful, you may be interested in purchasing the full-featured version marketed by Inso. Inso's Quick View Plus contains over a hundred different file viewing filters for word processors, spreadsheets, databases, fax files, bitmap and vector graphics. (These include IBM DisplayWrite, Legacy, Just Write, Professional Write, Lotus 1-2-3, Quattro Pro, d-BASE, r-BASE, Q&A, GIF, PCX, TIF, JPEG, CGM, EPS, CDR, and many others.) In addition to the drag-and-drop features available in Win95's Quick View, Quick View Plus allows you to print the contents of the View window, copy to the Clipboard, crop, and resize graphics, or transfer the formatted contents of a spreadsheet or word processing file to another Windows application.

Vertisoft Name-It

One of the problems with Windows 95's long filename feature is that it doesn't ordinarily work with older applications written for Windows 3.*x*. If you save a file with a name like *A Very Long Filename*, this is truncated for DOS and Windows 3.*x* applications and appears in their dialog boxes as AVERYL~1. Worse yet, some applications may create long filenames that aren't truncated properly for Windows 3.*x* applications to recognize. You may find files with spaces or other characters in their names that won't load into applications until you physically rename them to the 8.3 DOS format.

Vertisoft's Name-It is an application that provides relief for this problem. Its ability to add long filename recognition to old applications is more powerful than the similar feature in Norton Navigator. Name-It intercepts the system calls that bring up the old Windows 3. *x* File\Open and File\Save As boxes, substituting a Windows 95-style file list. For many applications, the substitution is automatic. For most others, a special Long Name button is added to the Windows 3.*x* file list box. When you click this button, a new Windows 95 file dialog opens, providing all of the long filename and right-click mouse options supported by real Windows 95 applications.

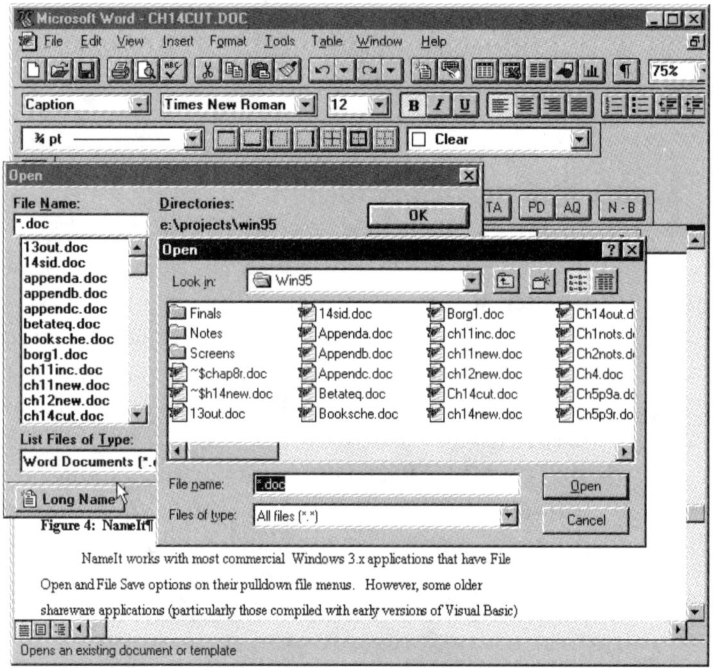

Name-It works with most commercial Windows 3.*x* applications that have File\Open and File\Save options on their pull-down menus. However, some older shareware applications, particularly those compiled with early versions of Visual Basic, make use of unconventional file lists. Name-It does not work with these programs.

Freeware and Shareware

The stockpile of shareware and freeware applications and utilities written for Windows 95 is expanding rapidly. It may be well worth your while to drop by some of the well-known online watering holes where programmers post their brain children.

If you're a member of CompuServe, visit Microsoft's Windows 95 forum and the WINNEWS forum sponsored by WUGNET, a national Windows user group organization. On The Microsoft Network online service, you'll find a Windows 95 software library in the Computers & Software category in the Microsoft Products\Windows 95 folder.

As we've mentioned in previous chapters, Microsoft maintains a free bulletin board download service and an Internet FTP site where additional software is available.

But for the most popular and innovative accessories for Windows 95, the hot place to look is the World Wide Web. The advantage of doing your file hunting with a Web browser is that you can often find much more than one-line descriptions and .ZIP files. Often, you'll see summaries of an application's capabilities or pointers to the home page for a shareware company. Microsoft also maintains a Windows 95 software library on its Windows 95 Web site at this address:

HTTP://WWW.MICROSOFT.COM/WINDOWS/SOFTWARE.HTM

A large assortment of 32-bit software is also available at this address:

HTTP://WWW.WINDOWS95.COM/APPS/

You'll find application folders there for Internet suites, Web browsers, mail and fax utilities, multimedia and graphics, cursors and screen savers, general utilities, productivity applications, and other goodies.

The basic policies governing shareware use remain fairly constant. Shareware programs can be had for the cost of the diskettes that contain them, or downloaded from an online source. You have a period of weeks or months to evaluate the software at your leisure. If you decide that you like what you see, a registration fee generally less than $100 will get you full documentation, technical support, and access to program enhancements.

The Association of Shareware Professionals is an organization that exists to monitor program quality, protecting both authors and consumers. If you find a READ.ME file included with a package that proclaims the author a member of ASP, you have several guarantees:

- You won't be getting a "crippled" package that deliberately disables program features.
- The package has been tested to meet certain standards of quality.
- The authors won't suddenly skip town when you need technical support.

Windows 95 PowerToys

This collection of Windows 95 utilities is authored by the Microsoft programmers who administered the Windows 95 beta program. It is not officially supported by Microsoft, but it is well worth having, since it was designed specifically to correct the most annoying deficiencies in Windows 95 that were reported by the more than 400,000 people involved in beta testing the product.

The PowerToys consist of the following utilities:

CABVIEW A desktop extension that adds a QuickView filter for Microsoft's compressed cabinet archives (.CAB files) that contain Windows 95 components and drivers. When CabView is installed, you can "QuickView" any .CAB archive to open a display window of its contents. Any file included in the .CAB archive can be dragged directly to the desktop, eliminating the necessity for running the EXTRACT.EXE utility, discussed in Chapter 2.

CONTENTS MENU An extension to Win95's right-click context menus. When it is installed, right-clicking on any folder brings up a new Contents option that opens a cascading display of the folder's contents.

CD AUTO-PLAY EXTENDER/FLEXI CD Adds Win95's CD autoplay feature to data and multimedia CDs, as well as audio CDs. Also provides quick taskbar button to control playback of audio CDs.

EXPLORE FROM HERE Allows you to quickly open the Explorer to any designated drive or directory.

QUICKRES Allows you to change the color-depth of the screen display on-the-fly, eliminating the need to restart Windows 95 when you switch from 256 to 16 million colors.

ROUND CLOCK Features an analog clock, similar to the one in Windows 3.1, but round instead of square.

SHORTCUT TARGET MENU Allows you to view and modify all the Properties of an object by right-clicking on its desktop shortcut.

XMOUSE Allows you to open objects simply by pointing at them with the mouse, instead of clicking the button. This one gets its name from the fact that the mouse works that way in the Unix X Windows graphic environment.

TWEAKUI This PowerToy is a collection of useful Control Panel extensions that deserves a section of its own. (In fact, you'll find one for it at the end of Chapter 4.) It allows you to change the speed of pop-up menus, change mouse double-click and drag speed, toggle animated folder display on and off, control the appearance of desktop shortcuts, eliminate special Microsoft utility icons from the desktop—Network Neighborhood, Inbox, the Microsoft Network, and Briefcase—or copy these special icons to folders. TweakUI also lets you quickly create desktop templates for any file on your hard disk (see Chapter 4), and automatically set startup boot options (see Chapter 6).

The PowerToys can be downloaded from the Microsoft FTP site or the Microsoft BBS Download service, or from the PowerToy Web page at:

HTTP://MICROSOFT.COM/WINDOWS/SOFTWARE/POWERTOY.HTM

You can download each module separately, or get the whole group in one compressed file.

Installing the PowerToys

After you download the PowerToys in their compressed format, follow these steps:

1. Create a folder for the PowerToys.

2. Copy the compressed PowerToy files you've downloaded into the folder you just created.
3. Double-click the compressed PowerToy files in the folder you've created to unpack the archives and copy installation files to your hard disk.
4. Examine the READ.ME files and install the PowerToys that you want to use. Right-click the .INF file icon for each PowerToy (these icons look like notepads with a little yellow gear on each), then choose Install from the pop-up context menu options.

If you decide that you don't like a PowerToy and want to remove it, open the Add/Remove Programs object on the Control Panel, find the PowerToy listed on the Install/Uninstall tab, and click the Add/Remove button.

Drag and File, Drag and Zip

Drag and File comes to your rescue by providing the full functionality that was formerly available in the Windows 3.1 File Manager, plus some new Win95 bells and whistles. It can horizontally and vertically tile file windows, view directory listings by file extension, and display side-by-side listings for two drive partitions. There's more. It can customize confirmation preferences for COPY/MOVE/DELETE, perform file operations on a group of filtered items, or configure and edit application/file associations, supporting Win95's long filenames and right-click mouse options. Drag and File also includes an augmented toolbar, and pull-down menu functions that hook into Win95's Quick View and Network Sharing features. It can tag/untag selected directories and files, sort in ascending or descending order, print, launch programs, find files, display multiple filtered file lists and set custom confirmation options for each window.

A companion program, Drag and Zip, turns the interface into a full-featured archive manager, allowing you to compress and decompress files on the fly with your chosen compression utility, drag and drop files into and out of zipped archives, and convert zipped archives into self-executing files, simply by right-clicking the mouse.

Drag and Drop/Drag and Zip is the brainchild of Bay Area Shareware Programmer Dan Baumbach, who is also a past ombudsman of the Association of Shareware Professionals. Both the Windows 95 and the Windows 3.1 versions of these utilities are available through CompuServe or at Baumbach's (Canyon Software) Web page.

The Future

The products we've listed here are only a smattering of the software products that will soon be available for Windows 95. Corel Systems' CorelDraw, Adobe's PageMaker and Photoshop, Borland's Delphi 32 and Paradox, and Delrina's Communications Suite and Cyberjack are all shipping now or are on their way, with many more packages to come.

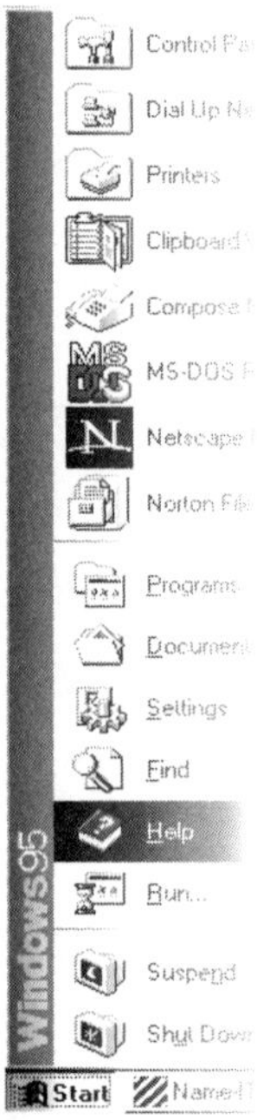
Printers
Settings
Find
Help
Run...
Suspend
Windows95
Start

chapter 15

About CPUs, the System Bus, and Other Hardware Standards

- The difference between various 386- and 486-level CPUs

  Upgrading to Pentium

- Why VESA (VLB) and PCI motherboards are better than ISA motherboards
- Hard disk standards

  Enhanced IDE vs. various flavors of SCSI

- Video standards and your display card

  Color-depth, bus speed, and onboard RAM

- Sound cards and CD-ROM drives

  What to look for

- Tape drives, flopticals, and removable media
- Communication protocols
- Printers and printer standards

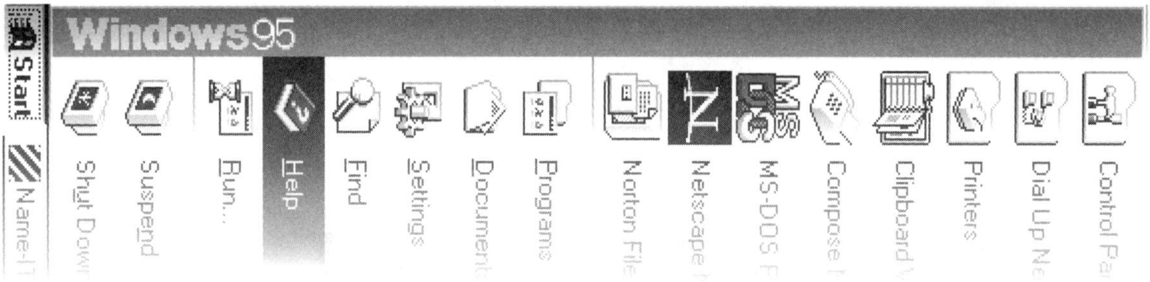

THIS and the next chapter intend to help you understand the relationship between your computer's hardware and Windows 95. You'll find condensed, "Byte-sized" information that other books about Windows 95 never seem to mention.

This chapter helps builds your hardware literacy for Intel-based PCs and gives you some technical grounding on performance issues associated with common PC standards. You'll also get some explanations and PC acronyms and shopping-list jargon. If you don't care much about the whys and wherefores of PCI, VESA, EIDE, SCSI, 16-bit/32-bit/64-bit hardware, and so on, you may prefer to skip to Chapter 16, which can help you decide whether your current system is adequate for running Windows 95. That chapter also discusses various upgrade options for buying new systems, improving existing systems, and choosing individual components.

CPUs and Bus Standards: Choices, Choices

The 386 and 486 CPUs that drive the majority of older, Intel-based machines make use of the same hard-wired instruction set. A series of name extensions, such as SX, SLC, DX, DX/2, and DX/4, is used to further describe the capacities of these processors.

The suffix SX has a totally different meaning when applied to 386 CPUs than it does for 486 processors. In connection with a 386 CPU, the suffix SX was used to denote a processor designed for the now obsolete ISA (industry standard architecture) data bus. This meant that although the processor itself could execute 32-bit instruction code, the data was processed and fed back to RAM and system peripherals in 16-bit chunks compatible with the limitations of the motherboard's internal architecture. This is one reason (along with slow execution speed) that Windows 95 is incompatible with 386SX machines.

In connection with 486 machines, SX has nothing to do with the instruction processing bandwidth. Instead, it means that the CPU includes no built-in math coprocessor. The math coprocessor (referred to in previous generations as the 80287 or 80387 chip) provides special support for the CPU to perform certain arithmetic calculations at a much higher speed. The high-speed calculations performed by the math coprocessor affect the performance of math-intensive applications like spreadsheets and CAD design applications. The absence of the math coprocessor in 486SX systems has little or no effect on the performance of basic operating system functions and simple business applications. However, the 486SX CPUs included in most low-budget machines also had low clock speeds of 16 to 25MHz. So, although these machines will run Windows 95, they are not really desirable hardware platforms.

DX, as applied to 386 CPUs, indicates a fully functional 32-bit processor that supports 32-bit data transfer to RAM and over an appropriately designed peripheral bus. Microsoft claims that Windows 95 will run on a machine with a clock speed as low as a 386DX 20MHz CPU, but performance on such a machine will be even worse than on low-end 486SX units. In practicality, a 486DX CPU with a clock speed of 33MHz is probably the minimum-level processor you should consider for use of Windows 95 as anything other than a novelty exhibition.

SLC denotes a set of 486 processors, designed by IBM, that run approximately 10 to 15 percent slower and cheaper than their DX equivalents at the same clock speed. SLC processors are designed with a minimal 1K internal data cache (compared to 8K in 486DX CPUs, and 16K in most Pentium units). 486SLC machines are more desirable than SX machines at comparable clock speeds.

The clock speed (ranging from 25 to 130MHz on current machines) controls the speed at which machine instructions are executed within the CPU. It does not necessarily represent the speed of the computer's system peripheral bus, although it can and usually does on older ISA machines. More recent systems often make use of special clock-doubled and clock-tripled CPUs that operate at a multiple of the bus speed.

DX/2 or DX/4 appended to a 486 CPU denotes a processor that performs internal calculations at a high clock speed, but delivers data to memory and the system bus at a lower speed. The popular 486DX/2 66MHz CPU executes internal instructions at a clock speed of 66MHz, but delivers data to the bus at a clock-speed of 33MHz. Just to confuse things, DX/4 usually denotes a clock-tripled CPU rather than one which is quadrupled. A 486DX/4 100MHz CPU processes internal instructions at a clock speed of 100MHz and usually delivers data to the bus at 100/3 or 33MHz, rather than 100/4 or 25MHz.

Pentium is the Intel Corporation's registered trademark for what would have been called the 586 generation of CPUs. Pentium processors are currently manufactured in 60, 66, 90, 100, 120, and 133MHz flavors. Intel also offers a special 83MHz overdrive Pentium processor, designed as a plug-in upgrade for existing 486 machines. This overdrive CPU and others in the Intel line all include special voltage converters to accommodate the differences in 6- and 3.3-volt motherboard designs. (See Chapter 16 for more information on Intel's line of plug-in CPU upgrades.)

What About the Pentium Floating Point Bug?

The famous Pentium glitch, an addition error that cropped up primarily in floating point calculations, led to a minor consumer crisis in trust for the Intel Corporation last year. The problem manifested itself in the performance of division operations carried out to a precision of seven or more significant figures. After first denying the existence of the bug, then denying its importance, Intel eventually decided simply to replace all Pentium CPUs free of charge upon request by any customer with a defective unit.

One quick way to find out if your Pentium processor has this glitch is to open a spreadsheet or the Windows calculator and perform this arithmetic computation:

```
(4,195,835 / 3,145,727) x 3,145,727
```

The answer should, of course, come out to 4,195,835. If, instead, you get a result like 4,195,579, then your system has the Pentium floating point bug. Public bulletin board systems have many diagnostic utilities that also detect this problem.

If you consider the Pentium floating point error a potentially serious problem, you can get a variety of bug-fixes. On the World Wide Web, you can find out about your options by going to HTTP://WWW.INTEL.COM/IAL and selecting the Microprocessor option. By FTP, you can go to FTP.INTEL.COM and download the file COMPLR.TXT from the directory PUB/IAL/PENTIUM. On CompuServe, you can "GO INTELARCH" and download the file COMPLR.TXT from the Pentium processor library "Pentium® Proc." Or you can just call Intel and request information.

If the whole affair seems like altogether too much ado about nothing, bear in mind the following unsubstantiated rumor culled from Pentium discussion groups on the Internet: Intel named the chip the Pentium instead of the 586 because, when the new processor added 486 + 100, the sum came out 585.9999996. (Or maybe not.)

Non-Intel CPUs

Within the broad lower limit of getting up to a minimum 33MHz 486DX-based machine, you have quite a bit of latitude. You're not stuck with one manufacturer (Intel) or one standard ISA bus structure. AMD and Cyrix Corp. offer clone 486 CPUs, often at bargain prices. There are also RISC-like CPUs that perform like a full Pentium in most respects. All these alternatives provide sensible upgrade paths without the horrendous cost that earlier Pentium upgrades entailed. Pentium-level and fast 486 processing have become economical and practical upgrade possibilities, even when expenses must be pared.

Clone "586" and Other "P-Class" CPU Options

It's usually the case—about the time the leading edge of some technology slides into the middle of the state-of-the-art curve, both money-saving clones and mainstream technology alternatives appear. Pentium-class CPUs and motherboards are no exception.

The first Pentium CPU clone boards are not true clones of Intel-based boards. Instead, they use an Nx586 chip from NexGen that achieves Pentium-like speed by using a reduced instruction set—in other words, the chip is a RISC alternative to Pentium. The RISC approach results in a chip that is not pin-compatible with the Intel chip, but considering its lower prices—typically $500 to $750 less for a NexGen-based motherboard than for a true Pentium board—this lack of physical compatibility may not be much of a problem. In any case, NexGen promises to provide its own CPU upgrade path.

Catching the Right Bus

If you're considering some kind of system upgrade, one concern to keep uppermost in mind is the data bus used by the motherboard for system peripherals. The hottest and fastest ISA video cards and disk controllers on the market are feeble compared to ordinary, inexpensive counterparts designed for motherboards with a VESA local bus (VLB), or PCI bus. These bus enhancements can be identified by the special 32-bit peripheral slots provided for them on the motherboard. When video or hard disk data is transferred from the CPU to a compliant controller over an enhanced bus, noticeable performance benefits result—more than 400 percent of what is possible on older, ISA systems.

The VESA Local Bus (VLB) Option

Windows 3.1 drove a need for faster graphics displays back in 1992, which led to the original VESA display standard. (VESA stands for the Video Electronics Standards Association.) The VESA standard adapted a special 32-bit slot on the motherboard to act as a logically separate data bus between the CPU, memory, and peripheral boards. Unlike a standard 16-bit ISA peripheral, a VESA card could run at the CPU's I/O speed—usually 33MHz—on a 486-based machine.

It was an ideal solution to the grindingly slow speed limits of ISA display adapters—the data throughput zoomed from 3-5MB per second to around 30-50MB per second, a tenfold increase for the cost of a simple board modification and a cheap connector. (In theory, the VLB bus can actually handle data streams of up to 130MB per second, but as any engineer will tell you, theory isn't practice.)

If you expect to stay with a 486 board over a fairly long time—for example, if you're upgrading multiple 486 machines in an office setting—you will save money and still realize quite good performance by sticking with a VLB motherboard. Make sure such boards have at least two VLB slots, however, since the local bus connector has long since stopped being used exclusively for graphics. You'll find VLB controllers for hard disk drives and other peripherals as well as graphics adapters, so two or three VLB slots constitute a practical minimum.

The PCI Option

The peripheral component interconnect (PCI) standard is rapidly replacing VLB on new motherboards. So unless you're convinced you'll never upgrade peripherals for your current system, ultimately you're likely to find VLB limiting. VLB versions of popular video and disk controller cards are still being manufactured, but not for very much longer. New I/O peripherals will require a motherboard not tied to yesterday's standards.

So if you do expect to buy additional peripherals during the near to middle future, it will be worth it to spring for PCI slots instead of VLB, even though they are marginally more expensive. If you need to justify it to the bean counters or to your spouse, just take a look at the life cycle of computer equipment.

The PCI standard has taken over the Pentium market so thoroughly that PCI designs are rapidly coming also to dominate newer PC peripherals. For that reason, even though VLB is theoretically faster than PCI, given a choice, PCI slots in a new motherboard will serve better over a longer period of time.

PCI is also a standard designed to support a broader range of peripherals, multiple processors, plug-and-play (P&P) peripherals, and multimedia applications that you won't find in VESA systems.

How PCI Works

PCI is a processor-independent bus that works on PCs, Power PCs, and other CPUs. The architecture—chiefly authored by Intel—is officially sanctioned as a standard by Microsoft and a consortium of other industry leaders. Most major manufacturers now support it.

A PCI motherboard typically has three or four open PCI slots on the motherboard plus one or two built-in PCI controllers for IDE (Integrated Drive Electronics), EIDE (Enhanced IDE), SCSI (pronounced "scuzzy" and short for Small Computer System Interface), or network peripherals. The PCI slots coexist with the ISA or EISA bus, which has expansion slots of its own. ISA and EISA boards can plug into ISA or EISA slots, while high-speed PCI boards plug into a PCI slot.

ENOUGH SLOTS? (PCI/VESA COMBO-SYSTEMS) If you're concerned about the number of available slots on your motherboard, you may be tempted to purchase one of the cheap, popular hybrid models that include both VESA and PCI slots. These systems also give you a chance to ease into the PCI bus gradually, since you can cycle your existing VLB peripherals into the machine. However, you may want to resist the temptation and avoid these systems. The reason? Although integrated VESA/PCI models make it easy to migrate your existing peripheral cards, they usually run anywhere from 15 to 40 percent slower than an all-VESA or all-PCI system in disk access and graphic processing. Generally, an all-PCI system runs a bit faster than an all-VESA system. The price difference between VESA and PCI versions of the same graphic card is usually negligible. PCI disk controllers tend to be a bit more expensive than their VESA counterparts.

tip *if you do decide to buy an all-PCI motherboard, look for one that includes a built-in floppy/IDE controller and/or built in serial and parallel ports. Otherwise, you may not have enough slots to transfer existing ISA peripherals like sound cards, network adapters, internal modems, and so on.*

An advantage of PCI is that it provides plug-and-play capability, meaning it automatically identifies and configures for PCI cards at startup. When PCI is integrated with an ISA bus, you usually have to tell the CMOS only about IRQs in use by ISA cards; PCI takes care of the rest.

Mastering the Bus

PCI also supports bus mastering. That means add-in boards can process data independently of the CPU and access the computer's memory and other peripherals on their own. This releases many otherwise lost processing cycles to the CPU and can result in much higher efficiencies—which translates to better performance.

How many peripherals a PCI bus can handle depends on loads, which in turn depend on electrical characteristics like inductance and capacitance. A normal bus can handle 10 loads, of which the governing PCI chips use three. That leaves seven for peripheral devices like controllers and graphics adapters. A controller built onto the motherboard uses one load while one that plugs into an expansion slot uses 1.5 loads, so the motherboard design can make a significant difference in expandability.

Working at its own speed slows PCI data transfers down a bit, relative to the fastest VLB I/O rate, but that bare fact is misleading. Keeping a clock speed separate from the processor's fits PCI architecture better to the faster clock speeds of Pentium chips. A fixed speed may make PCI not a "true local bus" in the sense of sharing its I/O directly with the processor. However, sophisticated logic and buffering keep PCI boards from suffering the speed penalty you might expect as a result. In fact, a PCI peripheral will usually run faster than the equivalent VLB device.

Plug-and-Play—or Is it Plug-and-Pray?

Microsoft Windows 95 is the first operating system compatible with the plug-and-play standard. That figures, since Microsoft and Intel are the ones who pushed the standard into being. Plug-and-play is an important advantage, but it requires peripherals aware of plug-and-play to fully exploit it.

You don't need P&P hardware to run Windows 95, of course, but you'll find that new peripherals with this capability will be much easier to install and maintain. For support specialists—especially in companies with hundreds or thousands of PCs under their purview—the P&P standard should save many personnel-hours, which corporate bean counters will appreciate. P&P will also be a boon to the small businessperson who will find it less necessary to call on technicians for help all the time.

The Windows 95 implementation of plug-and-play was called *plug-and-pray* by early skeptics, but it has settled into a fairly reliable technology. Here are the key features:

- Plug-and-play devices can attach to most buses including ISA, VLB, PCI, and EISA.
- Compatible connectors include PCMCIA, SCSI, IDE, serial port, parallel port, and monitor.
- Installing, loading, and unloading all device drivers is automatic.
- You can make on-the-fly configuration changes, meaning you can dock a laptop, plug in a modem, or insert a PCMCIA card, to cite three examples, without rebooting.
- Support is built in for many third-party devices, including CD-ROM drives, assorted video cards, and hundreds of modems.
- Windows 95 will notify drivers and applications of configuration changes, which means that smart software can react dynamically to changes.

For complete reliability, the P&P expansion architecture requires a P&P compatible BIOS plus new hardware that can work with it perfectly, not something anyone with good sense would offer to guarantee. Still, all three major BIOS vendors are aiming for designs flexible enough to resolve potential conflicts reliably, and the fine-tuning gets better all the time. For your system to be fully plug-and-play compliant, the BIOS should specifically support the Microsoft/Intel Plug-and-Play Standard, version 1.1. At present, this BIOS is to be found in a relatively small number of machines. Notebook manufacturers will probably be the first to jump on the bandwagon, and you can expect to see a Plug-and-Play 1.1 BIOS on most machines released in 1996.

note *Even if your machine does not have a plug-and-play BIOS, Windows 95 is capable of automating a large number of configuration chores. The protocols for both PCI and PCMCIA include independent plug-and-play support. Your PCI and PCMCIA peripherals will probably be recognized and configured correctly under Windows 95 without a P&P BIOS present in the system. (See Chapter 16 for more information on notebook computers and PCMCIA.)*

Detection of older (or "legacy") hardware is more hit-and-miss, though Windows 95 does try to detect and autoconfigure that type of hardware as well. Given fully compliant hardware and software, Windows 95 tracks installed devices and manages their resource usage dynamically. It's a good system, one that old-time PC jockeys will appreciate for the work it saves, though Apple Macintosh users have been known to sniff that a five-year-old still can't master it in ten minutes.

caution *Even with P&P, you'll need to exercise caution about plugging in or removing any internal devices without turning off the power. Some notebook docking stations and PCMCIA peripherals (now referred to by Microsoft as "PC Cards") are designed to let you do this, but most PC peripherals are not. The voltage transients can damage devices that plug directly into the internal bus.*

Hard Disks and Disk Controllers

Two hard disk interfaces are now commonly implemented in Intel-based PCs. IDE (Integrated Drive Electronics) is the cheapest and most widely used standard. The SCSI (Small Computer System Interface) standard is a faster, trickier implementation favored on high-end systems. The hard disk standards of the '80s—MFM (Modified Frequency Modulation), RLL (Run Length Limited), and ESDI (Enhanced Small Device Interface)—are still supported to a limited degree under Windows 95. However, systems that use these hard disk interfaces may not perform as well and are more likely to experience various compatibility problems.

The type of hard drive you buy for your system, especially if it's an internal drive, is determined by the interface used by the disk controller. With SCSI drives, the SCSI host adapter or motherboard SCSI chip will determine the speed. With IDE, there's considerably more choice involved, and you can get more storage for somewhat less money. That's particularly good news if you're working with a constrained budget, since 32-bit PC applications demand much more disk space than their 16-bit counterparts. On the other hand, SCSI drives allow fast, easy access to large disk partitions, and up to seven drives can be daisy-chained and accessed through a single controller.

Let's review the options in closer detail.

The IDE Option

For some time, IDE will probably remain the interface of choice for internal devices like internal hard drives, in part because it is easy and inexpensive to implement as part of the motherboard. The key to its success lies in the fact that it keeps so much of the circuitry internal to the disk, itself. Moving most of the interface from the bus and add-on boards into the storage device didn't add much to the cost of the drive. This technique also drove down the cost of assembling and marketing whole systems.

This "keep it internal" approach is fundamental to the IDE standard. But in the past two years things have been getting slightly more complex. The original IDE standard resulted from a collaboration between Western Digital and Compaq Computers and was readily adopted by other manufacturers. However, when Western Digital recently developed its enhanced (or "EIDE") standard, some other drive makers balked.

EIDE vs. Fast ATA

Seagate Technology, a larger driver maker than Western Digital, has coined its own acronyms of Fast ATA and Fast ATA-2 to compete with EIDE. Both terms refer to the PC interface between the CPU and the hard drive. By most other names, it's still IDE.

Both EIDE and Fast ATA offer the following features:

LOGICAL BLOCK ADDRESSING A scheme that allows DOS and Windows 95 to recognize IDE partitions up to 8.4GB in size, well above the ordinary IDE limit of 528MB.

ENHANCED DATA TRANSFER RATES Rates operating up to a maximum of 16,000KB per second, four times better than the ordinary IDE limit of 3300KB per second. (For this enhanced mode system to work, the drive must be used in conjunction with a 32-bit VLB or PCI controller card.)

MULTISECTOR READ AHEAD Sometimes referred to as *block mode*, this feature permits the controller card to read multiple sectors of a drive simultaneously, improving average seek time.

MULTIWORD DMA MODE ADDRESSING A new technology for faster data transfer through direct memory access.

Where EIDE differs from Fast ATA is in its scope. EIDE allows additional devices, such as CD-ROM and tape drives, to coexist with hard drives through a single controller unit. It also provides two interface connectors instead of one, allowing you to connect up to four drives to a single EIDE controller unit.

Today's IDE drives and controllers almost universally use some of the EIDE improvements. Many systems provide an EIDE host interface on the motherboard, so that you can plug in extra, optional components like CD-ROM drives.

EIDE and Fast ATA or Fast ATA-2 drives overcome one of the original IDE specification's most serious problems—a size barrier. The original IDE spec permits you to store no more than 528MB of data. The EIDE approach uses logical block addressing (LBA), in which the first block of storage is addressed as block O and succeeding blocks are numbered sequentially until the last block is used. There's no logical upper barrier. LBA has always been used for SCSI drives, but it's new—and a significant improvement—for IDE devices.

For most practical purposes, EIDE and Fast ATA are interchangeable. Drives designed by manufacturers pushing Fast ATA can be used interchangeably with EIDE controllers, and vice versa.

Drive Speeds and PIO

The main speed benefit of Enhanced IDE is its Programmable I/O (or PIO) Modes 3 and 4. But some motherboards don't permit you to exploit the speed benefit of the enhanced standard. If your EIDE system doesn't allow you to mix and match PIO modes, a faster drive is limited to the transfer mode of the slower drive. For instance, if you pair an IDE PIO Mode 2 drive with much faster PIO Mode 3 drive, both may have to run in Mode 2. The reason is that older IDE controllers must use the same mode for all devices on the same channel. Most newer motherboards and controller cards allow you to set the PIO transfer mode for the master and slave drives independently.

The SCSI option

SCSI systems have always been notoriously hard to tame on the PC platform, even though Mac users have long sworn by (instead of at) them. Windows 95 and plug-and-play make SCSI much easier to use than before, and it keeps getting easier as new drivers are written. Under Windows 95, vendors can simply create a "miniport driver," that is, an INF file that essentially plugs a SCSI card right into the generic Windows 95 32-bit driver. It eliminates the need to create a brand new driver from scratch for the new system and guarantees compatibility right out of the gate. Needless to say, vendors are creating these INF files very quickly, so if you already have a SCSI card, call your vendor to locate the needed INF miniport driver.

If your peripheral—CD-ROM drive, removable hard disk controller, or the like—is already hooked into your computer by SCSI, it's not a problem. You can use the old 16-bit drivers under Windows 95, though you might contact those vendors for upgraded versions. If you buy a new SCSI card, Windows 95 supports more than 70 models right out of the shrink-wrap, and the number is growing.

The Evolving SCSI Standard

The problem with SCSI, and what caused so much blue language to float out of PC user offices, was primarily how hard it was to manage multiple interrupts, I/Os, IDs, termination, and all other SCSI arcana. If you needed to call for tech support—well, everyone knows what an ordeal that can be. Best to have a brown-bag lunch and a reserve supply of patience on hand. A telephone headset or speaker phone can help a lot.

But plug-and-play has promised to change all this for the PC world, and the major SCSI card makers are taking the promise seriously. Adaptec and Future Domain, two heavyweights in the field that recently consolidated into one when Adaptec bought out its rival, have P&P ISA SCSI kits that make installing new SCSI peripherals painless, provided they're P&P ready. And the Adaptec version, known as ReadySCSI, can even recognize and help configure legacy SCSI peripherals automatically. The Adaptec PCI SCSI Master kit includes a Fast SCSI bus-master host adapter that can support 7 external SCSI-2 devices with the ease of SCSI in the Mac world.

Adaptec has successfully promoted a generic driver called ASPI, which makes for good interoperability. Anyone's SCSI card should be able to drive most manufacturers' SCSI hard drives and other devices. And SCSI is easy on you—to add a device, you just plug it into a blank socket on the SCSI ribbon. With P&P, SCSI becomes even easier—Windows 95 manages the settings automatically.

IDE on the other hand is seeing a welter of competing standards, as large (1GB and larger) hard drives become more common. There's EIDE from Western Digital, but other makers are pushing alternative "next-generation" IDE standards and there's no guarantee EIDE will be the dominant survivor. SCSI will likely take over as the standard of choice, at least with external add-ons, because of its speed and flexibility.

Types of SCSI Adapters

You can pick from various SCSI adapter types, of which only the first two were official standards as of late 1995:

SCSI-1 Data transfers are limited to 5000K per second.

SCSI-2 This standard extended the upper limit to 10MB per second and is currently the most commonly used SCSI interface using fast or wide data transfers.

FAST SCSI This interim solution boosts SCSI 2 data transfer by using a 10MB-per-second synchronous burst-transfer rate.

WIDE SCSI Wide SCSI uses a data path wider than 8 bits—either 16 or 32 bits. This technique also boosts data transfer to 10MB per second.

FAST WIDE SCSI As the name implies, these products combine Fast and Wide into what is usually marketed as Fast Wide SCSI. It provides burst synchronous transfers of 20MB per second by using a 16-bit data path. A 32-bit Fast-Wide SCSI board could theoretically achieve burst transfers of 40MB per second, but the technology is too expensive to market effectively for desktop systems. (Some high-volume network solutions with 40MB-per-second burst transfer technology are just beginning to appear.)

SCSI-3 The standard was not yet official in late 1995, but like the v.34 telecommunications standard, it was already supported in its interim form by numerous SCSI manufacturers. When finally approved, SCSI 3 will support the plug-and-play standard and transfer data at rates of 20MB per second or faster.

SCSI-3 has other compelling advantages over earlier SCSI standards. It will allow up to 15 SCSI peripherals per host adapter, compared with eight (including the adapter itself) for SCSI 2. Some vendors will add Fast-20 capability, allowing burst transfers of 20MB per second on 8-bit buses and 40MB per second across Wide (16-bit) paths. Also, the SCSI-3 standard will define new high-speed serial interfaces that may provide transfers as fast as 200MB per second, though such devices will be expensive and probably not common anytime soon.

By Many Another Name

Vendors call the different SCSI combinations a variety of marketing names, and usage is not standardized. If you see "Fast SCSI" on a box, you can pretty much expect it to follow the SCSI-2 specification, since SCSI-1 has no "Fast" modes, but even so, vendors prefer a label like "Fast SCSI-2" in order to underscore the SCSI-2 compliance. Similarly, "Wide SCSI" and "Wide SCSI-2" will usually mean the same thing, at least until SCSI-3 comes into its own.

SCSI-3 hasn't been around long enough to generate different labels. Still, various manufacturers including Adaptec, Conner, and Seagate say they will market SCSI-3 under an "UltraSCSI" label. So the proliferation of labels continues.

tip *The inconsistency in labeling can lead to shopping problems. For example, vendors sometimes use "Wide SCSI" to signify 20MB-per-second Fast Wide support, but you can't count on it. Such a label may mean exactly what it says, that is, the product may offer only Wide (but not Fast) SCSI transfers at 10MB per second. Make sure a SCSI device you're considering actually meets your needs before you pull out the checkbook.*

The EIDE/Fast ATA storage technology is moving so fast we won't try to set rigid rules on where to find the best buys. But EIDE drives in the 1GB range were going for less than 40 cents a megabyte toward the end of 1995, with data access speeds and transfer rates equal to all but the very fastest SCSI drives. Also, the EIDE drive specification has done away with the 528MB limit imposed by the original IDE standard, making it practical to go for the speed and simplicity of the EIDE interface even with huge drives.

On the minus side, EIDE is still limited to internal devices unless you're comfortable running unshielded ribbon cable outside the system box (an approach that invites data loss). If your mini-tower is out of room, you'll need to go external, with a SCSI host adapter. Going with SCSI is not a great financial sacrifice, since SCSI drive prices have also dropped to under 50 cents per MB. That makes large SCSI drives quite affordable, and low prices for high-performance host adapters like the AdvanSys card described earlier make SCSI an increasingly attractive alternative.

Video Standards and Your Display Card

Some basics: If Windows 95 is going to be your operating environment, any graphic card that you use should support a 32-bit bus standard: either VESA or PCI. If your current motherboard holds only an older, 16-bit ISA card, consider upgrading the motherboard or buying a new system. Don't buy a new 16-bit ISA display card. The 32-bit VESA or PCI bus increases display speed in Windows (or OS/2) by a factor of more than 10. This is noticeable on a subjective level if you do any kind of prolonged work.

The color-depth you need for your applications will tell you how much video RAM you'll need on your graphic card. For business applications and basic graphics, 256 colors are really all you need. If you work with color images that use 65,000 or 16 million colors, you'll need a graphics card that holds more display memory. The rule for determining how much memory is needed is this: multiply the horizontal and vertical pixel resolutions by the color-depth. Color-depth is measured in powers of 2. 16 colors equals 2^4, requiring 4 bits per pixel (.5 bytes). 256 colors require 8 bits (1 byte) per pixel. 65,536 colors require 16 bits (2 bytes) per pixel and 16.7 million colors require 24 bits (3 bytes) per pixel. So if you run Windows at 800×600 with 256 colors, you need 800×600×1 bytes or 480 kilobytes of onboard video RAM. A video card with 1MB onboard and a high-color RAMDAC chip can display 16.7 million colors at a 640×480 pixel resolution. To display 16 million colors at 800×600, you need a card with 2MB of onboard video RAM.

note *Even though you can find 1MB cards that will handle 16 million colors (as just described), you'll probably see better performance with cards that have a 2MB default configuration. The reason is that dedicated 2MB cards use the additional memory to speed up the display. The threshold for expanding to a 4MB card is the need to display 1024×768 pixels in 16.7 million colors. Some high-end color publishing graphic engines can add V-RAM up to 128MB or more and support resolutions of over 1600×1200 pixels. Beyond a certain point, more RAM equals more speed, not just higher resolution or more colors.*

Most VESA and PCI display cards currently process data at two standard internal transfer rates: 32- and 64-bit. The Imagine 128 card from Number Nine Graphics is an example of a card that handles data in 128-bit chunks. As we are going to press, 192-bit PCI video cards are just beginning to make their appearance. This internal bandwidth is one factor in determining the card's data transfer rate. Other factors are the type and quantity of memory on the card and the type of accelerated chipset that the card uses. A basic 32-bit card using 2MB of DRAM memory transfers data at about 100MB per second. The Imagine 128 with 4MB of V-RAM transfers data at about 500MB per second. For standard business applications running with 256 colors, a transfer rate of 100MB per second should be adequate. Higher screen resolutions and color-depths create more physical pixel data that must be transferred from the CPU.

The individual chipsets used by many PC video cards often contain additional tricks to speed up performance. The type of memory used for Video RAM also affects performance. DRAM chips used in less expensive video cards must go through additional clock cycles to reset and transfer data. VRAM memory can deliver data to the screen and reset portions of the card in a single cycle. The difference between cards using DRAM and VRAM becomes apparent when you use a newer, high-resolution monitor that demands a high vertical refresh rate.

The last (but not least) important factor in evaluating a video card is the software the vendor supplies with it. Some manufacturers have a reputation for issuing blazing fast hardware along with frustrating, buggy drivers that either don't run or won't install. Some manufacturers issue video cards with the bare bones drivers necessary to make them run while others include easy-to-use utilities for switching resolutions, calibrating color, or creating a "virtual desktop." On the high-end side of the corporate PC curve, new applications that lean heavily on graphics are coming in at amazing speeds. Videoconferencing and kiosk-level multimedia graphics are both prime examples. If you expect to deal with graphics at this level, you can't really work effectively with a simple graphics card anymore. You need a local-bus graphics accelerator that is memory-heavy and able to handle 1280 by 1024 or (better) 1600 by 1200 pixel resolution at 16.7 million colors.

The same basic rules hold true if you work with computer-aided design or create multimedia programs. You'll need first-rate graphics programs and equipment, and it won't pay to skimp.

Sound Cards

There was a time when a PC sound card seemed like just a frilly sort of add-on, not something that anyone who is "serious" about computing would be terribly concerned with. The advent of multimedia changed all that. Now it's common for e-mail messages and memos to contain voice recordings and other sound effects, and missing the content of such additions can distort a message's meaning. That's just one example, on the business side. That's not to mention all the games it would be much less enjoyable to play without the music and sound effects. (But "serious" computer users don't play games—do they?)

Multimedia hit PC computing with an impact similar to that of fast modems—it changed the way users perceived the potential of their systems. A sound card is essential to CD-ROM-based multimedia applications. In fact, the two are so closely tied that many CD-ROM drives come with a sound card that provides the CD-ROM controller interface.

While CD-ROM multimedia products helped bring sound cards into the mainstream of PC use, sound cards have now become central to many practical uses. Newer applications include on-board radio and TV reception, no-hands telephone stations, digitized answering machines, narration in business presentations, multiuser "white board" work sessions, and portable advertising and product promotions, among many others. There is even a specialized keyboard offered with a speaker on each side to provide stereo sound. (It's SC&T International's $200+ SMSK-200 model, and features on-keyboard sliders for balance, tone, and volume. The input jack accepts input from portable CD-ROM drives for those who lack a sound card.)

Picking the Right Sound Card

Technically, a sound card is just an expansion board designed to record and play back sound, providing its signal output to speakers or an external amplifier. Like consumer-oriented sound products, there's a huge range of available price and quality. Where consumer products range from, say, a small "boom box" to full-scale home entertainment centers, the range of available options in sound cards is quite broad. Here are the basics.

You can get sound cards in both EIDE and SCSI models, and there is not much difference in sound quality between them at the better end of the quality curve. The cheaper "no-name clone" cards are not SCSI, of course.

Good, Better, Best

If you didn't care about sound quality, you wouldn't want a sound card in the first place. You'd be satisfied with your tinny old beach resort boom box, and after all, a PC already comes equipped with an internal speaker. Who needs more?

But if you do care, bear in mind that getting a sound card is like buying a home sound system: You pretty much get what you pay for, and if you stint too much on price, you'll pay a penalty in sound quality. As you invest more in quality, you'll get more options and more flexible bundled software, as well as better sound quality. The best cards offer wavetable MIDI synthesis and CD-quality digital audio playback and can easily handle high-fidelity audio CD output from your CD-ROM drive. Less expensive boards use only FM synthesis, which has a lower sound quality, but can still play audio CDs.

Judging the Products

When considering a purchase, pay attention to the maximum sampling rate, the sampling size, and what record-and-play options a card offers. Also check a card's compatibility modes. Here are more details:

SAMPLING SIZE AND RATE For good sound quality, insist on a board that can handle sampling rates of 11.025, 22.05, and 44.1KHz in both 8- and 16-bit sample sizes. A musical passage playing in 16-bit samples at a 44.1KHz rate through good-quality speakers sounds every bit as good as a home sound system, though the power limitations of your PC's power supply will necessarily limit the power you can pump to the speakers. If you use the sound board output to feed an external amplifier or a set of headphones, the sound quality of 44.1KHz, 16-bit sampling will be as good as your external sound system provides, with no penalty in quality for having come from a PC CD-ROM drive.

COMPATIBILITY All but the most highly specialized sound cards are built for compatibility with at least one of three standards: Sound Blaster, Ad Lib, and Windows. If you plan to try more than just the applications that come in the box with the card, be sure your card supports all three standards. This is especially important if you expect to mix DOS and Windows applications. If you can't get a card that supports more than one of the standards, bear in mind that some software (especially DOS games) only knows about Creative Labs' Sound Blaster, so at minimum, make sure your card has a Sound Blaster compatibility mode.

SPEAKERS Pay attention to the speakers that come with the card. As with a home sound system, you'll waste your money if you don't get speakers good enough to reproduce the sound signal faithfully, without distortion. A good set of speakers starts at around $100, but if you want high fidelity sound, be ready to pay $200 or more. Good speakers will have built-in tone and balance controls, so you can set the sound level independently of the sound card and software. Of course, if you're on a budget you can also get dime-store quality speakers for under $30, but if you have sensitive ears, they won't thank you for the resulting assault on your senses.

BUNDLED SOFTWARE Any sound card will come with programs and drivers designed for it. At the upper end of the curve, the software can get quite interesting. For example, the Creative Labs Sound Blaster AWE32 model comes with a business-oriented text-to-speech module and is bundled with a Cakewalk Apprentice music sequencer program. You can expand its range of MIDI instruments with a series of what the manufacturer calls "software sound fonts." Other top-of-the-line cards come with similar software applications.

RECORD/PLAYBACK MODES Good-quality sound cards can handle 16 or more simultaneous voices, and wave-table synthesis. Not all cards offer both record and playback stereo modes; check that if it's important to you.

CD-ROM Drives

CD-ROM drives became an important mainstream computing tool when they stopped being solely the province of gamers and people who need megabytes of clip art and other desktop publishing resources. Since the advent of the affordable CD-ROM-based reference set, you can use them to quickly look up just about anything, without wasting acres of hard drive space on static data files. If you expect to work or play at all with multimedia, large graphical files and programs, or a large, static database, a CD-ROM drive is fast becoming an absolute necessity. Here are some things to keep in mind when getting one.

What to Look For

CD-ROM drives come in flavors of single, double, triple, quad (4×), and sextuple (6×) speed.

The original, single-speed CD-ROMs are not often seen in retail channels anymore. They passed data at 150K per second or less and only received the name "single speed" when the next, double-speed generation came in with a 300K-per-second transfer rate. Triple-speed drives handle data at 450K per second, while quad-speed drives top out at 600K per second. The newest 6× models handle data at 900K per second.

At a minimum, start with the MPC 2 specification, which calls for a double-speed drive, and get a quad-speed drive if you can fit it into your budget. Most CD-ROM drives now on the market are quad-speed, but the 6× standard is quickly taking over. (Triple-speed drives never caught on and have all but disappeared, since they offered relatively little performance benefit considering their high price.)

Whether to get a quad-speed or hold out for a 6× CD-ROM drive depends upon how you expect to use it. For many multimedia and reference titles, or for loading new software, even a double-speed drive is good enough, but bear in mind that it's not a good long-term solution. Quad-speed drives are dropping in price as they are being replaced, and they run CD-ROM applications like games much more smoothly. That makes them the best choice unless you're counting pennies.

tip *Data transfer rates aren't the only factor to consider. Access time also counts for a lot. The MPC 2 specification allows a maximum access time of 400ms, but don't get anything slower than a unit with 200ms access time or faster. You can get access times as low as 150 to 175ms in quad-speed drives, and the Teac 6X drive claims a 110ms seek time. Such speeds make a tremendous performance difference.*

The Right Interface

To integrate a CD-ROM drive into your system, you'll need to pick an interface. Until recently your choices were limited to proprietary interfaces (from Sony, Panasonic, and Mitsumi) supplied on most sound cards, or standard SCSI (requiring a SCSI host adapter) from any of a dozen companies. Many sound cards are starting to offer onboard SCSI connectors, which are the best choice, and some new systems are also including Enhanced IDE as basic equipment—another safe industry standard. Usability extras to look for include a headphone jack, front panel controls (so you can play CDs without fussing with software programs), and bundled software for programming audio CD play.

CD-R (Recordable CD-ROM) Drives

Now that CD writers are coming down in price (with models now available for under $1500), CD-ROMs are also being used to back-up huge disks. You can do a generational backup of a 1.2GB hard drive on a couple of CD-ROM blanks for around $20, and have what amounts to a permanent record. A CD-ROM also can transfer huge files between offices, to multimedia clients, and the like—they let you avoid spending hours tying up phone lines to transfer, for example, sets of graphic images or multimedia programs by modem when next-day physical delivery of a CD-ROM will do. CD-ROMs are not much subject to damage by the shipping process, unlike magnetic media. And, finally, a CD-ROM drive is now common equipment. People at the receiving end are much more likely to have one than, for example, a high-density floppy or digital audio tape drive.

The CD-R technology is advancing fast, but to get the best use out of it, you need a SCSI card. Smooth data transfer is critical when writing to a CD, and the slightest hitch can make a $10 CD blank good for nothing much but throwing across the parking lot.

Although CD-ROM writing drives are not a threat to backup tape drives and the like, they do make ever-increasing sense for purposes of data transfer now that nearly every new PC comes with a CD-ROM drive for reference CDs and games. A half-gig hard drive can be backed up to a single CD-ROM, which holds up to about 650MB of data. Copying data to a CD-ROM is much faster than copying to an equivalent floppy drive or tape system, at least at present. Once copied, data on the CD ROM can be transferred—copied—quickly to another machine. Large graphic or desktop publishing files can be transported to printing service bureaus, and there are no lingering questions about what size or type of tape drive the destination machine may be equipped with.

As efforts continue to make different platforms (yes, that means Macs and PCs) mutually compatible, there are no cross-platform compatibility problems with CD-ROMs. As long as the CD recording drive conforms to international CD standard ISO 9660, the resulting CD-ROM can be read on either platform.

Removable Hard Drives

As an alternative to the fixed, and fixed-capacity hard drive, various firms have marketed removable-media hard drives that let you switch hard drive platter cartridges in a way similar to switching traditional floppy disks. In particular, the Alliance Peripheral Systems, Inc. MobilStor SyQuest product line gained fame for its 100 to 270MB removable hard drives.

Removable hard drive devices are generally a lot slower than SCSI or EIDE hard drives, often being rated in MB per minute rather than MB per second for data transfer rates—not at all what you'd want for a system's primary disk drive. But they can back up large databases or whole systems and be put away for storage without using up a drive bay. They also work well for passing large files around an organization that has standardized on one manufacturer and one size of removable device. Since the cartridges can be passed around, and many newer portable drive designs can plug into a system's parallel port, the cartridges and drives are almost perfectly transportable from machine to machine.

Unfortunately, removable hard drives also have long been quite expensive—but that is changing fast. Some newer models of removable hard drive are coming out with much higher capacities and lower per-MB prices. For example, one model by Iomega Corp., maker of the floppy-based Zip drive (see next section), uses 1.3GB Winchester hard drive cartridges. Called the Jaz, the drive unit costs about $600 and each removable 1.3GB cartridge costs about $130. That's a dime a megabyte, folks, if you discount the price of the drive itself. The drive is a SCSI-2 device, but if you haven't got a SCSI-2 card you can get a special Adaptec SCSI controller just for the Jaz, for about $55. Users with large systems to back up, large files to distribute, or a need for portable high capacity storage will find this technology very attractive.

The disadvantage of most such systems is that they are too slow to use for primary hard drive storage, though that is changing. The Iomega device just described can be used as a bootable drive and claims 17ms access time, much faster than the original hard drives of 10 years ago, if slower than the 12ms accesses of typical EIDE drives. Data transfer rates even for the Jaz are still only about a third of a normal EIDE drive, however.

Floppies, Flopticals, and Assorted Other Media

Forget the venerable 5.25-inch floppy drive that revolutionized file distribution when IBM introduced the 1.2MB high density diskette. That size is almost a thing of the past, unless you have thousands of the old diskettes in your computer hutch and are determined to put them to use. Right now, programs are distributed almost exclusively on 3.5-inch 720K or 1.44MB diskettes, but even that is about to change. Some online information services are sending out software on CD-ROMs now, using the extra capacity to hawk specialized services or show samples of the kinds of multimedia files available to members. And Microsoft is making the transition very quickly to CD-ROM distribution of their largest programs. On floppies, the Redmond giant is using a new high-density DMF format that a standard 3.5-inch drive can only read, not write to.

What then is taking the place of the old floppy disks? It's not settled yet, but floppy-based portable storage technology is going in the predictable direction of more data in the same or less space. What follows is a quick overview of some of what's out there; for a more comprehensive look, check the ads in a current *Byte Magazine*, *Computer Shopper*, or some other PC-oriented journal.

- Iomega Corp. has had trouble meeting demand for a $200 floppy-based "Zip Drive" whose 100MB removable media costs $20, a storage cost of ten cents per meg if you expense the initial drive cost separately. With a data transfer rate of 60MB per minute, the SCSI version is about three times faster than the parallel port version. You can get a special $55 Adaptec SCSI card to drive it if you don't already have SCSI (or you can get a generic SCSI card instead, for about the same price, so you can daisy-chain more SCSI devices on the system). For maximum portability between systems, you'll want the parallel port version even though it is slower. The unit has a separate AC power adapter.
- Compaq Computer Corp., 3M Corp., and Matsushita-Kotobuki Electronics Industries have joined forces to introduce a 3.5-inch 120MB floppy drive that can also read standard 720K and 1.44MB disks. The new floppies can replace about 83 1.44MB disks, making both program installation and backups more convenient. The drive was expected to cost about $200 at first but to drop sharply in price soon thereafter.

- Teac offers a 1.44MB floppy and quad-speed CD-ROM drive in a single, half-height combo unit. This should gladden the hearts of desktop and mini-tower system owners who want an internal CD-ROM drive but can't find a place to put it. The unit uses a proprietary Teac CD-ROM interface but separate, standard floppy drive connectors.
- Panasonic also makes a combo CD-ROM drive and 5.25-inch rewritable optical drive.

Tape Drives and Other Sequential Storage

The thing about tape drives is that they are sequential instead of random access storage devices. That means it's impossible (except through pure luck) to access a specific file quickly; the tape must wind, and rewind, and take what can seem like hours to find the data or files you need. For that reason, tapes are used almost exclusively to back up hard drives. To a lesser extent, they are sometimes used to standardize the software on multiple office machines, but that kind of use runs into another problem with sequential storage media—they're slo-o-o-w. If you've ever twiddled your thumbs while a backup tape drive copied 150MB of data, you'll appreciate just how slow a tape feels once you're accustomed to the speed of random access.

With huge hard drives becoming the norm rather than the exception, the venerable QIC-80 backup tape drive is starting to look a bit small even though it stores over 200MB per cartridge. If you have a multidrive system with storage measured in gigs instead of megs, switching tape cartridges during a backup session can feel like the old "floppy shuffle" when drives pushed 80MB capacities but were still being backed up on 1.2 or 1.44MB floppies. It takes time and accurate labeling or you're in trouble if you ever have to restore.

Still, at this point tape backup units are a mature technology, and for the price of an old QIC-80 drive ($200 to $250) you can get tape systems that put upwards of 700MB compressed data on a single cartridge. It may take awhile, but as long as it can plug away at a backup unattended overnight, or in the background while you do something useful, the speed isn't all that important. It's mostly used for emergencies anyway; for quick, interim backups of data and other work files, floppies are still the media of choice.

Most tape drives use the floppy controller to transfer data, so you can't use floppies while doing a backup. For most users that is not really a terrible drawback, since you make a backup after, not before, you use floppies to install new software. In any case, systems that hook into the parallel port can get around that problem—if in fact it is a problem for you.

A worse drawback is that the floppy controller limits data throughput to floppy rates, but again, you don't buy tape drives for the blinding speed in the first place.

If it is speed you want, and you must use tape, you can get some very fast drives. At the high end of the spectrum, for around $4000, you can get a half-inch streaming tape backup system from APS Technologies that handles about 2.5MB per second, using parallel recording techniques. The SCSI-2 unit needs a fast computer (preferably Pentium) and a high-performance PCI, VL-Bus, or EISA SCSI controller. APS Technologies says the unit is aimed at high-end desktop units, but with a cartridge capacity of 20GB of compressed data, it's suitable for enterprise network backups too.

Extend Your QIC-80 Tape Life

If you're one of the millions of users who bought a QIC-80 tape drive back in the days of standard 120 to 250MB hard disks, you don't necessarily have to either replace it or resign yourself to long waits between shuffling tapes. You can get 30 to 40 percent more data onto a DC2120XL Ximat-formatted mini-cartridge, using an $80 (list) 3M Upgrade Kit. If you have an older Colorado Jumbo 250 or parallel port drive, you can expand the drive's capacity to 350MB simply by purchasing the latest versions of Colorado Systems' DOS and Windows tape backup utilities.

Forcing 350MB of compressed data into a former 250MB data space makes for a cheap upgrade that may not eliminate having to use multiple tapes in a backup, but can cut way down on the number of tapes needed. And it can save money better used for other purposes.

Upgrade to the Travan Standard

Travan is a new cartridge design by 3M that's a bit larger than a standard DC-2000 style mini-cartridge but holds 750 feet of tape. A Travan cartridge is somewhat trapezoidal in shape, with the larger end at the rear, so the front end mechanical heads, rollers, and so forth are the same size as those used for a DC-2000. That has two important benefits. First, a Travan drive is backward compatible; it can read and write to the DC-2000 or QIC-80 tapes you've already accumulated. Second, it can cram more tape into the back of the cartridge. In fact, it accommodates a longer stretch of tape that is 0.31 inch wide, instead of the traditional quarter-inch size. The result is a drive that can use either your old QIC-80 or DC-2000 tapes or the newer, higher capacity tapes, and that with compression can cram 800MB onto a single cartridge.

It's still slow and noisy, of course. That seems to be inherent in tape drives. But at least it will back up most or all of a standard large drive unattended; you won't have to hang around waiting to change tapes.

Other Tape Alternatives

For around $800 to $1200, you can get a digital audio tape (DAT) drive capable of recording 2 to 4GB of data on a cartridge. These devices are especially well suited to making unattended network backups overnight. They are generally fast and reliable, and some of the vendors also offer automatic tape changers that let you truly leave the driving to the backup software.

However, for less money you can now get a quiet CD-R recording CD-ROM drive that copies at SCSI-2 speeds on CD media that are not sensitive to magnetic fields and, once recorded, have an estimated 10-year shelf life. The CD-R technology is still developing, but if you can wait for automatic changers to come to market, this may become a better alternative to large standard tape or DAT drives.

note *A NEC multidisc 4X CD-ROM changer can also be used as a method for accessing and managing your series of CD-R backups. Share it on the network and you have access to 3.5GB of archive data. (The changer holds seven disks at 650MB each.)*

Modems

The task of maintaining compatibility with a variety of modems has long rested on the shoulders of the communications application. And although most modems conform to the Hayes-modem standard AT command set, there are almost as many deviations as there are modems—buy a new modem, reconfigure your application. For 32-bit applications, Windows 95 changes that.

While 16-bit applications will continue to work with modems pretty much as they did under Windows 3.1, 32-bit applications will be able to take advantage of the new Telephony API (TAPI). Windows 3.1 offered UNIDRV to ease printer support; Windows 95 tries to do the same for modems with its new Unimodem modem driver. This driver works with both TAPI and VCOMM (a Windows 95 low-level communication driver that provides hooks into communication devices such as modems, LPT ports, and COM ports). Unimodem takes the TAPI commands from communications applications and translates them into AT commands (or whatever command the modem understands).

A modem vendor can support the driver by writing a simple text or .INF file. Within this file will be the command strings necessary to communicate with the modem, and other specifications such as modem name, manufacturer, capabilities, and initialization commands. Windows 95 includes built-in support for hundreds of modems. With newer models, the manufacturer and model number can be detected and installed automatically.

The Alphabet Soup of Connection Protocols

Currently, the most universal standard for modems to talk to each other at 9600bps and above is called, v.32. (This is a protocol system designed by the International Telecommunication Union-Telecommunication, formerly known as the CCITT.) If your modem is equipped with the v.32bis feature, it can send and receive data at the higher rate of 14,400bps.

The MNP, v.42, and v.42bis extensions that some modems feature are additional compression and error-correction algorithms. They don't affect the raw bytes-per-second capacity of your modem, but they can improve reliability and compress data to increase the transfer rate.

U.S. Robotics offers an additional protocol in its modems called HST (high speed technology). The USR HST protocol allows proprietary connection at 14,400, and 16,800bps to another U.S. Robotics HST modem. Many BBS systems still use USR Dual Standard modems that can switch between v.32 and HST when they answer a call.

V.32terbo is an interim communication protocol developed by Bell Laboratories. It allows connections at 16,800bps and 19,200bps with other modems that support this standard. Since V32terbo doesn't require a faster processor to implement, it is currently being offered as a low-cost add-on to existing v.32bis products.

The newest modems available on the marketplace are capable of connect speeds up to 28,800 and even 33,600bps. The official protocol for communication at this speed, developed by the ITU-T, is called v.34. This standard was ratified in the Fall of 1994. Modems that use it have become fairly entrenched in the marketplace over the past year. Before the arrival of v.34, an interim protocol known as V.FC (or V.FAST) was built into a number of high-speed modems. The problem with V.FC is that modems from different manufacturers that use slightly dissimilar versions may be incompatible with one another. This means that a "Zoom" V.FC modem may not be able to connect to a "Supra", or a "Practical Peripherals" V.FC modem at speeds above the common speed of 14,400bps. If you are hunting for a new modem now, you should look for one that supports both v.34 and V.FC. U.S. Robotics offers an excellent line of modems that can accommodate all of the current telecommunication protocols being used.

note *if you're buying a new modem, you might do well to select a model that has an upgradable Flash BIOS. In the old days, in order to upgrade a modem from one standard to another, you had to order special chips, open the case, and perform minor surgery. Modems based on Flash BIOS technology can be upgraded to new protocol standards simply by downloading and running an executable installation file. The newest wrinkle in v.34 technology has been added recently by U.S. Robotics to their Courier and Dual Standard models. These models now support a maximum connection rate of 33,600bps, instead of the 28,800bps which is tops for most other brands.*

ISDN

ISDN is a technology that allows telephone connection rates more than four times faster than conventional modems through special, leased telephone lines. ISDN is gradually getting more support and is more widely available than ever before, but there are still three barriers to wider adoption of the technology. There is still a lack of good installation and diagnostic utilities; most ISDN products are difficult to set up and get working correctly with other equipment. Setting up line parameters with the telephone company is part of the problem and will get worse as more devices using different providers compete for the ISDN line. Standards-based compression is another technology needed to help ISDN gain "critical mass." Many vendors use proprietary compression schemes, but they are of limited usefulness because most telephone company switches only support 56Kbps per channel. The third problem is state Public Utilities Commission (PUC) regulation. Some understand the importance of intelligent ISDN tariffs, but many continue to lag and others, such as California, are using schemes that effectively raise rates.

Printers

Computers at one time were touted as the route to the paperless office, but as everyone knows by now, the ultimate effect was really to make it easy to compose and print more stuff on more paper in less time. As the capabilities of PC programs have evolved, so have the printers that make the output semipermanent. The ubiquitous dot matrix and daisywheel models of the

'80s have given way to inexpensive bubble-jet and ink-jet models that deliver better print quality and more production features at competitive prices. The warhorse Hewlett-Packard LaserJet Series II printer of the '80s has been replaced by newer models that print faster and support easier-to-handle font technologies and higher output resolutions. The Adobe PostScript language, mainstay of desktop publishers, has also undergone substantial revisions that eliminate common printing errors, and make it possible to reproduce more complex graphic images with a smaller amount of dedicated printer memory.

Printer Control Languages

To control your printer you must tell it what to do in a language that it understands. With laser and ink-jet printers there are two languages used almost universally: PCL and PostScript.

PCL

Short for printer control language, PCL was devised by HP to control its LaserJet series of printers. Intended for general business printing, PCL was designed originally to print letters and numbers, and to allow printing of small, postcard-sized graphics. It was these capabilities that led to the LaserJet's replacement of the daisywheel printer in the business world. The PCL Level 4 language was implemented in Hewlett-Packard models (notably the HP LaserJet Series II) up until about 1990. It contained no internal support for the scaleable, outline fonts commonly used by today's applications (although a PCL-4 printer can render Microsoft TrueType fonts in a rasterized, bitmap format). A new implementation called PCL-5 replaced the previous version of HP's printer language in models dating from the LaserJet Series III. HP PCL-5 printers include a series of resident scaleable fonts, analogous (though not completely equivalent) to the fonts resident in printers that support Adobe PostScript.

POSTSCRIPT

PostScript is a mathematical, descriptive language, originally devised by Adobe Systems, Inc., for printers meant to produce publishable output from layouts created under the Aldus PageMaker desktop publishing program (now also owned by Adobe). PostScript was included, originally, only in LaserWriter printers manufactured by Apple. Eventually, the Apple LaserWriter became popular on Intel-based PCs, as well. (The advent of a number of "PostScript-clone" languages in the late 1980's eventually persuaded Adobe to license its code to third-party printer manufacturers.) PostScript printers are more sophisticated devices than PCL printers. They produce a wider and richer number of half-tone images, and can more easily scale bitmap and vector images, rotate text in different directions, and provide more precise support for printing color images. Current PostScript printers from Apple and other vendors contain an implementation called PostScript Level 2. PostScript Level 2 is an improved version of Adobe's original printer language that speeds page output (always the flaw-in-the-ointment with graphic images under PostScript Level 1). PostScript Level 2 also makes it possible to process and print more complex vector curves with less printer memory than what was previously required.

As laser and ink-jet printers have become more powerful and more standardized, it has become more common for printers to include support for both PostScript and PCL. If, for economic reasons, you must select a printer that supports only one or the other language, you should know that PostScript printers tend to need more memory to achieve the same printing speeds, because they must do a great deal of computation. On the other hand, a PCL-specific printer is unable to interpret and print graphically precise Encapsulated PostScript, or EPS, files of the sort still preferred in the desktop publishing world.

Windows 95 includes drivers both for PCL and for PostScript printers, based on the published standards for each type of printing. Most laser printers (and a growing number of ink-jet and bubble-jet models) even on the lower end of the price curve have an operating mode capable of interpreting either control language. The manual that comes with the printer will generally specify which mode is best to use with that printer.

Dot Matrix Printers

Dot matrix is the oldest PC printing technology still in common use. Most dot matrix printers require the use of manufacturer-specific control codes, although compatibility with the Epson printer language is incorporated in many models. To the extent that a *de facto* dot matrix printer control language exists, it is probably the one used by Epson printers. Dot matrix printers do not generally support PostScript or PCL image processing, although clever programmers have produced software filters that can add this capability. (These emulation utilities are recommended only for dedicated hackers with lots more time available than money.)

Dot matrix printers mimic the printing action of a traditional typewriter, in which the reverse image of a letter is hammered against an inked cloth or plastic ribbon, which in turn transfers the letter's image to a piece of paper underneath. When a line of letters has been printed, the paper is scrolled up to a new line and the process is repeated. A dot matrix printer substitutes 9 or 24 individually moved pins for the typewriter's solid image keys. The pins are hammered selectively against the ribbon to produce a letter's image on the paper. The printing head doesn't have to swivel or turn in order to print a different letter image, but instead gains speed by simply pulling down a different set of pins to produce a different letter.

Advantages of dot matrix printing include low cost of consumables (ribbon cartridges are very inexpensive and these printers can use low-grade paper, keeping typical costs down to less than a penny a page) and, as mentioned before, the ability to print through several sheets of NCR or carbon paper to produce duplicate images in a single pass. A serious disadvantage is the resulting jagged letter images, since only 9 or 24 pins are used to generate the image. "Near letter quality" can be produced by making the print head take the time to hammer each letter image several times in slightly different positions, eliminating the worst of the "jaggies," but a dot matrix won't reproduce the quality of a typed letter or a 300-dpi (dot-per-inch) laser page.

Also, the physical hammering against the ribbon and paper is noisy and can be truly distressing in an office environment (and it can wake the baby—or the dead—at home). Higher resolution, quieter bubble-jet printers are selling for not much more than dot matrix printers, so there's no very good reason to buy a new dot matrix printer anymore.

Monochrome Ink Jet and BubbleJet Printers

Not many people realize it, but the market-dominating HP InkJet and the Canon BubbleJet printers were codeveloped by the two firms, and the technology is almost identical. There is very little technical difference between them, though Canon later put a bit more effort into enhancing the "explosions" at the print head that produce the tiny ink particles projected onto the paper by a BubbleJet printer. The Canon's finer particles permit slightly higher printing resolutions, but the disparity is not so great that a casual eye can see the difference. The most significant difference between the two printers is who owns the trademark to the name. HP owns InkJet, and Canon owns BubbleJet.

The differences in resolution are going back and forth anyhow, since HP has announced it will make a 1200-dpi InkJet printer. Photo-quality images are 2400-dpi, but even at half the photo resolution, you really cannot easily tell the difference. (Most current InkJet and BubbleJet printers print at a resolution of 300 dpi, or a hybrid 300 horizontal by 600 vertical dpi for text-based material.)

Both printer types work by spraying tiny jets (or bubbles) of ink from cartridges onto very finely focused spots on the paper surface, mimicking the action of a 24-pin dot matrix printer but at immensely greater resolutions. Unless you examine the output of a standard, 300- or 600-dpi jet-style printer with a strong magnifying glass, it looks like a standard printed page.

InkJet printers manufactured by Hewlett-Packard retain compatibility with the PCL standard built into its laser models. Some ink-jet and bubble-jet models also include PostScript interpreters, or the ability to use PostScript cartridges.

How Color Jet Printers Work

Color jet printers produce their colors using either three-color or four-color printing. A good color printer also will have a separate black-only cartridge for use when color isn't necessary. Four-color printers mix black, cyan, magenta, and yellow cartridges to get their color, while three-color printers use only cyan, magenta, and yellow. To get black, a three-color printer mixes its colors to create what is called composite black, but this uses up the ink and doesn't always produce a clean black color. Go with a four-color printer if you can.

Resolution

Color printers at the pricey end of the curve offer high-resolution color graphics modes. For example, the Epson Stylus Color and Canon offer 720 dpi printing while the HP DeskJet 660C prints at 600 dpi. It takes special paper to achieve those resolutions, however. All current color printers can achieve a lower 300×300 or 360×360 resolutions with more than enough clarity and color-depth for everyday printing jobs. Higher resolutions are slower and more ink-intensive, so even if you have them, you probably won't find yourself using them very often.

Laser Printers

They work like this: Laser printers have a diode laser to project a beam against a spinning mirror, which flashes the beam at a rotating drum coated with a photosensitive layer. Where the beam hits, the photosensitive chemical changes its electrical charge, and fine ink powder called *toner* adheres there electrostatically. It is then fused directly to the paper with heat. The heating element, moving parts, and laser diode all take power to run, and they generate noticeable heat, but recent power-saving technology is helping to alleviate that problem.

In the world of monochrome printing, laser printers and somewhat less expensive bubble-jet printers dominate even the home market, with the two overlapping at the low end of the laser and high end of the bubble-jet price range. Laser printers are generally preferred when speed matters, since they can print an entire page at a time instead of a line at a time like the ink jets. Laser printers generally manage 4 to 12 ppm (pages per minute), compared to a typical jet printer output of 1 to 2 ppm—though recent ink-jet models are achieving speeds of up to 7 ppm at standard resolutions.

The present main advantages of black-and-white laser printers in a world of color jet printers is the low cost of operation and the relatively high output speed. It is still best for high-speed printing in a networked environment, for example. If that sort of printing is what you need, a laser printer may be the way to go. High-end lasers also are preferred for extremely high output quality approaching that of typesetters.

Color Laser Printers

Color came relatively late to laser printers, and it is still very expensive but starting to become available to the middle market ranges. A typical color laser printer costs more than $3000 and does not produce output all that much better than a $500 Canon BubbleJet printer. For truly high-quality color printing you need to go to the expensive techniques—dye sublimation, thermal wax transfer, and the like. Or you can have the color-critical job printed by a service bureau.

Multifunction Printers

The next big wave in printers seems to be in multifunction devices just hitting the markets. Combination printer-fax-copier-scanner devices have been on the market for some time, but they have tended to offer nothing better than 200 dpi and to require physically changing switches or even toner cartridges in order to change function. This is now turning around, and some very good small-office/home-office multifunction printing devices are now coming onto the scene.

Moving On

In this chapter, we've attempted to provide you with a basic hardware vocabulary to help you become a canny hardware consumer. In the chapter that follows, you'll find some simple shopping advice tailored for those who must make purchasing decisions on both a personal and corporate level.

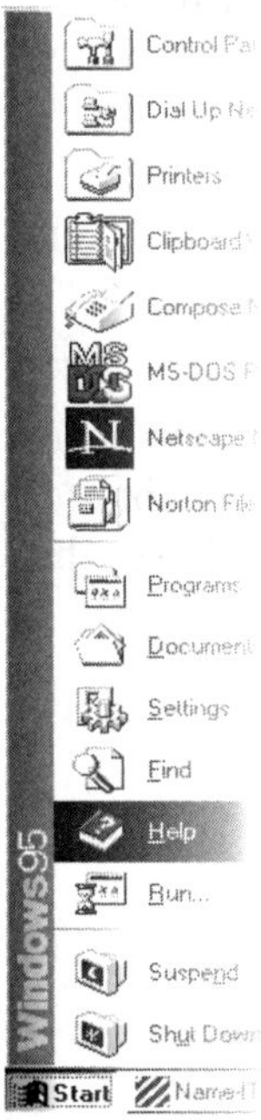

Control Pa
Dial Up Ne
Printers
Clipboard
Compose
MS-DOS
Netscape
Norton File
Programs
Document
Settings
Find
Help
Run...
Suspend
Shut Down
Windows95
Start

chapter 16

Hardware Questions and Upgrade Strategies

- Measuring system performance
    - Do you really need to upgrade?
- What to soup up first
- Upgrading old hardware
- Guides for buying a new system
- Windows 95 and mobile computing
    - Notebooks and PCMCIA peripherals
- Component upgrading strategies

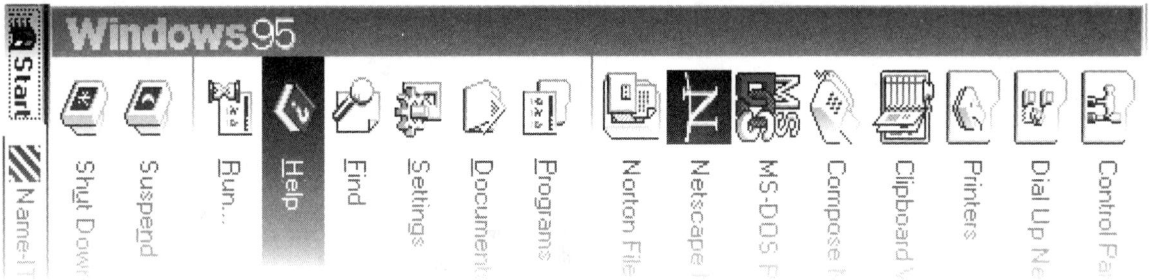

IT'S a simple fact—Windows 95 will work better on newer, more generic hardware. That's not to say, however, that Windows 95 won't perform satisfactorily on your older ISA 486 machine with 8MB of RAM. In fact, the authors of this book are a bit divided on that point. One of us feels that an 8MB ISA machine is all that's necessary for light Windows computing chores. The other is a multitasking junkie, who likes to have three or four projects simultaneously open on the desktop while constantly sending and receiving e-mail. Heavy multitasking takes more RAM, to avoid the bottleneck of constant reads and writes to virtual memory on the hard drive.

In this chapter, we help you evaluate your own hardware situation with regard to Windows 95. We outline several productivity scenarios and match them with some minimum hardware requirements. We also provide guidelines for upgrading your current machine, or buying a new system. By the way, if you're coming into this chapter, cold, you may want to flip back to Chapter 15, occasionally, for clarifications of acronyms and PC hardware jargon. In this chapter we toss around references to ISA, PCI, and the rest of the alphabet soup, assuming that you have the necessary background knowledge to absorb and weigh our consumer advice.

It Was Fast Enough Before

To upgrade the hardware or not to upgrade for Windows 95—that's a legitimate question for which there isn't really a simple universal answer. You don't need a fast Pentium with a gazillion MB hard drive to run Windows 95 effectively, but having one doesn't hurt. One thing is clear:

holdouts who are still tapping away on 286/386 machines with 40MB hard drives can forget about running Windows 95 at all—unless they're willing to tap the bank account enough to buy a new system.

Most users fall somewhere between those extremes, and between the extremes is where you need to apply some judgment. Probably the most vexing judgment call belongs to those whose systems have been fast enough for Windows 3.1, but have fallen off the leading technological edge. What if your system works well, but is several years old—is it now time to upgrade?

For example, if you currently depend on a 486 ISA system, should you keep using it or upgrade to a 32-bit VESA or PCI system? Should you get the cheaper and more abundant VESA local bus, selecting 32-bit VESA peripherals, or switch to a PCI system? If you move to a PCI system (with the peripheral replacements this entails), should you get a cheaper, fast 486, or a high-end Pentium machine? What about systems that combine PCI and VESA slots on the same motherboard; is this an economical way to protect your investment in VESA components?

PCs allow so many configurations that such questions could continue indefinitely. The fine points of hardware selection will depend on what you want and need, determined by your productivity environment, and the equipment you're starting out with. First let's look at the issue of whether you need an upgrade at all.

Microsoft claims you can run Windows 95 on a 386DX with 4MB of RAM and 20MB of hard disk space, but if you've tried it you'll probably conclude the 386DX minimum was dreamed up by Microsoft's marketing department, not by any computer user or realistic engineer. Strictly speaking, Windows 95 will run—barely—on a 386-based machine. But it can feel like one of those bad dreams in which you run as fast as you can, but you're up to your neck in molasses. It's not something to try when you're awake, unless you're ready to spend lots of time at the water cooler between programs.

If you do need or want the Windows 95 enhancements, but you're running a 386, be ready to price a system upgrade to, at minimum, a 33MHz 486DX-based motherboard. Windows 95 is actually designed for Pentium-level 32-bit processing, and there's a huge performance penalty on 386-based systems that you just won't want to pay.

Measuring Performance (What Should You Soup Up First?)

The ultimate test of your system's performance is your contentment with the response of the PC as you run through your daily applications. Here are the general areas you should consider:

CPU/MEMORY The time it takes to complete internal program tasks. Do you get irritated watching the Win95 hourglass, or sitting through lengthy "Please Wait" messages?

HARD DISK/CD PERFORMANCE Time expended in loading programs, switching between programs, and loading or saving files.

I/O SUBSYSTEM When you use your modem to upload or download files, or browse online information, are you comfortable with the response? Are you satisfied with your printer's page output speed?

VIDEO PERFORMANCE Do your programs have a snappy subjective feel? When you pull down a menu, select a new page, or modify a picture, does the screen quickly reflect the commands you enter with the mouse and keyboard?

MONITOR Is the text on your screen crisp, clear, and easy to work with? Are the colors consistent and solid? Is the display flicker-free?

In taking inventory of your system, some commercial and shareware benchmarking utilities can help you flag individual components that are overdue for replacement. Benchmark programs can be used to deliver both absolute and relative performance statistics. For instance, to measure the performance of the disk subsystem, Coretest is a time-honored freeware utility that can still accurately reflect the data transfer rate and average seek time of your hard disk. Available on CompuServe and most bulletin boards, Coretest is useful in helping you to determine whether enhanced 32-bit data transfer features are actually working on your system. Coretest also measures average seek time. (Which by contemporary standards, should be below 15ms to be considered good, and below 10ms to be considered very good.)

Torque is a freeware Windows video benchmark written by PC programmer Steve Gibson, of SpinRite fame. It was written explicitly to defeat the cheating that video card vendors do on other, more generic tests. Torque directly measures the number of pixels per second that a video card can transfer from memory to the screen or between two screen locations. A high score on this test means your video card is ideal for manipulating bulky, multicolor images in packages like Micrografx Picture Publisher, Adobe Photoshop, and so on. Typically, Torque will show a drastic dropoff for low-end cards tested between 256-color and 16.7 million-color modes.

Torque also shows the performance differences between video cards using DRAM, and the faster, more expensive VRAM. Typically, on low-end monitors, with a vertical refresh rate of 60 to 70Hz, there is little difference between DRAM and VRAM cards. With high-end monitor/card combinations that support a refresh rate of 72 to 80Hz, cards with VRAM memory show a significant increase in performance, especially in high-color graphic modes.

Speedy (SPEEDY.ZIP) is another rough-and-ready video benchmark that may predict your graphic card's performance as a multimedia device. Speedy measures a number of hardware and software (Windows GDI) video functions, delivering an aggregate Speedmark total in its central Window. Typically, a score of 10 to 25 on this benchmark indicates that your video card will deliver fairly good support for a typical business application environment, and multimedia playback will be acceptable in 8- and 16-bit color depths. A score higher than 25 indicates that you probably have a card with an onboard acceleration chip for Windows, and can expect excellent across-the-board performance. A Speedy score of under five may be a warning that your video card will deliver sluggish performance, and may not satisfactorily play back digital video.

Windsock (WINDSOCK.ZIP) is a venerable utility available on CompuServe and local bulletin board systems. This utility runs under Windows 3.*x* or Windows 95, performing CPU, disk, video and memory benchmarks. Results in each area are rated on a scale from "Poor" to "Superb." Since the tests were written for Windows 3.*x*, and include comparisons with 386 machines, the evaluative ratings must be taken with a grain of salt. However, Windsock's quantitative numerical ratings are useful in comparing your system to the included scores for a series of 486 machines. If your machine racks up astronomical scores on Windsock, you should not be unduly impressed, but if, on the other hand, your machine scores significantly below the results in the sample database, you may want to give some thought to replacing weak components. The documentation for Windsock explains how to pinpoint video scores to track down the aspects of performance related to CPU speed, and the aspects related to your video hardware.

Upgrading Older Equipment

In general, here's what to bear in mind if you're considering an upgrade.

486 OR PENTIUM CPU Given sufficient RAM (12 or 16MB, usually), a faster or more capable processor would come next. As discussed in Chapter 15, a 386-based CPU simply does not handle 32-bit code very well, and Windows 95 is based in part on 32-bit code. Switching to a 66MHz 486DX/2, 100MHz DX/4, or a Pentium from 83 to 133MHz, will produce dramatic improvements. The move from a fast 486 to a low-end Pentium will probably not make as big a difference as would adding memory above 8MB, up to about 32MB.

FIGURE 16-1

Windsock measures four important aspects of your system's performance.

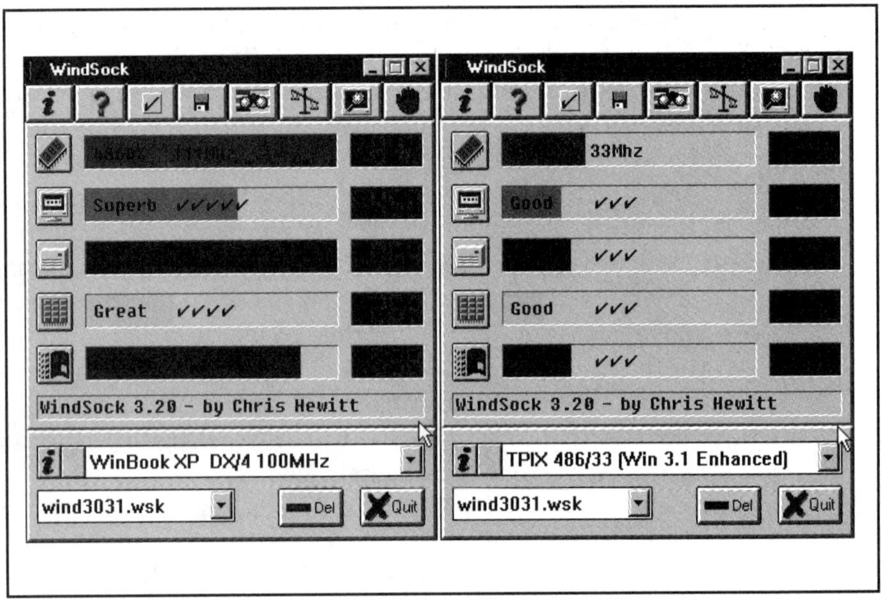

PCI OR VESA LOCAL BUS MOTHERBOARD WITH EXTERNAL CPU CACHE If you already have a 486 system that uses an older ISA motherboard, consider a motherboard replacement. A 32-bit 486 motherboard is an inexpensive upgrade. In many cases, you can simply transplant a 486 CPU from your older ISA motherboard to a new PCI or VESA model, or ask your local clone salesperson to do it for you. The performance gains you'll see with 32-bit hard disk and video access are well worth the price of this modest upgrade. An external CPU cache (not the same as the internal cache built into your CPU) is helpful because normal RAM is simply too slow to handle data at the speeds required by 386 or better CPUs. On a 486, make sure you have at least a 64K external CPU cache, and 256K would be even better. Adding more than a 256K cache offers only diminishing returns.

MEMORY Given a machine with a 486 33MHz DX or 25/50MHz DX/2 CPU, and 4MB of RAM, additional memory comes before everything else. You will see an astonishing difference in performance if you move from 4 to 8MB of RAM. If you can boost it to 12 or 16MB, you'll see an even better performance leap. From there, the upgrade to 24MB or 32MB will not produce as dramatic results, but would still be worth doing if you work with RAM-eaters like multimedia animators or CAD systems. If possible, stick with 72-pin SIMMS when buying memory, since they are the undisputed standard now. (If your motherboard uses older, 30-pin SIMMS, consider the possibility of a motherboard upgrade, since any additional memory you purchase of this type will be unusable on your next system.

LARGER, FASTER HARD DISK Windows 95 uses hard disk space as an extension of its working RAM, and 32-bit programs are inherently bigger than 16-bit ones. For both reasons, if you don't usually have at least 60MB free on your hard drive, consider purchasing a larger, faster hard drive. It's a buyer's market right now for Enhanced IDE (EIDE) drives. The addition of a new EIDE drive and 32-bit controller may boost your current data transfer rate by more than 400 percent. Fast Wide SCSI drives are even faster! (See Chapter 15 for more details on EIDE and SCSI drives.)

GRAPHICS ADAPTER If you have enough RAM, a good motherboard, and a large, fast hard disk, next take a look at your video card. Adding a 32-bit or 64-bit video adapter can make a huge difference in the speed at which windows on your screen are redrawn, giving your applications a snappier feel. (You'll notice this particularly with desktop publishing and image editing software.) For playing multimedia animations, upgrading older VGA cards may be mandatory. One MB of on-card RAM is enough for 256-color SVGA displays. At higher resolutions or with deeper colors, 2MB or more will serve better. Most good video cards now ship with at least 1MB of video RAM plus sockets for onboard memory expansion.

BIOS UPGRADE As plug-and-play (P&P) add-ons become more prevalent, some vendors and manufacturers are making BIOS upgrades available. If you expect to purchase and install more peripherals, or if you're upgrading multiple PCs to run Windows 95, upgrading them to a P&P BIOS can pay dividends in saved time and configuration effort.

note *Certain older 486 models may require a BIOS upgrade to run Windows 95 at all. A file called HARDWARE.TXT, placed in the WINDOWS directory after installation provides detailed information.*

HIGH-SPEED MODEM If you're still telecommunicating with a 2400 bps dinosaur, now is the time to step into the information age. A 14,400 bps integrated fax/modem is enough to connect you to text-based information services for business purposes, but if you plan to take advantage of the World Wide Web, and other developing Internet technologies, you should consider upgrading to at least a 28,800 v.34 fax/modem.

CD-ROM DRIVE If you don't already have a sound card, consider an integrated sound card/CD-ROM kit with a SCSI interface. This will save you a bus slot, and allow you to add other SCSI peripherals, later. (Some inexpensive card and drive combos only allow SCSI support for the CD-ROM; be sure to check this point before buying.) Multimedia kits with proprietary CD interfaces work, but they are also closed-end upgrades. If you intend to use the CD-ROM drive infrequently, consider buying an external model which you can simply remove and attach to your stereo system to play audio CDs until you need to install an office suite.

SOFTWARE UPGRADES Program publishers are scrambling to upgrade their products to 32-bit code. For many applications the upgrade may not be worth the price, but for some it is essential. The same goes for major file management utilities. You may also want to make the necessary investment to upgrade memory-intensive applications like graphics, multimedia, and large databases.

UPGRADED DISPLAY The monitor is a large part of your computer workplace. If you run several programs at once or use high-screen resolutions, or perhaps work with large spreadsheets, a 14-inch monitor makes a miserable tool. Larger monitors—15 or 17 inches—have come down in price and are well worth the investment, once the rest of your system is in good tune.

Some Tips on Upgrading Your Existing System

Here are a few general cautions about upgrading an existing system. They may help you avoid spending money on strategies that won't work well when the aim is to make Windows 95 work faster and better.

If you're using a DX/2-66, 486-based system, it should run Windows 95 just fine, if you've installed enough memory. Many sources say 8MB of RAM is enough, but that may still bog down the machine when you're using Microsoft Exchange, or connecting to the Microsoft Network. You'll be happier with 12MB or more of RAM if you like to give your machine a workout. Windows 95 strongly prefers lots of RAM to run in.

Don't spend money on peripheral upgrades for an older, ISA system. As with 30-pin SIMMS chips, this upgrade money would probably be better earmarked for a new, 32-bit motherboard. If you're thinking about a faster disk controller or video card for an ISA system, consider replacing the motherboard at the same time. If you're thinking of a peripheral upgrade for a VESA system, consider buying a PCI motherboard, instead, and PCI peripherals. While VESA systems are quite common now, they won't be when you do your next upgrade. To cycle today's hot new video card or SCSI adapter into your next system, go PCI whenever your budget permits.

Are you tempted to try plugging in a faster processor on the same motherboard? It is true that sometimes you can just change a jumper or two and plug a faster processor in—but sometimes it's not that easy. Most older

486 systems use a 6-volt bus, while newer CPUs use a 3.3-volt system. Maybe the voltage is adjustable, but quite likely it is not, and you don't want to put 6 volts on a 3.3-volt CPU. Special CPU upgrades that address this problem are available, but they're often almost as expensive as integrated motherboard/CPU components.

note *Intel now markets a series of overdrive plug-in processors that will convert 386 and low-end 486 machines to high-end 486 or Pentium CPUs. Intel's literature claims these upgrades are more effective than replacing your motherboard, but we believe this is not always the case.*

The time to consider plug-in CPU upgrades or processor-on-an-expansion-card hardware is if you need to upgrade a large number of older 386 machines in an office. In this situation, stopgap, plug-in CPU upgrades can help you avoid busting the budget. But even then, if you own a slew of 286s, avoid the temptation to leapfrog the processors. Replace the entire systems, and use the 286 machines for office e-mail centers, or take the tax deduction and donate them to a school.

If you have a 386 ISA (standard) computer, consider either sticking with Windows for Workgroups version 3.11 or upgrading to a minimum hardware system of the sort described in this chapter.

FIGURE 16-2 *The Intel overdrive plug-in 83MHz Pentium processor, with automatic voltage adjustment*

See Chapter 15 for more information about upgrading individual system components.

Buying New Systems

Buying a complete new system is a simple alternative to motherboard and component upgrades. Many well-integrated systems are available at very good prices from a variety of sources. What's right for you probably depends upon your productivity environment and a balance between the need for an extremely good price and the need for support from the vendor.

The average quality and reliability of PCs is increasing. Even if you plunk down your money at random, these days, you're likely to get a machine that generally works. But there are differences in hardware quality that can make your computing experience more pleasant once you're aware of them. (Not to mention saving you the frustration of having to call the vendor and send the box back for upgrades when this or that component won't do what you thought you paid for.) We figure that if you decide to bite the bullet and buy a new computer, you might as well learn the consumer canniness to select a machine that performs well and has the power to bear your productivity load for awhile.

Here are some issues to consider.

You can get serviceable, low-end complete systems—a 486DX/4 100MHz system, say, or a Pentium 75MHz machine with a 14- or 15-inch monitor—for $1000 to $2000, depending upon how much flexibility and computing power you're willing to give up. At the high end, where power users and resource-stretching programs reside, expect to pay $3000 to $4000 for a complete system, including best-of-class peripherals. That's a lot of money in some environments, such as a 50-machine warren of desk cubicles where the equivalent of 19th-century clerks type memos or provide product support. But $4000 is cheaper than what you'd have to pay to upgrade, piece by piece, an old 386 with a 13-inch green monitor into a power user's Pentium box.

If you're buying a new, first system for Windows 95, consider the long-term advantages of springing for a Pentium-level system with 16MB (or at least no less than 12MB) of RAM. Even 100MHz systems based on the Intel Pentium are "mainstream" now, with 133MHz machines available and 75MHz Pentiums coming into the market at commodity prices. Clone "586" processors also are driving the price down for Pentium-type motherboards. The 486 is definitely on the wane.

When it comes to notebook computers for mobile Road Warriors, the picture is slightly different. These units are more expensive than desktop machines, and a 486DX2/66 or 486DX4/75 with 12MB of RAM may serve you adequately. See the section on Win95 and mobile computing later in this chapter for a thorough discussion of issues that pertain to running Windows 95 on the road.

If you're an entry-level buyer on a budget looking for a desktop machine, a DX4/100 system with a less expensive AMD CPU may make good sense. A DX4/100 with 16MB of RAM performs almost as well as a Pentium 90 system with 8MB of RAM and it still costs considerably less. The penalty is that the machine will become obsolete sooner.

Picking the Right Supplier

When buying a whole system, your chief concerns are to get the components you need (preferably from known manufacturers with a compatibility track record). You'll also want flexibility for upgrades if that is a probable future strategy, and local technical support. The place to start is by picking a supplier that can help you meet these needs.

There are many good suppliers of new whole systems.

SMALL LOCAL VENDORS Though a local reseller's prices may not be rock-bottom, a local business will usually provide support at no extra charge for at least a specified period of time. Such vendors also can make fast decisions regarding per-unit price if you buy more than one system, an advantage over large retailing operations. For sales of under ten or so units, the advantages of local support may far outweigh the advantages of lower prices that include little or no support from large retailers or warehouse operations. One working rule to apply here: stick with vendors who've been in business at the same address and phone number for at least a year. That's about the time it takes for reliable mom-and-pop businesses to sort themselves out from unprincipled, cut-rate clone dealers.

LARGE RETAIL OPERATIONS These are the large department stores and warehouse operations where you can pick up complete systems at bargain basement prices. Some mass-marketed systems, such as those made by Packard-Bell, have profoundly affected how PCs are sold to consumers. There are two main disadvantages to using these channels—they almost always lack support after the sale, and after-sale flexibility may suffer. Expansion slots may be limited, you probably won't be able to switch out a motherboard, add new hard disks, video cards, and so forth.

MAIL ORDER AND ONLINE CHANNELS Mail-order firms, including Internet and other online order channels, often provide excellent values in both packaged systems and components. The larger mail-order firms (Dell, Gateway, ZEOS, etc.) have become well established and stand behind their products. Mail-order vendors are also likely to include good deals for bundling software (productivity applications and utilities) with the systems they sell. Make sure to request the documentation and floppy disks for these added value options. If you order computer systems or components by mail, use a credit card. That way you have the leverage of canceling the sale if the product is unsatisfactory. Take care if ordering online by credit card, however, since—despite some vaulting claims of security by various Internet software publishers—security problems still exist for financial transactions made over the Internet.

"GROW YOUR OWN" SYSTEMS If you've been using a PC for some time and have a lot of the components you need, you can often build your own system from a combination of old parts and new components. Most standard computer cases don't care what kind of motherboard they contain, and it is not terribly difficult to install a new one that makes use of your existing components like memory or I/O cards. You can often save money by building your own systems, on a small scale, at least. It is not often practical for situations involving multiple systems.

Mobile Computing with Windows 95

This section addresses the concerns of Win95 Road Warriors: whether you should become one, or stick with Windows for Workgroups on your notebook machine. Your choice depends largely on your personal computing needs and the power of your existing notebook hardware. With the right notebook, an upgrade to Windows 95 is eminently desirable. The added features and ease-of-use of the new operating system can simplify your day-to-day computing tasks. But if you must make do with a less powerful, 4MB notebook with a small hard disk, you're better off sticking with Windows for Workgroups.

For newer, more powerful systems, Windows 95 really makes life easier. Advanced power management, auto-installation of PCMCIA cards, hot docking to a workstation, automatic network connections, and convenient e-mail and fax management are all present in the operating system, waiting to be exploited. Windows 95 mostly eliminates the need to fidget with third-party software for CD-ROMs, SCSI devices, and PCMCIA socket services. Just pop a PCMCIA modem, controller card, or added memory into a socket and Windows 95 magically detects it. Plug a notebook into a docking station and the system configuration is automatically swapped to recognize new ports, peripherals, and network connections.

FIGURE 16-3 *The WinBook XP 100MHz DX/4 notebook and docking station*

In addition to the auto-configuration advantage for PCMCIA hardware, Windows 95 offers a number of software benefits for computing on the road:

DIAL-UP NETWORK/DIRECT CABLE CONNECTION Dial into the Internet on the road, or connect via modem to a network server through TCP/IP, Novell IPX, or Microsoft NetBEUI protocols. Direct Cable Connection lets you set up a two-computer LAN with your desktop machine, sharing files and printers through a simple parallel cable.

BRIEFCASE Briefcase lets you quickly synchronize local and remote directories. You can edit files copied from your desktop machine and have the changes copied automatically back to the host machine the next time you connect.

DEFERRED PRINTING You can work offline with a network printer. When you're not connected, you can still print as many jobs as you like. The output is stored in a spool directory on the notebook. The next time you connect to your desktop machine, the jobs are automatically queued and spooled to the printer.

HOT DOCKING Hot docking is dependent upon a plug and play BIOS. If your notebook computer has the current Microsoft/Intel plug-and-play BIOS, it will automatically reconfigure itself whenever you plug it in to or remove it from a docking station. Older notebooks can *cold-dock*. (This means you must power down the system and reboot each time you connect or disconnect from a docking station.)

Hardware Requirements for Win95 Mobile Computing

A top-range Road Warrior notebook suited to Windows 95 will have 12 to 16MB of onboard RAM, a 486DX/4 100MHz or faster processor, PCMCIA Type II and III slots, and a 500MB hard disk.

Your notebook may also include an internal modem, sound card, and built-in SCSI support (or access to a docking station equipped with a CD-ROM drive). The nicest of these machines include built-in CD-ROM drives, 32-bit video processing and/or 32-bit disk access implemented through a VESA or PCI system bus.

Notebooks unsuitable for Windows 95 includes older machines with 386 CPUs, non-VGA displays and configurations with less than 8MB of RAM, and small hard disks (less than 200MB).

This leaves a large number of computers in between the desirable top-range and the incompatible bottom-range configurations. A mid-range 486 notebook with 8MB of RAM is functional for basic computing tasks under Windows 95, but it may have difficulty taking advantages of some of the operating system's bells and whistles. Application performance may also be a bit sluggish.

The mid-range group of notebooks consists of 486SX 25MHz to 486DX 50MHz units configured with 8MB of RAM and older ISA video and disk controllers. Many of these machines don't offer specific support for multimedia. They have no built-in sound cards, SCSI ports, or other CD-ROM support. If your notebook has a 486 CPU, 8MB of RAM, and a small hard disk, you may use it to derive some satisfaction out of Windows 95. The absence of a sound card or CD-ROM support can be remedied, in some instances, by the addition of PCMCIA peripherals (now referred to by Microsoft and Intel as *PC Cards*).

While writing this book, we tested Windows 95 on a Toshiba Satellite 2400CT notebook (an older model with a small hard disk). Prior to installing Windows 95, we ran Stac Electronics' Stacker 4.0 disk compression package to expand the amount of available hard disk space from 340MB to almost double that amount. Windows 95, itself, will occupy from 65 to 140MB of storage space. The "Portable" Win95 configuration you can select during installation excludes features like the interactive tutorials, multimedia files, Microsoft Network, and Microsoft Exchange e-mail and fax support.

If you want to keep these features upgrading an existing Windows for Workgroups configuration, allow a minimum of 120MB, total, for the new operating system. This estimate allows for future software upgrades. (If you're a Microsoft Office user, remember that 15 to 20MB of space under the WINDOWS directory is occupied by the plug-in utilities and drivers installed with Excel, Word, and so on. If you're not an Office user, subtract 15MB from the required total. But remember that Novell Perfect Office, or Lotus SmartSuite may fill that space right back up again.)

Making Room on a Small Hard Disk

If your notebook's hard disk has a storage capacity of 200 to 350MB, disk compression software makes Windows 95 a more viable option. Using disk compression slows down performance, but if you want to take Windows 95 on the road, you can probably live with this. Most users will probably want to select Microsoft's DoubleSpace rather than Stacker. Stacker creates more disk space, but DoubleSpace is included for free in both MS-DOS 6.*x* and Windows 95. Windows 95 reads and writes to DoubleSpace drives through a 32-bit, protected-mode interface. This is faster than Stac's real mode compression.

If you're willing to spend another $49, you can purchase an enhanced version of DoubleSpace in Microsoft's Windows 95 Plus Pack. The enhanced DoubleSpace in Microsoft Plus! has compression capability that closely matches Stacker's. Microsoft Plus! also includes the added value of Microsoft's Internet Connectivity kit. (See Chapter 14 for more information on Microsoft Plus!.)

You should be aware that Stacker compression does work with Windows 95, and Stac Electronics now has an upgrade version (Stacker 4.1) that includes support for Win95's long filenames. Stacker 4.0 works, but you can't use its built-in defragmenter without destroying Win95 long filenames. Win95's built-in ScanDisk utility can repair file errors on a Stacker drive, but it can't repair compression errors. Stacker 4.1 is still a 16-bit real-mode compression system, but it runs considerably faster under Windows 95 than Stacker 4.0.

note *You should probably not use disk compression software on any partition intended to store and play back .AVI video files, unless you have a Pentium 90 or faster CPU.*

Installation Issues/CD-ROM Support

The Toshiba Satellite CT-2400 has a built-in SCSI port, which allows an external CD-ROM drive to be used for program installation and multimedia.

Some computers include no built-in SCSI support but allow access to a CD-ROM drive through a PCMCIA SCSI adapter.

Some notebooks can be plugged into a docking station, designed by the manufacturer, which may include a built-in CD-ROM drive. The WinBook XP notebook, which we also tested, plugs right into such a docking station.

If your notebook does not include implicit CD-ROM support, you have other alternatives for installing Windows 95:

- You can install from floppy disks.
- If you have access to another computer with a CD-ROM drive and to a portable file transfer utility, you can connect your notebook to the machine with the CD-ROM via a serial or parallel cable. Create a Win95 installation directory on the notebook's hard disk and use your file transfer utility to copy the Win95 directory from the CD-ROM to the notebook. This installation directory will occupy about 35MB of hard disk space on the notebook. You can then install (and subsequently update) Windows 95 from the local installation directory you've created.

note *If you use the DOS Interlink program to transfer the installation files from one machine to another, an additional step is involved. Interlink doesn't recognize CD-ROM drives. But you don't have to let that stop you. You can copy the Win95 installation directory locally from the CD-ROM to a directory on that machine's hard disk. Interlink will see this directory, allowing you to transfer it via cable to your notebook's hard disk.*

Working with PCMCIA SCSI

If you have a portable, external CD-ROM drive, but no SCSI support on your notebook, a PCMCIA SCSI card may be the solution to your problems. These cards cost from $250 to $350, and if you get the right one, Windows 95 will automatically recognize it as soon as you plug it in. The trick, here, is that if you haven't installed Windows 95 yet, you'll need to use the third-party software provided by the vendor to recognize the CD-ROM drive before installing Windows 95. This probably won't be completely automatic, but it usually works if the vendor's drivers were designed to support your notebook. Or you can install Windows 95 first from floppy disks or through the CD-to-hard disk file transfer method.

Once Windows 95 is up and running, you can plug a supported card into a PCMCIA slot and it will be recognized automatically. We found this to be true with the New Media Bus Toaster SCSI Card. We plugged it in, attached

FIGURE 16-4

The Megahertz XJ-2288 PCMCIA modem, with X-JACK connector

it to an external CD-ROM, and the next time the system booted, it was ready for action.

PCMCIA Modems

The XJ-2288 28.8K PCMCIA modem provided to us by Megahertz, Inc. also installed itself effortlessly when inserted into a Type II slot. You should experience similar, trouble-free modem installation, provided the second serial port address (COM2) is vacant on your notebook.

The WinBook XP notebook we tested normally ships with an internal 14.4K modem set up for COM2. When the MegaHertz modem was first inserted into this computer, Windows 95 attempted to set it up for COM3 (as it should). The problem was that the default interrupt assigned to the modem became IRQ10. This was fine for the 32-bit telecommunication applets bundled with Windows 95, but none of our DOS and Windows 3.*x* applications worked, since they were programmed to recognize only IRQs 3, 4 and 5. Fortunately, there was an easy solution. There was no reason to leave two modems active on the system, so we removed support for the WinBook's internal modem through the computer's CMOS settings. The next time Windows 95 booted, the PCMCIA modem was assigned to the conventional COM2/IRQ3 address and all was well.

If you plan to use a notebook as a multimedia machine, it may be worth your while to spend a little extra money and buy one with an active-matrix color display, rather than the default dual-scan display. The dual-scan display panel is adequate for business applications, but does a mediocre job of rendering video for Windows. You can, of course, simply plug a standard SVGA monitor into the notebook for movie watching. Most notebooks can handle a 1024×768 pixel external noninterlaced display with 256 colors or 800×600 with 65,000 colors, although they may be restricted to 640×480×256 colors on the internal display panel.

The Bottom Line

The bottom line on Windows 95 and mobile computing is that it's probably worth your time and trouble to install the operating system on a current machine that meets the minimum hardware requirements. You don't have to wait for next year's models with plug-and-play BIOS, CD-ROM, and PCI bus implementations. The operating system's built-in support for PCMCIA peripherals provides plug-and-play for notebooks, right now. The e-mail and fax support, network support, and pleasant, semi-intelligent interface all combine to ease the burdens of a traveling Road Warrior.

Component Upgrading Strategies

For many people with existing systems, the way to get good performance out of Windows 95 may not be to buy another PC. It may make more short-term economic sense to optimize the usefulness of systems you already own. Getting acceptable service from existing systems is likely to be especially important in business environments, where replacing capital equipment without counting the cost is rarely an option. This section reviews some issues linked to individual component performance.

Changing the Primary Drive

If you buy a new hard drive to supplement what your system already has, chances are good it will be larger and faster than your current drive. If so, you may want to make it your system's primary hard drive, the one from which the system boots and runs Windows 95. Since you can only use one primary, bootable partition on a system, switching boot partitions gets a bit tricky. Here's a procedure that won't have you scratching your head in the middle of the night, wondering how to get the silly computer running again:

1. Install the new drive as secondary (use jumpers or switches in accordance with the manufacturer's instructions).
2. Boot to Win95.
3. FDISK the new drive from Win95 to create a primary partition.
4. Format the new drive from Win95, using the /SYS option.
5. Use the Explorer to copy everything from the old to the new drive.
6. Some system files will be in use, so copy the WINDOWS directory last, by itself.
7. Create a Win95 floppy boot disk, if you don't already have one. Be sure to copy FDISK.EXE to this disk from the WINDOWS \COMMAND directory.
8. Shut down the computer.
9. Reset jumpers to set the new drive as primary and the old drive as secondary.
10. Swap the physical position of the new drive and old drive on the data ribbon cable.
11. Boot to a command prompt from your startup floppy. Run FDISK to set the primary partition on your new disk to active.
12. Boot Windows 95 from the new drive. If this procedure allows you to successfully start Windows 95, reformat the old drive.
13. If you run into a problem, reboot from the floppy disk and press F8 at boot time to get a menu. Then check to make sure that *all* WINDOWS directory files have been copied successfully from the old drive to the new one. You may find that some system-level files were not transferred successfully. If so, copy them over and try again—the problem may be solved.

If this procedure doesn't work (although in most cases, it should), you may need to return to your original disk configuration if you wish to preserve your original Windows 95 configuration.

Monitors

For full plug-and-play compatibility, your monitor must comply with two standards—DDC1 and DDC2B. Given such a monitor, make sure your new graphics adapter is also compatible. You'll then be able to switch screen resolutions on-the-fly—lower resolutions for simple text work, higher resolutions for the huge spreadsheet or deep-color-resolution multimedia tasks, for example.

A 17-inch monitor or larger feels comfortable at 1024×768 resolution. To get 64,000 colors takes 1.5MB of RAM, so put 2MB video RAM on your card. To achieve a flicker-free screen resolution of 1280×1024 pixels, your monitor should support a vertical refresh rate of at least 72Hz, and a horizontal refresh rate of 35 to 45KHz. To achieve a screen resolution of 1600×1200 pixels, you should use at least a 17-inch monitor, capable of an 85Hz vertical refresh rate and 45KHz to 55KHz horizontal refresh rate.

Video Cards: The Right Card for Your System

Earlier, we mentioned that a 15- or 17-inch monitor makes high-definition or true-color screens much more practical to work with. The monitor you have, and the screen resolution and color depth you need for what you do at the PC, determine what kind of video card you'll need. The card's ability to handle the screen well determines how well you'll like the results.

tip *To avoid flicker, get a card that can handle a vertical refresh rate of at least 70Hz at all resolutions (75Hz is better). And look for models supported by Win95's built-in screen drivers.*

As with everything else on a PC, it's partly a matter of personal preference, and partly a matter of matching the video card to the rest of your hardware. Next are some personal style considerations when buying a graphics card.

Let the Resolutions Rule

For higher resolutions or deeper colors, a 64-bit or better card would be preferable. And unless you expect to keep using your current VESA local bus motherboard for quite some time, go with PCI.

Let the screen resolution you need determine what graphics card to buy. For most users, 800×600 is just about the highest comfortable resolution on a 15-inch screen. On a 17-inch screen, most people find 1024×768 comfortable. With larger screens and higher resolutions you can run more windows, or see larger chunks of a spreadsheet or database at once. You also can get more icons and more readable text on the screen at one time.

Here are some variables to keep in mind when buying or upgrading your video system, depending upon the resolutions and applications you'll be using:

- If you're using an old (by which we mean, say, pre-1990) video board, it won't play multimedia very well. These older cards usually had an 8- or 16-bit bus bandwidth with not much onboard video memory—256 or 512K. For smooth multimedia, you need at least a VESA local bus (VLB) graphic card with a meg or more of memory unless you already have a very fast pre-VLB board.
- If you do have a fast pre-VLB board, such as an ISA Diamond Stealth card, it'll do the job for awhile, especially if you're saving for a new PCI system down the road. The main thing to remember is that you'll have to do a sort of balancing act. For example: if you have a VLB system now, but plan to move next to a PCI mother board, you may not want to spend $200 or more for a 64-bit VLB video card for your current system, since you'll just have to give it away, when you upgrade to PCI.
- As with most things involving a computer, you may be able to crank an older video card up enough to do the job awhile longer by adding memory—in this case, video memory. Add enough DRAM (you don't really need VRAM or other video-enhanced memory unless you work with 24-bit color at high resolutions) to bring a board up to 1MB.

tip *Video memory comes in two flavors: VRAM and DRAM. If you use 1024x768 at 256 colors or fewer, stick with DRAM. For working at higher resolutions with greater color depth, get the faster, dual-ported VRAM.*

For other configurations, see the following table:

Resolution	Colors	Memory Required
640×480	256	512K to 2MB
640×480	32K to 16M	1MB or 2MB
800×600	256	512K to 2MB
800×600	32K to 16M	1MB to 2MB
1024×768	256	1MB to 2MB
1024×768	32K to 64K	2MB to 4MB

Resolution	Colors	Memory Required
1024×768	16M	4MB
1280×1024	256	2MB to 4MB
1280×1024	32K to 64K	4MB
1600×1200	256	2MB to 4MB
1600×1200	32K to 64K	4MB

The next section briefly covers some things to bear in mind when working with the most demanding types of graphical applications.

Working with Multimedia Applications or CAD

On the high side of the corporate PC curve, new applications that lean heavily on graphics are coming in at amazing speeds. Videoconferencing and kiosk-level multimedia graphics are both prime examples. If you expect to deal with graphics at this level, you can't really work effectively with a simple graphics card anymore. You need a local-bus, accelerated graphics card that is memory-heavy and able to handle 1280×1024 or (better) 1600×1200 pixel resolution at 16.7 million colors. The same basic rules hold true if you work with computer-aided design or create multimedia programs. You'll need first-rate graphical programs and equipment, and it won't pay to stint.

Multimedia and CAD programs are notoriously demanding on graphics adapters. The requirements are about the same for both types of work, so we'll lump them together here. To handle the required level of graphics, your system will need to perform at high levels in all respects—and the primary focus must be on the video.

If you're a professional graphics specialist of any type and using Windows 95, forget about using a VLB accelerator and go straight to a fast Pentium-class machine with PCI graphics card and 16 (or, better, 24) MB of main RAM. Augment that with at least 4MB of VRAM on the graphics card. For raw speed, look for a board with 128-bit direct pathways to video RAM and digital-to-analog converters. If a board that far forward on the technological curve does not seem essential, at least get a 64-bit board for the more demanding graphics apps. Anything less and your work will seem to crawl across the screen.

Adding I/O Cards and Peripheral Devices

Look for plug-and-play compatible devices that will be detected by Windows automatically when you use the Install New Hardware Wizard. The Win95 Configuration Manager (part of the VMM32 virtual memory manager) can gather device information from the PCI bus including IRQ, I/O port address, and other details about your hardware. This information is used to install new hardware and eliminate the interrupt conflicts that used to crash the system and drive users crazy.

Insist on high-speed serial ports with 16550AF UARTs, or better. Many current PCI motherboards have this feature built in, along with parallel ports that conform to the new enhanced parallel port (EPP) standard. An EPP improves the speed of your printer output.

If you're buying a SCSI controller card, ask the vendor whether the particular size and configuration of your SCSI hard drive is supported in the card's BIOS.

If you're buying a new EIDE controller, try to get one that supports the new PIO Mode 4 drive transfer rate. A good EIDE controller should also include two drive interfaces, supporting a total of 4 EIDE peripherals. Look for a card that allows you to manually enable, disable, or change the IRQ and port addresses for the secondary controller interface. This feature may be useful in resolving configuration problems. Many EIDE controllers are also now being sold as combination I/O units that also include onboard serial, parallel and game ports. If you buy a combination unit, look for one that features high-speed serial ports and bi-directional, or EPP support on the parallel port.

If you're buying an internal fax/modem unit, if possible, get one that allows you to adjust the IRQ and port address configuration through software settings.

See Chapter 15 for more specific information on modems, printers, removable hard disk media, tape backup devices, and other peripherals.

The final section of this book is a series of appendices devoted to reconciling software and hardware conflicts, networking information, and other choice nuggets of information that should be useful to you on your Windows 95 odyssey. If you've read this far, congratulations! You are now a full-fledged Windows 95 guru. We hope you think it was worth the effort.

Printers
Settings
Find
Help
Run...
Windows95
Start

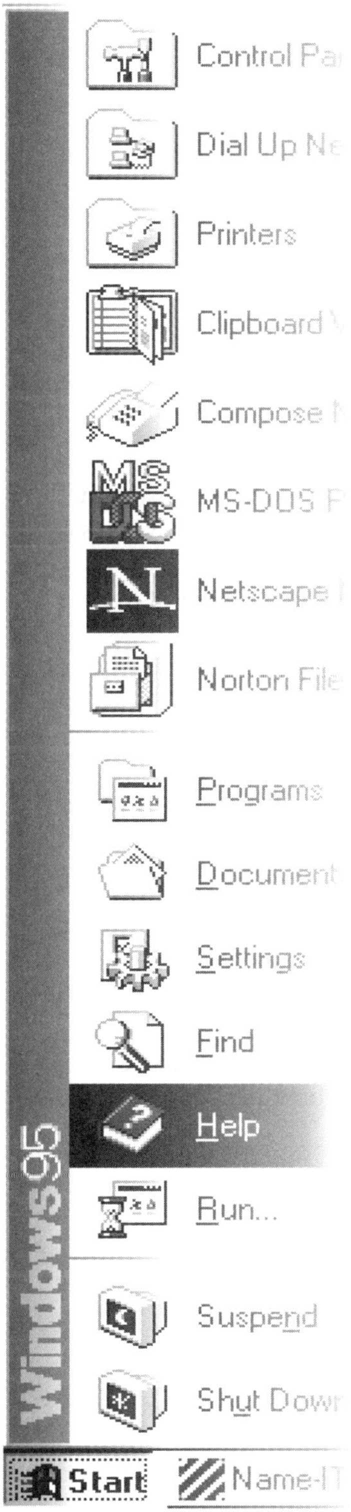

appendix A

Installation and Configuration Tips

- Preserving dual boot options
- Server-based Win95 installations
- Post-installation tips
- Win95 Service Pack update

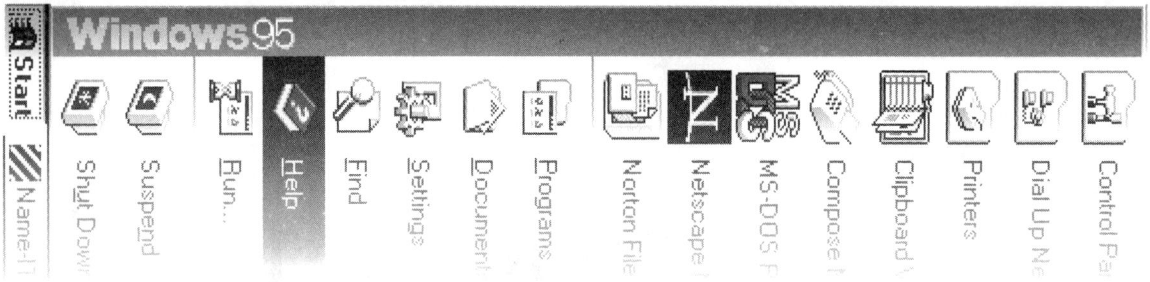

WINDOWS 95 is flexible. It can easily be made to coexist with previous versions of DOS, Warp OS/2, Windows NT, or all of these systems on the same hard disk. If you want to set up multiple operating systems easily, the installation order can often be critical to saving you a lot of extra effort. Here's a rundown on the general strategic order.

Preserving Dual Boot Options During Win95 Installation

If OS/2 is to be one of the operating systems on the hard disk, install it before Windows 95 or Windows NT, so that it won't wipe out the dual boot features built into these operating systems. If you must install OS/2 after Windows 95 or Windows NT has been set up, then make sure that you place it in a separate disk partition, and select the option to create an OS/2 Boot Manager partition. Do not install OS/2 to share a partition with Windows 95 or Windows NT. You may elect to install OS/2 in either a FAT or an HPFS disk partition. If you choose the HPFS partition, then files stored on this partition will be visible under Windows NT, but not under MS-DOS or Windows 95.

Windows 95 should generally be installed on a computer after any installation of OS/2, but before any installation of Windows NT. If you have installed OS/2 in an HPFS partition, you will need to make sure that one FAT partition containing a previous version of DOS is also ready and available through OS/2's Boot Manager menu. You will simply choose that partition when the computer starts, boot to DOS, and proceed with the Windows 95 installation as outlined in Chapters 2 and 3. (You can ignore the warning messages displayed by the Windows 95 Setup Wizard that OS/2 will become inoperable—provided you install Windows 95 and OS/2 in separate partitions.)

When Windows 95 has been successfully installed on your hard disk, the OS/2 Boot Manager will be temporarily disabled. The system will boot directly into Windows 95. You can restore the OS/2 Boot Manager simply by opening a DOS command prompt under Windows 95, and running the FDISK utility. From FDISK, choose option 2, Set active partition. On the next FDISK screen, you will see a listing for a small non-DOS partition, one to two megabytes in size. Enter the number in front of this partition to make it the active boot partition, and exit FDISK. The next time your computer starts, the OS/2 Boot Manager will reappear, allowing you to select either OS/2, or the partition that formerly launched DOS but now launches Windows 95. When you are running in the OS/2 operating system, you can use the OS/2 version of FDISK to modify the Boot Manager menu, if you like, changing the name of the DOS partition to "Windows 95."

If Windows NT is to be one of the operating systems on the hard disk, it should generally be installed last. Start Windows 95, and press F8 to bring up the Windows 95 boot menu. Select the option to boot to a DOS command prompt, rather than loading the Windows 95 desktop. Next, run the Windows NT setup program, making sure to choose a different directory from the one that contains Windows 95. You can install both Windows 95 and Windows NT on the same disk partition.

note *If you are installing the CD-ROM version of Windows NT, you will have to make sure that your Windows 95 CONFIG.SYS and AUTOEXEC.BAT files contain the real-mode drivers necessary for DOS to recognize your CD-ROM drive.*

When you install Windows NT, make sure to select the option that allows Windows NT to dual boot back to the previous operating system. After installation is completed, you can set the Windows NT default to start either Windows NT or the previous operating system, which in this case happens to be Windows 95.

If you are a rare, must-have everything user who has also installed OS/2, then the boot order that results from following the procedure we've just outlined is to open the OS/2 Boot Manager, allowing you to select between OS/2 and another operating system. If you choose the other operating system, the Windows 95 dual boot option that you installed previously, will have been replaced by the Windows NT dual boot option that you installed subsequently. When you choose the "other operating system" from OS/2 Boot Manager, the Windows NT dual boot menu will appear, giving you the option to go straight to Windows NT, or select NT's "other operating system" option, which will start Windows 95.

Special Dual Boot Setup for Windows NT/Windows 95

What if Windows NT was the first operating system on your hard disk, and you want to install Windows 95 over it, retaining access to both operating systems?

If Windows NT has been installed first, use the following procedure for adding Windows 95 to your computer:

1. Ensure that the computer is configured to dual boot between Windows NT and DOS.
2. Start the computer using the DOS operating system.
3. Remove the read-only attribute from the BOOTSECT.DOS and BOOT.INI files in the root directory, by typing the following:

   ```
   ATTRIB -R BOOTSECT.DOS
   ATTRIB -R BOOT.INI
   ```

4. Copy the BOOTSECT.DOS file to BOOTSECT.SAV.
5. Run Windows 95 Setup, installing into an existing Windows 3.*x* directory or into its own directory, but not into a directory that contains Windows NT system files. For example:
   - If there is a SYSTEM32 subdirectory in the WINDOWS directory on the computer, then Windows NT has been installed in the same directory as an earlier version of Windows. In this case, you cannot upgrade the configuration to Windows 95. *You must install Windows 95 in a new directory.*
   - If a computer running Windows NT 3.1 does not already have Windows installed, Windows 95 must be installed into an empty directory.
6. Remove the read-only attribute from the BOOTSECT.DOS file in the root directory.
7. Rename the BOOTSECT.DOS and BOOTSECT.SAV files by typing the following:

   ```
   REN BOOTSECT.DOS BOOTSECT.W40
   REN BOOTSECT.SAV BOOTSECT.DOS
   ```

8. Use a text editor to modify the BOOT.INI file to add Windows 95. For example:

```
[BOOT LOADER]
TIMEOUT=30
DEFAULT=C:\WINNT

[OPERATING SYSTEMS]
C:\WINNT="WINDOWS NT"
C:\BOOTSECT.DOS="MS-DOS V6.22" /WIN95DOS
C:\BOOTSECT.W40="WINDOWS 95" /WIN95
```

At system startup, the Windows NT dual boot menu appears, allowing you to select Windows 95 as a startup option.

remember *If your computer has any NTFS partitions, they are not available locally from within Windows 95.*

Server-Based Setup

The server-based setup procedure for Windows 95 (available in the ADMIN\NETTOOLS directory on the Windows 95 CD-ROM, but not with the floppy disk version) provides the following options, which were not available in past versions of Windows:

- Computers that start from the local hard disk can run a shared copy of Windows 95 from the server.
- Computers with floppy disk drives that start locally from a floppy disk and then connect to a server can run a shared copy of Windows 95.
- Diskless workstations that remote boot (sometimes called RIPL or remote IPL) from Novell NetWare version 3.*x* and 4.0 servers can run a shared copy of Windows 95.

Server-Based Setup can only be run from a computer that is currently running Windows 95 or Windows NT. You cannot run Server-Based Setup from Windows 3.1, Windows for Workgroups, or MS-DOS. If you want to use Server-Based Setup to create setup batch scripts or to create home directories for running shared copies of Windows 95, you must run Server-Based Setup under Windows 95. If you run Server-Based Setup under the

Windows NT operating system, you can only use this program to install the Windows 95 source files in a shared directory.

Server-Based Setup is not installed automatically with Windows 95. The files that make up Server-Based Setup are uncompressed files in the ADMIN\NETTOOLS directory on the Windows 95 compact disc. The following files are required for Server-Based Setup:

NETSETUP.ADM	NETSUSRC.INF
NETSETUP.DLL	POLEDIT.EXE
NETSETUP.EXE	RPLIMAGE.EXE
NETSETUP.INF	SETUPX.DLL
NETSETUP.LAY	SUWIN.INF

A network administrator can install Server-Based Setup on a local computer running Windows 95. To do this, insert the Windows 95 compact disc in your CD-ROM drive and switch to the ADMIN\NETTOOLS\NETSETUP directory. Then enter **COPY NETSETUP.* C:** at the DOS prompt.

Post-Installation Tips

The following are the most common things users will probably want to do to optimize Windows 95 immediately after installation:

1. Right-click and open the Start Menu. Drag a copy of the MS-DOS Prompt icon to the first level.
2. Open the Add/Remove Programs object from the Control Panel and install useful accessory features that were not included in your setup: Clipboard Viewer, Document templates, Quick View and System Resource Meter under Accessories, Dial-Up Networking and Direct Cable Connection under Communications, Backup under DiskTools, and Microsoft Fax.
3. Make a Startup disk if this wasn't done during installation. Open Add/Remove Programs to the Startup Disk tab and click the Create Disk button.
4. Adjust your video resolution above the default 640×480. Open the Control Panel Display object to the Settings tab and use the Desktop area slider.
5. Install your modem if this wasn't done during Setup. Open the Modems object on the Control Panel, and click the Add button.

6. Install and configure Microsoft Exchange to manage faxes and e-mail on the Microsoft Network, CompuServe or the Internet. See Chapter 10 for detailed instructions.
7. Install your printer if this wasn't done during Setup. Open the Printers folder under Settings in the Start Menu, and click the Add Printer button.
8. If you intend to use Win95's Dial-Up Networking feature to connect to the Internet, open the Control Panel Network object and make sure that the Microsoft TCP/IP protocol for Dial-Up Networking has been installed in the Components list. See Chapters 4 and 10 for details on how to add this component, if you don't see it in the list.
9. Check the configuration for CD-ROM speed. Open the Control Panel System object to the Performance tab, click the File Settings button, and select the CD-ROM tab. If Win95 has configured the default to Single Speed Drives, select the "Optimize access pattern" drop-down list, and choose a setting appropriate for your CD-ROM drive. You can also adjust the Supplemental Cache size on this screen.
10. Open the Control Panel System object to the Performance tab and examine the settings for File System and Virtual Memory. If these settings do not say 32-bit, you are not getting optimum Windows 95 performance. You may be using a third-party disk compression utility, or have unnecessary real-mode drivers present in CONFIG.SYS. You can improve performance by switching to the Win95 DriveSpace compression program and removing any unnecessary device drivers for your disk controller.
11. Examine your CONFIG.SYS and AUTOEXEC.BAT files for the presence of real-mode drivers designed to manage a SCSI disk controller, a CD-ROM drive, or a sound card under DOS/Windows 3.*x*. These drivers may be unnecessary under Windows 95 and needlessly waste memory. See Chapter 7 for instructions on how to replace real-mode DOS drivers with Windows 95 protected-mode drivers.

Miscellaneous Tips and Tricks

The following is a short additional collection of neat Windows 95 configuration and productivity tips that we discovered in the course of compiling this book. We hope you find them useful, too.

Bypassing the Startup Screen

As most users know, you can bypass the Windows 95 startup screen, if you want to monitor the processing of your CONFIG.SYS and AUTOEXEC.BAT files by pressing ESCAPE after the "Starting Windows 95" message appears on the screen. You can disable the startup screen permanently by editing the MSDOS.SYS file located in the root directory of your boot drive. To edit the MSDOS.SYS file, you must first disable its read-only and hidden file attributes.

Once MSDOS.SYS is visible and editable, open this file in Notepad, and add the following parameter in the [Options] Section.

```
[Options]
LOGO=0
```

To restore the startup screen, change this setting to

```
LOGO=1
```

Changing the Startup, Exit, and Shutdown Screens

You can customize the default startup, exit, and shutdown screens for Windows 95 with any image editor capable of saving files in Windows .BMP format. By default, the Windows 95 startup screen is a file called LOGO.SYS, located in the root directory of your C drive. The Exit and Shutdown screens are files called LOGOW.SYS and LOGOS.SYS, located in your WINDOWS directory. Although Microsoft gives these files a .SYS file extension, they are really Windows Bitmap (.BMP) files with a resolution of 32×0400 pixels and 256 colors. You can edit any of these three screens, by renaming them with the .BMP extension and loading them into Microsoft Paint. Or you can make your own customized screens from any bitmap image. First, rename the original Microsoft screens (REN LOGO.SYS LOGO.MS; REN LOGOW.MS LOGOW.MS, and so on).

Next, edit or create the new screens in Paint at a resolution of 320×400 pixels×256 colors. Save these files as LOGO.BMP (in the root directory of drive C), and LOGOW.BMP and LOGOS.BMP (in the WINDOWS directory). Next, rename the new LOGO files from the .BMP to the .SYS extension. The next time you start Windows 95, it will use the new screens instead of the defaults.

note *If any of your customized screens is saved at an incorrect resolution, Windows 95 will simply ignore it. If no LOGO.SYS file is present in the root directory of Drive C, Windows 95 returns to the default startup screen, because it is also embedded in another system startup file.*

Changing the Win95 Host Drive and Boot Directory

Sometimes, if there is insufficient space to place Windows 95 on drive C, or if your previous version of Windows resided on a different drive, the installation process splits Windows 95 files between two partitions. The bulk of the operating system is installed in the WINDOWS directory on drive D or drive E, but a series of critical startup files is placed in a WINDOWS directory on drive C. This can sometimes be inconvenient. You can actually combine the two WINDOWS directories into one and enter the appropriate startup information into MSDOS.SYS. If Windows 95 is split between drive C and drive D on your computer, simply copy all of the files from the C:\WINDOWS directory into D:\WINDOWS. When you do this, make sure that all of the hidden files are copied, such as SYSTEM.DAT and IFSHLP.SYS. Once the files have been copied, open MSDOS.SYS in a text editor and make the following changes in the Paths section:

```
[Paths]
HostWinBootDrv=D
WinBootDir=D:\WINDOWS
```

Once these changes are made, you can overwrite or delete the WINDOWS directory on drive C that was formerly used by Windows 95. Instead, you can use C:\WINDOWS to contain Windows NT or Windows 3.1.

note *If the bulk of Windows 95 is installed on a compressed drive, the installation is split deliberately between two partitions to facilitate updating configuration files. You may want to proceed with caution in combining directories on a system that uses DriveSpace or Stacker.*

Windows 95 Easter Egg

Windows 95 wouldn't be a real Microsoft product, without its secret, embedded "egg." Most Microsoft products (including Office and Windows) have this undocumented feature that plays music, shows a cartoon, or displays a scrolling list of thank you acknowledgments to the package's development team.

If you want to see the Windows 95 Easter Egg, use the following procedure:

1. Right-click on the desktop, and select Folder from the New menu. In the name field, type the following exactly as shown. (The egg is case-sensitive!)

```
and now, the moment you've all been waiting for
```

2. Press ENTER. Then, right-click on the folder again. Select Rename from the context menu, and type the following exactly as shown:

```
we proudly present for your viewing pleasure
```

3. Again, press ENTER, right-click on the folder, select Rename, and type the following exactly as shown:

```
The Microsoft Windows 95 Product Team!
```

4. Double-click the folder to open it. The animated list of production credits and music will begin.

note *The Microsoft Easter Egg doesn't work with certain types of high-resolution graphic adapters, notably those with Western Digital and S3 chipsets. If you have one of these graphics cards and want to see the show, you will first have to reset your system to the standard 640×480×16 display driver. Open the Display object from the Control Panel, select the Settings tab, click the Change Display Type button, and then click the Change button next to Adapter Type in the next configuration screen. If you do this, be sure to make note of your original video configuration so that you can restore it after you've seen the "egg show."*

Restarting Windows 95 Without a Warm Boot

Select Shut down, and click the Restart Computer option. Then, while holding down the SHIFT key, click Yes. Windows 95 will now restart without executing a complete warm boot.

Using the ERU System Backup Utility on the Win95 CD

Although Windows 95 is fairly stable and reliable, it can simply refuse to start if the System Registry (or Registration Database) becomes corrupt. The System Registry consists of two files called SYSTEM.DAT and USER.DAT located on your Windows 95 host drive. Although Windows 95 automatically backs these files up each time you start the operating system, a problem that corrupts the original files is very likely to be transferred to the backup copies (.DA0 files) as soon as you reboot the system.

To avoid this problem, Microsoft has included an emergency recovery utility on the Windows 95 CD. To preserve a reliable backup of your system registry and other critical startup files, run the program called ERU.EXE, located in the OTHER\MISC\ERU directory on the CD. (This utility is not available in the floppy disk version of Windows 95, although it can be downloaded from Microsoft's FTP site over the Internet.) ERU allows you to designate a drive and directory to store a spare copy of the System Registry, WIN.INI, SYSTEM.INI, CONFIG.SYS, AUTOEXEC.BAT, and DOS command kernel.

In the event of a Windows 95 startup failure, all you need to do is boot to a DOS command prompt, change to the directory you've created, and run the ERD.EXE restore utility placed there. You can choose to restore any or all of the backups of your vital files, as shown here. The files will be recopied to their default locations on your hard drive.

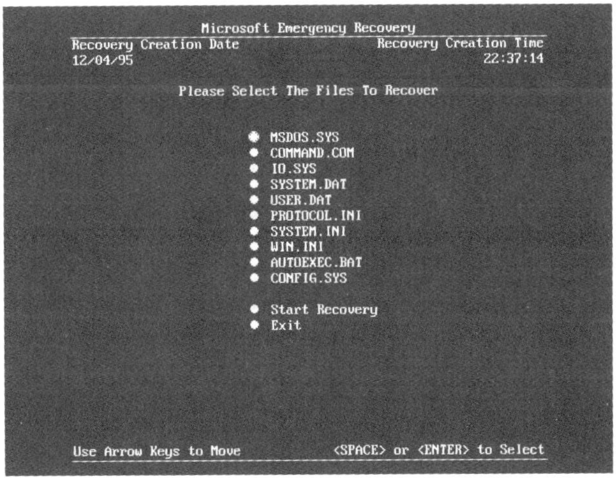

Windows 95 Service Pack Update #1

Microsoft has recently released the first Service Pack update for Windows 95. It consists of a number of individual component updates, new system drivers, and patches for known Windows 95 problems. The Service Pack is distributed in the form of a series of archived modules that can be unpacked and installed from directories on your hard drive. Perhaps the most significant upgrade in the package is the Microsoft Internet Explorer, version 2.0. This component adds the final version of Microsoft's World Wide Web browser to your desktop (overwriting the earlier version bundled in Microsoft Plus!) and adds Internet mail management to the Microsoft Exchange Inbox. The Service Pack also contains a protected-mode client shell for Novell NetWare version 4.0, as well as other network enhancements that allow users to take full advantage of Novell's directory services.

Here is a complete list of upgrade components:

INTERNET EXPLORER, VERSION 2.0 Adds or updates Microsoft's World Wide Web browser and adds Internet mail capability to Inbox.

DATA LINK CONTROL (DLC) PROTOCOL Allows network administrators to add protected-mode support for 32-bit and 16-bit applications used to access IBM mainframe and IBM AS/400 computers.

ENHANCED PASSWORD CACHE SECURITY UPDATE Addresses security issues, strengthening the encryption used for Windows 95's Password Cache. This component uses a 128-bit encryption key to replace the previous 32-bit module. PWL files created under the previous version are automatically upgraded.

UPDATED FILE AND PRINT SHARING SECURITY This driver upgrade addresses a security problem for users who make shared resources available over Microsoft or Novell NetWare networks. It will prevent other network users from obtaining read-only access after the System Administrator has logged off, and will correct problems with SAMBA, a shareware UNIX network client.

SERVICE FOR NDS (NETWARE DIRECTORY SERVICES) A 32-bit Novell 4.0 shell that allows full access to Novell NDS servers. The following features are included:

- Integrated login to NetWare 4.*x* servers
- Full support of NetWare 4.*x* login scripts
- The ability to use Network Neighborhood to browse the directory tree
- Full support for 16-bit NDS-aware programs written for MS-DOS or Windows using documented calls from the NetWare Client SDK

WINDOWS 95 SHELL UPDATE A patch to SHELL32.DLL that lets you browse Netware Directory Services from the Add Printer wizard and resolves a problem with attempts to copy a file onto itself over the network.

WINDOWS 95 OLE 32 UPDATE This update addresses file management behavior discovered in Microsoft Word, Microsoft Excel, and Microsoft PowerPoint for Windows 95, versions 7.0.

IRDA (INFRARED DRIVER) This driver adds support for the Infrared Data Association standard for wireless connectivity. It will let users establish remote connection to various peripherals (keyboards, printers, networks, etc.) without using cables.

UPDATES FROM WINDOWS 95 DRIVER LIBRARY A number of basic system drivers for Windows 95 have been updated, and will be available in the Service Pack. These include:

- Audio drivers for AST Research, Creative Labs, and DigiSpeech
- Display drivers for 8514/A compatible display adapters; ARK; ATI Technologies mach64 CT Driver Version 4.01; Avance; Diamond Viper, SpeedStar, and Stealth; Matrox MGA Millennium; Number 9; Trident; and VGA, plus a new QuickTime multimedia driver
- Modem drivers from QDS and Rockwell, plus an update to Microsoft's UNIMODEM TAPI driver
- Mouse driver from Mouse Systems, Inc.
- Network drivers from 3Com, Compaq, DCA, DEC, Everex, HP, ICL, Intel, Microdyn, NCR, OliCom, Proteon, Racal, Realtek, SMC, SysKon, Tulip, UB, Xircom, and ZDS
- Printer drivers for use with DEC, Lexmark, LPT, and Tektronx printers
- UPS (universal power source) driver update from APC
- Updated storage drivers from Adaptec, Compaq, IOmega, Qlogic, Rancho, and WD

This Service Pack update is available from Microsoft upon request, and can also be downloaded from the Microsoft FTP and Windows 95 World Wide Web sites.

Printers
MS-DOS
Programs
Settings
Find
Help
Run...
Suspend
Windows95
Start

appendix B

Using RegEdit for Fun and Profit

- The mysteries of RegEdit explained
- Changing the default Setup drive
- Turning folders into thumbnail bitmap viewers
- Creating document templates

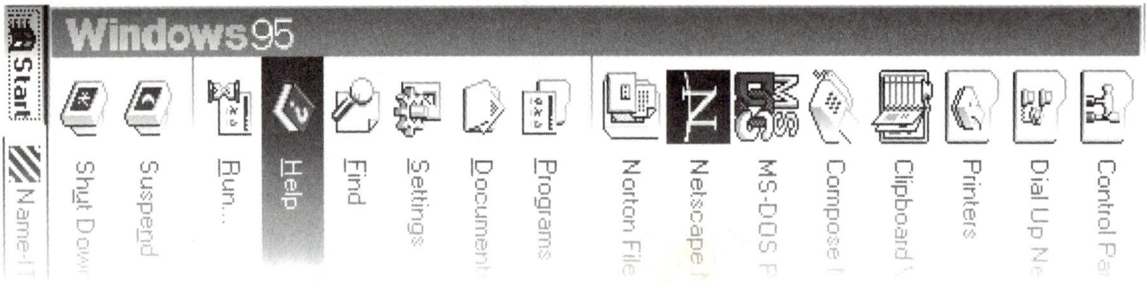

In Windows 95, the System Registry plays a much larger role than it did in previous versions of Windows. Large portions of the WIN.INI and SYSTEM.INI files that used to control the configuration of the system don't exist anymore. Instead, the wide array of configuration parameters that used to be written to these files are automatically shuttled to the System Registry. One consequence of this shift is that users who seek to customize Windows 95 must either learn the basics of browsing and modifying the registry or be at the mercy of hackers and shareware authors to do the job for them.

We've already detailed some of the changes you can make to bend the Windows 95 desktop to your will. In Chapter 4, we showed you how the TweakUI utility developed unofficially by the Windows 95 programming team enhances the Control Panel. In Chapter 14, we also provided a brief description of the other utilities in the Windows 95 PowerToy suite. Most of these applets enhance control of the desktop and add new features by placing specific entries in the flexible System Registry.

In Chapter 5, we provided a RegEdit command summary and showed you how to export and import either the whole registry, or selected portions. Here, we'll provide a more advanced look at some of the other useful things you can do with Microsoft's registry browsing tool.

Backing Up Your Registry Settings

Before you start making modifications in the Windows 95 System Registry, first preserve a backup copy of the current version. The registry is stored in a file called SYSTEM.DAT, stored in your WINDOWS directory. Additional information is stored in a file called USER.DAT. Although Windows 95 makes nominal backups of these files called SYSTEM.DA0 and USER.DA0, in actuality these backups are frequently overwritten and unusable in the event that problems arise in the original files. Refer back to Appendix A for instructions on using the Microsoft Emergency Recovery utility to make a reliable registry backup set.

The Mysteries of RegEdit Explained

Once you've backed up the registry files, add the RegEdit utility (located in the WINDOWS directory) to your Accessories folder, or launch it from the command line. You'll find that it opens into two screen windows. On the left, you'll find six main folders that may contain thousands of settings and system control options:

- **HKEY_LOCAL_MACHINE** keeps track of the installed hardware and software on the computer. This is the section where alternate configurations for docked and undocked notebooks are stored.
- **HKEY_USERS** is the portion represented by the USER.DAT file in your WINDOWS directory. It keeps track of the desktop configuration, network configuration and individual user profiles.
- **HKEY_CLASSES_ROOT** and **HKEY_CURRENT_USER** affect file associations and current user information. These are the sections we'll be most interested in editing.
- **HKEY_CURRENT_CONFIG** stores the current display and printer settings.
- **HKEY_DYN_DATA** stores system performance parameters. For instance, the menu speed-up options offered in the TweakUI Windows 95 PowerToy modify data in this section.

On the right you'll find individual data entries corresponding to each registry key in the left pane.

The six main branches of the registry can be opened to display subfolders and settings by toggling the + and – signs to the left of each folder icon, as shown here:

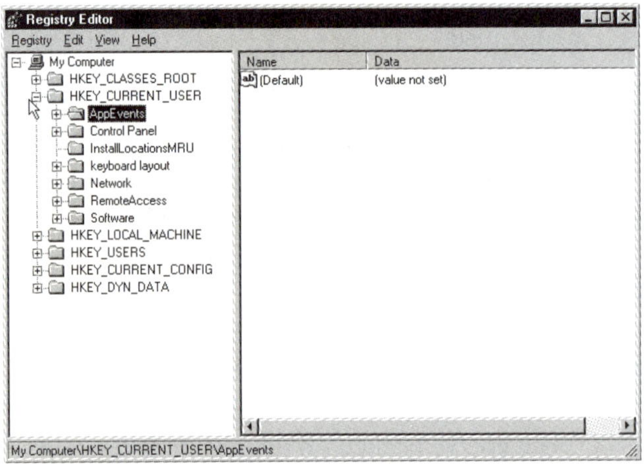

RegEdit has three pull-down tool menus, and a fourth Help menu. We saw in Chapter 5 that the options on the Registry menu can be used to import and export selected portions of the registry contents. The Edit menu options are used to create new registry information, modify existing information, or search for the location of specific registry information. The View menu lets you control the display of the two RegEdit windows. You can also adjust this display, simply by left-clicking the mouse on the dividing bar between the two status windows and moving it to the right or to the left.

The folders on the right side of the dividing bar are referred to as *keys*. The entries on the left side of the dividing bar are String Values, Binary Values, and DWORD Values.

You can examine any information in the registry by selecting a folder or subfolder key in the left window and pressing the TAB key to see associated string information in the right window. To return to the key in the left window, press SHIFT-TAB.

Using RegEdit

Now that we've bent our minds a little in acquiring an understanding of the RegEdit interface, let's use it to perform some useful chores.

Changing the Default Setup Drive

If you're a Windows 95 road warrior with no CD-ROM drive, you may have discovered the useful trick of installing Windows 95 and updating system configuration by simply copying the contents of the floppy Setup disks or of the Win95 CD folder to a directory on your hard drive. Or you may have plugged into a borrowed CD-ROM drive to do the initial setup, and then want to make modifications to the configuration on the road. Windows 95 remembers the source drive and directory you use for the initial setup. This can be annoying if you want to update your system configuration from another location that contains the necessary installation files.

For instance, let's say that you've plugged into a network or a borrowed CD-ROM drive to install Windows 95, and then diligently copied all of the setup files to a C:\WIN95 directory on your hard drive. Now, when you use Add/Remove Programs or Add New Hardware, the system always complains that the installation drive can't be found, and forces you to browse around for a new file source location.

You can use RegEdit to change the SourcePath file location to any drive and directory you want. Select the Find command on RegEdit's Edit menu and search for a value called SourcePath, as shown here:

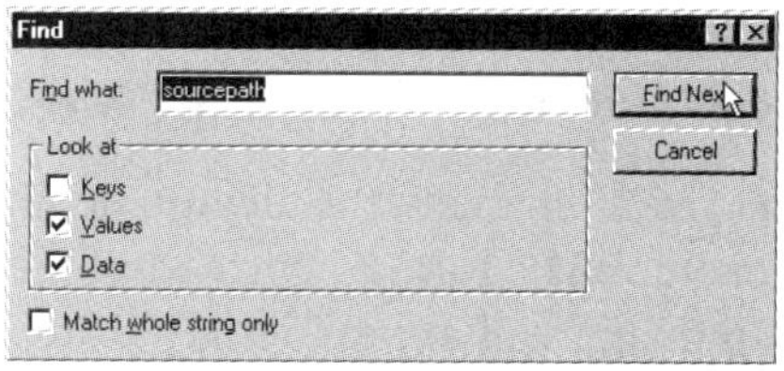

You can deselect the Keys and Data search boxes.

When the first SourcePath entry is found on the right, press SHIFT-TAB to see its associated key on the left. If the first associated key is for Microsoft Plus! Setup, or some other application, press F3 to continue searching. The next occurrence of SourcePath will probably be associated with the Windows\CurrentVersion\Setup key. This is the value you want to change. You'll notice that the data value in the right display window lists the original drive and directory that you used to install Windows 95.

To change the default SourcePath, highlight the SourcePath name in the right display panel again and select the Modify command on RegEdit's pull-down Edit menu:

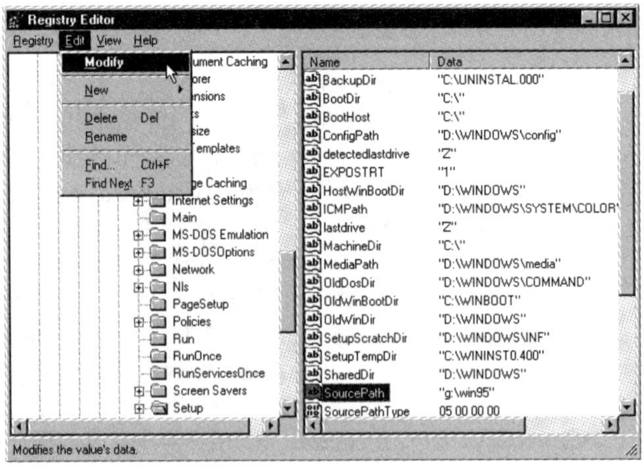

Enter the new drive and directory in the Value Data box that pops up and click OK. The next time you need to make a system change, Windows 95 will automatically look for driver files on the drive and directory you've entered.

Note that if you have stored the installation files for Microsoft Plus! on your hard disk, you can modify the Microsoft Plus! SourcePath, as well.

Turning Folders into Thumbnail Bitmap Viewers

This trick changes the default icon display for graphic images in the Microsoft .BMP format. Instead of displaying a generic BMP icon, each bitmap image will appear in My Computer or Explorer or on the desktop with a thumbnail representation of the picture it contains.

For this trick, we'll also add another RegEdit feature to our repertoire. Instead of manually searching through and modifying the System Registry, we can write a script that will do it for us automatically.

To make .BMP file icons display thumbnails of their contents, enter the following script into Notepad and save it as THUMBNAIL.REG.

```
REGEDIT4
[HKEY_CLASSES_ROOT\Paint.Picture\DefaultIcon]
@="%1"
**end of Thumbnail.reg**
```

To import this change into the System Registry, open the Run box on the Start Menu and enter the command: REGEDIT THUMBNAIL.REG. Restart Windows 95 and you'll find that icons for .BMP files and shortcuts to .BMP files now display on the desktop as thumbnails of the bitmapped images they represent, as you can see here:

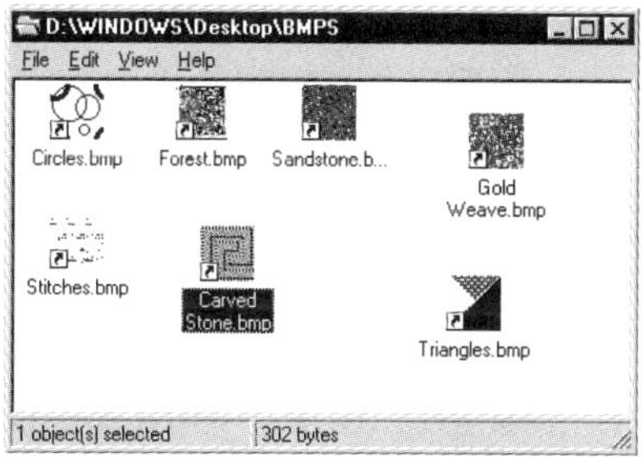

You could also have searched manually for the Paint.Picture key in the left RegEdit display pane and modified the DefaultIcon value. If a third-party installation program has reassociated the .BMP bitmap file type with an application other than Microsoft Paint, this trick won't work. You'll have to find the key for the new application assigned to the .BMP extension, or else try opening the Add/Remove Programs object and successively remove and reinstall Paint. This will restore the original Windows 95 file association for .BMP images.

Creating Blank Document Templates

In Chapter 4, we mentioned that the TweakUI PowerToy for Windows 95 has the ability to automatically convert any document on your hard drive into a desktop template. The following section shows you how to do this trick without TweakUI.

Template documents can be created in My Computer\Explorer or on the desktop by right-clicking and selecting the New option from the pop-up context menu. To add more blank, new templates to the pop-up list, you must first create an association for the document type to an application in My Computer\Explorer.

1. Open My Computer, select View\Options\File Types, and click the New Type button.
2. Enter a description of the file type and a file extension. (For example, let's assume we're creating a template for WordPerfect 5.1 for DOS. We enter WordPerfect in the description box and .W51 in the file extension box.)
3. Click the New button under Actions. Enter Open in the Action dialog box, and select the application used to perform the action.

For this example, we'll enter C:\WP51\WP.EXE. Click OK and exit the Options menu.

4. Now open RegEdit. Expand the HKEY_CLASSES_ROOT section, by clicking the + sign to the left of the icon. Pan down to and select the .W51 extension, which has just been created.
5. Add a new key to .W51 and title it "ShellNew." (Select New\Key from RegEdit's Edit menu.)
6. Select the ShellNew key and add a new string value. Title it "Nullfile." To do this, select New\String Value from RegEdit's Edit menu:

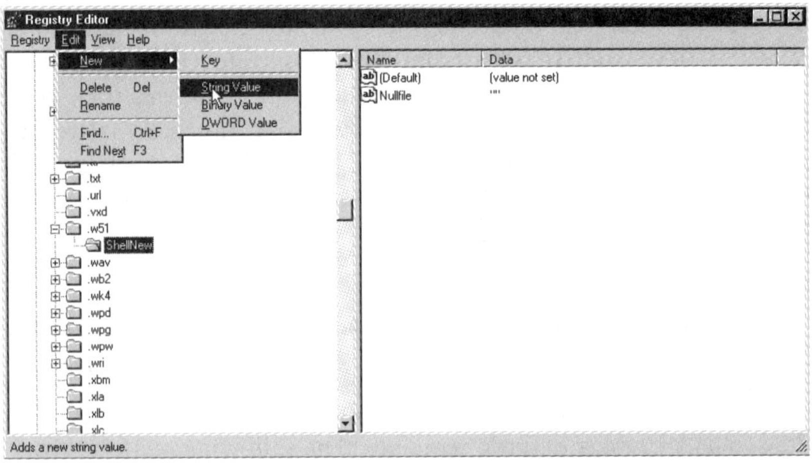

7. Close RegEdit. A new option to create blank WordPerfect documents has been added to the templates on the Desktop\New menu and to the File\New menu in My Computer\Explorer. You can now use the New Template feature to create a dummy WordPerfect object on the desktop or in a folder. (Right-click, point to New, and select it from the template list.) After the object appears on the desktop or in a folder, double-click it to open a blank, new WordPerfect document.

Creating Formatted Document Templates

A slightly different twist in RegEdit lets you make new templates linked to formatted documents. For example, let's add a template for WordPad that creates a formatted letterhead document. By default, Windows 95 installs a vanilla .TXT template and opens a blank document in Notepad. We can do better than that.

The SHELLNEW directory under your WINDOWS directory is used to store dummy documents for template shortcuts created by Windows 95. We'll create a letterhead in WordPad. You can also use this trick to create templates for other applications: a Microsoft Word document, a presentation template for PowerPoint, or a publication page in PageMaker. After we create the WordPad letterhead, we'll save it to the SHELLNEW directory under a new file extension. This will avoid conflicts with WordPad's already-registered .RTF association. Finally, we'll set up a program association for the new file extension and use RegEdit to add the association to Windows 95's list of available document templates.

1. Unhide the WINDOWS\SHELLNEW directory. Open My Computer or Explorer and make sure that the View option has been set to Show All Files. Right-click the SHELLNEW directory under WINDOWS, select Properties, and deselect the "hidden" file attribute checkmark.
2. Now, open your application of choice and create a formatted document to serve as a template. Figure B-1 shows one created in WordPad.

FIGURE B-1

A letterhead template for a busy M.D.

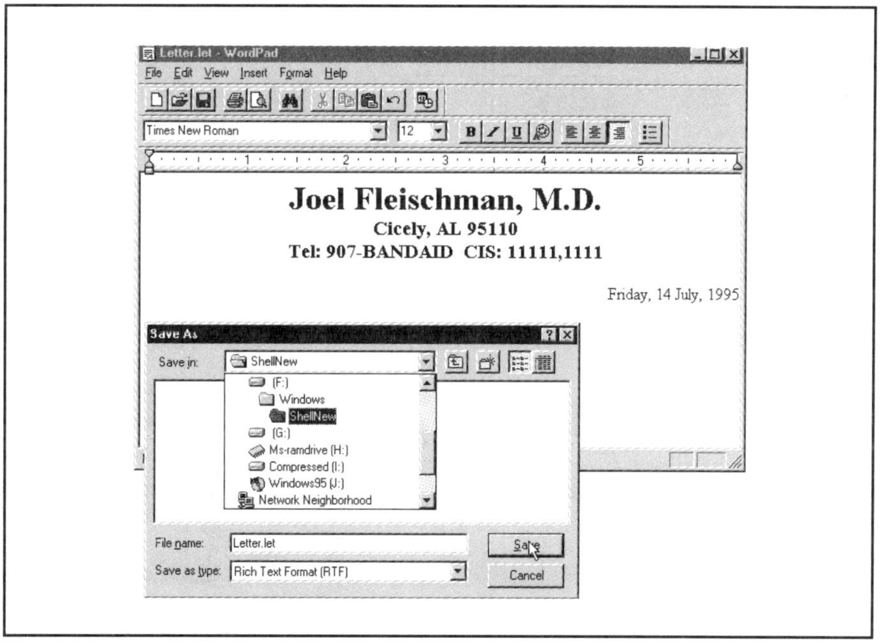

3. Save the formatted template with a new file extension. For our example, we'll use the extension .LET, saving the file in the WINDOWS\SHELLNEW directory as LETTER.LET.
4. Open My Computer or Explorer and create a file association for the new .LET extension. Use the procedure described in the previous example; enter Letterhead in the file description box, and .LET in the extension box in the Add New File Types window.
5. Click the New button under the Action window, enter Open in the Action dialog box that pops up, and enter the path to the associated application in the "Application used to perform action" dialog box. In this case, use the browse button, or type in the following:

```
[D:]\PROGRA~1\ACCESS~1\WORDPAD.EXE "%1"
```

note *In WordPad, the %1 parameter following the program name has to be enclosed in quotation marks, as you can see in Figure B-2. This is also true for Microsoft's Paint application. For most other DOS and Windows applications, the %1 parameter is entered directly after the application name without being enclosed in quotes.*

FIGURE B-2

An "Open" option is configured for the new .LET file type.

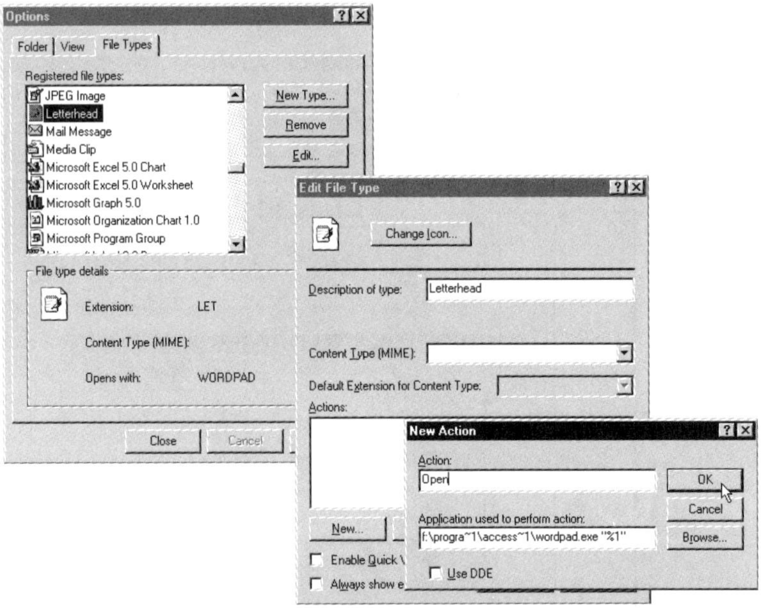

6. Click the OK button, and back out of the File Types\Options menu.
7. Now open RegEdit, and find the newly created .LET extension in the HKEY_ CLASSES_ROOT section. (You can use the Find command on the Edit menu.) Select the .LET extension and create a new key titled SHELLNEW, as you did for the previous template exercise.
8. This time, under the .LET\SHELLNEW key, add a new string value titled Filename.
9. After Filename appears in the RegEdit window, right-click it and select Modify, or choose Modify from the Edit menu. Enter the name of the template file you created in step 3 in the Value data box, in this case, **LETTER.LET**.
10. Click OK and close RegEdit.

As in the previous template exercise, you've added a new template to the list that appears when you select File\New from Explorer or right-click New on the desktop context menu. From now on, you can select Letterhead from the list of templates: A new letterhead document will appear on the desktop or in a designated folder. Double-click this object, and a new instance of your pre-formatted letterhead opens in WordPad, allowing you to type a new letter.

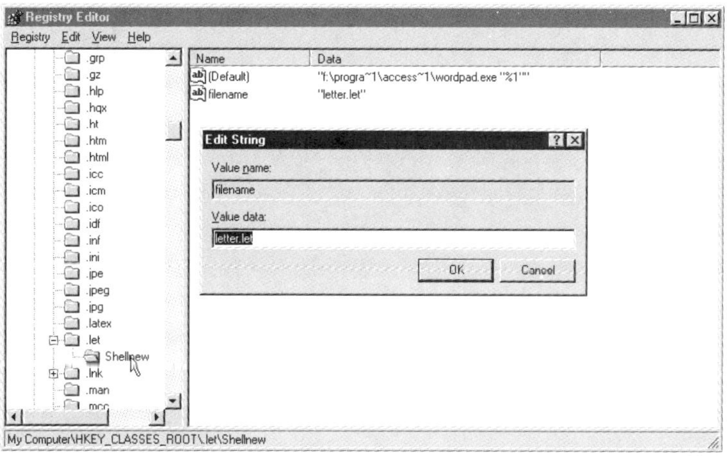

FIGURE B-3 *Our template document, LETTER.LET, is now associated with the .LET file type we've created.*

You can create as many new letterhead documents as you like from the template, editing and saving each with a new name and location.

The two procedures we've just outlined can be used to create new desktop templates for any DOS or Windows application, either to open a blank document or to create new documents containing preformatted content.

appendix C

Addresses and Online Resources

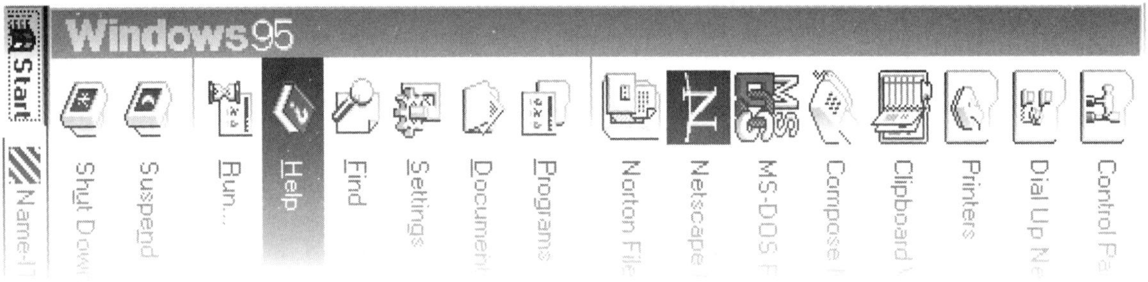

A

ADOBE Systems
1585 Charleston Road
Mountain View, CA 94039
Telephone: 415-961-4400
BBS: 206-623-6984
CompuServe Forum: Go ADOBEAP
World Wide Web: HTTP://WWW.ADOBE.COM/SOFTWARE.HTML

American Megatrends, Inc. (AMI Atlas PCI Motherboard)
6145-F Northbelt Parkway
Norcross, GA 30071
Telephone: 800-828-9264; 404-263-8181
World Wide Web: HTTP://WWW.MEGATRENDS.COM

Ares Software (FontMinder, Font Chameleon)
P.O. Box 4667
Foster City, CA 94404
Telephone: 415-578-9090
BBS: 415-286-8879

Canyon Software (Drag and File, Drag and Zip)
1537 Fourth Street, Suite 131
San Rafael, CA 94901
Telephone: 415-453-9779
World Wide Web: HTTP://WWW.CANYONSW.COM

CDRP, Inc. (Chestnut CD-ROMs)
P.O. Box 360
Cambridge, MA 02141
Telephone: 617-494-5330

Delrina Communications Corporation (Communications Suite, Cyberjack)
895 Don Mills Road
500-2 Park Centre
Toronto, Ontario
Canada M3C 1W3
World Wide Web: HTTP://WWW.DELRINA.COM;
HTTP://WWW.CYBERJACK.COM

Helix Software (Netroom, Hurricane, Discover Professional)
47-09 30th Street
Long Island City, NY 11101
Telephone: 800-451-0551; 718-392-3100

Inso Corporation (Quick View Plus)
401 North Wabash, Suite 600
Chicago, IL 60611

Intel Corporation (CPU upgrades, motherboards)
2300 Mission College Boulevard
Santa Clara, CA 95052
Telephone: 800-321-4044
CompuServe Forum: Go INTELFORUM
World Wide Web: HTTP://WWW.INTEL.COM/PROCS

InterSoft International, Inc. (Netterm Telnet)
P.O. Box 218794
Houston, TX 77218-8794
CompuServe ID: 72060.2331

Ipswitch, Inc. (WS_FTP32)
267 Hillwood Street
Martinez, GA 30907
Telephone: 706-780-2671

McAfee Software (VirusScan 95)
2710 Walsh Avenue
Santa Clara, CA 95051
Telephone: 408-988-3832
BBS: 408-988-4004

Microsoft Corporation
1 Microsoft Way
Redmond, WA 98052
Telephone: 206-882-8080
Windows 95 Tech Support: 206-635-7000
Microsoft Network Online Service Support: 800-386-5550
CompuServe Forum: Go WIN95
Bulletin Board Download Service: 206-936-6735
Win95 World Wide Web: HTTP://WWW.MICROSOFT.COM
/WINDOWS
Internet FTP Site: FTP.MICROSOFT.COM (FTP\DATA)

Netscape Communications, Inc. (Netscape Personal Navigator)
501 E. Middlefield Road
Mountain View, CA 94043
Telephone: 415-528-2555

Pacific Commware, Inc. (TurboCommander, TurboExpress I/O Board)
180 Beacon Hill Lane
Ashland, OR 95720
Telephone: 800-856-3818; 541-482-2627

QUALCOMM Incorporated (Eudora E-Mail)
6455 Lusk Boulevard
San Diego, CA 92121-2779
Internet FTP Site: FTP.QUALCOMM.COM

Quarterdeck Corporation (QEMM, MagnaRAM, WinProbe, CleanSweep, Internet Suite)
13160 Mindanao Way, 3rd Floor
Marina del Rey, CA 90292
Telephone: 800-683-6696; 310-309-3700
CompuServe Forum: Go QUARTERDECK
World Wide Web: HTTP://WWW.QUARTERDECK.COM

Symantec, Inc. (Norton Utilities, Norton Navigator, Norton Antivirus)
10201 Torre Avenue
Cupertino, CA 95014
Telephone: 800-441-7234; 541-334-6054
CompuServe Forum: Go SYMANTEC
World Wide Web: HTTP://WWW.SYMANTEC.COM

Toshiba Computer Systems Division
P.O. Box 19724
Irvine, CA 92619
Telephone: 714-583-3925

Touchstone Software Corporation (Win95 Advisor)
2124 Main Street
Huntington Beach, CA 92648
Telephone: 714-969-7746

Vertisoft Systems, Inc. (Remove-It, Name-It)
Four Embarcadero Center, Suite 3470
San Francisco, CA 94111
Telephone: 415-956-5999

WinBook Computer Corporation
1160 Steelwood Road
Columbus, OH 43212
Telephone: 800-468-7502

The Wollongong Group, Inc.
1129 San Antonio Road
Palo Alto, CA 94303
Telephone: 800-872-8649; Canada: 519-747-9900
E-mail: pcsales@twg.com
World Wide Web: HTTP://WWW.TWG.COM

Internet Resources

Windows 95 Home Pages
World Wide Web: HTTP://NAUTILUS.UTMB.EDU/WIN95/WWW.HTM

Windows 95 HQ: Steve Jenkins
World Wide Web: HTTP://WWW.WINDOWS95.COM

Windows 95 Annoyances: Creative Element
World Wide Web: HTTP://WWW.CREATIVELEMENT.COM /WIN95ANN

WinServe: Tim Hall
World Wide Web: HTTP://WWW.WINSERVE.COM

Index

B

C

E

J

K

L

M

N

Q

R

T

U

V

X

Y

Z

Leaders of the Pack

The Internet Health, Fitness & Medicine Yellow Pages

by Matthew Naythons, M.D. with Anthony Catsimatides
$22.95 U.S.A.
ISBN: 0-07-882188-6

The Internet Yellow Pages Third Edition

by Harley Hahn
$29.95 U.S.A.
ISBN: 0-07-882182-7

The Internet Science, Research & Technology Yellow Pages

by Rick Stout and Morgan Davis
$22.95 U.S.A.
ISBN: 0-07-882187-8

The World Wide Web Complete Reference

by Rick Stout
$29.95 U.S.A.
ISBN: 0-07-882142-8

NetLaw: Your Rights in the Online World

by Lance Rose
$19.95 U.S.A.
ISBN: 0-07-882077-4

The Internet Complete Reference Second Edition

by Harley Hahn
$32.95 U.S.A.
ISBN: 0-07-882138-X

To Order, Call Toll Free 1-800-822-8158

By Mail: Osborne/McGraw-Hill Order Services, P.O. Box 545, Blacklick, OH 43004-0546, FAX 1-614-755-5654

OSBORNE
McGRAW-HILL